D1284777

The Heart of Hamlet

YOU WOULD PLUCK OUT THE HEART
OF MY MYSTERY . . . (III, iii)

REPORT ME AND MY CAUSE ARIGHT
TO THE UNSATISFIED. (V, ii)

THE HEART
OF HAMLET

The Play Shakespeare Wrote

WITH THE TEXT OF THE PLAY
AS EDITED BY PROFESSOR GREBANIER

BERNARD GREBANIER

Thomas Y. Crowell Company
NEW YORK · ESTABLISHED 1834

For

CONSUELO URISARRI FORD

He that hath wings, let him soar;
Mine is the heart at your feet
Here, that must love you to live.

Preface

IN WRITING *The Heart of Hamlet* my only objective has
been to restore comprehensibility to the play which few—with the
exception of some critics—would deny being the crowning glory of
the English-speaking stage. I hoped for the attention of every sort
of reader: the general cultivated reader, the addict of the theater,
the director, the actor, the student of Shakespeare, the student of
literature, and the professional Shakespearean scholar. I was as anxious to procure the ear of all as to meet the challenge of the last-
named.

This edition of *The Heart of Hamlet* is to be distinguished from
the edition made available for the general public and the people of
the theater by virtue of the fact that it contains the text of the play
with my notes and comments on the text. This is an edition for the
special student, the scholar, the director, and the actor. It includes
these innovations:

I introduce in many places emotional cues and stage directions,
and take the liberty of italicizing certain words of the dialogue, in
an effort to elucidate given moments of the drama, and the meaning
of lines and speeches. Here I hope to help reader and actor arrive
at once at what is meant.

I discuss in footnotes some of the important dramatic issues.

I cite at crucial moments critical opinion at great variance with

vii

mine. These quotations taken together with pages 55–131 (where every conceivable theory advanced about the play as a whole and its characters has been summarized) provide a fairly exhaustive compendium of opinions on *Hamlet*.

In short, this edition provides as well, I trust, an efficient acting-version of the play.

It will not escape notice that I have had to take exception most often to the commentary of Wilson, Kittredge, and Adams, and to the version of the play presented in Olivier's movie. Such was inevitably the case. Wilson's *What Happens in Hamlet* (often referred to as a classic) and his edition of the play have been held as ultimate authorities for a quarter of a century; the prestige of Kittredge and Adams has been second only to his. While I am able to agree with these gentlemen on certain details, I am in profound disagreement with all three in what seems to me most essential. Where they err, I think, is in hardly ever remembering that *Hamlet* is a play, and, moreover, that it was its author's concern to be true to what is fundamental to human nature. As for Mr. Olivier, his sincerity, enthusiasm, and vast abilities are beyond dispute; he has given us several of the greatest performances of our time; but his *Hamlet*, I feel, did his genius no credit. His movie has exerted and is likely to continue to exert enormous influence on most people's notions as to what Shakespeare meant; unhappily there is little of Shakespeare in that production, and it was part of my task, though a very small part, to show as much.

BERNARD GREBANIER

Contents

The Heart of Hamlet

UNLESS EXPERIENCE BE A JEWEL, THAT I HAVE PURCHASED
AT AN INFINITE RATE.

The Merry Wives of Windsor, II, ii

I *The Jewel of Experience: in Explanation*

HAD I HAD the foreknowledge to seize the occasion, I might
have spared myself years of confusion. But how, at seventeen, was I
to imagine that *Hamlet* would thereafter be in any way important
to me?

The experience was one to prove Wilde to have been talking
merely common sense when he insisted that life imitates art. Mr.
Rocco, my barber, in his simplicity had never heard of *Tom Jones*,
and I in my seventeen-year-old complexity had heard of it but had
not yet read it. Nevertheless, as he sat by my side one night at the
theater, Mr. Rocco unconsciously aped one of the most hilarious
passages in Fielding's novel.

I had saved up enough money to take my girl to a performance
of *Hamlet*. At the last minute she had decided to quarrel with me,
and refused to go. That night in the barber's chair I bitterly com-
mented on the instability of women; to my surprise, Mr. Rocco,
scissors poised in air, offered to accompany me instead so that the
ticket might be used. In a way I can no longer recapture, this seemed
to my adolescent mind like exquisite revenge, and I agreed.

My companion amply made up for the mediocrity of the performance. He had never heard of the play, he could have under-

stood little of its language, but I doubt if anyone ever enjoyed a performance of *Hamlet* more. Throughout the evening he sat on the edge of his seat, now and again throwing me a look of anguished apprehension. Beads of perspiration decked his troubled brow—and these were by no means due entirely to the heated atmosphere of the gallery or the season. And then—this, lovers of Fielding, I swear is truth!—when the Ghost appeared in the Queen's chamber, Mr. Rocco cried out, "Look out!" After the final curtain, exhausted and exalted, he exclaimed, "Wasa damn good! *Molto simpatico e naturale.* Geesa, I wasa scare!"

Had I only known that night that I was not to become, after all, a great pianist! Had I only guessed that talking and thinking about *Hamlet* were to be daily occupations for most of the rest of my life! What an opportunity I let slip when I failed to ask Mr. Rocco what the play meant to him, what precisely had evoked his pity and fear! I might then and there have started re-discovering Shakespeare's *Hamlet*. That it meant something very exciting and very clear to Mr. Rocco his actions eloquently testified. He found it, moreover, *simpatico* and *naturale*.

But everyone knows that *Hamlet* is a good play—everyone, apparently, but Mr. T. S. Eliot. If it were not a good play, actors would not forever be reviving it, and audiences would not be crowding theaters to see it even when Mr. Evans or Mr. Olivier assumes the title role. Unhappily, only the professional scholars have told us what the play is supposed to mean, and what they have told us makes confusion worse confounded.

I managed to pass safely into my early twenties without becoming a victim of that confusion, for *Hamlet,* during that interim, was the last thing I was thinking about. My thoughts, such as they were, were indeed far removed from all matters academic or anything associated with Shakespeare on a certain fateful afternoon in 1926 when Professor Lewis Freeman Mott, chairman of the English department of the college which was to graduate me in a few weeks, stopped me in a corridor to ask me an amazing question. Would I be interested in conducting a course in Shakespeare?

This esteemed scholar could have had no idea how astounding his offer was. At the moment he made it I had not the slightest intention of becoming a teacher of Shakespeare or of anything else.

My only purposes connected with college were to be done with institutions of learning forever. Indeed, a few days earlier, the final speech required of me in Public Speaking had been devoted to a scorching attack on the teaching profession, during which I did not omit quoting Shaw's truism on those who teach. Nor had I any idea of how I could have earned the good opinion of a man so universally held in awe as Professor Mott, for in his classes I had had little to say —unless I could say it in writing.

It may be for the reason that to a boy the incense of flattery is of all fragrances the most enchanting that I managed to answer him, on my way through the flooring, in the affirmative. But there were other incitements, too, to my seizing the opportunity of immediate employment—some practical, the chief one eminently romantic. On the promise of this position I was married in a few days. And so my education began that week.

My next obligation, plainly, was to transform myself into a scholar. Paderewski's laurels, which up to the time of that fatal interview I had intended snatching, could rest on his snowy head: he was safe from me now. I had more pressing problems to face. Up to this point I had taken my college studies quite insouciantly. I had been merely an omnivorous reader of literature, an enthusiast for great books with an unconquerable distaste for homework. Registered in a course on the Age of Pope, I would be too deep in Dostoievski to have time for Addison; another semester, Addison would prove irresistibly fascinating when I was supposed to be reading Tennyson. My reading had been exclusively for pleasure—a habit which to date I have rarely been able to correct. I had read a great deal, in several literatures, but I had read very few of the books about books—of the kind I have since written myself.

Developing more scholarly methods in my literary pursuits thus became quite suddenly a matter of self-preservation. For not many college teachers have entered upon their careers with the disadvantages I encountered on my first day of teaching.

My Shakespeare class was composed entirely of young men who had been my fellow students only three months before. Some of them were annoyed, some were indignant, at having to sit under me; others considered the situation a huge joke. All of them were determined to make things as difficult as possible. It was obvious that I could expect a steady barrage of questions all semester. Since that first class no other has been hard to teach.

I felt myself challenged. With the foolhardiness of youth I began the course with the most challenging of all the plays. I had been working at *Hamlet* for an entire summer in anticipation, and was impatient to begin the contest. While resolved to be brave, I nevertheless did not forget that part of valor which is discretion. One thing I had learned from going to college: it is possible for a teacher to go through a course without once expressing a conviction of his own; such a lecturer was even held by the students he bored to be very scholarly—scholarly, in fact, in proportion to his ability to bore. Scholarship, it seemed, was a matter of culling bushels of quotations from the critics to fling at one's students. I therefore was prepared, after a summer's intense note-taking, to engulf the opposition: I had copybooks filled with theories on *Hamlet* by Goethe, Schlegel, Coleridge, Ulrici, Werder, Klein, Bradley, Stoll, Eliot, and Freud. I atoned for not having any theories of my own by presenting a profusion of the theories of others; for a brief hour I basked in a light of awe because of my references to Freud and Eliot, the two newest gods on the horizon. But I did not enjoy that respect for long.

A sorry state of affairs soon developed. As I proceeded to read the text of *Hamlet* with my students, the theories which I had faithfully collected and whose number I was still busy augmenting had the lamentable tendency of canceling one another out. It was, of course, very easy and even exciting to use one theory, as we advanced line-by-line through the play, as a cudgel with which to belabor another theory. But by the time we had finished the fifth act, neither I nor my students had the faintest idea of what the play was about. Many of the theories were attractive and had an apparent validity; all, taken together, proved that not one was acceptable. I had been far too thorough, as my sometime fellow students did not omit pointing out.

Before it fell to my lot to teach *Hamlet* again I had the intervening nine months to add to my knowledge of scholarship on the play. The prodigy I then delivered to my classes died the same death. I tried the same procedure, except that I quoted more critics. At the final curtain I knew less about *Hamlet* than ever.

When at the end of my third year's teaching I had followed the identical approach with equal futility, it seemed time to be a little wise. There was no denying any longer the fact that the more I knew of other men's *Hamlet* the less I knew about Shakespeare's. Further scholarly opinion could be of no help. If, to end the dilemma, I decided to adopt one theory out of hand and let the matter rest, which should I choose? How could one decide among the claims for respect of such men as Samuel Johnson, Goethe, Coleridge, Werder, or Bradley? And what of all that enlightened medical opinion, when the doctors looked at literature? Dared one be so unmodern as to turn one's back on the subtler, more titillating interpretations of Freud and his school—beckoning behind half-opened doors from dim chambers peopled by the psychopathic? And what was to be answered to the doggedly unromantic scholarship beginning to emerge out of the level topography of the American Middle West, from men who calmly averred that the reason Hamlet fails to kill the King any earlier is that such an act would have ended the play before the last act? Or—most dreadful of all possibilities—could the untamable T. S. Eliot be right (in those days who could have guessed he would become an Old Master?) when he hinted that *Hamlet* is a bad play after all? "We must simply admit that here Shakespeare tackled a problem which proved too much for him," Mr. Eliot had not long before declared.[1]

It was at this point that my memory of Mr. Rocco came to the rescue. I must now try to be simple and sincerely interested in the play itself, like my old barber, and let the work speak to me without anyone else's help. If an illiterate barber could understand the play, why should I permit scholarship to befuddle me?

I decided therefore upon an experiment. The fourth year I explained to my classes my current dilemma and confessed frankly that I had no idea what the play actually said. I told my students that if we cooperated I thought we might discover what Shakespeare intended us to understand, provided we read *Hamlet* with no preconceptions. George Bernard Shaw says that one of the troubles with mankind is that we are forever distressed to find that our pail contains dirty water, but that we never throw out the dirty water before dipping into the clear well. "We persist," he says, "in pouring the clear water into the dirty; and our minds are always muddled in consequence." Well, I was resolved to throw out all the dirty water I had scooped up, before dipping into the clear water of Shakespeare himself.

This time my class read *Hamlet* as though we were all an audience at the first day's performance in Elizabethan London. We tried to have no ideas about what the play would unfold, and took up each scene in order, speculating only on what we had already read, and charting carefully what we had thus far discovered, scene by scene. Very early the work began to take shape, and to my stupefaction the story became entirely clear, the characters began to breathe, all the incidents fell into place, and at the conclusion I felt I knew exactly what Shakespeare had meant to convey. As I took stock of what I now comprehended, I recognized that it was in agreement at various points with the strictures of this or that commentator. But to my horror I also realized that the meaning the play now had amounted in its totality to a new theory! The hero himself was a completely different kind of man from any he had been described as being—a man at last quite intelligible and in no way strange,*

* For having come to the conclusion that Hamlet is quite intelligible, Sarah Bernhardt was sneeringly dismissed when she enacted the role. "In her defense of her reading of the part, she said she thought Hamlet a simple character, and one critic remarked, 'Need we say more than that?' Meaning to say, the remark put her out of court." [2] I was born too late for the privilege of seeing her performance. There is, of course, nothing very inviting in the prospect of seeing any woman masquerading as Hamlet—least of all when she is "dressed and got up like the pictures of young Raphael." [3] And while I strongly feel that during a Shakespearean performance in any other language

> My native English now I must forgo,
> And now my tongue's use is to me no more
> Than an unstringed viol or a harp,
> Or like a cunning instrument cased up,
> Or, being open, put into his hands
> That knows no touch to tune the harmony;
>
> > *Richard II*, I, iii, 160 seq.

nevertheless to have missed the Bernhardt Hamlet is probably to have been robbed of an important experience. Her intelligent defense as well as several other details of her performance imply a comprehension in many respects far in advance of most commentators.

however brilliant. I was appalled to find that I had stumbled upon a new theory when my only desire had been to understand Shakespeare. Stout Cortez—or even Balboa—silent upon a peak in Darien, could not have been more stunned.

Now the question which I had sought to answer, "What was the author saying when he wrote the work?" is a question which rarely agitates directors in our theater. On that subject Mr. Eric Bentley, who for freshness of vision has few peers among scholars of modern drama, in a stimulating chapter on "Doing Shakespeare Wrong" has cogent things to say. He does not forget the contributions of the last few decades in abolishing the ponderousness of earlier twentieth-century productions. That called for abolishing. The Shakespeare one saw on the boards in my youth was more oppressive than impressive—an endless march of ever-changing painted sets, pompous oratory, and elaborate costumes. The reaction against this heavy style, however, as Mr. Bentley accurately perceives, has been to have "no style at all." The moderns tend to say, "Let Shakespeare speak for himself," and profess to have no theories about producing him. Their basic assumption, observes Mr. Bentley shrewdly, is fallacious, for they pretend "that an entirely negative performance *could* be given." The modern director often feels he is doing enough for the play if he maintains an uninterrupted pace, and is sure the actors "are seen and heard" and do "not bump into each other." Many performances are content to be "merely decorative." No one seems interested in achieving clarity of meaning. Of Miss Webster, who has often directed Shakespeare, Mr. Bentley says, "A fog surrounds her Shakespeare"; and he notes that in the Olivier film of *Hamlet* "the story was not told (they thought that we knew it or that it doesn't matter)." [4]

Mr. Bentley is, of course, entirely right. How can Shakespeare be "allowed to speak for himself" if the directors and the actors do not know what he is saying? Whatever they deliver—be it sense, nonsense, or chaos—they inevitably become during the performance the only means by which the author can address us. Obviously, the first step in directing even a merely adequate performance of a play must be the seeking of some knowledge of the play's meaning.

But there are directors and actors who are in a worse position than those "moderns" of whom Mr. Bentley justly complains—if a worse position be possible. And they are those worthies who are, these days, chiefly occupied in racking their ingenuities to give a new twist to a Shakespearean play. The one factor they deem totally irrelevant to their conceptions is what Shakespeare might have meant. With them novelty alone is the criterion of merit. The more far-fetched the invention, the more credit they think they earn. Yet it is a truth as old as Longinus that "ugly and parasitical growths arise in literature from a single cause, that pursuit of novelty," which even in his time was "the fashionable craze of the day."

During the Winter of 1949, for example, New York saw a brilliant piece of acting on the part of the Malvolio in an otherwise indifferent *Twelfth Night*. But however clever as an exhibition of the art of acting, it was not the Malvolio Shakespeare had created. After complimenting the actor sincerely on his skill in projecting *an* interpretation of the role, I mildly protested that in making Malvolio far too sympathetic he had created a character both at variance with the text and quite destructive of the comic effect of the Malvolio story; he exclaimed, "I'm delighted to hear you say that! I deliberately altered Malvolio to a well-meaning, kindly, if too fussy old dear. As the snob Shakespeare painted him, I found him unbearable."

Recently another well-known actor was telling me of his experiences on the road with *The Merchant of Venice*. Orthodox Jews, he informed me, conduct a service for the dead when one of their children marries out of his faith. Bent on innovation, my actor-friend introduced a scene of that kind to fill out the story of Jessica's elopement and "emphasize Shylock's piety"! He went further: acting Shylock himself, he thought up a wonderful new effect. When Shylock, crushed by the reversal of fortune, was about to make his final exit, the actor paused in the doorway and held out his arms to suggest crucifixion! I asked how successful the new ideas had proved. He answered without a glint of humor, "You know—I just couldn't put it across. Shakespeare stacked the cards too much against Shylock!"

In the 1957 season a prominent director had a new brainstorm. We were convinced that *Measure for Measure* was laid in Venice instead of in Vienna—after all, both cities begin with a V! Since the play is listed among the comedies, everyone was desperately funny. The audience dutifully laughed at Isabella, Angelo, and the Duke—

though, to be fair, only half-heartedly—although an unfunnier work than this acidulous play, which runs over with sublime and somber poetry, has never been written. Best of all, the sets (as they could never have been in Vienna or London) were made up of long strips of Venetian blinds, and the stage crew had the merriest time of anyone, effecting a change of scene by opening and shutting them with a fine snap. It was more like a carnival, of course, than the performance of a masterwork of dramatic satire. But few minded that: the production was "so original."

When it comes to presenting *Hamlet* it is possible that most actors and directors even feel obliged to introduce some novelties to justify the production. Take the case of Mr. Olivier's cinema version, where any number of innovations were introduced. I mention only one striking instance. In the last scene the Queen was made to seize the poisoned chalice with the deliberate purpose of committing suicide. The actress very well conveyed the idea that she knew the drink would prove fatal; she was warning her son by this act of self-sacrifice not to partake of the cup himself. In the play Shakespeare wrote (Mr. Olivier omitted much of it), the Queen is an unknowing victim when she drinks; moreover, such an act of sacrifice would have been impossible to Shakespeare's shallow Gertrude. The film's director, of course, might consider that objection quite beside the point. Certainly no critic saw fit to make the objection.

Apparently nothing is now of less moment than the author's conscious intentions. (In some quarters it is only the author's *unconscious* intentions that are respected. Naturally only the author is disqualified to have an opinion about *them*.) If innovation is to be the criterion of excellence, why need so able a man as Mr. Olivier have refrained from ingenuity? By this date, however, the most daring of all innovations would be to present *Hamlet* from the dramatist's point of view.

At the very outset of this study, then, we are confronted with a basic issue: what is the function of the interpreter? Self-expression has been exalted in our century, with the help of progressive education, to the degree that the vaporizing of an idiot is held (democratically) to merit as much attention as the sober reflections of an Aristotle. "Because," we are reminded, "everyone is entitled to his"

—one should say "their"—"opinion." The average reader would much rather tell you his reactions to *Hamlet* than study the play for what Shakespeare meant. The college student of our time apparently can hardly wait to finish the first chapter of a novel before flinging the book aside to "discuss" it with his friends. One pictures the lad in a dither as he turns to the first page, asking himself, "I wonder what I'm going to think about this!" He never will ask, "What is Flaubert trying to say to me?" but only, "What am I going to be saying about Flaubert?"

It is not out of keeping with the times, therefore, that public interpreters should rarely penetrate beyond their own feelings when they take upon themselves the performance of a masterpiece. It is a forgotten concept that an actor or a musician ought to be the humble servant of the creator's purposes. (Certain of the New Critics go so far as to maintain that the creator's purposes are irrelevant.) Since audiences will flock to see a popular star (these days, preferably a popular cinema star) in no matter how deplorable a play, or to hear a virtuoso in no matter how trivial a program, writers and composers tend to degenerate into mere handmaidens to the performer's personality. In recent years, when leading actors have murdered some of Shakespeare's best plays, it has been the pastime of dramatic critics to hold Shakespeare responsible for production failures. *Macbeth*, they have told us, is after all only a cheap melodrama—overlaid, it is true, with some good poetry; *Twelfth Night* is a hodgepodge of improbabilities wholly impossible to manage (*Death of a Salesman*, of course, is not!); *As You Like It*, a favorite butt, is unactable rot. How sad that the gifted Miss H., the talented Mr. E., the inspiring Miss C. should waste their incomparable abilities on dated rubbish! *

* Even so sensitive a critic as Mr. John Mason Brown could say of *Twelfth Night* that, although "thousands, fortunately, still delight in seeing the comedy," he himself "would feel more relief than grief" at the prospect of never seeing it again. Mr. Wolcott Gibbs behaved on the same occasion with elaborate condescension toward the play, and pretended to find *Twelfth Night* indistinguishable in plot and dramatis personae from *As You Like It*. Mr. Gibbs, one of the most brilliant and astute of critics when the subject was contemporary drama, was almost insufferable in parading his boredom with Shakespeare; he almost never

For any individual, on stage or in the audience, to exalt his own reactions above the creator's intentions is a strange kind of conceit. Surely Mr. Toscanini held his unrivaled place among conductors in our century because it was Haydn, Mozart, Beethoven, or Wagner he gave us—never Toscanini. It was clearly his ambition always to approximate the performance for which the composer himself would have wished. Mr. Stokowski in his day has drawn more thrilling sounds from the strings than Mr. Toscanini cared to evoke, and has been more exciting at certain moments of a composition. But the moment passed, and a self-respecting music lover could only be ashamed for having been gullible enough to be pleased even momentarily with such sensationalism, once he recovered his sense of proportion. An interpreter like Stokowski gives us himself rather than the composer. The actor, scholar, or critic surely owes it in all humility to Shakespeare to be the dramatist's Toscanini, not his Stokowski.

But where are the Toscaninis among Shakespearean directors and actors? Mr. Olivier proved himself one of the very greatest interpreters of our age with his magnificent impersonation of Oedipus years ago, and almost equalled that feat anew with his cinema version of *Henry V*. For these two performances alone he is entitled to profound respect and thanks. Alas! his effeminate Dane is far from

---

failed to commiserate with the actors who were trapped by the dullness of a Shakespearean vehicle. Sometimes the critics are downright offensive. When Mr. Robeson gave his handsome-looking and entirely meaningless performance of Othello, one rapturous reviewer praised him for rescuing the work from musty obscurity; "What was *Othello*," he cried, "before Robeson played it?" In truth that season it became impossible to utter a syllable on Miss Webster's production because everyone's social conscience seemed involved; not to have adored Mr. Robeson's Othello was tantamount to being enrolled in the Ku Klux Klan. Not being a snob, one would have been willing, though we were at war, to have had a German or a Japanese take the role if he made some attempt to be the Othello Shakespeare created. If Mr. Robeson had any idea at all of what he was doing, he seemed to think he was playing Uncle Tom. As for Shakespearean criticism in the metropolitan papers and monthlies, a study of it should prove rewarding to anyone nurturing both a love of Shakespeare and a bilious temper.

Shakespeare's Hamlet, and sadly distorts the plot of the play itself. Mr. Gielgud as director and actor gave us a work of perfection in *The Importance of Being Earnest;* in the movie of *Julius Caesar* his brilliant Cassius lifted the film out of ineptitude; in a minor role in the movie of *Richard III* his great acting made Mr. Olivier's appear merely extraordinarily clever: in 1959 his ebullient Benedick was Shakespeare's scintillating hero himself. Earlier he demonstrated himself to be a performer of the truest genius when he gave *Hamlet;* rarely has there been a display of such virtuosity on the stage. But his Hamlet was not admirable as an interpretation of *Shakespeare's* hero. In every scene Mr. Gielgud was thrilling; but there was no architecture to the play as he gave it. He would have been hard put to it to describe what manner of man his Hamlet was when all the hero's conduct was taken into account. Mr. Gielgud, in short, was Shakespeare's Stokowski, not his Toscanini.*

In this matter of indifference to the creator's purposes, the theatrical designers are as great sinners as the actors. A celebrated designer dismissed objections to his gloomy sets for Macbeth's castle as irrelevant. Shakespeare makes it quite clear that the castle is pleasant and inviting. Granting that the sets were impressive in themselves and might have served superbly for *Dracula*, I objected that they belied the dramatist's express descriptions. The artist, however, affirmed his right to ignore the playwright's demands and follow his own imagination. It did not concern him that it must be highly ludicrous to hear Duncan exclaim:

> This castle hath a pleasant seat; the air
> Nimbly and sweetly recommends itself
> Unto our gentle senses

as the King looks up to an edifice so terrifying that anyone normally constituted would have chanced the dangers of a savage forest rather

---

* Nevertheless, Miss Margaret Webster, Mr. Robeson's director, can say: "There is not one 'right' Hamlet with all the others wrong!" [5] She insists that Shakespeare would never have pinned his actors down to any given interpretation; to stipulate one, she says, would be asking not for acting but for "a system of mathematics." These fashionable (if odd, for a director) opinions are expressed in a volume entitled *Shakespeare Without Tears*!

than spend a night in so murderous-looking a dungeon. Was not the effect Shakespeare planned far subtler than obvious Gothic horror? Later Mr. Orson Welles presented Macbeth's dwelling as a subterranean cave, chill and damp from the constant trickling of water down the overhanging rocks! But the bearskins and Valkyrie helmets of the cast must have been sufficient protection against influenza!

Already, because of the popularity and frequent revivals of Mr. Olivier's movie, every semester I find myself having to disabuse my students, who are uniformly convinced that Gertrude's drinking of the potion in the last scene is suicidal in intent. Who can calculate the wrong ideas which irresponsible direction and acting instill in the public concerning these plays? Among the cardinal matters in *Hamlet* to be understood correctly, there is one concerning which I for years cherished the wrong conviction. A remarkably exciting performance of Gertrude, witnessed in my student days, was responsible for completely detouring me from the true path of the tragedy's plot. The actress had powerfully conveyed the notion that the Queen had been a partner in the murder of her first husband; her guilty looks lingered so many years in my memory that they long delayed my understanding that Gertrude is completely unaware that Hamlet's father met his death through murder. When I came to know the actress personally years later and jestingly spoke of her error, she said (with the tongue of actors!), "My dear, I hadn't the slightest idea of *what* I was trying to project. I make it a rule to look as though I *did* understand what I am doing. Actually, my chief worry was that, although I was *years* younger than the woman playing Ophelia, they had insisted on a make-up for me that added decades to my appearance!"

In our times there has been a more disturbing tendency to introduce into the plays overtones, not only un-Shakespearean, but thoroughly nasty as well. During the "Get thee to a nunnery" speeches in his uncut *Hamlet*, Mr. Evans encircled Ophelia in a passionate embrace while he hoarsely whispered the lines between kisses on her neck—thus suggesting elements of pathology overlooked even by the doctors. In a movie presenting a sequence from the last scene of *Othello*, Mr. Ronald Colman, enacting the Moor, was seen kissing Desdemona most tenderly and with much passion while he choked the life out of her. Just what violence these highly original ideas work upon Shakespeare's tragic conceptions, no one seems to have questioned. Is a tradition in the process of being originated to transform Shakespeare's tragic figures into the likenesses of inmates escaped from a psychopathic ward?

The Freudians, of course, have been busy with Shakespeare.* We need not now deal with their observations on *Hamlet.* But it may here be remarked that ever since Freud discovered an Oedipus complex in the Prince, the scene in Gertrude's chamber has been presented in a fashion to make one squirm. To this revolting procedure more than one reputed scholar has given his benediction.

When stage performances thus follow the lead of "authorita-

* Why not? After all, they think, the artist and the neurotic are cut from the same piece of cloth: "The neurotic is an artist become effeminate, and the artist, a neurotic who has become more manly" 6—including, no doubt, Emily Dickinson, Elizabeth Barrett Browning, Christina Rossetti, Edna St. Vincent Millay, and Willa Cather! The noted analyst Brill avers that all poets remain "on a pregenital level," since poetry is an oral outlet because it is but "a chewing and sucking of nice words and phrases" (poetry, obviously, is never concerned with ideas); and even when a few poets do "progress to the genital state of development," they "nevertheless show the result of fixation in the oral, urethral and anal-sadistic stages of the libido development." 7 (How lucky are the stars of the average citizen, who escapes the horrors attendant on the composition of poetry!) Freud himself, eloquent on *Hamlet,* did not neglect the other plays. *Macbeth,* for instance, is basically a study of contrasts between sterility (Macbeth had no children) and fecundity (Banquo had a son).8 Later psychoanalysts are more beguiling. Samples: "Shakespeare's women are his mother—Gertrude, Lady Macbeth, Desdemona, Juliet, the Shrew." 9 (What a composite portrait!) Desdemona is an almost masculine woman, as shown in Othello's greeting her as "O my fair warrior!" (no humor allowed!); she is a good example of "female penis envy . . . the regret of the female child that she does not have a sex organ equal to that of the boy. . . . No analyst will fail to recognize a typical expression of this penis envy in the behavior and the words of Desdemona as Othello reports them: *Still the house affairs would draw her,* etc. Desdemona's penis envy is expressed not only in her wish to be a man as brave and noble as Othello, but also in the fact that she *takes the scarcely concealed initiative in the courting*" 10 !!!

tive" commentators, it is difficult to quarrel with the good intentions of the director. Theoretically it is the business of the scholars to light the path for Shakespearean performers. Alas, in practice scholarly vagaries often lead performances into quagmires. A dreadful example may be found in what has happened as a result of a proposal of Professor J. Dover Wilson, acknowledged as legislator in matters Shakespearean. For no very good reason, Wilson found the *Get thee to a nunnery* scene as printed in editions of *Hamlet* up to 1935 utterly puzzling.[11] In a book that has since been taken as Gospel, he makes an absurd suggestion which nearly all directors of *Hamlet* have adopted, to the further confusion of matters.

It will be remembered that in the second scene of Act II, Polonius assures the King and Queen that he has made a great discovery: Ophelia's rejection of Hamlet's love has been responsible for the Prince's strange conduct, and Hamlet, repulsed,

> Fell into a sadness, then into a fast,
> Then to a watch,* thence to a weakness,
> Thence to a lightness, and, by this declension,
> Into the madness whereon now he raves.

Polonius goes on to offer to prove his theory. While Hamlet is walking there in the lobby some time soon, he can arrange to "loose" Ophelia to the Prince; Polonius and the King, meanwhile, can hide behind the tapestry and listen to the conversation.

Professor Wilson insists that, in order to explain Hamlet's later treatment of Ophelia, the Prince must overhear this little plot. Just before the lines in question (II, ii, 162-4), therefore, he inserts a new stage direction:

> Hamlet, disorderly attired and reading a book, enters the lobby by the door at the back; he hears voices from the chamber and pauses beside one of the curtains, unobserved.[12]

It should be added that Professor Wilson regards this not as a new stage direction but as the "restoration" of a lost one.

Gielgud immediately availed himself of this new piece of busi-

* sleeplessness.

ness in his presentation of *Hamlet* and, since the Gielgud production, most directors have followed suit, so that it is highly probable that most playgoers now think that this "overhearing" by Hamlet of Polonius' plan was Shakespeare's own intention.

This is not the place to go into the gratuitousness of Professor Wilson's "restoration," or into how hopelessly confusing it renders the scene it intended to clarify—Hamlet's interview with Ophelia. Mr. Gielgud's own experience of Hamlet's "overhearing" is eloquent of the fatuity of the device. "I do not think it clarified the meaning sufficiently to warrant the trouble we took with it at rehearsals," he says. ". . . I was continually struck with the feeling when playing this scene that if Shakespeare had meant Hamlet to overhear something, he would surely have made it clear in the text [i. e., other than in a—'restored'—stage direction]. The play has much spying in it . . . but in each case it is Hamlet who is spied upon. I think it unlikely that Shakespeare would weaken this characteristic feature of his play by making Hamlet spy on, or overhear, any other character before the more important point of his enemies' spying on him had been definitely registered with the audience." [13] Everything Mr. Gielgud says here is sound, though the failure of his experiment seems unknown to his successors. Hamlet's enemies spy upon him; if Hamlet were also to "overhear" them, eavesdropping would become a tendency in the play, and a note of the ludicrous would thereby inevitably intrude upon the tragic mood. Esthetically Professor Wilson's "restoration" is indefensible, for it makes Hamlet's eavesdropping *accidental*—unlike the spying to which he is subjected. Noble tragedies (see Chapter II) do not rely upon such accidents for serious consequences. Here such a one would be a cheap trick, especially if it could furnish, as Professor Wilson says it does, "the mainspring of the events that follow." [14] *

This case is but one of many in which Shakespearean scholar-

---

* Such tricks are acceptable in comedy—Shakespeare uses them deliciously in *Much Ado About Nothing*. There is, of course, an "overhearing" scene in *Othello*, but there the Moor *agrees* to eavesdrop on Cassio and Iago; it is by plan, not accident. Moreover, Othello "discovers" nothing from what he hears; his mind is already poisoned, and the conversation to which he listens only confirms what he already believes.

ship has operated in the direction of distorting Shakespeare's meaning.

If, then, I wish to sponsor publicly a theory of *Hamlet*, it is only out of a profound conviction that the theory describes what Shakespeare intended the play to mean. Could I not anticipate his approval of this book when we meet in the Elysian Fields, so far as I can safely anticipate anything, I would destroy it before it ever saw the light of publication.

This view of *Hamlet* has been tested by the challenge of many generations of alert students in my classes. At the beginning I was worried enough at having to teach a *Hamlet* like no one else's, and was conscious of how silly that must appear in a young man. It fell immediately to my lot to teach Shakespeare every semester, summers included (until teachers' salaries were a little improved), from that time on. And every semester the experimental method only validated and fortified and made more real the meaning which had revealed itself. After a while it became clear that this interpretation of *Hamlet* must be for me the correct one. Three decades have elapsed since that first experiment, and while I have been able to add details and to deepen immeasureably the dimensions of the play in my understanding, I have found no reason to alter the original conception in its larger outlines. Indeed, it has become firmer with the years. In a whimsical mood, Alfred Drake, one of my old pupils and now a bright star on Broadway, once complained that he had to pass up a chance to do *Hamlet* in New York because he could never do any *Hamlet* other than the one he studied with me, and despaired of convincing any director to try it. In his dressing rooms all over the country he has been converting a generation of young actors, and they have succumbed. During a recent run of *Kismet* for several seasons, many in the cast were instructed by him in a line-by-line reading of the play, and when Alfred went to London to re-create his great success in *Kismet*, he started converting young English actors in the company too.

I am no longer a young man, and no longer self-conscious about having a totally new view of *Hamlet*. It is time, therefore, for me to go to print. I feel that this new-old *Hamlet* of Shakespeare's is a far more stirring and exalted play than the stage in my time has seen. I shall never cease to admire the genius of Mr. Gielgud or of the late John Barrymore in their performances; acting could not be more admirable than was theirs—but it was not Shakespeare's *Hamlet* they gave us. The play Shakespeare wrote is a far more important work than directors and commentators have depressed it into seeming to be.

There is yet another service I aspire to perform for the world's greatest poet. Is there anyone who does not admire Shakespeare? But, ah, how many do not love him, the most lovable of all the world's poets! It is a curious fact that two kinds of people know and love him: the simplest and most untutored folk everywhere, and the most cultivated. All over the world people who can barely read their native languages know and love Shakespeare; countless Italians who would not dare approach the Papa Dante they worship by name, are familiar with Shakespeare in Italian translation. Needless to say, the most refined tastes in literature can never be satisfied if he is excluded. But the vast majority of Shakespeare-idolators really love him not at all. What crimes the grammar schools and high schools have committed against him! How thoroughly the schoolma'ams have alienated all possible interest in the most rewarding of all writers! They speak of him as if he were a combination of *Self-Help* and *Poor Richard's Almanac*. (What will happen to the plays now that the comic books have been encouraged to aid the educational process, one shudders to think.) They debase the dramas into horrid little Sunday-school exercises: *King Lear* teaches one to be kind to one's father, and *Hamlet* to be true to one's self. One almost wishes for a dictator's fiat forbidding the teaching of Shakespeare below the college level. How is it possible to make comprehensible to immature minds the most adult writing ever penned? What high-school teacher, for example, could succeed in making a murderer credible as the hero of a tragedy for his students, even if he was unusual enough to know that Brutus is the central character in *Julius Caesar?* To make anything like a story out of the work for the youngsters it is common to transform Antony (sometimes Caesar) into the hero and Brutus into the villain; what happens to poor Cassius in the process is too painful to relate.

Yet, in more than thirty years of college teaching I have found that every young man and woman old enough to have observed a little of life can be depended upon to love Shakespeare once the plays are given a chance to speak for themselves. I have never taught a boy or girl who did not capitulate to Shakespeare's magic. It is the schoolma'ams who have been killing interest in him. It is their large group—they who have eyes and see not—which goes to the theater to see Shakespeare in the same spirit in which many go to church—not at all religiously, I mean, but out of a sense of duty to be performed. Shakespeare is not to be approached as a divinity, but as the human being who possessed the warmest humanity on record. He is not to be read as though he were an Immanuel Kant. He is better than that. He is the world's greatest poet and dramatist, and he knew more about human relationships than anyone who has ever written about them; and we can learn more about other people and ourselves through an understanding reading of him than we could gather in ten lifetimes of personal experience. But we must come to him with some experience to begin with; and, above all, unless we come with our humanity ready to be touched and exercised, it is better not to come to him at all.

I know of a simple man, a stockbroker in Wall Street, who has read very little. But some years ago he discovered Shakespeare. And in him he found compensation for all the catastrophic harassment of a life that has been peculiarly bitter. He carries around in his pocket a little black loose-leaf notebook into which he has carefully copied out his favorite passages. He lovingly weighs and tests a passage for months before it is admitted into his golden thesaurus. And he has confessed to me that he feels lost unless his little book is in his pocket, for he counts on it every day to nourish his spirit. I imagine that the "other service" I wish to perform with this volume will be understood when I say that I hope this study will make my broker-friend seem not at all odd but very wise.

Naturally, one apologizes profoundly for daring to believe that one understands *Hamlet* thoroughly. Really, once the dirty pail of water is emptied, the water in the well will prove quite clear. First, then, we must see how muddied the water actually is, in the chapter entitled *Confusion Worse Confounded*; after that, in *The Cloak of Night Plucked Off* we shall empty the muddied water a little at a time; thereafter we shall draw from Shakespeare's own clear well. Before we do any of this, however, since we seem these days to have forgotten the flavor of pure tragedy, we had better drink of its fresh springs, so that we may keep with us the taste of the waters we mean to carry home. This we do in the next chapter, *Melpomene*, where we shall dig through current misconceptions of tragedy and literary techniques, aided by the tool of many a sharp footnote, until our springs begin to bubble.

It is to the average well-read man and woman that the address is made, unhampered by the heavy load of Shakespearean commentary. I am anxious, inevitably, for the ear of the scholar as well; but of him I must ask the enormous task of forgetting what he thinks he knows until I have done with my case. And for the case—which is Shakespeare's, not mine—I ask indulgence if *Melpomene* is minded to quote the authority with which he may be all-too-familiar.

I shall not conceal from the reader of the following pages, however I may try, that *Hamlet* has come to be for me the most important work to be understood in the world of literature. It is certainly the richest and most profoundly rewarding creation of the human spirit. No one can read it understandingly without reaping endless personal benefits. I feel that the accumulation of scholarship on *Hamlet*, to shift my image, has effectively

enclosed with stone,
with double stone and triple

this treasure-hoard, and I conceive that my chief task must be to demolish these walls so that the treasure may be reached. I do my predecessors the credit of believing that they too were moved by a similar desire to reach to Shakespeare's play itself. I expect them to forgive me if I have used their arguments as implements of destruction. All weapons that can afford one entry through those impregnable ramparts I gladly seize.

REFERENCES IN CHAPTER I

1. T. S. Eliot, *The Sacred Wood* (London, 1920), p. 98.
2. M. Baring, *Sarah Bernhardt* (Hamburg, 1934), p. 133.
3. *Ibid.*
4. E. Bentley, *In Search of Theater* (New York, 1953), pp. 116, 117, 118, 120, 121.
5. M. Webster, *Shakespeare without Tears* (New York, 1942), p. 103.
6. I. Bergler, *The Writer and Psychoanalysis* (New York, 1954), p. 11.

7. A. A. Brill, "Poetry as an Oral Outlet" (in *Psychoanalytical Review*, XVIII, No. 4, Oct. 1931).

8. S. Freud, *Collected Papers* (London, 1924–5), Vol. IV, pp. 318–44.

9. D. E. Schneider, *The Psychoanalyst and the Artist* (New York, 1950), p. 266.

10. T. Reik, *The Secret Self* (New York, 1952), pp. 60–61.

11. J. D. Wilson, *What Happens in Hamlet* (New York, 1936), p. 103.

12. J. D. Wilson, *Hamlet* (Cambridge, England, 1936), p. 43.

13. R. Gilder, *John Gielgud's Hamlet* (New York, 1937), pp. 51–52.

14. Wilson, *What Happens in Hamlet*, p. 108.

SOME INNATE IMPULSE TO . . . NOT LET HUMAN DIGNITY
DOWN AT A PINCH KEPT HIM RESOLVED TO HOLD ON.

C. E. Montague, *Action*

II Melpomene: the Nature of Tragedy

A DISTASTE for all tragedy is sufficiently common among the vulgar. "Life is depressing enough," runs the platitude; "why go to the theater to be reminded of the fact? Give us Abbott and Costello or the Marx Brothers." Yet people of some sensitivity, while not necessarily eschewing low comedy, do find gratification in tragedy. They do not go to it to be depressed—that would be an idiotic exercise for anyone!—but because they find themselves, at the end of a good tragedy, emerging from the theater in a mood of chastened exaltation, a mood which makes life seem not less sad but more understandable and easier to bear—a mood which would be very difficult to define, had not Aristotle already so perfectly defined it.

Now, it is not implied that one who is enthralled by *Oedipus Tyrannus* could not delight in the antics of the Brothers Marx. The demands of the human spirit are—luckily for the arts!—extensive. No one who willingly suffers with Lear will therefore the less enjoy roaring at Falstaff's ribaldry another day. There is nothing anomalous in a man's being elevated by *Parsifal* on Good Friday and anticipating eagerly a performance of *The Bartered Bride* a week later.*

* Thus (*Patience*):
　　"DUKE. Tell me, Major, are you fond of toffee?

It is precisely because the tragic summons into play the most exalted capacities of the human spirit that it has been traditionally approached in a holy-day disposition.

We rightfully expect, the point is, from each of the multitudinous experiences available to us, the reward uniquely pertaining to it. The pleasures of a cool swim on a hot day defy analogy with the pleasures of a tennis match; those of champagne with those of a planked steak. We do not seek from painting what we receive from music. We no more expect to procure from Leonardo what we receive from Rubens than we expect to procure from the *Mass in B Minor* what we receive from *The Marriage of Figaro*.

If as a result of its peculiar resources no one of the arts can deliver the same meanings and comforts as another, and if because of the inevitable circumscriptions imposed by subject and technique no two works in the same art (or by the same artist) can convey identical meanings, it is none the less true that the comic spirit and the tragic spirit have each its own qualifications, and these cut across the limits of the various arts. Plainly, there were affinities of purpose in the creation of *Much Ado About Nothing*, the Overture to *The Barber of Seville*, the *Would-Be Gentleman*, certain paintings of Hogarth and Breughel and Teniers, *Vanity Fair*, some of Beethoven's *Scherzi*, and *The Importance of Being Earnest*. The affinities are perhaps even stronger in *King Lear*, Beethoven's *Eroica*, *Paradise Lost*, the paintings on the ceiling of the Sistine Chapel, Miss Cather's *A Lost Lady*, and the *Saint Matthew Passion*.

MAJOR. Very!

COLONEL. We are all fond of toffee.

ALL (the Dragoons). We are!

DUKE. Yes, and toffee in moderation is a capital thing. But to *live* on toffee—toffee for breakfast, toffee for dinner, toffee for tea—to have it supposed that you care for nothing *but* toffee, and that you would consider yourself insulted if anything but toffee were offered to you —how would you like that?

COLONEL. I can quite believe that under those circumstances, even toffee would become monotonous." [1]

For "toffee," read tragedy, melodrama, satire, comedy (high or low) or farce.

That is, we anticipate from the tragic, whatever the art or particular work, a characteristic response. If we miss this response, we have been cheated of our due. Dreiser could call his novel *An American Tragedy*, Mr. Miller could present *Death of a Salesman* as a new kind of tragedy, Mr. Inge's *Come Back, Little Sheba* may have been hailed as a stirring tragedy—but moving though they may be, sincere as they unquestionably are, saddening or depressing as they have been found, tragedies they are not. For they do not fulfill the high function of tragedy, which, as Aristotle understood, is to provide for us "through pity and fear" the "proper purgation of these emotions."

It is to be hoped that no one will deem it stranger that Aristotle, because he lived twenty-three hundred years ago, could have precisely stated for all times * the purpose of tragedy than that Archimedes should not much later have discovered, as the world acknowledges he did discover, the fundamentals of hydromechanics on the famous occasion when he took a bath. Indeed, there is nothing at all odd in the fact that an "ancient" Greek should have understood the function of tragedy, when we remember how vital a part of civic life the witnessing of tragedy was to an Athenian.

Aristotle lived in an era peculiarly favorable, even for a man of his extraordinary sagacity, for the statement of eternal principles concerning tragedy. He was not in the position of that notorious German savant who wrote a disquisition on the elephant.† He did not

* One must defend oneself against the contemporary tendency to consider everything written before 1950 outdated. One is no longer astonished to find a pair of critics say of a masterful story and its author that he "died in 1928 but this story . . . is as vital as when it was written." [2] This in 1953! Accelerate this tempo a little and a man may expect his literary reputation "may outlive his life half a year."

† Though it can hardly be possible, there may be some fortunate who has not heard one of the many versions of this celebrated tale. If so, it seems only fair to deprive him herewith of that felicity: A number of eminent representatives of various cultures were asked to write a treatise on the elephant. The Englishman bade his man pack his traps, went off to Africa, lived with the elephant and hunted him; after six months he returned to England and wrote a book entitled *Elephant-Hunting in Africa*. The Frenchman went to the *Bibliothèque Nationale*, where he spent two

have to evolve the principles of tragedy or decide out of hand what they ought to be. He lived in the age immediately following the enormous dramatic productivity that had begun with Aeschylus and continued with Sophocles, Euripides, and their contemporaries, who had been providing the Athenian citizens with their yearly experience of spiritual purgation. All he had to do, therefore, was to ask himself: What are the basic attributes of tragedy as exhibited in the works of these masters? What, despite the wide differences of their approaches to tragedy, had they all understood tragedy to be? Aristotle had only, thus, to deduce from many masterworks (the vast majority of which have been lost to us) just what is the *sine qua non* of tragedy—and that he managed to perfection.

To begin with, Aristotle implies quite plainly what constituted the role of tragedy in the life of the Athenian citizen. Tragedy had had a long and important history as a rite connected with the worship of the god Dionysus; by the time of the Golden Age in Athens, when the plays of Aeschylus and Sophocles were presented in the Theater of Dionysus, and tragedy, as Aristotle says, had found at last its "natural form," its function was both religious and medicinal. It would be fair to say that the ceremony of attending the tragedies in Athens during the festival of Dionysus was the religious equivalent of the Hebraic-Christian practice of fasting on the Day of Atonement or during Lent. The citizenry of Athens came to the theater on those days to achieve *katharsis*, purgation. The Athenian way of achieving spiritual cleansing was, of course, basically opposed to the Hebraic-Christian. The latter involves self-condemnation, the acknowledgment of personal sin, the beating of the evil back into the breast; the Greek, letting the sin flow out of one's system, the getting rid of the evil by affording it a channel through which to depart. (It is difficult to refrain from the conviction that psychiatrists might have starved from lack of patients in those days!)

Doubtless in more primitive times this purgation was achieved

---

industrious years, after which he published a two-volume work, *bien documentée*, entitled *L'Éléphant et Ses Amours*. The Jew, naturally, wrote a treatise on *The Elephant and Zionism*. The German simply went home, asked his *frau* to make him a huge pot of black coffee, sat at the dining-room table, and there, the story concludes, *out of his inner consciousness* he evolved an elephant.

through the unlimited license then endorsed during the Dionysian revels. But by the time of Aeschylus such merely animal methods were no longer adequate, and tragedy provided the perfect vehicle for the rite of *katharsis*. Then the Athenian went to the theater to participate in the tragic deed of some noble hero or heroine (tragedy rises above even the difference of sex); as he watched and hearkened he *became* Oedipus or Clytemnestra or Creon or Electra or Eteocles —he suffered with each, he experienced heroic passions, he fell spiritually as each hero or heroine fell—yet he remained safe in body and secure from guilt in soul. He became blind vicariously with Oedipus, but still had his own eyes; he helped direct Orestes' sword with Electra but himself rested innocent of the worst of all crimes, a mother's murder.*

* If the modern skeptic finds it difficult to accept the possibility of a whole population's being as aesthetic-minded as we here imply, let him recall the incomparable architecture, the hundreds of great tragedies and sculptures produced under the patronage of these people. Let him remember that it was Aeschylus, the sublimest poet among the tragedians, and Sophocles, the sublimest dramatist, to whom this populace with its applause most often awarded the coveted prize. There is no way of accounting for it, but despite our own empirical knowledge of the shabbiness of popular taste, we cannot deny that in that age the Athenians were an astonishing people. (Though still among the most charming people in the world, one can no longer say the same for their taste. Paying lip-reverence to their classical culture, they are now much more interested in their dull Byzantine past. As for their apprehension of beauty—! One will find the Acropolis fairly clear of Greeks on most days; they are busy trotting visitors off to see and admire an atrocity decorating the grave of a maiden buried in their Cemetery Number One, the work of a modern sculptor, depicting the lady lying near death on her couch, the folds of the sheet being so realistic that they seem actually to have been used a week! Around this horror crowds are always to be seen gaping in astounded delight.) The story of Sophocles' trial could have been true nowhere else and in no other era. The ninety-year-old dramatist was sued by his son, in an attempt to break Sophocles' will in favor of his illegitimate son's family, on a charge of his being mentally incompetent. In answer, the great old man simply read in court a passage from the masterpiece on which he was then engaged, *Oedipus at Colonus*, the tribute to Colonus, his native town. The court was so much moved by the magnificence of the poetry that the case was dismissed at once, and Sophocles

And such must always be the function of tragedy. We all accumulate poisons from the inescapable frustrations of daily living; our disasters are wont (and for this we might offer thanks) to be only petty and mean; we are not allotted the scope for expending ourselves on noble issues; we do not experience grand catastrophes, and thus venoms overflow within us and quench the inner light. We come, then, to tragedy for purgation from our spiritual ills. By participating in a noble tragedy such as our life does not afford, but Hamlet or Lear or Oedipus do enact, we come away chastened and cleansed, better prepared to take up the burdens of the day.

To speak in this manner is to speak of the social import of literature with validity. In truth, it is only when the arts fulfill their aesthetic obligations that they *can* be socially useful. We once knew a cellist, member of a string quartet, who professed despair, as was fashionable in the late 'thirties, over his inability to coordinate his "social conscience" with his music. How, for instance, was he to make a *Razoumovsky Quartet* contributory to social progress? When we were beginning to tire of these impasses of his and of his masochistic cries of *mea culpa*, we were struck with the perfect solution for his dilemma—though he considered it merely flippant. "If you really want to help the progress of humanity," we offered, "why don't you learn to play the cello better than you do?"

There has been much nonsense written in the twentieth century by critics who have given their economic, sociological, psychoanalytical—and most absurd of all—"Marxist" interpretations of the arts. What they have had to say may or may not be a contribution to economics, sociology, psychoanalysis, or history—but it is worse than irrelevant to the arts, worse even than merely vulgar. Worse, for it has been responsible for innumerable acts of mayhem against the arts and artists alike. Aesthetically-minded people are more, not less, sensitive to calls upon their conscience from the sufferings of humanity. It is easy to distract them from the creative fields in which

---

carried home in honor to his dwelling. Where else could this have happened but in the Athens of his day?

Public taste, of course, has not at all times been at low ebb. It is well to remember that with the Elizabethan butcher, baker, and candlestick-maker, Shakespeare was the most popular playwright of the day.

they labor, with the reproof: "Is this a time to be concerned with such irrelevance as beauty?" That is a question which might just as appropriately have been asked of Dante, Watteau, or Brahms. For in what era have not suffering, carnage, and deprivation been abroad? Luckily for the world, such men have usually understood that there is sustenance man is always in need of, quite as much as of bread—sustenance they could endow us with only by cultivating unapologetically their best gifts. They have known that the riches they pour out for us must be for more than one era. It is not that one denies the possible value of making posters, marching songs, or bitter plays which will move men to picket for the thirty-hour week and higher wages. We all approve of decreased taxes, adequate defense, better sanitation, and municipal housing—and for such ends comedy and satire can agitate. Tragedy cannot. It does something more important. When high-minded creators, pushed to the wall by this class of critics, do less nobly than they could in order to propagandize against a social ill, let them consider whether the temporary disease they would cure is more pressing than that unceasing accumulation of spiritual frustrations that every man and every woman harbors within, and for which tragedy and the tragic spirit are the best anodynes. Even when we conquer the moon, as it seems we must, these frustrations will continue to require easement—in all probability, more than ever.

As for the various sociological interpretations of tragedies extant, how can such commentary illuminate or facilitate by a jot the experience for which tragedy is created? Of what avail is it to relate *Othello* to Shakespeare's economic status, personal marital experiences, social class, subconscious involvements? The purposes for which *Othello* exists are in no way affected by such knowledge; for, to begin with, and to end with, *Othello* fulfills the purposes of tragedy. It can therefore, for every man and every woman, purify the spirit, give insight into life, and bestow courage for the tensions of living. For these are the function of tragedy, and surely no nobler service is performed by any other kind of human activity. If this be error and upon us proved, we never writ nor no man ever suffered.

And these things it can do only by operating, as Aristotle observes, through the agency of the individual audience's emotions of pity and fear. Pity is self-explanatory. But what is this "fear," this *phobos?* The word used to be translated as "terror"; but nowadays "terror" is too much associated with sliding panels and disappearing staircases to be serviceable. This fear, which might perhaps be better rendered into modern English as "awe," is double: awe at man's insignificance in the face of the vast complexity, over which he can exercise no control, of God, Nature, and society—a complexity in the face of which he seems so puny and helpless; and awe, too, at the seed of divinity in man which, despite his very insignificance, prompts him to stand up against adversity, and will not allow him to bend his neck accommodatingly to the axe suspended over him.

A hero who is the victim of the forces operating upon him, who can be crushed by adversity, and who bows before the axe threatening him, may inspire pity but never fear. If Hamlet, however noble, were only the victim of the evil circumstances enmeshing him, and were discomfited by them to the extent that he could neither cope with nor combat them (this is perhaps the most popular of all misconceptions of his character), he would be no tragic hero, for he could inspire no awe, and hence would belong not in the glorious company of Oedipus, Lear, and Othello, but in that of Dickens' Little Nell. Mr. Butcher, although making an exception of Hamlet because he accepts the popular view of that hero's make-up, well says of the character of the tragic hero that it must have "in it some vital and spontaneous force which can make and mold circumstances. . . . It is of the battling, energetic type," and he agrees that "most" of Shakespeare's heroes are of this kind: "strong and dominant natures, they are of a militant quality of mind." [3]

Pity is not enough for the tragic sentiment—that is the error too many aspirants to tragic writing have not been at pains to circumvent. Pathos, which is easier to evoke than awe, does not by itself provide the tragic *katharsis;* unaccompanied by fear, it tends to depress, not cleanse. It is, moreover, but a step from mere pity for the victim to indignation against his oppressor; and when indignation intrudes powerfully the tragic sentiment is murdered. To be much inflamed against a villain, or society, or things in general—to be greatly indignant—is to be deprived of the curative effects upon the spirit of tragedy's purgation. There are occasions when we ought to be inflamed, no doubt—but they can never be the occasions when we can also be cleansed within. To say, as one must, that *An Ameri-*

can Tragedy and *Death of a Salesman* fall short of their pretensions is to question neither the power of their indictment nor their possible social usefulness; they simply do not rise to the dignity and unique function of tragedy. (Their authors' hopes that somehow these works might manage to encompass both indictment and tragedy have proved vain. The finished creation, like one's children, has a distressing way of being what it is, one's intentions notwithstanding!) The difficult task of combining tragedy and indictment depends for its success on a very delicate balance between these normally opposing elements. Ibsen, who rarely attempted pure tragedy, contrived this balance admirably in *Ghosts*. From this example alone it is possible to deduce that the secret lies in going no further than implication when one indicts in tragedy. In *Ghosts* our prime concern is neither with venereal disease nor the tyranny of the moral values of the past, but with the fall of Mrs. Alving, whose attempts to stand up against those specters are blasted by her own defects of character.

There is, let it be repeated, room for all kinds of expression, and a dramatist may prefer to write a play in the spirit of burning indignation or mockery or gentle raillery, but such a play is bent upon providing something more and a good deal less than the tragic *katharsis*. Ibsen and Chekhov have few peers among world dramatists, and there is no more reason why Ibsen should not have chosen to write *The Wild Duck* in a vein of ironic indictment or why Chekhov should not have chosen to write *The Cherry Orchard* in the comic spirit, than that Shakespeare, because he had written *Hamlet*, need have resisted penning the indignant arraignment of moral hypocrisy of *Measure for Measure*. This is not to charge these plays with artistic inadequacy; *The Wild Duck* is Ibsen at his greatest, *The Cherry Orchard* is beyond need of anyone's praise, and *Measure for Measure* for its poetry alone must ever be priceless. It is merely to remind one that none of them has been conceived in the vein of tragedy. Indeed, *Measure for Measure* and *The Wild Duck* are far more bitter than tragedy must ever attempt to be.

The merely pathetic, then, is not enough—not enough, that is, to solace the human spirit. Indeed, the pursuit of the merely pathetic is likely to skirt dangerously near the boundaries of the sentimental (i.e., false sentiment) and often falls over into it. The borderlines were not always clear, for instance, to so great an artist as Dickens. *Bleak House* is a great tragic novel if only because it contains Lady Dedlock; *The Old Curiosity Shop*, on the other hand, is vitiated into sentimentality because it contains Little Nell. It is related of Wilde that when someone asked him whether he had not been profoundly affected by the demise of Little Nell, he answered that a man must have a heart of stone who could read those pages without dying of laughter. Thus, mere pathos may have so little dignity as to defeat its own ends. Pity without fear cannot make for tragedy.

Now, as we have implied, the pity and fear required of us, the audience, are expressed chiefly during the course of our self-identification with the hero of a tragedy. As we attend the tragedy, *we* must be Lear, Electra, or Hamlet, so that at the conclusion we may feel that us the play

> with new acquist
> Of true experience from this great event
> With peace and consolation hath dismissed,
> And calm of mind, all passion spent.[4] *

This hero, as Aristotle knew, must have certain qualifications, or else this self-identification on the part of the audience cannot take place. He cannot be a completely "virtuous man brought from prosperity to adversity," for that would only excite indignation—or, as Aristotle puts it, "it merely shocks us." Nor can he be a "bad man

---

* These famous lines, perfectly expressing the audience's ideal reaction to the fall of a tragic hero (in this play, Samson), were dictated by one of the earliest of the moderns to understand truly the meaning of Aristotle's words. Indeed, Milton, in the Foreword to *Samson Agonistes*, strongly emphasizes the curative, the medicinal function of tragedy when he says of tragedy that it "hath been ever held the gravest, moralest, and most profitable of all other poems (i.e., forms of literary composition); therefore said by Aristotle to be of power by raising pity and fear, or terror, to purge the mind of those and such-like passions, that is to temper and reduce them to just measure with a kind of delight, stirred up by reading or seeing those passions well imitated. Nor is Nature wanting in her own effects to make good his assertion: for so in physic things of melancholic hue and quality are used against melancholy, sour against sour, salt to remove salt humors."

passing from adversity to prosperity," for that "possesses no single tragic quality"—we should be indignant here too, though for quite different reasons. Nor can he be an utter villain whose downfall we witness, for at that we should rejoice. The kind of hero with whom alone we can identify ourselves is one extreme in neither virtue nor vice, a man essentially good, whose misfortunes are brought about "by some error or frailty"—*hamartia*, as the Greek has it, the famous "tragic flaw" of literary parlance. "The single Greek word *hamartia*," as Mr. Lane Cooper reminds us, "lays emphasis upon the want of insight within the man, but is elastic enough to mean also the outward fault resulting from it." [5]

That is to say, the hero of a tragedy must be to a considerable extent the author of his own doom; he must fall because of some basic moral weakness. (Aristotle's word for "character" is *ethos*; as he sees it, character in tragedy means "moral constitution.") The hero of a tragedy, in other words, never falls only because of circumstances, Fate, or Destiny, but chiefly through some species of personal ethical blindness. No one can possibly identify himself with a man or woman who suffers catastrophe only through some accident. By definition an accident is a happening that cannot be anticipated, and must therefore necessarily be left out of account. An accident is an occurrence that can be explained by no ordinary human logic, in which we are accustomed to move from cause to effect. When a man suffers accident the cause is outside his control and we cannot put ourselves in his place. For these reasons, in a world of ever-recurring accidents we are all compelled to live as though they did not occur; if we were not, in dread of the unpredictable we should never dare to step out of our houses—indeed, should never dare move from a chair, which, moreover, would have to be discreetly placed well out of the possible descent of a chandelier.

There is no misconception more prevalent than the vulgar one which credits the classic Greek tragedies with exhibiting the remorseless operation of Fate. Many careless textbooks have perpetuated this untruth, and book reviewers are forever describing some modern work showing the agency of blind Destiny as being in that respect "like a Greek tragedy." Poor Oedipus is always being subpoenaed as an analogy for the hero of such a book. In point of fact, no tragic hero is more completely the author of his own doom than Oedipus; he builds his own funeral pyre log by log, impelled as he is by his *hamartia*, his tragic flaw—overweeningness, heedlessness, wilfulness.

Consider his actions, as they are revealed to us in the play. Raised by the king and queen of Corinth as their son, he was disturbed at a feast by a drunkard's slighting insinuations about his origins. Oedipus begged the King and Queen to reveal the facts of his birth, but their answers were so evasive that he journeyed to the oracle to learn the truth. But, characteristically, the oracle answered a question he had not asked, and it spoke of his murdering his father and committing incest with his mother. Horrified at these words, in order to escape such a fate Oedipus vowed never to return to Corinth. Although virtuous, Oedipus was however also an exceedingly heedless man. Since he had consulted the oracle only because he was unsure of his parentage, he could, if completely rational, also have taken care, to avoid the terrible future prophesied, never to kill any man old enough to be his father and never to mate with any woman clearly older than himself. Yet before long, refusing to clear the road for Laius' carriage, he slew his father in a fit of wrath; and soon thereafter he recklessly allowed himself to be wedded to the widowed Jocasta, his mother. It is beside the point that he did not know either to be his actual parents. He had been given sufficient warning for him to have avoided both deeds.* Read in any other light than through these facts, which are a part of Sophocles' play, *Oedipus Tyrannus* will never mean what its author intended or its original audiences understood. Oedipus a victim of Fate would not be a tragic Oedipus, only a pathetic one.†

* There is nowhere a more brilliant study of this play than in Professor H. D. F. Kitto's *Greek Tragedy* (2d edition, revised, London, 1950), pp. 135–41. He says, "Sophocles is not trying to make us feel that an inexorable destiny or a malignant god is guiding the events."

† The same sort of admonition must be made about *Romeo and Juliet*, a play almost universally misunderstood. The fault here is somewhat Shakespeare's. He was still near the beginning of his career, was writing his first good tragedy, and unsure of himself (as the verse's alternation between lyrical sublimity and fumbling fatuousness demonstrates). In this play he toyed with the idea of setting a prologue before each act, but apparently gave up after writing only two—which he

Since accidents do occur they are naturally represented in tragedy. They could hardly fail to be. For, in a manner of speaking, everything that happens to an individual, everything that occurs without his first having willed it, is an "accident," whether it be the unheralded appearance of a human being at one's threshold or the lateness of the morning train. But such accidents, whatever their consequences—and we are aware that the tardiness of a train may be but the first of a series of destructive events—in tragedy must be represented (if they contribute to the catastrophe) as cooperating with the hero's tragic flaw. For instance, the lateness of a train may contribute to tragic catastrophe if we feel it is our hero's characteristic fault that, knowing the undependability of the company's services, he made no provision for the contingency of lateness. Or, the sudden appearance of another human being at the threshold may contribute to our hero's fall if we feel that some aspect of their relationship is owing to a defect in our hero's character. In short, in a tragedy it is the hero's personal shortcoming which starts the rocks tumbling down the cliff; and accidents of time and place may convert the inconsequential falling of a few rocks into a destructive avalanche. Tragedy ever reminds us that each man lives in a world over which his control begins abruptly to cease in the area contiguous to the exterior side of his own skin. It *is* disastrously unlucky that Desdemona loses the handkerchief precisely when she does lose it: her handkerchief lost on any other day might have caused no trouble at all; on that particular day Othello because of his tragic flaw has already allowed his mind to be poisoned against her. But, on the other hand, were Othello other than he is and she other than she is, no catastrophe need have ensued because of that loss. It *is* disas-

---

would have done wisely to remove; they are of no consequence to the tragedy. Unhappily the first prologue speaks of Romeo and Juliet as "a pair of star-crossed lovers," and the phrase has been taken up by criticism without regard to the transactions of the plot. It is a far better play than the words imply. If the love of Romeo and Juliet were crossed only by their evil stars, they would be merely victims of circumstances, not tragic figures, as they are. They would be two well-meaning weaklings with whom we cannot possibly identify ourselves. As it is, the work clearly exhibits them falling as a result of the tragic flaw they both share —heedlessness.

trously unlucky for Macbeth (and for Duncan too!) as well as for Lady Macbeth that the King comes to stay at their castle on that of all nights: on any other occasion Macbeth might not have been steeled for the bloody deed; on that night he was prepared to murder. On the other hand, people do accept the hospitality of those whom they have benefited, arise without a gash the next morning, hale and hearty, and leave their hosts in no danger of the electric chair. In tragedy, the hero's tragic flaw sows a wind that reaps the whirlwind.

The classic tragic flaw, the *hamartia* exhibited by the heroes and heroines of Greek tragedy, is some species of rashness, or as Mr. Butcher tentatively states it, an "error of judgment arising from a hasty or careless view of the special case; an error which in some degree is morally culpable, as it might have been avoided." [6] For us "overweeningness" or "heedlessness" is the most satisfactory designation in our language for the rashness found in the classic tragic hero.* Tragedy reminds us, because of the fatal overweeningness of the hero, of the necessity of remaining modest before the gods. We must never for a minute forget, no matter how favorable appearances may be to us, that we can hardly manage ourselves, much less the rest of the world. The tragic hero is a man whom we admire, often love, but who at a crucial moment—even as you and I

* Mr. Butcher would probably not be quite satisfied with either word. He knows that Sophocles' *Oedipus Tyrannus* was in Aristotle's judgment the ideal tragedy,[7] and therefore feels that any description of *hamartia* must be one to account for the hero of that play—a view in which we heartily concur. But, incredibly enough, this great scholar actually can say of Oedipus: "His character was not the determining factor in his fortunes. He, if any man, was in a genuine sense the victim of circumstances." [8] Hence, Professor Butcher decides that the meaning of *hamartia* cannot be, after all, limited to "either a defect of character or a single passionate or inconsiderate act," [9] and must include the possibility of an error for which the hero is not responsible.[10] Thus the door is opened to mere accident as the cause of the tragic catastrophe, and hence to the banishing of all possible self-identification with the hero. The conception of *Oedipus Tyrannus* earlier discussed in this chapter brings the play into uniformity with the rest of Greek tragic drama, as it unquestionably must have been for Aristotle, who admired it above all other tragedies.

—forgets discretion, has the illusion that he can manipulate a course of events just because he chooses to view them a certain way. Oedipus is brave, fearless, and generous, but he is utterly reckless about his own conduct; because he *intends* to avoid the crimes predicted by the oracle, he feels foolishly safe and takes insufficient precautions to prevent their commission. The oracle is no more responsible for the crimes he commits than the three witches are for Macbeth's murdering Duncan. Oracle and witches are simply the voice of the vast complex of affairs, full of pitfalls for all of us, the voice that warns us to moderate our wilfulness and live with intelligence. Catastrophic for us if we feel so superior to the world's chances that we disregard the warning or prefer to interpret it as a signal to plunge ahead wherever our will would lead us! Indeed, as the truth narrows inch by inch closer to Oedipus, we see him questioning himself less than ever; rather, that characteristic overweeningness of his makes him turn against Creon, who only wishes him well, and against sightless Tiresias, whose only guilt is that he sees the truth to which Oedipus (though in possession of his eyes) blinds himself. For all his qualities, Oedipus is a stubborn man who cannot be prevented from destroying his own peace. Such a man is Lear, who out of similar stubbornness turns against Cordelia and Kent, who love him most, just because they speak truth too bluntly to be palatable to his bad temper. Such an overweening man is Othello; pure of soul, if ever man was, lofty in principle, courageous, wholly unselfish and unassuming, he yet permits himself to forget all he has reason to know his wife to be ("My life upon her faith!"),[11] and, having lost his judgment, allows his overwrought emotions to lead him to disaster. This overweeningness destroys Romeo and Juliet; we are not disposed to hold it against them when first love precipitates them into recklessness, as we cannot hold it against Lear, Othello, and Oedipus that they are overweening, for these are beings who evoke our affection, not our censure; but we are forced to recognize, if we understand Shakespeare's play correctly, that had Romeo and Juliet taken a few pains to conciliate their families, who were all too ready to make peace, their love might have ended happily.

It is interesting to observe that we can identify ourselves only with men and women who have such flaws, and not at all with a flawless character. It is not only because we know privately how imperfect we are. It is rather because a flawless man, if he suffers catastrophe, having no error that can bring about his doom, can fall only through forces external to himself, i.e., by accident or Fate. As graphic illustration we may consult the difference in our feelings about the deaths of Paris and Romeo in the same play. Romeo is far from perfect. Before he meets Juliet, he is obviously insincere, a mooncalf in love with love, affected—is saved from being a bore, indeed, only because his faults are so common to youth. Paris, on the other hand, is an entirely attractive character, and remains so throughout the play. A lesser artist, since our sympathies are to be with Romeo, would have made a rival lover something of a villain. But Shakespeare has strengthened the pathos by making us feel that, barring the fact that she does not love him, Juliet might do much worse than marry Paris. His love for her is beyond question; he is respectful to Capulet; he is forbearing at Friar Lawrence's cell when Juliet is almost rude to him, and answers her curtness with gentlest affection; he is overwhelmed with grief at the news of her supposed death; and the depth of his affections is to be gauged by his quietly going to pay his obsequies with perfumed water, flowers, and devotion when she has been entombed, and vowing to continue these services to her memory nightly thereafter. He is killed only because he wishes to protect the sanctity of the dead from what he conceives to be the vengeance of a Montague. He is innocent of a single unpleasant trait or deed. He knows of no marriage between the lovers, is even unaware they have met. He is a person entirely sinned against, a fact untrue of Romeo. And yet we cannot identify ourselves with Paris because, entirely admirable though he is, he is only a victim of circumstance. While with Romeo, who is less ideal than Paris, we can identify ourselves because he is the author of his own doom, because he possesses a tragic flaw. This paradox is quite characteristic of true tragedy.

There are other qualifications for the tragic hero besides this *hamartia*. Though most of the subjects of Greek tragedy were taken from the treasuries of mythology, Aristotle wisely observes that tragedy need not confine itself to traditional stories. But, because of the plays he knew, he suggested that the tragic hero should be one "highly renowned and prosperous." This dictum was perverted during the English Restoration to mean only high social rank, and in that distorted garb fathered many a dull so-called Heroic Tragedy in which the hero owned no distinction beyond his being a prince and nourishing a propensity toward pompous oratory—a man unable to arouse any sympathy. A man of social eminence with the soul of a mouse cannot be tragic. No one is a candidate for tragedy just because his name appears in the *Almanac de Gotha* or the *Social Register*—a fact no one there listed will deplore. The heroes "highly renowned and prosperous" of Greek lore were, of course, men and women of position, but they were renowned even more for their personal accomplishments and qualities. We must, therefore, in consequence of literary experience since then, modify Aristotle's suggestion to include men and women, whatever their rank in society, who are *above the average in personal qualities*. Thomas Hardy's Jude, though of humblest origin, is a true tragic hero by power of his unconquerable thirst for learning and a larger life, the unyielding search for which raises him above his fellows. Social position is not a basic requirement for a tragic hero; what is essential is an internal quality which sets him apart from the herd— which makes him, in short, not bend his head to the axe, as the average man will do. The same spiritual superiority of his heroes in Conrad's novels rates these stories among the noblest tragic works in fiction, perhaps the best in English in the last three-quarters of a century—those simple, sometimes even rough, souls who when adverse fortune corners them prefer to go down to disaster rather than part with a few rags of personal honor, all they have to cover themselves with in their dolorous pass. The death of these men is a loss to the world; the world is poorer for their falling from its ranks. So, while Jude and Lord Jim are tragic characters, Dreiser's Clyde Griffiths and Mr. Miller's Salesman are not, because, though we pity them, their fall involves no loss to humanity, no awe. With the tragic hero something more than himself goes down to defeat.

For this reason we may add that a hero with inner qualities above the average is likely to be a more impressive one if he comes from an important place in society. Such a man involves the destinies of more lives than his own. A tragic hero of rank carries along with him to ruin more than can a man from humbler walks of life. The death of Abraham Lincoln, for example, was a greater tragic fact (for North and South) than the death of any Union or Confederate soldier. Milton had in Samson the perfect symbol for the tragic hero, who when he brings the edifice down upon his own head also causes general ruin. A hero of lofty place is also more tragic because he falls from a greater height; a fall from ten stories is bound to be more catastrophic than one from a doorstep. The fall of an eagle weighs more with us than the fall of a sparrow. As the Gentleman says of Lear:

> A sight most pitiful in the meanest wretch,
> Past speaking of in a king! [12]

Shakespeare's tragic heroes all satisfy both requirements. They are all men and women superior to the average; and Lear is a king, Macbeth becomes one, Cleopatra is a queen, Hamlet is a prince, Coriolanus and Othello are the very props of the state, Brutus is the cause of civil war, and Romeo and Juliet are the offspring of Verona's two leading families. These two attributes will also be found in the tragic figures who stand close to the central character in importance: Cassius is second only by personal choice to Brutus, Desdemona is the daughter of a leading senator, Lady Macbeth becomes a queen, Cordelia is first a princess and then a queen, and Antony (of *Antony and Cleopatra*) is one of the twin pillars sustaining the world.

Now, since self-identification on the part of the audience with the hero is the root of the cathartic experience in tragedy, how, it may be asked, is one to identify oneself with a man who, unlike ourselves, is above the average? The naturalists * since Zola have indeed maintained that it is with the average man that audiences can more readily identify. Isn't he more like ourselves than General Othello, Prince Hamlet, or King Lear? Isn't his very mediocrity closer to our own experience? Zola, Dreiser, James T. Farrell, Arthur Miller (we exempt the hero of his fine tragedy, *A View from the Bridge*),

---

* We employ the term despite the objections of some current practitioners of naturalism to being designated otherwise than as realists. They consider "naturalism" an insult. But some word is surely called for to distinguish the method of a Flaubert from that of a Zola, that of a Willa Cather from that of a Dreiser.

William Inge, and their peers have valiantly labored to keep their heroes within the dimensions of averageness and mediocrity. Not only their heroes but their heroes' experiences are run-of-the-mill, within the petty scope of our own everyday experiences. On the face of it, logic would seem to indicate that you and I can more easily be the Salesman or Clyde Griffiths than Prince Hamlet or King Lear. But this is not actually the case, for at least two reasons, one psychological, the other aesthetic.

For a very human cause, no individual can identify himself with an average man as hero. What normal human being ever thinks of himself as average? We may know that the trivialities of our own lives will not bear objective representation; modesty, for instance, bids us remember that the occasion on which we missed a step and sprained an ankle could be a dramatic one only to ourselves. But just the same we are all aware of stately potentialities for tragedy, all kinds of noble capacities which the world ignores in us but to which, given the opportunity, we would rise. What unattractive woman but sees in the mirror somewhere in her face a hint of beauty? What cringing coward but knows that when the right moment strikes he will seize occasion? We are all endowed with "one grace, one wonder at the least," which saves us from undifferentiating submergence in the sea of the general. To ourselves none of us is mediocre. And hence, those convincingly average people created by the naturalists we view with an almost impersonal kind of sympathy. Those men and women are pathetic, perhaps—but they cannot be ourselves because they lack our dimensions, our potentialities. As for the sub-average creations of Mr. Steinbeck and Mr. Erskine Caldwell, there is, of course, no possibility of our identification with them, and they loom most real when they figure comically, as they do, for instance, in *Tobacco Road*.

Another reason why we cannot identify ourselves with the hero of the naturalists proceeds from aesthetic considerations. As we have observed, a completed creation, just because it has its own entity, takes on a life of its own, always something in excess of its author's intentions. The distinction between realism and naturalism is that the realist *selects* his materials from everyday reality while the naturalist, traditionally concerned with the representation of average people, studiously presents quasi-scientifically the sense of *all* the facts of everyday reality. Thus the naturalist achieves his reality by surrounding his characters with a thousand little details of everyday experience. We see from which side of the bed our hero rises, so to speak, observe the tone of the water after he has made his ablutions, note the brand of toothpaste he uses, and so on— these facts being important for our comprehension of his life. This is that spirit of scientific documentation which Zola called for and which his followers have strictly adhered to. Yet, strangely enough, our familiarity with the persons of these stories, as the work makes its leisurely way to its conclusion, grows more and more remote, and the figures become less and less realizable. Only the details take on vividness, not the people connected with them. That is why the *Iliad* is a greater book than *For Whom the Bell Tolls*, despite its paraphernalia of gods, goddesses, and antique warfare. Priam pleading for his son's remains voices the grief of all stricken men in time of loss, and Hector taking leave of his wife speaks with the tongue of all men saying farewell. In Mr. Hemingway's novel there is no single occurrence of such moving universality; the events of his story belong to our day, his gods are our gods, and his warfare our warfare, but from his characters we stand, however well-wishing, aloof; they end by being little more than names to us.

It is the persons with whom we identify ourselves; we can identify ourselves with any happenings only if we can identify ourselves with the person to whom they occur. It matters not whether there are ghosts or witches in the world; what does matter is how Hamlet and Macbeth behave (that is, how *we* behave) in encountering them. It is beside the point to ask whether any girl is likely to procure the perfect husband by his correct choice among three caskets; what is to the point is that Shakespeare makes that experience entirely real because Portia and Bassanio are real. Now, the reader of the naturalistic novel, while the details are accumulating *en masse*, is by degrees being further and further cut off from self-identification. *An American Tragedy* is utterly successful in depicting a thoroughly average young man, raised in an average environment in a particular part of the West, going to work in a particular Midwestern city and having characteristic experiences of average boys in such an employment, getting into the difficulties in which average boys entangle themselves, escaping to an average community in a particular part of New

York State, and there falling into a pattern leading to disaster. I accept the picture * but it means little to me personally because the accent has been placed upon his environment, and I have lived in totally different environments. None of the experiences of Clyde's youth and adolescence were mine; I knew no such parents, no such teachers, had no fellow bellhops, never associated with factory girls, never nursed as a glamorous ideal canoeing on the lake with small-town "aristocracy" or playing bridge with them. That is, I do not associate myself with the man of whom I must remember that he gets up on the left side of the bed and uses toothpaste X, when I myself get up on the right side of the bed and use toothpowder Y. The very precision of the details excludes me.

Now, realism as practised by Jane Austen, Balzac, Tolstoi, Flaubert, Dickens (at his best), Thackeray, Meredith, Hardy, Henry James, Miss Cather, and Mr. Faulkner (among others) avoids this dehumanizing process. The very act of selection, though the material is taken from everyday experience, by omitting these particularizing details tends to elevate the characters above the realm of the average, makes them lifelike but larger than life—as they ought to be—places them with the universal rather than the commonplace; and, as Aristotle observes, it is the business of the literary creator to "express the universal." Without respect to tragedy, it will be seen that the characters created by Ibsen and Chekhov, both realists, are not

* But I reject its indictment of American justice. Dreiser is outraged that, though Clyde did not murder Roberta but only (wanting her dead) *allowed* her to drown when he could have saved her, his hero should have capital punishment visited upon him. A monumental second volume is devoted to retracing the events of the story as a powerful arraignment of the law. But it makes little difference that Clyde is technically innocent; he surely is as morally culpable of a death he could easily have prevented as if his hand had pushed Roberta under the waters. His excuse, the excuse of mediocrity, that he just did not save her but certainly did not actually kill her, alienates us from sympathy, and we cannot share Dreiser's indignation at the miscarriage of justice. The real failure of this novel is demonstrated by the fact that Roberta, in despite of the author, manages to be something of a tragic figure because of the quality of her love for Clyde. Her rising to tragedy disqualifies him as a tragic figure. If we identify with her, we must take sides against him.

deluged by minuteness of detail; their figures are universal. Emma Bovary emerges not as a commonplace woman but as a woman whose tragic failing is common to all women; Flaubert's severe selectivity in recording her life has made her universal; as a result we recognize in Emma's disaster that any woman who allows the characteristically feminine dissatisfaction with the attainable to have free rein will plunge herself and all connected with her into misery. Much the same may be said of Anna Karenina and Miss Cather's Lost Lady, both creations of superb realists. With these women all men and women can identify themselves, for they are not typed but universal. The great persons of literary creation are both entirely themselves and at the same time so deeply rooted in our common humanity that they are we too.

From our vantage point the old quarrel between romanticism and realism has no meaning. "The Poet is not an Historian," says Aristotle. It is the business of the historian to record what has actually happened, the particular event; it is that of the man of letters to deal with what "in a given situation might well happen—a sequence of events that is possible," [13] i.e., possible in the sense of being credible. Romanticism and realism are therefore merely matters of preference dictated by the creator's own temperament—which, in truth, may itself so vary that the same author may produce at different times pieces of realism and romanticism, as was the case with Flaubert, Ibsen, Hauptmann, Hamsun, and Strindberg. For the purposes of literature it matters not whether a writer's plot is the fiction of his imagination or the product of his experience and observation of everyday living—provided that he knows men and women as they are—of the past or of the present, set in the country or set in the town. Both romanticism and realism have justified themselves by their creations; by their fruits we know them to merit equal praise. Shakespeare's plays and Flaubert's *Madame Bovary* would be enough to make argument superfluous, and readers of judgment turn to both schools with equal enthusiasm. For the *reality* of the plot has nothing to do with whether its locale be in an impossible Forest of Arden or an actually existing Lyons or London, its time an imagined sixteenth century or an observed twentieth. "A sequence of events which, though actually impossible, looks reasonable should be preferred by the poet to what, though really possible, seems incredible," says Aristotle.[14] Daily, events occur which would be impossible to make credible in the telling, yet the genius of a Shakespeare can make the advent of Hamlet's father's ghost an experience of fear-inspiring reality. We will accept any story as real, no matter how related or unrelated to our own experience, if it offers the characters the opportunity to behave in universal human fashion, for with that we can always identify ourselves. We all have occasion to encounter ghosts, though they come not from beyond the grave, who appear before us to lay upon us their own stern behests.

And thus the great persons of literature are not only lifelike; they take on more reality than life itself. We come to know Shakespeare's Beatrice, Hamlet, Othello, Desdemona, Iago, Isabella, Cordelia, Kent, and Coriolanus better than we know our own brothers and sisters. For we know these exciting beings completely, could predict how they would behave in a given situation. We can be sure, for instance, that if Beatrice had been Othello's wife no tragedy could have ensued; she would have ridiculed him into rationality with a barrage of well-aimed sarcasms until he spoke his suspicions, which she would have summarily routed with merriment; before she was through with him, he would have been on his knees begging forgiveness. Isabella, on the other hand, would have turned on him in blazing moral indignation and shamed him into sense; Cleopatra would have ensnared him with her enchantingly perverse moods until he drowned his thoughts in passionate embraces. We can be sure, too, that Hamlet in Othello's place would have been quicker to suspect Iago than Desdemona; that Kent, with his blunt loyalty to those he loves, would have pierced through the villain's lies. We know that Desdemona, for all her exquisite delicacy, would have answered Lear not in Cordelia's style, which threw the aging monarch so completely off balance that he lost all perspective, but in the manner she answered Brabantio, which answer, despite the folly of the question, saved her father's face before the assembled court. Benedick would never have looked at Ophelia twice, though Claudio would have adored her; Hamlet, with Portia at his side, would have solved his problems without catastrophe to her or himself. We know these people completely; our brothers and sisters, whom we ought to know better than them, have a way—alas!—of behaving quite unpredictably. The flesh-and-blood reality of the great creations of the literary masters is, indeed, one of the chief solaces in life for us. So long as we share with them our common humanity, none of us can ever be alone.

None of the world's writers can offer that solace to the extent that Shakespeare does; no other writer exercises our sense of oneness with our fellow human beings in as lively a way as he. It is for this reason that all the scholarly knowledge in the world will not bring the student within sight of Shakespeare if he come unaccompanied by his common humanity. The call upon that common humanity is not, as in Milton, opulently orchestrated with thrilling literary reference; one returns from Milton rewarded in direct proportion to one's previous saturation in the sea of the world's great books. Literary reference plays an almost negligible role (though no knowledge is negligible when reading him) in the apprehension of Shakespeare; in him the appeal is always based upon experiences common to human relationships.* The simplest of Italian barbers who can honestly find *Hamlet* a play *molto simpatico* basks more surely in the warmth of Shakespeare's sun than the most ponderous of scholars who cherishes no passion for literature beyond one for sources, dates, editions, and commas. Naturally, all that kind of knowledge can lead one all the closer to Shakespeare—provided one also brings along his heart. It was the great Bradley himself who, with his vast erudition, could speak with admiration of "that native strength and justice of perception, and that habit of reading with an eager mind, which make many an unscholarly lover of Shakespeare a far better critic than many a Shakespeare scholar." [15] †

---

* It is here that the professional scholars are always erring. Their enthusiasms over the "findings" of their researches impel them constantly to blind themselves to meanings in Shakespeare which are obvious enough in the light of ordinary human relationships, in favor of bloodless interpretations which bring the poet closer to his contemporaries and sources but further away from what is eternally true in human nature.

† These words, prefatory to one of the few monumental volumes of Shakespearean commentary, never palatable to a certain type of "scholar," are probably with relief thrown with the book into the discard by such as pronounce Bradley's brilliant volume "superseded" by later "findings." He is far too perceptive ever to be superseded; and

Having cleared some ground, as we now approach Shakespeare's work we must make it plain that we are not interested in appraising either him or *Hamlet*. A man must be a fool to stand in front of Pike's Peak and say, "I like you," or stick out his tongue and say, "I don't like you." Pike's Peak will be there long after this little man is forgotten, and so will Shakespeare and his *Hamlet*. We can choose only either to be blind or to see. And it is not the people who love the arts most who are forever appraising them; rather they are too busy experiencing the arts to have much patience with talk about them. They are too busy listening to Beethoven to participate in the recurrent epistolary warfare in the *Times* arguing the greater merits of the *Third, Fifth, Seventh,* or *Ninth Symphony;* they probably feel as they listen to each that *it* is the greatest, or rather that each symphony, having a complete and perfect life of its own, is as great as it need be. (And they probably feel, too, that nothing disqualifies the *Sixth* or the *Eighth* either.) This weighing of comparative greatness among things superlatively great is the most absurd of follies. Criticism and discussion are defensible only to the extent that they can enrich the experience of the work of art. Such alone is the apologia for whatever bypaths of criticism we feel obliged to trace in this work.

There remains before we come to *Hamlet*, now that we understand the nature of tragedy, to consider briefly what may be said of Shakespeare's practice in writing tragedy.

Though there is little likelihood that Shakespeare could have known Aristotle's *Poetics*, we find him in all the principles we have drawn therefrom thoroughly Aristotelian. When we consider how utterly different were the history, technique, and theatrical requirements of the Athenian drama, we are all the more struck with the timeless truth of Aristotle's deductions, so that in these fundamentals Shakespeare's tragedies illustrate them as completely as do Sopho-

---

when he is wrong he never loses one's respect. His delicate appreciation of Shakespeare's tragic power and his own scope will both survive centuries of new scholarly discoveries about dates, editions, and sources. We find ourselves in total disagreement with his view of *Hamlet*— though nothing better has ever been written upon *Lear* than his lectures —and we love him even for his errors, for he writes like a poet himself, and with the vivacity born of love for his subject.

cles'.* If Aristotle could have known Shakespeare's tragedies, he might have gone further than Ben Jonson, and said to him:

> I will not lodge thee by
> Euripides, bid Aeschylus to lie
> A little farther off, to make thee room:
> Thou art a monument without a tomb.[17]

But can we single out any tendency, can we phrase any philosophy implied in Shakespeare's tragedies when they are considered as a whole, as surely as we can for great world dramatists like Aeschylus, Sophocles, Euripides, Molière, Ibsen, and Chekhov?

Two qualities are obviously to be found in his plays—comedies, histories, and tragedies alike—and these are: an infinite compassion for human beings and an incomparable understanding of the operations of the human soul. He has made us comprehend the involved processes which motivate so bloodchilling a scoundrel as Iago † no

---

* From this generalization we exclude Shakespeare's very early and inept *Titus Andronicus*. Some scholars deny his authorship of a work so repellent in plot as this. But the master's hand is to be discerned (though unsteady) in its often by-no-means contemptible verse. (Shakespeare's verse, like Shakespeare's understanding, was far less Elizabethan than Shakespearean.) There should be nothing shocking that the world's greatest poet-dramatist should have written one of the world's worst plays before he was mature enough to write so many of the world's best. Most of Milton's earliest verse is dismal, as he himself was well aware when, at twenty-four, he deplored his lack of "inward ripeness." [16] Yet *Paradise Lost* is nonpareil in narrative poetry. These instances, which could be multiplied (e.g., Shelley, Whitman, Beethoven, Wagner), are a proof of how much self-discipline and growth are involved in the highest expressions of genius.

† Among his villains there are only two whose wickedness is not explained—Goneril and Regan, more like harpies than normal flesh and blood. It is of no avail to say of them flippantly that they are incomprehensible because they are women. Shakespeare knew what he was creating, and he needed these two horrors to complete his gallery of portraits. Anyone who has lived with any thought in the twentieth century must acknowledge that here and there we meet with a creature, like a Hitler or a Stalin and the demons who clustered about them in mutual sympathy, whom no psychological theory can explain, incarnations of

less than the almost saintly forbearance of a Helena. Dostoievski has often been mentioned as more nearly Shakespeare's peer than any other writer in this compassion and this comprehension, and surely the great Russian has few equals in these respects. But an important difference exists between the two. Dostoievski's compassion, vast as it is, has a moral unbalance at its root: he is so anxious to understand evil that before he is through with it he has banished it as a kind of human delusion; he washes it away in tears—is, in short, at basis a sentimentalist. Shakespeare, even when weakest, in his early plays, is not once guilty of sentimentality; no writer is more completely free of that taint. (It would never have occurred to him, for example, to select a prostitute as the saintliest of his women.) Ever careful to account for evil, in so far as it can be accounted for, and eager to understand it, he never confuses good and evil. Evil is never depicted by him as only good intentions gone astray. We may have every understanding of the wickedness of Iago or Edmund, may even a little pity them, but we have never any doubt that they are a menace nor do we cease wishing to see their wickedness thwarted. The sanity of distinguishing both between what is good and what is evil, and between the cause of evil and the evil itself, is fundamental in Shakespeare's view of the world. And it is fundamental to a healthy functioning of the body politic; without it all must be chaos.* We must learn to understand what we can of the causes of evil; we must exercise ourselves to help abolish these causes, in so far as they can be abolished, but the evil itself must be punished if

---

evil as they seem to be. To the indignant devotee of professional psychology one merely observes that whatever could be said about the factors which "condition" a Hitler could be said about countless others who in no way resembled him: men born the same year, in the same kind of house and street in the same city, to parents of comparable temperaments and income, brought up during the same crucial years, subject to the same disillusionments and deprivations. Many of these others became not Hitlers but his victims.

* The anthropologists have copiously demonstrated to us that what is an evil in one culture may be a good in another. But they have also thereby proved—a conclusion some of them evade—that every society *has* a good and an evil, that ethical distinctions are *sine qua non* to the existence of the race.

we are to survive. We may understand that the gangster-killer may be somewhat a product of the slums (choosing thus to overlook the bright ornaments of society who grew up in the same districts), but we do not therefore hand him a machine-gun and say, "Go ahead, my boy, we understand your impulse to murder!" We must be busy clearing slums but we must also safely remove the killer.

This unmatched compassion and this limitless understanding are not peculiar, however, to the tragedies. What then do we find in the tragedies? Those plays are corrupted by the schools into little moral sermons. *Macbeth*, a favorite victim, is everywhere perverted into a lecture on the dangers of ambition. Ambition is, of course, not necessarily wicked. It is evil only when it spurs men, as it does spur Macbeth, to work evil; but it also provokes some men to noble acts from which thousands reap benefits. Macbeth's *hamartia*, although universally so described, could not then be ambition; no one could take exception if his ambition led him to hope for elevation by the exercise of his military talents, in the fashion which saw his appointment to Cawdor. His tragic flaw is an overweeningness, a recklessness of consequences and the prices he must pay for his acts, even though he knows what these will be like—a heedlessness which moves him to give free rein to his ambition through murderous acts, through means he should firmly reject. Shakespeare's profound wisdom disinclined him from propounding such abstract saws as that "honesty is the best policy," or "ambition is wicked." Honesty, generally, is good. But if a doctor announced to a woman that her husband had six months to live, knowing that his words would kill her, the goodness of his honesty would be open to question. Shakespeare, quite to the contrary, everywhere demonstrates that he feels with his Friar Lawrence:

> For nought so vile that on the earth doth live
> But to the earth some special good doth give,
> Nor aught so good, but, strained from that fair use,
> Revolts from true birth, stumbling on abuse:
> Virtue itself turns vice, being misapplied,
> And vice sometime's by action dignified.[18]

No one better knew than Shakespeare the bottomless truth of the dictum, "By their fruits ye shall know them." He does not imply that love, for instance, is either good or bad. It is good in so far as it transforms Romeo and Juliet overnight from a callow youth and an insipid girl into two adults of passion and glowing imagination; but it is bad in so far as it makes them reckless. One might as well *accuse* them of love as Macbeth of ambition. Love is good in that it causes Cleopatra and Antony to rise majestically above their egotisms and opportunisms; but it is bad in that it makes them heedless of the road they travel together. One cannot make any moral generalizations about love, honesty, patriotism, and so on—only about the particular acts which they motivate.

Nor can we pretend that Shakespeare's tragedies exhibit the triumph of the virtuous. He knew that there is no neat distribution of rewards and punishment in this world, as was the case with Archibald the All-Right's Gentle Jane, who "was good as gold,"

> And when she grew up she was given in marriage
> To a first-class earl who keeps his carriage!

and his Teasing Tom who "was a very bad boy,"

> The consequence was he was lost totally,
> And married a girl in the *corps de bally!* [19]

Shakespeare knew that such is but wishful thinking about life. Rather do we witness, as we must in life, the prolonged success of the Iagos, Edmunds, Gonerils and Regans, Siciniuses and Junius Brutuses; and, what is more anguishing, the heartbreaking sufferings of the Hamlets, Othellos, Lears, and Cordelias. Indeed, Shakespeare's tragic figures suffer all out of proportion to their faults, as they would in life. For merely possessing a bad temper and stubbornness did ever man suffer more than Lear?

The neoclassical period of English literature, committed by its narrow interpretation of ethical values to the doctrine of "poetic justice," was mightily disturbed by Shakespeare's failure to reward the good. It approved, rather, the morality of Richardson in *Pamela, or Virtue Rewarded*, in which Lord B., after vainly chasing Pamela over six volumes in an attempt to seduce her, in the end rewards her endurance by marrying her. The neoclassicists were, therefore, pleased when Tate revised *King Lear* to restore Lear to his throne at the conclusion and marry Cordelia, spared death, to the deserving

Kent. This travesty of Shakespeare's tragedy won the approval even of Samuel Johnson; and this was the version the public saw on the boards for something like a century and a quarter. But Shakespeare would have no traffic with these facile dispensations of justice. He had deliberately, in writing *Lear*, altered the original ending, which found the king once more in possession of his kingdom, to make it a true tragedy. He knew that we are never granted in life a gold star for every act of good conduct or sacrifice, nor are the wicked always rapidly checked in their careers. Sometimes in his tragedies a man of noble deeds (Brutus, Hamlet, Othello), sometimes a man of wicked deeds (Macbeth) goes down to ruin.

But, nevertheless, there is a meaning in the conclusions of his tragedies. If the man fighting on the side of goodness does go down to ruin at the catastrophe of a tragedy, so do those who act in behalf of wickedness. Hamlet is dead, but so are Claudius, Gertrude, Polonius, and Laertes. Othello and Desdemona die, but Iago is to suffer death by torture. Lear and Cordelia perish, but so do Cornwall, Regan, Goneril, and Edmund. And when the smoke clears after the general disaster, who remain in command of the ruined field to build life anew? Almost always exclusively the forces for goodness.* Hamlet is dead, but the well-balanced Horatio and the courageous Fortinbras carry on; Othello dies but a wiser Cassio continues; Lear is dead but Kent and a sager Albany and Edgar survive; in *Macbeth* the forces for right are plainly triumphant; in *Romeo and Juliet* the rival families outdo each other in offering peace and atonement at the end. The world is thus left in the capable hands of the good, and all that has been evil has perished in the fall of the hero.

In other words, Shakespeare seems to be saying that although the good man may go down to defeat, goodness itself cannot. This is the peculiarly Shakespearean version of *katharsis*. Shakespeare's tragic endings remind us that overweeningness may hurl the noblest to the dust, but he bids us also not despair about the world, only to look into ourselves. For goodness, he knows, in the long run,

---

* The exceptions are the "Roman" plays, where Shakespeare, limited by well-known history, seems to have chosen a tragic ending consonant with the type history-play.

though the struggle be protracted and arduous and may seem momentarily to fall to the evil, cannot be extinguished. He seems to imply what Milton later expressly states:

> Virtue may be assailed, but never hurt,
> Surprised by unjust force, but not enthralled,
> Yea even that which mischief meant most harm,
> Shall in the happy trial prove most glory.
> But evil on itself shall back recoil,
> And mix no more with goodness, when at last
> Gathered like scum, and settled to itself
> It shall be in eternal restless change
> Self-fed and self-consumed: if this fail
> The pillared firmament is rottenness,
> And earth's base built on stubble.[20]

Evil, as so many poets have insisted, can in the event only prove temporary, for it carries the seeds of its own dissolution within itself.

What then? If life has meaning, Shakespeare seems to say, it is in the living of life itself, in participating, as we must, in the struggle

> Where evil wars in that design immense
> With good, the gear of God's beneficence.

REFERENCES IN CHAPTER II

1. W. S. Gilbert, *Patience*, I.
2. J. Greene and E. Abell, *Stories of Sudden Truth* (New York, 1953), p. 80.
3. S. H. Butcher, *Aristotle's Theory of Poetry and Fine Art* (New York, 1951), pp. 351–2.
4. *Samson Agonistes*, 1755—end.
5. L. Cooper, *Aristotle on the Art of Poetry* (Ithaca, 1947), p. 40.
6. Butcher, *op. cit.*, p. 318.
7. *Ibid.*, p. 320.
8. *Ibid.*
9. *Ibid.*
10. *Ibid.*, p. 321.
11. *Othello*, I, iii, 296

12. *King Lear*, IV, vi, 208–9.
13. Cooper, *op. cit.*, p. 31.
14. *Ibid.*, p. 80.
15. A. C. Bradley, *Shakespearean Tragedy* (London, 1929), p. 2.
16. "On His Having Arrived at the Age of Twenty-Three," 7.
17. Ben Jonson's "To the Memory of My Beloved Master William Shakespeare," 19–22:

> *I will not lodge thee by*
> *Chaucer, or Spenser, or bid Beaumont lie*
> *A little farther off, to make thee room:*
> *Thou art a monument without a tomb.*

18. *Romeo and Juliet*, II, iii, 17–22.
19. W. S. Gilbert, *Patience*, II.
20. *Comus*, 588–598.

HE THOUGHT HE SAW A BANKER'S CLERK
  DESCENDING FROM THE 'BUS;
HE LOOKED AGAIN, AND FOUND IT WAS
  A HIPPOPOTAMUS.
"IF THIS SHOULD STAY TO DINE," HE SAID,
  "THERE WON'T BE MUCH FOR US!"

HE THOUGHT HE SAW AN ALBATROSS
  THAT FLUTTERED ROUND THE LAMP;
HE LOOKED AGAIN, AND FOUND IT WAS
  A PENNY POSTAGE-STAMP.
"YOU'D BEST BE GETTING HOME," HE SAID,
  "THE NIGHTS ARE VERY DAMP!"

Lewis Carroll, Sylvie and Bruno

III Confusion Worse Confounded: "Hamlet" and the Critics

WHATEVER DIFFICULTIES *Hamlet* now presents emanate largely, though not entirely, from the confusion attending the interpretation of its hero's character and objectives. No other play of Shakespeare's revolves so completely about the central character as does this. To see Hamlet otherwise than as Shakespeare intended him to be is to mistake the meaning of the entire play. It is a great misfortune that the commentators, with the best will in the world, have fairly succeeded in obfuscating the dramatist's intentions. To make one's way through the conflict of their opinions is to understand (*durch Mitleid*) perfectly Lucifer's hazardous voyage through Chaos:

                                                a dark
        Illimitable ocean without bound,
        Without dimension, where length, breadth, and height,
        And time and place are lost; . . .
        . . . . amidst the noise
        Of endless wars . . .
        For hot, cold, moist, and dry, four champions fierce
        Strive here for mastery, and to battle bring
        Their embryon atoms; they around the flag
        Of each his faction in their several clans,
        Light-armed or heavy, sharp, smooth, swift or slow,
        Swarm populous, unnumbered as the sands. . . .
        . . . To whom these most adhere
        He rules a moment; chaos umpire sits. . . .[1]

The reader may, then, wish to spare himself the kind of experience which could bedevil the Devil himself. He who must run
as he readeth may choose to skip this section: in this we allow the
critics and scholars to speak for themselves, and in the following
section we answer them with chapter and verse. Yet it would be a
pity to miss the sport. And, unless the reader possesses absolutely
no ideas about Hamlet, he is bound to scent the whiff of his own
somewhere in the millefiori nosegay here culled.

It will be cold comfort to the cultivated general reader to know
the state of current scholarship, but to give him his bearings he ought
in all fairness to be apprized of it. It is true enough that there is an
atmosphere of emotional stability (often deceptive) about the writings of twentieth-century literary scholars which makes earlier commentary seem in comparison rather flighty. A kind of Germanic
doggedness to be concerned only with the facts, and to employ them
logically, characterizes the newer commentaries and provides an
air of sobriety particularly welcome after some of the romantic
nonsense vented in the nineteenth century. Modern criticism, one is
expected to feel, though certainly duller, is safer. There has been,
indeed, an enormous amount of investigation in our time into literary
sources, dates, editions, and historical analogy. All of this should be
to the good, and could be, if this enthusiastic digging away at the
mound of facts did not result in a situation as unsatisfactory as the

"unscientific" procedures of earlier commentary. Facts are helpful and cannot be ignored, but they are also capable of wild over-interpretation. For example, because it has been proved that in Elizabethan literature a man in love is occasionally shown as being slovenly in dress, innumerable scholars take that discovery as proof that Shakespeare causes Hamlet to appear before Ophelia with his "stockings fouled, ungartered," and wrinkled simply to indicate, by use of a theatrical convention, that Hamlet is in love with her. Now, if the matter of the play pointed to such an interpretation of the incident (as it does not), this convention would certainly reinforce the scene. But the unfortunate habit of our scholars is to use such an isolated scholarly discovery to prove their contentions about the play as a whole. It will not do to conclude that because a few of Shakespeare's contemporaries used such a convention to convey a meaning, Shakespeare necessarily used it for the same meaning, particularly when we must thereby exclude a sounder, simpler, more human interpretation of Hamlet's clothes being disordered. Twentieth-century scholarly conviction that Shakespeare could never have meant more than his contemporaries, reduces him from the stature that every unscholarly admirer knows him to possess.

Nineteenth-century commentary was, in short, too much the victim of imagination working without regard to the facts; twentieth-century commentary is too much in love with isolated facts and too much the victim of an almost total lack of literary imagination. There is something absurd about the contempt of academic scholars, which is as great as a woman's for last year's fashion in dresses, for any speculations older than a couple of decades. The pseudo-scientific search for newer facts about sources, dates, editions, and historical analogies thus would rate only the newest crop unearthed as possessing value. Professional scholars seem often more interested in answering one another than in writing their learned articles to enrich anyone else's experience of literature.* It is a state

---

* We still recall the words of one of our professors, a man of renown in his field, during the ancient days of our graduate study: "I cannot understand the complaint of so many young scholars that they cannot find new subjects to write about; they seem to feel that everything's been done. All I have to do is pick up any issue of a learned

of mind that unhappily cooperates with prevailing conditions in the academic world. College professors of English are expected intermittently to turn out "learned articles" in order to maintain their jobs or advance their salaries. The result is that they seem mutually to have agreed to operate in a hermetically sealed chamber from which the general public is excluded—too often the poets they write about are excluded too. Such scholars contrive to rule over a private empire to which only the "specialist" is admitted, and to which the well-read lover of literature is not anxious for a passport. Indeed, this lover of literature, if he has a creative imagination, need not even apply—for in that closed realm nothing is more suspect than creativeness. There it is common to sneer at the critical vision of a Coleridge, Hazlitt, Arnold, or Pater, and at the generous enthusiasms of a Shelley or Swinburne—on the grounds that these men were only creators, not scholars. It is true that the facts at our disposal were not at theirs, and that therefore these men did make (inevitably) certain errors; but it is also true that, with all his "mistakes," Coleridge remains to date about many matters the keenest critic Shakespeare ever had—and even his mistakes are interesting and part of literature itself. There is nothing odd in that a great poet should have deeper insight into another great poet than a scholar writing either for reasons of bread and butter or to chase the bubble of scholarly reputation.* As for the rapturous endorsements of a Swinburne, whose taste was ever vitiated by them? At worst they are touchingly amusing; at best their magnanimous passion for literature is healthily contagious. There is surely less harm in overpraise of a good thing than myopic unawareness of its merit. Too much modern scholarship has

---

periodical like the *P.M.L.A.* or *Englische Studien,* and I always find so much to disagree with, that I'm all set to write a half-dozen articles myself." Even Professor J. Dover Wilson's *What Happens in Hamlet* owes its genesis, by the author's own admission, to this frame of mind. In his dedication he tells of reading by chance an article on the play by W. W. Greg in *The Modern Language Review* and of how, after re-reading it, he realized that he "had been born to answer it." [2]

* With the exception of Aristotle and Longinus the roster of the world's great critics is the roll of some of the greatest creators of literature: e.g., Plato, Horace, Dante, Ben Jonson, Dryden, Addison, Johnson, Lessing, Goethe, Coleridge, De Quincey, Arnold, Pater.

degenerated into the picking of fleas by scholars from one another, or even looking for them where they are not. It is all a vast dedication to the wrong ends, for facts can be of invaluable use to true literary criticism. But they are utterly useless without literary imagination or when they are employed without reference to the basic truth that literature must ever be a representation of the life that is lived by men and women.* There are, happily, scholars who do not forget this.

The situation understood, we are ready to plunge into the thick of the fight over *Hamlet*. First, however, a few admonitions are in order:

¶ Some of the opinions quoted are entirely fallacious; some are partially true; some stand on the threshold of truth but do not enter. Let no one, in desperation, seize upon any single view because it seems as good as any other. For that will bring no satisfaction to the earnest seeker after Shakespeare's meaning. None of these opinions will exactly fit *Hamlet*, and we can be content with nothing less than perfect conformance of the theory we accept to the play Shakespeare wrote.

¶ We can do no more than give examples of typical interpretations. For each we quote, rest assured there exist others varying but slightly from it.

¶ We present what we believe to be all the leading interpretations in one chapter for the very reason that we are not primarily interested in answering any one of them. We should like to avoid the picking of fleas from our colleagues' theories; we wish to understand the play for what it says in itself. Too many critics have fallen into the error of beginning with the Prince himself and *then* going to the play of which he is a part. If we present opinions which we hope will provide some amusement, it is largely to get them out of the way, though we shall be glad to acknowledge with gratitude our indebtedness for an idea or two we pick up in the process.

* A well-known scholar, commenting on a brilliant historical novel, said in admiration, "An enormous amount of research must have gone into this work. But what courage it must have taken to put it all together to make a novel!" Lucky for scholars that authors do not lack this courage. Otherwise on what could scholarship feed?

¶ We undertake to make all plain in due course. There is nothing bewildering in *Hamlet,* once we clear the road to it.

It should be remembered, to begin with, that there was not always a "*Hamlet* problem." The vogue of finding one did not commence until the eighteenth century, when the drama was nearly a century and a half old. *Hamlet* was plainly a great favorite very early in its career, as the number of its known printings testifies—testimony which is amplified by the recorded admiration [3] of several contemporaries of Shakespeare. An able study of older *Hamlet* criticism clearly proves that the play was widely known throughout the seventeenth century [4] (at the opening of which it was written), but nowhere implies that during that popularity there was any doubt as to the meaning of the play. The Earl of Shaftesbury, no Shakespeare idolator, could say complacently early in the eighteenth century that of all its author's plays *Hamlet* "appears to have most affected English hearts, and has perhaps been oftenest acted of any which have come upon our stage," and that its plot is one "naturally fitted to move horror (i.e., fear) and compassion." [5] This guess of Shaftesbury's has been made good by Mr. Hogan, who shows statistically that 358 performances of the play were given in London between 1703 and 1750—the largest number for any Shakespearean play.[6]

It is, of course, possible that actors and directors, impelled by their willingness to sacrifice a play for the greater exhibition of personal talents, may have been to some extent responsible for inaugurating the difficulties—we see them doing as much in our own time. But there certainly has been one force at work in the distortion of *Hamlet*'s meaning. No student of the scholarship on the play can fail observing how much each age and intellectual climate have perverted this masterwork to suit the prejudices of the epoch. Shaftesbury praises *Hamlet* for conforming to standards Shakespeare never dreamt of considering. Johnson raps its author over the knuckles for failing to meet much the same standards. Goethe makes its hero another Werther, Coleridge an early-nineteenth-century Romantic, the Germans make him very German, and the Freudians into a perfect candidate for the clinical couch.

Unfortunately, the English theater could not maintain a direct

tradition from Shakespeare to us that in any way resembles the manner in which the *Comédie Française* at Paris has inherited the acting traditions directly from the days of Corneille, Molière, and Racine.*
In England the growth of Puritanism in the generation following Shakespeare's death resulted in the gradual withdrawal of the public's support from the theater. Even when they were a small minority, the Puritans of Elizabeth's day were untiring in their attacks on the stage and their efforts to have the giving of plays prohibited. At length, with the majority of the populace now in their ranks, they were strong enough to close the last of the Elizabethan playhouses by Parliamentary edict in 1642. The evidence is that this last surviving theater would soon have had to shut its doors in any case, for there was too small an audience left to keep them open. During the Cromwellian Commonwealth few plays were given anywhere in England for the public. And when, in the next generation, drama was revived with the opening of first one, then a second theater (only one of which ever managed to thrive at the same time) in London, for the entertainment of the limited circle of the Court—the

* When the actors of Molière's theater and those of the rival *Hôtel de Bourgogne* combined, the *Comédie Française* was born, its first patents being issued in 1685. Thus it came into direct succession of the acting traditions of the two theaters with which Corneille, Molière, and Racine had been intimately connected[7]—Molière himself, of course, being the presiding genius and leading actor of his troupe. The result is that the audience at the *Comédie* today probably see their classics performed as the authors intended them to be, because of the unbroken continuity of the companies. Strangers, indeed, have been known to remark that there is something almost Chinese in the conventionalized gestures and attitudes, tempi, and movements of the French classics as seen at that theater, and marvel at how identically actors seem to interpret the same role. They do not quite understand that so far as the spectators' interest in the actors is concerned, it centers not at all on possible new interpretations, which would only shock the audience, but on proficiency in acting technique—to find a new delicacy or power in a well-known gesture, look of the eye, or lift of the voice. There devotees sit on the edge of their seats, hands poised for applause, in anticipation of certain moments of which they know not only the speeches but the stage direction by heart, and the precision in the rendering of which they are prepared to appraise.

body of the public still absenting itself—the line of Elizabethan acting traditions was lost.

In an age so spectactularly different in tastes, interests, morals,
morale, and philosophy as the Restoration, those traditions, had they
been available, would probably have carried little weight with either
actors or courtly audience. The court of Charles II or James II had
little or no respect for the most characteristic among Shakespeare's
many gifted contemporaries, and were glad enough to think those
"barbarians" might die of neglect. For Shakespeare alone did they
make exception; but only a man of Dryden's stature preferred not
to speak of him condescendingly. Pepys, immortal for his mediocrity, is a sure barometer for the average taste of the time. He thinks
Romeo and Juliet the "worst [play] that ever I heard in my life,"
and after a performance of *A Midsummer Night's Dream* takes an
oath that "I . . . shall never see [it] again, for it is the most insipid,
ridiculous play that ever I saw in my life"; a monstrous travesty of
what pretended to be *Macbeth*, however, charms him by the "variety
of dancing and music." The Restoration was too busy aping the
French in dress and the grand manner, too anxious to cultivate the
salon version of the classical, to feel comfortable in Shakespeare's
open spaces.

It is true that one playwright-manager bridged the period from
the closing of the theaters in 1642 to the opening of the Restoration
playhouses less than two decades later, Sir William D'Avenant. It
is also true that D'Avenant was pleased to float the rumor that he was
Shakespeare's illegitimate son, in an era when no one seemed to mind
branding his mother a harlot to get himself a little extra distinction
in the world. Born the son of decent tavern-keepers (the name then
was Davenant) whose hostel Shakespeare sometimes visited, he may
even have been named for the dramatist—although the name of William is not sufficiently exotic among Englishmen for us to jump to
that conclusion. At any rate, D'Avenant was five when Shakespeare
retired from the stage, and ten when he died—an age too tender even
for a genius (which D'Avenant emphatically was not) to acquire
from the master any profound knowledge of Shakespeare's conceptions of his works, even had the latter felt inclined to bestow it
on a six-year-old darling of a pigmy size. Moreover, during the
Restoration D'Avenant became very much the man of the new age,

as his mangling of *Measure for Measure, Much Ado About Nothing, Macbeth,* and *The Tempest* (the last with Dryden's cooperation) abundantly proves. Gosse calls him the "debaser" of the stage and deems his influence "wholly deplorable." [8] It was under his influence that Betterton and his fellow actors of the Restoration took over the French style and that the theater began to be buried under elaborate scenery.* D'Avenant is assuredly too slender a thread on which

* Yet, because of his reputed relationship to Shakespeare and the fact that he knew the theater before the Puritan prohibition, it is generally assumed that he passed on Elizabethan tradition to the new age. The Restoration Court, on the other hand, everyone agrees, was notably unreceptive to the Elizabethan style. Without setting out to do so, Mr. Hazelton Spencer, in his thoroughly documented study of Restoration adaptations of Shakespeare, *Shakespeare Improved,* makes out a perfect case against the notion of D'Avenant as a sort of belated Elizabethan.[9] Consider just a handful of D'Avenant's literary crimes (all of them stimulated by a desire to accommodate the new taste): He took Beatrice and Benedick out of *Much Ado* and put them into his perversion of *Measure for Measure,* making Benedick Angelo's brother; [10] in the same work he did not hesitate to change Claudio's superb lines,

> Ay, but to die, and go we know not where
> To lie in cold obstruction, and to rot,
> This sensible warm motion to become
> A kneaded clod, and the delighted spirit
> To bathe in fiery floods or to reside
> In thrilling region of thick-ribbed ice,
> To be imprisoned in the viewless winds
> And blown with restless violence round about
> The pendant world, or to be worse than worst
> Of those, that lawless and incertain thought
> Imagine howling—'tis too horrible . . .

to

> Oh Sister, 'tis to go we know not whither.
> We lie in silent darkness, and we rot;
> Where long our motion is not stopt; for though
> In graves none walk upright (proudly to face
> The stars) yet there we move again, when our
> Corruption makes those worms in whom we crawl.
> Perhaps the spirit (which is future life)

to hang the continuance of Shakespearean tradition. All the evidence is to the contrary.

It is quite possible that, unlike their compeers of the French classic stage, English-speaking actors have always felt, as Miss Webster does, that it is more important for actors and directors to exploit their own personalities than to interpret the dramatist's creation. Perhaps our difficulties with Shakespeare really owe their ori-

> Dwells salamander-like, unharmed in fire:
> Or else with wandering winds is blown about
> The world. But if condemned like those
> Whom our incertain thought imagines howling. . . . ; [11]

in his version of *Macbeth* he did not scruple to introduce songs like this:

> Black spirits and white,
> Red spirits and gray;
> Mingle, mingle, mingle,
> You that mingle may.
> Tiffin, tiffin, keep it stiff in,
> Fire drake Puckey, make it lucky:
> Liar Robin, you must bob in. . . . ; [12]

and he was responsible (Mr. Spencer proves) for the dreadful 1676 publication of *Hamlet,* a version "ruthlessly cut." [13] Among the omissions are Polonius' advice to his son, his scene with Reynaldo, Hamlet's encounter with Fortinbras' army, Hamlet's first soliloquy, his soliloquy after the Player's speech, and his speeches to his mother in her closet after the Ghost's disappearance. [14] Among the mutilated lines in this *Hamlet* a few samples will indicate the conscienceless hand of the adapter:

> Is sicklied o'er with the pale cast of thought

becomes

> Shews sick and pale with thought;

and

> In hugger-mugger

becomes

> Obscurely to inter him. [15]

Was this the man who could be interested in passing on to Betterton Shakespeare's own *Hamlet?*

gins to what theatrical folk have done with his texts. Of one thing we can be sure: by the time we come to the great Garrick, *Hamlet* was well on its way to becoming something quite different from what its author had envisioned. Johnson says, to us amazingly, that "the pretended madness of Hamlet causes much mirth"—a point of view which few modern audiences would share, but which seems to justify Mr. Mathew's conclusion that *Hamlet* in the mid-eighteenth century was performed "not as a Tragedy but as a Tragi-comical Pantomime in the Classical sense." [16]

In any event, it was more than a century before anyone recorded any difficulties in understanding this ever-popular play. Once the difficulties were raised, however, the winds of criticism began to augment in rage until they stirred up tempests and hurricanes to vie with those in the third act of *Lear*. To make an orderly presentation of this hurly-burly is not easy. But it is possible to state that the storms have raged over two questions above all others: 1. Is Hamlet's conduct that of a sane man? 2. Why does he delay killing the King? We shall consider these first.

HAMLET'S SANITY

Not to be Gilbertian, we may nevertheless agree at the outset that four attitudes are the only possibilities on the question of Hamlet's sanity: (1) Hamlet is insane, or (2) Hamlet feigns insanity, or (3) Hamlet feigns insanity at times and is actually insane at others, or (4) Hamlet is perfectly sane and never pretends to be otherwise. All but the last have been stoutly upheld.

"THE MAD PRINCE"

In the seventeen-forties Aaron Hill observed that "besides Hamlet's assumed insanity, there was in him a melancholy, which bordered on madness" [17]—melancholy being at the time as fashionable a "disease" as allergies are today. Some years later Dr. Akenside remarked to George Steevens, the Shakespeare editor, that "the conduct of Hamlet was every way unnatural and indefensible, unless he were to be regarded as a young man whose intellects were in some degree impaired by his own misfortunes." [18] These appear to be the earliest expressions advancing the theory of Hamlet's mental illness. Ever since Dr. Ferriar in 1813 was sure the hero's character "can only be understood" on the principle of latent lunacy,[19] the medicos have been busy with Hamlet,[20] eager to prove him insane. It is an inviting theory, for it comfortably explains in anyone's conduct whatever seems otherwise difficult of explanation. In Hamlet's case (and the doctors have made it a case!), it would cozily leave nothing to be accounted for.

Among the doctor-critics we are particularly devoted to two: Dr. Ray and Dr. Bucknill. Dr. Ray sheds light upon the subject in a magazine fitly named *The American Journal of Insanity;* like other colleagues he feels Shakespeare wrote with the authority of a brain specialist and was not "guided solely by intuition. He unquestionably did observe the insane." [21] So good a medico was Shakespeare that "Hamlet's mental condition furnishes in abundance the characteristic symptoms of insanity in wonderful harmony and consistency. . . . [22] On the supposition of his real insanity we have a satisfactory explanation of the difficulties which have received such various solutions." [23] Dr. Ray's solution recommends itself as a procedure to simplify life: if anybody's conduct strikes you as inscrutable, dismiss the man from your thoughts by labeling him a lunatic. The worthy doctor is particularly troubled about a scene which has upset many a commentator—Hamlet's "remarkable interview" with Ophelia, a scene which, he says, has "proved a perfect *pons asinorum* [bridge of asses]," though we fear Dr. Ray is ready to join the braying throng. "Some regard his treatment of Ophelia as unnecessarily harsh and unfeeling. . . . If Homer sometimes nods, so may Shakespeare. Others think that Hamlet's love for Ophelia was but lukewarm after all. . . . The most natural * view of the sub-

---

* "Natural, n. . . . 3. One born without the usual faculty of reasoning or understanding; a fool; an idiot.

> This drivelling love is like a great *natural*, that runs lolling up and down to hide his bauble in a hole.
> *Romeo and Juliet*, II, iv, 95."—*The Century Dictionary,* Vol. V.

Also, as an adjective: " 'Truly,' said I, 'the turn is so natural either way you have made me almost giddy with it.' "
Addison's "Ned Softly the Poet" (*Tatler*, 163).

ject—that which is most readily and obviously suggested—relieves us of all these difficulties, and reveals to us the same strong and earnest significance which appears in every other scene of the play. If Hamlet is really insane . . . then his conduct is what might have been naturally expected." [24]

But we have a special fondness for Dr. Bucknill. Hamlet, he says, "offers as tests of his sanity that his pulse is temperate, that his attention is under command, and his memory faithful, tests which we are bound to pronounce as fallacious as could be offered. . . . The pulse in mania averages about fifteen beats above that of health; that of the insane generally, including maniacs, only averages nine beats above the healthy standard. . . . That a maniac would gambol from reproducing in the same words any statement he had made is true enough in the acute forms of the disease; but it is not so in numberless instances of chronic mania, nor in melancholia or partial insanity. . . . Indeed, the possessor of the most brilliant memory we ever met with was a violent and mischievous maniac. He would quote page after page from Greek, Latin, and French classics. *The Iliad* and the best plays of Molière in particular, he seemed to have at his fingers' ends." [25] One reads this and the doubt is raised in the unmedical mind as to whether or not they had confined the right person to the padded cell.

But not all in the profession are so coldly clinical. Dr. Ray, you will have remarked, gave evidence of a romantic side to his character as soon as Ophelia's name came up. Dr. Conolly, however, is almost a poet: "In his conversation with Ophelia his words and conduct are simply those of a man distempered. . . . There is no reason and no excuse except the sad excuse that he is not in his perfect mind. To suppose him feigning is impossible. No man, however, resolved to act a cruel part, could be supposed to listen to words of trust sincerely spoken by a gentle woman, diffidently addressing him, and returning him the gifts he had in happier hours presented to her with honeyed vows, without casting away all predetermined simulation, and clasping her to his heart." [26] The tender rhetoric reveals the doctor's noble heart; I wish that my own physician had some of Dr. Conolly's romantic warmth—his bills might, in consequence, be more tolerable! O, Ophelia, in the desire to be just to thee, how many crimes have been committed in thy name against Lord Hamlet! Even the bear, Sam Johnson, with asperity said of your lover that he played "the madman most" when he treated you "with so much rudeness, which seems to be useless and wanton cruelty." [27]

With such good effect, apparently, did the faculty discourse on the symptoms of Hamlet's madness that by 1871 Dr. Stearns could say, "The majority of readers of the present day believe that Hamlet's madness was real." [28] This may indeed have been the case, considering that we find the editor Hudson, well-known for his sensitive comments on and squeamish expurgations of Shakespeare, confessing that after twenty years of reflection he is forced to the conclusion: "In plain terms, Hamlet is mad." [29]

It was probably inevitable that the legal profession, not to be outdone by its ancient rival, should make its pronouncements too. Mr. Watts brings Hamlet before the bar for the murder of Polonius, tries him, and as prosecutor, defender, judge, and jury decides that the Prince must be given by any true Britishers the verdict of "not guilty . . . on the ground of insanity"; Hamlet's sentence is "to be detained during Her Majesty's pleasure." [30]

Men of letters have by no means been loath to follow in the cry of the doctors. Lloyd believes that the very warning Hamlet "gives of his purposed simulation" of madness "may be but one of the cunningness of the truly insane." [31] This is a fairly common view.[32] Thus, George Henry Lewes: Hamlet "may be really mad, and yet, with that terrible consciousness of the fact which often visits the insane, he may 'put an antic disposition on' as a sort of relief to his feelings." [33] Mr. J. Dover Wilson's idea bears, as we shall see, a certain resemblance to this. Some, including several already cited, ascribe Hamlet's madness not to a latent lunacy but to his being unhinged by his interview with the Ghost.[34] *

Such, oddly enough, is the view taken in that work now gen-

---

* Indeed, young innocents these days are encouraged to take this position, if anything so cloudily expressed can be said to take a position; in her *Children's Shakespeare* Miss Nesbit explains to her juvenile readers: "The shock of seeing and hearing his father's ghost made him feel almost mad, and for fear that his uncle might notice he was not himself, he determined to hide his mad longing for revenge under a pretended madness in other matters." [35]

("Her style was anything but clear . . ."—*The Three Voices*.[36])

erally held the most authoritative on *Hamlet*. Mr. J. Dover Wilson believes too that Hamlet is rendered by his talk with the Ghost unstable,[37] though the tendency was earlier manifested, and that later in the play the Prince feigns madness: "This passage of a hundred lines (i.e., after the Ghost's disappearance in the first act) exhibits Hamlet in a state of extreme emotional instability, and with an intellect tottering on its seat. Furthermore the 'antic disposition' has manifested itself on three separate occasions before Hamlet ever refers to it at all. . . . Shakespeare wishes us to feel that Hamlet assumes madness because he cannot help it. The tragic burden has done its work, and he is conscious that he no longer retains perfect control over himself. What more natural than that he should conceal his nervous breakdown behind a mask which would enable him to let himself go when the fit is upon him?"[38] In short, the Ghost has left his son in the "pitiable condition" of a complete nervous collapse.[39] * The pioneer psychoanalyst, Dr. Jones, feels that Shakespeare depicted "with faultless insight" Hamlet caught in the toils of "psychoneurosis," which implies "a state of mind where the person is unduly, and often painfully, driven or thwarted by the 'unconscious' part of his mind, that buried part that was once the infant's mind and still lives on side by side with the adult mentality that has developed out of it and should have taken its place."[40] He finds himself much in accord with Mr. J. Dover Wilson.

Mr. W. W. Greg considers Hamlet the victim of hallucinations, the Ghost's narrative being but a "figment" of Hamlet's brain;[41] Mr. Kemp varies this view by branding the Ghost a liar, and arguing that not Claudius but Horatio was the murderer of the late king;[42] Mr. Leech thinks Hamlet pathologically incapable of revenge[43] since he is "at least on the borderline of madness."[44] Mr. Mathew deems him

---

* In a discussion of tragedy it is unnecessary for us to make fine medical distinctions between such losses of self-control as madness, nervous breakdown, neurasthenia. The actual differences among these (if medicine *has* decided what they are!) are beside the point. All these and shades thereof amount to the same thing so far as the cardinal literary question is concerned. And that question is simply: "Is the hero responsible for his acts?" A madman, a psychopath, a neurotic, or a victim of a nervous breakdown, all, obviously, are not to be held accountable for what they do, and hence cannot serve as tragic heroes.

half-mad: "He was more mad than he thought he was though more sane than some other people believed [45]—whatever that means. For Mr. G. Wilson Knight, Hamlet's behavior towards Ophelia is once more the proof of madness: "This is no mock-madness. To see it as such is to miss the power of the central theme of the play"; Hamlet walks alone "within the prison of mental death." [46]

Some have pronounced Hamlet the type manic-depressive [47] or "cyclothymic"; [48] some the neurasthenic [49]—even going so far as to explain the composition of the play as owing to Shakespeare's nervous condition because of his father's death and Essex's execution, [50] or, like the other tragedies, to the painful events in Shakespeare's life; [51] some find him only temporarily insane; [52] some insane only with Ophelia.[53] One writer thinks him mad only as a result of being "too long at the university" [54] and thus developing into a kind of perennial sophomore (which would offer grim horizons to college teachers if administrations these days did not eject students who show propensities towards a protracted tenancy). Another is convinced that the proof of Hamlet's lunacy is that he is a perfect logician and tries to use "the essential principles of logic" excessively [55]—which, it seems, only a madman does. (We may have here an explanation, at least, of why madmen continue, happily, to be in a minority. But does it mean that hereafter one ought to be extremely chary of dealings with one's colleagues, the professors of logic?)

The great Bradley stands somewhere outside these opinions, holding, as he does, that the root of Hamlet's character is melancholy, which he thinks "from the psychological point of view . . . is the centre of the tragedy." [56] But, he warns, " 'Melancholy,' I said, not dejection, nor yet insanity. That Hamlet was not far from insanity is very probable. His adoption of the pretence of madness may well have been due in part to fear of the reality." [57] Bradley, however, with that literary refinement so characteristic of him, also warns: "But the psychological point of view is not equivalent to the tragic." [58] Unfortunately, he did not sufficiently hearken to his own admonishment, as we shall see.

Many scholars, while rejecting Bradley's detailed account, accept *Hamlet* as a study in melancholia; [59] to Mr. Knight this disease makes of Hamlet "a dark and dangerous force"; [60] Professor Adams feels that the play "involves a study of melancholia," though he feels that to be incidental to the main subject: "a study of the *disillusionment* of an idealist." [61]

A man must have considerable cheek, one surmises, to suppose that because of all this manufactured confusion Shakespeare himself could not have answered the question as to whether Hamlet is to be understood as mad or sane. Yet it was no one less than Barrett Wendell who maintained as much.[62] Even Mr. Granville-Barker is convinced that Shakespeare nowhere makes clear whether Hamlet is mad or not, and that the dramatist deliberately causes his hero to speak of his mental condition equivocally: "The thing itself is a riddle. He attempts no answer. Nor need he"; [63] and Mr. Trench thinks that "even Shakespeare perhaps found it hard to understand him." [64] Professor Schücking finds, however, that only near the end of the play does Hamlet provide the answer, when he shows himself practically *"non compos mentis."* [65] Were it not patently unjust one might be tempted to ask Mr. Mark Van Doren if he does not also believe Shakespeare uncertain about what he was trying to create. In a series of chapters remarkable for insight on the various plays, Mr. Van Doren on *Hamlet* alone—except for his delightful prose—is disappointing; for he manages in the midst of much clever summary of opinion and brilliant phraseology to avoid taking any point of view at all: "It has been said of Hamlet that something in his genius renders him superior to decision and incapable of act, and it has been pointed out that he dominates the busiest of all known plays. Both views are right. His antic disposition has been analyzed as a symptom of abnormality and as a device for seeming mad. Neither theory is without support. He has been called the best of men and the worst of men. One judgment is as just as another." Mr. Van Doren cites the various theories as to what it is that engages Hamlet's "deepest attention," and decides "Any of them will do." [66] Obviously, Shakespeare's Hamlet must have been to the playwright one man, not a monstrous composite of all critical opinion! To go further, with the other gentlemen, and ascribe to the creator vagueness of intention, is to deny the very basis of the creative process. A man creates only because he has something very definite to impart, and it would be odd that of all the world's masterpieces *Hamlet* should be the exception!

We ourselves—need we say?—are convinced that Hamlet is perfectly sane.

HAMLET FEIGNING MADNESS

Of course, almost from the beginning of the discussion, as the arguments to prove Hamlet mad were being advanced, there was no lack of contenders proving Hamlet's insanity to be only feigned. Many, indeed, thought him so plainly feigning madness that there was no need of arguing the point. Samuel Johnson was one of these, and there have been many others down to the dawn of our present century.[67] As Mackenzie put it, as early as 1780, "The distraction of Hamlet is clearly affected through the whole play, always subject to the control of his reason, and subservient to the accomplishment of his designs." [68] Although there has been some tendency in recent scholarship, as we have seen (notably in the writings of Messrs. Greg and J. D. Wilson), to revive the idea of Hamlet's mental instability, chiefly through subtle psychiatric analyses, comparatively few commentators in our time feel it urgent to prove that Hamlet feigns insanity. Most scholars now calmly take that view for granted,[69] though occasionally it has been said that for Hamlet so to conduct himself proves rather "impolitic." [70]

But in many quarters it is assumed that Hamlet's playing the madman is the very root of the plot. Professor Lewis, after an examination of Shakespeare's sources, states this conviction in the most powerful terms: "The pretence of madness was the starting-point from which Hamlet's character was evolved, and it may well have determined the whole course of its development." [71] Professor Stoll inaugurates part of his discussion with: "The lively lunacy that Hamlet now assumes is indispensable to the plot." [72] And Professor Kittredge says even more explicitly that "Hamlet's motive for acting the madman is obvious. We speak unguardedly in the presence of children and madmen; . . . and so the King or the Queen may say something that will afford the evidence needed (i.e., by Hamlet) to confirm the testimony of the Ghost"; [73] but, Professor Kittredge adds, this device decided upon by the Prince "on the spur of the moment," does not prove successful, and Hamlet learns nothing he needs because of it. Vaguely allied to this view is the explanation that Hamlet's purpose is to "gain time." [74] Mr. Hazelton Spencer sees the hero's "biding his time" through pretended lunacy as simply an old convention of the revenge-play which Shakespeare was glad to employ.[75]

Hamlet's motive for feigning madness has had other ascriptions than Professor Kittredge's. One nineteenth-century critic thought that the "masquerade . . . pleased a misanthropic humor,—it gave him shelter and a sort of escape from society." [76] James Russell Lowell felt that since "Hamlet *drifts* through the whole tragedy" and "never keeps on one tack long enough to get steerage way . . . the scheme of simulated insanity is precisely the one he would have been likely to hit upon, because it enabled him to follow his own bent, and to drift. . . . It enables him to *play* with life and duty, instead of taking them by the rougher side, where alone any firm grip is possible." [77] That the feigned insanity serves the important function of easing "the mental suffering" under which Hamlet labors because of his long delay [78] is Professor Adams' opinion.

Considering the dramatist's possible motives in having Hamlet assume madness, Professor Stoll holds that the device "arouses suspense—we apprehend and dread the Prince's betrayal of his purpose." [79] On the other hand, it is sometimes held that Shakespeare's intentions were to provide comic effects,[80] such too having been Samuel Johnson's notion.

There is surely no need for us to multiply instances. The odds are overwhelming that the reader, at this point, at least, conceives Hamlet to be a man who (for one reason or another or for no reason) assumes the guise of lunacy. While we have not always been able to guess precisely which interpretation an actor thought he was conveying to the audience, when the intent has been at all clear every one of the many Hamlets we have seen on the stage has exhibited the hero as pretending insanity. We still remember Mr. John Barrymore flicking off Rosencrantz and Guildenstern with a well-calculated wave of the hand, while rolling his eyes maniacally. (This Mr. Olivier could not do in his cinema version since he completely omitted Rosencrantz and Guildenstern from the plot!) We still can see Mr. Evans, at the approach of the same unfortunate pair, murmuring, "O, here they come!" while he took a lock of his hair, brushed it over his eyes, and took on the look and conduct of a zany.

No, we need not multiply instances for any view so widely

adopted. But we are by no means through with the matter. It is curious that not many commentators have asked themselves just what Hamlet's assumption of the role of madman does accomplish for the plot of this play. Professor Stoll, indeed, remarks in passing that that conduct in the old *Hamlet* story has more reason for being introduced than in the play Shakespeare wrote [81]—a point made more emphatically years ago by Büchner.[82] Mr. Robertson goes further in deeming the feigned lunacy a downright defect in the tragedy; Shakespeare, he argues, unwisely retained from his sources both the revelations of the Ghost and the assumed madness of the hero; one or the other could have made his play healthy enough, but each makes the other superfluous, and consequently Shakespeare never succeeded in unifying both elements into a convincing drama.[83]

Now, the conviction that Hamlet plays the madman has received powerful endorsement from the study of Shakespeare's sources. Of them we must here take some knowledge.

The Elizabethan dramatists seized upon their plots where they found them, there being no inhibiting copyright laws. The London theater played much the role in providing literary entertainment that the movie palace (should one now say the television set?) does today for the general public. If a story was well-liked that was excuse enough for its being converted into a play; if an old play had been popular that was enough reason for reworking it into a new one within a few years; just so, a novel or play that is popular today inevitably finds its way to the screen, the leading difference being that now authors collect royalties for use of their plots. Like his fellows, Shakespeare rarely troubled to invent a new plot. What is astonishing is that he could contrive to create vibrant life out of the dull sources he chose; the originals of some of his most moving creations vary from the stupid to the disgusting. For the exercise of his genius apparently almost any plot was good enough to set in motion his imagination.

For his *Hamlet* the possible sources were two; there can be little doubt that he availed himself of one or the other or both. Some eight years before the composition of his play there already existed (we do not know for how long) a drama familiar to the public, on the same subject. We do not have any copies of this older play, and it would prove a jewel beyond price if a copy should suddenly come to light. But we know, just short of certainty, that this play was written by Thomas Kyd; aside from documentary evidence pointing to his authorship, we know from his epochal *Spanish Tragedy* that Kyd's tastes in drama would have drawn him to the old Hamlet story for its blood-and-thunder possibilities—which, moreover, he would have employed in a manner far different from Shakespeare's. We also know from contemporary Elizabethan reference that this old play had provoked mirth among the judicious because of its recurrently appearing Ghost's crying "like an oyster-wife" in a hollow voice, "Hamlet, revenge!"

We do possess, however, a tale from the French, which was indubitably the source for the old play, and may very well have been Shakespeare's source too, despite the salient differences between his tragedy and the tale—for Shakespeare did not hesitate to change his originals to any extent. The tale appeared in Belleforest's *Histoires Tragiques* (1576); there exists an English translation of it under the title of *The Hystorie of Hamblet*, printed in 1608,[84] some five years after Shakespeare's play first appeared in print. Whether or not there had been earlier publication of the translation it is impossible to say; in any case Shakespeare might very well have read Belleforest's French.

Scholarly judgment, on the whole, has been that Kyd's play was Shakespeare's immediate source, and there is sufficent reason to think so. But since the play is not extant, it is impossible to make any comparisons between it and *Hamlet*. It is, however, not specious to comfort oneself with the thought that in Belleforest's tale we have substantially the same story (except for the Ghost) that Kyd must have told. Kyd was never guilty of any psychological interest or insight in the handling of his characters, and was concerned only with external dramatic effects; he would have been little incited to alter Belleforest's story in any important details. With the addition of one of those fearsome ghosts of his, he had a plot perfect for a man of his tastes.

What was this plot? We thus briefly summarize Belleforest's tale:

¶ The King of Denmark bestows the rule of a province upon two brothers, Horvendile and Fengon (Shakespeare's Hamlet's father and uncle, respectively). Piracy being the fittest employment for men of spirit in those days, Horvendile becomes "the most renowned pirate" then scouring the seas; the King of Norway in envy challenges him "to fight with him body to body" and Horvendile kills him in combat. The King of Denmark, delighted with his brave warrior, gives him his daughter Geruth (Shakespeare's Gertrude) as a bride. Fengon, jealous, decides to murder his brother, who presumably has become King when his wife has inherited the throne. "Having secretly assembled certain men, and perceiving himself strong enough to execute his enterprise," Fengon falls upon Horvendile with his band, *while his brother is banqueting with friends,* and slays the King. Fengon has already seduced Geruth; but she is so popular with her subjects that the people quickly forgive Fengon his crime when he explains that he has killed Horvendile to protect Geruth from being slain by her spouse. "Boldened and encouraged by such impunity," Fengon now proceeds to marry Geruth, "whom he used as his concubine during good Horvendile's life," thus being guilty of "a two-fold impiety"—"incestuous adultery and parricide murder."

¶ Now, Horvendile's son, Hamblet, *"perceiving himself to be in danger of his life . . . and assuring himself that Fengon would not detract the time to send him the way his father Horvendile was gone,* to beguile the tyrant in his subtleties" hits upon the plan of "counterfeiting the madman with such craft and subtle practices," that he appears to have "utterly lost his wits." He is determined, if he lives long enough to attain "to man's estate," he will "not long delay the time to revenge the death of his father." *His assumed lunacy succeeds in defending* "his life from the treasons and practices of the tyrant, his uncle." But Hamblet reveals so much intelligence behind his seeming insanity, that the King decides to employ a lady of easy virtue to seduce the Prince and discover what is troubling him. For this end certain courtiers are appointed "to lead Hamblet into a solitary place within the woods," whither they conduct the "fair and beautiful woman." But Hamblet has been warned by a friend; and the lady herself, being in love with Hamblet, helps foil the plot.

¶ Fengon's next move against his nephew is to have one of his councilors secretly hide in Geruth's chamber behind the arras to hear what speeches might pass between Hamblet and his mother. But Hamblet suspects a trick, and counterfeiting a fit of lunacy, he begins to "come like a cock beating with his arms" upon the hangings of the room; "whereby feeling something stirring under them," he cries, "A rat, a rat!," thrusting his sword through the cloths, and pulls out "the councillor half dead," makes "an end of killing him," and cuts "his body in pieces." He now turns on his mother and upbraids her for marrying and defending the murderer of his father; he also confesses that his insanity is feigned and explains why. She is so much overjoyed to find her son truly sane that she honestly repents, and agrees to do nothing to betray his secret or interfere with his taking vengeance on his uncle.

¶ Fengon next manages to send Hamblet to England with secret letters to the English King requiring the death of the Prince. But Hamblet, while his companions are asleep, reads the letters, and counterfeits others which order the death of the two messengers and also request that the King of England marry his daughter to Hamblet. The English monarch is pleased with Hamblet, puts the messengers to death, and gives his daughter to the Prince.

¶ The following year, just as the Danish court is celebrating Hamblet's funeral, the Prince appears. He encourages everyone to drink to excess. When the courtiers are all drunk, he brings down the wall-hangings upon them, fastens the cloths to the floor so that no one can escape, and sets fire to the hall, thus destroying his foes. The King having withdrawn into his chamber, Hamblet follows him there, and severs Fengon's head from his body, crying: "This just and violent death is a just reward for such as thou art: now go thy ways, and when thou comest in hell see thou forget not to tell thy brother . . . that it was his son that sent thee thither with the message, to the end that being comforted thereby, his soul may rest among the blessed spirits, and quit me of the obligation that bound me to pursue his vengeance upon mine own blood." Attracted by the flames, the people gather, and Hamblet reveals the truth, supported by his mother's public confession and repentance. His oration so much moves the Danes that he is proclaimed king.

¶ After his coronation he goes to England to fetch his wife, but the English King plots Hamblet's death. Warned in time, Hamblet kills this foe, and returns to Denmark with two wives. There, assailed by another uncle, Wiglerus, and betrayed by his second wife, Hamblet is slain. His treacherous widow marries the enemy Wiglerus.

What appalling nonsense! one is tempted to cry. That is usually one's reaction to the originals which inspired Shakespeare to write his masterpieces. But the very inferiority of those fables causes one to marvel all the more at the genius which could see in them the raw materials for the exploitation of his talents.

Now, we must note some important relationships between this tale and Shakespeare's tragedy:

¶ Plainly, though we need not concern ourselves with most of them, Shakespeare made many changes in the details of the plot (e.g., Hamlet's age, his marrying in England, his revenge on the entire court, the manner of his death; the Queen's permanent repentance, her survival at the end; the character of Ophelia's prototype and her actions, etc.) as well as numerous additions.

¶ There is no Ghost in the tale. That character, we may depend upon it, was added by Kyd, who adored introducing supernatural inciters to vengeance; Kyd may have taken the hint, it seems to us, from Hamblet's last speech to Fengon.

¶ There is no play given by Hamlet before the King and Queen. There was no occasion in the tale for his so doing—nothing for him to prove or discover.

¶ But what is of extreme importance to us is that in the tale:

¶ 1. Hamlet's father is murdered openly at a public banquet. There is no reason to believe that Kyd would have altered this fundamental, for it would have provided him with exactly the kind of "big scene" of blood letting violence he was addicted to. (In Shakespeare's play *the root of the whole story* is that Hamlet's father was murdered *secretly*.)

¶ 2. Hamlet feigns insanity for a very good reason: to protect his life against his uncle. (In Shakespeare's play Hamlet has no such motive; Claudius would be glad to live peaceably with his nephew.)

The first of these points will be considered later in the correct place, but we may here observe that this change is one to make of Shakespeare's *Hamlet* a totally different story.

The second, however, is germane to the question of Hamlet's feigning insanity. It is not until, late in the play, the King finds himself threatened by Hamlet's conduct (after the presentation of the play before Claudius and the court) that he takes any measures against the Prince's life, and then purely out of self-protection. Until then, Claudius does all he can to make friends with his nephew. Hamlet, therefore, has in Shakespeare's plot no reason for pretending to be mad. The commentators, therefore, have been reduced to finding reasons outside the plot for his assuming madness. The critics, one and all, seem to agree that when Hamlet urges Horatio and Marcellus, after his interview with the Ghost, to swear never to reveal what they have seen

> How strange or odd soe'er I bear myself
> (As I perchance hereafter shall think meet
> To put an antic disposition on)
>
> I, v, 170–72

what he is saying is something like: "No matter how incredibly I may seem to be behaving, since, for example, I might think it expedient hereafter to pretend I am crazy. . . ." (These lines, we are sure, mean nothing of the kind. See pp. 141–47.) It is this passage which is the basis for interpreting Hamlet's conduct throughout the remainder of the play as an assumed insanity.

But listen to Samuel Johnson. With that vexing mixture of bottomless good sense and impoverished imagination so characteristic of him, he once wrote words which brought him to the very threshold of the truth: "Of the feigned madness of Hamlet there appears no adequate cause, for he does nothing which he might not have done with the reputation of sanity." [85] How true! And what a pity that Johnson could not have gone a step further in his thinking!

If Hamlet, indeed, *does* nothing that he might have done as a sane man, why then—. Why then, it is not enough to say critically with Professor Stoll that the feigned insanity makes better sense in the old Hamblet tale than in Shakespeare, or to complain with Mr. Robertson that it ruins Shakespeare's play. Nor is it enough to assume, because feigned insanity is an element in the old story, that Shakespeare need have incorporated it in his play; if he could change the whole meaning of the plot by having Hamlet's father murdered secretly, he was quite capable of discarding the feigned insanity as useless to his conception.* It is, rather, high time to be rid of this incubus of an idea that Hamlet pretends to be insane, which is more responsible than any other delusion for distorting the play Shakespeare wrote.

The truth is—why should we longer hesitate to say so?—that in *Hamlet* as Shakespeare wrote it, the hero is neither mad nor feigns insanity at any time. He is perfectly sane and never pretends to be otherwise. Of this the evidence will be presented hereafter.

HAMLET'S PROCRASTINATION

Hamlet "cannot bring himself to kill Claudius." [86] The liveliest part of the discussion on the play has centered around this point. Hamlet, in the view of many scholars, makes only "poor excuses for delay"; [87] he is forever appealing to his brain to fabricate reasons for "still further delay." [88] Indeed, "delay," some assert, "is the essence of the plot," [89] which is generally felt to be "a study in indecision." [90]

For a long time the reasons for this delay were traced, as might be expected in a tragedy, to a defect in the hero's character.

---

* Nothing can be proved by reference to what Shakespeare's audience would have expected. The scholars here would have it both ways: on the one hand they try to explain away "inconsistencies" on the grounds that Shakespeare was using inherited materials which he could not manage to work satisfactorily into the body of his play, materials he could not discard because the audience was familiar with an old plot; and, on the other hand, they account for the very significant alterations Shakespeare was ever making in the plots he adopted, on the grounds that plays were given in such swift succession in the many Elizabethan theaters, that the audiences could never have kept track of the plots!

It is interesting, in this connection, to remember how variously the Greek tragedians manipulated stories which were familiar to *every member* of their audiences. (Compare the three Electra plays, for example.)

Mackenzie, author of the lachrymose *Man of Feeling*, who specialized in downtrodden innocence, seems to have been the inaugurator (in print) of the earliest of the "subjective" explanations of the tragedy—the sentimental notion that Hamlet is too delicately constituted, too sensitive to commit an act of violence such as vengeance requires: "We see a man who in other circumstances would have exercised all the moral and social virtues, placed in a situation in which even the amiable qualities of his mind serve but to aggravate his distress and to perplex his conduct." [91]

But it was the name of the great Goethe which has given most authority to this view. A sizeable part of his most important novel, *Wilhelm Meister*, is given over to a consideration of Hamlet,* and he thus strikingly expounds his theory of the hero's character:

> "The time is out of joint: O cursed spite,
>   That ever I was born to set it right!

"In these words, I imagine, will be found the key to Hamlet's whole procedure. To me it is clear that Shakespeare meant, in the present case, to represent the effects of a great action laid upon a soul unfit for the performance of it. In this view the whole play seems to me to be composed. There is an oak tree planted in a costly jar which should have borne only pleasant flowers in its bosom: the roots expand, the jar is shivered. A lovely, pure, noble, and most moral nature, without the strength of nerve which forms a hero, sinks beneath a burden it cannot bear and must not cast away. All duties are holy for him; the present is too hard. Impossibilities have been required of him,—not in themselves impossibilities, but such for him. He winds and turns, and torments himself; he advances and recoils, is ever put in mind, ever puts himself in mind; at last does all but lose his purpose from his thoughts, yet still without recovering his peace of mind." [92]

---

* Which fact may be responsible for the tradition of introducing the endless passages of "intellectual discussion," those dreadful *longueurs*, in the German novel. Thomas Mann won considerable acclaim for these pretentious stretches of dullness in his works.

It will be no news that there are few forces at work in society equal in power to that of fashion. People have not hesitated to go as far as suicide when suicide has been fashionable; not so very long ago there was, indeed, a wave of suicides because of a song variously named as "Black Sunday" or "Blue Monday"; all over the Western world it was *à la mode* to buy a recording of it, go home and play it, and then kill yourself—though it is hard to know why, unless you were a lover of music. But even the boldest and most original minds in any given epoch are subject to the influences of fashion without being aware they are. How much of Dante's love for Beatrice and Petrarch's for Laura, despite the terrible sincerity of these poets, was owing to the medieval traditions of courtly love which urged a bard give his heart to a woman he had no thoughts of possessing, and to whom he remained faithful while he and she married some one else? How much of Byron's life is owing to its peculiar circumstances, and how much to the model of the Storm-and-Stress antisocial hero of his period, which Byron may be said to have incarnated? How much of our own F. Scott Fitzgerald's self-destruction to his personal weakness, and how much to the fashions of the Jazz Age? No one can answer these questions because these men no less helped make the fashion than became victims of it.

The excessively sensitive, easily crushed type of hero was epidemic in the Romantic Movement, and Goethe himself was considerably responsible for the vogue. His youthful indiscretion, the novel *The Sorrows of Young Werther*, achieved a huge success, and because of its hero it became a sign of personal superiority that a man could be so delicately fabricated as to be hurt at every turn of experience.* By the time Goethe had finished his *Wilhelm Meister*, he bitterly regretted *Werther* and rejected its insipid hero, seeing him for the absurdity he was. It was a matter of deep chagrin to the greatest of the Germans that he continued to be known as the author of *Werther* even after he had given the world *Faust*. Nevertheless, when he looked at Hamlet, he himself fell victim to the mode he

---

* *Werther* too started an epidemic of suicides. For a time it was *de rigeur* to follow the lead of its hero, and you had hardly any soul at all unless one fine day you were found with a pistol in one hand, a copy of *Werther* opened at the appropriate passage in the other, Werther's waistcoat on your corpse, and a bullet through your silly head.

had helped create, and conceived Shakespeare's hero in his imagination as another Werther, an exquisitely and morbidly sensitive youth unable to cope with the world.

Actually, although it is Goethe who foisted this sentimental Hamlet upon the world, that Hamlet, like Werther, was already "in the air." The seeds for such characters had been sown by the sentimentalists who flourished side by side with the rationalists of early eighteenth-century England. (The well-balanced Addison, for example, had such a partner in Steele.) Goethe, like so many young literary men of his generation in France and Germany, was an Anglomaniac, madly in love with these English sentimentalists, and deeply influenced by them. It is impossible to say what Englishmen had begun the process of inventing a sentimental Hamlet, but it has only recently become evident by the publication of Boswell's *London Journal* that a "too sensitive" Hamlet was already being talked about not only before the composition of *Wilhelm Meister* but a whole decade even before the creation of the prototype Werther himself.

Boswell records under the date of April 6, 1763 in his journal (seventeen years before Mackenzie's words on Hamlet) a conversation with the celebrated actor, Thomas Sheridan (not to be confused with the playwright Richard B. Sheridan): "He gave us, however, a most ingenious dissertation on the character of Hamlet. . . . He made it clear to us that Hamlet . . . is . . . a young man of good heart and fine feelings who had led a studious contemplative life, and so become delicate and irresolute. He [Shakespeare] shows him in very unfortunate circumstances, the author of which he knows he ought to punish, but wants strength of mind to execute what he thinks right and wishes to do. In this dilemma he makes Hamlet feign himself mad, as in that way he might put his uncle to death with less fear of the consequences of such an attempt. . . . His timidity being once admitted, all the strange fluctuations which we perceive in him may be easily traced to that source. . . . He endeavors to stir up his languid mind to a manly boldness, but in vain. For he still continues backward to revenge, hesitates about believing the Ghost to be the real spirit of his father, so much that the Ghost chides him for being tardy. When he has a fair opportunity of killing his uncle, he neglects it and says he will not take him off while at his devotions, but wait till he is in the midst of some atrocious crime, that he may put him to death with his guilt upon his head. Now this, if really from the heart, would make Hamlet the most black, revengeful man. But it coincides better with his character to suppose him here endeavoring to make an excuse to himself for his delay. . . . In short, Sheridan made out his character accurately, clearly, and justly."

Boswell, himself one of the most sentimental of men, as the amorous passages in his life amusingly demonstrate, obviously liked this sentimental view of the Prince. The actor Sheridan, who may or may not have fathered the view, was a sentimentalist too; he employed, he said, the poems of Ossian as one would "a thermometer" to "judge the warmth of everybody's heart." At any rate, his analysis of Hamlet is substantially like the Hamlet which Mackenzie, Goethe, Schlegel, and Coleridge each much later "discovered." Goethe, being a man of genius, impressed his Hamlet upon the world, until it was superseded by Coleridge's variation. Later in the nineteenth century a French scholar could say witheringly: "Let us put aside altogether the notion that Hamlet . . . was in the mind of his creator the type of the German race. . . . People here [i.e., in France] are . . . inclined to make a Werther out of Hamlet." [93]

Goethe's position has been in our century firmly restated by Mr. Trench: "Made for a philosopher, he [Hamlet] has been put into the situation of a politician; made for a moralist, he is required to be a manslayer; suited for the production of theory and idealism, he is asked by Fate to produce energy and practical efficiency." [94] This attitude, even more recently, has been echoed by Mr. Fergusson: Hamlet is "defenceless and uninstructed in the midst of life," [95] and also by Mr. Neilson, who finds the Prince to be "a person more unfitted for the task allotted to him" than any hero on record,[96] and who believes the end of the play to show that Hamlet's "mind and heart are bruised. His youth is maimed." [97]

In 1946 this Hamlet was able to satisfy the criteria of *le dernier cri* in literary fashions, Existentialism; it was said that Hamlet is not "existent but rather . . . passing through an existential phase"; but at a certain point "his values are translated from 'reason' to 'absurdity' "; finally, "at the end the focus shifts"—his earliest attitude of " 'absurd sensibility' " has been changed to " 'normal' sensibility" and he sees that "the existential insight was after all delusion." [98] We should hope *anyone* would see that!

"TOO IRRESOLUTE"

Such oversensitive and professionally incapable men, though uncurrent nowadays as heroes, were very dear to the Romantics. It is therefore not surprising that quite independently of each other a German and an Englishman should have simultaneously conceived identical theories of Hamlet in this vein. Unhappily, Coleridge felt called upon to defend himself against the charge of plagiarizing Schlegel.[99] He need not have bothered; the temper of the times rendered such an occurrence beyond the province of the accidental. It is much more astonishing that quite independently of each other Messrs. James and Lange (if we were correctly taught) should, as psychologists, have conceived simultaneously the fascinating notion that when you see a bear, you first run away and *after that* are frightened! We accept the coincidence of that discovery readily enough, though we are glad to say that we have never had the opportunity of testing its validity.

Schlegel, whose version was the earlier in print, described Hamlet as procrastinating because he was too irresolute to act: "Hamlet has no firm belief either in himself or in anything else. From expressions of religious confidence he passes over to sceptical doubts. He believes in the ghost of his father when he sees it; and as soon as it has disappeared, it appears to him almost in the light of a deception. He has even got so far as to say, 'There is nothing either good or bad but thinking makes it so.' The poet loses himself with his hero in the labyrinths of thought, in which we find neither end nor beginning. . . . A voice commissioned . . . by heaven from another world demands vengeance for a monstrous enormity, and the demand remains without effect. The criminals are at last punished . . . by an accidental blow, and not in a manner requisite to announce with solemnity a warning example of justice to the world." [100]

It is Coleridge, however, who by the brilliance of his exposition has given the world that conception of the hero's character which is still (unfortunately) the most universally accepted by the general public. Shakespeare wished, he says, in our hero's character "to exemplify the moral necessity of a due balance between our at-

tention to the objects of our senses, and our meditation on the workings of our mind,—an *equilibrium* between the real and the imaginary
worlds. In Hamlet this balance is disturbed: his thoughts, and the images of his fancy, are far more vivid than his actual perceptions, and
his very perceptions, instantly passing through the *medium* of his
contemplations, acquire, as they pass, a form and a color not naturally
their own. Hence we see a great, and almost enormous, intellectual
activity, and a proportionate aversion to real action. . . . Hamlet is
brave and careless of death; but *he vacillates from sensibility and
procrastinates from thought, and loses the power of action in the
energy of resolve.*" [101] *

An analysis radiantly phrased! But an analysis true, not of Hamlet, but of Coleridge himself. Poor Coleridge! No one, during his
greatest creative years, less understood the distinction between imagined and actually written books. If only we could somehow recapture from the air the hundreds of finished masterpieces he talked
into it! Has any other poet so firmly maintained a claim to im-
mortality on the basis of so little an accomplishment?—one completed poem (*The Ancient Mariner*), two fragments (*Kubla Khan*
and the first part of *Christabel*), and some splendid passages in a
handful of pieces (as in *Dejection* and *Frost at Midnight*).† For
him it was always so much simpler to imagine a book, to resolve to
do it, than to sit down and write it.

Like the public, innumerable scholars follow Coleridge's interpretation.[102] Dowden finds Hamlet "disqualified for action by his
excess of the reflective tendency, and by his unstable will." [103] Mr.
E. K. Chambers describes the hero's situation as "the tragedy of the
intellectuel, of the impotence of the overcultivated imagination and
the over-subtilized reasoning powers to meet the call of everyday
life for practical efficiency"—for him Hamlet, whose "real interest
is all in speculation," is "the academic man, the philosopher, brought
suddenly into the world of strenuous action, and proving himself

---

* The italics in the last sentence are ours.
† Yet, for all that, who would exchange *The Ancient Mariner* or
either of those two fragments for nine-tenths of the *Collected Works*
of that Wordsworth he so catastrophically worshipped—who, that is, except the schoolma'ams? For, O the difference to them!

but the clay pot there." [104] Hamlet is depicted as "a habitual dweller in his own thoughts," [105] as coming to catastrophe because "he thought too much," [106] as having his will power atrophied by "his power to think," [107] or because he has a genius for inaction,[108] or because he can act only in his imagination.[109] Another "existentialist" believes that Hamlet does not act because "he is the sage who has penetrated or thinks he has penetrated to the very essence of being, the essence of living, and who therefore, understanding the futility of all activity, settles into the calm of inaction." [110]

Slight variations are played upon this theme: Hamlet exercises his passion in words rather than deeds; [111] his will is broken "through an abnormal development, not only of the reflective but of the emotional faculties"; [112] he is the type "undeveloped poet who adds to all he thinks and feels the spirit of a nimble and passionate imagination," remaining the while "silent,* reserved, meditative," and "unaccustomed to action, untrained in its struggles"; [113] his defeat is that of the type artist, who fails because it is his nature to be impractical; [114] he is the victim of a conflict due to the fact that he was born an active Dane but educated at the University to be a reflective German.[115]

For some he is irresolute because he is the idealist who loathes the world of actuality,[116] and becomes perverted into an "embittered and passionate" pessimist.[117] Or, he is no idealist at all but a convinced fatalist: he is convinced of "man's impotence against an all-powerful providence"; [118] he surrenders fatalistically all "his personal responsibility" to act; [119] experience teaches him at last no longer to be passion's slave but to be resigned.[120] Or, he was always a pessimist; [121] though inwardly a "volcano." [122] For all his "intellectual keenness" Hamlet's "aimless weakness," in the catastrophic outcome, "spreads around far more misery than the most inconsiderate violence." [123]

Among the more diverting of the refinements of Coleridge's view are the convictions: that Hamlet "did not *lose* his mind but *found* it" in the revelation of his father's murder, though in the shock of "that discovery he forgot a crime and ignored a duty"; [124]

---

* Surely silence has by no one else been achieved with so many words!

that his trouble was not in thinking too much but in thinking the wrong way; [125] that he opposed life itself and rejected all its activities; [126] that so far from being in any way noble or philosophical, he was simply a blundering, mouthing ideologist.[127] *

A measurement of the wide acceptance of Coleridge's conception of the hero as the irresolute thinker is the fact that Professor Butcher in his great work on Aristotle's *Poetics* feels it necessary to modify the Aristotelian concept of a tragic hero (as well as his own healthy understanding of Shakespearean tragedy) to accommodate this view: "Much more rarely, as in Hamlet, can character become dramatic by an intellectual and masterly inactivity which offers resistance to the motives prompting ordinary men to action. . . . There is in Hamlet a strenuous inaction, a *not*-acting, which is in itself a form of action. . . . [However,] most of Shakespeare's characters, like the heroes of Greek drama, are strong and dominant natures, they are of a militant quality of mind." [128]

And so they are!

"TOO MELANCHOLY"

We have already noted the commentaries which describe Hamlet not so much as a lunatic as a victim of melancholia. Some scholars ascribe to this melancholy the cause for Hamlet's delay in killing Claudius. Just as there are clearly affinities between the Goethe—"too sensitive" theory and the Schlegel-Coleridge—"too irresolute" view, so there are affinities between the latter and this notion of Hamlet's procrastinating through melancholy. For this explanation

* George Bernard Shaw's Hamlet was a variation of Coleridge's too, though, naturally, with a Shavian twist: Hamlet "is a man in whom the common personal passions are so superseded by wider and rarer interests, and so discouraged by a degree of critical self-consciousness, which makes the practical efficiency of the instinctive man on the lower plane impossible to him, that he finds the duties dictated by conventional revenge and ambition as disagreeable a burden as commerce is to the poet. Even his instinctive sexual impulses offend his intellect; so that when he meets the woman who excites them he invites her to join him in a bitter and scornful criticism of their joint absurdity." ("The Saturday Review," October 2, 1897.) By the way, not all poets have found commerce a disagreeable burden, as Shakespeare's biography very specifically indicates.

the chief spokesman has been the eloquent Professor Bradley, who partly accepts and partly rejects the Coleridgean concept.

He agrees that "even if the view (i.e., Coleridge's) itself does not suffice, the *description* given by its adherents of Hamlet's state of mind, as we see him in the last four Acts, is, on the whole and so far as it goes, a true description. The energy of resolve is dissipated in an endless brooding on the deed required." [129] But the theory as a whole "degrades Hamlet and travesties the play," for Hamlet "at any *other* time and in any *other* circumstances than those presented would have been perfectly equal to his task." [130] If he stands helpless before his duty, "the direct cause was a state of mind quite abnormal and induced by special circumstances—a state of profound melancholy." [131] The melancholy induced the excessive reflection, and the latter was but a symptom of the inaction. "The moral shock of the sudden ghastly disclosure of his mother's true nature," [132] made clear by her hasty marriage, has sunk "his whole being towards annihilation"—and in the midst of this disgust with life, Hamlet is commanded by the Ghost to wreak vengeance. "His soul leaps up in passion to answer this demand. But it comes too late. It does but strike home the last rivet in the melancholy which holds him bound." [133] And it is this melancholy which "accounts for the main fact, Hamlet's inaction." [134]

Mr. Knight carries the idea even further. Hamlet, as he sees him, endures intense soul-sickness and melancholia.[135] "The symptoms are, horror at the fact of death and an equal detestation of life, a sense of uncleanliness and evil in the things of nature; a disgust at the physical body of man; bitterness, cynicism, hate." [136] Hamlet does not avenge his father's death not out of hate of bloodshed, "but because his 'wit's diseased'; his will is snapped and useless, like a broken leg." [137] He does not kill Claudius for that would not have brought his father back to life, nor given life to Hamlet "who had so long lived in Death," nor "have altered the Universal Scheme. To Hamlet, the universe smells of mortality." [138] "In the universe of this play. . . he is the only discordant element, the only hindrance to happiness, health, and prosperity: a living death in the midst of life." [139]

Professor Adams agrees that disillusionment leads to Hamlet's melancholy.[140] Miss Campbell also believes Hamlet not naturally melancholy, but made so by grief, a grief "that renders him dull, that effaces memory, that makes him guilty of the sin of sloth." [141] But there are those who believe Hamlet's character to be fundamentally melancholic.[142] To bolster that contention, parallels have been cited between Shakespeare's lines and various quasi-scientific works on melancholy; one scholar is convinced that the dramatist employed Dr. Timothy Bright's *A Treatise of Melancholie* (1586) as a textbook to supply his hero's traits; [143] another confidently declares: "That Hamlet is to be accepted as essentially a melancholic can no longer be in doubt, now that contemporary sources dealing with this type . . . have been explored." [144] While others argue that the Prince is the typical Elizabethan melancholic,[145] one scholar demonstrates that Shakespeare has rather pre-envisioned the conception of melancholy later to be propounded by Kant; [146] and there are those who think Shakespeare's understanding of this disease was worthy of a brain specialist.[147] Hamlet's melancholy is described as purely psychic,[148] and as resulting in a serious monomania of pessimism.[149] But one commentator remarks that if this melancholy does cause Hamlet to procrastinate, it is allied to his "conscientious scruples against blood revenge." [150]

And that new perspective brings us to our next theory.

"TOO MUCH THE MAN OF MORALS"

It was inevitable, one supposes, that someone would start a school of criticism to explain Hamlet's delay in terms of moral scruple, though of all "explanations" this exceeds all others, even the Freudian, in silliness.

Ulrici began it. "Even when Hamlet has assured himself of the King's guilt by the device of the play," he says, "he still hesitates, and forms no resolve; he is still beset with doubts and scruples,—but preeminently *moral* doubts and *moral* scruples! Most justly. Even though the King were trebly a fratricide, in a *Christian* sense it would still be a sin to put him to death with one's own hand, without a trial and without justice. In Hamlet, therefore, we behold the Christian struggling with the natural man and its demand for revenge, in a tone rendered still louder and deeper by the hereditary prejudices of the Teutonic nations. The natural man spurs him on to immediate action, and charges his doubts with cowardice and irresolution; the Christian spirit . . . draws him back, though still resisting. He hesitates, and delays, and tortures himself with a vain attempt to reconcile these conflicting impulses." [151]

This view has, of course, been widely enough endorsed.[152] "Hamlet's responsibility is to his own conscience. . . . Why should a man like Hamlet, noble of nature, gentle, thoughtful, scrupulous, eager to believe the best of his fellows—" asks Quiller-Couch, "why should such a man *not* shrink from the deed?" [153] "His higher nature," agrees a scholar, "will not allow him to commit murder." [154] His inner promptings are to kill Claudius, but Hamlet triumphs over them, avers another, and will not act in violation of his conscience as he must do if he obey the Ghost's behest.[155] Hamlet, in all these opinions, is too much the Christian to kill anyone.

The point is sometimes made with a certain diminution of ethical loftiness of tone: the task appointed Hamlet is beneath his dignity, the world being too pernicious a place for him to stoop to take vengeance in it; [156] or, Hamlet's struggle is a cornerstone in the history of the law's evolution, for his battle is between the old morality of blood revenge and the new *legal* method of allowing the law to punish offenders; [157] or, he is a man caught between the values of two worlds, the medieval and the modern.[158] (A pretty idea.) Sometimes a little quaintness intrudes: Hamlet's problem is to discover a way of committing the great sin of murder without sinning; [159] or, it is to avoid seeming to kill the King for the purpose of seizing the throne, since Hamlet is the heir apparent; [160] or, he solves his inability to overcome his scorn of the world by refusing to take part in its affairs and turns to amateur theatricals instead.[161]

Before proceeding, the gentlemen may prefer to take off their hats (if wearing a hat is their normal dress for reading a book) and the ladies to cover their heads. For now, as we come to recent opinion in this Hamlet-too-much-the-Christian vein, the subject takes on a religiosity and a grandiloquence which are calculated to be awe-inspiring. We are about to pass from variations on Hamlet's mere scrupulosity to loftier measures. You may read what immediately follows in the same spirit which prompts some people to go see and hear *Parsifal* on Good Friday—as a substitute for attending church, though we cannot guarantee that either exercise will satisfactorily settle the destiny of your immortal soul. Now we hear not how Hamlet is too moral to kill, but how he has been divinely appointed to commit murder.

Hamlet, we read, is concerned only with the Eternal and cannot be bothered with personal vengeance; for paramount to the tragedy is "the conception of Omniscient Providence controlling the destinies of men." [162] Professor Craig sees the whole play as a spiritual struggle for the hero before he is ready for his holy mission to kill Claudius: "Before a man can act effectively he must master his own soul." It is for this reason that Hamlet procrastinates. "All men hesitate to take up arms against a sea of troubles. . . . All the blame bestowed upon Hamlet as a procrastinator rests squarely on the shoulders of all men, and they know it." [163] (We hope, reader, that you will henceforth cease making Hamlet *your* scapegoat!) And Mr. Fergusson adds to these heavy harmonies a somber tone: Hamlet does accomplish "some sort of purgatorial progress for himself and Denmark." [164]

The anthem swells, and we behold Hamlet becoming transformed into a kind of combination Parsifal-Kundry to Denmark's Amfortas. (On second thought, gentlemen, we think you had *better* take off your hats.) To provide the dark organ-pedalling as a background for this hymn of regeneration, Miss Spurgeon, having studied the imagery of the play, notes that the typical figure employed in *Hamlet* to describe the condition of Denmark is the ulcer or tumor. Hence she concludes that "the problem in *Hamlet* is not predominantly that of the will and reason, of a mind too philosophic or a nature temperamentally unfitted to act quickly: he [Shakespeare] sees it pictorially *not as the problem of an individual at all*, but as something greater and even more mysterious, as a *condition* for which the individual is apparently not responsible, any more than the sick man is to blame for the infection which strikes and devours him, but which . . . relentlessly annihilates him and others, innocent and guilty alike. That is the tragedy of *Hamlet*, and it is perhaps the chief tragic mystery of life." [165] (This *is* harder than bezique!)

Denmark being thus foully decayed, Hamlet's business therefore is not to kill the King but to "cleanse the world of the virulent poison that has entered it." [166] (One feels like hushing into shame the less noble commentators who say, in a manner dangerously near laissez-faire or allez-au-Diable, that Hamlet knows he *cannot* reform the world of its rottenness, feels there is not enough point to killing the King, and hence refrains from doing so.[167])

But Mr. Roy Walker and Mr. S. F. Johnson soar to sing golden hymns at heaven's gate. The latter says of Hamlet that "he is the instrument of an inscrutable Providence to whom man is of more value than many sparrows," and that before he dies Hamlet arrives "at an attitude that bridges the gap between the real and the ideal and transcends the conflict between appearance and reality." [168] Mr. Walker wings even higher, for he believes of Hamlet that "only in his weaker moments did he conceive his duty to be no more than the murder of his uncle. His innermost consciousness was struggling towards the realization of order in human affairs." (The round has come full circle. Now instead of Hamlet's problem being connected with the killing of Claudius—as the play, if *that* has any authority in the matter, would seem to imply throughout—that issue is purely incidental to Hamlet's purposes.) Hamlet's waiting to kill the King "was the waiting which is a struggle to attain the divine spontaneity in which humanity is transfigured into the image of a divinity that shapes our ends." [169]

We feel somehow lacking in duty that we cannot here summon a rumble of kettledrums and the bright blare of trumpets to render more sublime the period of these uplifting organ tones. But we cannot. We only pause to admire that the business of killing a man, even though that man be a king, can be made to figure symbolically as so holy an enterprise. It is disconcerting to reflect that assassination can be transmogrified once more in our own times into a sacred rite. How did Frazer ever allow himself to omit Hamlet from the voluminous instances of *The Golden Bough?*

We also pause to wonder what this rigmarole has to do with authentic drama.

"TOO COMPLEX-RIDDEN"

Now we need a new music as the formidable company of psychoanalysts looms on the horizon—something like the obscene wind-effects Strauss so cannily employs in *Tyl Eulenspiegel*, perhaps. But maybe, after all, we may stay with the organ *—for we are informed

---

* Psychoanalysts, note this interesting *lapsus calami.*

of one of these authorities that the division between the
the obscene is not so sharp as we have imagined, that the
s   may be "connected by an invisible navel string with the
coarse sexual, with what people call the obscene." [170]

Again we move from theory to theory by gradation. The distinguished psychoanalyst Ernest Jones singles out Ulrici, inaugurator of the "too scrupulous" theory of Hamlet's procrastination,
as the first critic to take an intelligent approach, since Ulrici was
the earliest to stress the hero's "internal conflict." [171] Presumably
Ulrici thus opened the first portal leading to the twilight regions of
Hamlet's unconscious, where complexes have a merry time of it in
the dark.

By concentrating on Hamlet's preoccupation with his mother,
some of the more purely literary scholars have helped pave the
road for the psychoanalysts. "Hamlet's inertia derives partly at least
from his reaction to his mother's re-marriage," says one.[172] He is
interested much less in killing the King than in the salvation of the
Queen, offers another.[173] But the road is immeasurably widened by
the half-timid concession of some that "unconscious" elements may
be basic to the understanding of the tragedy. Professor Tillyard
stoutly defends the detection of "unacknowledged motives," for
the "world of *Hamlet* is one in which the unexpressed motives are
likely to count." [174] Mr. Clutton-Brock goes further and boldly
states that Hamlet's unconscious mind shrinks from killing Claudius
because he is eager above all to *forget* his father's murder as well as
his mother's second marriage; [175] to take vengeance would be to
stamp on his memory what he is eager to obliterate from it.

But these harmless flirtations with Freudianism are as nothing
to the bold deeds of the professionals. It was the master himself who
began a magnificent onslaught on the subject—and that was, says
Doctor Jones, as it should have been: Hamlet's problem is the
"Sphinx of modern literature," and it was only "fitting" that the
man who solved the riddle of the "Theban one" (i.e., by inventing
the Oedipus complex) should have "solved the riddle of this
Sphinx" [176] *—Sigmund Freud.

* Would it be too much temerity to remark that Oedipus was certainly the one man on record who could not be accused of harboring

Let us, however, listen to the words of the master. Hamlet, he says, can do almost anything except kill the man "who did away with his father and has taken his father's place with his mother." Instead of loathing Claudius, he feels self-reproach because he knows himself in wish to be "no better than the murderer" he is supposed to punish.[177] Hamlet has long felt the incestuous urge towards his mother and his feelings are "hysterical" because Claudius has done what he himself has always wished to do, killed Hamlet's father and mated with Gertrude. And that is the reason why Shakespeare was impelled to write the play, for it is a presentation of his own complexes at the time of composition. *Hamlet* was written immediately "after the death of Shakespeare's father (1601)," * and the confused feelings disturbing Shakespeare himself at the time were mirrored in Hamlet's father-hate and mother-fixation. In another work, however, Freud, although repeating the imputation of an Oedipus complex to Hamlet, comes to different conclusions about the author's role in the composition of *Hamlet*. There he notes that the name "William Shakespeare" is probably a pseudonym to conceal the identity of Edward de Vere, Earl of Oxford (whose vogue as author of Shakespeare's plays has somewhat displaced the claims of the Baconians), who "lost a beloved and admired father while he was still a boy, and completely repudiated his mother, who contracted a new marriage soon after her husband's death."[178] †

Freud is fascinating on the incidents in *Hamlet*. Nothing is more diverting than his analysis of the manner in which Hamlet's father was killed, as re-enacted in the pantomime before Claudius. The dropping of poison into the monarch's ear "can only be explained by the latent sexual meaning. . . . The poison stands for sperm. . . . The ear is the reception chamber. . . . The double meaning given it bespeaks the sadistic conception of coitus" formed by a child in the course of its sexual investigations. Hamlet identifies himself with the murderer, not only because Claudius has killed

---

an Oedipus complex? The Greek Oedipus had no opportunity to acquire complexes of any kind towards the woman he married.

* In 1601 Shakespeare was a mere child of thirty-seven, and had been a father himself several times! But that is probably irrelevant.

† There is nothing in history to match the calm certainty of your psychoanalyst. He has his answer, whichever way the facts seem to turn.

Hamlet's father, as the Prince has yearned to do himself, but also as the "deputy of the parental sexual activity." [179] Hamlet, therefore, cannot kill the man with whom he unconsciously identifies himself. Indeed, he "actually revels" in the murder of his father which Claudius has committed for him.[180]

Now, you may wonder what Shakespeare would think of all this. The answer is that that would not at all matter. A Freudian disciple, after repeating the Oedipus complex charge against our hero, and ascribing the delay to the fact that "the murder of his father was a deed" Hamlet had "long harbored as a design in his unconscious," adds that Shakespeare himself "was not conscious of this hidden" motive,[181] and after all why should he be? "Poetry should not be too apparent, lest its beauty change into atrocity." [182] As Emil Ludwig says in a burst of understandable indignation: If "Shakespeare could regain life long enough to read Freudian explanations, scales would fall from his eyes and he would—in the role provided by that even greater master of the drama, Freud—exclaim: 'At last I understand my Hamlet!' " [183] There is no reason to suppose, however, that Mr. Ludwig's irony could mitigate by a degree the Olympian calm of the Freudians. They would simply assure him he had spoken literal truth—unconsciously, of course.

Doctor Jones' emphasis is more on Hamlet's horror at the Queen's incestuous marriage than at his father's murder,[184] and the scholarly Mr. Walley also believes that the Prince finds his mother "more reprehensible" than Claudius, that he would rather take vengeance on her, but, being asked only to kill Claudius, is thereby prevented from taking action.[185] Again and again it is insisted that Hamlet's chief trait is his incestuous love for his mother,[186] that his conscious mind hates the King but his "subconscious blindly identifies his own personality with the lover of his mother." [187]

Quite recently a leading psychoanalyst has taken an even bolder stand. What if the late king had not been murdered? What would Hamlet be like then? The answer: Even if Hamlet's father had died a natural death, and even if Gertrude had not remarried, Hamlet would still feel hostile to his mother. And this is the process by which he arrives at his hostility: Father's death "has removed the superior rival for Mother's love"—i.e., Father himself. Those "repressed infantile wishes" for sexual commerce with Mother threaten now to emerge. "Here is the occasion to take the place of Father" as Mother's lover. But the conscious mind rejects the idea, and Father's figure is as a result glorified, while Mother becomes the object of "antagonism and resentment" as a measure of self-protection from temptation on the part of the son. The more Hamlet is impelled to assume his father's place, the more his resentment against his mother will grow.[188] Obviously, the *manner* of Father's death, therefore, could not materially alter Hamlet's essential frustrations.*

Doctor Jones has his own slant on Hamlet's reasons for not being able to kill Claudius. Hamlet hates the King, but it is the hatred of one jealous "evil-doer towards his successful fellow." He can never denounce Claudius with the same passion with which he upbraids his mother because denunciation of the King would only "stimulate to activity his own unconscious and 'repressed' complexes. . . . In reality his uncle incorporates the deepest and most buried part of his own personality, so that he cannot kill him without also killing himself." [190]

Doctor Stekel has truly a new notion, however. Hamlet, according to him, cannot kill Claudius because the Prince has too many doubts about his origin. "Who could vouch that Hamlet is not his uncle's son if his mother was intimate with him before the father's death? Thus, Hamlet would kill his own father if he were to take revenge on his uncle for the death of his official father." [191] Considering Hamlet's age, this notion would lend an air almost of respectability to Gertrude's adultery, when its long life is calculated. And as for Claudius, how his passion must have grown with the decades! Why should we even consider Hamlet's procrastination in the face of Claudius'? Why should Hamlet's few months claim our attention when we think of the patient years in which Claudius must, according to Stekel's view, have waited to do the deed? The possibilities become more engaging every minute. This thirty years

---

* With becoming modesty, this author concludes these speculations: "If this discussion can be considered at all as an original, analytic contribution to the Hamlet problem, it may deserve that title only as a by-product of the curiosity of a psychologist who sometimes goes astray in his thoughts when he explores the yet undiscovered recesses of the human mind." [189]

of procrastinating on Claudius' part make him a marvelous subject for psychoanalytical inspection (why has *he* been overlooked?), and one feels that one would like to know more about him.

> Who was his father?
>   Who was his mother?
> Had he a sister?
>   What of his brother?
> Or, was there a dearer one
> Still, and a nearer one
>   Yet, than all other?

Before departing, however unwillingly, from the companionship of this exciting school of commentators, the reader might be interested in two little variations on the Freudian theme. One of them takes us momentarily into pediatrics: Shakespeare's parents had five children between Shakespeare's third and sixteenth years, and that is why he has made Hamlet procrastinate; that delay embodies the adult's reviving his "three-year-old's intense reactions" to the first of his mother's pregnancies and births.[192] The other, original enough, makes Hamlet feel unconsciously far from hostile to Claudius, who is for him a second "protective" father; while Claudius is alive Hamlet is thus saved from indulging his desire to possess the Queen; what Hamlet would prefer to do is commit *matricide*. Because he is not up to that, he procrastinates. Not until the Queen is dead will he be able to carry out the Ghost's injunctions to kill his father's slayer; once Gertrude has drunk the fatal drink, however, Hamlet, freed at last of his incestuous obsession, can kill the King." [193]

We have heard rumors of the existence of a "homosexual" rather than an "Oedipus complex" explanation of Hamlet's dilemma, but have been unable to track one down. Here and there, of course, the Freudians have thrown out a vague remark to the effect that there "is something homosexual" in Hamlet's conduct while they are busily expounding the "Oedipus" theory. What is adorable about psychoanalysis is that you can always prove anything you like from any given body of facts. We therefore, to supply the deficiency, submit a "homosexual theory" of Hamlet—since in all fairness to those of that persuasion they should not be thus ruthlessly excluded—based on the same evidence employed to prove the "Oedipus" contention:

1. Hamlet had an unnatural love for his father (as witness his glowing references to him) and hence always resented his mother, wishing to be in *her* place. This would neatly explain his rejection of Ophelia quite as well as the Oedipus argument that he gave her up because of his mother. Hence, too, his hatred for Claudius, who killed the man Hamlet loved. He delays because people of his sexual orientation shrink from action.

2. Or, he secretly loves Claudius, too, and cannot for that reason kill him. To strengthen this view there is, besides his rejection of Ophelia, his suspicious closeness to Horatio, who is very virile. One might also bring in the fact that he speaks much more courteously of Laertes than he does to his sister.

3. Or, since homosexuals are notoriously attached to their mothers, Hamlet has always hated his father, is glad he is dead (though *not* for "Oedipus complex" reasons) and is really grateful to Claudius for the murder. Naturally, being a man of honor, Hamlet cannot *consciously* admit his gratitude or attraction to his uncle, and hence speaks bitterly of him, while taking no action against him. Etc.,etc.

It is probably wrong to jest about the "Oedipus complex" version of Hamlet, however, for the Freudians have made it no laughing matter. The damage they have wrought the play is incalculable. Their notions have taken firm hold of the stage (and screen), and ever since the Gielgud production every representation of the play on Broadway has adopted this view; the scene in Gertrude's closet has been made (notably in Evans' and Olivier's performances) to crawl with incestuous overtones. As a result many playgoers must by this time feel that such was Shakespeare's meaning. Moreover, the Shakespeare scholars themselves, almost without being aware of it, have now for decades over-emphasized Hamlet's closeness to his mother. For that one holds the performances of the play responsible. But it is a false and vicious reading of the play's meaning, and it is high time that there be an end to it.

We draw some faint comfort from the complaints of one psychoanalyst, who feels that actors now lift these "Oedipus" stirrings into the realm of the conscious! He objects to the Olivier movie on the grounds that this Hamlet, having read the accounts of Freud and Jones, has accepted and absorbed them "not wisely but too well." [194] The Prince, thus, addresses his mother as though she were his sweetheart, and the incestuous barrier between them begins to disappear; they are ready at any moment to embrace as lovers. Olivier, in sum, did not permit his feelings to *remain* in the realm of the unconscious, where they should be left—they were all too plain. The analyst observes cryptically that although he believes the "Oedipus complex" theory correct, "I do not believe an actor should act the part according to this or any interpretation." (He ought to be well pleased with most Shakespearean performances.)

At any rate, whether for reasons of *submerging* the incest back into the unconscious, or for any other reason, one would thank future Hamlets to forget Freud and mother fixations, and behave a little more normally with Gertrude. In his dealings with her, Hamlet has incitements enough to act with passion of quite another variety.

OTHER VOICES, OTHER LUNES

There are, naturally, some "subjective" explanations of Hamlet's adjournment of vengeance which fit into none of the classifications we have looked at.

At least once it has been maintained that Hamlet is a woman, brought up as a man, and in love with Horatio [195]—a theory that would seem to account for Hamlet's reluctance to kill Claudius and to marry Ophelia. The idea was incorporated long ago into a German movie,* with a Scandinavian actress playing Hamlet, and there was,

---

* In 1920, Asta Nielsen enacting the role of the heroine-hero. In all fairness to that production, however, it should be added that (unless memory is playing tricks) there was no pretense that it was Shakespeare's story which was being presented.

Before this film and Mr. Olivier's, there were a number of cinema versions of *Hamlet*, none of which we have been able to see. Messrs. Mander and Mitchenson's delightful photographic record, *Hamlet through the Ages* (London, 1952), is running over with all kinds of entertaining facts on past productions of the play; and to it we are indebted for many of the following facts (pp. 2, 3, 8, 24, 33, 37, 52, and 65). Among the film versions were:

indeed, something quite Wagnerian about the affair; as Hamlet fell in death and all her lovely hair tumbled loose and revealed itself for the first time, one was reminded of that incomparable moment at the opera when Siegfried, having pierced through the Magic Fire, undoes the corselet from the sleeping form of the well-padded Valkyrie, beholds her capacious bosom, and staggers back, crying (quite superfluously): "This is no man!"

(On the other hand, one writer stoutly maintains that Hamlet ought always be portrayed as wearing a beard.[196])

1. In 1900, a French filming of the last scene in the play, with Sarah Bernhardt in the title role.

2. In 1907, a French filming of the Ghost scenes in Act One.

3. In 1908, an Italian version of the same.

4. In 1910, a French film of the entire story, with Jacques Grétillat as Hamlet.

5. In 1910, the first English film.

6. In 1911, a Danish film, with Alwin Neuff as Hamlet.

7. In 1913, an English film, starring Forbes Robertson.

8. In 1914, an American film, with James Young as Hamlet, and Clara Kimball Young as Ophelia.

Sarah Bernhardt is, of course, still remembered for her impersonation of Hamlet, but she was by no means the first actress to undertake the role. Mrs. Siddons was apparently the first female Hamlet (1777), and the novelist-actress, Mrs. Inchbald, soon followed her lead (1780); neither of these ladies, however, chanced a London performance. The first time that city saw a female Hamlet was in 1796, when Mrs. Powell enacted the role; New York first saw the attempt in 1819, when Mrs. Bartley made it. Among many other female Hamlets, there have been Charlotte Cushman (1851), Alice Marriott (1861), Mrs. Bandmann-Palmer (1895), Clara Howard (1899), Eva Le Gallienne (1937), and Esmé Beringer (1938).

There have been other strange *Hamlets*. There was a celebrated *Dog Hamlet* in the early nineteenth century, in which a gifted dog followed Hamlet around throughout the course of the play, and in the last scene pinned Claudius to the floor while Hamlet killed the King.

In the pages of the present study, references to the "film version" of *Hamlet* are, of course, to Mr. Olivier's only. That is likely to be the only one with which readers have any acquaintance, and it is, moreover, bound to be on view for some time to come.

There are other accounts of the procrastination. At complete odds with Schlegel and Coleridge's too-thoughtful Prince, George Santayana finds Hamlet totally irrational: "He acts without reflection, as he reflects without acting. At the basis of all his ingenuity . . . lies this act of inexplicable folly: that he conceals his discovery, postpones his vengeance before questioning its propriety, and descends with no motive to a grotesque and pitiful piece of dissimulation." [197] Professor Lewis thinks Hamlet's delay the fruit of his pretended madness.[198] A recent writer conceives the hero as more devoted to rant than to action.[199] Another thinks Hamlet's inaction owing to his inability to understand himself.[200]

The "To be or not to be" soliloquy has caused many commentators to emphasize the Prince's concern over death. Doctor Jones sees Hamlet's struggle as "at heart one long despairing fight against suicide." [201] Mr. Masefield, too, believes that he prefers death to action.[202] But Mr. John Middleton Murry makes Hamlet's *fear* of death the mainspring of the plot: " 'To be or not to be' verily is the question." The Ghost has implanted "in Hamlet's soul that utterly new horror of death which will for a time prevent him from taking revenge." Shakespeare has Hamlet put off vengeance for two reasons: his fear of that "something after death" of which the Prince speaks, and the Christian ethics which bids him "resist no evil." But it is the former which "is the main dramatic motive of delay." [203]

It has also been suggested that the reason we cannot decipher the causes of Hamlet's inaction is that they keep changing throughout the play. "The causes of Hamlet's long delay are complex; the center of gravity, so to speak, shifts from act to act, from scene to scene. New complications arise." Shakespeare preferred "we should decide for ourselves" what the leading motives may be, so that we may have a deeper sense of the complexity of all human emotions.[204] But elsewhere this vagueness of intent is felt to be a fault: the hero having no ostensible reason for postponing vengeance, the dramatist attempts to cover up the weakness of his plot by Hamlet's frequent self-reproaches.[205] It is also held that the delay was meant to be a puzzle,[206] a mystery.[207]

The Prince is described as "the most complete failure" on record.[208] He inherits his "weakness, his self-abandonment" from his mother, his "foolhardy courage" from his father; and his "passion for crooked ways" and his love of "intriguing" from his uncle.[209]

He is a fatalist, crippled in action by the conflicts of his personality—his trust and distrust of logic, his emotional make-up, and his affectionateness.[210] He is "the philosopher, who realized that life was not worth having," for it is basely gross, fit only to be rejected by the noble of soul.[211] Yet Mr. Madariaga has depicted him as "egocentric"—a man of "Borgian mind" with "utter disregard" for the feelings of others—a man who believes all things "permissible to the powerful for the sake of power." [212]

Hamlet is "the apotheosis of the Fool," according to the dramatist's depiction of that vocation.[213] He is also the typical esthete and a warning "illustration of how such imbeciles fare," when faced with practical duty; he is "morally contemptible" like all esthetes—heartless to Ophelia (whom he is eager to corrupt), to his friends, and to Polonius.[214]

The trouble with Hamlet is that he doesn't know his Bible intimately enough; such men are doomed to failure.[215] He is an eleventh-century Catholic prince who might have been saved and successful had he consulted a "spiritual adviser." [216] He is a typical product of Renaissance learning as dispensed at the University of Wittenberg, and rendered by it unable to deal with the world; his fellow student Horatio suffers from the same incapacity.[217] His conflicts are the product of the *Kultur* of the Elizabethan age.[218]

Nor have Hamlet's physical disabilities been overlooked. He ails from a fatty degeneration of the heart, and he procrastinates because of his "too too solid flesh." [219] He is "a fat neurasthenic, half evil, half imbecile." [220] So judge an American and an Italian; but a more charitable Frenchman, while granting his excess weight, is sure it did not harm him in any way.[221]

Hamlet was no melancholy Romantic, but "first and last and always the gentleman," who learned to control his passions.[222] He was also a confirmed celibate.[223] He was a constable; for that is what his name means, and Shakespeare uses the word symbolically.[224] He was, in addition, probably a Hindu; for his conviction that to exist is to suffer is clearly drawn from the *Bhagavadgita*.[225]

While we are on the subject of the character of Hamlet, we

should take note of some of the commentators who, without reference to the question of his procrastination, discover Shakespeare himself in his hero.

To a certain extent every creator, even so detached a writer as Shakespeare, inevitably puts something of himself into his creation—even when, unlike Byron or Keats, he has no taste for writing autobiographically. To write well he must identify himself with his characters, each in turn, and see what they do and say from their point of view. No one has ever managed this process more perfectly than Shakespeare. And M. Courdaveaux, after dismissing various theories concerning Hamlet's make-up, has Shakespeare very reasonably describe the manner of Hamlet's conception: "To what end do you argue in this fashion and impute to me depths of thought I never possessed? It may be I am a great poet and an admirable arranger of stories for the theater, but I was never the profound philosopher you paint me. . . . As for the topic which so much concerns you, I found in the *Tales* of Belleforest a story which struck me as being dramatic, and I tried to use it in the theater, as I have done with countless others . . . Instead of the wild half-sorcerer the legend supplied, I began making out of Hamlet a gentleman of my own day, the flower of Queen Elizabeth's courtiers, with all the intellectual culture of the sixteenth century. Then, by a process familiar enough to poets, I gave to this intelligent man, refined by education, sentiments I myself acquired by nature and events. Suffering from men and events, I have used the situation of my hero to put into his mouth the vexations and disillusionments of my own heart." [226]

But not all have been content with so moderate and reasonable an approach to the world's most completely objective writer. Taine insists that "Hamlet is Shakespeare," and that in the hero "Shakespeare has painted himself." [227] So, too, feels Mr. Figgis.[228] One critic says that Hamlet is "a full-length portrait of Shakespeare's mind"; [229] another, of his inner self; [230] yet others, of Shakespeare in his everyday life,[231] of his own nature,[232] of his own misfortunes.[233] (The last commentator also adds, as if to square accounts, that Shakespeare is not only the author of his own plays but of the works attributed to Bacon as well.) Hamlet is what Shakespeare "might have been if he had not written the play"—it was his sublimation of the "super-ego and the impulses of the id." [234] Doctor Jones goes, of course, much further, and in a long chapter psychoanalyzes "The Hamlet in Shakespeare" via the play, finding in it abundant proof, backed by the *Sonnets*, of the dramatist's bisexuality.[235]

Allied to the search for the autobiographical in Shakespeare's work is the modern pastime of discovering portraits of his contemporaries in the play. Although a harmless enough sport, it strikes us as of all occupations the most futile. Even if any of these findings could be accepted, they can contribute nothing of literary import; they cannot by an iota elucidate the plays as drama, as poetry, as comedy, or as tragedy. It is perfectly true that Shakespeare frequently makes reference to contemporary events; that was because he conceived himself to be a modern writing about modern (or rather, eternal) values, rather than historical ones, no matter where or when his locale; the butcher, the baker, and the candlestick-maker, moreover, who were his audience, would have a livelier sense of the reality of the play's transactions if it were peppered with references familiar to all of them. It is also true that every creator naturally draws upon his observation and knowledge of the people around him. But all that constitutes something quite different from the supposition that he who created not for an age but for all time should have found it worth the trouble to give us full-length portraits of this or that Elizabethan courtier. In any case, even had he taken that trouble, it could hardly matter to us now when we approach *Hamlet*. Whatever value the tragedy has for us has nothing to do with the lives of Essex, Leicester, or James VI of Scotland.

Like Mr. W. H. of the *Sonnets*, Hamlet has been identified both with Southampton [236] and Pembroke.[237] Because of the Essex rebellion and the fall of Elizabeth's last favorite, many have found in the Prince a portrait and defense of him [238]—though, confusingly, some make an analogy between Laertes' storming of Claudius' palace (in which Hamlet had no hand) and Essex's abortive attempt to do the same to Elizabeth's. One writer also concludes that Claudius is Leicester; [239] another believes the whole work a memorial to the ill-fated Essex; [240] another, a combined tribute to Essex and Marlowe with some self-portraiture superimposed.[241] Hamlet has also been thought a portrait of James I by a considerable number of scholars; [242] one commentator adds that Gertrude is Mary Stuart; Claudius, Bothwell; and Ophelia, Anna Douglas; [243] another very ingeniously reasons in this fashion: Hamlet calls Claudius a "pajock" (peacock), i.e., Jacob, i.e., James—Hamlet is "hambled," i.e., "the lamed one"—Laertes is "leo(lion)-heart"—Ophelia is "Mephisto-ophelia." [244] Hamlet has also been identified with Bacon (who is, naturally, the author of this and all of the other Shakespearean plays), Horatio with Shakespeare, and Fortinbras with James.[245] *

Hamlet has, finally, been called the typical Jew, a portrait of "a people bleeding from the heart at the injuries inflicted by the wickedness of the world." [246]

For the sake of completeness we must include at least one specimen from the so-called "Marxist" critics. These guileless folk have a simple time of it; according to them, until very recent days "progressive" writers have forever been demonstrating the fall of the feudal order and the rise of the middle class. (Why anyone should lift a pen to reiterate the demonstration none of them explains.) We know of one lecturer on *Hamlet* who describes Hamlet's indecision as a symbol of the decaying feudal order and Fortinbras' purposefulness as a symbol of the rising middle class. (Ophelia is "feudal lyricism"—which "is pretty but I don't know what it means.") He considers it beside the point that Fortinbras, whom he makes to represent the leading concept of the play, appears (in one of the longest plays ever written for the stage) for about five minutes *in toto*.

It is a simple exercise, as we have said. To indulge in it, you do not have to bother reading the books you discuss: any digest of the World's Best Books will satisfy your needs. For in any story someone is likely to be going up, and he will be the middle class, and someone going down—you've guessed it!—he is the decaying feudal order.

Mr. Morrow thus eloquently places Shakespeare in the vanguard

---

* In R. C. Churchill's fascinating study of "the attempts which have been made to prove that Shakespeare's works were written by others," *Shakespeare and His Betters* (Bloomington, Indiana, 1959)—and these others include Bacon, Raleigh, Essex, Cecil, Burton, Southampton, Shirley, Derby, Rutland, Barnard, Devonshire, Stirling, Oxford, Florio, Marlowe, Queen Elizabeth, and various "groups" of the forementioned!—we read how Hamlet has been claimed as a portrait of Raleigh (pp. 72, 106); Burton (p. 77); Bacon (p. 77); Derby (pp. 106, 182); Rutland (pp. 91, 106); Oxford (p. 106). Mr. Churchill demolishes all this nonsense very ably (pp. 121–223).

of social progress: "It was the middle class, then, whose advance meant the advance of civilization. . . . It fought, however selfish its aims, against all that stood in the way of expansion, all the impeding powers of the feudal world. . . . When all is said of Shakespeare the fact remains that in expressing this class he belonged with the movement forward." [247] It is to be hoped that Mr. Granville Hicks will blush at the words he once wrote as preface to this criticism: "Bourgeois critics"—lovely phrase!—"Bourgeois critics, schooled in doctrines of the sanctity of art, talk about the irrelevance of Marxism to literature. . . . Most critics seem unaware that the stirring events of Queen Elizabeth's reign constituted a crucial episode in the conflict between capitalism and feudalism. Certainly they do not perceive the effect that this struggle—a class struggle—had on Shakespeare's choice of themes, and they will be shocked to discover that . . . he was, in his treatment of his themes, unmistakably a partisan." [248] Mr. Morrow acknowledges that Mr. Hicks' "stimulating comments have done much to give . . . what merit" his work has.[249] Ah, the fatality of rushing into print, the permanence of the printed word!

SOME SENSE AT LAST

There remains a small group of *Hamlet* critics whom we may call the "objective" school because they look for the reasons of Hamlet's delay not in his personal shortcomings but in the circumstances of the story itself.

They all share one very serious defect: they attempt to account for Hamlet's fall entirely in terms of the situation in which the hero finds himself, and thus they unwittingly rob the drama of any claims to authentic tragedy; their Hamlet becomes only a victim of arbitrary Fate, a man without the necessary tragic *hamartia*, and consequently not a tragic hero. (In fact, one of our leading Shakespearean scholars, partial to this school, but forgetting first principles, has declared: "If *Hamlet* is not a tragedy of external circumstance there never was one." [250] To which one is obliged sadly to reply, "There never was.")

But this school of "objective" *Hamlet* scholars has done the play the great service, unfortunately insufficiently heeded these days, of drawing attention to the actual material of the drama, from which the "subjective" interpretations have wandered too far afield, pre-occupied (as they are) with trying to understand Character without reference to the Plot. There is no aspect of tragedy upon which Aristotle more insists than the basic nature of Plot. Literature being an imitation of life, "the primary objects of artistic imitation are human beings in action, men performing or doing something"; for Aristotle the distinguishing trait of drama is that it "directly presents the actions of men." Hence, Plot takes precedence even over Charac-ter in tragedy, "for tragedy is an imitation, not of men, but of an ac-tion and of life, and life consists in action." Plot is the organization of the action, and hence characterization must accommodate the Plot, not Plot the characterization. The "objective" critics have the virtue of keeping their eyes on matters connected with the Plot of *Hamlet*. If we cannot accept their comments as satisfactorily complete be-cause they sin in the opposite direction and tend to overlook Char-acter altogether and the relation of the tragic flaw to the catastrophe, we are nevertheless indebted to them for stressing certain factors in the story which must not be dismissed.

F. W. Ziegler, a celebrated actor, was the first to note an im-portant element in the play. Hamlet plans to give the piece before the King in the hopes that Claudius' guilt will become publicly evi-dent. "If the King's occulted guilt unkennel itself, Hamlet's sword must be plunged in the murderer's heart. If the royal bodyguards do not instantly cut him down, which is to be expected, he will cer-tainly have to justify the assassination of the King before a legally constituted court." And all Hamlet then could bring in as evidence would be the corroboration of Horatio and Marcellus that they had seen a ghost.[251] Such testimony would hardly exonerate Hamlet from what must appear a case of clear regicide—*if* the attending court allowed him to live long enough to have a trial.

This is an observation that makes sense. It reminds us that al-though *we* believe Claudius guilty of the murder of Hamlet's father, none of the persons of the drama besides the murderer (and possibly one other being) even suspects that there has been a murder. The rest of Denmark, including—be it said at once—the Queen, believes that the late monarch died a natural death, and has no reason to be-lieve otherwise. These facts we ought to bear in mind throughout the play.

Another fact of equal importance we are likely to overlook. In our times, when the only surviving European dynasties are political figureheads, we are inclined to think of kings as we do of other human beings. Though elevated in position, they no longer inspire the terror that was theirs when they were held to possess "divine right." In the seventeenth century regicide was more than a matter of killing another man; it was a sacrilegious act—as England later discovered when, after its legally constituted Parliament voted the execution of Charles I, Europe rocked with horror at what it deemed a deed of blasphemy. To recapture the sense of the divinity which did hedge a king, one has only to read one of the finest of Stuart dramas, *The Maid's Tragedy*, written by Shakespeare's gifted fellow playwrights, Beaumont and Fletcher. This play contains at least one scene of such dramatic intensity as would be enough to make the fortunes of any play today—did it not also contain a twist of plot, perfect for its times but unacceptable to ours, which would mar the entire tragedy for a modern audience. The hero, a brave warrior, is married by the King, quite beyond his expectations, to the most ravishingly beautiful woman at court; to wed her, he abandons his betrothed. After the wedding ceremony he discovers upon the very first night that his bride will never sleep with him: the marriage, which the world believes his reward, is but a ruse to cover her secret love affair with the King, and to provide a father for the King's illegitimate children when they are born. *We* should expect him to rush with his sword to exterminate the treacherous monarch. But our hero is a contemporary of Shakespeare's. What does he therefore do? He indeed rushes to the monarch with his sword, but only to kneel before him and to plead that his betrayer slay *him*, exclaiming:

> As you are mere man
> I dare as easily kill you for this deed
> As you dare think to do it. But there is
> Divinity about you that strikes dead
> My rising passions; as you are my king,
> I fall before you, and present my sword,
> To cut mine own flesh, if it be your will.[252]

This, as reflected in many plays, is the light in which Shakespeare's fellow citizens saw kings. And the proof of it is in *Hamlet*, too. In the final scene, even after Laertes has revealed to the whole court that Claudius is to blame for both the poisoned cup which has killed Gertrude and for the plot which enabled the naked blade to deal Hamlet his mortal hurt, when Hamlet thereupon flings himself at the King to stab him, the court reacts, as it were, by conditioned reflex:

> ALL.   Treason! Treason!
> V, ii, 320

They would have had that reaction to the killing of their King no matter what Laertes had just exposed.

In assessing Hamlet's problem of vengeance, then, we must begin by taking into account the almost insuperable difficulty facing the Prince when he attempts, singlehanded, the life of a king. This Shakespeare's audience would have understood as too obvious to require underlining. We are likely, however, to be unaware of it.

The German critic Klein advances us another step in the realization of the fundamentals of the plot: "The tragic root of this deepest of all tragedies is secret guilt. . . . Here the brother in sleep, far from all witnesses or the possible knowledge of any one, is stolen upon and murdered. And how murdered? . . . Murder most secret, murder, as it were, in its most primitive shape, murder invisibly committed; . . . a thief-like murder, such as they only commit who steal a crown. The victim himself is all unconscious. . . . For this deed of blood there is no human eye, no human ear. The horror of this crime is its security; the horror of this murder is that it murders discovery. . . . The son has no other certainty of the unwitnessed murder than the suspicion generated by his ardent filial love, the prophecy of his bleeding heart, 'O my prophetic soul!' *—no other conviction but the inner psychological conviction of his acute mind; no other power of proving it but that which results from the strength

---

* This is a serious slip. When Hamlet exclaims these words after the Ghost identifies the murderer, it is absurd to interpret them as meaning that he has always suspected his uncle of the crime. Up to this interview with his father's spirit, Hamlet has had no idea that his father died an unnatural death. The line means merely that he feels now his old hatred of his uncle has a real basis.

of his strong, horror-struck understanding. . . . Vengeance is impossible, for its aim hovers in an ideal sphere. It falters, it shrinks back from itself, and it must do so, for it lacks the sure basis, the tangible hilt; it lacks what alone can justify it before God and the world, material proof." [253]

That this commentary is on the right track—as far as it goes—is obvious once we remember that *Shakespeare took the pains to change the original version of the story*, as we have noted, so as *to make the murder of Hamlet's father not an open act of assassination*, publicly committed and therefore known to the world, *but secret, hidden from everyone's knowledge*, apparently impossible to bring charges against. The change, as we have also already remarked, is such as to alter the whole meaning of the story. It is urgent that we remember that Shakespeare's plot is constructed on the premise of *secret* murder.

It was Karl Werder who most significantly elaborated Klein's position. He reminds us that Hamlet's task involves more than stealing upon Claudius and killing him. "To a tragical revenge there is necessary punishment, to punishment justice, and to justice the vindication of it before the world. And therefore, Hamlet's aim is not the crown, nor is it his first duty to kill the King; but his task is justly to punish the murderer of his father, unassailable as that murderer is in the eye of the world, and to satisfy the Danes of the righteousness of this procedure. . . ."

We interrupt the quotation to reinforce this cardinal point. The Ghost's only injunction to Hamlet concerning the taking of vengeance against Claudius is:

> But howsoever thou pursuest this act,
> Taint not thy mind
>
> I, v, 84–85

—which, lowered into prose, means something like this: "But in whatever way you carry out this act of vengeance against Claudius, be careful that you manage it without injuring your soul": in other words, "be sure that your deed be an act of justice, not murder." In *Hamlet* itself, as we shall see, we behold the differences between an act of private reprisal or spite (such as Laertes is anxious to perpetrate) and an act of justice (such as Hamlet is enjoined and wishes to perform). They have nothing in common. An act of justice must be one that the world, knowing the facts of the case, can understand as such.

That Hamlet is mightily concerned, when he has at last killed Claudius, that what he has done be correctly understood by Denmark, his world, as justly done, is eloquently demonstrated during the last minutes of the play. He has, after Laertes' death, but three brief speeches allotted him while the venom is working its mortal way in his blood, and these last utterances of his are largely given over to his anguished desire that everything be explained. In the first of them he addresses the astonished court:

> You that look pale and tremble at this chance,
> That are but mutes or audience to this act,
> Had I but time—as this fell sergeant Death
> Is strict in his arrest— O, I could tell you—
> But let it be. Horatio, I am dead;
> Thou liv'st. *Report me and my cause aright*
> *To the unsatisfied.*
>
> V, ii, 345 seq.

It is his paramount thought as he is dying. Now Horatio attempts to follow him in death, but he dashes the poisoned cup from his faithful friend's hand, and he has but one reason for doing it:

> O God, Horatio, what a wounded name,
> *Things standing thus unknown,* shall live behind me!
> If thou didst ever hold me in thy heart,
> Absent thee from felicity a while
> And in this harsh world *draw thy breath* in pain
> *To tell my story.*
>
> V, ii, 355 seq.

And with his last breath, a few moments later, still troubled with the importance that the world understand his acts, he says:

> So tell him, with the occurrents, more and less,
> Which have solicited—
> [i.e., *Tell Fortinbras all the happenings which*
> *have incited—*]
>
> V, ii, 368–9

He was about to add "my acts" but life fails him. He has only four words more: "The rest is silence," and with them he dies. The catastrophe is complete: Hamlet meets death without knowing whether what he has done will ever be understood. And the critics, on the whole, have seen to it that it should not.

Let us return to Werder. He is speaking of the earlier part of the tragedy: "But it is the difficulty of producing this evidence (i.e., against Claudius), this proof, the apparent impossibility of convicting the guilty person, that constitutes the cardinal point in *Hamlet!* And therefore killing the King *before* the proof is adduced would be, not killing the guilty, but killing the *proof;* it would be, not the murder of the criminal, but the murder of Justice! It would be truth that would be struck dead, through such an annihilation of its only means of triumph; the tragic action would degenerate into the action of mere brutes; a strange, outrageous, brutal blow across the clear eyes of the understanding would be this senseless stroke—for which the critics are so importunate!" * [254]

Werder's view, while it does not furnish a thorough understanding of the drama and fails to account for much that happens in it, is essentially healthy and corrective of much nonsense written about *Hamlet.* It affords an intelligent point of departure for examining the progress of the action, by affirming fundamentals that would have surely been deemed obvious enough by early audiences unencumbered by the weight (since Mackenzie) of more than a century and a half of commentary. Although not sufficiently respected for its undercurrent of good sense (perhaps because all German criticism has been rendered suspect by a prevailing heavy-handedness and mysticism), Werder's theory has been endorsed by a number of respectable scholars. [255] The limitation of his criticism is that, despite

* Thus much, discounting a certain Teutonic floridity, Werder speaks to the point. But a great deal of what follows in Werder is not so good. As we have noted, the argument fails to make Hamlet a tragic hero by keeping him a victim; Werder, like Klein, must be pronounced inadequate in some of his conceptions, in many details of his exegesis, and in his concept of Hamlet's character. Some of his lacks are due to his readiness to take for granted Hamlet's feigned insanity. He has a hard time of it relating that to the plot, and proving it natural and essential to the story.

sound premises, it avoids keeping a fresh, unprejudiced eye on the actual events which form the plot.

THE PLOT'S THE THING? NO, THE SOLILOQUY!

In the next two chapters, where, respectively, we answer the confusion-makers and then outline the play as we believe Shakespeare understood it, we shall keep our bearings by never losing sight of the Plot. At this late date one would think it axiomatic that in drama worthy of the name, it is plot which "is the first principle and, as it were, the soul of a tragedy; character holds second place." [256]

Nevertheless, despite this unexceptionable observation of Aristotle's, Professor Stoll, who has founded something of a school of his own in Shakespearean criticism these past decades, declares: "We have no right . . . to interpret the character by way of the plot." [257] Mr. Johnson, who calls Professor Stoll "the most considerable critic of Shakespeare since Bradley," says of him that he has undertaken "to re-establish the integrity of the work of art . . . and to define the primary meanings of the play in terms of the time and place of their composition and production." [258]

Of the latter procedure we have already said that although it is indispensable it is full of hazards too. Shakespeare was in every quality and understanding immeasurably beyond his fellow Elizabethans. While much in his plays can be illuminated by an understanding of Elizabethan manners and beliefs, in and out of the theater, it is always dangerous stubbornly to insist that Shakespeare was never more than just another dramatist of the age. The bromide that "all writers cannot help reflecting their age" is true enough—but only to a degree. The great writer has ever been one who is better than his age; his greatness, indeed, is always in direct proportion to his having outdistanced the notions of his contemporaries. Professor Stoll, by never seeing Shakespeare as more than an Elizabethan, ends by diminishing him to the size of his smallest fellow playwright and audience.

As for the former attribution, it strikes us as a careless description of Professor Stoll to say that he tries "to re-establish the integrity of the work of art." It is a fact that Professor Stoll has always seen, as one should see, the dramas as plays written for the stage, not only for the library; but he seems unwilling to view Shakespeare's masterpieces as more than highly successful popular entertainment. And between art and mere entertainment—particularly in the instance of tragedy—the gaps are very considerable. Professor Stoll sees little more in *Hamlet* than a clever and not-too-well-thought-out rewriting of an old play. "Prompted by his usual opportunism," Shakespeare, he feels, turned "to account" the popular traditions of the revenge play.[259] The audience was familiar with "feigned madness as an artifice and a natural employment of the revenger," not only in the old play on *Hamlet*, but in other revenge plays as well. He therefore "passed lightly, carrying his audience with him, over the reasons for it." [260] Shakespeare simply "kept Hamlet as he found him, only manipulating him more deftly. The audience were accustomed to the revenger beating about the bush but reproaching himself for it." [261] Hamlet's delay, in short, is only due to the Elizabethan convention of the revenge play, hence cannot be related to any defect of the hero's character or situation, and need not be questioned by us. The inference is that since Shakespeare had five acts to fill up, Hamlet could not take his revenge until the last scene, or the play would be over too soon. (Professor Spencer, on the other hand, remarks on *Hamlet's* extraordinary length, and observes ruefully: "Nearly all of Shakespeare's plays have proved too long for the endurance of most audiences. . . . Why Shakespeare, who almost lived in the theater, habitually wrote in excess of its requirements is a pretty question." [262] Even if the reproach were just, it would show Shakespeare as something more than a conformer to Elizabethan standards!) To keep the audience interested, according to Professor Stoll, Shakespeare used the soliloquies as a stop gap until the revenge should take place at the end; the soliloquies are, therefore, a vital part of the play's narrative.

We are thus asked to think of the soliloquies, which by nature are not action but only speech, as basic to the story. Tragedy in this way becomes not a representation of life, of men in action, but a species of oratory. Such an idea makes of the dramatist a mere patcher of monologue and dialogue, a disguiser of inadequate plot material! Professor Stoll in his anxiety to restore Shakespeare to the Elizabethan stage also exiles him from the company of the world's greatest creators, where people infinitely less informed than Professor

Stoll know he belongs. It is *not* true that Shakespeare "kept Hamlet as he found him." When Shakespeare altered the elder Hamlet's murder to a secret one, he changed everything in the story's base, and was bound therefore to change everything accordingly in the hero's character and conduct. To deny him the intelligence of understanding that much about his profession is to make of him a bungler or Professor Stoll's successful opportunist. If he had been merely an opportunist he need have changed nothing in his source. He obviously had his reasons for making so vital an innovation in the story's premise; he obviously intended to write a quite different dramatic study from that afforded by the traditional Hamlet plot. And change that plot he did—in many significant ways. On that plot we had better keep our eye. Character *is* to be understood in terms of plot (Professor Stoll will forgive my preferring Aristotle's authority in this cardinal matter to his)—except, of course, in the work of a bungler or a cheap entertainer. What is the value of scholarship's familiarizing itself with the old Hamlet story if it is never willing to ask the meaning of Shakespeare's divergences from it? Would anyone dare assert that Shakespeare kept *any* of his great tragic figures "as he found him"? What has his Othello in common with the original Moor who commissioned the ensign to beat Desdemona to death with a sandbag, and then proceeded to help his officer pull down the ceiling over her to make her death seem an accident? What has his Lear in common with the mildly pathetic Lear of the old play, or Macbeth with the Scot of the chronicles? And yet from none of their sources did he make so basic a deviation as in the case of *Hamlet*.

Moreover, if Hamlet does procrastinate, it is inevitable that we should ask why, and not be content to answer that Elizabethan revengers generally delayed. To accept so prosaic a reply is to forget that tragedy is an imitation of the actions of men as we know men to be. One can only sympathize with Professor Stoll's desire to banish the vapid kind of Shakespeare-idolatry which owns no wish to understand what it adores, with his will to put an end to irrelevant sentimentalizing over the plays; one values the impulse which causes him to keep his attention on the *Hamlet* that was intended by its author to be acted on the boards. But *Hamlet* has always been more than engaging theatrical entertainment. We must never forget that it is a play or that it was the work of an Elizabethan; but we must also not divorce it from universal human experience, which all great tragedy mirrors. *Hamlet* was certainly the creation of a man who knew his theater; but that man was also the world's greatest dramatist and the world's greatest poet. And when he composed *Hamlet* he composed a great tragedy.

HAMLET, THE PLAY

Unluckily, it has often been other than that to commentators. Voltaire, steeped in neoclassical taste, found it "vulgar, barbarous," and was sure it would be deemed "intolerable by the lowest populace of France or Italy," for despite some "sublime passages," its plot is utterly revolting.[263] (Those populaces continue to prove his prediction wrong.) To a German it is an unintelligible work because of the superfluity of its incidents and the inconsistencies of its characters.[264] Halliwell-Phillipps came to despair of "meeting with any theories that will reconcile its perplexing inconsistencies." [265] (He might have done better to forget the theories and let the play speak for itself!) Papini thought most of the drama incoherent.[266] Mr. Robertson has always stressed the failure of *Hamlet* as a work of art,[267] and has insisted that Shakespeare must be viewed as "first and last an adapter . . . of other men's plays," finding this truism to be nowhere "more obvious than in *Hamlet*." [268] Another scholar, of like mind, ascribes Shakespeare's failure to his having continually changed his intentions during the course of *Hamlet*'s composition.[269]

What many of the critics think of the work as a whole has already been revealed by the quotations we have made from them. There are other scattered pronouncements: *Hamlet* is a tragedy not of excessive thought but of "defeated thought," a herald of the modern illness of uncertainty; [270] it is a study of the contradiction between appearance and reality; [271] it is a tragedy only because of the numerous corpses accumulating during its action, for to Shakespeare tragedy meant violent death.[272]

Finally, there are those unhappy, and hopelessly inartistic, commentators who look only for symbolical, allegorical meanings in a work of art. To one of them the whole play is a symbol, and "every character is besteeped in deepest fumes of foul concoction from the nethermost hells of human life." [273] To another, Hamlet stands for

Little Faith, Horatio (Ho-ratio) for Reason, Claudius for Natural Understanding, Polonius for Memory, Laertes for Learning, Francisco for Peace, and Bernardo for Desire.[274] *Hamlet* is represented as an allegory on three modern types of men: the one who thinks too much (Hamlet), the one who thinks too little (Laertes), and the ideal combination of thinker and man of action (Fortinbras).[275] Again, Hamlet is Spiritual Aspiration, Gertrude Emotion and Desire, Claudius Worldly Reason, Hamlet's father Intuition, Horatio Mistrust, Ophelia Experience, Polonius Worldly Wisdom * and Laertes Vanity.[276] More ingenious: the letter "h" being an aspirate, it stands for the "breath" of life; it is significant that only Hamlet, Horatio, and Ophelia have that letter in their names, for they are the only characters in the play that stand for life; Ophelia (*ope* plus *helios*) is Sunshine; Hamlet (*H* plus *am* plus *let*—*H* is the breath of life, *am* is the verb *to be*, *let* is *to hinder*—put them all together and they spell —no, *not* "mother," but)—Humanity Hindered.[277] Again, Hamlet figures allegorically as Truth, the court as Falsehood;[278] or Hamlet and Horatio both represent the New Philosophy as taught in the dramatist's day at Cambridge.[279] *Hamlet*, though its author was unaware of it, is a perfect solar myth.[280] Once more Ho-ratio is Reason, but this time Francisco is FRANCIS baCOn, the author of the play;[281] on the other hand, Shakespeare's having performed the role of the Ghost for his company proves that he was a ghost writer for Bacon.[282]

The play is a defense of Roman Catholicism [283] and an attack on the new Protestant faith, Hamlet's father being the old religion; Gertrude, England wedded to the new corrupt Protestantism (Claudius); and Hamlet, the youth of England torn between loyalties to both.[284] It is also a revolt *against* Roman Catholicism,[285] the "Marxist" view being likewise that Shakespeare was "hostile to the Catholic Church and the English feudal class allied with it." [286] That *Hamlet* was a pure expression of the Protestant Revolt is thus elaborately exposed by a German scholar: the Ghost is the Spirit of Christ, Ho-ratio (again!) is Melanchthon-Reason, Hamlet is Lutheranism,† Claudius the Papacy, Laertes Erasmus, and the Poles are the

* !!

† Why, in England?

Devil defeated by both Hamlet's father and Fortinbras; England is now free to establish the new religion.[287]

When, in the next chapter, we bring our answers to the analyses cited of Hamlet's character and conduct, we shall be pardoned if we do not notice these allegorical idiocies. *Hamlet* has nothing to do with this rubbish. It does not hanker after mystical meanings. It is only one of the world's greatest tragedies, taking its place beside its creator's tragic masterpieces. It is also his most ambitious and brilliant intellectual undertaking, the most brilliant in the history of dramatic literature.

REFERENCES IN CHAPTER III

1. *Paradise Lost*, II, 891–909.
2. J. D. Wilson, *What Happens in Hamlet* (New York, 1936), pp. 1–7.
3. M. Chute, *Shakespeare of London* (New York, 1949), pp. 229–30.
4. P. S. Conklin, *A History of Hamlet Criticism 1601–1821* (New York, 1947).
5. Anthony, Earl of Shaftesbury, *Characteristics* (London, 1732), Vol. I, p. 275.
6. C. B. Hogan, *Shakespeare in the Theatre* (Oxford, 1952), p. 460.
7. See F. Brunetière, *Les Époques du Théâtre Français* (Paris, 1892).
8. E. Gosse, "D'Avenant" in *Encyclopedia Brittanica* (11th ed., Cambridge, England, 1911), Vol. VII, p. 852.
9. H. Spencer, *Shakespeare Improved* (Cambridge, Mass., 1927), pp. 136–91.
10. *Ibid.*, p. 138.
11. *Ibid.*, p. 146.
12. *Ibid.*, p. 162.
13. *Ibid.*, p. 176.
14. *Ibid.*, pp. 176–77.
15. *Ibid.*, pp. 178–82.
16. F. Mathew, *An Image of Shakespeare* (London, 1922), p. 245.
17. Cited in H. H. Furness, *Hamlet* (Philadelphia, 1918), Vol. II, p. 235.
18. G. Steevens, *The Plays of William Shakespeare* (London, 1778), Vol. X, p. 413.
19. J. Ferriar, *An Essay towards a Theory of Apparitions* (London, 1813), p. 114.
20. E.g., G. Farren, *Observations on the Laws of Mortality and Disease* (London, 1829), pp. 12 seq.

L. M. Griffiths, "Hamlet's Mental Condition" in *Shakespeariana*
VI (1889), pp. 467–77.

A. O. Kellogg, *Shakespeare's Delineations of Insanity, Imbecility
and Suicide* (New York, 1866), pp. 36–65.

B. N. Oakeshott, "Hamlet: From a Student's Notebook" in *West-
minster Review* CXLVII (1897), pp. 669–78.

21. I. Ray, reprinted in *Contributions to Mental Pathology* (Boston,
    1873), p. 485.

22. *Ibid.*, p. 506.

23. *Ibid.*, p. 509.

24. *Ibid.*, p. 517.

25. Sir J. C. Bucknill, *The Mad Folk of Shakespeare* (London, 1867),
    p. 111.

26. J. Conolly, *A Study of Hamlet* (London, 1863), p. 110.

27. S. Johnson, *The Plays of Shakespeare* (London, 1765), Vol. VIII,
    p. 311.

28. C. W. Stearns, *The Shakespearean Treasury of Wit and Knowledge*
    (New York, 1860), p. 352.

29. H. N. Hudson, *Shakespeare: His Life, Art, and Characters* (Boston,
    1879), p. 252.

30. N. Watts, *Was Hamlet Mad? A Legal and Metaphysical Study*
    (London, 1888), pp. 25–26.

31. W. W. Lloyd, *Critical Essay on Hamlet* (London, 1856), p. 332.

32. E.g., G. Hookham, *Will o' the Wisp* (Oxford, 1922), pp. 123–
    28.

33. G. H. Lewes, *On Actors and the Art of Acting* (London, 1875), p.
    137.

34. E.g., B. Nicholson, *New Shakespeare Society's Transactions*, Part II
    (1880–85), pp. 341–69.

    F. T. Wood, "Hamlet's Madness" in *Notes and Queries* CLX
    (1931), p. 7.

35. E. Nesbit, *The Children's Shakespeare* (New York, 1938), p. 81.

36. Lewis Carroll, "The Third Voice" in *The Three Voices*.

37. J. D. Wilson, *op. cit.*, pp. 91–94; 111–12; 135; 205–29.

38. *Ibid.*, pp. 91–92.

39. *Ibid.*, p. 90.

40. E. Jones, *Hamlet and Oedipus* (New York, 1949), p. 69.

41. W. W. Greg, "Hamlet's Hallucination" in *Modern Language Re-
    view* XII (1917), pp. 393–421.

    ———, *A Book of Homage to Shakespeare* (ed. by I. Gollancz),
    (Oxford, 1916), pp. 179–80.

42. L. Kemp, "Understanding Hamlet" in *College English* XIII (Oct., 1951), pp. 9–13.

43. C. Leech, *Shakespeare's Tragedies* (Oxford, 1950), p. 80.

44. *Ibid.*, p. 82.

45. F. Mathew, *op. cit.*, p. 243.

46. G. W. Knight, *The Wheel of Fire* (Oxford, 1930), p. 23.

47. H. Somerville, *Madness in Shakespearean Tragedy* (London, 1929), pp. 17–40.

48. J. H. E. Brock, *The Dramatic Purpose of Hamlet* (Cambridge, England, 1935).

49. E.g., C. von Schröder, *Wille und Nervostät in Shakespeares Hamlet* (Riga, 1893).

50. K. Rosner, *Shakespeares Hamlet im Lichte der Neuropathologie* (Berlin, 1895).

51. J. Bing, "Veien til Hamlet" in *Edda*, L, pp. 39–55.

52. E.g., L. Campbell, *Tragic Drama in Aeschylus, Sophocles and Shakespeare* (London, 1904), pp. 194–217.

53. E.g., H. Becque, "Der Wahre Hamlet" in *Magazin für Literatur* XXXVII (1908), pp. 587–91.

54. (Anon.), "The Very Cause of Hamlet's Lunacy" in *Scribner's Magazine* XLIC (1908), pp. 122–23.

55. T. L. Davis, "The Sanity of Hamlet" in *Journal of Philosophy* XVIII (1921), pp. 629–34.

56. A. C. Bradley, *Shakespearean Tragedy* (London, 1929), p. 127.

57. *Ibid.*, pp. 120–21.

58. *Ibid.*, p. 127.

59. E.g., L. L. Schücking, *The Meaning of Hamlet* (translated by G. Rawson) (Oxford, 1937), p. 33.

60. G. W. Knight, *The Imperial Theme* (London, 1951), p. 111.

61. J. Q. Adams, *Hamlet* (Boston, 1929), p. 195.

62. B. Wendell, *William Shakespeare* (New York, 1894), pp. 250–62.

63. H. Granville-Barker, *Prefaces to Shakespeare; Hamlet* (London, 1948), p. 56.

64. W. F. Trench, *Shakespeare's Hamlet, a New Commentary* (London, 1913), p. 115.

65. L. L. Schücking, *op. cit.*, p. 166.

66. M. Van Doren, *Shakespeare* (New York, 1939), p. 190.

67. E.g. (Anon.), "Sarah Bernhardt on Hamlet's Madness" in *Poet Lore* XII (1900), pp. 148–49.

    C. H. Burr, Jr., "Hamlet Once More" in *Poet Lore* III (1891), pp. 615–26.

E. Dowden, *Shakspere* (New York, n.d.), p. 122.

A. Meadows, *Hamlet: An Essay* (Edinburgh, 1871), p. 10.

68. H. Mackenzie, *The Mirror* 100 (1780).

69. E.g., J. Q. Adams, *op. cit.*, p. 217.

E. K. Chambers, *Shakespeare: a Survey* (London, 1925), p. 185.

E. E. Stoll, *Shakespeare and Other Masters* (Cambridge, Mass., 1940), pp. 110; 114.

W. J. Tucker, *The College Shakespeare* (New York, 1932), pp. 185–220.

70. M. Huhner, *Shakespeare's Hamlet* (New York, 1952), p. 2.

71. C. M. Lewis, *The Genesis of Hamlet* (New York, 1907), p. 75.

72. E. E. Stoll, *Shakespeare and Other Masters* (Cambridge, Mass., 1940), p. 144.

73. G. L. Kittredge, *Hamlet* (Boston, 1939), p. xiii.

74. E. A. Schell, "Hamlet, the Tragedy of Inaction" in *Methodist Review* XCI (1909), pp. 877–89.

75. H. Spencer, *The Art and Life of William Shakespeare* (New York, 1940), p. 314.

76. (Anon.), "On the Feigned Madness of Hamlet" in *Blackwood's Magazine* (Oct., 1889), p. 452.

77. J. R. Lowell, *Among My Books* (Boston, 1870), pp. 218 seq.

78. J. Q. Adams, *op. cit.*, p. 230.

79. E. E. Stoll, *Art and Artifice in Shakespeare* (New York, 1951), p. 118.

80. E.g., J. Corbin, *The Elizabethan Hamlet* (London, 1895).

81. E. E. Stoll, *Shakespeare Studies* (New York, 1942), p. 114.

82. A. Büchner, *Hamlet le Danois* (Paris, 1878).

83. J. M. Robertson, *"Hamlet" Once More* (London, 1923).

84. This will be found conveniently reprinted in H. H. Furness, *Hamlet* (Philadelphia, 1918), Vol. II, pp. 91–113, and other printings of this Variorum Edition.

85. S. Johnson, *The Plays of Shakespeare* (London, 1765), Vol. VIII, p. 311.

86. J. Masefield, *William Shakespeare* (London, 1930), p. 158.

87. J. Q. Adams, *op. cit.*, p. 250.

88. *Ibid.*, p. 275.

89. J. M. Robertson, *The Genuine in Shakespeare* (London, 1930), pp. 94–96.

90. A. Nicoll, *Studies in Shakespeare* (New York, 1928), p. 82.

91. H. Mackenzie, *loc. cit.*

92. J. W. von Goethe, *Wilhelm Meister* (translated by T. Carlyle) (Boston, 1851), Vol. I, Book V, p. 295.

93. V. Courdaveaux, *Caractères et Talents* (Paris, 1867), p. 305.

94. W. F. Trench, *op. cit.*, p. 115.

95. F. Fergusson, *The Idea of a Theater* (Garden City, 1953), p. 143.

96. F. Neilson, *Hamlet and Shakespeare* (New York, 1950), p. 79.

97. *Ibid.*, p. 86.

98. W. Sypher, "Hamlet: The Existential Madness" in *Nation* CLXII (1946), pp. 750–51.

99. S. T. Coleridge, *Shakespearean Criticism* (ed. by T. M. Raysor) (Cambridge, Mass., 1930), Vol. I, pp. 18–19.

100. A. W. Schlegel, *Lectures on Art and Dramatic Literature* (translated by J. Black) (London, 1815), p. 193.

101. S. T. Coleridge, *Essays and Lectures on Shakespeare* (*Everyman Library*) (New York, 1930), pp. 136–37.

102. E.g., H. Baumgart, *Die Hamlet-Tragödie und ihre Kritik* (Königsberg, 1877).

     G. F. Bradby, *Short Studies in Shakespeare* (New York, 1929), pp. 133–95.

     H. Bulthaupt, "Hamlet" in *Dramaturgie des Schauspiels* (Leipzig, 1902), Vol. II, pp. 289–334.

     D. Dorchester, "The Character of Hamlet" in *Methodist Review* LXXIV (May, 1892), pp. 390–404.

     E. Ganz, *Vermischte Schriften* (Berlin, 1834), Vol. II, pp. 270 seq.

     F. Hahne, "Das Hamletproblem" in *Germanisch-romanische Monatsschrift* V (1913), pp. 442–56.

     C. M. Ingleby, *Shakespeare, the Man and the Book* (London, 1877), Vol. I, pp. 120–36.

     S. Lee, *A Life of William Shakespeare* (New York, 1917), pp. 353–65.

     A. Nicoll, *op. cit.*, p. 82.

     T. Salvini, "Hamlet" in *Erklärungen und Betrachtungen über einige Werke und Charaktere, W. Shakespeares* (Berlin, 1882), pp. 219–48.

     ———, "My Interpretation of Hamlet" in *Putnam's Magazine* III (Dec., 1907), pp. 352–55.

     C. Semler, *Shakespeares Hamlet* (Leipzig, 1879).

     E. Wolff, "Hamlet und Sein Ende" in *Frankfurter Zeitung* 154, 156 (June 5 and 7, 1901).

103. E. Dowden, *op. cit.*, p. 121.

104. E. K. Chambers, *op. cit.*, pp. 181, 182, 183.

105. H. Coleridge, *Essays and Marginalia* (London, 1851), Vol. I, p. 153.

106. C. Clark, *A Study of Shakespeare* (Stratford, 1926).

107. B. R. Conrad, "Hamlet's Delay—a Restatement of the Problem" in *Publications of the Modern Language Association* XLI (1926), p. 687.

108. A. Symons, *Dramatis Personae* (Indianapolis, 1923), pp. 309–16.

109. O. Rank, "Das Schauspiel in Hamlet" in *Imago* IV, p. 41.

110. P. Arnold, "Les Raisons d'Hamlet" in *Les Lettres* I (1945), p. 123.

111. K. Fischer, "Shakespeare's Hamlet" in *Kleine Schriften* V (1896), p. 206.

112. F. S. Boas, *Shakespeare and His Predecessors* (London, 1896), pp. 384–408.

113. S. A. Brooke, *Ten More Plays of Shakespeare* (New York, 1927), pp. 91–138.

114. R. Wolf, "Hamlet, or the Artist's Defeat" in *The Measure* (Jan., 1926), pp. 13–14.

115. L. Barnay, "Zur Darstellung des Hamlet" in *Deutsche Revue* (Jan., 1901), pp. 103–08.

116. J. E. Baker, "The Philosophy of Hamlet" in *Essays in Dramatic Literature* (Princeton, 1935), pp. 455–70.

117. A. Doering, *Shakespeares Hamlet* (Hamm, 1865), p. 34.

118. L. L. Schücking, *op. cit.*, p. 167.

119. H. B. Charlton, *Shakespearean Tragedy* (Cambridge, England, 1948), p. 103.

120. T. Spencer, *Shakespeare and the Nature of Man* (New York, 1949), p. 108.

121. R. Berthelot, *La Sagesse de Shakespeare et de Goethe* (Paris, 1930), pp. 37–39.

122. F. T. Vischer, *Kritische Gänge* (Stuttgart, 1861), p. 89.

123. F. Kreyssig, *Vorlesungen über Shakespeare* (Berlin, 1862), Vol. II, p. 263.

124. O. W. Firkins, "What Happened to Hamlet?" in *North American Review* CCXII (Sept., 1920), pp. 393–403.

125. H. B. Charlton, *op. cit.*, pp. 93, 102.

126. G. W. Knight, *The Imperial Theme* (London, 1951), p. 101.

127. K. Bleibtreu, "Ueber Hamlet" in *Die Gegenwart* LXXV (1909), pp. 124–26.

128. S. H. Butcher, *Aristotle's Theory of Poetry and Fine Art* (New York, 1951), pp. 351–52.

129. A. C. Bradley, *op. cit.*, p. 106.

130. *Ibid.*, p. 107.

131. *Ibid.*, p. 108.

132. *Ibid.*, p. 118.

133. *Ibid.*, p. 120.

134. *Ibid.*, p. 122.

135. G. W. Knight, *The Imperial Theme* (London, 1951), p. 107.

136. *Idem*, "Hamlet's Melancholia" in *The Wheel of Fire* (London, 1930), p. 25.

137. *Ibid.*, p. 26.

138. *Ibid.*, p. 33.

139. Knight, "An Essay on Hamlet" in *The Wheel of Fire* (London, 1930), p. 44.

140. J. Q. Adams, *op. cit.*, pp. 196–199; 225–228.

141. L. B. Campbell, *Shakespeare's Tragic Heroes: Slaves of Passion* (Cambridge, England, 1930), p. 115.

142. T. Gessner, "Von Welchen Gesichtspunkten ist Ausgezehen," etc. in *Jahrbuch der Deutschen Shakespeare Gesellschaft* XX (1885), pp. 228–81.

143. M. I. O'Sullivan, "Hamlet and Dr. Timothy Bright" in *Publications of the Modern Language Association* XLI (1926), pp. 667–79.

144. L. L. Schücking, *op. cit.*, p. 27.

145. E.g., H. Nicolai, " 'Ecstasy' und 'Passion' " in *Germanisch-Romanische Monatsschrift* XXIII (1935), pp. 36–67.

146. T. Klein, "Hamlet und der Melancholiker in Kant's Beobachtungen" etc. in *Kant-Studien* X (1905), pp. 76–80.

147. G. Dumas, *États Intellectuels dans la Mélancholie* (Paris, 1894).

148. G. Wagner, *Hamlet und Seine Gemüthskrankheit* (Heidelberg, 1899).

149. H. Frank, *The Tragedy of Hamlet* (Boston, 1910).

150. A. H. Tolman, "A View of the Views about Hamlet" in *Publications of the Modern Language Association* XIII (1898), pp. 155–84.

151. H. Ulrici, *Shakespeare's Dramatic Art* (translated by A. J. W. Morrison) (London, 1846), p. 218.

152. E.g., W. Arndt, "Hamlet, der Christ" in *Die Zukunft* XVI (Aug. 8, 1896), pp. 275–79.

    M. F. Egan, *The Ghost in Hamlet and Other Essays* (Chicago, 1906), pp. 141–69.

    G. Liebau, *Studien über W. Shakespeares Trauerspiel Hamlet* (Bleichrode, n.d.), pp. 1–16.

    W. F. Whitlock, "Hamlet—a Character Sketch" in *Methodist Review* LXXX (1898), pp. 881–98.

W. B. Wright, "Hamlet" in *Atlantic Monthly* LXXXIX (1902), pp. 686–95.

153. Sir A. Quiller-Couch, *Shakespeare's Workmanship* (London, 1919), pp. 196–97.

154. E. D. Beery, " 'The Tempest,' the Sequel to 'Hamlet,' " in *Arena* XVIII (Aug., 1897), pp. 254–61.

155. H. Ford, *Shakespeare's Hamlet: a New Theory* (London, 1900), p. 106.

156. A. von Berger, "Hamlet" in *Dramaturgische Vorträge* (Vienna, 1890), pp. 244–61.

157. J. Kohler, *Shakespeare vor dem Forum der Jurisprudenz* (Würzburg, 1883), pp. 181–228.

F. Rubinstein, *Hamlet als Neurastheniker* (Leipzig, 1896).

158. (Anon.), "Sweet Prince" in *Nation* CXL (June 26, 1935), pp. 729–30.

159. G. R. Foss, *What the Author Meant* (London, 1932), pp. 12–26.

160. D. Figgis, *Shakespeare* (London, 1911), p. 213.

161. G. Wolff, *Der Fall Hamlet* (Munich, 1914).

162. E. Venable, *The Hamlet Problem and Its Solution* (Cincinnati, 1912), p. 102.

163. H. Craig, *An Interpretation of Shakespeare* (New York, 1948), p. 187.

164. F. Fergusson, *op. cit.*, p. 145.

165. C. F. E. Spurgeon, *Shakespeare's Imagery and What It Tells Us* (New York, 1935), pp. 316–20.

166. H. R. Hutcheson, "Hamlet's Delay" in *Shakespeare Newsletter* I, 19.

167. P. K. Guha, *On Two Problems in Shakespeare* (London, 1926) and H. Türck, *Faustus-Hamlet-Christus* (Berlin, 1918), pp. 210–90.

168. S. F. Johnson, "The Regeneration of Hamlet" in *Shakespeare Quarterly* III (July, 1952), pp. 206–07.

169. R. Walker, *The Time Is Out of Joint* (London, 1948), p. 152.

170. T. Reik, *The Secret Self* (New York, 1952), p. 110.

171. E. Jones, *op. cit.*, p. 45.

172. C. Leech, *op. cit.*, p. 117.

173. W. B. D. Henderson, "Hamlet as a Castiglionean Courtier" in *The McGill News* XV (June, 1934), pp. 15–34.

174. E. M. W. Tillyard, *Shakespeare's Problem Plays* (Toronto, 1949), p. 156.

175. A. Clutton-Brock, *Shakespeare's Hamlet* (New York, 1922), pp. 45–46.

176. E. Jones, *op. cit.*, p. 22.

177. S. Freud, "The Interpretation of Dreams" in *The Basic Writings of Sigmund Freud* (New York, 1938), p. 310.

178. *Idem, An Outline of Psychoanalysis* (New York, 1949), p. 96.

179. E. Ludwig, *Doctor Freud* (New York, 1947), pp. 238–39.

180. *Ibid.*, p. 240.

181. S. Lorand, *Psychoanalysis Today* (New York, 1944), p. 377.

182. *Ibid.*, p. 378.

183. E. Ludwig, *op. cit.*, p. 242.

184. E. Jones, *op. cit.*, p. 61.

185. H. R. Walley, "Shakespeare's Conception of 'Hamlet,'" in *Publications of the Modern Language Association* XLVIII (Sept., 1933), p. 796.

186. E.g., E. Wulffen, *Shakespeares Hamlet, ein Sexualproblem* (Berlin, 1913).

187. H. Somerville, *op. cit.*, pp. 17–40.

188. T. Reik, *op. cit.*, p. 29.

189. *Ibid.*, p. 32.

190. E. Jones, *op. cit.*, p. 88.

191. W. Stekel, *Compulsion and Doubt* (New York, 1949), Vol. II, p. 606.

192. E. M. Sharpe, "An Unfinished Paper on Hamlet" in *International Journal of Psychoanalysis* XXIX (1948), Pt. II, pp. 98–109.

193. J. C. Moloney and L. Rochelein, "A New Interpretation of 'Hamlet'" in *International Journal of Psychoanalysis* XXX (1949), pp. 92–107.

194. T. Reik, *op. cit.*, p. 19.

195. E. P. Vining, *The Mystery of Hamlet* (Philadelphia, 1881).

196. A. Luther, "Hamlets Bart" in *Bühne und Welt* VIII (1902), p. 664.

197. G. Santayana, "Hamlet" in *Life and Letters* I (June, 1928), p. 25.

198. C. M. Lewis, *op. cit.*, p. 83.

199. D. R. Godfrey, "The Player's Speech in 'Hamlet'" in *Neophilologus* XXXIV, pp. 162–69.

200. J. J. Lawlor, "The Tragic Conflict in 'Hamlet'" in *Review of English Studies*, New Series I, pp. 97–113.

201. E. Jones, "The Oedipus Complex as an Explanation of Hamlet's Mystery" in *American Journal of Psychology* XXI (1910), pp. 72–113.

202. J. Masefield, *op. cit.*, p. 162.

203. J. M. Murry, *Shakespeare* (New York, 1936), pp. 202–03.

204. W. W. Lawrence, "Hamlet and Fortinbras" in *Publications of the Modern Language Association* LXI (Sept., 1946), p. 698.

205. J. M. Robertson, *The Genuine in Shakespeare* (London, 1930), pp 96–98.

206. J. D. Wilson, "Hamlet" in *Six Tragedies of Shakespeare* (London, 1929), p. 75.

207. O. Smeaton, *Shakespeare, His Life and Work* (New York, n.d.) (Everyman Library), pp. 338–62.

208. W. Leighton, *The Subjection of Hamlet* (Philadelphia, 1882).

209. R. Zimmermann, *Studien und Kritiken zur Philosophie und Aesthetik* (Vienna, 1870), p. 96.

210. J. Owen, *The Five Great Skeptical Dramas of History* (London, 1896), pp. 277–348.

211. N. Cartwright, *The Prince and the Offered Crown* (London, 1879), pp. 9–45.

212. S. de Madariaga, *On Hamlet* (London, 1948), pp. 13, 16, 18, 19.

213. (Anon.), "Hamlet as a Fool" in *Atlantic Monthly* LXXXIV (1899), pp. 285–87.

214. J. C. Collins, "Old and New Lights on Shakespeare's 'Hamlet'" in *Contemporary Review* LXXXVIII (1905), pp. 649–64.

215. A. H. Ames, "Hamlet from the Standpoint of Theology" in *Methodist Review* LXXV (May, 1893), pp. 369–79.

216. W. Devlin, "A Catholic View of Hamlet" in *American Catholic Quarterly Review* XXXII (1907), pp. 239–50.

217. K. Meier, "Kleine Studien" in *Dresdener Anzeiger* (1904), pp. 11–23.

218. J. Wihan, *Die Hamletfrage* (Leipzig, 1921).

219. E. V. Blake, "The Impediment of Adipose, a Celebrated Case" in *Popular Science Monthly* XVII (1880), pp. 60–71.

220. G. Papini, *Four and Twenty Minds* (New York, 1922), pp. 186–97.

221. J. Derocquigny, "L'Embonpoint d'Hamlet" in *Revue Anglo-Américaine* (1920–7), IV, pp. 527–29; V, p. 96.

222. G. R. Elliott, *Scourge and Minister* (Durham, 1951).

223. J. L. Sullivan, "Something Touching the Lord Hamlet" in *Commonweal* XV (Dec. 30, 1931), pp. 243–44.

224. K. Dietrich, *Hamlet der Konstabel der Vorsehung* (Hamburg, 1883).

225. A. Pfungst, "Hamlet—der Inder" in *Frankfurter Zeitung* (Sept. 15, 1906).

226. V. Courdaveaux, *op. cit.*, p. 323.

227. H. Taine, *Histoire de la Littérature Anglaise* (Paris, 1866), Vol. II, p. 254.

228. D. Figgis, *op. cit.*, p. 320.

229. J. H. E. Brock, *The Dramatic Purpose of Hamlet* (Cambridge, England, 1935).

230. K. Götz, *Das Hamlet-Mysterium* (Speyer, 1903).

231. J. A. Chapman, *Papers on Shakespeare* (New York, 1932), pp. 1–39.

232. F. Harris, *The Man Shakespeare* (London, 1909), p. 7.

233. E. Reichel, "Hamlet als Gelehrter" in *Magazin für Literatur* LXIX (March 31, 1900), pp. 324–31 and (April 7, 1900), pp. 356–58.

234. E. Sharpe, "The Impatience of Hamlet" in *International Journal of Psychoanalysis* X (1929), p. 272.

235. E. Jones, *Hamlet and Oedipus*, pp. 101–126.

236. F. Mathew, *op. cit.*, p. 236.

237. A. Döring, *Hamlet* (Berlin, 1898).

238. E.g., H. Conrad, "Hamlets Familie" in *Jahrbuch der Deutschen Shakespeare Gesellschaft* XVI (1881), pp. 274–323.

———, "Shakspere und die Essex-Familie" in *Preussische Jahrbuch* LXXIX (Jan., 1895), pp. 183–229.

A. Guthmann, "Hamlet als Neurastheniker" in *Berliner Wochenschrift* III, p. 60.

V. McNabb, "Is Hamlet Autobiography?" in *Catholic World* C (1915), pp. 754–66.

G. Rhys, "The Real 'Hamlet'" in *Nineteenth Century* LXXIII (May, 1913), pp. 1031–39.

239. K. Bleibtreu, *op. cit.*, pp. 101–04.

240. E. S. Le Comte, "The Ending of Hamlet as a Farewell to Essex" in *English Literary History* XVII, pp. 87–114.

241. C. Norman, *So Worthy a Friend: William Shakespeare* (New York, 1947), pp. 233–37.

242. E.g., W. P. Johnston, *The Prototype of Hamlet* (New York, 1890). L. Winstanley, *Hamlet and the Scottish Succession* (Cambridge, England, 1921).

243. K. Silberschlag, "Shakespeares Hamlet" in *Jahrbuch der Deutschen Shakespeare Gesellschaft* XII (1877), pp. 261–89.

244. P. Heinrich, *Die Namen der Hamlettragödie* (Leipzig, 1904).

245. R. Rice, *The Story of Hamlet and Horatio* (London, 1924).

246. S. Meisels, "Judenhamlet" in *Populär-wissenschaftliche Monatsblätter zur Belehrung über das Judentum* (Frankfort, 1901), Vols. VII & VIII, pp. 150–55.

247. D. Morrow, *Where Shakespeare Stood* (Milwaukee, 1935), p. 82.

248. *Ibid.*, pp. 9–10.

249. *Ibid.*, p. 5.

250. H. Spencer, "Hamlet's Soliloquies Uncut" in *London Times' Literary Supplement*, (Sept. 21, 1933), p. 631.

251. F. W. Ziegler, "Hamlet's Character," quoted in H. H. Furness, *op. cit.*, Vol. II, p. 278.

252. Beaumont and Fletcher, *The Maid's Tragedy*, III, i, 238 seq.

253. L. Klein, *Berliner Modenspiegel*, quoted in H. H. Furness, *op. cit.*, Vol. II, p. 297.

254. K. Werder, *Vorlesungen über Shakespeares Hamlet*, quoted in H. H. Furness, *op. cit.*, Vol. II, pp. 358, 368–69, 370.

255. A. W. Brotherton, "The Real Hamlet and the Hamlet Oldest of All" in *Poet Lore* XVI (1905), pp. 110–30.

   H. Corson, "Hamlet" in *Shakespeariana* III (1886), pp. 337–352.

   Dr. Damme, "Warum Zaudert Hamlet" in *Preussische Jahrbücher* LXVI (Sept., 1890), pp. 247–70.

   A. Gelber, *Shakespeare'sche Probleme* (Vienna, 1891).

   J. O. Halliwell-Phillipps, *Memoranda on the Tragedy of Hamlet* (London, 1879).

   E. Legouis, "'Hamlet' de Shakespeare" in *Revue des Cours et Conférences* (1909–10), series 1, pp. 681–89; series 2, pp. 30–40.

   W. J. Rolfe, "Introduction" to Werder's *The Heart of Hamlet's Mystery* (New York, 1907), pp. 1–38.

   H. Traut, *Die Hamlet-Kontroverse im Umrisse Bearbeitet* (Leipzig, 1898).

256. S. H. Butcher, *op. cit.*, pp. 27–29.

257. E. E. Stoll, *Art and Artifice in Shakespeare* (New York, 1951), p. 101.

258. S. F. Johnson, *op. cit.*, p. 187.

259. E. E. Stoll, *Art and Artifice in Shakespeare* (New York, 1951), p. 92.

260. *Ibid.*, p. 93.

261. *Ibid.*, p. 94.

262. H. Spencer, *The Art and Life of William Shakespeare* (New York, 1940), p. 309.

263. Voltaire, *Théâtre Complet* (Geneva, 1768), Vol. II, p. 201.

264. R. Benedix, *Die Shakespearomanie* (Stuttgart, 1873), pp. 274–90.

265. J. O. Halliwell-Phillipps, *op. cit.*, p. 7.

266. G. Papini, *op. cit.*, pp. 186–97.

267. J. M. Robertson, "Is Hamlet a Consistent Creation?" in *Free Review* (July, 1895).

268. J. M. Robertson, "The Naturalistic Theory of Hamlet" in *Criterion* III (Jan., 1925), pp. 172–92.

269. G. F. Bradby, *Short Studies in Shakespeare* (New York, 1929), pp. 133–95.
    See also T. S. Eliot, *The Sacred Wood* (London, 1920), pp. 87–94.
270. D. G. James, *The Dream of Learning* (Oxford, 1951).
271. J. Paterson, "The Word in 'Hamlet'" in *Shakespeare Quarterly* II (1951), pp. 47–55.
272. J. V. Cunningham, "Tragedy in Shakespeare" in *English Literary History* XVII, pp. 36–46.
273. H. Frank, *The Tragedy of Hamlet* (Boston, 1910), p. 236.
274. M. Knights, *Shakespeare's "Hamlet" Interpreted* (London, 1893).
275. W. W. Crane, "The Allegory in 'Hamlet'" in *Poet Lore* III (Nov., 1891), pp. 565–69.
276. G. B. Finch, "The Play of 'Hamlet' from a Theosophic Point of View" in *New Shakespeare Society's Transactions* (1880–86), pp. 150–1.
277. S. G. Preston, *The Secret of Hamlet, Prince of Denmark* (Cincinnati, 1897), p. 165.
278. M. J. Wolff, *Shakespeare, der Dichter und Sein Werk* (Munich, 1913), Vol. II, pp. 99–142.
279. J. Darlington, "Hamlet" in *Irish Ecclesiastical Record*, Series 4, V (May, 1899), pp. 417–26.
280. S. Korner, "'Hamlet' as a Solar Myth" in *Poet Lore* III (April, 1891), pp. 214–16.
281. E. Bormann, *Das Shakespeare Geheimniss* (Leipzig, 1895).
282. P. Woodward, "Ghost in his Own 'Hamlet'" in *Baconiana*, Series 3, IX (1911), pp. 43–49.
283. W. J. Tucker, *op. cit.*, pp. 185–220.
284. J. Spanier, *Der "Papist" Shakespeare im "Hamlet"* (Trier, 1890).
285. E. Gerkrath, *Der Dramatische Meisterwerk des Protestantismus* (Berlin, 1918).
286. D. Morrow, *op. cit.*, p. 35.
287. N. Krieger, "Prolog zu Shakespeares 'Hamlet'" in *Anglia* LIV (July, 1930), pp. 168–78.

O NIGHT, WHICH EVER ART WHEN DAY IS NOT!
O NIGHT, O NIGHT! ALACK, ALACK, ALACK!
A Midsummer Night's Dream, V, i

THIS COLD NIGHT WILL TURN US ALL TO FOOLS AND MADMEN.
King Lear, III, iv

THE DEEP OF NIGHT IS CREPT UPON OUR TALK.
Julius Caesar, IV, iii

WHY, HERE WALK I IN THE BLACK BROW OF NIGHT
TO FIND YOU OUT.
King John, V, vi

THE CLOAK OF NIGHT BEING PLUCKED FROM OFF THEIR
BACKS,
STAND BARE AND NAKED. . . .
Richard II, III, ii

IV *The Cloak of Night Plucked Off: Reason and the Critics*

IN EVERY PLAY there are things said, things thought, and things done. Of these the most important are the things done. ("The primary objects of artistic imitation are human beings in action, men performing or doing something."—Aristotle) [1] Other forms of literary composition may simply narrate or describe the actions of men; it is in the direct presentation of these actions that drama is distinguished from the novel, the short story, narrative poetry, and the essay. The very word *drama* comes from the Greek verb *dran, to do* or *to act*. Hence, to understand a play we must focus our attention primarily on the things done during the course of the plot. Things thought and said must be interpreted according to the light thrown upon them by the action of the play.

Further, in a drama of even the feeblest psychological insight our interpretation of the things said is subject to what is actually being thought. Not to be too arbitrary, we may affirm that our comprehension of a play begins with the transactions of the plot; with them in mind we pierce through the words spoken to what the characters are actually thinking, for without the action we should not know how to understand the words. For instance, when Iago says to Othello: "My lord, you know I love you" (III, iii, 117), we are not to interpret the words on their face value, we are not to believe that Iago's bosom overflows with welling affection for Othello or to prepare ourselves for deeds of kindliness and generosity. Rather, since this is a play, we first recollect that Iago is at the moment busy destroying Othello (the action), and next realize (since this is a play of psychological depth) that he speaks these words only because he is gloating over his growing success in winning power over the Moor. Thus, when we analyze a drama, we must first place emphasis on the thing being done, next, the thing being thought, and—in view of these—last, the thing being said. In our daily living, could we always manage to gauge people with the same precedence we should be living with perfect discretion.

Unhappily, a vast bulk of Shakespearean commentary is nullified by the predilection of scholars to base their theories on things said. They take a passage out of context with the action, and build upon a single passage (sometimes a single line or two) their interpretation of the whole play, and then squeeze the entire work into the theory, no matter how bad the fit. These Procrustean habits require lopping off entire sections of the action; if any given scene proves inconvenient to the theory it is ignored as if it were not there.

A good example is the widespread view of Antony (in *Julius Caesar*) as a beautiful unselfish character, a view which completely leaves out of account his scene with Octavius and Lepidus (IV, i), wherein all three are revealed as cold-blooded politicians who think of Rome only as a pawn in the game of personal power. Begin and end your understanding of Antony with his "Friends, Romans, countrymen" speech (III, ii), and you have your heroic Antony of popular conception, the invention of generations of schoolma'ams. But in the scene of the meeting of the triumvirate, shortly after, Antony figures as an unprincipled scoundrel: first we see him coldly appointing who is to be butchered and who not, and agreeing out of policy to the death of his own nephew; then, as soon as Lepidus quits the room, we observe him losing not a minute in urging Octavius to agree to the liquidation of Lepidus too:

> This is a slight unmeritable man,
> Meet to be sent on errands. Is it fit,
> The threefold world divided, he should stand
> One of the three to share it?
>
> IV, i, 12 seq.

Octavius reminds Antony that he has agreed to Lepidus as one of the three to share the rule of the world; Antony replies that his agreement was merely political expediency: Lepidus is needed for a while as one needs an ass to help bear burdens, but

> having brought our treasure where we will,
> Then take we down his load and turn him off,
> Like to the empty ass, to shake his ears . . .

Cynicism cannot go further, and it is part of Antony's portrait. Now, if this scene disturbs your notions of him, just pretend that it isn't in the play. Or, if you are of the temper of some intransigent but subtle-minded commentators, read that scene with your preconceptions, not for what the action reveals, but with the purpose of forcing the lines to accommodate your theory of Antony. On the other hand, you can choose to begin your study of his character at the beginning of the play, and watch well his relationship to the other persons of the drama; this will give you the man Shakespeare created, and you will find him a creature whose moral constitution you would hardly hold up as an exemplar for your son.

Shylock, one of Shakespeare's most misunderstood characters, has been distorted out of all proportion by this Building on Quotations. Isolate the "Many a time and oft" and the "Hath not a Jew eyes?" passages (I, iii, 107 and III, i, 61) from their proper places and you are ready to come forth with, what Shakespeare never intended, a noble defense of the Jews and a Shylock who is the "tragic representative" of his race. On the other hand, fasten on Gratiano's slurs during the trial scene (IV, i, 364; 379; 398) and you have what was even further from Shakespeare's purpose, a denunciation of the Jews and a Shylock portrayed in a spirit of such anti-Semitism as periodically moves some rabbi to demand the play's total suppression. But if you are interested in Shakespeare's intentions, you will prefer to take Shylock from the moment you first meet him, judge him and everyone else by what they do, and follow through the play; at the end you will have a Shylock completely different from either of these, and a Shylock, moreover, of quality and import.

Of all of Shakespeare's works none, of course, has suffered more than *Hamlet* from this old sport of Building on Quotations. Goethe, we have seen, erected upon an unimportant couplet his sentimental notion of a too-delicate hero; Schlegel upon an equally inconsequential remark his too-thoughtful Hamlet. (These lines, "The time is out of joint . . ." and "There is nothing either good or bad . . . ," are unimportant and inconsequential not in the intellectual but in the *dramatic* sense. Consider when, where, and to whom they are addressed and they have no bearing, you will see, on the plot's development, and hence very little on the character's.) Choosing, hit or miss, a passage enables one to prove almost anything about a Shakespeare play.*

* Shall we? Very good! Ladies and gentlemen, we herewith present you with the evidence that *Hamlet* is concerned with the one matter thus far overlooked, the Irish Question, which in Shakespeare's day was very much a *burning* one. (See Spenser's *View of the Present State of Ireland,* urging the "reducinge that salvage nacion to better gouerment and cyvillitie.") Our proof is based not on one quotation but two. (This should really, to follow tradition, be put in an appendix; appendices are as popular with Shakespearean scholars as they are in operating rooms of hospitals.)

After seeing the Ghost, Hamlet answers Horatio's "There's no offense, my Lord," with

> Yes, by Saint Patrick, but there is, Horatio!
>
> I, v, 136

—calling to witness not an English or a Danish saint (*are* there any Danish saints?) but *the patron saint of Ireland!* As we have seen, some scholars maintain that *Hamlet* espouses the Catholic cause—dangerously unpopu-

If we are to understand *Hamlet* we must be patient in our anxiety to understand its hero. We must take the advice of the King in Lewis Carroll's *Alice:* "Begin at the beginning and go on till you come to the end: then stop." [2] Few critics bother to do any of these three things. The beginning of the consideration of any good play

---

lar in our dramatist's day—but it is now clear that they have not been bold enough in their speculations. Here we see Hamlet *secretly* espousing the Irish cause, most dangerous cause of all. Now we can better interpret that "prison house" where Hamlet's father is "doomed for a certain term . . ."—that abode a description of which "would harrow up" one's soul (I, v, 10–16). Obviously, Hamlet's father is living in exile in Ireland—his situation curiously similar to that of Dean Swift, as apt quotation could quickly demonstrate, who described that land in even less complimentary language.

We do not know, of course, what Hamlet privately proceeds to do after this revealing outburst, for Shakespeare keeps it a secret too, thus adding to the dimension of his play (see page 71, above); he wishes it to be a mystery. (Let those who would construe that as a defect remember how *Finnegan's Wake*—Irish too!—gains by being a *little* mysterious.) At any rate, whatever Hamlet's shenanigans (an Irish word? Does not "hugger-mugger" of IV, v, 84 have a Gaelic ring too?) may be, he has developed so close an understanding with Ireland's guardian that not long after, when he finds Claudius praying, he addresses the saint in accents the most intimate:

> Now might I do it, Pat!
> III, iii, 73

as he whips out his sword. The nickname indicates that he is by this time on terms of greatest familiarity with Saint Patrick, who, with an Irish sense of fun, it may be assumed, will not take umbrage.

It is true the last quotation would require two slight changes in typography—one comma and one capital. The line is usually printed "Now might I do it pat." But such trifling alterations are nothing to Shakespearean scholarship. Many of the reputed would consider such tamperings as beneath notice, they themselves not having hesitated to change the very words (which we have not offered to do) or their traditional meanings, or even the plot itself (as by gratuitous interpolation of stage directions), etc. And as for modifying punctuation—!

This "Irish theory," but sketchily presented here, will soon receive the attention it merits. Correspondence informs us that the world may must be a consideration of its plot. No idea is more underlined in *The Poetics* than this one.* Naturally, when a good play is in progress we are as much interested in the characters as in the plot, and in some plays more so. But it is only within the mold of a strong plot that character can sustain interest, for in drama it is through action that character must reveal itself. "Dramatic action," says Aristotle, "is not with a view to the representation of character: character comes in as subsidiary to the action." [3] It is significant that he particularly praises *Oedipus Tyrannus* as the outstanding instance of the subordination of character to plot; this is the one play most admired by the world among the Greek tragedies for its powerful characterization! And he was right, of course. In no play is the hero's character revealed more progressively as the action progresses; you will find that you could not cut from the play one speech without jeopardizing the entire structure.

---

anticipate three monographs elaborating the argument: *Noch Eine "Hamlet"* by Herr N. D. B. Reinaberg; *Hamletje* by Professor B. N. D. Ebirgenär; and a work by Dr. Granrieeb of the Punjabi University (we regret that we cannot decipher *his* title). We are also warned that the indefatigable Monsieur B. D. N. Baniergré will issue his *"Hamlet" et la Liberté irlandaise* not distantly; in it he threatens to demolish the argument. No doubt he will simply make it an occasion for advancing, as usual, the case for the Bourbon pretender to the French crown.

* And none is more sadly in need of revival today. Contemporary drama is largely indifferent to plot. In the United States, where theater has been far more stimulating during the last few decades than in England, the situation is all the more vexing. It is true that Mr. Anderson and Mr. Williams have restored to the English-speaking stage a poetry which has been long exiled from it, and that some of their fellows have recovered a healthy contact with the realities of experience. But illogical or mangled plots remain the vogue. The justified success of plays like *The Member of the Wedding* are in despite of their feebleness of construction. Miss McCullers' play was infused with authentic poetry, but in her brilliant novel of the same name she had the materials for a very fine, possibly a great, play, had she taken pains to create a plot. Plays with a sound plot are becoming so rare that a leading New York critic seriously suggests that plot may be an outmoded requirement in drama. When the drama no longer requires plot, paintings will no longer require color or sculptures shape.

When, therefore, in the next chapter, we present Shakespeare's *Hamlet* as we believe its author intended it to be understood, we shall begin with the plot. In the present one, we must use the same procedure in answering the leading theories already noticed. We must make our frame of reference what actually happens in the play.* If the dramatic action is at variance with a theory, that is enough to nullify the theory. And any theory which cannot be illustrated by reference to the plot must be branded irrelevant.

HAMLET ALWAYS SANE

On the question of Hamlet's sanity we can be brief. Hamlet is not insane, *nor does he ever pretend to be insane.* You will remember Samuel Johnson's astutely observing that the Prince does nothing in the play which he could not have done without the reputation of insanity. That is truer than the Great Lexicographer realized. Shakespeare nowhere shows Hamlet pretending lunacy.

Maintaining this, we are in a difficult position. The normal proceeding when the question of anyone's sanity is raised is to prove not the sanity but the insanity. Everyone is presumed to be acting sanely unless he can be shown to be acting otherwise. No one is called upon to prove that he is sane; it is only on evidence of abnormal behavior that he is to be thought not sane. In the case of Hamlet what we must insist upon, in all fairness, is the rejection of the legend that he assumes the role of a madman, a legend foisted upon him by commentaries; we must become freshly acquainted with him as Shakespeare conceived him. As normal human beings we must assume that he too is normal and is behaving normally, unless he gives evidence of behaving otherwise. He will be found acting not once in a way to arouse our suspicions.

At this point the reader is no more asked to accept in advance that Hamlet's conduct is that of a perfectly sane man than to adopt any other of the views we have quoted. He is asked only to observe

* Mr. William Bliss in his *The Real Shakespeare: a Counterblast to Commentators*, a zestful work no lover of Shakespeare should ignore, devotes a chapter of boundless good sense to a refutation of Mr. J. Dover Wilson which he ironically entitles "What Does Not Happen in Hamlet." [4]

Hamlet carefully. If, remembering performances or prejudiced readings of *Hamlet*, he finds it impossible to image Hamlet as a hero always behaving sanely, he is requested to be patient until, in our later discussion, he comes upon the scene (or scenes) causing him concern. He must not at this juncture indulge in the game of Building on Quotations by asking, "How about the time Hamlet says—?" If he will wait until we reach that moment, he is likely to find that the question will already have answered itself. Our chief problem, in the meantime, is to maintain order. At the present all that is asked is his assent to this reasonable proposition: If Hamlet can nowhere be shown to be conducting himself like a madman, he must be accounted as neither mad nor pretending to be mad.

The reader must also turn deaf ears to all those weighty commentaries which irrationally insist that because the old Hamlet story contained a hero who feigned insanity to protect his life, Shakespeare necessarily caused his hero to do the same—even though in our play, for more than half of its duration, Hamlet's life is in no danger. It is amazing that those scholars who have seen that Shakespeare's hero has not the reason of the old Hamlet for assuming madness have never asked themselves where in Shakespeare's play he does so. To have asked that question would have been to put literary sources to some use. Shakespeare was no cobbler of old shoes. He did *not* keep Hamlet "as he found him." Having removed the need for the pretended madness, he was capable of removing the pretended madness too. Once he determined to make the murder of Hamlet's father a secret one, he engaged to tell an essentially new story. Certain elements of the old plot, it is true, he did retain. It is characteristic of his methods that he should have kept what he could employ to advantage—not because, as the scholars vow, he was lazy, but because retaining from an old plot what he could for a new story presented an interesting challenge. (He stood in the same relation to his source as did the Athenian dramatists to the familiar stories of their legendry, retaining what was useful and altering what must be changed in accordance with the play's conception.) This meeting of challenges constitutes one of the chief pleasures of creation; every creator is, in a manner of speaking, a runner in a one-man obstacle race: he deliberately selects and places the hurdles to be overcome, and is exhilarated in overcoming them. The challenge is one of the great incentives to creation, as every creator knows. Shakespeare, it is true, did earn a good livelihood from his craft; but the scholars are foolish to deduce from that fact that he was exclusively concerned with supplying a market. They forget that he was also a sublime artist, and an artist creates for the fun of it too.

Now, the notion of Hamlet's feigning insanity has, as we have remarked, been rooted in one particular passage:

> so help you mercy,
> How strange or odd soe'er I bear myself—
> *As I perchance hereafter shall think meet*
> *To put an antic disposition on—*
> That you, at such time seeing me, never shall
>   note
> That you know aught of me,—this not to do,
> So grace and mercy at your most need help you,
> Swear.
>
> I, v, 169 seq.

"To put an antic disposition on" is generally assumed to mean, loosely, "to behave like a madman." Before we re-examine its meaning, let us agree: if nowhere we *see* Shakespeare causing Hamlet to conduct himself like a madman, we must insist that no actor has Shakespeare's authority to make him behave like one, when no moment of the action calls for lunatic behavior.

(If one wished to be sophistical, in academic tradition, and did not wish to re-examine the language of this passage—as we shall do in a few moments—one could say, noting that Hamlet nowhere does play the madman, that when Shakespeare had reached thus far in the composition of his play—the last scene of the First Act, where the passage occurs—he still thought he might use the feigned madness of the old Hamlet story, but then changed his mind. If that were the case—and it is not—there would still be no justification for interpreting the role as that of a man assuming insanity, since the action that follows exhibits no instance of his behaving that way. Suppose that the old Hamlet story told of a hero who decided to protect himself against his uncle by speaking only Greek thereafter, and suppose that Shakespeare's hero in the first act announced that henceforth in company he would speak only Greek. If thereafter the audience never heard the hero utter a word of that mellifluous tongue, the announcement would have to be dismissed as an impulse later reconsidered and never executed.*)

Before looking more closely at the crucial passage, let us recreate the circumstances in which the words are uttered. Hamlet has been alone with the Ghost. The Ghost has revealed the fact that Hamlet's father did not die a natural death, as everyone has believed, but was murdered by his own brother Claudius, who had first seduced the Queen to adultery. The Queen has not been accused by the Ghost as an accomplice in the murder, and henceforth among Hamlet's mental tortures will be his uncertainty of the full extent of her guilt. The Ghost has laid upon Hamlet two behests: in avenging his father's murder Hamlet is enjoined,

> . . . howsoever thou pursuest this act,
> Taint not thy mind, nor let thy soul contrive
> Against thy mother aught . . .
>
> I, v, 84–86

—i.e., manage your vengeance so that you do not jeopardize your own spiritual health—work an act of justice, not another murder—and spare the faithless Queen. The Ghost has made no stipulations as to how or when this vengeance is to be executed. With the approach of morning the Ghost has disappeared.

Surely, anyone who has seen Mr. Gielgud's performance can never forget how superb he was in the remainder of this scene: it was acting of sheer genius, and right in every detail. Here only, if anywhere in the tragedy, is Hamlet near nervous collapse:

> Hold, my heart,
> And you, my sinews, grow not instant old,
> But bear me stiffly up!

He staggers about, clasping his head between his hands as though the beating inside it would deprive him of his reason ("in this distracted globe"). To most men the narrative of the Ghost might have indeed proved too much: to hear that solemn voice from beyond the grave, the voice of a deeply loved father—to learn of the sufferings of that

---

* Mr. Olivier's cinema version avoided the issue altogether by omitting the entire passage.

spirit's endurance of the flames of Purgatory (I, v, 10–21) and the gloom of the night it is condemned to stalk—to hear of his mother's adultery, of his father's murder, of his hated uncle's criminality—to have the burden of vengeance thrust upon him—all this, without preparation, laid upon him suddenly—and to have the horrible tale cap the bitterness in which his father's death and mother's hasty marriage have already plunged him—even the mightiest of men might have been undone by such a stroke. But not Hamlet. Small wonder, however, that he reels; the world, whose foundations trembled at his father's death and began to shake at his mother's marriage to his hated uncle, has just tumbled about his ears.

But he is given no time for ordered reflection; before his whirling thoughts have spent themselves—in a mere twenty lines—Horatio and Marcellus are upon him. He has not even had time to recover some degree of self-control.

Only Mr. Gielgud has understood how ill-prepared Hamlet is at this moment to speak to anyone. He is bursting with what he has been told, and the lines prove that he is on the verge of disclosing everything:

MAR.	How is 't, my noble lord?
HOR.	What news, my lord?
HAM.	O, wonderful!
HOR.	Good, my lord, tell it.
HAM.	No, you'll reveal it.
HOR.	Not I, my lord, by heaven.
MAR.	Nor I, my lord.
HAM.	How say you, then, would heart of man once think it?— But you'll be secret?
HOR. & MAR.	Ay, by heaven, my lord.
HAM.	There's ne'er a villain dwelling in all Denmark—

He's about to add, "like my uncle." Characteristically, Hamlet, who has not had opportunity for one minute's consideration of his enormous task, is on the point of ruining everything. Human, all too human, he rushes to the comfort of sharing the burden of what he has heard. But, characteristically too, just in time he stops the torrent of his words. Mr. Gielgud conveyed all this marvelously: at the

end of the last line quoted, he suddenly ceased, looked in dazed be-
wilderment at both men, clapped a hand over his mouth to dam the
current, and staggered away almost drunkenly, while muttering

> But he's an arrant knave.

Words—anything to finish the sentence which he has nearly ter-
minated by a revelation that could have proved fatal to his cause.
Before he dare confide, he must have leisure to get his bearings.
Surely, this is precisely what Shakespeare intended.*

    Horatio, not remotely guessing what Hamlet has learned, is a
little offended at the latter's suddenly breaking off his confidence.
But Hamlet, perceiving the error so nearly committed, is evasive: he
has his business, they theirs; he wishes to be left to his. Then, because
gracious by nature, he sees that he is hurting his best friend by shutting the door against affection; he apologizes for his strange words:

> I'm sorry they offend you, heartily;
> Yes, faith, heartily.

The repetition indicates the sincerity of his regret at being unable to
tell his friend more as yet. *L'amitié ferme les yeux* and Horatio at
once reassures him:

> There's no offence, my lord.

Hamlet, a trifle calmer, contrives to atone to Marcellus too for the
sudden interruption of his confidences. He can vouch that this is "an
honest ghost"; but he must pray them both not to inquire further
into his dealings with it:

---

  * Nevertheless, it is not so generally understood. Kittredge describes
the passage as showing Hamlet speaking "flippantly of the Ghost and
its errand." [5] Adams finds these words to be "so much nonsense." [6] Wilson thinks them a parrying of the men's "natural curiosity by a piece of
'wonderful' news which tells them nothing." [7] John Barrymore's interpretation, wonderful in many places, was annoyingly consistent with
such views; he took each of the men around the shoulder, led them up
to the footlights, assumed a very conspiratorial air with "But you'll be
secret?", played up the suspense of what he was about to say, and delivered "But he's an arrant knave," as though it were all a great joke,
and moved off in handsome profile with an airy wave of his hand. It was
all very amusing, very flip—and rather revolting.

> For your desire to know what is between us,
> O'ermaster 't as you may.

And, having so nearly made a mistake himself, he pledges them to silence on what they have witnessed. Marcellus takes umbrage at being asked to swear on oath on the sword:

> We have sworn, my lord, already.

But Hamlet will not be denied, and insists. Unheard by the other two, the Ghost's voice echoes "Swear!" from underground; and Hamlet, still shaken, shifts his place to banish the sound from his still trembling ears. (It is not five minutes since the Ghost departed.) Horatio deems Hamlet's behavior "strange" only because he himself does not hear the ghostly voice.

At last the oath is proposed: They are never, no matter how incredibly Hamlet seems to be behaving—since hereafter he may find it necessary to act in a way that will seem odd—to fold their arms in an attitude implying private knowledge of him, or shake their heads sagely, or give out some doubtful phrase implying that they could say more if they chose to:

> so help you mercy,
> How strange or odd soe'er I bear myself—
> As I perchance hereafter shall think meet
> To put an antic disposition on—
> That you, at such time seeing me, never shall
> With arms encumbered thus, or this headshake,
> Or by pronouncing of some doubtful phrase,
> As "Well, we know," or "We could, an if we would,"
> Or "If we list to speak," or "There be, an if they might,"
> Or such ambiguous giving out, to note
> That you know aught of me,—this not to do,
> So grace and mercy at your most need help you,
> Swear.

And the two men take the oath.

Hamlet does not imply by

> As I perchance hereafter shall think meet
> To put an antic disposition on

that he may hereafter decide to play the madman—though universally that is the accepted meaning of these words.* The reasons against such an interpretation are more than one, and all cogent. And it is the better to gauge them that we have therefore been at pains to re-create the moment of drama in which the words are spoken.

¶ It is psychologically inconceivable that Hamlet could have decided upon so unusual and important a plan as playing the madman, when he has not had a moment's leisure to think of any line of future conduct. As we have seen, the entry of Horatio and Marcellus found him still whirling from his converse with the Ghost. The effort merely to check himself from revealing what the Ghost has imparted has consumed all his attention up to this point of the dialogue. He cannot humanly be thought capable of conceiving such an elaborate scheme in the maelstrom of his violent emotions during these few minutes.

¶ We do not see or hear Hamlet talking like a madman thereafter.

¶ Hamlet performs nothing and learns nothing during the course of the rest of the play as a consequence of assumed madness.

¶ The idea of assumed madness is dependent upon the meaning of the word "antic," in "To put an antic disposition on." Despite the universal misconstruction of this passage, the word "antic" has never meant "crazy" or "lunatic." The *Oxford English Dictionary* no-

---

* Kittredge: "A clear allusion to his purpose of counterfeiting madness." [8] But that device "adopted on the spur of the moment" proves "unsuccessful." [9] Adams: "He plans to act the madman." [10] Why? "We can only guess. His task seemed to call for a stratagem of some kind." But Hamlet fails "to use it to accomplish the great deed." [11]

Wilson: "Hamlet assumes madness because he cannot help it. . . . He is conscious that he no longer retains perfect control over himself. What more natural than that he should conceal his nervous breakdown behind a mask which would enable him to let himself go when the fit is upon him?" [12] This pretended madness "is the very salt of his (Shakespeare's) play . . . Imagine *Hamlet* without it, and most of the wit together with all the fun . . . would be lost." [13] (Why should wit and a sense of humor which are not masquerading as lunacy be less engaging?)

refer to Hamlet as a soldier; an actor might therefore with
justice take a fancy never to enter upon the stage withou
along a piece of cannon. (Hamlet, unquestionably, has
but we do not see him operating in that profession d
of the play.) Or the actor might, to be comple
always to come on stage leading behind him o
roo. There is nothing in the play to sugges
garoo, but there is nothing prohibiting
intelligence. Exactly the same can be
insanity.

These considerations do not
pect of the plot. After Poloniu
of the persons of the drama
sure Hamlet is deranged
and Guildenstern are
rumor, and the Kin
could be proved

Why is P
by the cou
unhappy
with e
has

It will be seen that the common denominator in all these meanings
is "grotesque." Remembering Shakespeare's willingness to use one
part of speech as another, we must still conclude after considering
all the definitions that the only possibilities among them for his use
of the word in this crucial passage are to be found in *b*, *c*, *g*, and *j*.
None of these implies even remotely the notion of insanity.

We have gone thus remorselessly into the matter to make it
clear that although actors continue to project a Hamlet feigning
madness, in so doing they impose a meaning upon the tragedy that
is not in it. It is true that Polonius starts a rumor that Hamlet is mad,
but there is no warrant to take the cue from that old fool. Others

as much
t dragging
been a soldier;
uring the course
ely original, prefer
n a leash a pet kanga-
the cannon or the kan-
their introduction—except
said for introducing feigned

, however, banish one important as-
comes to his absurd conclusion, some
do speak of Hamlet as mad. Polonius is
, Ophelia is made to think so, Rosencrantz
nformed so, the Queen chooses to accept the
(who knows better and would give much if it
that Hamlet is mad) pretends to think so.*
olonius' notion that Hamlet is mad taken up generally
t? When first we meet the Prince he is friendless and
, grief-stricken over his father's death; and fairly disgusted
everyone about him because of the speed with which his mother
remarried, the incestuous nature of that marriage, the readiness
the court to condone it, his dislike of his uncle, and the ease with
which his valiant father has been forgotten. Then at the end of the
first act he has his volcanic experience with the Ghost, hearing for
the first time that his father has been murdered and who the murderer (according to the spirit) is, and being pledged to vengeance.
That interview, in addition to conveying the shattering information
and laying upon him the heaviest of obligations, also raises questions
concerning the extent of his mother's culpability and the meaning of
the interview itself. After it, it is understandable that the most normal and convivial of men might seem something less than cheerful,
less than affable to the court which gives its support to the new king.
Remember that no one except the murderer (and, as we shall see,
possibly one other) knows that there has been a murder, that no one

---

* Wilson's Claudius is sure that Hamlet's derangement is "genuine
enough." [14] Wilson's proof? Claudius *says* so to others.

except Horatio and Marcellus (to neither of whom does it occur that he is mad) knows that he has had dealings with the Ghost. Denmark is satisfied with the reigning monarchs, and, like the rest of the world, prefers to have things agreeable. Hamlet's ungraciousness to the King and sarcasms to his mother and general unfriendliness will strike everyone as very shocking, odd, and unreasonable—everyone, that is, except Claudius, whose tortured conscience troubles him when Hamlet rejects his friendly overtures. In self-interest Claudius is obliged to encourage the general verdict that Hamlet's behavior is abnormal—is glad to do it. It leaves him the freer from any possible connection with it. And so Hamlet's reputation for being "transformed" grows, even while Claudius' inner fear is that his nephew may be all too sane.

In such an environment, alone (but for Horatio's understanding) in his knowledge of what the Ghost has revealed, of what he himself must find out, and of what he must manage to do, Hamlet has only to behave as any normal human being would behave in his circumstances to convince a Denmark, unaware and unconcerned, that he is queer. Who of us, if it were whispered abroad that we are not of sound mind, would not seem to furnish proof the livelong day to prejudiced observers uninformed of our problems, that we are indeed mentally unbalanced?

The point was shrewdly made in a Broadway hit of some years back, *The Shrike*. The hero of that melodrama, despairing of ever being rid of a vicious wife so that he can marry the girl he loves, has attempted to commit suicide. He no sooner recovers in the hospital than he sees the folly of his act, and is ready to come to grips with his many problems. But his wife, who would rather see him committed for life than free to go out into the world and have a decent life without her, manages the hospital staff so ably that he is soon under suspicion of being mentally unsound. Through her efforts he is put "under observation." After all, he is informed, "the doctors take most cases of suicide to be an inverted homicidal tendency. Do you know what that means? . . . You're a potential murderer in their eyes." [15] He is given the same kind of idiotic test that Polonius administers to Hamlet to try his sanity ("Do you know me, my lord?"—II, ii, 173): What is the capital of France? When did Roosevelt die? Subtract from a hundred by sevens.[16] Indignant at this stupidity, he is almost too revolted to answer, and vents his annoyance. But that tells against him. Knowing himself in his wife's clutches, he reacts as any normal human being would, with alternate anger and irony, his attempts at being calm varying with the sense of the hopelessness of his situation. He is in the desperate position of having to prove that he is not abnormal before the doctors will release him. Finally, in exasperation, when the psychiatrist has been convinced that this patient has been behaving rather too explosively, the trapped husband cries out to his wife in a burst of justified fury: "You've got to hold on tight to keep your balance here, Ann. Everything you say and do is reported. You are constantly watched. I shouldn't be getting excited now. If I'm seen, it will set me back God knows how long. You can't have normal human feelings here, Ann. Only continuous calm. Is that normal—for anyone?" [17]

It is exactly in the same kind of exasperation that Hamlet, who has heard a little too much of his supposed madness and now perceives that his mother excuses her own lechery by construing his home truths as lunacy, cries out to her:

> Ecstasy!*
> My pulse, as yours, doth temperately keep time,
> And makes as healthful music. It is not madness
> That I have uttered. Bring me to the test,
> And I the matter will re-word, which madness
> Would gambol from. Mother, for love of grace,
> Lay not that flattering unction to your soul,
> That not your trespass, but my madness speaks.
>   III, iv, 139 seq.

But up till then, except for several sardonic thrusts, he makes no attempt to convince those who think him mad that he is sane. How would he, how would anybody in his situation, go about proving his sanity? Is he to rattle off problems in arithmetic, relate facts of history, ask for an examination? The more he would protest his sanity, the more everyone would become convinced that he had lost it. Such indeed is his mother's reaction to the deeply earnest and eloquent speech we have just quoted! Besides, he is indifferent to their opinion; they are no friends of his. If they wish to think him

---

* i.e., madness.

mad, let them. It gives him more privacy, which is what he wants. But there is no place in the play where he makes the slightest effort to *confirm* them in their opinion of his madness—unless one be so dehumanized as thus to interpret his two ironic passages with the old fool Polonius. It would be too hard if one could not allow Hamlet, who has a magnificent sense of humor, to pull the leg of the dotard who is completely confident that the Prince is mad, and whose own brain is so vacuous.

Hamlet, then, behaves throughout with perfect sanity. We cannot interpret his indifference to other people's opinion of his conduct as a feigning of insanity.

HAMLET AND THE GHOST

Approaching the larger question of Hamlet's procrastination, we had better begin by understanding what part in the plot is allotted the Ghost. The revelations and behests of the Ghost inaugurate the first significant advance of the play's action. Upon them the plot firmly rests. If we fail to understand precisely the import of Hamlet's interview with the Ghost we cannot correctly understand his subsequent conduct.

In our salad days, when *Hamlet* was still a puzzle to us, we found ourselves particularly disturbed in our attempts to comprehend this specter. The spirit of Hamlet's father seemed to us to be discussed, by the characters who behold him, in language strangely unsuited to the late Majesty of Denmark. More than that, we felt thwarted by what appeared a major confusion: in the first scene Horatio and Marcellus decide to make their report to Hamlet with the express object of inciting the Prince to join them on the platform so that he may converse with the Ghost, whom they have both beheld—

> HOR. Let us impart what we have seen tonight
> Unto young Hamlet, for upon my life,
> This spirit, dumb to us, will speak to him.
> I, i, 169 seq.;

yet in the fourth scene they restrain him by main force when he wishes to follow the Ghost for just that very purpose—

MAR.   But do not go with it.
HOR.   No, by no means . . .
MAR.   You shall not go, my lord.
HAM.   Hold off your hand!
HOR.   Be ruled. You shall not go.

                                        I, iv, 62 seq.

Indeed, Hamlet is compelled to hurl them off so that he may do what they have brought him out into the night to accomplish. It was obvious that we did not know enough about Elizabethan ghosts.

It happened that at the time we were indulging a new enthusiasm which we had caught like a rash from that indefatigable collector of vampires, demons, and witches, Montague Summers, the author of *Demonology and Witchcraft, The Geography of Witchcraft, The Vampire, The Vampire in Europe,* and other fascinating studies. Living in the twentieth century, Mr. Summers, partly because of his wide reading and partly for reasons of temperament, came to believe devoutly in the reality of the Devil and a whole tribe of minor demons who spend their time decoying humanity into error; further, he became firmly convinced that to deny the existence of these devils is to deny the tenets of Christianity. He is deliciously exciting to read (no less in his choice polyglot footnotes than in his text)—a completely medieval intelligence operating, with a vast store of learning, in the midst of a modern scientific world. He, for instance, with all due allowances for hoaxes and pretenders, was sure that spiritualists and mediums do receive messages from the spirit world; only he identified the senders of the messages as minor devils busy, as ever, with the destruction of human souls. From the endless treasury of Mr. Summers' histories and examples we began to understand that while the world generally accepted the idea of a personal Devil, it was also generally believed that

                        the Devil hath power
            To assume a pleasing shape
                                II, ii, 628–29

—almost any shape his Satanic Majesty pleases.

In the midst of our necromantic-diabolic readings, we discovered that the Bodley Head Quarto series, edited by Mr. G. B. Harrison, had been publishing several volumes of early treatises referred to by Mr. Summers, and we hastened to purchase them. Among these little treasures was the reprint of the *Daemonologie* written by King James VI of Scotland (later James I of England) in 1587. This work of the bigot-king began to educate us in Elizabethan lore concerning ghosts.*

It is clear from the *Daemonologie* that a ghost may be none other than the Devil himself, masquerading for the occasion in the guise of a person familiar to the unfortunate mortal favored with the supernatural visit. James, who probably never once harbored an original idea in his cranium, was voicing accepted notions when he wrote the following passage:

> PHI. And will God then permit these wicked spirites to trouble the reste of a dead bodie, before the resurrection thereof? Or if he will so, I thinke it should be of the reprobate onely.
>
> EPI. What more is the reste troubled of a dead bodie,

---

* As a matter of fact, two enterprising studies of Elizabethan attitudes towards spirits had been made long before,[18] but Shakespearean scholarship had taken no cognizance of them, and we were at the time unaware that in them we might have learned more fully about demonology of the period. Until comparatively recently Professor Stoll was almost unique in having given any thought to the subject, when he insisted that Shakespeare's ghosts must be accepted by us on the same terms as Shakespeare's audience.[19] Since then a very few scholars have studied the subject, chief among them being Professor J. Dover Wilson in an important preface.[20] Mr. Wilson's later pages on "Ghost or Devil?" should also be mentioned as perhaps his best contribution in *What Happens in Hamlet* [21]—although we find his exegesis on the Closet Scene extravagant. More recently, Mr. R. H. West has gone thoroughly into pneumatology as exhibited in Elizabethan drama.[22] Nevertheless, few scholars now take the Elizabethan view of ghosts into account when discussing *Hamlet*, even though, as Mr. Wilson admirably states it: the Ghost in *Hamlet* "was a revolutionary innovation in the history of dramatic literature . . . The stock apparition of the Elizabethan theatre was a classical puppet, borrowed from Seneca, a kind of Jack-in-the-box, popping up from Tartarus at appropriate moments . . . It is one of Shakespeare's glories that he took the conventional puppet, humanized it, christianized it, and made a figure that his spectators would recognize as *real*." [23]

> when the Deuill carryes it out of the Graue to serue
> his turne for a space . . . ? . . . And that the
> Deuill may vse aswell the ministrie of the bodies of
> the faithfull in these cases, as of the vn-faithfull,
> there is no inconvenient; for his haunting with their
> bodies after they are deade, can no-waies defyle
> them: in respect of the soules absence. . . .
> Amongst the Gentiles the Deuill vsed that much
> . . . to discouer vnto them, the will of the defunct,
> or what was the way of his slaughter. . . . And to
> that same effect is it, that he now appeares in that
> maner to some ignorant Christians.[24]

To an Elizabethan, then, a ghost would stand in suspicion of being not the spirit belonging to the body in which it was clothed, but very possibly a devil that had for the occasion borrowed the use of that body. There are multitudinous proofs that such is the attitude of the characters in *Hamlet* towards the Ghost. Shakespeare was writing about this apparition in the manner that made most sense to his audience, and his very phraseology in all references to it was conditioned by popular belief. This frame of mind of the author accounts for what we had earlier felt to be a style of scant respect to that awesome presence.

Let us observe that phraseology. It is significant that although the Ghost appears dressed and armed in precise resemblance to Hamlet's father, the figure is normally referred to in a depersonalized word, not, as we should expect, in terms which would identify him as the late King. We take some of these expressions in the order in which they arise:

(I, i)	HOR.	What, has this *thing* appeared again tonight?	(21)
	MAR.	Touching *this dreaded sight*, twice seen of us	(25)
		. . . . if again *this apparition* come	(28)
		. . . . speak to *it*	(29)
	HOR.	Tush, tush, 't will not appear.	(30)

The Ghost enters.

MAR.	. . . . . . Look, where *it* comes again!	
BERN.	*In the same figure*, like the King that's dead.	

> MAR. ......Speak to *it*, Horatio.
> BERN. Looks *it* not like the King? Mark *it*, Horatio.
> (40–43)

> BERN. *It* would be spoke to.
> MAR.   Question *it*, Horatio.
> HOR. *What art thou* that *usurp'st* this time of night
> Together with *that fair and warlike form*
> In which the majesty of buried Denmark
> Did sometimes march? . . . .
> MAR. *It* is offended.
> BERN.   See, *it* stalks away!   (45–50)

To modern ears it sounds strange enough that they should all use the neuter in reference to the King's ghost, and even stranger that Horatio, recognizing the form of their late monarch, should ask, "What art thou?" If we know, however, that to them this may be a devil, all they say is clearly a reflection of their reservations concerning the Ghost's actual nature.

As the men continue talking, they never speak of the spirit as being that of Hamlet's father, but say:

> Is *it* not *like* the King?   (58)

> Our last king
> *Whose image* even but now appeared to us   (80–81)

The Ghost re-enters and Horatio addresses it:

> Lo, where *it* comes again!
> I'll cross *it, though it blast me*. Stay, *illusion!*   (126–27)

This would be the language of mere rant, if it were not that Horatio is aware he may be speaking to a demon who *could* blast him. He means exactly what he says. For the rest of the scene this kind of language continues.

In the next, when Horatio is reporting his experience to Hamlet, he does not say that he saw the late king, but rather:

> (I, ii)   A figure like your father   (199)

And Hamlet himself, loving his father as he does, none the less says:

> Did you not speak to *it?*   (214)

When the Prince agrees to join them that night he speaks words that ignorance would again pronounce bombast, but which we must understand as a realistic preparation for a projected encounter with a ghost:

> If *it assume my noble father's person*
> I'll speak to *it, though hell itself should gape.*   (244–45)

Later that night the Ghost appears before Hamlet, Horatio, and Marcellus; note the language the Prince employs in addressing the spirit; with all his adoration of his father, Hamlet as a rational human being has his reservation about ghosts too:

(I, iv)   Be thou a spirit of health or *goblin damned,*
          Bring with thee airs from heaven or *blasts from hell,*
          Be thy *intents wicked* or charitable . . .   (40–42)

Now we can understand why Horatio and Marcellus would prevent Hamlet's following the Ghost when it invites him "to a more removed ground," where they could not be present to protect him. Horatio puts his fears into plain English, which is to be taken literally:

> *What if it tempt you toward the flood,* my lord,
> *Or to the dreadful summit of the cliff* . . .
> *And there assume some other horrible form*
> *Which might deprive your sovereignty of reason* . . . ?
> (69–73)

In short, this could be the Devil up to his usual mischief, not at all the spirit of Hamlet's noble father. If it wishes to speak, let it speak in the presence of Hamlet's comrades.

But Hamlet does follow the Ghost, and alone. Presently, however, even he feels he has taken enough risks:

(I, v)   *Where wilt thou lead me?* Speak, I'll go no further. (1)

The Ghost speaks at last, and it seems to us that the actor interpreting the role could easily give dimension to the problem of the Ghost's identity by accenting the verb in the next line we quote. If it were merely a matter of exterior resemblance, Hamlet surely needs not to be informed who it is that addresses him. After thirty years of intimate acquaintance, no father appearing before his son remarks, "I am your *father*." But knowing the need of settling the doubts of Hamlet (and Shakespeare's audience), the Ghost reassures Hamlet:

> I *am* thy father's spirit.   (9)

With any other emphasis the line becomes idiotically superfluous.

After the Ghost disappears and Hamlet is joined by Horatio and Marcellus, he loses no time in informing his friend:

> Touching this vision here,
> It is an *honest* ghost, that let me tell you.   (137–38)

In the interval between this scene and the next time we see Hamlet he has had leisure to think over his situation. Naturally, with all his willingness to believe that it was his father's spirit with whom he has spoken, he owes it to his soul's safety to keep an open mind until he can prove the Ghost's reliability. Knowing nothing about Elizabethan pneumatology, Schlegel interpreted Hamlet's uncertainty as a symptom of irresolution: "He is a hypocrite towards himself; his far-fetched scruples are often mere pretexts to cover his want of resolution. . . . Hamlet has no firm belief either in himself or in anything else . . . ; he believes in the ghost of his father when he sees it, and as soon as it has disappeared it appears to him almost in the light of a deception." On the contrary, Hamlet's doubts about the Ghost are a symptom not of weakness, but of *strong-mindedness*, a determination to know exactly where he is going. When he has decided to give the play before Claudius, he means exactly what he says, and his words are again to be taken, not as an excuse, but in their literal meaning:

> The spirit that I have seen
> *May be the devil; and the devil hath power*
> *To assume a pleasing shape; yea, and perhaps . . .*
> *Abuses me to damn me. I'll have grounds*
> *More relative than this.* The play's the thing
> Wherein I'll catch the conscience of the King.
>   II, ii, 627 seq.

Hating Claudius, Hamlet must guard himself against a readiness to believe him guilty. The Ghost may have been an evil spirit, and therefore one of Hamlet's chief motives in arranging to give the play is to determine whether or not the apparition did house his father's spirit. If Claudius prove unaffected by the performance, the Ghost may be dismissed as a devil indeed.

The play is given with success (to a degree), and at last the all-basic question is settled for Hamlet:

> O good Horatio, *I'll take the ghost's word* for a thousand pound.

III, ii, 297

He never raises the question again, and we are here a little past the middle of the tragedy.

Obviously, then, Hamlet's need to decide about the identity of the Ghost forms one of the ground elements of the plot during the first half of the play. And an Elizabethan audience would have quickly understood the justifiability of his doubts, would have understood them to be precisely what he describes them to be. It would never have occurred to anyone in Shakespeare's theater to imagine, as later commentators have done, that Hamlet was merely making excuses to rationalize delay.

The Ghost, therefore, is one of the persons most essential to the plot. Precisely because specters have more or less passed out of the horizons of a post-Darwinian world, are we obliged to rediscover what Shakespeare's audiences would have assumed concerning them. It is our only hope of discovering accurately Shakespeare's meaning. Yet that vital knowledge has been ignored by all but a few scholars. Without it, it is impossible to put ourselves in Hamlet's place. Unhappily, much of the commentary on *Hamlet* is invalidated by all kinds of irrelevant and uninformed speculation about the effect of the Ghost's injunctions upon the hero. Many have interpreted the Ghost as a kind of embodiment of Hamlet's lunacy. Mr. Greg, as we have noted, has argued that the Ghost is but a "figment" of Hamlet's brain, in the teeth of the fact that the apparition has been encountered two nights by Francisco and Bernardo before the drama opens (see I, i, 33), and is twice beheld by Horatio and Marcellus, the second time when Hamlet himself is seeing this "figment."

Having reached this point, we need not trouble to answer Mr.

Greg further. When we dismissed the idea that Hamlet ever behaves irrationally, we were also dismissing the notion of his ever being actually insane or mentally unbalanced. But we should like to enforce a concept already advanced by us. No tragedy can have as a hero a man who is mentally unbalanced—whether he be the lunatic of the medicos, Mr. Greg's victim of hallucinations, Professor Bradley's victim of melancholia, or Mr. Wilson's victim of a nervous breakdown who "cannot help doing" what he does. The whole meaning of tragedy is involved in the personal responsibility of the hero for his fall, and a mentally unbalanced hero is innocent of any responsibility for his acts. Nor can we allow to slip by without protest those commentators like Messrs. Granville-Barker, Van Doren, and Lawrence who are content to think Shakespeare meant his hero to be a riddle and who even discover artistic dimension in such vagueness. To make a virtue out of confusion is not only in violation of the fundamental obligation of the arts to communicate, but it is also in defiance of our need of identifying the tragic flaw of the hero before we can apprehend the meaning of his fall. Without a clear comprehension of the hero's traits, there is no possibility of our participating in the experience for which tragedy is created.

Whatever may be said, therefore, about Hamlet's procrastination, it is now evident that Hamlet's doubts about the Ghost have nothing to do with that question.

HAMLET NOT TOO SENSITIVE, NOT TOO THOUGHTFUL, TO ACT

The simplest way to answer the Coleridge-Schlegel school of *Hamlet* criticism that the Prince is too much the thinker to act, as well as the Goethe school that he is too sensitive to avenge himself, is to take a rapid view of the things which happen in the play itself. Hamlet is, indeed, a thinker, a philosophical man, if you will; but he is not a professional philosopher—not the kind of man whose chief preoccupation in life is to wrangle amiably over abstract speculations on the nature of time, space, and being—the "To be or not to be" soliloquy notwithstanding! He is not, we mean, the Hamlet we are forever seeing on the boards, the great "brain," always making his entrance with arms folded in profound meditation—the professional thinker wandering about without his nurse.

Let us take a view of what Hamlet actually does in this play. Told of the appearance of a ghost resembling his father, he immediately arranges to join Horatio and Marcellus that very night in the hopes of meeting it too (I, ii). When the Ghost appears, he rejects the fears of his friends, brave men both, is powerful enough to throw off their restraining grasp, and follows the dread apparition, unconcerned about the mischief which may be awaiting him further down the road (I, v). He seizes his first opportunity to test the Ghost's veracity and at the same time to expose Claudius if he be guilty of murder; this opportunity he is quick to recognize when the Players arrive, and he is inspired to try the device of presenting a play at court (II, ii). He manages to present his play without impediment (III, ii). In the Queen's closet, to which he has come to castigate his mother, when Polonius cries out behind the arras, his sword is out and through the cloth in a flash; moreover, the thing he has come to do he continues to do, even with Polonius's corpse in the room (III, iv). His visit with his mother over, he drags off the body of the dead councilor and hides it himself (IV, ii). He greatly admires the courage and enterprise of Fortinbras' going forth with an army to fight merely on a point of honor (IV, iv). In the encounter with the pirate ship, en route to England, Hamlet boards the enemy alone, yet manages to win over the whole crew singlehanded, so that they are willing to take him back to Denmark (IV, vi). (He seems in this episode to be much more of an Errol Flynn kind of hero than the one we usually behold on the stage.) His worst foe, Claudius, implies quite clearly that Hamlet is a brilliant fencer (IV, vii, 103 seq.), and the Prince later leaps at the offer of a match with Laertes, an expert duelist (V, ii, 180 seq.). At Ophelia's grave, he jumps in after her brother and grapples fiercely with him (V, i, 280 seq.). And in the last scene, mortally wounded though he is, he has the prowess to rush at the King, stab him, force the remainder of the poisoned drink down his throat, and—after this mighty expenditure of effort —dash the cup from Horatio's firm hands (V, ii, 333 seq.).

From Ophelia we have learned that he is everywhere respected as a model courtier and soldier (III, i, 158), and at the finale it is a soldier's funeral which Fortinbras orders for him:

> Let four captains
> Bear Hamlet, *like a soldier*, to the stage,
> For he was likely, had he been put on,
> To have proved most royally.
>
> V, ii, 406 seq.

His reputation and his conduct have surely nothing in common with Goethe's delicate "vase" or Coleridge's ponderer—too sensitive or too thoughtful to act. Indeed, it may be questioned whether or not any man who remained inactive through excessive delicacy or excessive thought was ever occupied in acting to the extent and with the energy exhibited by the hero of this tragedy!

HAMLET NOT TOO MORAL TO ACT

Act Hamlet does, in short—and all over the premises. Nor is he in any way impeded by Christian morality, as Ulrici and others have maintained, or by that sense of a divine mission which has more recently been attributed to him. That Hamlet does believe he has an immortal soul is beyond dispute. That he is something of a Christian one must also agree. But just how much of one, must be left to the theologians. It is safe to assume that any divine taking a clear view of Hamlet's conduct and thought will agree that the Prince would never be a candidate for sainthood.

He kills Polonius by error. How grief-stricken is he at his act of mayhem? When the corpse comes tumbling forth, notice Hamlet's repentant tone:

> Thou wretched, rash, intruding fool, farewell!
> I took thee for thy better. Take thy fortune.
> Thou find'st to be too busy is some danger.
>
> III, iv, 31 seq.

And he turns back to continue chiding his mother. At the end of the scene, before he goes out "tugging in Polonius," his delicacy and Christian scrupulousness are once more evident as he says sardonically over the corpse:

> I'll lug the guts into the neighbor room.
> Mother, good night. Indeed this counsellor

> Is now most still, most secret, and most grave,
> Who was in life a foolish prating knave.
> Come, sir, to draw toward an end with you.
>
> > III, iv, 212 seq.

Motherly affection must indeed be blind to enable Gertrude presently to report to Claudius:

> > he weeps for what is done.
> >
> > > IV, i, 27.

Later, Hamlet sends Rosencrantz and Guildenstern to their death without scrupling for a moment to wonder whether they may not be innocent of any ill towards him. He suspects them, and that is enough for him. Horatio plainly hints that he may have been unjust, but Hamlet tosses aside the reproof:

> HOR. So Guildenstern and Rosencrantz go to't.
> HAM. Why, man, they did make love to this employment;
> They are not near my conscience.
>
> > V, ii, 56 seq.

His point of view towards his luckless erstwhile friends is that if their natures were too weak to survive being involved in his affairs, so much the worse for them:

> 'Tis dangerous when the baser nature comes
> Between the pass and fell incensed points
> Of mighty opposites.
>
> > V, ii, 60 seq.

He never pauses to ask whether they could have avoided being so involved. Not much Christian charity here!

Hamlet has killed Laertes' father, and is concerned about avenging his own, yet he can be so blind as to ask the young man indignantly:

> Hear you, sir,
> What is the reason that you use me thus?
> I loved you ever.
>
> > V, i, 311 seq.

Hamlet cannot understand why Laertes should feel hostile to his father's assassin!

But the most shocking moment of Hamlet's behavior from a Christian point of view is when he withholds his weapon from killing Claudius when he finds the latter apparently praying, lest so he send him straight to heaven. He will wait until he finds the King

> When he is drunk asleep, or in his rage,
> Or in the incestuous pleasure of his bed,
> At gaming, swearing, or about some act
> That has no relish of salvation in't,—
> Then trip him, that his heels may kick at heaven
> And that his soul may be as damned and black
> As hell, whereto it goes.
>
> III, iii, 89 seq.

You must accept Christian dogma to entertain such views, but you are also less than an ideal Christian to entertain them! And it is also a little more than absurd to construe, as some contemporary critics do, a hero who when angered can be as uncharitable as Hamlet into an instrument of God's for cleansing the world!

We do not mean, of course, to imply that, because he is less than a perfect Christian, Hamlet is to be viewed, as some few have viewed him, as morally contemptible. He does not have to be a saint to engage our sympathies. Indeed, it is questionable whether a saint could figure as the hero of a tragedy.

What we have adduced should make short work, too, of a Hamlet delayed by "unexpressed motives," by the operations of his subconscious mind (which phrase covers psychoanalytical commentary), or by his fear of death. An audience can follow a tragedy and participate in it only when the motives and mental processes are clearly demonstrated. As for a fear of death, every one of Hamlet's acts cited in the preceding pages gives the lie to that.

If Hamlet does not procrastinate because of excessive delicacy, thoughtfulness, moral scrupulousness, or involved complexes, and if he is neither mad nor ever feigns to be mad, what were the hero and the tragedy of Shakespeare's creation? We are ready to answer now.

REFERENCES IN CHAPTER IV

1. L. Cooper, *Aristotle on the Art of Poetry* (Ithaca, 1947), pp. 5–6.
2. L. Carroll, *Alice's Adventures in Wonderland*, Chapter XII.
3. S. H. Butcher, *Aristotle's Theory of Poetry and Fine Art* (New York, 1951), p. 27
4. W. Bliss, *The Real Shakespeare: a Counterblast to Commentators* (London, 1947), pp. 228–255.
5. G. L. Kittredge, *Hamlet* (Boston, 1939), p. 271.
6. J. Q. Adams, *Hamlet* (Boston, 1929), p. 217.
7. J. D. Wilson, *What Happens in Hamlet* (New York, 1936), p. 79.
8. G. L. Kittredge, *op. cit.*, p. 173.
9. *Ibid.*, p. xiii.
10. J. Q. Adams, *op. cit.*, p. 217.
11. *Ibid.*, p. 218.
12. J. D. Wilson, *op. cit.*, p. 92.
13. *Ibid.*, p. 95.
14. *Ibid.*, p. 118.
15. J. Kramm, *The Shrike* (New York, 1952), p. 147.
16. *Ibid.*, p. 109.
17. *Ibid.*, p. 131.
18. T. A. Spalding, *Elizabethan Demonology* (London, 1880).
    F. W. Moorman, "Shakespeare's Ghosts" in *Modern Language Review* I (1906), pp. 192–221.
19. E. E. Stoll, "The Objectivity of Shakespeare's Ghosts" in *Publications of the Modern Language Association* XXII (1907), p. 205.
20. J. D. Wilson, "The Ghost Scenes in 'Hamlet' in the Light of Elizabethan Spiritualism" in Lavater's *Of Ghosts and Spirites Walking by Nyght* (Oxford, 1929), pp. vii–xxxi.
21. J. D. Wilson, *What Happens in Hamlet* (New York, 1936), pp. 51–86.
22. R. H. West, *The Invisible World* (Athens, Georgia, 1939).
23. J. D. Wilson, *op. cit.* (New York, 1936), pp. 55–56.
24. King James the First, *Daemonologie* (Bodley Head Quartos) (London, 1925), pp. 60–61.

V Facts Are Stubborn Things: Shakespeare's "Hamlet"

WE NOW KNOW what the play and its hero are not, and therefore are well on the way to knowing what they are.

Let us, true to our dramatic principles, begin by examining the fundamental action of the play. What is most basic we italicize.

MURDER WILL SPEAK WITH MOST MIRACULOUS ORGAN: ACT ONE

(i) Horatio hears from Marcellus and Bernardo how an apparition has twice appeared to them; he is skeptical. *Suddenly the Ghost appears, in the perfect likeness of Denmark's late king.* Excitedly, Marcellus bids Horatio speak to it; as a scholar he possesses the vocabulary to address what may be a demon in language that will not offend. *But the Ghost will not answer,* and disappears. When Marcellus asks what can be the reason for the current haste in preparing for war, Horatio explains: the late king, challenged to open combat by the King of Norway, slew him and thus honorably won certain lands; now the latter's son, Fortinbras, is busy collecting an army to win back from Denmark the lands his father lost. Horatio breaks off as the Ghost re-appears, and boldly determines to face it, though it should "blast" him for his courage. In a kind of incantation, he powerfully conjures it to reveal its purposes. But the cock crows and the apparition vanishes. *Horatio suggests that they at once communicate their experience to Prince Hamlet.*

(ii) Before the convened Danish court, King Claudius expresses his grief—a little too urbanely!—over the recent death of his brother, the late king, and explains his hasty marriage to his brother's wife, Gertrude, as owing to the pressure of state affairs and the consent of the noblemen. He delegates two envoys to deal for him in the Fortinbras affair, and grants Laertes, son of his councilor Polonius, permission to return to France. Then, with elaborate display of affection, he addresses himself to his nephew, now his son, Hamlet, and gently upbraids him for still wearing mourning for his dead father. Claudius urges him to look on him as a father. Hamlet insultingly repulses the offer, ignores the King, and ironically assures his mother that his mourning is more than a matter of black attire and momentary tears. The King expresses his wish that Hamlet not return to the university, but remain at court; he informs the world that Hamlet is sole heir to the throne. Left alone, Hamlet expresses his revulsion at his mother's marriage, only two months after his father's death, to the man Hamlet hates most of all men. Moreover, this particular marriage is the more odious for being incestuous. Now Horatio and Marcellus come in. After welcoming with delight his old schoolfellow and closest friend, Horatio, *the Prince is told of the appearance of the Ghost. Hamlet, very much excited, promises to join them that night in hopes to see the Ghost. Even if it be a devil he will speak to it:*

> (If it assume my noble father's person
> I'll speak to it, though hell itself should gape . . .)

Hamlet can hardly wait for nightfall.

(iii) Laertes is about to leave for France; he urges Ophelia to mistrust Hamlet's attentions: it is unlikely that the Prince would think of marrying a commoner. Polonius comes in, and gives his son advice and a farewell blessing. Then he turns to Ophelia and questions her concerning Hamlet's conduct towards her, which he suspects as having dishonorable intentions. He ends by commanding her to cease all further communication with the Prince:

> This is for all:
> I would not, in plain terms, from this time forth,

> Have you so slander any moment leisure,
> As to give words or talk with the Lord Hamlet.
> Look to 't, I charge you.

Ophelia will obey.

(iv) The next midnight. *Hamlet awaits the Ghost* with Horatio
and Marcellus. *It appears. It is his father's form which confronts
Hamlet, but he knows that it may be a demon which he sees. He
therefore calls upon the aid of heavenly goodness before addressing
it:*

> Angels and ministers of grace defend us!
> Be thou a spirit of health or goblin damn'd,
> Bring with thee airs from heaven or blasts from hell,
> Be thy intents wicked or charitable,
> Thou comest in such a questionable * shape
> That I will speak to thee.

The Ghost silently indicates that Hamlet is to follow it, but Marcellus and Horatio urge him not to accompany it: such apparitions
have been said to tempt men to destruction. This spirit might

> assume some other horrible form

which could drive its victim into madness. But *Hamlet will not heed*,
and begins to go with the Ghost. His friends hold him back by main
force, but Hamlet hurls them off:

> (By heaven, I'll make a ghost of him that lets † me!)

and follows the Ghost.

(v) Hamlet, having followed the Ghost for some time, avers
that he will venture no further. *The spirit identifies himself as Hamlet's father, and reveals his murder at the hands of Claudius*, his own
brother, *who first had seduced the Queen to adultery*. Having described the manner of the poisoning, *the Ghost lays upon Hamlet the
burden of revenging this murder, and makes two injunctions: Hamlet is not to taint his mind in the pursuit of vengeance, and he is not
to contrive any punishment for the Queen. The Ghost makes ab-*

---

* i.e., inviting question.
† i.e., hinders.

*solutely no stipulation as to how speedily Hamlet is to achieve venge-
ance* or what method he is to employ: the important thing is that
vengeance must be worked in the spirit and manner of justice.
*The act ends with this scene, and since Hamlet has just learned of
his task, his conduct thus far raises, of course, no question of procrastination.*

THE PLAY'S THE THING: ACT TWO

(i) We learn that Laertes has been for a while in Paris. Polonius
sends his servant Reynaldo to spy on his son and find out how the
young man has been conducting himself. Ophelia enters in great
perturbation: Hamlet has just forced his way into her room and
frightened her by his garb, his silence, his intense study of her face,
and his sudden withdrawal. She assures her father that, as he has
commanded, she has been refusing to see Hamlet and to hear from
him. Polonius concludes from her account that her rejection of the
Prince has driven the young man mad, and he intends to report as
much to the King.
In the intervening time since the end of Act One, Hamlet has had
leisure to confide in Horatio and to think over *his problem,* the chief
aspects of which are, *first and foremost, the questionable reliability
of the Ghost,* which may have been a demon; *the apparent impossibility*—if the Ghost's word may be taken—*of proving a case against
Claudius,* since the murder was secret; *the need of settling the Ghost's
authenticity; and, if Claudius is indeed a murderer, achieving vengeance.*

(ii) The King has sent for Rosencrantz and Guildenstern, two
old schoolfellows of Hamlet. He tells them that the Prince has been
behaving very oddly recently, and beseeches them to discover what
is troubling their friend, and to do what they can to revive his spirits.
The ambassadors from Norway return with the good news that
Fortinbras has been forbidden by his monarch to prosecute the war
against Denmark. This business ended, Polonius at great length assures the King and Queen that Hamlet's strange behavior is due to
Ophelia's rejection of his love:

> I precepts gave her,
> That she should lock herself from his resort,

> Admit no messengers, receive no tokens.
> Which done, she took the fruits of my advice . . .

and as a result Hamlet has declined into a state of madness through frustrated love. Polonius promises to prove his theory if the King will fall in with his scheme: he will contrive a meeting between his daughter and the Prince, while he and the King eavesdrop. Hamlet now comes in; the King and Queen depart. Polonius endeavors to test the extent of Hamlet's "madness," but is himself routed by the exasperated Prince. Hamlet is now joined by Guildenstern and Rosencrantz, whom he at first greets with great joy. Soon he suspects, however, that they are acting as spies for the King, and he begins to treat them with contempt. Glad to clear the air, *they tell him that the company of players must soon arrive in town.* Hamlet is delighted at the prospect of seeing again some of his old actor-friends. The actors enter and are warmly welcomed by him; *he asks them to recite a passage from a play he particularly admires. During the recitation, Hamlet, struck by one of the lines, conceives an important plan.* As the players go out, *he delays their leader and requests a performance at court tomorrow of "The Murder of Gonzago,"* and says that he wishes to insert a few lines in the text. *The actor agrees.* Left alone, *Hamlet reveals that the play he has ordered contains a plot similar to the events outlined by the Ghost. When the play is presented tomorrow night, perhaps the similarity will so work upon Claudius that the King will publicly proclaim his guilt before the court:*

> I have heard
> That guilty creatures sitting at a play
> Have by the very cunning of the scene
> Been struck so to the soul that presently *
> They have proclaimed their malefactions.

And since the Ghost may have been a demon,

> (The spirit that I have seen
> May be the devil . . .)

and Hamlet must first be sure of the King's guilt, at the very least the performance will settle once and for all the authenticity of the

* i.e., at once.

Ghost and Claudius' innocence or guilt. This much Hamlet will learn by closely observing the King's reactions to the play. He may also learn something about his incomprehensible mother, and the extent of her guilt.

As the second act concludes, there is still no question of procrastination. Hamlet has seized the very first opportunity that has presented itself for procuring answers to some fundamental questions. Until he knows these answers, he cannot possibly know whether or not he has been misled by the Devil and is to murder an innocent man. He is therefore not chargeable with wasting any time either in the discharge of his filial obligations or in advancing the cause of justice. Also, there has been no occasion for his feigning madness.

EVERY FOOL WILL BE
MEDDLING: ACT THREE

(i) The next day. Guildenstern and Rosencrantz admit to the King and Queen that they have failed to determine the cause of Hamlet's distraction. *Polonius extends the Prince's invitation to attend the play tonight, and the King eagerly accepts.* When the others leave, Polonius places Ophelia where Hamlet is bound to meet her, thrusts a prayer book in her hand, and then conceals himself and the King so that they may overhear the encounter. Hamlet enters and delivers his celebrated soliloquy: it is the fear of what lies in wait for us after death that makes us endure the catastrophes of life. He now sees Ophelia, who astonishes him by trying to return his gifts to her with the accusation that he no longer loves her. Unable to believe his ears, he bitterly urges her, while she weeps, to flee the world's corruption and enter a nunnery. Suddenly, Hamlet is aware that they are being overheard. He is now infuriated with her, insults her as a hypocrite, and leaves in a rage. He is absolutely convinced that she is allowing herself to be used as a decoy by his enemies.

The King, emerging with Polonius, is convinced neither of Hamlet's madness nor of his love for Ophelia. Polonius suggests that Gertrude be asked to invite Hamlet's confidences while Polonius listens from a concealed place. The King agrees. *This day is the longest day of the play; it continues through the act and does not end until the fourth scene of Act Four.*

(ii) Later that day. *Hamlet* urges upon the players a natural, convincing performance of their piece, and *engages Horatio to watch the King's reactions carefully so that they may compare notes afterwards*. The court enters, Hamlet taking a place near Ophelia where he can study Claudius well. *The play is offered*, first as a brief pantomime, then in dialogue. *As it proceeds the Queen is not unduly affected by it; the King is mightily alarmed. But he is a strong man and does not break*, though Hamlet applies himself to make him do so. Noting Claudius' agitation, Polonius dismisses the actors, as the King staggers out, followed by the courtiers. *Hamlet is elated: the Ghost has plainly told the truth:*

> (O good Horatio, I'll take the ghost's word for a thousand pound.)

Horatio certifies Hamlet's observation of Claudius. Rosencrantz and Guildenstern come back to say that the Queen wishes a conference with her son. Hamlet treats them with contempt, and accuses Guildenstern of trying to play upon him as though he were an instrument. Polonius enters to repeat the Queen's summons. After teasing the old man, Hamlet agrees to see his mother at once. Left alone, Hamlet admits to being in a dangerously violent mood after his success:

> now could I drink hot blood,
> And do such bitter business as the day
> Would quake to look on.

(Only too true! In a few minutes he will indeed do such bitter business!)
In this interview with his mother, he must be calm:

> I will speak daggers to her, but use none.

(iii) In the King's chamber, immediately after the performance. Claudius informs Rosencrantz and Guildenstern that Hamlet must go, in their company, to England lest his lunacy become dangerous. *Polonius enters*, as they leave, *to assure Claudius that he will eavesdrop on Hamlet's talk with the Queen*. Alone, the King tries to pray, but cannot. *On his way to his mother's closet, Hamlet finds Claudius on his knees, is tempted to kill him on the spot*, but restrains his impulse with the consoling thought that when occasion will be ripe for the act he can choose a moment when Claudius' soul will be sure to go to Hell. Right now it is most important to speak to his mother.

(iv) In the Queen's closet, *Polonius* urges her to be severe with Hamlet, then *hides behind the tapestry*. Excitedly, *Hamlet* enters her room and at once *begins to pour out a torrent of accusation against her. She becomes frightened at his violence and calls for help. Polonius loses his wits and calls out too. Caught off guard by the commotion, Hamlet in a flash whips out his sword*, thrusts it through the hangings, *and kills the old man*. After the deed, he cries:

> Is it the King?

It was an act of sheer impulse. Had he reflected a moment, his intelligence would have assured him that it could not have been Claudius, whom he left praying in his own chamber only a few moments before.

Hamlet, when he sees whom he has killed, has no remorse, and turns back to castigate his mother with increased fury. At first she self-righteously denies any consciousness of having sinned:

> What have I done, that thou darest wag thy tongue
> In noise so rude against me?

But Hamlet compels her to confront the image of her licentiousness, until she sickens at the picture of what she is. His violence mounts. Suddenly the Ghost appears before him, interrupting his flood of accusation, and quiets him. Since Gertrude does not see the apparition, she concludes that Hamlet is talking to the empty air when he addresses the Ghost, that her son is truly insane, and that everything he has charged against her was, after all, but the raving of a madman. The spirit departs and Hamlet once more holds up the mirror for her to inspect her tainted soul. He does not realize, however, that he is now having no effect upon her—that she is now proof against self-examination, and luxuriating in the role of a mother sorrowing over her poor mad boy. *Hamlet understands that his killing of Polonius has called a halt to the pursuance of his revenge, and that Claudius now has an excuse for forcing him to go to England.* As he stands over Polonius' corpse he says ruefully:

> I will . . . answer well
> The death I gave him . . .

> This man shall set me packing.
>
> 176–77; 211

The play is now more than half over, and there is still no question of procrastination, still no occasion for pretended madness.

INDISCRETION SERVES: ACT FOUR

(i) The same night. The Queen at once reports Polonius' death to Claudius; she represents the deed as a product of Hamlet's lunacy. *The King determines to send Hamlet to England immediately,* and dispatches Rosencrantz and Guildenstern to find the corpse and convey his nephew to him.

(ii) Rosencrantz and Guildenstern come upon Hamlet, and take him to the King.

(iii) Hamlet is brought before the King, and after fencing with the King's demand for Polonius' body, reveals its whereabouts. *Claudius tells Hamlet that he must go to England at once for his own safety.* Prepared for this move, *Hamlet is by necessity compelled to agree.* With an insult, he takes his leave. Alone, the King reveals the fact that *the English sovereign has been commanded by letter to put Hamlet to death* upon his arrival in England.

(iv) Fortinbras is passing, by permission of Claudius, with his army through Denmark. Hamlet, on his way to the port, noting the example of this prince's courage, regrets with good cause his own behavior, now that he is being hurried off into exile. God

> gave us not
> That capability and god-like reason
> To fust in us unused.

When Hamlet forgot that divine faculty and acted on blind impulse in killing Polonius, he was guilty of

> Bestial oblivion—

behaving like an unreasoning beast.

Thus ends the longest day of the tragedy.

(v) Some days later. The death of her father and the exile of Hamlet have broken Ophelia's mind. She wishes to see the Queen, who prefers to be spared the sight of the girl's distress, but allows her to come in. Ophelia enters, and in her madness reveals the causes of her mental collapse. After she leaves, a messenger announces that Laertes, back from France, has collected a rabble which is storming the palace. Laertes enters and threatens Claudius because of Polonius' death. With admirable courage and ease the King quickly placates him, and convinces him of his own innocence. Ophelia returns. The sight of her madness overwhelms her brother with grief. In veiled language Claudius promises him satisfaction for the sufferings of his family:

> Be you content to lend your patience to us,
> And we shall jointly labour with your soul
> To give it due content. . . .
> And where the offence is let the great axe fall.

(vi) A sailor brings Horatio a letter from Hamlet, who has just landed in Denmark again. The message recounts how *on the second day of the voyage to England, the ship encountered a pirate. During the struggle, Hamlet boarded the pirate ship alone, won over the crew, and has been brought back to Denmark by them.* Hamlet asks Horatio to see that the King receive the letters he has addressed to Claudius, and desires his friend to hasten to meet him.

(vii) Claudius has found occasion to tell Laertes privately that it was Hamlet who killed Polonius; he assures him that before long he will hear satisfying news—i.e., from England, that Hamlet has been put to death. A messenger brings a letter from Hamlet to the King. Claudius is astonished to learn of Hamlet's return, which he attributes to his nephew's refusal to continue his voyage. The King wastes no time in speculation. *He plots with Laertes for Hamlet's death. Laertes is to challenge the Prince to a fencing match; instead of the sword with point and edge blunted, commonly used in such matches, Laertes will be equipped with one that is sharpened. Laertes not only proves amenable, but announces that he will anoint the sword with a deadly poison. To make sure of Hamlet's death, Claudius will also have prepared a poisoned drink for Hamlet* in case the plot for the match should fail. Gertrude comes in with the news that Ophelia has been drowned. Laertes breaks down at the report; he has a more powerful incentive for murdering Hamlet, for he holds him responsible for his sister's death too.

We are here at the end of Act Four. Still no procrastination, no feigned insanity. ———————

THE FELL SERGEANT DEATH: ACT FIVE

The next day is the last day of the play. ———————

(i) A sexton and his laborer-assistant are preparing Ophelia's grave. Hamlet and Horatio enter, and the Prince converses with the sexton, never guessing whose grave the latter is digging so light-heartedly. The funeral procession now winds its way through the churchyard, and Laertes angrily argues with the priest because Ophelia, on the suspicion of being a suicide, has not been accorded full rites of Christian burial. It is thus that Hamlet learns of her death. The Queen, scattering flowers in the grave, regrets that Ophelia did not live to marry Hamlet. Laertes, in a torrent of sorrow, leaps into the grave and asks to be buried alive with his sister. Hamlet, disgusted at this public display of grief, and himself shocked by the news that Ophelia is dead, jumps into the grave after him. Laertes starts grappling with him, and they are forcibly parted by the attendants. Hamlet upbraids Laertes for his ranting and protests that he has loved Ophelia more than any brother could. He dashes out, followed by Horatio. Claudius bids Laertes be patient by covertly reminding him that today is the day on which their revenge upon Hamlet will be accomplished.

(ii) Later the same day. Hamlet's unexpected return to Denmark is now more fully explained. *He tells Horatio of his discovering aboard ship Claudius' letter ordering his execution*, and how he substituted another letter demanding the slaying of Rosencrantz and Guildenstern. *Fate*, cooperating with Hamlet's intuitions, *has proved kind to him, and has given him another chance to further his plans for avenging his father. The document commanding Hamlet's death, now in his possession, is tangible proof that Claudius is a murderer.* Before the news of the death of his erstwhile friends can come from England, Hamlet concludes:

the interim is mine.

He expresses regret over his hasty anger with Laertes, for he now realizes the similarity of their cases: both have had their fathers slain.

Osric, a young fop, enters with the challenge to a rapier match with Laertes, which Hamlet accepts. Another lord enters to ask whether Hamlet prefers dueling now or some other day. Hamlet is ready for the match now, and sends back a message to the King full of double meanings:

> I am constant to my purposes; they follow the King's pleasure. If his fitness speaks, mine is ready, now or whensoever, provided I be so able as now.

Hamlet has the evidence to prove the King's attempt against his life. The match would be a splendid occasion for calling the court together, and he seizes the opportunity.
He is conscious of a vague foreboding of ill, and Horatio at once offers to have the match called off. But Hamlet refuses to give in to his premonitions.
The court now comes in. But when Osric offers the foils, *Hamlet does not trouble to inspect them or to notice that the one Laertes chooses is sharpened at the point.* The match begins, but Laertes, loath to carry out the dastardly scheme, fences halfheartedly. The King sends the poisoned cup to Hamlet, who bids the servant put it by till later. The Queen, excited by the match and ignorant of the contents of the goblet, drinks before the King can prevent her. *Laertes at last spurs himself and succeeds in wounding Hamlet.* The Prince now fights furiously. *During the scuffle they exchange rapiers and Hamlet soon runs Laertes through.* The Queen dies from the poisoned wine. *Laertes, dying too, tells Hamlet he has not much longer to live*—that the blade was envenomed—and reveals that Claudius is to blame. *Hamlet rushes at the King and stabs him with the envenomed rapier; then amidst the cries of "Treason!" of the assembled courtiers, he forces the poisoned drink down Claudius' throat.* As the venom is doing its fatal work on *Hamlet,* Horatio seizes the poisoned cup, but Hamlet dashes it from his hands, and *pledges his friend to live so that he may recount the facts to the world.* Hamlet names Fortinbras as his choice as successor to the throne, and dies. Fortinbras enters and orders a soldier's funeral for Hamlet.
The play is ended, and the question of procrastination still waits to be raised. Moreover, there has not yet been any occasion for Hamlet to feign insanity.

Keeping the plot in mind, let us for a moment scrutinize the time element in *Hamlet*. Act One consumes two successive days. Act Two, the third day of the action, begins sometime thereafter— some two months later, as we presently discover—time sufficient for Laertes to have been residing in Paris for a while. All of Act Three and the first four scenes of Act Four take place on the next day. The next scene begins the fifth day of the action, a week or so later, the interim accounting for the return of Laertes (on hearing of Polonius' death) and Hamlet (brought back by the pirate ship) to Denmark. Act Five is concerned with the next day, the last day of the action.

There are thus only two intervals of time in the play: two months between Act One and Act Two, and about a week between the fourth and fifth scenes of Act Four. These two lapses of time have no direct bearing upon the story and are left vague by Shakespeare for that reason. It is only by calculation that the reader will be aware of them at all. They are present only because it does take time to go from Denmark to Paris, does take time to return from there, and does take time to make even an interrupted voyage to England.

During the second of these intervals Hamlet is busy sailing first in the direction of England and then back to Denmark. Since the rest of the play shows no intermission of time, *it could only be between the close of the first act and the opening of the second that he might under any circumstances be charged with delay*. The remainder of the story takes place on three action-crowded days immediately (save for the shipboard interval) succeeding one another.

Now, in a play the central theme of which is delay or procrastination, it is obvious that the time element would have to be of cardinal importance. We should have to be aware constantly that the days are passing, that our hero is allowing time to slip through his grasp.* But in *Hamlet* the passage of time is deliberately kept in the

---

* Shakespeare knew well enough how to impress on his audience the sense of the hours' marching relentlessly by, when he wished to do so. In *The Tempest*, for example, we are never allowed to forget that the action takes place between two and six o'clock:

PROSPERO.   What is the time o' the day?
ARIEL.   Past the mid season.

background, far from our consciousness. For example, as regards
the only considerable interval, the time between Act One and Act
Two, we are nowhere informed during the entire length of the
second act just how much later than the second day of the action

---

PROS.   At least two glasses. The time 'twixt six and now
             Must by us both be spent most preciously.

                                             I, ii, 239 seq.

MIRANDA.   Alas, now, pray you,
             Work not so hard. . . .

FERDINAND.   O most dear mistress,
             The sun will set before I shall discharge
             What I must strive to do.

                                             III, i, 15 seq.

PROS.   For yet ere supper-time must I perform
             Much business appertaining.

                                             III, i, 95–96

CALIBAN.   Why, as I told thee, 'tis a custom with him,
             I' the afternoon to sleep. There thou mayst
                                   brain him . . .

                                             III, ii, 95–96

PROS.   At this hour
             Lies at my mercy all mine enemies.
             Shortly shall all my labours end.

                                             IV, i, 263 seq.

PROS.   Now does my project gather to a head.
             . . . . How's the day?

ARI.   On the sixth hour; at which time, my lord,
             You said our work should cease.

PROS.   I did say so,
             When first I raised the tempest.

                                             V, i, 1 seq.

PROS.   When I have required
             Some heavenly music, which even now I do,
             . . . . I'll break my staff.

                                             V, i, 51 seq.

PROS.   And in the morn
             I'll bring you to your ship and so to Naples.

                                             V, i, 306–07

this day is supposed to be. It is only on the next day, in the middle
of Act Three, that Ophelia gives the clue in a chance remark which
we hardly heed because of our concentration on the Mouse-trap
which is to be set before Claudius:

> HAM. For, look you, how cheerfully my mother
> looks, and my father died within's two hours.
>
> OPH. Nay, 'tis twice two months, my lord.
>
> III, ii, 134 seq.

At our leisure—for as Hamlet's little play is about to begin, who can
be bothered about such matters?—we make our reckoning, text in
hand: in Act One we were told that the late king has been dead two
months (I, ii, 138); if on this day in Act Three he has been dead
twice two months, fortified by a course in elementary arithmetic
we are able to multiply—twice two months makes four months; now
we cleverly subtract the two months of Act One from the four
months of Act Three, and we realize that two months have inter-
vened between Act One and Act Three. Model mathematicians, we
now note that Act Two took place on the day immediately before
Act Three, and therefore, this time subtracting one day from the
two months, we come to the brilliant discovery that Act Two began
some two months after Act One. The significant point, however,
must not escape us as we rejoice in our calculating powers: it is that
the lapse of two months between the first and second acts was of no
importance to Shakespeare, since he makes no mention of it until the
play is half over, and then in the most casual style imaginable. In
other words, the time element is of no consequence to the play—
which would certainly not be the case if procrastination were the
theme.

In terms of Elizabethan presentation, the matter may be stated
even more emphatically. The first publications of *Hamlet* were issued without any indication of the division of acts or scenes, for
the very good reason that the Elizabethan audience was unaware of
these divisions. There were no intermissions between acts, no curtains to terminate scenes; characters entered and made their exits,
scene followed scene, without a break. On Shakespeare's stage, therefore, the interval between the first and second acts would have had
practically no effect upon the consciousness of the audience, par-

ticularly when no mention was made during the course of Act Two of any specific passing of time.

As for these two months between Act One and Act Two, the only time Hamlet can by any stretch of the imagination be held to procrastinate—what shall be said of them? Well, no five-act play can be thought to have as its subject matter an idea which is never dealt with on the stage and is exhibited solely off stage *between* the conclusion of the first act and the opening of the second. That forms no part of the action; it is rather business that the dramatist wishes to throw out of consideration from his story. In short, the interim between the first two acts of *Hamlet* is there only because reasonableness requires it. The fact that Shakespeare was as vague as possible about it is plainly owing to his desire that we attach no significance to it.

Shakespeare's Hamlet, *then*, is not a play about a man who procrastinates * or a man who feigns madness. Neither appears in the

---

* One scene in *Hamlet* (III, iii, 73–96) more than any other has been fastened upon as a basis for the concept of procrastination—the brief scene in which the hero comes upon Claudius apparently in prayer—a moment of the drama that has bedeviled the perspective of many a commentator. Kittredge, who accepts the idea of feigned insanity (even though he admits that "the device . . . adopted on the spur of the moment . . . is unsuccessful" [1]), comes fairly close to the truth about Hamlet's procrastination; but alas! with this play a miss is as good as a mile. Realizing Hamlet's need of confirming "the testimony of the Ghost," he understands that up to the presentation of "The Murder of Gonzago" there is no delay on the hero's part. But directly after that, Kittredge thinks, when the Prince beholds the King on his knees, Hamlet is free to strike, knowing that the Ghost was honest. He observes that "the strenuous avenger Laertes would not have hesitated to plunge his sword into the King's back." [2] The reasons Hamlet advances for not doing this, avers this commentator, are not the true ones. "He does not really postpone his uncle's death in order that he may consign him to perdition. The speech is merely a pretext for delay." [3] According to Kittredge Hamlet here procrastinates because he "cannot butcher a defenceless man." He does not kill Claudius now, when he might be expected to, because "such an act is not in accord with Hamlet's nature and education." [4] (But Hamlet butchers a defenceless Polonius in a few moments, and Hamlet later sends defenceless Rosencrantz and Guilden-

work. It is not true, as Professor Stoll and others have argued, that
because delay is a convention of plot in the typical Elizabethan revenge play, we must therefore look for it inevitably in Shakespeare's
Hamlet. In this tragedy there is no procrastination, there is no delay.

---

stern to their deaths without a qualm in either case—and against none
of them does he harbor the grievance he holds against Claudius.)

Of course, if you are burdened with the misconception that the
theme of the tragedy is procrastination, you will naturally seize upon
this scene, for it is the only one during which the action shows Hamlet
failing to kill the King. For this reason Bradley considers it the "turning point of the tragedy." [5] But there are several cogent reasons (all of
them dramaturgical) why no great weight can be attached to anything
that occurs in this scene:

¶ To begin with, although four different dramatic situations are
developed in this scene—the interview with Rosencrantz and Guildenstern, with Polonius, the King's attempt to pray, and Hamlet's appearance—these happenings are so sketchily dealt with that the aggregation
amounts to only 98 lines—constituting one of the briefest scenes in the
play. Dramatic effectiveness requires any happening of importance to
receive a certain extensiveness of treatment. The audience must have
time to digest the event and be impressed by it if it has significance—as
witness Hamlet's interview with the Ghost, his scene after that with
Horatio and Marcellus, his listening to the passage from the *Dido* play,
his interview with Ophelia, the presentation of "The Murder of Gonzago." Though putting this little scene to several good uses, Shakespeare
fundamentally uses it as a "breather" in between the two most important scenes of the act: the most exciting scene of the play and the climax
of the plot, both of which are extended to lengths commensurate with
their importance.

¶ Hamlet does not appear in this scene until line 93, and then to
make but one speech of 23 lines.

¶ This speech is, moreover, a soliloquy. And in a good play, however engrossing a soliloquy may be, it can never determine the course
of the plot since nothing can *happen* during it.

As Hamlet enters on this scene, we are to understand that it is but
a matter of a few minutes since we heard his last soliloquy—no longer
than it has taken him to walk from one room in the palace to this corridor (represented on the Elizabethan stage by the inner stage at the rear)
adjoining the King's and Queen's private chambers. Hamlet pauses. The
King, his back to him, is at his prayers.

If the tragedy is not about the hero's fatal procrastination or delay, what then is it about? Having discarded all preconceptions, and having examined the plot and seen that it reveals neither delay nor feigned insanity, we are almost ready to decide what kind of

> Now might I do it pat, now he is praying.
> And now I'll do it.

There is but one action that can accompany those words: Hamlet whisks out his sword. We are not unprepared for this. A few minutes ago, he confessed himself ready to drink hot blood, to be in a dangerous mood. We shall not be unprepared either, a few minutes from now, when his sword is out again, thrusting a death-blow at the form concealed behind his mother's tapestries.

Why does he not kill the King now? (Masefield: Because of his characteristic and "baffling slowness." [6] Spencer: Because Shakespeare is not ready to end his play.[7] Tillyard: Because Hamlet doesn't really wish to kill Claudius. A true son of a murdered father would cut the murderer's throat even in a church.[8] Bradley: Hamlet "has no effective desire" to kill Claudius.[9] Kittredge: The entire soliloquy "is merely a pretext for delay." [10] Wilson: He rationalizes his sparing of Claudius to make delay "more palatable to him at the moment." [11]

The truth is that Hamlet now knows at last that the King is his father's murderer; every fiber in his body is straining to put an end to Claudius' hated existence, and Hamlet's hand is only too ready to do the deed. But he was never better launched than now upon his course of vengeance. His intelligence assures him that this is not yet the moment to kill Claudius. Though on the road to achieving proof of the King's guilt to show the world, Hamlet has not the proof yet. The rest of his speech, therefore, is his attempt to force himself to sheathe his sword again, unwilling as his hand is to obey his intellect. His words are not at all a pretext, an excuse for delay—but rather addressed to his inner violence. Be patient, be patient, he is telling his blood: the time will come when it will be right to strike, and when the time comes I shall choose the moment—not one like this, when the villain is making his peace with heaven, but

> When he is drunk asleep, or in his rage,
> Or in the incestuous pleasure of his bed,
> At gaming, swearing, or about some act
> That has no relish of salvation in 't—
> Then trip him, that his heels may kick at heaven,

man Hamlet is and to identify, as we must, his tragic flaw. But not quite yet. First, to be safe, let us stay with the plot a little longer.

THE CLIMAX OF *HAMLET*

To comprehend a play perfectly it is always necessary to know where precisely the climax is to be found. For the climax is the pivotal point of the plot, and, if the drama be the work of a capable playwright, one's analysis of the basic plot and the characterization must show up as true or false once the climax is correctly identified.

The climax of a well-constructed plot is the moment of action which determines the course of subsequent events towards a more or less inevitable conclusion. The climax settles the direction which the rest of the plot must take according to the laws of probability.

The climax may also be defined in terms of the characters of the story. At the beginning of any plot the persons of the drama stand in a certain relationship to one another. In a play worthy of the name, since there is action, movement, these relationships become

---

And that his soul may be as damned and black
As hell, whereto it goes.

These lines, by the way, have given great offence to the critics. (Hanmer: "This speech of Hamlet . . . [has] something so very bloody in it, so inhuman, so unworthy of a hero, that I wish our poet had omitted it." [12] Samuel Johnson: "This speech . . . is too horrible to be read or to be uttered." [13] Hunter: "In the whole range of the drama there is, perhaps, nothing more offensive than this scene. Hamlet is made to dote on an idea which is positively shocking." [14] Adams: "One of the most revolting sentiments in all Shakespeare." [15]) Anyone who knows Elizabethan literature ought to be aware that none of Shakespeare's contemporaries would have been greatly shocked by Hamlet's words. They merely prove that Hamlet is no milksop, that the blood in his veins is red, and that when he hates he hates thoroughly. At any rate, we need not be over-nice or subtle about this outburst. Hamlet means exactly what he says.

His mother waits and he must hasten to her. Hamlet's swift unsheathing of his sword warns us that it will not take much for his reason to lose control over his surging violence, after the success of his little play, and become engulfed by recklessness—as it does in a matter of moments.

altered during the progress of the plot.* The climax of the drama is
the happening which causes the greatest dislocation in the balance
established among the chief persons of the drama at the opening of
the plot.

Thus, the climax of *Romeo and Juliet* is the killing of Tybalt by
Romeo. Up to that moment there has been always the possibility of
happiness for the lovers, despite their difficulties. Romeo, we feel,
has had but to inform old Capulet that he is now his son-in-law, and
after some to-do over the clandestine nature of the marriage, Juliet's
father would have welcomed him into the family, having already
said of him:

> Verona brags of him
> To be a virtuous and well-governed youth.
> I would not for the wealth of all this town
> Here in my house do him disparagement.
>   I, v, 69 seq.

But once Romeo slays Tybalt, all hope for his marital felicity is
gone. The Prince has already decreed death to anyone fighting in
the streets; as Tybalt's slayer Romeo is doubly doomed.

A great deal of careless talk concerning the meaning of climax
has resulted generally in very slovenly thinking about an aspect of
dramaturgy of primary concern to the playwright. In grammar
school we were taught as a boy that the climax is the "high point"
of the story, the most intensely exciting moment of the plot; we had
drawn for us on the blackboard a long climbing line to represent the

---

* It is the lack of this alteration in the relationship of the characters
which would disqualify Plato's *Dialogues* as drama, which of course they
make no pretensions to being. But the *Dialogues* contain many important ingredients of superior drama which only too many plays lack:
they have characterization, brilliant dialogue, noble ideas, wit, gravity,
charm, and excitement. The characters, however, stand in the same relationship to one another at the end as at the beginning—except, of course,
on the ideational level. We might put the matter another way: the
Dialogues of Plato have no plot. And, to move from the sublime to the
sentimental, it is on the same grounds that most of the so-called plays
of Mr. Saroyan must be pronounced not plays at all; the persons of his
"drama" tend to experience no alteration in their relationships as established when first they are introduced.

rising action, and then at the climax a sharp angle from which the line swooped downward to show the falling action. In our adolescent mind, regularly nurtured at the nickelodeon, the climax came to be perfectly illustrated by the tense moment when the hero and the villain were struggling at the edge of the cliff; the villain fell off, and there began the descending action. In works of that sensational quality the moment of greatest excitement might indeed coincide with the climax, but it is not true that it necessarily does so or even usually does so in great tragedies. Such a coincidence of climax with point of highest excitement would tend to make the crucial deed far too theatrical for the purposes of the tragic experience. For instance, though exciting enough, the killing of Tybalt by Romeo is less tense a moment of drama than the killing of Mercutio, which immediately precedes it—and is the less tense because it follows so closely on the fatal wounding of Mercutio. But the death of Romeo's friend, although more exciting than the death of Tybalt, despite the fact that it *leads* directly to the climax, is not in itself the climax of the play. When Tybalt re-enters to fight with Romeo, difficult though it would be, the latter, if he were sufficiently heedful of his future happiness, could still say, "Tybalt, I cannot fight with you; I am married to Juliet, and you and I are now bound by ties which should promote our friendship, not our enmity." He might also remind Tybalt, as he did Mercutio and Tybalt a few minutes earlier, that

> the Prince expressly hath
> Forbid this bandying in Verona's streets
>   III, i, 91–92.

Instead he throws discretion to the winds, forgets Juliet and the life he might have with her, and is only conscious of the guilt he feels for Mercutio's death. We love him none the less for his youthful rashness, but once his sword runs Tybalt through, Romeo is headed straight and inevitably for catastrophe. Such is the typical act of the tragic hero at the climax of the drama.

Unfortunately, the hero-struggling-with-the-villain-at-the-edge-of-the-cliff attitude colors much of the discussion concerning the climax of *Hamlet*. The Mouse-trap presented before Claudius, Gertrude, and the Court is very probably, as Mr. Wilson enthusiastically describes it, "the most exciting episode in Shakespeare's greatest drama." [16] Certainly at no other part of the play are there so many

absorbing things to watch: Claudius' reaction to the little drama, and
Gertrude's too; Hamlet's eager anticipation of what may happen and
his close observation of the King and Queen; Horatio's careful attention; the reactions of the court to whatever is to be the conduct
of the King, the Queen, and Hamlet; Polonius' preoccupation with
Hamlet's apparent attentions to Ophelia; Ophelia's renewed hopes
in her lover's affection; and the Mouse-trap itself—a whole, complex
world of dramatic interest, presented all at once and yet in such a
way that we can enjoy every bit of it! There is, in all likelihood, no
scene in any other play in which the audience's pulses beat with such
wild excitement. None the less, there is no justification for Mr. Wilson's pronouncement that "The play scene is the central point of
Hamlet. It is the climax and crisis of the whole drama." [17] That
scene certainly advances the action with an enormous bound forward, and it *does lead* directly to the climax. But it is not in itself
the climax of the play. At its conclusion it is true that the fearful
possibility which reason has prevented Claudius from entertaining
is now a dangerous certainty: the King now definitely knows that
Hamlet is aware of his father's murder and the identity of the murderer; it is also true that Hamlet's uncertainty concerning the reliability of the Ghost has been settled. But despite this tightening of
the dramatic tension, Hamlet and Claudius—who are the central
figures in the tragic conflict (who else could they be?)—remain, for
all their greater enlightenment, in the same relationship they held at
the end of Act One. Ever since the Ghost's revelations, Hamlet has
been the pursuer and Claudius the pursued; the end of the play scene
finds them, though both fortified by more knowledge, in the same
roles. Hamlet is, to be sure, more the pursuer and Claudius more the
pursued now, but the Prince's task, though progressing, remains to
be accomplished. Moreover, there is the important puzzle still to
resolve for his peace of mind: what role has his mother played in
his father's death?

Mr. Wilson's view of the climax, if incorrect, is not absurd, for
the play scene (like Mercutio's death) is the most powerful event
leading to the climax. Other scholars, however, are egregiously in
error when they agree with Professor Bradley in seizing upon the
one little scene in which Hamlet might be shown as procrastinating,
the moment when he refrains from killing the kneeling Claudius, as

"the turning-point of the tragedy." [18] This "sixth soliloquy" has been described as for long being most widely accepted "as the crux of the play." The temptation to bolster the theory of delay by the one occasion where it might be said Hamlet does nothing is understandable. But, leaving aside the esthetic criterion of the folly of looking for the climax in a scene that in its entirety is given twenty-three lines, there remains the greater absurdity of expecting to find the climax in a soliloquy (Hamlet's only speech in this scene) in which nothing occurs but the pouring out of words. The soul of drama is action, and the climax (of all parts of the play) must be an action. Finally, Hamlet and Claudius are in precisely the same relationship to each other at the end of Hamlet's twenty-three lines as before he entered upon that scene. Nothing has changed; he has merely *not* killed the King yet. More importantly, his not killing the King *then* in no way affects the course of events—if we may be allowed to phrase so silly an idea.

But greater depths of ineptitude have been reserved for some recent scholarship. Mr. Johnson reports that there is a "speech that seems, by general consent, to have replaced Hamlet's sixth soliloquy (III, iii, 73–96) as the crux of the play; it is Hamlet's response to Horatio's suggestion that he avoid the fencing match with Laertes:

> Not a whit, we defy augury; there's a special providence in the fall of a sparrow. If it be now, 'tis not to come; if it be not to come, it will be now; if it be not now, yet it will come: the readiness is all." [19]

V, ii, 230 seq.

This general consent has largely been given by that school of critics which takes the quasi-religious view of Hamlet as an instrument of Providence in the assassination of Claudius, the task being to cleanse Denmark. Mr. Johnson, therefore, is of accord. "Hamlet felt, before he left Denmark, that all occasions informed against him;" [20] he comes back with a markedly changed attitude—"all occasions are informing for him now." [21] He is ready promptly to comply "with the pleasure and purpose of Providence." [22] Hence, the "defy augury" speech is the "crucial speech" of the play; [23] "in Act I he was a student prince; in Act V he is the ordained minister of Providence. In the intervening acts . . . as in the morality plays, the conflict between man's divine nature, embodied in the rational soul, and his bestial nature, embodied in the animal soul, brings him to the verge of despair, from which he is saved by the intervention of Providence." [24]

We confess a difficulty in summoning the patience requisite to the high seriousness of our inquiry when we are faced with such hyperbolic folderol as this. Everything about it is wrong. It transforms *Hamlet* from a great tragedy to a morality play of the Middle Ages; the pulse-stirring complexities and subtleties of a masterwork to the naive, if mildly effective, simplicity of *Everyman*, with which indeed this critic finds it has strong affinities; the creator from the most brilliant and successful dramatist writing for a virile, full-blooded age to a medieval monk tinkering on the stage with theological abstractions; the hero from the tragic framer of his own doom to a mere colorless "instrument." It also performs two unpardonable esthetic crimes: that of looking for the climax of one of the longest tragedies extant in the last scene (—in this instance the hero at the climax would seem to ascend yet higher from the edge of the cliff, down which the enemy-animal soul has just tumbled!); worse still, that of discoursing upon tragedy not as an imitation of life which must show men in action, but as though it were the function of drama statically only to exhibit changes of attitude on the part of the hero.* It is, moreover, sublimely indifferent to the very nature of

---

* Suggestion for the plot of a modern play built on these principles: Our hero, Cyril, living in the historic town of Banbury, is the victim of a mild case of kleptomania, despite a fundamentally moral nature. He is constantly torn between a desire for the ethical life and an irresistible compulsion to filch books from the shop of his uncle, the local bookseller, and Banbury tarts from the trays of his cousin, the baker. The case is further complicated by the fact that the baker and the bookseller, two avaricious bachelors, are very wicked men with a side line in the black market. Cyril is properly patriotic, and loathes the fact that these relatives of his should be responsible for the something that is rotten in Banbury. For the better part of four acts, Cyril is tortured by his hate of them, his shame of his own pilferings, and his worry over his steadily increasing avoirdupois, which (because of his raids on the tarts) begins to make locomotion difficult; we behold him warring between man's divine nature, embodied in Cyril's rational soul, and his bestial nature,

drama to look for the crux of a play in a speech, no matter how revealing, unallied to significant action.

With all these points of view there is a further shortcoming. In a great tragedy, since the hero falls through a defect of character, the tragic flaw must of necessity be in evidence at the climax; the deed which becomes the turning point of the plot must be an expression of his tragic failing. Thus, when Romeo at the climax kills Tybalt, his tragic flaw of rashness is clear. He even cries, as he draws his sword to fight him:

> Away to Heaven, respective lenity,
> And fire-eyed fury be my conduct now!
>
> III, i, 128–29

Instead of reasonably telling Tybalt of their new ties of kinship, he says in effect: "I here renounce the mildness which reflection would dictate, and surrender myself to fury to lead me now!"

---

embodied in Cyril's animal soul, until he is on the verge of despair, from which he is saved in the nick of time by Providence. In the middle of Act Four, a stroke of lightning burns the bakery to the ground with the baker in it. Occasions which have been informing against Cyril now inform for him. The source of tarts and the temptation therefor, as well as the black-marketeer, are all eliminated at once. In the Fifth Act, Cyril steps to the footlights and delivers a long "realizing" speech (Mr. Odets alone, perhaps, could do this full justice): he recognizes in the consuming shaft of lightning that divinity which is literally shaping his ends by saving him from a fatal *adiposis;* he realizes that with the evil cousin incinerated there remains only the wicked bookseller-uncle keeping the time out of joint in Banbury; he understands, now that occasion informs *for* him, that he must cleanse the town as the instrument of benign Providence; and he resolves (this is our climax) that whenever Providence sees fit to present the opportunity, his will be "a willing compliance with the workings of heaven." [25] His chance occurs later that same day. His uncle asks him to accompany him on the bus down to London; at the bankside Cyril pushes him into the Thames. Our hero returns to Banbury, having fulfilled his mission as the instrument of Providence, appropriates the bookstore, as the nearest heir, and suffers no more from kleptomania. A library now at his disposal, and the tarts a thing of the past, he gives his days and nights to the reading of Thomas Aquinas and Shakespearean commentary.

If the play scene is indeed the climax of *Hamlet*, what tragic flaw of the hero is there exhibited? *

The thoughtful reader may by this time have identified the climax of *Hamlet* for himself. A reading of our plot summary will plainly reveal it. There is obviously but one moment in the tragedy, but one deed of Hamlet's, which conditions unalterably the course of the remaining action—and that is his killing of Polonius (III, iv). At the instant he raises his sword to plunge it through the arras, he has been managing his cause very well. The Mouse-trap has indeed captured the horrible truth about Claudius, and Hamlet can banish forever his doubts concerning the Ghost. He is free to make further plans, knowing at last that he is on the right track. He has, moreover, caused Claudius to behave publicly in a way sufficiently suspicious to back whatever disclosures the Prince hereafter can make to Denmark. If he would reflect but for a fleeting second before his blade makes its rent in the cloth, he must know that whoever may have just cried out behind the arras, it cannot be the King, for him he has just left praying in the adjoining chamber. But he too, like Romeo, at the crucial moment throws respective lenity to heaven, and is willing to allow fire-eyed fury to be his guide now. Rashly he stabs the old man, not knowing who his victim is, and he pays heavily for his folly.

This deed reverses roles for Hamlet and Claudius. It is now the Prince who becomes the pursued and the King who can become the pursuer. Claudius, certain now of Hamlet's being a threat to his safety, is able (as Hamlet soon realizes, though too late) to hustle

---

* Apart from the fact that no tragic flaw of Hamlet's is illustrated by his giving of the Mouse-trap, Mr. Wilson might be at a loss to answer the question on other scores. To him "*Hamlet* is a tragedy, the tragedy of a genius caught fast in the toils of circumstance and unable to fling free." [26] In other words, Hamlet owns no tragic flaw, is not the author of his own doom, is only a victim of chance; and the play itself is rather a study in pathos than a tragedy, and its hero a first cousin to Little Nell. Elsewhere, however, Mr. Wilson says that it is a tragedy of "a great and noble spirit subjected to a moral shock so overwhelming that it shatters all zest for life and all belief in it." [27] If being overwhelmed by moral shock be some species of tragic flaw, how does the play scene evidence it?

the Prince off to England and remove him from the place where alone he can pursue his task of vengeance. Precisely when his position is most favorable, precisely when he has established the basis for a just revenge, Hamlet loses everything through one foolish act of recklessness.

If our principles hold fast—and they do—Hamlet has exhibited in this "rash and bloody deed" the tragic flaw which will bring him to catastrophe. His tragic failing is apparently some kind of recklessness? Incredible? No, merely true. Hamlet falls not because he is too timid, too sensitive, too thoughtful, or too scrupulous, but because he is too rash, too overweening, too heedless.

SOME QUESTIONS RAISED CONCERNING THE TRANSACTIONS OF THE PLAY

Before we come to discussing more fully Hamlet's character and the characters of the other people in the tragedy, it would be well to settle some other matters concerning what happens in the play itself. These matters have been subject to much misinterpretation too, sometimes because of unawareness of or insufficient attention to objective fact, sometimes because of a disoriented comprehension of the characters involved. Let us take these problems as they arise, act by act.

ACT ONE

*Why did not Hamlet succeed to the throne
upon his father's death?*

It has often been thought that Claudius' purpose in marrying Gertrude was "to steal the throne from Hamlet." [28] * At the least it

---

* Wilson goes much further: Claudius' "usurpation is one of the main factors of the plot"; [29]—though this scholar concedes that Hamlet's only two direct references to what he calls the Prince's "blighted hopes of the succession . . . occur very late in the play." [30] To bolster this view he is forced to distort Hamlet's first line, *A little more than kin, and less than kind,* into a reference to Hamlet's "disappointed hopes of the succession." [31] Actually the line simply means that because of the

is felt that "there is something amiss here: brothers do not succeed brothers, unless there is a failure in the direct line of succession." [32]

But there is nothing necessarily "amiss" in the succession. It is not true that "brothers do not succeed brothers, unless there is a failure in the direct line of succession"—at least it is not true in this play. It was the elder Fortinbras, King of Norway, whom Hamlet's father killed in combat; yet it is not his son, young Fortinbras, who now sits on the throne, but the latter's uncle, even though young Fortinbras is very much alive (I, i, 80–107; I, ii, 27–33).

It is interesting to remember (what everyone seems to have overlooked) that in the old Hamlet story Belleforest has *Hamlet's father rewarded for his services to the crown by being married to the King's daughter* (Shakespeare's Gertrude). This would patently mean that it was Gertrude, not Hamlet's father, who was heir to the throne—that while she lived the crown was safely hers, and that the Prince, in any case, could not rule while his mother was alive.

Nevertheless, it is true that we feel in Shakespeare's play, as indeed in the Belleforest story, that Hamlet's uncle is more than consort to the Queen, that he is very much the king, and that the rule is as much his as hers. It appears that Shakespeare thought of this throne as shared jointly by King and Queen—that the death of Hamlet's father left Gertrude still monarch, and that Claudius' marriage to her rendered him half-sharer of the crown. Is not this the true meaning of Claudius' words in his opening speech when he refers to his wife as

> The imperial jointress of this warlike state
> I, ii, 9?

The *Oxford English Dictionary* cites this line as the earliest use of *jointress* to mean "a widow who holds a jointure," [33] and the word is so glossed by Kittredge [34] and Wilson.[35] But since the *Oxford Dictionary* finds no previous example for such a meaning, its au-

---

marriage the King is more than Hamlet's uncle now, he is his stepfather too ("more than kin"); but though they are now more closely related they are not of the same kind, for the haste and the incestuous nature of the marriage prove Claudius to be less than human (a pun on "kind," which also meant "human").

thority in thus defining this usage is open to challenge. It would be both flat and undignified of Claudius to speak of his Queen as a widow who has been left an estate by the death of her late husband.

Shakespeare made "up his language as he went along—crashing . . . through the forest of words like a thunderbolt"; [36] habitually he transformed adjectives into nouns, nouns into verbs, verbs into nouns, and in general played havoc with grammatical tradition. The *Oxford Dictionary* quotes several examples earlier in date than *Hamlet* of the use of *joint* to mean "united or sharing with one another" —as early, indeed, as 1424.[37] In our play the night has already been described as "joint-labourer with the day" in the preparation for war (I, i, 78). Shakespeare apparently made a noun, *jointress*, out of this meaning of *joint*. If our guess is right, Claudius is saying of his Queen that she shares the throne of Denmark equally with him.

Further, there is evidence that, to a certain degree, consent of the nobility is required in Shakespeare's Denmark before the claimant can be officially recognized. In the last act, Hamlet speaks of his uncle as having

> Popped in between the election and my hopes;
> V, ii, 65

again, as he is dying, he says:

> I do prophesy the election lights
> On Fortinbras.
> V, ii, 366–67

Claudius plainly rules with the consent of those he governs, and has legally been accorded the "election" of the nobles. From this point of view, Claudius cannot be said to have deprived Hamlet of the throne by either force or chicanery. One feels that Hamlet will be next to rule, and that Denmark expects him to wait graciously and patiently, just as, doubtless, Norway expects young Fortinbras to wait until his uncle's death for the succession.

Claudius may be an interloper, but he is not a usurper. To insist with Professor Wilson that the question of the succession is a major issue with Hamlet and therefore fundamental to the plot, is to tamper with the very premises of the story. It is also hard to see how anyone can read the play with an open mind and conclude that

Hamlet is bitter because *he* has not been made king, however bitter he is to see the man he loathes on the throne; his mind dwells on wider perspectives than personal ambition. He is agitated by far nobler and far more tragic concerns than an impatience to rule Denmark.

In Mr. Olivier's movie the entire issue was avoided by omitting the "imperial jointress" lines and keeping Claudius intoxicated throughout the scene. Other interesting novelties: the courtiers applauded Claudius at the end of his first speech as though *they* were at a play; Claudius quite publicly showed his hatred for Hamlet, despite his sugared lines; presently he jealously tugged Gertrude away from Hamlet, whom she was busy mothering.

What function in the tragedy do Hamlet's soliloquies serve?

Of all of Shakespeare's heroes Hamlet is certainly the one most given to soliloquizing. It is so that we remember him. But since Shakespeare was a dramatist to his fingertips, this play is so powerfully constructed that, although we should be sorry to lose any of Hamlet's self-communings, the tragic impact of the plot in no way depends upon any of the soliloquies. By very nature of the soliloquy, nothing can happen during the delivery of one, and so the plot cannot be advanced by any one of them. Hamlet does not even come to one new decision during the course of any; if he did the play would be that much weakened, for a decision, being a dramatic fact, should evolve from a situation, not from oratory. Shakespeare's predecessors had used the soliloquy either to inform the audience of certain facts and situations, or for only the crudest kind of self-revelation by a character (akin to the silly confidences made in mid-Victorian melodramas by the villains to the audience, while they twirled their mustaches). But Shakespeare found a new use for the soliloquy. As we listen to one of his characters thinking aloud, he invites us to inspect the working of the man's soul. Often, as later in Browning's dramatic monologues, while we hear the character attempting to rationalize or justify his conduct, we understand him better than he is able to understand himself. It is thus that we see through the self-delusions of Shylock, Benedick, Iago, and Angelo while they are posturing to themselves—just as we do in the cases of that evil pair, the Duke of Ferrara and that lost soul who soliloquizes in the shadows of a Spanish cloister.

Hamlet, largely alone in a setting which is poisonous to him, must pour out his powerful feelings often to the empty air lest he suffocate from the attempt to stifle them. We must be careful, however, to take him no more literally than we do Shylock or Benedick. The soliloquies in our play have by the dramatist been carefully and subtly allied to the action of the play. The sane approach, therefore, to each of them is always first to ask, "What has occurred to cause this outburst?" There is always something that has happened to occasion it. Hamlet in his agony writhes and shoots off sparks of anguish in all directions as he unburdens his feelings; but he always winds back to the dramatic fact which has impelled him into coruscations of dissatisfaction with the world and himself. That dramatic fact, that happening, is always at the core of the soliloquy. And it is only in the light of that happening that we can rightly understand his words, his disgust, his self-tormentings, his often unjustified self-accusations. As he stands before us alone and murmurs,

> O that this too too solid flesh would melt . . .
> I, ii, 129

what recent events have caused the sudden outburst of anguish he now indulges? They are: the death of his father and the hasty remarriage of his mother.

Concerning that marriage everything is like venom to him, and we require no Oedipus complexes to understand his revulsion. Nothing is more common than that a young man or woman who has cherished the illusion that his parents were ideally happy should feel disgust at the spectacle of a mother or father's second marriage—a disgust strong enough if the marriage takes place two years after the death of a beloved parent; how much more powerful when the interval is only two months:

> A beast, that wants discourse of reason,
> Would have mourned longer!

Worse yet, the marriage of Gertrude and Claudius was incestuous.

Why is the Queen's second marriage incestuous?

Such marriages have been held incestuous from early times, and the fight to lift the ban on them has not yet been completely won in England, where until 1907 the marriage of a man with his deceased wife's sister was forbidden. The bill to permit such a marriage was first adopted in Commons in 1850, but the Lords rejected it the next year. It was brought before the legislature in '56, '58, '59, '61, '62, '66, '69, '70, '71, '72, '73, '75, '77, '78, '79, '80, '82, '83, '84, '86, '88, '89, '90, '91, '96, '98, and 1900.[38] No wonder the fairies in *Iolanthe* thought it necessary to send Strephon into Parliament so that he might "prick that annual blister, marriage with deceased wife's sister!" At long last, in 1907, the bereaved male was free to pay his addresses to his sister-in-law. But even today the woman who did what Gertrude has done would be legally guilty of incest.

ACT TWO

What was the meaning of Hamlet's appearance and behavior in Ophelia's room?

Ophelia does not at all understand the experience which has terrified her; nevertheless the account she gives of it (II, i, 77–100) makes what happened clear enough. Clear enough, that is, if in listening to it we have not abandoned our common humanity.

As she was sewing in her room, Hamlet suddenly appeared before her, hatless (hats were then normally worn indoors), his jacket open, his stockings soiled and fallen, his knees trembling and his face dead-white, and looking as if he had just gone through hell. He took her firmly by the wrist, stood back at arm's length and, with his other hand on his brow, began to study her face. At length, "a little shaking" her arm, he nodded thrice, with a sigh so deep that it seemed a sob. Then he released her, and, his glance still fixed upon her, found his way out of the room.

Every aspect of this unexpected visit is mysterious and frightening to the girl; her confusion has encouraged the scholars'. A. C. Bradley: "When Hamlet made his way into Ophelia's room, why did he go in the garb, the conventionally recognized garb, of the distracted *lover?* . . . His main object in the visit appears to have been to convince *others*, through her, that his insanity was not due to any mysterious cause, but to this disappointment (in love), and so allay the suspicions of the King." [39] (It is true, of course, that the Elizabethan lover was occasionally represented as careless in his dress.) J. Q. Adams: "This slovenliness in costume has usually been interpreted as the pose of the forlorn lover. . . . But Hamlet's physical appearance cannot be explained on this score. He has 'no hat upon his head'; the sad lover is invariably represented with his hat plucked low over his eyes. . . . Hamlet's slovenly and foul dress is what one should expect from a 'natural' or idiot; and as such it is in perfect keeping with his announced plan of putting on an 'antic' disposition." [40] J. D. Wilson: Hamlet's "mental instability," obvious enough in the preceding scene (with Horatio and Marcellus), here is shown to have "grown intense meanwhile." [41] G. W. Knight: This was "no mock-madness . . . Polonius sees the truth"; this was madness itself.[42] But if we think of Hamlet as a human being instead of as an automaton operating exclusively according to Elizabethan conventions, we shall find his motives and conduct comprehensible enough. The claims of scholarship are rightful, but so are the claims of human experience. When we examine a work of literature we must keep a just proportion between them; when a choice becomes necessary, we must allot precedence to human values. Let us consider the details of Ophelia's report:

¶ Why did Hamlet force his way into her room? Not to play the madman. Why should he wish to frighten his sweetheart with such capers if his objective were the King's opinion? He might more easily have appeared before his uncle as a lunatic, yet he never chooses to do so. Nor is it a symptom of real insanity that he appears before the girl he loves. The simple fact is, as we hear from Ophelia's own lips, that, as her father required, she has cut off all communication with the Prince:

> as you did command,
> I did repel his letters and denied
> His access to me.
>
> II, i, 108–110

Is it odd that he should have decided that he *will* see her, despite her avoidance of him—even if he must break into her chamber?

¶ Why was his dress disordered? Not because that disorder is—or is not—conventional for the sad lover or the melancholy man, as scholars have merrily argued pro and con. Why should he appear so before her only, that once, and never before *our* eyes? And not because that disorder would prove him mad. Why should he appear so before her and never before the King? Can we not understand by simply putting ourselves, as we are expected to do in a tragedy, in the hero's place? For some time her rejection of him has been torturing him; his mother's faithlessness has already caused him to stigmatize all women with frailty (I, ii, 147). Can we not conceive him, torn between his complicated worries over the Ghost's revelations and his bitterness at Ophelia's unexplained renunciation of him at a time when he most needs her love, flinging himself upon his couch without bothering to disrobe (though naturally without his hat on his head!), tossing about in anguished uncertainty—and then suddenly, with characteristic impulsiveness, jumping up, resolved to find out at once by confronting Ophelia without warning, whether or not she is such another as Gertrude? Can we not see him, full of this purpose, dashing to her room just as he was, his jacket half-opened, his stockings rumpled, his face white, his knees trembling, looking like a vision out of hell?

¶ How are we to interpret his actions in her room? He did not speak: he had come to see. Like most intuitive people, he was prepared to judge her by the way she looked when required to confront his gaze. It is an old prejudice of the race that innocent people always return our scrutiny with frank steady eyes, and that the guilty always shiftily look away.* And Hamlet had come to indulge this maggot. He held her firmly at arm's length to have a good look at her. He raised his other hand to his brow to clear away all other thoughts, a gesture common to men trying to concentrate on a problem before them. And how would Ophelia have reacted to Hamlet's study of her? Insecure herself, half convinced of the rumors floating about that Hamlet is unbalanced, easily frightened, she nat-

---

* A highly unreliable criterion. People often will look away out of shame for the brazenness of the inspector, or only because they have weak eyes. The hardened criminal is well-trained to outstare the innocent.

urally turned away in confusion and blushed—thereby seeming only too plainly to her lover to be guilty of falseness to him. He was only too much convinced of what he had feared, as his solemn nodding thrice betokens—a movement indicating the confirmation of his worst suspicions.* As he left the room, his eyes still fastened on her while he moved to the threshold, he carried with him the conviction that she had indeed abandoned him.

> *Hamlet at first greets Rosencrantz*
> *and Guildenstern with warmth;*
> *what causes the change in his attitude towards them?*

When his old schoolfellows first appear, Hamlet is delighted to see them, and exchanges some jovial ribaldry with them—the kind of harmless bawdry young fellows indulge when they meet, the overflow of excessive good health and animal spirits. The passage concludes:

> HAM.   . . . What's the news?
> ROS.   None, my lord, but that the world's grown honest.
> II, ii, 240-41

This pleasantry tinges Hamlet's merriment with bitterness again; he has good reason to know that Rosencrantz's "news is not true." And this sour note intrudes upon his warm and essentially gaily-intended:

> What have you, my good friends, deserved at the hands
> of Fortune, that she sends you to prison hither?

---

* Kittredge, however sees in the movement a weightier significance: "It is at this moment that Hamlet decides he must renounce Ophelia and give up all thought of marriage and happiness. To involve an innocent girl in such a revenge as he contemplates would have been a crime." [43] This sounds high-minded enough, but there is no evidence of such a renunciation on Hamlet's part, nor is it normal that any man facing the gravest of problems should therefore think of renouncing a woman's love at such a time. As for Kittredge's reason, why need Hamlet have involved Ophelia in his pursuit of revenge? Claudius managed to kill his brother without involving Gertrude. And Hamlet would more involve Ophelia in his revenge by rejecting her love if she loves him, than by accepting it.

(The subtle and deeply stirring dramatic values of the ensuing dialogue have yet to be projected on the contemporary stage. Directorial and scholarly blindness towards this powerful scene is owing to the reasonless preconception of Rosencrantz and Guildenstern as a pair of revolting traitors to their friend.)

Guildenstern and Rosencrantz have been warned by the King that Hamlet is "transformed" (II, i, 4–10). Here is already sad evidence. Has not Claudius shown his loving concern for Hamlet by summoning them to his side? They exchange glances as Guildenstern says with some astonishment:

> Prison, my lord?

Hamlet responds, without explaining:

> Denmark's a prison.

In relieving his heart he is mystifying theirs. Distressed at his unaccountable change of mood, they try to pass off the apparent irrelevance airily: if Denmark's a prison, the world must be one; has not Hamlet all a man could desire?

Imperceptibly Hamlet's feelings have altered: he has been thrust out of his pleasure at seeing his old friends into a recollection of his wretched circumstances. He attempts rather lamely to recapture his gaiety of a moment ago, but soon gives up. Let's go to the court, he suggests, for by my faith I'm not up to this discussion. Now occurs a most delicate and all-important moment of drama. At its commencement the two are Hamlet's dear friends; at its conclusion he has begun to divorce them from his affection forever. The men are on their way out, possibly arm in arm, when with easy cordiality Hamlet asks anew:

> But in the beaten way of friendship, what make you at Elsinore?

Poor Rosencrantz! Too fond of Hamlet to be skilful in deceit with his friend, he is in an impossible situation. If he is to help "restore" Hamlet to his former self, he cannot reveal the King's part in their being there. Had he merely replied:

> To visit you, my lord,

Hamlet's affection would in no way have become impaired. But he cannot speak with genuine innocence, despite the honorableness of his intentions, and so he tries to sound casual:

> To visit you, my lord; no other occasion.

That "no other occasion," that one phrase too much, becomes the slender thread with which Hamlet strangles their friendship, the thread which leads him from love of them to hatred, and thence inevitably to their own death. It is by such chance slips of the tongue as Rosencrantz's that a man's whole destiny may be altered. No one who had come merely to visit his friend would have added that "no other occasion." It is too innocent to ring true. At first Hamlet reacts only to the "to visit you," and responds with warm thanks. But while he speaks, he is pricked with the awareness that something in Rosencrantz's words has had a hollow ring, something which gives the lie to the other's seeming ingenuousness. And so, on a sudden impulse, Hamlet stops in his tracks and asks:

> Were you not sent for?

Dreadful to be playing the spy even in an apparently good cause! How can Rosencrantz look other than guilty at the demand of his friend, the random shot which has gone to the center of their embarrassment in his presence? His glance seeks Guildenstern's for support, while Hamlet, hot on the trail of discovery, halts their movement toward the exit, and presses for an answer:

> Is it your own inclining? Is it a free visitation? Come, deal justly with me. Come, come. Nay, speak!

As they continue to hesitate, his anger rises. At last Guildenstern speaks, and like his partner attempts to sound as guileless as his conscience assures him he has the right to feel:

> What *should* we say, my lord?

Unhappy pair! Hamlet misses nothing going on about him, catches every inflection of the voice, every glint of the eye, can almost see behind his back—and like all people so constituted is subject to immediate decisions of monumental importance on the frailest of grounds. To be but the twentieth part of one poor scruple less than

direct with such men is dangerous. For Rosencrantz and Guildenstern it proves fatal. Guildenstern's evasion is the knife that severs
them both from Hamlet's love. His mounting anger spurs his intuitions, and he guesses that Claudius and Gertrude have sent for
them, though he does not stop to consider, then or later, that his
friends may be entirely innocent of malice toward him, that their
objectives may do them no discredit. Foolishly, Rosencrantz protracts their reticence by one more brief evasion. Hamlet, seeing their
defenses weakening, pushes his query more forcefully, conjures them
by their long friendship to be "even and direct" with him. That plea
is irresistible: they are his friends. Shamefacedly they admit:

> My lord, we *were* sent for.

It is too late. Though now they are prepared to tell him everything,
he will not give them the chance. With augmenting irony he goes on
to tell *them* why they were sent for, before they can furnish him the
facts. In this way, he sarcastically assures them, they may preserve
their loyalty to the King and Queen—as though they were hirelings
of the crown. In his tables he has already inscribed them as traitors,
purchased, like the rest of Denmark, by Claudius.

> *How and when does Hamlet hit upon the idea*
> *of presenting the play before the King and Queen?*

Delighted at seeing the players, Hamlet has at once asked for
a "passionate" speech from a play on Dido and Aeneas. Hamlet begins the speech and, to ingratiate himself with the Prince, Polonius
compliments him on his delivery. But after the player continues
where Hamlet left off, the old man finds the speech "too long."
Hamlet, furious at the interruption, turns upon him in scorn, and
apologizes to the player: Polonius can be pleased only with something vulgar:

> he's for a jig or a tale of bawdry, or he sleeps: say
> on. Come to Hecuba.

But Shakespeare himself had a very important dramatic reason for
Polonius' interruption. Having dismissed it, Hamlet will turn with
augmented intensity to listen to the player. And it is the next line
which contains the phrase which gives Hamlet his all-important idea.

Shakespeare, by this device, both accounts for the impact of the line on Hamlet, and at the same time isolates the line by itself:

> But who, O, who hath seen the mobled queen—
>   II, ii, 525

recites the Player. Hamlet is struck forcibly by the phrase "mobled (i.e., muffled) queen." Muffled Queen! That phrase might, figuratively, describe Gertrude—muffled as she is from his view! What could one do to rip off the layers of "seeming" which conceal the true Gertrude?

Thus, while the Player proceeds with the speech, Hamlet's mind is busy with a scheme—the idea of giving his little unmasking play. The psychology of the evolution of his plan is brilliantly suggested, although it seems never to have been noted by commentators. Hamlet, because of that "mobled queen," thinks first of a means of penetrating to his mother's secret. Next it occurs to him that he can do better even than that—perhaps unmask the King too!

ACT THREE

What is the meaning of the
"To be or not to be" soliloquy?

Just before Hamlet enters (III, i, 56), Polonius has placed a prayer book in Ophelia's hand, shown her exactly where she is to walk as if in the midst of her devotions, and then has retired with Claudius behind the curtain at the back of the stage—the regular place for "overhearing" on the Elizabethan stage. When Hamlet comes in, he is at first oblivious of her presence, and delivers the most celebrated (and most completely misunderstood) of his soliloquies.

Doubtless it is too celebrated for its own good, despite the majesty of its utterance. Charles Lamb confessed that he could no longer "tell whether it be good, bad, or indifferent; it has been so handled and pawed about by declamatory boys and men, and torn so inhumanly from its living place and principle of continuity in the play, till it has become to me a perfect dead member." [44] It is also the passage probably responsible for the old lady's saying that she loves *Hamlet* because it is so full of quotations. It is also the point in the play where actors convey their conception of the hero to the pole opposite to Shakespeare's meaning by projecting visual grounds for the notion of an over-ratiocinating Hamlet: it is so often their pleasure to enter from the wings, one arm supporting the other, while the first two fingers touch the temple—a picture of the professional philosopher indulging in thought for the sheer fun of it—and then stand before the footlights to discourse, without provocation, upon life and death. It is here that the run-of-the-mill Hamlet has managed to stereotype the image of a ghastly rationalizing Prince, all brain and no body, into a likeness guaranteed to provoke laughter from the vulgar at any foolish mimicking thereof. In the popular imagination a "ham actor" is connected with this pose assumed by generations of Hamlets. Even the best of Hamlets tend to fall into the mold—though on a certain memorable occasion the comment of a highly remarkable cat should in all justice have been enough to smash it.

After his triumphant long run on Broadway, John Barrymore took the play to London. It chanced that there was reconnoitering off stage a certain cat whose name unhappily has not come down to us. A cat, but no ordinary cat—though it is doubtful that such a thing as an ordinary cat exists—a cat, in fact, of literary genius. When Barrymore entered for his soliloquy, supporting arm and fingers at the temple at approved angles, this same cat entered too, at a respectful distance, tail upright with delight. Hamlet was oblivious of the homage; the audience did its best not to titter. As Hamlet took his stand to plunge into heavy meditation, the cat scrutinized him first with some wonder. A very handsome Prince indeed—where had the stage ever seen a finer profile? A beautiful expressive voice. But what could be the meaning of the figure he was trying to cut? This was neither the accent of Christians, nor the stand of Christian, pagan, or man, it imitated humanity so abominably. Our intellectual cat had to decipher the puzzle. Quietly it walked to a spot directly in front of Hamlet, turned its back upon the audience, curled its tail about it, and gazed up in total astonishment at this strange being above it. It is not recorded whether the cat gave any voice to its critical opinion, but its posture and position were eloquent enough.

By this time the audience could no longer restrain its approving laughter. Caught in the middle of the soliloquy, Barrymore felt something amiss, looked down, and then raised his celebrated eyebrow indeed! With great tact, and a great deal more naturalness than earlier employed, he gently raised the critic, petted it, and quietly conducted it to the wings—where, no doubt, it was relieved to be among human beings again. This cat, which may very well have looked at more than one king, had never seen a prince so conducting himself, and let it be known to the world. What a pity that its critical judgment has not found dissemination! *

As we approach consideration of the "To be or not to be" soliloquy we are overwhelmed with concern: what apology can serve our turn for having the temerity to offer a new account of this celebrated passage? Well, to our business—*nec deus intersit nisi dignus vindice nodus!*

Almost universally Hamlet is conceived to be contemplating suicide in his opening lines.

> To be or not to be: that is the question,

is by almost everyone taken to mean: "to remain alive or not to remain alive: that is the question." Hamlet is deciding, says Malone, "whether he should continue to live, or put an end to his life"; [45] "he is meditating on suicide," says Bradley a century and a half later; [46] "again he is contemplating suicide," says Adams, "longing with infinite desire to make an end of his suffering with a bare bodkin"; [47] "he is thinking of suicide, as in the First Soliloquy," says Wilson [48] (who feels, with many others, that self-destruction is a daily impulse of Hamlet's), and observes in passing that this is the opinion of most scholars. This conception accords readily with the idea of Hamlet as a man suffering from melancholia, neurasthenia, nervous breakdown, weakness of will, pessimism, this complex or that complex. It is also a conception totally wanting in tragic dignity.

Having accepted such a reading of Hamlet's thoughts, many commentators have gone on to register complaint against Shake-

---

* Barrymore himself was the authority for the authenticity of this incident.

speare's artistry in this passage. Hamlet, as they understand him, proceeds in the next lines to state the alternatives of remaining alive or killing himself. They construe

> Whether 'tis nobler in the mind to suffer
> The slings and arrows of outrageous fortune

as a description of Hamlet's view of the consequences of living; and

> . . . to take arms against a sea of troubles,
> And by opposing end them

as a poetical elaboration of the idea of committing suicide. But, they ask, was not Shakespeare nodding when he wrote the second of these? How is it possible, they demand, to take arms against a *sea*? Shakespeare, they assert, surely confused images here.[49] To rescue Shakespeare from the imputation of failing in his craft of poet, many have come forward with suggestions. Some have proposed a "better" reading for the text's *sea of troubles* with such emendations as:

> a siege of troubles (*Pope*) [50]
> th' assay of troubles (*Theobald*) [51]
> assailing troubles (*Hanmer*) [52]
> the seat of troubles (*Bailey*) [53]—*this one rather Rabelaisian?;*

or would keep *sea* but alter *take* to *make:*

> make arms against a sea of troubles,

meaning "to swim against a sea." [54] Others, on their part, have leaped to defend the text: Hackett thinks the sea "is the *heart*—the fountain of existence"; [55] several others (with dubious intent) have observed that the Celts were known to resist the ocean flood with swords in their hands.[56] (The Danes, of course, are notoriously un-Celtic!) This is a pretty sad state of affairs. The emendations are all hideous; the defenses are no defenses. There is no escaping the conviction that *were* the traditional interpretation of the lines valid, Shakespeare must be accused of being slipshod—and at a most unpardonable moment. Moreover, *if* the traditional interpretation were valid, several other charges should also be brought against our poet:

1. The charge of being repetitious. If "the slings and arrows of outrageous fortune" be a description of the miseries of life, then why does he say it all over again four lines further on:

> The heart-ache and the thousand natural shocks
> That flesh is heir to?

[handwritten marginal notes: "1 F, death / 2 el three / 3 cent mg / 4 / 5 me moved from Wittenberg"]

2. If both these mean, even roughly, the same—to the weakening of both—the first must be pronounced as quite inflated for a description of the miseries of life, inflated and poetically insincere. The second is honest and effective. If the traditional view were correct he, apparently having bungled the expression once, tried it over again, this time successfully. But that is no excuse for a poet while both are allowed to remain.

3. If the question in "To be or not to be" is whether to live or to commit suicide, then (despite the grandiloquent tones of the "declamatory boys" and actors) Shakespeare is guilty of expressing that question as feebly as possible. In the phrase "To be or not to be" there is nothing poetic; the phrase is, indeed, abstract, prosaic, couched in the language of logic, not the emotions. Matters of life-and-death demand poetry at its most superb, most specific, most moving.

It does not, of course, occur to us that these charges can be seriously brought against Shakespeare. In our private Compleat Gentleman it is written: "When dealing with a creator of stature, one even not of Shakepeare's stature, particularly when dealing with him at the height of his powers, assume that any apparent confusion you encounter is not his but your own. Do not seek comfort by postulating printer's errors. First examine your own understanding of the work. Where lay *your* short-sightedness which may account for your confusion?" These rules hold even in the teeth of the unsupervised conditions under which Shakespeare's plays were printed and of the carelessness of Elizabethan printers. We dare not presuppose error unless we are faced with no meaning. If intelligible sense conflicts with our own theory, we had better re-inspect the theory, rather than hasten to suggest alterations in the text. In the case of this passage, are we to admit that, at the height of his career, and at a sublime moment of one of his chief masterpieces, Shakespeare is likely to be guilty of slovenliness and poetic ineptness? The question calls for a week's penance. Even at the beginning of his career, when he was subject to errors of taste, he could be over-extravagant as a poet, but never slipshod or sapless. It would be better if criticism remembered this.

Though most critics agree that the soliloquy is a product of Hamlet's contemplating suicide, not all interpret the first line to mean "to live or to destroy myself." Samuel Johnson saw the "question" as "whether, *after our present state*, we are to be or not to be." [57] J. Middleton Murry concurs with Johnson: it is the fear of something after death which "is the main dramatic motive of delay" in the tragedy.[58] Unable to make sense out of the imagery in the lines which follow, a few critics think that Hamlet speaks in a confused way to prove that he is insane: he knows his soliloquy is being overheard by the King.[59] (As though a soliloquy could be overheard in any but the most anemic play!)

Dowden and a couple of other scholars have been on the right track in rejecting the interpretation of suicide, but they have been either ignored or, as by Wilson, ruled out.[60] Nevertheless, Dowden came closer to the truth than anyone when he thus paraphrased "To be or not to be": "Is my present project of active resistance against wrong to be or not to be? Hamlet anticipates his own death as a probable consequence." [61] I. T. Richards considers that the opening line refers to Hamlet's intended killing of Claudius,[62] and he too comes closer to Shakespeare's meaning than the bulk of critics.

Let us begin with the question which we recommended earlier: what is the dramatic fact behind the present soliloquy? Tonight "The Murder of Gonzago" will surely "catch the conscience of the King" if he is guilty. If he prove so, Hamlet must outline at once a plan of action that will enable him to avenge his father. The Prince now stands on the very threshold of the crisis of his problem. The closer the great event approaches, the harder it is for him to wait. He speaks, therefore, somewhat from impatience; but he also speaks somewhat from awareness that beyond tonight's test of Claudius lie, it may be, heavy deeds for him to do—deeds of blood and death.

And so he enters upon the stage this crucial day with all kinds of conflicting thoughts pounding in his head. Shall I wait until tonight to discover the truth? If my play unmasks him as my father's murderer, what do I do next? Suppose he unmasks himself to me, but is clever enough to conceal the truth from the court, how will that help my cause? How can I be sure I can force him to announce his guilt to an unsuspecting world? How then do I bring him to justice? Justice! Why do I trouble myself with justice? ("Taint not thy mind!" said the Ghost.) Am I not asked the impossible when I am charged to wait until my cause is clear to the world? Why do I not kill this man at once—now? *

His first words, no one needs to be reminded, are: "To be or not to be." They are, we have said, colorless and abstract. Shakespeare wanted them so. There is no warrant for paraphrasing the first line into anything more concrete than "Is it (or, possibly, is this thing) to be or is it not to be—that is the question." What is this *it* or this *thing?* There can be no warrant for identifying it as more than some conclusion or decision Hamlet has just come to. What that conclusion or decision is, does not matter: all that we can determine from the lines that follow is that it has to do with the alternatives of waiting for the right moment to kill Claudius or killing him at once. (*To be*, for instance, might be the decision to wait or it might be the decision to kill now.) The rest of the soliloquy could not be more definite than it is; "To be or not to be" could not be more indefinite than it is. Shakespeare wishes, in short, to communicate neither more nor less than the fact that Hamlet has been debating with himself. What the subject of this debate has been, the lines immediately following make clear (or, rather, it is time that they should do so):

> Whether 'tis nobler in the mind to suffer
> The slings and arrows of outrageous fortune—

Were it nobler done of me, Hamlet asks, *to wait and suffer in my mind the hurts and wounds inflicted by the outrageous fortune which is mine?*—that wicked destiny which asks him to act under conditions impossible to a rational and honorable man—the uncertain authority which commands him to avenge—that ironic fate which

---

* If the reader decide that we have invented these thoughts for Hamlet, let him be patient until we have concluded the analysis of the soliloquy.

restrains him from avenging until he can prove what seems beyond proof—

> Or to take arms against a sea of troubles,
> And by opposing end them.

Or shall I rather, Hamlet continues, *throw to the winds the dictates of reason, no longer wait and suffer in the mind*—*shall I recklessly hurl myself into the midst of this impossible complex of events, like a man opposing the ocean with a puny sword, and put an end to the contest by engulfing myself in them, and bringing about my own destruction?*—shall he discard justice and reason, kill Claudius without more ado, and thus bring on the end of his problem, and thus, too, the end of himself?

> And by opposing end them. To die . . .

To kill Claudius now would be a swift solution of his troubles, an end to his anguish and doubts and to his waiting for the event, an end to his mental torture. But to kill Claudius would also be to meet his own death. Hamlet speaks of taking arms against a sea because he knows that to hurl himself recklessly upon Claudius, safe and protected by the good-will of Denmark, is as hopeless a gesture as would be an attempt to conquer the tumultuous ocean with a sword. Such an endeavor can end only in his own death. Far from thoughts of suicide, Hamlet is here meditating such reasonless precipitance as would involve his own death with his uncle's.

Having begun with a consideration of the wisdom of killing Claudius now, the soliloquy moves by natural gradation to the sphere of philosophical speculation. What does it mean "to die"?

> To sleep—no more,

Hamlet would assure himself. And if by "sleep" we mean an end to "the heart-ache" and the thousand "shocks" of living—ah, that would be

> a consummation
> Devoutly to be wished!

—a consummation (not of suicide! but) of taking arms against a sea of troubles. *Kill Claudius and win forgetfulness*. To die, to sleep— perchance *not* to forget, but to dream! There's the obstacle ("rub")! For who knows what dreams we may have once we have "shuffled off" the fuss of living ("mortal coil")? That is the consideration ("respect") that makes calamity so long-lived. Otherwise,

> who would bear the whips and scorns of time,
> The oppressor's wrong, the proud man's contumely,
> The pangs of disprized love, the law's delay,
> The insolence of office, and the spurns
> That patient merit of the unworthy takes,*

when he might be rid of all this with an unsheathed dagger ("bodkin")?

Though speaking philosophically, Hamlet is also a man, and his reflection is based upon his own experience. And this has been his experience: "the whips and scorns of time"—his having to be patient in his cause and bear the tortures of waiting and uncertainty; "the oppressor's wrong"—Claudius' seizing his father's throne and position of power; "the proud man's contumely"—the offensive haughtiness of the King's friends at court; "the pangs of disprized love"—Ophelia's rejection of his love; "the law's delay"—the endless waiting until one can bring a culprit like Claudius to justice; "the insolence of office"—all that he must bear at the hands of Claudius, and men like Polonius and Osric and (so he thinks) Rosencrantz and Guildenstern; "and the spurns that patient merit of the unworthy takes"—his entire situation, which requires of him patience, silence, and forbearing, while his enemy has everything his own way.

Who would bear, Hamlet asks, the burdens of this life, but that "the dread of something after death,"

> The undiscovered country from whose bourn
> No traveler returns, puzzles the will
> And makes us rather bear those ills we have
> Than fly to others that we know not of?

---

* Scholars are at one in considering these references to be impersonal and general. Madariaga says that these things "Hamlet could not possibly have suffered" since he is a prince; "Hamlet is here speaking in general terms." [63] Joseph speaks of these lines as "producing in the form of a series of rhetorical questions example after example of people not normally regarded as heroic, who endure life when they might easily make away with themselves." [64] We read a very personal meaning in Hamlet's words; in that light they are the more powerful, because more immediate.

These words touch so deeply upon our common feelings about death, it is small wonder the passage is revered.*

Hamlet concludes: it is just this kind of forethought ("conscience") which makes cowards of us all. And it is this consideration of the consequences of our acts which converts red-blooded action into pale brooding upon possible outcomes, and thus great enterprises often fail to be carried out.

*What is the explanation of Hamlet's treatment
of Ophelia in the scene which immediately follows?*

At the conclusion of the "To be or not to be" soliloquy Hamlet is suddenly conscious of Ophelia's presence (III, i, 88):

> Soft you now!
> The fair Ophelia!

He has just been confronting no less than eternity. His mood is a chastened one. And as he sees her quietly pacing back and forth intent upon her prayers, she seems like an angel herself, "so pure a thing, so free from mortal taint," that he murmurs gently:

> Nymph in thy orisons
> Be all my sins remembered! †

---

* Yet, chorus the critics, why does Hamlet say that no traveler returns from beyond the grave when he has seen his father's spirit?

Furness: The line was "an apparent oversight." [65]

Theobald: The Ghost came from neither Heaven nor Hell, both final resting-places, but from Purgatory, an intermediate place.[66]

Schlegel: The remark proves that "Hamlet could not fix himself in any conviction of any kind whatever." [67]

Wilson: "Hamlet has given up all belief in the 'honesty' of the Ghost, and . . . Shakespeare wrote the lines to make this clear." [68]

Joseph: "At this moment he feels that the Ghost is an 'illusion.' " [69]

Coleridge answered such absurd queries for all time—but with little avail:

> "If it be necessary to remove the apparent contradiction,—if
> it be not rather a great beauty,—surely it were easy to say,
> that no traveler returns to this world, as to his home." [70]

† The simple eloquence of these words has the very ring of spiritual peace. Nevertheless Wilson has a theory about this scene and he will

It is true that when he broke into her chamber he became convinced that she had renounced his love. But he still loves her, and is caught off guard; after his solemn meditations on life, he is so moved by her apparent purity and her beauty that it is his love which speaks for him.

---

not let the text speak for itself. "There is no warmth" in *The fair Ophelia*, he observes. "The touch of affectation in 'nymph' and 'orisons' (both pretentious words) and of sarcasm in 'all my sins' shows that Hamlet speaks ironically." [71] Old Sam Johnson's sensibilities were certainly more alert when he said of these same words, "This is a touch of nature. Hamlet, at the sight of Ophelia . . . makes her an address grave and solemn, such as the foregoing meditation excited in his thoughts." [72] As for Wilson's seeing only irony in *fair, nymph, orisons* and *all my sins!*:

1. *fair:* Silvia, in the song, is

> Holy, fair and wise
>> *Two Gentlemen of Verona*, IV, ii, 41;

in the same song it is asked,

> Is she kind as she is fair?
> For beauty lives with kindness;

the enamored Biron cries of his love,

> I'll prove her fair or talk till doomsday here
>> *Love's Labour's Lost*, IV, iii, 274;

Bassanio says of beloved Portia,

> And she is fair and fairer than that word
>> *The Merchant of Venice*, I, i, 162;

and Lorenzo of his beloved Jessica,

> And fair she is, if that mine eyes be true
>> II, vi, 54;

Orlando of his Rosalind,

> Carve on every tree
> The fair, the chaste, and unexpressive she
>> *As You Like It*, III, ii, 9–10;

Othello, when his love for her is overpowering his determination to kill that love, exclaims in anguish to Desdemona that she is

> so lovely fair and smell'st so sweet
> That the sense aches at thee.
>> *Othello*, IV, ii, 68–9.

Poor Ophelia, miserable at the role forced upon her by her father, incapable of speaking for herself, eagerly seizes upon the sweetness of Hamlet's first words, and inquires after his health. He thanks her, and adds a little dispiritedly, "Well, well, well." She too, her question has implied, has credited the rumors about his "transformation." And now the unhappy girl in her desperation tries an expedient that she trusts will heal the widening breach between her and her lover. It is the only thing we ever see her do on her own initiative—and how tragically unwise of her to do it! Her logic is touchingly feminine, but of the kind the male intelligence never apprehends at the moment of challenge. Unknown to her father she has brought with her some gifts Hamlet has given her in the past, and these she now presses into his hands. Too dutiful a daughter, timid and repressed, she dare not explain to her lover how far her heart is from the obedience with which she has followed her father's commands. She hopes that the sight of these little treasures, tokens of

---

All the men quoted above speak with deepest affection; presumably it is only Hamlet who uses the word without warmth.

    2. *orisons:* It is the simple and innocent Juliet who says to the Nurse,

> I have need of many orisons
> To move the Heavens to smile upon my state
>   *Romeo and Juliet*, IV, iii, 2–4;

and in the simplest of scenes Milton's Adam and Eve in love of God,

> Lowly they bowed adoring, and began
> Their orisons, each morning duly paid.
>   *Paradise Lost,* V, 144–45.

For no reason, in Hamlet's mouth the word becomes "pretentious" and therefore ironic.

    3. *nymph: The Century Dictionary* uses our passage to illustrate the meaning: "A young and attractive woman; a maiden. (Poetical)" [73]

    4. *all my sins:* That this should be construed as ironic is most astounding of all. Barring saints, has any Christian felt so pure that his sins need not be remembered in the prayers of an innocent girl?

The reason for these distortions is Wilson's conviction that Hamlet has overheard Polonius' plotting to "loose" Ophelia to him, and therefore knows Ophelia has been planted where he has found her. Because of this untenable theory Wilson is forced to be deaf to the rapt tone of Hamlet's exclamation.

Hamlet's affection, will somehow so work on him that he will find means to rescue her from her wretched situation, and place her safely under the protection of his love. It is a completely womanly inspiration, not too dissimilar from that which prompts Desdemona, when she is convinced she has lost Othello's love, to bid Emilia:

> Prithee, tonight
> Lay on my bed my wedding sheets.
> *Othello*, IV, ii, 105–6

Hamlet, reacting as a man will react, is so far from understanding Ophelia's motives that he looks upon the return of the gifts as a gesture of her final rejection of his love (remember that he has been denied access to her and that his letters have been either unanswered or returned), and he murmurs in a pained voice:

> No, no!
> I never gave you aught.

(In reading the commentators on this scene, one must learn to sit like Patience on a monument. Kittredge, like Ophelia, knows that Hamlet *did* give her these presents, and so concludes that Hamlet is now talking "as insanely as he knows how. Ophelia replies with the gentle firmness which one might use to a refractory child." [74] Madariaga is sure that Ophelia, a licentious girl, has not at all obeyed her father; she has not only seen Hamlet, but has also admitted him to her bed. The proof? Had she refused to see her lover, "she would not return the trinkets alleging that 'rich gifts wax poor when givers prove unkind.'" [75] Her earlier salute, *How does your honour for many a day?*, "proves that her door has remained open" to him, but that he is now too bored to wish to see her anymore. [76] Adams believes that her saying she has wished to redeliver his gifts "is an obvious falsehood"; Hamlet, suspicious at this, answers, "on his guard," that he never gave her aught; "producing the jewels," she continues "acting the part laid out for her . . . repeating words supplied by her father, as well as acting out an insincere scene contrived by him." [77] [As if this frightened girl could act out any part! She has been stationed at her post like an automaton by Polonius, who usually treats her like one, and left on her own, which is why she undertakes to "return" the gifts; Polonius and the King are not interested in what she says to Hamlet, but what he says to her. Polonius is busy trying to prove that Hamlet is mad because of love for Ophelia.])

What Hamlet has given her he refuses to take back. Moreover, to accept them would be to grant his consent to the termination of their love, and that he is not willing to do.

But obvious-minded Ophelia takes him literally. She knows "right well' that he has made these presents to her (she is convinced her lover is truly unbalanced), and she knows too the sweet words with which they were offered. If his love is gone ("their perfume lost") she does not wish to keep his gifts.

Is there a more universal device among women than to provoke a lover's protestations of passion by accusing him of not loving? Shakespeare was familiar enough with it. Beatrice, for instance, who has more intelligence in her little finger than Ophelia possesses in her cranium, is not above this archness; when she would have Benedick kill his good friend Claudio, and he refuses, she has only to say:

> There is no love in you
> *Much Ado About Nothing*, IV, i, 295

and he is ready to change his mind. Lady Macbeth, no modest Griselda, when Macbeth shows signs of weakening in his determination to kill Duncan, cries in highly feminine fashion:

> From this time
> Such I account thy love.
> *Macbeth*, I, vii, 38

If women can do this to incite their men to murder, it should not be surprising that Ophelia would hope by calling Hamlet's love into question she can incite him to work the miracle to free her from her misery.

But Hamlet reacts as a man will react. Men, being cruder than women, are more dangerously fond of logic; a woman has small patience with that kind of thinking. A man reasons from A to B, from B to C, and so on until he painfully reaches Z. A woman begins at Q, is next at H, but reaches Z long before him; she is the best refutation of Euclid's claims that the shortest distance between two points is a line which is straight. And, what is apropos to our scene, when a man says Yes, his meaning is Yes; by No he means No. To a woman Yes and No have quite different significations than this. Not that she means No by Yes. She means something that has a little of No in it and also a little of Yes—something between the two extremes, a locus the mental vision of the male cannot discern. In the regions of these subtle shadings of meaning, of airy indecision, women seem to be most at home, and men most at a loss. If a young woman tells her lover that she wishes never to see him again, he is likely to think that she wishes never to see him again. And he will stay away, taking to bourbon, poetry, or wakeful nights, as his nature dictates. Then, if he meet her by chance a few doleful days later, she will in all likelihood upbraid him for not telephoning this long while, reflecting caustically on the quality of his affection; if bewilderingly he protests, "But you said—!" she will toss her head in annoyance at his slow-wittedness, possibly adding, "And they say you're intelligent!" *

These differences between the mental processes of men and women make for much of the charm of life but for tragedy too. Hamlet has not been allowed to see Ophelia or to hear from her, and now she accuses him of not loving her any longer. Smarting from the wounds of disprized love, he cannot believe his ears. Is it possible she can pretend to be speaking sincerely? Dare she accuse *him* of renouncing their love?

Ha, ha! Are you honest?

(The word had more connotations in Shakespeare's day. The line also implies: If you can, knowing what you have done to me, speak this way, are you really as virtuous and chaste as you look?) Her accusation has thrown him off, and bitterness intrudes into his tone. You are beautiful, he exclaims, and therefore dangerous, and if you have any honesty in you,

* We are aware that some ultra-feminists (should they not be called "masculists"?) will be indignant at the imputation of any differences between men and women—unless the differences are adduced to prove the superiority of women. Nature, nonetheless, continues to behave as though there were differences. Completely agreeable to equal rights for women, we yet cry with that gallant French senator, "*Vive la différence!*"

> your honesty should admit no discourse to your beauty
> . . . For the power of beauty will sooner transform hon-
> esty from what it is to a bawd, than the force of honesty
> can translate beauty into his * likeness.

Hamlet is angry now, but chiefly with himself. He is lashing himself for not remembering what her treatment of him has been, for having allowed himself to be ensnared by her apparent innocence, the maiden holily engaged in her orisons.

Terrified at his change of tone, which she does not understand —his reaction is so much unanticipated by her, so far from her hopes! —she begins to weep, and tries confusedly to fathom his words. His bitterness increasing, her only refuge is in her tears. Seeing which, Hamlet is of a mind to construe them as hypocritical too. Now for the first time he talks with irony, shooting at her:

> This was sometime a paradox.

Oh, but of course, of course—he means to say—you do not catch my meaning! You *will* play the injured innocent to the last, won't you? Then he adds with all the hurt of thwarted love:

> I did love you once.

Confounded, disappointed, unable to help herself, she sobs:

> Indeed, my lord, you made me believe so.

Like most men, he cannot bear to see the girl he loves in tears, no matter how unjust or unreasonable she has been. Hamlet, naturally, guesses Polonius' part in the straining of their relationship, though he has no way of telling how loyal or disloyal her heart may be to himself. It is all too involved; he knows he cannot count on her rebellion against her father, and is therefore no less bitter. The case seems hopeless. He will make it easier for her, at least, by shouldering the blame and himself disclaiming love for her. Partly out of wounded pride, partly out of pity for her, he murmurs:

> You should not have believed me . . . I loved you not.

* its.

With no thought of the agony she has been causing him, sunk in her own unhappiness, she takes his words in their literal sense:

> I was the more deceived.

Her tears drain him of his anger. He has only overwhelming pity for her, but knows not how to help her. Blindly male, he would require some small sign that she desires his love; the pathetic hint she has just given him has been completely misread by his masculine self-absorption. He knows only that he has been patently rejected, and he has compassion for her inability to stand up against the forces working on her.

In this mood he bids her flee the world and her corrupting environment. Why should she cooperate in continuing the propagation of the vile human race? Better for her to enter a convent. He is himself honest, as men go, yet he knows himself, as representative of the species, to be capable of the most hideous of crimes.

> We are arrant knaves all; believe none of us. Go thy ways to a nunnery.*

---

* It is here that Wilson's theory (that Hamlet overheard Polonius scheming for this interview) leads him, with the most honest intent, to an interpretation that is downright revolting. Because there are extant a few examples of the usage of the word *nunnery* in Elizabethan slang to mean "whore house," Wilson advances the idea that Hamlet is here bidding Ophelia join a house of ill fame. Because, he says, Hamlet is convinced that Ophelia has agreed to trap him, he comes "very near to calling Ophelia a prostitute to her face." [78] Sad to relate, none of Wilson's suggestions has been more enthusiastically endorsed by Shakespearean scholars than his glossing of this word. Everywhere it is now considered established fact that such is the meaning of word and passage. *The Oxford Dictionary* does list the word as a cant term for "a house of ill fame" for 1593 and 1617.[79] But its meaning in the familiar sense of "a convent" or religious house for nuns goes back to 1275. *The Oxford Dictionary* lists it as so used in 1290, 1305, 1330, 1386, 1389, 1425, 1440, 1450, 1470, 1483, 1523, 1538, 1548, 1550, 1571, and 1577; and the quotation under 1602 to illustrate the same meaning quite properly is our line from *Hamlet*.[80] With such an impressive record the word in all conscience may be thought to have been used by Shakespeare in this

These words have the ring of a bitter-sorrowful-pitying farewell.

But suddenly Hamlet asks,

Where's your father?

Clearly, when Hamlet asks that, he must know that Polonius is within earshot. Yet, an unbiased reading of all that has preceded this question makes it equally clear that nothing Hamlet said until now shows any awareness of his being overheard. (If Wilson's theory were correct, indeed, and Hamlet did know of the eavesdroppers all the time, "Where's your father?" must have been one of the first remarks he would have addressed to Ophelia, not, as it is, one of the last.)

The Barrymore production presented this moment as Shakespeare must have intended it. Hamlet's "Go thy ways to a nunnery" was rightly interpreted as a farewell. After it, Hamlet abruptly turned away from the weeping Ophelia and began to leave the stage. Now, in that production the background of this scene was designed as a series of massive columns; behind one of them Claudius stood concealed, behind another, Polonius. During Hamlet's discourse with Ophelia, Polonius had intermittently been peeking out from behind his column to see what was going on—a piece of business entirely in keeping with his character. This time Hamlet's sudden move to leave caught Polonius unprepared. He bobbed quickly back again, but not quickly enough to escape Hamlet's catching a glimpse of him; moreover, a few inches of Polonius' robe lay unretrieved along the base of the pillar. In a flash, Hamlet looked to Ophelia (who was unaware of what had passed), back to the column,

---

normal sense too. There is not one solid reason which rules out that likelihood.

Before Wilson, when the word was understood to mean "a convent," the reasons assigned for Hamlet's advice have been quaint; most critics, of course, have resorted to real or assumed madness as the explanation. But Adams, whose Hamlet in his "sick, melancholy brain" thinks that Claudius has designs upon Ophelia's virginity, thus paraphrases the line quoted above: "Believe no man. All men are bent on seducing women. So do not believe the next man—Claudius—when he tells you he loves you, for assuredly he will be trying to deceive you." [81]

back to Ophelia again, and then in perfect fury shouted, "Where's your father?" It was a difficult piece of directorial timing, executed to perfection.

It would seem that until Mr. Gielgud adopted Professor Wilson's suggestions it was fairly traditional to stage the scene as Barrymore did.[82] The conception certainly was a creditable adaptation of the situation as it must have been staged in the Elizabethan theater. Polonius, concealed behind the curtains of the inner stage, would, one conceives, being Polonius, have thrust his head through the openings of the cloth now and again, would have been a little too late in withdrawing it on Hamlet's sudden move to exit, and might easily have not had time to pull back the skirts of his robe after him. It is precisely the self-assured *gaucherie* you would expect of Polonius.

Now Hamlet is enraged indeed, and it is in a rage that the rest of his words are addressed to Ophelia. The question he puts to her he little looks to be granted an honest answer to now. Spiritless, browbeaten Ophelia dares not tell the truth, and mumbles, "At home, my lord." Hamlet's fury sweeps to its apex, but because of that admixture of pride and vanity without which no man seems able to breathe, it is probably a fury largely directed at himself. At first he had been trapped into looking upon her as though she were a saint; then her return of the gifts portrayed her as a flirt; but his bitterness over that he had allowed to dissolve at the spectacle of her tears; and when he was just now about to leave her, it was with great pity for her. What a fool he has been! How he has permitted himself to be victimized by his love of her! How he has played into the hands of her dotard father!

First it is to the old man that he directs his insults, letting him know he is now aware of his hiding place:

> Let the doors be shut upon him, that he may play the fool nowhere but in's own house!

And he turns to go with a savage, "Farewell!" Poor Ophelia, ignorant of Hamlet's discovery and unable to account for the violent change in his voice from his sorrowing "Go thy ways," is now certain he is mad, and, calling upon the heavens to help him, weeps more bitterly than ever. Her tears now only evoke his cold wrath, and he returns to pour his anger over her. It is in a far different tone that he repeats, "Get thee to a nunnery." With another farewell he moves off, but comes back—the lines powerfully mirror his complete exacerbation—to spit out:

> Or if thou wilt needs marry, marry a fool; for wise men know well enough what monsters you make of them.

Once more he begins to tear away ("To a nunnery, go, and quickly too. Farewell!"); once more Ophelia invokes the heavenly powers to restore him to sanity. All this is to him undiluted hypocrisy—her tears, her pretending to think him mad, her calling upon the heavens for help—all this nauseates him as being so much unconvincing display, and he comes back for the last time to tell her so. He knows enough about female deception:

> God has given you one face, and you make yourselves another. You jig, you amble, and you lisp and nick-name God's creatures.

I'll have no more of it! he cries, it is too infuriating! Finally, he calls out to whoever may be concealed behind the hangings:

> I say, we will have no more marriages. Those that are married already, all but *one*, shall live!

and dashes out.

Not a syllable of what he has said has upon it any marks of madness. Once aware of Polonius' presence, however, Hamlet was no more capable of considering Ophelia's dilemma than he was of being fair to Rosencrantz and Guildenstern, from the moment they became treacherous in his eyes. To be evasive with him is to be guilty of whatever his intuitive nature suspects. But much as we pity Ophelia her incapacity, we do not blame Hamlet. That she chooses to obey her father rather than be just to her lover, wins more sympathy for him than for herself. Even the younger, innocent, inexperienced Juliet would rather have heard that her father, mother, and Tybalt were all dead than Romeo banished (*Romeo and Juliet*, III, ii, 114–125).

Why is Hamlet's going to England
mentioned several times?

Shakespeare's reasons are purely dramatic. The first time Claudius mentions it is after he emerges from eavesdropping on Hamlet and Ophelia (III, i, 177):

> he shall with speed to England,
> For the demand of our neglected tribute—

perhaps a change of air will improve Hamlet's health and temper. Here Claudius apparently has no more nefarious intentions than to remove his nephew from the court awhile. He is strong-minded enough to resist believing that Hamlet could possibly know about the murder. He may hope that Hamlet's hostility is owing only to the marriage. In all events, a vacation from home might bring back a more agreeable nephew from England. When we hear the King's plan, we feel fairly certain that Hamlet would refuse to go.

The second time Hamlet's going to England is mentioned is when Claudius, having revealed himself as a murderer during "The Murder of Gonzago," commissions Rosencrantz and Guildenstern to get Hamlet to accompany them to England (III, iii, 1–7). This time we are convinced that Hamlet will never agree to leave Denmark now that his line of action is taking direction.

Why have these references been made? For a powerful reason. When Hamlet plunges his sword through the cloth into Polonius' body (III, iv, 24)—the climax of the plot—the full impact of this tragic error comes upon us as we realize: Now Hamlet will have to go to England! He himself quickly estimates the consequences, when he says to Gertrude,

> I must to England   (200)

and a few lines further mutters over Polonius' corpse:

> This man shall set me packing   (211).

His rash deed has ruined his revenge, and delivered him into the hands of his foe. The King can order him to England—now with murderous purposes, of course:

> Hamlet, this deed of thine, for thine especial safety,
> . . . must send thee hence
> With fiery quickness; therefore prepare thyself . . .

In Hamlet's brief but acrimonious answer to this, the point is grimly and finally driven home:

HAM. For England?
KING.   Ay, Hamlet.
HAM.   Good!
KING. So it is, if thou knew'st our purposes.
HAM. I see a cherub that sees them.

                                        IV, iii, 42–50

What is the meaning of the word "idle"
in Hamlet's line: "I must be idle" (III, ii, 96)?

Just before "The Murder of Gonzago" is to be given, Hamlet is busy talking to Horatio and enlisting his aid. Sometime after his interview with the Ghost, Hamlet has told his friend of the Ghost's account of the late King's death; now he asks Horatio to fasten upon Claudius' face during the performance with all his powers of perception. If the King's hidden guilt does not "unkennel" itself, it *is* a damned spirit which they have seen. Horatio pledges his full cooperation. With a flourish, the Court begins to enter. Seeing the King and Queen approaching, Hamlet leaves his friend's side with:

> I must be idle.

This has become, for no reason, a crucial line among commentators. To support the theory of assumed madness, the word *idle* is usually glossed to mean "crazy"—that is, Hamlet is supposed to be telling Horatio that he must now "act the madman again, since the others are coming." Thus Kittredge.[83] Wilson says that the words mean "I must assume my antic disposition." [84] * Even André Gide was hoodwinked by the commentaries to render the line in his translation of the play in this bald fashion:

> A présent je dois faire l'idiot.[86]

* This distortion goes back to the mid-nineteenth century when Delius and Staunton gave it that interpretation.[85]

Our own contribution to the discussion is revolutionary: we insist that by *idle* Shakespeare meant "idle," i.e., "unoccupied or inactive." His plays are running over with lines in which the word is used in this modern sense.*

When Hamlet says to Horatio "I must be idle. Get you a place" he simply means that he does not wish Claudius to find him in close conference with his friend; it is important that the King have no suspicions of any kind, and therefore he wishes Claudius to find him being merely idle, unoccupied, not up to anything, before "The Murder of Gonzago" begins. It is that simple.

No doubt the perverted glossing of *idle* is a product of the scholars' trouble with the conversation which now follows with the King. In it, they have decided, Hamlet proceeds to talk sheer non-

* Thus, for a brief sampling: 1. Othello, in recounting his history to Desdemona, had occasion to speak of vast caves *and deserts idle*. (*Othello*, I, iii, 140)—these deserts were certainly not crazy! 2. Ford says to Mistress Page concerning his wife: *As idle as she may hang together for want of company* (*Merry Wives*, III, ii, 13). 3. Menenius speaks of how the "body's members" rebelled against the belly for remaining *I' the midst of the body, idle and unactive* (*Coriolanus*, I, i, 102). 4. In the same play Valeria comes to coax Virgilia out of her house with: *Come, lay aside your stitchery. I must have you play the idle housewife with me this afternoon* (I, iii, 75–6)—she is not inviting her to play the lunatic! 5. During his quarrel with Cassius, Brutus says scoffingly to him that his threats *pass by me as the idle wind* (*Julius Caesar*, IV, iii, 68).

The only example scholars have been able to cite to justify glossing *idle* as "crazy" is when Goneril speaks to her steward of Lear as:

> Idle old man
> That still would manage those authorities
> That he hath given away!
> *Lear*, I, iii, 16–18

This is as unjustifiable a perversion of the meaning [87] as the attempt in *Hamlet*. Lear's mind has not yet begun to collapse—he has not yet had any contention with his viper daughters. Goneril is merely shrewishly accusing her father of having nothing better to do with his time than make a nuisance of himself. There is no example in Shakespeare of a use of the word *idle* to mean "crazy." It meant "doing nothing, unemployed," as long ago as the year 950.[88]

sense. As a matter of fact nowhere in the play does he speak with livelier and more dramatic pertinancy. Claudius, of course, does not follow Hamlet's meanings—because the King has no notion of Hamlet's purposes in presenting the play. The Prince speaks to him in double meanings, the real significance of which is clear only to himself—and to us, if we are alert. But it is absurd to pretend that this double-talk is a manifestation of pretended lunacy, when everything said is so powerfully cogent and apropos.

Anxious not to raise any suspicions in the King's mind, Hamlet, one would suppose, would try to be gracious and agreeable with him—particularly since Claudius obviously takes the invitation to the play as a gesture of friendliness. But Hamlet cannot pretend friendship for this man; more dangerously, he cannot refrain from relishing his private knowledge with elaborate sarcasm. The King asks, politely, how things are with him:

> How fares our cousin * Hamlet?

Hamlet feigns that the word *fare* was intended in the sense of *eat*, and replies that he is doing very well indeed, that like the chameleon —as it was then thought—he can live on nothing but air:

> I eat the air, promise-crammed.

Like the chameleon, he means privately, I am sustained by the air— and the air just now is crammed with the promise of my unmasking your guilt.† He continues:

> You cannot feed capons so.

Claudius treats him, Hamlet means, encircling him with diplomatic politeness, as though he had lost his manhood. The promise in the

---

* relative.

† Moberly: "The King had promised him that he should be next to himself; but Hamlet ought to have been first in the realm." [89] Kittredge: Hamlet's line is intended to give weight to the belief "that disappointment about the kingship is the cause of his insanity." [90] Wilson: " 'I am tired,' says Hamlet, 'of being fed with mere promises of the succession.' " [91] This is indeed pulling things out of the air. The issue of the succession to the crown has not even been mentioned thus far in the play.

air when fulfilled may soon prove to Claudius that Hamlet is not the emasculated creature he seems to think. The King, following none of these subtleties, replies:

> I have nothing with this answer, Hamlet; these words are not mine.

Hamlet's answer, No, nor mine now, means, of course, that now that the words have been uttered, they no longer belong to him. But it is possible he means more than that. Were the pleasures of sarcasm worth the risk he has taken? It has surely been impolitic of him to say this much. Even if the King has not understood, he may very well have begun to feel a threat behind Hamlet's words—and it is above all important that Claudius be not put on guard right now. It may be because Hamlet perceives he has said too much that he turns his back upon the King and begins to tease Polonius.

> *Why do the players present "The Murder of Gonzago"*
> *in pantomime before beginning to enact it?* (III, ii, 145)

The reason is, again, purely dramaturgical. Shakespeare's scenario will require Claudius' staggering out in the *middle* of the performance, if he is to prove to Hamlet and Horatio that he is a murderer. But if the performance is thus to be cut short, how is the audience to know what in the play unkennels the King's guilt? It was to provide the audience with a knowledge of the play's plot, that Shakespeare hit upon the device of a brief dumb-show as a kind of short cut. The audience must be informed of the play's similarity to the Ghost's narrative.

> *How is it that Claudius, having seen*
> *in the dumb-show what the plot of the play is to be,*
> *allows the dialogue to proceed?*

This ought to appear a hopelessly unimaginative query, but it is a matter that has been endlessly worried over by commentators—with some truly astonishing answers.* In Mr. Olivier's movie the

---

* Greg, deducing that Claudius remains calm during the pantomime, concludes that his lack of agitation exonerates Claudius as a murderer; the Ghost's story was not a message from the other world but a "figment

director apparently felt it to be a serious difficulty, which he solved by omitting all of the dialogue portion, and keeping Claudius busy kissing Gertrude's hand, so that he missed the first part of the pantomime.

Let us consider the scene from the point of view of stage performance. How would Claudius, unprepared for Hamlet's trap, humanly react? Naturally, to be gracious as a response to Hamlet's "friendly" invitation to the performance, he will watch with attention. Is it psychologically acceptable that in one instant he should note the similarity of the little play to his own misdeeds, and rise, scream, and rush from the room? That is what the posing of the question we are considering implies. If it were so acted, the audience would never grasp the import of his reaction; for dramatic effectiveness, it is necessary that Claudius' terror should mount by degrees until it reaches the breaking point.

That grading of his reactions is also true to the psychological facts. Let us not forget that the dumb-show is very brief, that it takes but a few minutes to present. As it begins, Claudius watches it with no more concern than he would observe any other play. There is nothing in the demonstrations of love between the Player King and Player Queen that need disturb him. Only in the middle of the dumb show does the Poisoner enter.

It is when the Poisoner "pours the poison in the King's ears" that Claudius will start. Quickly he will look about him—Gertrude and the courtiers are calmly observing the play (Gertrude knows nothing about any poisoning); next he will glance quickly at Hamlet—who, all as quick, is pretending to be elaborately absorbed in the performance. No, Claudius will tell himself, I must be mad to think there is anything in this but coincidence. How could Hamlet possibly have staged this to unnerve me? Not he, not anyone in Denmark (except, perhaps, one other) knows my crime. It is fantastic

---

of Hamlet's brain." [92] To answer this Wilson wrote a whole book which intends to prove that Claudius is unaffected by the dumb show only because he is not watching it: at the time he is busy talking to Polonius and Gertrude.[93] Gray thinks Claudius does not realize Hamlet's connection with the performance.[94] Lawrence decides that the dumb-show is an artistic blunder on the part of the author, since it warns the King; he concludes that Shakespeare did not write that part of the play.[95]

that I allow myself to find a special meaning in this play. I must not be stupid. This is only a play.

Claudius is a strong man, and he soon realizes that, whatever may be the import of his nephew's invitation to this piece, all he has to do is sit tight and say nothing until the play is over. It is simply a matter of enduring until the end of the performance. That, he feels, he can manage. Before he has reached this conclusion in his thoughts, the brief pantomime is over. He looks about again, at Hamlet, at Gertrude, and the court. Everything seems in serene accustomed order.

Hamlet, on his part, perceives that this is no weak adversary. The King, whatever his reactions, is contriving to keep a diplomatic silence. Out of the corner of his eye Hamlet has noted, of course, Claudius' searching looks. This is a good beginning, Hamlet thinks, and to cover the interval between the dumb-show and the opening of the play's dialogue, he smothers his excitement by concentrating on Ophelia, and thus somewhat reassures Claudius. The fact that she can ask,

> Will they tell us what this show meant?

indicates that the pantomime has been so brief that no one in the room has completely digested it. (The audience, however, having heard the Ghost's narrative, has absorbed it rapidly enough.) Because of its brevity, Claudius might very well be asking himself whether he is not allowing his fancy to run riot in supposing that the play has been meant to afflict him. Hamlet is busy with Ophelia; the rest are all absorbed in the entertainment. He will know better, he decides, as the dialogue unfolds. In the meantime, he braces himself; he has only to control himself until it is all over.

As the dialogue of "The Murder of Gonzago" proceeds, Hamlet realizes that Claudius will never break unless he can force him into speech. Once he can make the King break the dam of silence, Hamlet is sure he can cause Claudius to give himself away. What, moreover, is the meaning of the Queen's placidity? How much does she really know? Hamlet must do something to make them both speak. He feels Claudius' eyes studying him intensely during the dialogue, and knows the King is overwrought. Ostentatiously ignoring him, Hamlet looks straight at Gertrude, and shoots at her:

> Madam, how like you this play?

Quite impersonally she replies with the criticism:

> The lady protests too much, methinks.

(The touch is perfect. Sentimentalists like Gertrude never see themselves as they are: if they did, they could not bear to live.)

But Hamlet's arrow has lodged where he meant to aim it—in the King's bosom. Claudius gathers from Hamlet's question that his own growing alarm may be perhaps fully justified. Despite himself his anxiety unseals his lips; the tension is too much for him, and before he knows what he is doing he is asking Hamlet:

> Have you heard the argument? Is there no offence in 't?

This is what Hamlet has been waiting for. For the first time he looks directly at the King and cries:

> No, no! They do but jest, poison in jest; no offence i' th' world!

Now Claudius is certain. By some miracle Hamlet has found out his secret. But how? He holds on to the sides of his throne to master himself, and once more, despite himself, as in a hideous nightmare, he hears himself speak. Exultantly, Hamlet now speaks with lightning rapidity. The King's nerves are overstrained: he must break them. Also, he must fill in the time until the Player Poisoner enters; the performance must not be stopped. Hamlet gives the screw several powerful new turns: his answer to Claudius is brilliantly sinister. The play? It's called "The Mouse-trap." How? By figure of speech. But it's a story of murder done in *Vienna* (not Denmark!). The victim's name was *Gonzago* (not Hamlet!); his queen's *Baptista* (not Gertrude!). With a little patience your Majesty will see how it works out. It's a knavish piece of work. But your Majesty and the rest of us—we have free souls—why should we be disturbed by it?

The Poisoner enters. Here Hamlet counts on the King's breaking. As the actor prepares to speak, Hamlet looks away from Claudius, delivers some rapid jests at Ophelia, and bids the actor plunge into his speech. When the Poisoner pours the venom into the Player King's ears, Claudius can bear it no longer, and begins to crack. Knowing he has exposed himself to Hamlet, he rises. Wildly, Hamlet spits out at him anything that comes into his head, in the hope that Claudius will publicly damn himself.

It is Polonius who stops the performance, and perhaps thus saves the King from overtly blurting out the truth. Why should it be he who comes to the King's rescue? Brokenly, the King staggers from his throne, calls for lights, and stumbles out. His self-mastery, though not enough to conceal the truth from Hamlet, has protected him from saying anything incriminating in the presence of his wife or the courtiers.*

Why does the Ghost re-appear in Gertrude's closet? (III, iv, 103)

In a rash fit, Hamlet has killed Polonius. He turns from the corpse to speak harshly to his mother:

> Leave wringing of your hands. Peace! Sit you down,
> And let me wring your heart . . .

As he proceeds in his castigation of her, there is an air of desperateness in what he says, as of a man fighting at the last ditch. While he speaks, he is aware that he has just committed an irremediable error —a fact he eventually puts into words—and he hurries on as though he has no time to waste. As he talks, all his hatred for Claudius, all the poison engendered in him by her marriage, begins to spill out. The fury of his words momentarily forces Gertrude to confront herself. Seeing that his attack is making some impression on her ("O Hamlet, speak no more!"), he renews his furious denunciation of Claudius as a pickpocket who stole the unguarded crown. Hamlet is at the apex of his rage when the Ghost appears.

Usually it has been assumed that the Ghost's purpose is to spur Hamlet out of his delay. With a procrastination theory in mind, a hasty reading of Hamlet's lines would seem to lend weight to such an interpretation:

* In the Olivier movie the court, more interested in watching Claudius than the play, seemed to understand the King's guilt too. The courtiers became infected with Claudius' fright, and general pandemonium ensued. To complete the riot, Hamlet seized a torch and scared the entire assemblage out of the chamber.

> Do you not come your tardy son to chide,
> That lapsed in time and passion, lets go by
> The important acting of your dread command?

But we have seen no procrastination, no delay—and now that the play is much more than half over it is too late to look for it. When Hamlet accuses himself as "lapsed in time and passion" he is giving two reasons why he has failed to carry out the Ghost's "dread command":

1. Circumstance ("time") * has made it difficult to bring Claudius to justice, the conditions with which he has had to cope having impeded honorable vengeance;

2. His having allowed *passion* to take his reason prisoner, when he rashly killed Polonius, has thwarted his cause and canceled all the gains made on this very night.

The Ghost's answer is in but two lines:

> this visitation
> Is but to whet thy almost blunted purpose—

* In Shakespeare *time* often means "circumstance," as Wilson, oddly enough, has pointed out.[96] E.g.,

> I know love is begun by time
> *Hamlet*, IV, vii, 112;

> The truth you speak doth lack some gentleness
> And time to speak it in.
> *Tempest*, II, i, 137–8;

> O time most accurst,
> 'Mongst all foes that a friend should be the worst!
> *The Two Gentlemen of Verona*, V, iv, 71–2;

> We shall write to you,
> As time and our concernings shall importune.
> *Measure for Measure*, I, i, 56–7.

And *lapsed* is used by Shakespeare to mean "arrested":

> only myself stood out;
> For which, if I be lapsed in this place,
> I shall pay dear.
> *Twelfth Night*, III, iii, 35–7.

This is, apparently, the only other time Shakespeare uses the word.

words which, if read carelessly, would seem (and are so construed) to reprove Hamlet for causeless delay. But viewing them—as commentators have never viewed them—with an eye to the image the poet had in mind, they mean exactly the opposite of the accepted notion. Hamlet's purpose has become "almost blunted." The figure is of a sword or blade. How do our knives become blunted? From too little or too much use? Certainly, as every housewife could tell, from overuse. The Ghost accuses Hamlet not of having done too little but of having done far too much. He is referring not to his son's mental attitude, but specifically to the murder of Polonius—an act which, by excessive use of his sword, has blunted the edge of Hamlet's revenge. To recapitulate: Hamlet asks, Do you come to chide me because I have allowed my emotions to put fetters on my revenge? The Ghost replies, Yes, you have dulled the blade of vengeance by your thoughtless use of your sword.

There remains the fundamental question as to why Shakespeare caused the Ghost to appear at this particular juncture. If his purpose was, as is universally assumed, to have the Ghost jog Hamlet into action after unreasonable delay, why just at this time? Why in Gertrude's chamber, since the Ghost chooses not to be seen or heard by her? Obviously there must be some other reason, and if we remember that this is a play it is not hard to find. After the folly of killing Polonius, Hamlet was driven into desperation by that error —as his lines eloquently show—that desperation expressing itself in mounting violence against his mother. Earlier tonight he has vowed to speak daggers to her but to use none—vowed it because he was well aware how easy it would be to use them—but after the murder of the old man he approaches steadily to the brink of new folly and violence. At the apex of Hamlet's fury, as we have said, the Ghost *intervenes* to warn Hamlet and to calm him. He has permitted himself enough violence in this room, and it is of this that the Ghost has reminded him. In another moment might he not have done violence to Gertrude too? The rest of the Ghost's brief speech (his only one in this scene) is intended to pacify the overwrought Prince, and bring him to deal more reasonably with the Queen:

> But, look, amazement on thy mother sits.
> O, step between her and her fighting soul.

> Conceit * in weakest bodies strongest works.
> Speak to her, Hamlet.

Nothing in the play is more touching than the loving concern for this unworthy woman which the Ghost has carried even beyond the grave. Ironically, even with his superterrestrial wisdom, the spirit knows little about Gertrude. She is indeed in a fit of amazement, but not (as the Ghost supposes) because of contrition over her past guilt.

Having decided that Hamlet is mad when he, at his father's behest, speaks his first gentle words to her,

> How is it with you, lady?

she pityingly asks him,

> Alas, how is 't with *you*
> That you do bend your eye on vacancy
> And with the incorporal air do hold discourse?

In anguish, as yet unaware that she neither beholds nor hears his father, Hamlet points out to her that pale form, whose very looks and cause would be enough to make stones capable of feeling for him. And to the Ghost he cries to cease bending his gaze on him lest pity for his father

> convert
> My stern effects; then what I have to do
> Will want *true color;* tears perchance for blood.

These lines have never been correctly explained, perhaps for the reason that it has been forgotten that the word *color* in Shakespeare's day (and for two centuries earlier) meant "allegeable ground or reason." [97] It was used in that sense earlier in the same act by Polonius, in talking to Ophelia, as he gives her the prayer book (III, i, 45):

> That show of such an exercise may color
> Your loneliness.

Such is its meaning when Cleopatra upbraids Antony:

* imagination.

> Nay, pray you, seek no color for your going,
> But bid farewell and go.
> *Antony and Cleopatra*, I, iii, 32–3

What Hamlet is saying to the Ghost is: Pity for you could easily turn aside the sternness of all I yet must do—I've but to look at you to cast all caution to the winds again, and kill your wicked brother without further ado—then such a premature act would lack the grounds by which I could justify it ("want true color")—and there would be many tears to shed thereafter for the blood that recklessly I should spill.

Hamlet now tries to make his mother see the Ghost as it steals away—but she can see no apparition.*

* There is on (what claims to be) record a statement of what Shakespeare thinks of people like her! A quite amazing, though not at all fascinating, book, *Shakespeare's Revelations* by "Shakespeare's Spirit, through the Medium of his Pen, Sarah Taylor Shattford" (The Torch Press, New York, 1919). The foreword to this compendium, signed:

> SHAKESPEARE in Spirit
> Through my treasured clairaudient, Sarah; the only medium through whom I, as spirit, have worked at words.
> Dictated by the spirit August 14th, 1919

informs us that as regards the reviler of spiritualistic mediums, Shakespeare wishes "here for the rest of time . . . to brand the culprit who defames, underestimates the instrument through which his work is accomplished . . . Avaunt dissembler." (The last phrase bespeaks the author of *Macbeth!*) Among all sorts of things the volume contains a series of maxims, which might have been mouthed by some half-witted cousin of Lear's Fool: "Pigs and sows have no need of gloves." "Poke a hornet's nest if you want to be stung." "The future is just ahead. Today was yesterday. Tomorrow will soon be today" (pp. 12–23). If Shakespeare's prose seems to have undergone an alteration "on the other side," no less can be said of his verse. He seems to have been reading Wordsworth, though without much profit:

> "Fourteen summers have passed since I saw England.
> These have I counted on my two hands.
> Lest you should think I have no hands
> Being Shakespeare's shade, then let me say
> I have the SAME hands which were mine,
> Even those hands defects. [*sic*]" (p. 65)

ACT FOUR

What lies behind Ophelia's distributing
the flowers in her madness? (IV, v, 175 seq.)

It is a great pity that the world has abandoned the language of
the flowers (though some remnants of it have been kept alive by
the enterprise of florists), that charming old convention which attached a special meaning to each variety of bloom; the modern
audience in the theater is bound to miss most of the subtlety of this
scene, in which Ophelia distributes to Claudius, Gertrude, and
Laertes the imaginary blossoms which her disordered fancy conceives she has culled.

Lacking Shakespeare's direction, we cannot declare with absolute positiveness the identity of the person Ophelia addresses in
each of her phrases. But a knowledge of the meaning of each of the
flowers she has to offer and of the history of the King, Queen, and

---

He has, however, kept up with the times, as in his poem "Democracy":

> "A land all free whose people rule themselves;
> A Nation all united in one cause . . ." (p. 33)

Since some of these compositions were dictated in New York, we need
not be surprised at Shakespeare's "The Yankee's Prayer," in which a
World War I soldier laments having to kill a "Hun" in battle, and concludes:

> "If I must kill my brotherman
> For this world's liberty.
> I'll do my duty like a man;
> As every soldier must—
> Then, as we say in the U. S. A.:
> 'In God We Trust.'" (p. 358)

(There is something Elizabethan in this punctuation!) But to come back
to the association which reminded us of this volume, Gertrude's blindness to the Ghost, hearken to Shakespeare's spirit on "Ghosts":

> "The wraith of death men speak of sneeringly,—
> Recalling in a joke its sight or name;
> But when they find these ghosts are just as they,
> They'll ponder long the way through which they came."

(p. 35)

Laertes, makes it possible to be fairly accurate. To Laertes she gives rosemary (for remembrances) and pansies (for thoughts—the name of the flower itself having come from the French pensée, "thought"). To Claudius she offers fennel (for flatterers), columbine (for cuckoldry, because of its horn-like shape), and rue (for sorry memories). She sets aside some rue for herself too. To Gertrude too she gives rue, but with this qualification:

> O, you must wear *your* rue with a difference.

She also gives her a daisy (for dissemblers), and concludes that she would like to give her some violets too (for faithfulness) but there are none to give, since her father died.* In each case her choices are wonderfully appropriate. The mysterious and sudden death of their father has given Laertes occasion for much thought (pansies) and remembrance (rosemary). (Rosemary, by the way, was in use at Elizabethan funerals.) The King has flattered (fennel) many during the late King's lifetime—Gertrude, Polonius, and the courtiers; he has been an adulterer (columbine); for that reason and even more because he is a murderer, he has his fill of sorry memories (rue). Ophelia herself has sorry memories (rue) of Hamlet and her father. But those (rue) of the Queen are different from her own because Gertrude was not a victim but a sinner, and different from those of Claudius because Gertrude was innocent of murder. The Queen, as

---

* Naturally, the critics have had a merry time with this passage. Staunton: She confounds Laertes with Hamlet and therefore gives the rosemary to him.[98] Steevens: *You must wear your rue with a difference* refers "to the rules of heraldry, where the younger brothers of a family bear the same arms *with a difference*, or mark of distinction." [99] (Obviously Steevens thinks the remark addressed to Claudius, not Gertrude.) Dyce: "Does Ophelia mean that the daisy is herself?" [100] Kittredge: She may give the daisy to the King or Queen.[101] Wilson: She keeps the pansies for herself.[102]

No one seems to think, with us, that Ophelia first gives rue to the King, then sets some aside for herself, and then offers the rest to the Queen. But the text, as will be seen, justifies our reading. We prefer, moreover, to think of her as addressing each of the three present in turn, one at a time—a more charming stage action than if she kept whirling around, back and forth, from one to the other.

an adulteress, was a dissembler (daisy) to her first husband. As for the violets of faithfulness, they withered when her father died; Hamlet's murder of Polonius, which has put an eternal bar between him and her, and his going away, have put an end to all the faithfulness the world held for her.

Does Ophelia recognize each of the three as she bestows her floral gifts? At the moment her clouded mind is clear enough as to whom she is addressing—else there were no possibility of the very pointedness of the flowers' meanings.

But the most interesting question of all has never been raised. How does it happen that Ophelia knows all these things—Claudius' treachery, his and Gertrude's adultery, and the murder itself? In the twentieth century, with our greater knowledge of psychological processes, we are in a better position than our predecessors to appreciate the depth of Shakespeare's insight. Ophelia's references to the past of Gertrude and Claudius seem to come from the darkest recesses within her, as from a hidden knowledge that she has never dared allow to pass her lips. We may well imagine that a girl permitted as few liberties as she has been would in Polonius's household be treated as though she were not there during the discussion of the world's affairs, her father and brother fully confident that what she heard was safe with her. She has heard talk of Gertrude's adultery, she has even overheard talk about the murder! If Polonius could know of that crime, he must have been somewhat a partner in it. It is this passage which satisfies us that Claudius was indebted to him in the murder of the late King.

As for Ophelia, what a glimpse we now have of the frustrated life of the poor girl—of all that she had heard and was not supposed to know—of all the terror and misery of her thoughts that she could never express! If we were impatient with her earlier, we can only have the greatest pity for her now.

ACT FIVE

*Why did Shakespeare introduce
the gravediggers into his play?*

The roles of the two gravediggers were enacted by two clowns in Shakespeare's company. The public liked to have clowns in plays, and it is only too obvious to observe that here they are being used for comic relief. All of which is true and well known. But it does not explain why Shakespeare waited until the last act to bring the clowns in.*

His reason, we believe, was predominantly an esthetic one. For the first three acts of the tragedy the tone of this play has been achieved through an interweaving of the tragic and the comic. The comic has been of two kinds: the intellectual, witty toying with words and ideas of Hamlet; and the broadly humorous befuddled meddling and slow-wittedness of Polonius. With the death of Polonius the source of the latter kind of comedy has been removed from the play. In the hurry of the brief fourth act, with its rapid succession of scenes, there was no room or need for broader comic effects. But now Shakespeare is faced with the esthetic problem of maintaining the tone established everywhere else in the play.

The problem is perhaps more clearly seen with reference to painting. No skilled painter would be content to paint the portrait of a lady in which his subject wore a ruby brooch upon her dress and allow that small area of red to be the only one in his picture. Such a solitary patch of vivid color would be enough to ruin any canvas. To bring the brooch into tone with the rest of the work, he would possibly give hints of its color in various places on her robe, and would almost certainly blend ruby-red into the background of the picture.

So Shakespeare, having affirmed the broadly comic as part of the tone of his play, must find new sources for it now that Polonius

* On a rainy night the reader might be diverted by a perusal of N. J. Symons's psychoanalytical interpretation of the graveyard scene, in which all references are given specifically sexual meanings. It is not possible to quote extensively from this engaging monograph, as one is tempted to do, because book publishers do not appear to allow themselves the license of vocabulary accorded the psychoanalytical journals. But to give some idea of this exegesis, suffice it to report that according to it: the "digging" is a sexual symbol; the first skull is symbolic for Gertrude; the first and all the other skulls also are symbolic for Hamlet's father; Hamlet himself is the "real gravedigger" (in a sexually symbolic sense); Ophelia is identified in Hamlet's unconscious with his mother because of his "repressed thought that both women were 'bitches,'" and in *my Lady Worm* Hamlet schizophrenically "equates Gertrude-Ophelia as 'worm.'" [103]

cannot supply it. And for his fifth act he invents a new source for each of its two scenes: in the first we have the gravediggers, in the next the absurd Osric. Thus the play will continue to its conclusion without any dilution of the established tone.

His solution of the problem is admirable beyond praise. With his incomparable power for making many virtues out of one necessity, he not only maintains the tone he has set, but also contrives to vary the broad comic effect itself. Polonius, the gravediggers, and Osric is each a species of clown in his own right; but there is a wide range of difference in their clownishness. In the case of the gravediggers, like the drunken porter in *Macbeth* and the Fool in *Lear*, they deepen the tragic effect. We laugh at their idiocies, but as we laugh a chill goes up and down our spines, and our sense of horror is augmented. While we are diverted at their stupidities, we are aghast that they can be so vulgarly callous to the awful solemnity of death, that they can jest in its presence, that anyone can sing a silly ditty while he is going about such work.

But it is Horatio, with his omnipresent good sense, who reminds us that, since we cannot dispense with gravediggers, we cannot demand that they be squeamish about their employment:

> Custom hath made it in him a property of easiness.
>
> V, i, 75

How should the scene of the fencing match be staged?

This is a matter of considerable moment. Were the King not to be impeded by the table before him and his distance from the fencers, Gertrude's life need not be forfeit. In the Elizabethan theater, the King and Queen as they took their places in all likelihood sat upon their thrones in the inner stage, and before them would have stood a table upon which the stoups of wine were set. (The inner stage was the only part of the stage that could be curtained off; consequently it was only there, while the curtains were closed, that thrones or any furniture could be prepared for an ensuing scene.) The match itself took place on the stage proper. Before the match begins, Hamlet handsomely apologizes to Laertes before the whole court (V, ii, 237 seq.). Who but a man with the blood of Polonius flowing in his veins could resist the honorableness of amends like these:

> Let my disclaiming from a purposed evil
> Free me so far in your most generous thoughts,
> That I have shot mine arrow o'er the house
> And hurt my brother.

—and then and there renounce his vile plot against the other's life? But Laertes evades a direct answer. Osric, in charge of the foils, begins to distribute them. He must surely have been instructed to make certain that Laertes procures the envenomed, sharpened rapier. To help him at the moment of choice, Claudius deliberately distracts Hamlet's attention from the proceedings by engaging him in conversation:

> KING.   Cousin Hamlet,
>   You know the wager?
> HAM.   Very well, my lord.
>   Your Grace hath laid the odds o' the weaker side.

(Here again Hamlet is speaking with double meaning. The King is backing him in the match, and on the surface Hamlet means to imply that theirs is the weaker side. But in his other meaning, he and the King form opposing sides. Thinking of his coming vengeance, he insinuates—not at all referring to the match—that Claudius' side, which the King imagines must remain triumphant, will soon be seen the weaker, and Hamlet's the stronger. Hamlet is so well pleased to exercise his wit in this private quibble that he pays scant attention to the choice of rapiers.)

It needs only Osric's eye to lead Laertes to the choice of the deadly weapon. Hamlet, apparently, picks the first rapier to hand. Thus at a most critical minute Hamlet is betrayed by the same heedlessness which caused him to kill Polonius. Under normal conditions no fencer would think of examining all the foils to be sure none of them is deadly; but these are not normal conditions. It is catastrophic that Hamlet can have forgot it was Claudius who arranged the match. Claudius announces that to honor his nephew he will throw a fine pearl ("an union") into the wine cup. He drinks to Hamlet's health. The match begins. In the first bout Hamlet scores a hit. Seeing his nephew doing too well, Claudius wastes no time in slipping the poison into the wine, and sending the goblet down to Hamlet. The tension of this scene is wonderful. Hamlet puts off the cup-bearer with the remark that he wishes first to play the next bout. He scores another hit. The Queen, delighted at his prowess, quits her place in the inner stage to play again the loving mother—this time fatally. She comes to him and affectionately wipes the perspiration from his brow. Then, excited at what appear signs of reciprocated affection in him, she takes the drink from the servant standing by. Claudius cries:

> Gertrude, do not drink!

He dares say no more, and she is too far from him to be intercepted. His impulse must be to clear the space between them and seize the goblet—but that would expose him. There is nothing he can do in that flash of time. His machinations have turned against him and rob him of the possession he prizes most, his wife. She insists upon drinking, and then, to our consternation, she offers the cup to Hamlet. He says

> I dare not drink yet, madam; by and by.

and we breathe with relief.

Laertes realizes that now there is no time to expend, for the Queen must soon show the effects of the poison. Hamlet has noticed that Laertes has been fencing halfheartedly:

> Come, for the third, Laertes; you but dally.

Laertes puts forth his best effort and wounds Hamlet.

The last minutes of the match have elicited a variety of comment and exposition. Samuel Johnson's remark is astonishing: "The exchange of weapons is rather an expedient of necessity than a stroke of art"; [104] from which we can only conclude that in Garrick's day the interchange of weapons between Hamlet and Laertes was made to appear an accident—in defiance of common sense and dramatic values. (It is agreeable to report that we have not always seen the business directed that way.) The direction of the First Folio is not very explicit:

> *In scuffling, they change rapiers.*

The attempts of critics to make it more so vary from the quaint to the mad. Seymour thought that Hamlet, disarming Laertes "with a quick and strong parry," courteously hands his own weapon to Laertes while innocently picking up the latter's, and that Laertes has no choice but to accept it.[105] Adams' view is much the same: Hamlet's proffer of his own rapier is an example of the hero's "magnanimous behavior." [106] Tieck was particularly elaborate: The rapiers are kept on the table, according to him; the men choose their weapons, fight for a time, and then return them to the table, conversation occupying "the pause between rounds"; the King commissions Osric or some other hireling to change the position of the rapiers on the table, for Claudius is as anxious to see Laertes dead as he is to destroy his nephew.[107] Elze believed that the interchange of weapons is by accident; both fencers are too much excited to mark which weapon they seize.[108] Tom Taylor had Hamlet throw Laertes a foil "but, by mistake" retain "the one he had disarmed him of." [109] Marquard, finding supernatural influence everywhere in the play, suggests that the interchange is "the work of spirits." [110]

What all these gentlemen failed to see is that the exchange must be a *deliberate* one on Hamlet's part *because he has been wounded*. Had Laertes been fighting with the usual bated weapon, Hamlet could not have received a cut. Once he feels the sting of the wound, although unaware of the venom on the point of Laertes' rapier, he will in a second realize that he has been treacherously dealt with, and will see to it that he comes into possession of his opponent's rapier.

The conclusion of the match has been presented in many different ways, but we have never seen it done so convincingly as by John Barrymore. Hamlet and Laertes closed, separated; then Laertes, crying

Have at you now!

made a successful lunge and wounded Hamlet lightly on the breast. Hamlet was about to continue the contest, but paused. To his astonishment he felt himself cut. He put his hand to his breast, and it came away with blood upon it. He did not deem the wound more than trivial, but was precipitated into a rage by the realization of foul play, that Laertes' sword was not bated. Now with full fury he fought with one objective: to beat Laertes' rapier out of his grasp. Claudius, seeing all that had been occurring, tried to stop the match—but he could reach them no more than he could his wife. This is clearly what Shakespeare meant.

With maniacal energy Hamlet beat the foil from Laertes' hand. Laertes stooped to pick it up, but Hamlet quickly put his foot upon it, with elaborate irony offered Laertes his own foil—nobody but John Barrymore could do this to perfection!—and slowly and sardonically grasped the rapier Laertes had been using.

As the fight is renewed with savagery, the Queen falls, faint from the poison, and Hamlet runs Laertes through. Thus the latter dies very quickly, as much from the sword-thrust as from the poison, whereas Hamlet, having been but scratched, dies more slowly from the workings of the venom.

The first to go is the Queen, whose last words are a warning to Hamlet of the drink. Not knowing his minutes are numbered, the Prince leaps at once to the task of vengeance: calling for the doors to be locked, he cries:

> Treachery! Seek it out!

We suggest, but do not insist, that at this line Hamlet should reach into his doublet to extract the document ordering his death in England, as a prelude to revealing Claudius' guilt. (This would be, of course, a radical innovation—but we feel it may very well have been what Shakespeare meant.) But Laertes' next words prevent his proceeding, for he learns, and begins to feel, that his time is running out:

> Hamlet, thou art slain;
> No medicine in the world can do thee good,
> In thee there is not half an hour of life . . .
>
> 325 seq.

There is no time for Hamlet to unearth beginnings. Hearing that the point has been envenomed, Hamlet dashes to the King and stabs him with the deadly weapon.*

---

* To clear the air, one ought to list here some of the crimes perpetrated by the Olivier movie during the last minutes of the tragedy:

1. When Gertrude drinks of the wine she knows it to be poisoned;

REFERENCES IN CHAPTER V

1. G. L. Kittredge, *Hamlet* (Boston, 1939), p. xiii.
2. *Ibid.*, p. xiv.
3. *Ibid.*, p. xv.
4. *Ibid.*, p. xiv.
5. A. C. Bradley, *Shakespearean Tragedy* (London, 1929), p. 136.
6. J. Masefield, *William Shakespeare* (London, 1930), pp. 163-4.
7. H. Spencer, *The Art and Life of William Shakespeare* (New York, 1940), p. 315.
8. E. M. W. Tillyard, *Shakespeare's Problem Plays* (London, 1950), pp. 146-7.
9. A. C. Bradley, *op. cit.*, p. 135.
10. G. L. Kittredge, *op. cit.*, p. xv.
11. J. D. Wilson, *What Happens in Hamlet* (New York, 1936), p. 246.
12. H. H. Furness, *Hamlet* (Philadelphia, 1918), Vol. I, p. 281.
13. *Ibid.*, p. 283.
14. *Ibid.*, p. 281
15. J. Q. Adams, *Hamlet* (Boston, 1929), p. 275.
16. J. D. Wilson, *op. cit.*, p. 139.
17. *Ibid.*, p. 138.
18. A. C. Bradley, *op. cit.*, p. 136.

---

she calls Hamlet's attention to her drinking so he may observe the consequences; her death by suicide is an act of self-sacrifice to save her son from the envenomed goblet.

2. At Hamlet's line, *Treachery! Seek it out*—delivered by Mr. Olivier as *"Seek it ou-ou-out!"*—the hero rushes up a staircase to a balcony overlooking the scene, and jumps therefrom in fine Fairbanks style to stab the King. (It is recorded that in filming this scene, the Claudius insisted on having a stand-in for this moment. A professional strong man was fitted into the King's robes. But "even strong men have their limits; this one was knocked unconscious and lost two teeth."[111])

3. The important line, *Treason! treason!* is omitted.

4. Horatio makes no attempt to die too.

5. There is no Fortinbras. His concluding speech is given to Horatio.

6. At the very end, there is a long procession down steps, then up, up, interminably up; Hamlet's corpse is carried past the Queen's vacant bed (subtle!), then further up, to the top of the battlements. Why? Are we to conclude that Hamlet's body will presently be hurled fathoms below onto the rocks bordering the sea?

19. S. F. Johnson, "The Regeneration of Hamlet" in *Shakespeare Quarterly* III (July, 1952), p. 192.
20. *Ibid.*, p. 199.
21. *Ibid.*, p. 203.
22. *Ibid.*, p. 205.
23. *Ibid.*, p. 204.
24. *Ibid.*, p. 206.
25. *Ibid.*
26. J. D. Wilson, *op. cit.*, p. 39.
27. *Ibid.*, p. 43.
28. J. Q. Adams, *op. cit.*, p. 184.
29. J. D. Wilson, *op. cit.*, p. 34.
30. *Ibid.*, p. 30.
31. *Ibid.*, p. 34.
32. *Ibid.*, p. 31.
33. Vol. V, p. 598.
34. G. L. Kittredge, *op. cit.*, p. 139.
35. J. D. Wilson, *op. cit.*, p. 38.
36. L. P. Smith, *On Reading Shakespeare* (Chautauqua, 1933), p. 71.
37. Vol. V, p. 597.
38. *Encyclopedia Britannica* (11th Edition) (Cambridge, England, 1911), Vol. XVII, p. 756.
39. A. C. Bradley, *op. cit.*, pp. 155–6.
40. J. Q. Adams, *op. cit.*, pp. 222–3.
41. J. D. Wilson, *op. cit.*, p. 111.
42. G. W. Knight, *The Wheel of Fire* (London, 1930), p. 23.
43. G. L. Kittredge, *op. cit.*, p. 178.
44. C. Lamb, *Works* (London, 1870), Vol. III, p. 88.
45. H. H. Furness, *op. cit.*, p. 205.
46. A. C. Bradley, *op. cit.*, p. 132.
47. J. Q. Adams, *op. cit.*, p. 251.
48. J. D. Wilson, *op. cit.*, p. 190.
49. E.g., W. J. Birch, "Hamlet III, i, 59" in *Notes and Queries*, Sept. 12, 1885.

   J. B. Wilmhurst, "Hamlet III, i, 59" in *Notes and Queries*, Nov. 28, 1885.
50. H. H. Furness, *op. cit.*, p. 207.
51. *Ibid.*
52. *Ibid.*
53. *Ibid.*

54. Pourquoi Pas, "Dickens' Emendation in 'Hamlet' III, i, 58" in *Notes and Queries*, July 29, 1911.

55. H. H. Furness, *op. cit.*, p. 208.

56. E.g., F. J. Furnivall, "The End of Hamlet's 'sea of troubles'" in *Academy* XXXV (May 25, 1889), p. 360.

57. H. H. Furness, *op. cit.*, p. 205.

58. J. M. Murry, *Shakespeare* (New York, 1936), p. 202.

59. E.g., J. M. Street, "A New Hamlet Query" in *Poet Lore* XX (1909), pp. 468–78.

   C. M. Street, "To be or not to be" in *Poet Lore* XXV (1914), pp. 461–72.

60. J. D. Wilson, *op. cit.*, p. 190.

61. E. Dowden, *Hamlet* (London, 1928), p. 99.

62. I. T. Richards, "The Meaning of Hamlet's Soliloquy" in *Publications of the Modern Language Association* XLVIII (Sept., 1933), pp. 741–66.

63. S. de Madariaga, *On Hamlet* (London, 1948), p. 63.

64. B. Joseph, *Conscience and the King* (London, 1953), p. 114.

65. H. H. Furness, *op. cit.*, p. 213.

66. *Ibid.*

67. *Idem*, p. 214.

68. J. D. Wilson, *op. cit.*, p. 192.

69. B. Joseph, *op. cit.*, p. 116.

70. S. T. Coleridge, *Essays and Lectures on Shakespeare* (London, 1907), p. 150.

71. J. D. Wilson, *op. cit.*, p. 192.

72. H. H. Furness, *op. cit.*, p. 215.

73. (1901) Vol. V, p. 4047.

74. G. L. Kittredge, *op. cit.*, p. 211.

75. S. de Madariaga, *op. cit.*, p. 42.

76. *Idem*, p. 47.

77. J. Q. Adams, *op. cit.*, p. 254.

78. J. D. Wilson, *op. cit.*, p. 193.

79. Vol. VI, p. 264.

80. *Ibid.*

81. J. Q. Adams, *op. cit.*, pp. 238–9, 258.

82. J. D. Wilson, *op. cit.*, p. 131.

83. G. L. Kittredge, *op. cit.*, p. 220.

84. J. D. Wilson, *op. cit.*, p. 198.

85. H. H. Furness, *op. cit.*, p. 236.

86. A. Gide, *Hamlet* (New York, 1945), p. 141.
87. J. D. Wilson, *loc. cit.*
88. *Oxford English Dictionary*, Vol. V, p. 23.
89. H. H. Furness, *op. cit.*, p. 236.
90. G. L. Kittredge, *op. cit.*, p. 220.
91. J. D. Wilson, *op. cit.*, p. 169.
92. W. W. Greg, "A Critical Mousetrap," in *A Book of Homage to Shakespeare* (ed. by I. Gollancz) (Oxford, 1916), pp. 179–80.
93. J. D. Wilson, "The Parallel Plots in 'Hamlet' " in *Modern Language Review* XIII (1918), pp. 129–56.
94. H. D. Gray, "The Dumb-Show in 'Hamlet' " in *Modern Philology* XVII (1919), pp. 51–4.
95. W. J. Lawrence, "The Dumb-Show in 'Hamlet' " in *Life and Letters* V (Nov., 1930), pp. 330–40.
96. J. D. Wilson, *Hamlet* (Cambridge, England, 1936), pp. 213–14.
97. *Oxford English Dictionary*, Vol. II, p. 638.
98. H. H. Furness, *op. cit.*, p. 346.
99. *Ibid.*, p. 348.
100. *Ibid.*, p. 349.
101. G. L. Kittredge, *op. cit.*, p. 264.
102. J. D. Wilson, *Hamlet* (Cambridge, England, 1936), p. 226.
103. N. J. Symons, "The Graveyard Scene in 'Hamlet' " in *The International Journal of Psychoanalysis* IX (Jan., 1928), pp. 96–119.
104. H. H. Furness, *op. cit.*, Vol. II, p. 146.
105. H. H. Furness, *op. cit.*, Vol. I, p. 448.
106. J. Q. Adams, *op. cit.*, pp. 329–30.
107. H. H. Furness, *loc. cit.*
108. *Ibid.*
109. *Ibid.*
110. *Ibid.*, Vol. II, p. 292.
111. F. Barker, *The Oliviers* (Philadelphia, 1953), p. 309.

OFF WITH THY MASK! SWEET SINNER OF THE NORTH; THESE
MASKS ARE FOILS TO GOOD FACES, AND TO BAD ONES THEY
ARE LIKE NEW SATIN OUTSIDES TO LOUSY LININGS.
Dekker and Webster, *Northward Ho!*, V, i

VI *Dramatis Personae: Sounding Through Their Masks*

THUS FAR we have examined the play, emphasizing plot
and action, without imposing upon our analysis preconceived interpretations of character. Knowing what we now know, we can at
last safely turn to the persons of the drama.

PRINCE HAMLET

We have a rough idea of the hero's tragic flaw. Through a consideration of the plot and action we know what he is not, and more
than a little of what he is. If we refuse to wander afield from the
play, it shall not be difficult to describe Hamlet as Shakespeare
created him.

We already know, for instance, that so far from being a shrink-
ing violet or a creature of meditation who acts only in his imagination, he is an extraordinarily active man, a man who finds it easy to
act—as witness: his following the Ghost despite his friends' admonitions, his immediately conceiving the plan for the Mouse-trap on
the first possible occasion, his effective presentation of it, his killing
of Polonius, his unsealing the King's commission to England and
substituting of other orders, his boarding the pirate ship alone, his

winning over the pirates to his bidding, his grappling with Laertes in the grave, his eager acceptance of the challenge to fence, his violent attack on Laertes once he knows he has been tricked, his savage killing of Claudius. We also know that he is thought of not only as a scholar and courtier but as a soldier too, and that it is as a soldier that Fortinbras thinks of him.

Hamlet is thirty years of age. This fact, despite wrangling of scholars over it, is settled by a passage in the play; since it is the only reference to the matter in the entire work, Shakespeare's own words must be considered final and authoritative, and there can be no appeal from them. In the last act the gravedigger informs Hamlet that he took up his profession "on the very day that young Hamlet was born" (V, i, 160); a few lines further on, he adds that he has been working at it "man and boy, thirty years" (177). This poses an even simpler problem in arithmetic than the one we have already so triumphantly solved. (Why so many scholars, no youngsters themselves, are dismayed that Hamlet, who is young, can be thirty, is no less astonishing than shudder-causing to consider. As for Hamlet's being a student at the university, as he and Horatio have been when the play opens, there is nothing strange in that. Until fairly recently universities were not trade schools but institutions of learning. Scholars attended them not to acquire the means of earning a livelihood, nor even to become better citizens, but only to learn. Learning was then an end in itself—a concept now deemed medieval in educational circles (educational authorities do travel in circles)—and the immediate objective was the enrichment of the knowledge of the individual. Even today, of course, one finds many a grey-head among the student population of universities.)

What does Hamlet look like? Certainly he is a man of energetic figure, not at all the wispy creature we so often see upon the boards. It is too ridiculous that when he speaks of his "too too solid flesh" (I, ii, 129) the actor should have barely enough to keep him warm—that when the Queen fears he will lose the match with Laertes because "he's fat, and scant of breath," the Hamlet before us should look like the ghost of a ghost, whom a puff of wind could blow away. Not that we suggest that either of these lines proves the Prince to be corpulent—that would be absurd for a young tragic hero, equally absurd for a man we are to think of as a soldier, an expert fencer, the glass of fashion and the mold of form. A hero of normally athletic frame venting his disgust with the human race in a fit of revulsion against his mother's remarriage might well deem any flesh too solid; and a fencer out of practice and even a trifle heavier than he has been might be too fat and short of breath for the alertness required in the match. Nothing more is conveyed by the two passages.

Aside from the testimony of Hamlet's activities, we have another clue to his physique—a clue that in itself would not be decisive, but which may be considered proof of the justice of what has been said. Shakespeare, writing for his own troupe, knew in advance which actors would assume the various roles he was creating. He knew, while he was composing *Hamlet*, that Burbage, the great actor who impersonated many of Shakespeare's heroes, would enact the title role. It would be almost unavoidable that the dramatist should, as he evolved the character of Hamlet, have conceived him in the figure of Burbage. And from Burbage's portrait we know him to have been a man of powerful frame. And while in life we would grant, on intimate acquaintance with the person, that a man of powerful physique could actually be timid, or too sensitive, or too thoughtful, or too scrupulous, or complex-ridden, on the stage such qualities can best be communicated by a man delicate—even effeminate-looking—such a Hamlet as unfortunately we usually see. The audience looking at an energetic, muscular figure on the boards will naturally expect him to exhibit energetic, muscular qualities. And these Hamlet possesses.

To reject the idea of a too sensitive, too thoughtful, too scrupulous Hamlet, however, is not to deny him his extraordinary brilliance of intellect. It is a by-product of the specialization which has narrowed every phase of modern life that we take for granted that the hero of the football field avoids the library as he would a leper colony, and that the lover of books will never be found in the stadium. And, indeed, such is by and large our experience. But it was not always so. The Renaissance gentleman held quite as much as the ancients the doctrine of a sound mind in a sound body. His newly recaptured enthusiasm for the riches of human experience, after the long centuries during which only the life after death had been thought worthy of attention, prompted him to encompass as much of it as he could, and to exercise his faculties to their fullest. The depth and the breadth of Hamlet's character make him, far from the melancholic or the neurotic, almost the most magnificent embodiment in literature of the Renaissance ideal. Where shall be found a more splendid expression of this ideal than his rapturous phrasing of it:

> What a piece of work is a man! How noble in reason!
> How infinite in faculty! In form and moving how express
> and admirable! In action how like an angel! In apprehension how like a god! The beauty of the world! The paragon of animals!

> II, ii, 316 seq.,

where a completer tribute to the endless potentialities of man to make *this* life abundant and beautiful? It is the more significant of Hamlet's make-up that he delivers this apostrophe, from the deepest founts of his nature almost in despite of himself, at a moment of great bitterness; and if he adds:

> And yet, to me, what is this quintessence of dust? Man
> delights not me,

it is because he has just become convinced that two of his oldest friends have treacherously sold themselves to Claudius' employ.

When we insist that Hamlet is an athletic man of strong body, therefore, we no way imply that his frame is any more powerful than the intellect it houses. Hamlet, indeed, is probably the most admirably intellectual of the world's tragic heroes. His interests are everywhere; he is at home in the world of books, of sports, of music, of speculation, and on the battlefield,* to mention only a few spheres

---

* This universality is the only respect in which it is safe to say he mirrors his author. Among the endless facets of Shakespeare's genius, the limitlessness of his zest for knowing everything about life is one of the most compelling. It is everywhere stamped upon his very vocabulary. Although few of us seem aware of the fact, we all go about giving autobiographical hints to the world during the communications of the day. A man who perpetually uses the phrase "high-brow" labels himself; no person of culture would think of using it. A man who instinctively praises

of his knowledge. This universality is reflected in his uncommon respect and enthusiasm for words. He uses them with the genius and heady delight of a great poet. Whereas for Polonius words are traps in which he is always getting snared, impediments over which he is forever stumbling, for Hamlet they are important realities. He

---

some accomplishment with "That was a home run!" and describes a situation of his own with "There was I, sitting in the bleachers," is plainly a man who spends time in, or thinking about, the ball park. A man who speaks of others as "an Ajax in strength," "a Prometheus in endeavor," "a Thersites in gall," portrays himself a bookworm; the man who talks always of "fouling the scent," "clearing the jump," or "putting to ground," when men and women are his subject, is clearly a fox-hunter. Our crop of jitterbugs wore its mad distortions of the language as a banner. Just so we must conclude from Shakespeare's vocabulary that he must have been driven by the most powerful curiosity about every aspect of human experience to observe life more closely than anyone who has ever written.

The English language is more than three times larger in its vocabulary —that is to say, more than three times richer—than any other European tongue. If the cultivated reader, unaware of the statistics, were asked which writer in our language has drawn most copiously from that wealth, which author has the largest vocabulary, his answer would probably be—and it would be a shrewd one—Milton. But he would be incorrect. Milton employs, in truth, a vast vocabulary second only—to Shakespeare's, which is something like twice as great in extensiveness. This fact is truly astonishing, for the inexhaustible erudition and marvelously complex subtlety of Milton's diction would seem to grant the palm to him at first glance; Shakespeare only rarely uses such Milton-like phraseology as:

> the multitudinous seas incarnadine;

rather are lines like these far more characteristic of his style:

> We are such stuff
> As dreams are made on, and our little life
> Is rounded with a sleep.

His vocabulary is essentially simple. Its vastness is a product of the matchless variety of human endeavors from which he draws his images. What is most astonishing is the depth of knowledge he demonstrates in every human activity to which he refers. We ourselves are convinced, for example, that he knew music intimately, as a musician would know holds them up to the light to glory in their form and color. For him they are more than the vestment for ideas, they are also inspiring sources for new ideas. Language, in the wretched circumstances in which he finds himself, is as much comfort to him as music can be to the musician. And that is why, with no one but Horatio to talk to, he pours out the torrent of his soliloquies—in a flood and power such as Shakespeare has allowed no other of his tragic heroes.

It is this brilliance of his intellect which is responsible for much of the confusion of the commentaries. His mind works with lightning rapidity and hurries on from idea to idea. No one about him is anywhere near being his equal, and Horatio is the only one who always understands what he is talking about. Hamlet *always* speaks to the point, *always* talks sense—though expressing it too dazzlingly for his hearers' comprehension. Feeling himself surrounded only by enemies and those in the hire of his enemies, save for one friend and a few honest soldiers, he is too contemptuous of his foes, too indifferent of their opinion, to be plain and homely in his drift, too enamored of words to resist toying with them. It is thoroughly characteristic of him that he is forever using them with double meanings —one for himself, one for his interlocutor; he is not only unconcerned that he speaks beyond the comprehension of the court, he is in this way able to ease his inner torment by venting his scorn of a parcel of time-servers. The others, not following his meanings, find it all the more convenient to explain away their slowness of wit by deeming him mad. But it is surely inexcusable that the scholars, instead of deciphering what he says, should, like Polonius, interpret his flashing brilliance as madness, real or feigned. Hamlet is witty, ironic, sardonic throughout the play—even, at times, because of his speed, cryptic—but he never says anything that for all its brilliance is not perfectly rational and thoroughly logical and appropriate to the moment he says it. One needs the greatest alertness to keep up

---

it. Over the years students qualified by knowledge and experience to make such studies have written treatises for us which proved they were satisfied that Shakespeare was an expert sailor, an expert lawyer, an expert hunter, an expert gardener, an expert in real estate—and each made out an extremely convincing case. Shakespeare's universality, even more than Hamlet's, is almost incomprehensible, however, to the narrowness of the modern mind.

with him, it is true. But that fact renders him not abnormal, only superior to the normal.*

We have said that he is certainly not a professional philosopher, who discourses for the pleasure of it on abstract concepts—nothing could be more disastrous in drama than such a character given free rein!—but he is a highly philosophical man. That is to say that, like Portia, who in this respect is his counterpart and to a degree shares his basic philosophy, he never starts a train of speculation for its own sake, but rather, like her, is stimulated to speculation by events and experiences. Returning to her home after the trial, Portia observes a light in her house, remarks upon it, and follows it with a philosophical reflection, since that is her turn of mind:

> That light we see is burning in my hall.
> How far that little candle throws his beams!
> So shines a good deed in a naughty world.
>   V, i, 89 seq.

Thus, too, works Hamlet's mind—but with a difference. Because he is a man of powerful energies, a man indeed of violence when aroused, he does not pause to make the observation of the event, but begins with the speculation which the event arouses. You will find embedded in the turmoil of his soliloquies the occasion which causes the violence, but it is always the conclusion which comes first. Thus, in his first soliloquy, he opens with:

> O, that this too too solid flesh would melt,
> Thaw, and resolve itself into a dew!

and goes on to express his disgust with the world:

> How weary, stale, flat, and unprofitable,
> Seems to me all the uses of this world,

and only after that comes the event which occasions this revulsion: his mother's callously marrying so soon after his father's death:

> That it should come to this!
> But two months dead!
>   I, ii, 129 seq.

* One is aware, of course, that being superior to the norm would render him thoroughly abnormal in the view of some psychologists.

This is the pattern of every one of his soliloquies: first the idea, then the occasion for it. And he soliloquizes in this fashion because his is a volcanic nature, and because in his case the soliloquy is the release for his pent-up feelings. What is important to remember is that, as a philosophic man rather than a philosopher, he is always spurred to powerful reflection by a happening. If we wish to understand him and the play, we must, since this is drama, interpret his soliloquies not literally but in terms of the situations which occasion them.

Since his express conduct is the fundamental part of the tragedy, it is a gross superficiality to follow the lead of the commentators in looking for Hamlet's own philosophy of life in the bitter outporings of his soliloquies. Their dramatic function is to show us his inner ferment. But a man who loves life very much might be the first to say, "I'm sick of it. I wish I were dead," when suddenly someone very close and dear to him behaves in a way that makes all he thought of that individual an empty illusion. To know how Hamlet feels about life we must watch not what he says about it so much as what he does living it. Look at him in this way, and you will find him not melancholy, not complex-ridden, not pessimistic, not even disillusioned basically—but a healthy, vigorous man, much in love with life, who, given the slightest opportunity, is happy, cheerful, companionable, and kind.

It is not in his many bitter reflections that we are to look for his fundamental view of life, for those are always inspired by the disenchanting conduct of those closest to him, but rather in speeches such as his beautiful apostrophe to the nature of man. If we are to judge him under the circumstances when occasion allows him to react normally, according to the inclinations of his own temperament —that is, when he is dealing with people who give him no cause to distrust them, we shall find him remarkably high-minded and generous. Of all his utterances there is perhaps one that gives us the clearest index to how Hamlet would live, given decent surroundings: when he asks Polonius to see that the actors are "well bestowed" and "well used" (conceiving shrewdly that Polonius may be counted upon to treat them shabbily, as his inferiors), the old man responds:

> My lord, I will use them according to their desert,

and Hamlet retorts angrily:

> God's bodykins, man, better. Use every man after his
> desert, and who should scape whipping? Use them after
> your own honour and dignity. The less they deserve, the
> more merit is in your bounty.
>
> II, ii, 546 seq.

This is akin to the principles by which Portia lives; as she phrases
them:

> Though justice be thy plea, consider this,
> That in the course of justice none of us
> Should see salvation. We do pray for mercy,
> And that same prayer doth teach us all to render
> The deeds of mercy.
>
> IV, i, 198 seq.

But Portia is surrounded by men and women of goodness and kind-
ness, and she is free to allow her philosophy to blossom in all she says
and does. Hamlet, encircled by knaves, can be himself only with
comparatively few.

He not only takes unconcealed delight in the company of any
human being he has no reason to distrust—and no pessimist or disillusioned optimist would do this—but also puts such people at their
ease with ready grace, never stands on ceremony with them, never
behaves like the self-conscious prince addressing the commoner, is
indeed remarkably democratic in his dealings with them. These traits
are exhibited at once on his first encounter with Horatio:

> HAM. Horatio!—or I do forget myself.
> HOR. The same, my lord, and your poor servant ever.
> HAM. Sir, my *good friend. I'll change that name with
> you* [i.e., servant].
>
> I, ii, 161 seq.

Then he turns to Marcellus to say:

> I am *very* glad to see you.
> I, ii, 167

When, at the conclusion of the scene, Horatio, Marcellus, and Bernardo leave, it is with the formal "Our duty to your honour." But Hamlet, indebted to them for their act of friendship, corrects them:

> Your *love*, as mine to you.
>   I, ii, 254

His is the rare grace of the truly patrician mind which knows how to put others on the footing of equality without condescension. There are many such touches throughout the play. After his interview with the Ghost, when he has sworn Horatio and Marcellus to secrecy, they stand aside for him to precede them out; first he thanks them for their help with great sincerity:

> With all my love I do commend me to you.
> And what so poor a man as Hamlet is
> May do, to express his love and friending to you,
> God willing shall not lack.

and then refuses to allow them to attend him as inferiors:

> Let us go in together.
>   I, v, 184 seq.

Again, when Rosencrantz and Guildenstern first appear, his great pleasure at seeing them is openly expressed:

> My excellent good friends! How dost thou, Guildenstern? Oh Rosencrantz! Good lads, how do ye both?
>   II, ii, 228 seq.

His great capacity for enjoyment is manifested at their first mention of the Players; he is full of excited enthusiasm:

> He that plays the king shall be welcome . . .

and he plies his schoolfellows with questions about them:

> What players are they? . . .
> How chances it they travel? . . .
> Do they hold the same estimation they did . . . ?
>   II, ii, 332 seq.

And when the actors arrive his cordiality and joy are unfeigned:

> You're welcome, masters, welcome all. I am glad to see
> thee well. Welcome, good friends. O, my old friend! Thy
> face is valanced since I saw thee last; com'st thou to beard
> me in Denmark? What, my young lady and mistress!
> By'r lady, your ladyship is nearer heaven than when I
> saw you last . . .
>
> II, ii, 440 seq.

Hamlet has serious shortcomings, yet no hero has more endearing traits. Though, in his first fit of anger against Laertes' extravagant display of grief at Ophelia's grave, he fails to remember that
the young man has cause enough to resent him, when calm reflection reminds him of the facts Hamlet has the dignity and courage to
admit his fault to Horatio (V, ii, 75 seq.), and soon makes public
apology to Laertes before the entire Court:

> Give me your pardon, sir. I've done you wrong,
> But pardon't, as you are a gentleman.
>
> V, ii, 237–38

Our respect for his integrity is the greater because he makes this
beautiful amends to a man who is prepared to kill him by treachery.

His capacity for affection is profound and untainted by the
bitterness of his circumstances. His open cordiality to Marcellus,
Bernardo, and the actors proves how quickly he warms to those who
deal honorably with him. It is the conduct of Rosencrantz, Guildenstern, and Ophelia which drives him to suspect them. With her he is
most loath to be suspicious, indeed, and for all her stupidity and his
harsh words his love for her never alters. It is no bar to the love
he bears her and his desire to marry her that she is a commoner. The
commonplace Polonius and Laertes, who in Hamlet's place would
never be so indifferent to disparity of rank, can only think that
Hamlet's purposes must be dishonorable. But social differences are
of no consequence to the Prince, when he loves.

His friendship with Horatio, his one solace, is one of the great
beauties of the play—not to be missed because it is understated. As
is common with men, the two need few words to express it, and
Hamlet only once feels the urge to put it into words (III, ii, 59 seq.),
and then most eloquently. A look, a phrase, suffices for communicat-

ing the complete understanding between them; nor does Horatio hesitate gently to inform his friend when he believes him in the wrong. Though quiet, it is one of the great friendships of literature, and is itself a demonstration of Hamlet's capacities for the richest of lives.*

If Hamlet, therefore, pours out bitter words it is not because his nature is warped. On the contrary, his bitterness is only the expression of the frustration of his powers for delight, good health, activity, and affection—of his having to check, because of the situation he is in and the corruptibility of those he has loved best, his deepest impulses to love and to lead a full, wholesome life. It is the bitterness of the dynamic personality straining at the bonds imposed upon it, of the affectionate nature that must withhold its warmth, and instead of loving must distrust.

In terms of his situation how are we then to describe his tragic flaw, the *hamartia* which will hurl him to destruction? We have already identified it as a species of rashness,† and thus placed him in

---

* It is a matter for serious consideration whether the institution of friendship, the noblest of human relationships, is not now on its way out, its demise under Freudian auspices. As *The New Yorker* put it some years ago, things are getting so bad that two men no longer dare to go away together for a weekend without taking along a woman. In these naughty times, it already takes considerable courage to maintain the relationship. For some curious reason, anyone may hate any member of the same sex without incurring the suspicion of abnormality; it is pathological only to feel affection. Hamlet and Horatio must inevitably fall under the axe, when psychoanalysis gets around to them!

† To estimate how distant we are from the commentaries, let us quickly review critical opinion on Hamlet's tragic flaw. Stoll says he has none; he "has no tragic fault . . . —like Romeo's his fault is not in himself but in his stars." [1] Walley agrees: "He is a good man overthrown by evil through no particular fault of his own." [2] Spurgeon implies the same: the problem of the tragedy "is not the problem of an individual at all"; [3] Fergusson adopts this view. [4] (None of these explains how, lacking a hero with a tragic flaw, *Hamlet* qualifies as tragedy.) We have noted that Hamlet's tragic failing according to Goethe is extreme sensitivity; according to Coleridge and Schlegel, excessive intellectualization; Bradley, melancholia; Ulrici, moral scrupulosity; the psychoanalysts, a complex. (Klein and Werder found the root of the tragedy outside the hero's

the company of the classic tragic heroes of world literature—Clytemnestra, Oedipus, Electra, Creon, Phèdre, Mrs. Alving, Lady Dedlock, Brutus, Othello, Macbeth, Lear, Cleopatra, Jude the Obscure, Eustacia, Emma Bovary, and the Lost Lady—all great souls who fall through heedlessness, each in his own way.

By temperament nothing is easier for Hamlet than to act; his powerful nature propels him into action on the slightest challenge. But his problem is such as is hardest for a man so constituted: to wait, to be patient until he can prove that the Ghost spoke the truth, and, having settled that, to build his case against Claudius so that vengeance will be plainly an act of justice before the world. His own strong-mindedness makes him fully aware of the course he must choose, and he exhibits a degree of self-control remarkable for a man of his volcanic impulses. So far from being the hero who cannot whip himself into action, he is the tragic figure that *can* act readily, but *who must not*—until the moment be ripe. It is heartbreaking to witness the extent to which his mind *does* triumph over his energetic nature, the extent to which he *does* hold the impulse to act in leash; his self-control is truly heroic. But great as it is, it is not enough. Prescisely when he is beginning to reap the harvest of his hard-won patience, he forfeits everything by his unconsidered killing of the man behind the arras, Polonius—as it turns out. This act of sheer impulse has negated the value of all he has suffered and accomplished, and, moreover, has tendered his fate into the hands of his enemy.

Hamlet is well aware of his tragic rashness of temperament. His admiration for Horatio is based upon his friend's better balanced nature:

---

character, in his environing circumstances.) One critic finds Hamlet lacking all passion for action;[5] another, lacking all emotion.[6] Another accuses him of desiring to be too perfect;[7] a lady thinks the cause of his disaster his determination never to marry.[8] Masefield finds him too wise to act, since in Hamlet's world action would be fruitless.[9] Adams thinks "the young Prince possesses to a fatal extent *idealism regarding human nature*": his tragic fault is a "too easy faith in human nature."[10] And Campbell believes that because Hamlet is inconsolable for his losses, "his grief is of the sort that renders him dull, that effaces memory, that makes him guilty of the sin of sloth."[11]

> for thou hast been
> As one, in suffering all, that suffers nothing,
> A man that Fortune's buffets and rewards
> Hath ta'en with equal thanks; and blest are those
> *Whose blood and judgment are so well commingled*
> *That they are not a pipe for Fortune's finger*
> *To sound what stop she please. Give me that man*
> *That is not passion's slave,* and I will wear him
> In my heart's core . . .

III, ii, 70 seq.

How different from himself, whose blood is ever at war with his judgment! Nor does Hamlet need any other to apprize him of the fatality of his rash murder of the old man; he sees it at once—when the deed is irremediable. And, as he is being hurried off to England, he puts the blame where it is due—his failure to use his head when it was most important to do so:

> Sure, He that made us with such large discourse [i.e.,
>   *power of reasoning*],
> Looking before and after, gave us not
> That capability and god-like reason
> To fust in us unused.

IV, iv, 36 seq.

Yes, it was his duty to look before and after, and in truth he did so astonishingly well for such a man. But in his situation, any loss of reason, any impulsive act invites destruction.

Well, fate is kinder than he has title to expect. An impulse causes him to go through the papers of Guildenstern and Rosencrantz, and there he discovers the palpable proof of Claudius' criminality that he requires. In his account of the adventure to Horatio, completely forgetting that it was rashness which once ruined his cause and might easily have brought about his own death, he hymns rashness because this time it resulted in a benefit:

> Rashly,—
> And praised be rashness for it; let us know
> Our indiscretion sometimes serves us well
> When our deep plots do pall . . .

V, ii, 6 seq.

His experience should have taught him otherwise. Once again the stars are auspicious; he has a second, even a better chance to carry out his task, despite his tragic error. But as he speaks we tremble for the issue: what can be hoped for a man who is glad to be rash? He is, as usual, too ready

> to take arms against a sea of troubles.

And our fears are only too just. He accepts the offer to fence with Laertes. Rashly forgetting that Laertes has no reason to wish him well, and that the King, now his bitter enemy, who has already practised against his life, is the sponsor of the match, Hamlet omits inspecting the foils.

As we have said, no lover of the sport would inspect them. What tennis player examines the ball before it comes his way, to see that it is stuffed with hair, not with dynamite? Ah, but what tennis player accepts an invitation to the match from his deadliest foe? Or, if he did, would it not be wise of him to inspect the balls, unsportsmanlike though it be? Hamlet, in his excitement over the in-incriminating document in his possession, is heedless again, and forgets the resourcefulness of his adversary—this time, fatally. And so, though he presently executes his task, he does so at the needless cost of his life.

This rashness of his is, of course, allied to his best qualities—his strength, his courage, as made demonstrable on the many occasions when he leaps into action. It is allied, too, to his indifference to the esteem of the court, his willingness to let them think what they please of his sanity. It is a by-product, as are his wit, irony, and toying with words, of his excessive good health, his strong animal spirits.

But, as in life our defects are usually the other side of our best qualities, it is also allied to his worst faults. Because of it, Hamlet, so gracious and just, can be unpardonably unjust. Once he has decided that Guildenstern and Rosencrantz have been sent for by Claudius, he never pauses to ask whether they may not be acting out of true friendship to him, whether their motives may do them no discredit. It is enough for him that his intuitions tell him that they are guilty, and he sends them to a death they certainly have not merited—as Horatio sees may be the case—and he does so without any regrets. The same quickness of temper which makes his discourse scintillate, prompts him to rapid decisions that can be grossly unfair. Thus, too, we listen in amazement as, at Ophelia's grave, he exclaims indignantly to Laertes:

> Hear you, sir,
> What is the reason that you use me thus?
> I loved you ever.
>
> V, i, 311 seq.

Because he is aware of having always thought only well of Laertes, he can forget that he has killed the young man's father, and that in reason Laertes might hate him as much as he himself hates Claudius.

It is a character with grave faults.* But its beauties are so extensive that there is copious room even for such shortcomings. It is a character of great scope, and such defects as are in it are commensurate with the virtues.

Before leaving the Prince, we think it interesting to note that there are three young men in the play in a similar circumstance—and perhaps so placed by the dramatist that we might gauge Hamlet's character the more accurately—Hamlet, Laertes, and Fortinbras. Each has had a father killed and each assumes the filial duty of avenging that death. In circumstances Hamlet is closer to Laertes: their fathers have been murdered secretly, or in a manner that is kept from the world. Fortinbras' father was killed in open combat by the late king of Denmark; the world knows the manner of his death, and Fortinbras is free to seek revenge when he collects an army to march against Denmark (I, i, 80 seq.). In character, however, Hamlet is closer to Fortinbras, and would act with his directness and honor. But he is not free, like him, to engage upon his task. Not having the low traits of Laertes, Hamlet is unwilling to go about achieving vengeance in the former's contemptible manner. Polonius' son is so much concerned about what the world will think

---

* Some, among whom we do not wish to be numbered, would consider Hamlet's occasional adventures into ribaldry as a failing too. Mercutio is even looser of tongue than he, and no one has ever held it against him. The license with which he and Hamlet sometimes speak is harmless, more a symptom in a young man of excessive vitality than an index of licentious character.

of him if he does not at once kill someone—almost anyone—in return for his father's death, that he has not a thought for justice or honor. Unlike Hamlet, he can cry:

> Conscience and grace, to the profoundest pit!
> I dare damnation. To this point I stand,
> That both the worlds I give to negligence,
> Let come what comes; only I'll be revenged
> Most thoroughly for my father.
>
> IV, v, 132 seq.

Though not a saint, Hamlet, when he is conscious of what he is doing, will not give the next world to negligence, nor will he damn his immortal soul; he desires justice as well as vengeance. Laertes is first ready to kill Claudius; having no greater motive than personal satisfaction, he is easily quieted by the resourceful King, and won over to a plot against Hamlet. No method is too nefarious for him; he would be willing "to cut his throat" even "in the church"; and he is quick to second Claudius' plan of an unbated sword with the suggestion of envenoming its point. These are short cuts to achieving an eye for an eye, but they are not such as Hamlet's noble nature would ever permit him to employ. If he were as luckily placed as Fortinbras, he would behave as does the Norwegian Prince; being situated as Laertes is, it is impossible for him to deal treacherously like him. Thus Hamlet stands between the two, a nobler Fortinbras situated as Laertes is situated, and unwilling to behave as Laertes would behave.

KING CLAUDIUS

For the dramatic contest, a hero of such dimension calls for an opponent worthy of him, and in Claudius Shakespeare has equipped Hamlet with a by-no-means contemptible adversary.

It is true, as Professor Adams observes, that Hamlet describes him as a "satyr," a "bat," a "filthy moor," a clown, and a toad, but we are not to fall into the trap with this commentator by calling this "abundant evidence that he is unattractive, even repulsive." [12] So, too, Professor Bradley, on Hamlet's authority, says of Claudius that "he had a small nature. . . . He was a man of mean appearance—a mildewed ear, a toad, a bat; and he was also bloated by excess in drinking. People made mouths at him in contempt while his brother lived." [13] Such is indeed Hamlet's portrait of him, but we should be as unwise to take the Prince's word for the picture, as to believe Claudius when he describes Hamlet to Laertes as malicious. Hamlet, unconcerned with being fair to his two old friends, Rosencrantz and Guildenstern, will certainly be less so to the man he loathes. Mr. Masefield adds a touch unprovided by Hamlet when he says the King "fears intellect," [14] thus making him akin, for no reason, to Julius Caesar. This ugly, drunken butcher has become all too familiar on the stage, and there are good grounds for being sure that Shakespeare had no such person in mind when he created Claudius.

Gertrude, the last woman to run to adultery, was driven to it obviously by powerful physical attraction to her late husband's brother. To explain to the audience how such a conventional-minded woman could be compelled to indulge so inhibited a relationship, Claudius must be handsome, or at least attractive enough to make evident his sexual magnetism. A few critics have been fairer to him. Professor Jones wisely rejects Hamlet's prejudiced testimony, but he overstates the case by saying: "When Hamlet goes 'mad,' Claudius does everything that a reasonable and kindly man could be expected" to do.[15] Kindly towards Hamlet, Claudius certainly never feels. Professor Kittredge, much closer to Shakespeare's intention than most, on the other hand, goes much too far: "King Claudius is a superb figure. . . . His intellectual powers are of the highest order. He is eloquent . . . always and everywhere a model of royal dignity. . . . Intellectually, then, we must admit Claudius to as high a rank as Hamlet himself." [16] The truth is that there are few men in world drama whom we can admit intellectually to as high a rank as Hamlet.

But Claudius is a highly intelligent man, capable, attractive, and well-fitted to rule a kingdom. Professor Bradley, allowing a disparity between the King's physical and mental attributes, grudgingly admits: "He is not without respectable qualities. As a king he is courteous and never undignified; he performs his ceremonial duties efficiently; and he takes good care of the national interests." [17] We can put the case more strongly. Denmark is well-satisfied to have him on the throne. When Guildenstern says to him:

> We both obey,
> And here give up ourselves, in the full bent
> To lay our services freely at your feet,
> To be commanded.
>
> II, ii, 29 seq.

he is no more vilely selling his soul to the devil than are Voltimand and Cornelius, sent on a well-managed embassy to Norway, when they say:

> In that and all things will we show our duty.
>
> I, ii, 40

Such, with public reason enough, are the sentiments of the entire court. We have no cause to believe that as a monarch he is inferior to the late king. Hamlet's father was a brave warrior and a scholar; but Claudius by skillful diplomacy keeps his country out of war. He speaks with elegance, courtesy, and intelligence, and it is easy to see why he is well liked. Such a man, of course, makes Hamlet's situation the more desperate. A bloated clown would render his case easier.

Claudius, for all his ability, if not debased and ignoble, is not, however, a noble character. The root of his criminality seems to be a completely materialistic nature, rarely touched by spiritual values; his is the temperament most at home in politics. He has thirsted for the power and riches of this life, and has been undeterred by principle in achieving them in the directest way possible. Having dispatched his brother and married the Queen, he is quite anxious to live on good terms with Hamlet—not out of any kindliness towards him—but because if the Prince is willing to be affable, life will become completely agreeable for the King. He neither fears nor loves Hamlet, indeed must be well aware (intelligent as he is) of Hamlet's intense dislike of him; but a happy, well-contented stepson is all he needs to lay the disturbing memory of his brother's murder. It is for this reason that he perseveres in trying to win the Prince's good will and makes it clear that Hamlet is heir to the throne. Not that he particularly desires Hamlet's affection. But if Hamlet lives apparently at peace with his family, the world will the sooner forget the rapidity of Gertrude's remarriage and its incestuous nature.

Murderer though he is, he is not the worst of men. There *is* a kind of man who seems beyond all hope of salvation, the self-deceiving criminal, the hypocrite who is swift to lay the responsibility for his own evil at the door of others—such a blood-chilling creature as Shakespeare created in Angelo (in *Measure for Measure*). Claudius conceals very well from the world his criminality, but he plays no tricks with himself. When he is on his knees trying to pray to God for forgiveness, he knows full well that the miscreant cannot be forgiven while he clutches firm the prize for which he sinned. His terrible honesty at this moment wrenches our hearts with a twinge of compassion for him, and he somewhat merits it. He, at least, is the superior of those who fancy they can cheat Heaven by mouthing empty words of prayer, when in his misery he exclaims:

> But O, what form of prayer
> Can serve my turn? "Forgive me my foul murder"?
> That cannot be; since I am still possessed
> Of those effects for which I did the murder,
> My crown, mine own ambition, and my queen.
> May one be pardoned and retain the offence?
>   III, iii, 51 seq.

If he is not noble, there is a part of his life which partakes of nobility, and that is his love for his wife. It is very plain that he wished to marry Gertrude not for the crown alone but because of his love for her. He says as much to God, when he is baring his soul and its motives. It is the simple truth which, with the embarrassment of one man confessing his love of his wife to another, he delivers to Laertes, when the younger man asks him why, if Hamlet, as Claudius has said, "pursued" the King's life, Claudius took no measures against his stepson:

> The Queen his mother
> Lives almost by his looks; and for myself—
> My virtue or my plague, be it either which—
> She's so conjunctive to my life and soul,
> That, as the star moves not but in his sphere,
> I could not but by her.
>   IV, vii, 11 seq.

The testimony to the truth of this red-faced confession is everywhere in the play. You will notice that not once during the entire course of the drama does Claudius ever say a disparaging thing concerning Hamlet to the Queen. Moreover, Hamlet in their presence is untiring in his insults to the King; Claudius may bite his lip, but his answer to the Prince is always polite. He even pretends to construe the offending remark as a cordiality. A clever man, his motives, as with all of us, are mixed; his forbearance with Hamlet—publicly—can only redound to his credit and Hamlet's obloquy. But there is no doubt that his forced patience is also born of his desire to spare his Queen any hurt.

The priggish may point out that the tie between Claudius and Gertrude is a purely physical one. But aside from the question as to whether or not a purely physical tie exists anywhere except on the theoretic plane, even if such a love is not of the highest kind, it is love which is between them, and, Shakespeare plainly feels, such a love is better than no love at all. It certainly deserves being measured by its fruits, and Claudius' considerateness of Gertrude is the one truly elevated aspect of his character. He has spared her all participation in, all knowledge of her first husband's murder, and he continues sparing her by suppressing his growing hatred of Hamlet so that she need not be torn between her love for both of them. He definitely limits his own freedom of action against the Prince through his protectiveness of his wife, and for her sake bears the brunt of Hamlet's public derision—a difficult task for a man of his strong character.

Claudius, of course, unlike the others, at no time thinks Hamlet mad, though it is practicable for him to go along with the rumor. With the unquiet mind of the murderer, he interprets Hamlet's hostile conduct as indicating that the Prince may by some unimaginable means know more than he should. Claudius would give anything to be resolved on this point. Once the Mouse-trap reveals how much Hamlet does know, Claudius is quick to plan removing his enemy. And then his foe's own blunder gives him his perfect opportunity of ending the threat to his own security, and he at once seizes it.

QUEEN GERTRUDE

Shakespeare's portrait of the Queen is one of the most brilliant depictions in literature of the sentimentalist. Gertrude is a well-meaning, superficial woman of quick but shallow emotions. Her chief desire is to be happy and see everyone around her contented; like all sentimentalists she is touched by the distress of others but is quite unequal to the smallest of personal sacrifices that might be of help to them. Thus, she is so far superior to Polonius and Laertes, that she anticipates with pleasure Hamlet's marrying a "good girl" like Ophelia, even though she be a commoner; she is gentle and kind with the girl—until she is in trouble. At the news that Ophelia has become demented, Gertrude's first reaction is:

> I will not speak with her.

And when she is told the girl's "mood will needs be pitied," answers in self-protection:

> What would she have?
>   IV, v, 1 seq.

Gertrude does not wish to be unnerved by the sight of Ophelia's distress. Once Ophelia is safely dead, however, she can afford the luxury of tender rhetoric:

> Sweets to the sweet; farewell!
>   (*Scattering flowers*)
> I hoped thou shouldst have been my Hamlet's wife.
> I thought thy bride-bed to have decked, sweet maid,
> And not to have strewed thy grave.

Her love for her son is genuine enough, as far as it goes. She cannot understand why, with everyone else resigned to his father's death, he protracts his mourning—all of two months! She reminds him that "all that lives must die," that death is "common." When Hamlet bitterly throws the phrase back at her:

> Ay, madam, it is common,

she completely misses his savage irony, and asks, in her obvious-minded way:

> If it be,
> Why seems it so particular with thee?
>   I, ii, 72 seq.

If only Hamlet would be sensible, is her feeling—if only he would be pleasant to his new father and forget the old, how charming life could be!

She is a soft creature, and affectionate—when the cost is not too high—and would like to see Hamlet marry for her own sake as well as his. She is delighted that her husband has sent for Guildenstern and Rosencrantz on the pretense that they may cheer their old friend and "draw him on to pleasures." Her son's invitation to attend his play she welcomes as a symptom that he is recovering from sullenness, and she eagerly takes up the role of the indulgent mother.

One can imagine that she must have had her bad moments during her late husband's life whenever she had occasion to reflect on her infidelity to him; she is not the kind of woman who could be very happy in sin. But things always turn out for the best! Her husband luckily relieved her of a moral problem by dying, and she was able to marry her lover. It must have been with a sigh of thankfulness that she took on again the mantle of respectability. One can be sure that by the time the drama begins, she has quite forgotten her adultery, though it ended but two months earlier. This would explain her amazing conduct while the Mouse-trap is being presented. She watches it, personally unaffected, as she would watch any other mildly diverting entertainment, and Hamlet learns nothing about her guilt from her reactions. Knowing nothing of a murder, she naturally draws no analogy between the slayer of the little play and Claudius. But we should expect a woman of any depth to be startled by the close similarity to her own experience of that of the fickle Player Queen's. Gertrude fails to see herself reflected. How should this tale of adultery apply to her? The Player Queen is disloyal in her love, and she herself is a respectable married woman! She is so unmoved by the proceedings that Hamlet, foiled in his plan so far as she is concerned, is forced to ask during the performance:

Madam, how like you this play?

And with the calm of an impartial observer she answers:

> The lady protests too much, methinks.
>
>   III, ii, 239–40

She has the impenetrable hide of your true sentimentalist.

When the Mouse-trap has upset Claudius in some way she does not fathom, she intends giving her son a sorrowful lecture on his filial ungraciousness. Hamlet's violence, however, frightens her out of the dramatics she has planned. Then after the shock of Polonius' death, horrifying to her gentle nature, she is forced by Hamlet for a few brief moments to listen to his torrent of accusation, and the worst of all her experiences commences: she is face to face with the unbeautiful truth about herself. Nothing is less endurable than his relentlessly holding up the glass for her soul; and in terror she cries out:

> O, speak to me no more!
> These words like daggers enter in mine ears.
> No more, sweet Hamlet!
>
>   III, iv, 94–96

Suddenly the Ghost appears, and Hamlet holds discourse with what is apparently the vacant air, pointing out the figure that is invisible to her. Her terror ceases, and she murmurs:

> Alas, he's mad!
>   III, iv, 105

—and one can almost hear her adding silently, "Thank God!" He's mad, and everything that he has said is a product of his madness. Nothing he has charged her with was really true—the likeness of that depraved woman he has so powerfully delineated is no portrait of her. Those dreadful words of his were only the ravings of a lunatic. She can forget them now. Rather she can luxuriate in a mother's concern for her poor son and his ruined mind!

It is almost unbearably pathetic to see, as Hamlet proceeds in his efforts to wake her conscience, torturing himself the while, how deluded he is in thinking he is making the slightest impression on her. He does not suspect that she has already forgotten his bitter charges, is already deaf to his renewal of them.

> O Hamlet, thou hast cleft my heart in twain,
>
>   III, iv, 156

she weeps, and he imagines that her heart is broken to see how vile she has been. What she means, however, is that her mother-heart is cracked to witness how far gone is her poor son's mental sickness. As she wrings her hands over his plight, she has inwardly returned to her hitherto-undisturbed self-complacency.*

THE FAIR OPHELIA

Shakespeare's portrait of Ophelia is perhaps the most interesting depiction in world drama of a thoroughly uninteresting young woman. She has been compared with various of his other heroines, but actually he has drawn no one like her, except possibly Hero (of *Much Ado*), and even she has a few flashes of spirit. These two, alone among his women, resemble the type English heroine. The others are truly astounding in the modernity of their conception. One looks in vain for such flesh-and-blood creations as his in the whole range of the English novel (with the exception of the girls of Jane Austen and a very few of Dickens) up to the time of Meredith. How wishy-washy seem the traditional modest maidens to be found in the pages of Richardson, Fielding, Scott, and Dickens—a procession of heroines almost interchangeable—when measured with Juliet, Portia, Beatrice, Rosalind, Viola, Olivia, Isabella, Desdemona, Lady Macbeth, Cordelia, Helena, Cleopatra, Imogen, Hermione, Perdita, and Miranda, how vapid and colorless! No wonder that in exasperation with those English Patient Griseldas Thackeray created his little rogue of a Becky—and then fell victim to the tradition when he conceived his Amelia! Shakespeare's girls are real women, full of charm and warmth and intelligence, most of them witty and

* Though commentaries have been scant on Gertrude, she has had her share of critical distortions—all the way from the scholar who maintains she is a queenly woman who never committed adultery,[18] to the feminine admirer who is convinced that in the last scene she deliberately commits suicide, drinking of a cup she suspects to be poisoned in order to warn her son against drinking too.[19] This absurd notion was incorporated into Mr. Olivier's movie version, with what permanent damage to the play we can tell only when we know whether future productions will make it traditional, as they may. Gertrude, of course, had no way of knowing that the drink was envenomed.

gay too. Ophelia is the exception. She is the quiet, modest, submissive, spiritless fair creature dear to the heart of English fiction. Unhappily such girls do exist (though, luckily, in diminishing numbers —one of the few improvements of modern times); many parents have assiduously educated their girl-children to be that sort of "good" girl. And since they do exist, Shakespeare may very well have felt that he needed Ophelia to make his gallery of women complete. She is, moreover, the perfect foil for his hero, the perfect heroine for his story. Anyone less insipid would have dimmed the brightness of his hero and tempered the bitterness of the circumstances in which Hamlet is involved.

If you wish to convert a healthy child into Ophelia's kind of pliant creature without will, the approved method is to suppress every one of her normal impulses as soon as she manifests it, every symptom that she may be thinking independently of your direction. To make her good, as you define goodness, you render her incapable of expressing an emotion (beyond weeping, of course, which you will commend as proper to modesty), incapable of an original thought or motion. Your child, thus trained, will be thoroughly marketable in the marriage mart; you also ensure an uneventful life for her and a maddeningly dull one for her spouse.

In this technique of rearing such a maiden, Polonius has been past master—like all fathers who prefer libertines for sons and nuns for daughters. He has her completely bullied. She is accustomed to delivering up to him her most private thoughts. She allows him to intercept her mail without demurring—fancy what would occur if anyone dared tamper with letters addressed to Portia, Beatrice, or Isabella! But Ophelia cannot imagine rebelling or even objecting. She listens to his endless sermons—and when he becomes short-winded, her brother takes up where he left off. She listens to both with docility, and thinks them very knowing in the ways of the world. The one concern they have is that she keep her maidenhead intact until she is safely married; that is their (and how many others'!) conception of keeping a maid virtuous. They succeed. She always does as she is told, and follows her father's commands to the letter— at the price of her happiness. She has come to be utterly dependent on his management of her life. Without it she is lost. She never says a truer word than, when her father asks if she can be such a fool as to think Hamlet sincere in his honorable professions, her honest admission:

> I do not know, my lord, what I should think.
>
> I, iii, 104

That is her customary frame of mind. She has been taught to place no stock in her intuitions, to form no judgment of her own. Her heart tells her that Hamlet's love is true and honorable; but if her brother and father both assure her that it cannot be, she finds it safer to credit them.

It has been asked how so brilliant and vital a man as Hamlet could possibly love a girl as vapid as Ophelia. Ah! If one could answer that, one could also answer why in life A marries B, why X loves Y. Such disparities between men and women in love are only too common. Probably the last mystery science will ever solve is the cause of love.

About Ophelia commentary has been almost as lunatic as about her lover. Of course, most men have not really approved of such high-spirited and intellectual girls as Shakespeare usually created; Beatrice, for instance, has come in for a great deal of disparagement because of her blazing wit; and some critics have been appalled at the possibility of any man's marrying so irrepressible a woman. Ophelia, therefore, has had her particular devotees; it is to be feared that there are still too many insecure men who idealize her sort of nincompoop. Samuel Johnson speaks of her as "the beautiful, the harmless, and the pious," [20] censuring Hamlet for his treatment of her. In the nineteenth century she is described as "like an artless, gladsome, and spotless shepherdess. . . . The world . . . is not worthy of her." [21] The Germans, who prefer her type as excellent material for a worthy *hausfrau*, have adored her. One of them says that in her he sees "a gentle violet, a truthful, modest German girl, a completely Nordic woman's temperament—poor in words, shut up within herself, not knowing how to express with her lips her deep rich heart. She is akin to Cordelia and Desdemona. . . . She is thoroughly German, old German, in her family relationships." [22] There is little quarrel, then, as to the passivity of her character; the only difference would seem to be whether or not one can admire it. Few of her admirers, however, go so far as to count her losing her mind as another grace: "There is something very poetical in Ophelia's sharing her Hamlet's destiny,—even in the very form,— a mind diseased,—in which it has come upon him. Her pure and selfless love reflects even this state of her beloved; no cup is so bitter but that if it is poured out for him she will drink it with him. Nay, she, the gentle, unresisting woman, drains to the dregs that which his masculine hand can push aside (at least for a time) when he has but tasted it. United as their hearts were by love, this madness of Ophelia brings her closer * to Hamlet than any prosperity could have done." 23 Greater love than this hath no woman for her lover: that she become insane to keep him company!

It is rather around the matter of "Hamlet's treatment of Ophelia" that the discussion has raged. Nothing in the history of the criticism of this play astonishes more than that this should be a mysterious issue, for nothing is made plainer in the tragedy itself. Nevertheless, Professor Wilson perfectly reflects critical opinion when he says, "The attitude of Hamlet towards Ophelia is without doubt the greatest of all the puzzles in the play, greater even than that of the delay itself." 24 It is the part of the drama that most disturbed Professor Bradley, too, who found it impossible "to account for the disgusting and insulting grossness of his language to her," 25 and who says again, "I am unable to arrive at a conviction as to the meaning of some of his words and deeds, and I question whether from the mere text of the play a sure interpretation of them can be drawn"; 26 the conclusion forced upon this eminent scholar is that Hamlet's love for Ophelia "was not an absorbing passion." 27

The most common view, however, is that Hamlet has loved Ophelia sincerely, but that his mother's swift marriage after his father's death has poisoned his feelings towards the entire sex, and it is for this reason that Ophelia becomes, as Goethe describes her, "Forsaken, cast off, and despised." 28 Hartley Coleridge puts the case thus: "Hamlet loved Ophelia in his happy youth, when all his thoughts were fair and sweet as she. But his father's death, his

---

* Ophelia's madness must certainly have given demonic strength to their love if it could bring them closer—when we remember that during the period which witnessed her loss of mind and her death, he was away at sea.

mother's frailty, have wrought sad alteration in his soul, and made the very form of woman fearful and suspected. His best affections are blighted, and Ophelia's love, that young and tender flower, escapes not the general infection." [29] Such a view cooperates (as does that of the psychoanalysts, that "he rejects Ophelia" because of his Oedipus complex), of course, with a conception of Hamlet which we have already thrown into the discard: a Hamlet morbid, melancholy, and neurotic. It is based usually on his outburst, during his first soliloquy:

> Frailty, thy name is woman!
> I, ii, 146

But it will be noted that he does not say that Frailty's name is Ophelia; that is to say, it is of his mother he is thinking and speaking when he delivers that line. And there is no reason why a young man of wholesome mind who is properly disgusted with his mother's licentious conduct should transfer that disgust to his sweetheart without occasion.

Another widely accepted view is that Hamlet rejects Ophelia because he must give all his energies, all his thoughts, all his attention to the task of vengeance. A mid-nineteenth-century critic phrases it: "There could be no sterner resolve than to abandon every purpose of existence, that he might devote himself, unfettered, to his revenge; nor was ever resolution better observed. He breaks through his passion for Ophelia, and keeps it down, under the most trying circumstances, with such inflexible firmness, that an eloquent critic has seriously questioned whether his attachment was real." [30] Gervinus elaborates the conception by interpreting the "Get thee to a nunnery" scene as "the farewell of an unhappy heart to a connection broken by fate; it is the serious advice of a self-interested lover, who sends his beloved to a convent because he grudges her to another, and sees the path of his own future lie in hopeless darkness." [31] Sometimes Hamlet's "rejection of Ophelia" is put on a less self-conscious base; as Schlegel expresses it, "he is too much overwhelmed with his own sorrow to have any compassion to spare for others." [32]

However convincing such rejection may sound in the abstract, however conceivable on the part of an emotionally unbalanced man, it is perfect nonsense, in terms of human experience, to think it possible to a healthy young man. No normally constituted lover renounces love because he has a great problem to deal with. It is precisely in such crises that the male is most in need of a woman's affection; the greater the problem the greater will be his urge to rely upon the consolation of such affection. It is simply not human to think of Hamlet as giving up Ophelia because he must concentrate on avenging his father—and, moreover, nothing of the kind is said or demonstrated in the play.

Several critics have thought that Hamlet has seduced Ophelia,[33] and Tieck gives a peculiarly unpleasant version of that: "The poet has meant to intimate throughout the piece that the poor girl, in the ardor of her passion for the fair prince, has yielded all to him. The hints and warnings of Laertes come too late. . . . At the acting of the play before the court, Ophelia has to endure all sorts of coarseness from Hamlet before all the courtiers; he treats her without that respect which she appears to him to have long forfeited." [34] It is to be hoped that this piece of nineteenth-century morality will make the reader shudder, and think his own era not so bad after all.

Other odd explanations of the Hamlet-Ophelia relationship have been advanced. Quiller-Couch observes that in the old Hamlet story the prototype of Ophelia was a prostitute: Shakespeare altered her character to make her innocent, but made her act as though she were a loose woman.[35] (An extraordinary feat in drama!) Adams imagines that Hamlet thinks "Claudius has foul designs upon the innocence of Ophelia." [36] Almost the extremest of these positions is Wilson's: Hamlet "treats Ophelia like a prostitute" [37] because she agreed to trap him for Polonius and the King; this Wilson thinks the only solution to "the greatest of all puzzles in the play."

It has remained, however, for a Spanish critic to push this hectic view of the Hamlet-Ophelia relationship to the limits of incredibility. Madariaga, whose Hamlet is a monster of monomania, exclaims: "The idea that Hamlet could be in love with anybody but himself is incompatible with Hamlet's character [38] . . . Hamlet was at no time in love with Ophelia," [39] nor was she ever in love with Hamlet, the proof of her emotions being her "acquiescence in her father's designs." [40] Merely through the call of the flesh, Hamlet and Ophelia have "strayed into intimacy without much depth of love." [41] They are two sophisticates who have loaned each other the use of their bodies for mutual pleasure, and Ophelia has "been free enough with her favors" to the Prince, who by this time is largely bored with her.[42] (Had the play been a Restoration comedy, this interpretation might make some sense—provided, of course, that even in that period the dramatist had been someone other than Shakespeare.)

The only correct answer to the question as to why Hamlet rejects Ophelia is the same as the answer to the question as to why he procrastinates: *he doesn't*. We confess that to us "the greatest of all puzzles" about the play is how this particular question ever became a puzzle. Certainly Shakespeare could not have been clearer.

What happens is not that Hamlet rejects Ophelia—such a move would never occur to him—but that, as any young man would interpret her conduct, Ophelia rejects Hamlet. *Shakespeare devoted an entire scene* (I, iii), and several additional passages, in exposition of the fact. Nothing else develops in that scene but the departure of Laertes—a matter of no dramatic importance, which could have been managed by report or even taken for granted when Polonius later sends Reynaldo to spy on him. But Shakespeare uses the scene of Laertes' departure to further our comprehension of the rift to come between Hamlet and Ophelia. About to leave for foreign parts, Laertes lectures his timid sister, warning her that she must suspect Hamlet of evil designs upon her maidenhead. The pusillanimous Ophelia assures him quite sincerely:

> I shall the effect of this good lesson keep
> As watchman to my heart.   (45–6)

And she means it. There are never subtle shadings in the discourse of Ophelia: her simple speech is the expression of a simple mind. Though Laertes is no way gifted to understand either the heart or the head of a man like Hamlet, his sister is so habituated to being directed by her father and brother that she is at least willing to weigh his counsel. Now Polonius comes in to repeat the lecture. When Laertes has left, the old man turns upon her, and we are witness to the bullying process by which he has stamped all vitality out of her:

> I must tell you
> You do not understand yourself so clearly

> As it behoves my daughter and your honour.
> What is between you? Give me up the truth.   (95–8)

He laboriously seconds Laertes' certainty about Hamlet's wicked intentions, and pooh-poohs Hamlet's vows of love as well-tested traps to ensnare a green girl—as he knows from his own experience:

>   I do know,
> When the blood burns, how prodigal the soul
> Lends the tongue vows.   (115–17)

She, as ever, does not know what to think, and so Polonius makes up her mind for her. She is to have nothing more to do with Hamlet.

Being what she is, the spiritless girl faithfully obeys him. Two months later he is able to report to his monarchs that she has locked herself from Hamlet's "resort," admitted "no messengers," received "no tokens," and handed over to her father his letters, one of which he proceeds to read aloud, with critical asides, to Claudius and Gertrude (II, ii, 107 seq.).

No explanation given him, no communication answered, what is Hamlet to think of Ophelia but that she has found it suddenly expedient to break with him, at a time when he has no friends at court? He feels that she has renounced him when most he needs her love, that she is a time-server like her father, that she finds it advantageous to avoid him while he is surrounded by enemies. It is to be sure of this judgment that he forces his way into her room, as he must do if he is to see her at all. There, frightened by his abrupt entry, so unlike his normal courtly behavior, she is too much pulverized by her father's threats to explain to Hamlet why he has not seen her, why she has not been able to write to him. Because of Polonius' orders, she stands before him petrified into silence, and confused. Her confusion, naturally, certifies Hamlet's worst fears.

Then as ever, under her father's thumb, she allows herself to be used as a bait so that Polonius and the King may overhear what Hamlet may have to say to her. It is their first meeting in a long time, with the exception of his anguished storming of her room. This is the crisis of their relationship, and it is Ophelia's complete want of courage which makes the encounter catastrophic to both of them. The poor creature, trapped by Polonius' tyranny, hopes somehow that the gesture of forcing into Hamlet's hands his former gifts will cause him to understand what she knows not how to put into words without disobeying her father. She is the forlorn maiden waiting in her prison tower to be rescued by her fair knight, who does not even know she is there. Alas! such maidens, who cannot make clear their needs, are likely to wait forever for their rescuer.

Knowing her father is listening to all she says, what can she do in her impotence but weep bitterly, weep because her lover does not guess the heavy burden she bears, weep because she cannot tell him, weep because he does not contrive to rescue her from it? Most of Shakespeare's heroines would never have been so unreasonably obedient to their father as to find themselves in such an impasse. But all women expect the unintuitive male to understand without explanations—to know that a rejection is not necessarily a rejection, that a situation is nothing like what it appears to be. Having no clue to her two months' avoidance of him, despite his quick-wittedness, Hamlet can only conclude that she is playing a hypocritical game with him—at a court of hypocrites.

From this time on he naturally tries to kill his love for her, but he never succeeds in doing so. How deep his love remains, we witness at her funeral. It is truly ludicrous to have to consider the to-do raised by criticism over "the disgusting and insulting grossness of his language to her in the play scene." A few bawdy jests lightly tossed off (and mixed, it is true, with some withering sarcasms because of her having trapped him earlier that day, as he thinks)—partly the product of his excitement at the performance of "The Murder of Gonzago," partly an attempt to appear gay enough to disarm any possible suspicions of Claudius'—why should they be construed so heavily? Ophelia accepts them in the merry vein in which they are intended—that much may be said for her—and seems even pleased at Hamlet's sallies as signifying his recovery of high spirits. Though assuredly a "nice girl," if ever there was one, she understands his bawdry very well, and gives no token of being really offended with it. She reproves him almost with an embarrassed titter which shows that she is quite pleased with him—in a way that women often do at such moments. Moreover, the standards for decency were quite different in the days before Puritanism so much altered the English character. Many of Shakespeare's most exquisite heroines deliver themselves of ribaldries that would have made a Victorian damsel feel obliged to faint only to hear. Certainly no one would censure the morals of Portia or Beatrice because they own a robust sense of humor; and Desdemona listens to the "indecencies" of Iago without making a scene, but rather encourages him to continue with his merriment. Ophelia, even though her speech (until she loses her mind) would satisfy the most rigid Victorian code, as an Elizabethan would have been accustomed to taking ribald merriment in her stride. That she was by no means unfamiliar with it is proved by the fact that in her madness she sings a song of such bawdiness as matches anything Hamlet says. Obviously she has not only heard the ditty, but memorized it as well. This is a stupid point to have to discuss, and one leaves it willingly.

Her misery over her situation, over her lover's madness (thus she accounts for his severity towards her), and then over her father's death and Hamlet's exile proves too much for her weak spirit to bear, and she loses what little mind she ever had. Without her father's commands she hardly knows how to live. It is in her madness that she at last touches us with deep pity. Shakespeare nowhere shows himself a sublimer artist than in the manner in which he gives us to understand during the ravings of her disordered mind how fearful was her life in her father's household—through the fragments of her vagrant thoughts we read the dreadful subjection of her days, all the dread things she has overheard, all the unspeakable things she knows but has had to suppress within herself lest they leap into the light, all the terrible cost of her filial obedience. Shakespeare's genius enabled him to reveal the mysterious workings of the unconscious mind in the "mad scenes," centuries before the Freudian theories, and not in the dangerous clinical manner of the psychoanalysts, but, like the true artist, as an imitation of life as it is lived.

It should be observed, by the way, that the madness of Ophelia might readily have settled the question of Hamlet's reputed madness or feigned madness. As Shakespeare shows us her loss of mind, we find it much resembling the madness of Lear and the pretended madness of Edgar—these three examples clearly exhibiting Shakespeare's method of representing insanity on the stage. All three appear more or less fantastically garbed, all three speak without order or logical sequence, all three are unaware (except for moments of clarity) of the identity of the people they address. That fact alone should deal the death-blow to any wisp of a suspended judgment on the question as to whether or not Shakespeare intended the Prince to be understood either as mad or feigning madness. Hamlet's dress is the normal dress for mourning, his remarks are always to the point and flow in recognizable order, and he is always very much aware of to whom it is he speaks, much more aware than his interlocutor (or often the critic) remotely guesses!

POLONIUS

With the exception of the Prince himself, Polonius and Rosencrantz and Guildenstern are the persons of the drama most frequently misrepresented on the stage.

Actors interpret Polonius either as a charming old man, running over with sound opinion, and an affectionate, indulgent father; or as a pleasant but somewhat befuddled councilor, with the best of intentions in the world. Among the critics the most extreme tribute paid to him has been that of Tieck: "I see in Polonius a real statesman. Discreet, politic, keen-sighted, ready at the council-board, cunning upon occasions, he had been valued by the deceased King, and is now indispensable to his successor." [43] As regards the old man's intelligence, even Samuel Johnson's famous "dotage encroaching on wisdom," though nearer the truth, is a characterization far too generous. That Polonius did serve the late King is an indication that he may once have possessed some ability; but it must have been entirely in the realm of politics. He has the kind of mind, often to be met with in the business and professional worlds, that by its shrewd concentration upon material successes achieves its goal at the cost of everything else. He is devoid of warmth, humanity, and affection (except for his son), and gives symptoms of never having known a spiritual impulse in his life. A career of making all his acts subservient to self-advancement has in the end deadened even his practical cunning. At the age we meet him he is certainly indispensable to no one. Nothing is left of his ability and shrewdness but a few tags, a few catch-phrases, to which, even when they do express some grains of truth, he pays scant heed in his own demeanor. It is he, for example, who utters the celebrated:

> brevity is the soul of wit
>   II, ii, 90

—a profound truth; but no character in Shakespeare is so long-winded as Polonius. He is always threatening to be brief, is always about to sum up in a few words—and continues to harangue his audience by the hour.

We never encounter him doing a wise or creditable thing, or giving anyone intelligent counsel. He is, in short, a dotard of the most limited horizons, a clumsy fool who stands in his own light. Understanding the world from his own unenlightening experiences, he is honest enough in refusing to believe that Hamlet could possibly wish to marry anyone so far below him in rank as Ophelia. Though Hamlet's intentions were entirely honorable, and even the Queen approved her son's choice, Polonius in Hamlet's place would never have made such a disadvantageous match.

He is very well pleased with his own feeble mind, however, and thinks he knows the answers to all questions. His inability to follow the speed of Hamlet's intellect is merely evidence to him (and many critics) that the Prince is "far gone." Besides being an ass, he is, of course, a time-server, always the friend to the party in power, with the keen scent of politicians for which way the wind is blowing.

It is probably an uncritical admiration for the well-known advice he gives Laertes before his son's departure for Paris which is responsible for Polonius' reputation for wisdom. That passage has been memorized by generations of unhappy school children, as though it were an ideal guide to the good life. Listened to carefully, however, though containing a few acceptable platitudes, it turns out to be admirable enough as precepts for getting on in the world; but the man who followed it would certainly be cheated of experience's richest rewards. Yet the phraseology of this speech has echoed down the centuries—for no good reason. What has been the point of mouthing

> And it must follow as the night the day
>   I, iii, 79

as though it were the sublimest instead (as Shakespeare intended) of the emptiest of images, a perfect reflection of the obvious-mindedness of the dotard who speaks it? In the advice there are, as we have said, some truisms, but such platitudes

> so extreme in date,
> It were superfluous to state!

Keep the friends you have tried; do not be running after new ones; dress well but not gaudily—even a dunce knows that much. But the passage taken as a whole contains nothing admirable.

> This above all: to thine own self be true

sounds noble enough—until you realize that in context it can only mean, "Be true to your own material advantage; see to it that you line your pockets well." For Polonius advises: Do not go about letting people know what you really are thinking; let others confide in you and express their opinions as much as they wish—but keep your own counsel. Avoid getting into a quarrel, but once you are in it see that you win (no matter, apparently, whether you are in the right or the wrong). Remember that clothes make the man. Never lend money; that is the way to lose money and friend. Never borrow money; that discourages habits of thrift.

Such guidance will do for those who wish to make the world their prey, but it is dignified by no humanity. Who can live humanly without ever borrowing or lending? Is one to turn his back on his best friend in an hour of need? Will the sensible man grieve when he has lost what he took to be a friend because of a loan made him? Does he not rather congratulate himself at having made a good investment, no matter what the sum, at having paid little for so important a discovery? Polonius, naturally, can give to his son only the crass philosophy which molded his own career. (How different is the precept of the noble Countess of Rousillon, who is able to hold as a model to her son a father quite other than Polonius—who need only remind him what he owes to his line, when she would teach him how to live:

> Be thou blest, Bertram! and succeed thy father
> In manners as in shape! thy blood and virtue
> Contend for empire in thee; and thy goodness
> Share with thy birthright! *Love all, trust a few,*

> *Do wrong to none:* be able for thy enemy
> *Rather in power than use;* and keep thy friend
> *Under thy own life's key.*
>   *All's Well That Ends Well,* I, i, 70 seq.

Like everyone else in the play, Polonius's character is to be gauged by the way he behaves. He bullies his daughter, crushing every spark of life out of her. He sends a spy after his son to discover just what the young man is up to in Paris (II, i). His emissary, in order to draw out the Danish colony in Paris, is himself to slander Laertes first. He is to describe him as "very wild," addicted to what Polonius thinks the "usual slips" of youth. Such as gambling? inquires Reynaldo. Yes, answers Polonius—gambling, or drinking, or swearing, or quarreling, or frequenting houses of prostitution. The servant, finer than the master, is astounded that he must so besmirch Laertes' character. But to Polonius these vices are to be expected of the "fiery mind"—he remembers his own youth! Reynaldo is not to go too far, however; he is not to represent Laertes as a *steady* patron of bawdyhouses. And why all this invention? Because, Polonius assures his man,

> Your bait of falsehood takes this carp of truth:

some Dane will be sure to come forward with the information that he has indeed seen Laertes gambling, or drunk, or quarreling, or entering "a house of sale—*videlicet,* a brothel." Having learned this, Reynaldo is to allow Laertes free rein. One cannot but conclude that Polonius is less worried that his son may be leading a vicious life than that it may not be vicious enough.

He is, in short, a notable upholder of a double standard for men and women. Ophelia is to make her prime concern retaining her virginity; Laertes may drink, swear, quarrel, and patronize the prostitutes—all in moderation. These vices would prove his son a youth of spirit. There is, unluckily, many a Polonius among fathers, suppressing his daughters' simplest human impulses, but eager to encourage his sons to be what he likes to think of himself as having been, a reckless young devil. Having learned nothing from life, having given nothing to it, their hope is to have their sons follow in their footsteps, to learn no more and give no more.

Polonius' most obvious trait is, of course, his tendency to become lost in words, the index of a befuddled brain which cannot follow through with an idea, which inevitably loses the thread in a labyrinth of verbiage. He might be considered, indeed, almost entirely a comic character were it not for the darker side of his nature which prevents our taking him too lightly. But his mental confusion, his being forever trapped by language, is certainly laugh-provoking. He is like an athlete practising on one of those treadmills which require one's running fast if one is to stay in the same place. So Polonius puffs away at words; the more of them he employs, the less he advances what he is trying to say. He could be said to sound like a walking thesaurus, if his words were not so dull, for he is unable to express the simplest notion without the aid of many synonyms. The more his phrases pile up, the less he contrives to say. Thus, while he is reporting his theory of the cause of Hamlet's "madness," he begins with the premise that the Prince is mad. Although Claudius and Gertrude are both prepared to grant him that, Polonius must embellish the idea—can no more put it aside than if it were glued to him:

> I will be brief. Your noble son is mad.
> Mad call I it; for, to define true madness,
> What is't but to be nothing else but mad? . . .
> That he is mad, 'tis true; 'tis true 'tis pity,
> And pity 'tis 'tis true. . . .
> Mad let us grant him then; and now remains
> That we find out the cause of this effect,
> Or rather say, the cause of this defect,
> For this effect defective comes by cause. . . .

Words, words, and nothing! At last he comes to Ophelia, and again he begins by announcing a truth no one would dispute:

> I have a daughter;

even this, however, he cannot allow to pass without some addition:

> —have while she is mine.
>   II, ii, 92 seq.

The stupidity of this old fossil is excruciatingly funny. His dullness is in complete contrast to, and thus makes a perfect foil for, Hamlet's lightning-like rapidity; Hamlet's mind is all light and his is all fog.

One can understand, nevertheless, why some critics have felt that Polonius is "indispensable" to Claudius, despite the folly of his suggestions. It will be noted that the King always seems to be complimenting him quite effusively. Such, at first, would seem very odd behavior on the part of a man as clever and strong-minded as Claudius, whom one would expect only to be irritated at the constant attendance of a pedantic fool. Why does he even tolerate the old buffoon, who must be a sore trial to his patience? Why is he forever at pains to smooth him down? To Laertes Claudius says before the whole court:

> The head is not more native to the heart,
> The hand more instrumental to the mouth,
> Than is the throne of Denmark to thy father.
>
> > I, ii, 47 seq.

This is fairly extravagant praise, considering the intelligence of the speaker and the dim-wittedness of the subject. Later, to Polonius himself he says:

> Thou still hast been the father of good news.
>
> > II, ii, 42

In the middle of the old man's recital of Ophelia's obedient rejection of Hamlet's communications, Polonius invites the offer of another bouquet, and it is forthwith presented to him:

> POL.   What do you think of me?
> KING.   As of a man faithful and honorable.
>
> > II, ii, 129-30

And again:

> POL.   Hath there been such a time—I'd fain know
>   that—
>   That I have positively said, " 'Tis so,"
>   When it proved otherwise?
> KING.   Not that I know.
>
> > II, ii, 153 seq.

Why should Claudius be so anxious to please him? Why should he choose to retain him as his counselor at all? The obvious answer (and in light of it, we may justly interpret Polonius' quoted remarks as a reminder to the King of his indebtedness to him) is that the old man's position under Hamlet's father must have borne considerable weight in winning the election of the crown for Claudius. So much we take for granted about this time-server.

But do not Polonius' words remind Claudius of a deeper indebtedness? Does not Claudius retain the old man's services because he has no other choice?

There is a certain amount of evidence in the play which would point to Polonius' being rather worse than an old bore and time-server, to his being more nefarious than his white hairs would suggest. Why should Claudius, for example, after the Mouse-trap has revealed to him that Hamlet knows of the late king's murder, run so great a risk as to commission Polonius' listening behind the arras in Gertrude's chamber, when the King must know that Hamlet will speak of that murder to his mother? Why should he *allow anyone* to hear that tale? Why should he put the possession of such knowledge—even if it were only to be taken as a rumor not to be credited—in the hands of Polonius—why, unless Polonius already knows all about the murder, unless nothing he could hear would be news to him? In short, was not Polonius an accomplice in the murder of Hamlet's father? Such a deed as Claudius committed is almost impossible to manage singlehanded. Who would have been in a better position to assist him, who readier (in exchange for future favors) to assist him, than Polonius? It is entirely within the possibilities of his character that the old councilor should have been a partner in arranging the slaying, and it would explain Claudius' endless and otherwise incredible patience with him. And it would explain too the King's willingness to have Polonius an audience to Hamlet's talk with Gertrude; Claudius is certainly not the man to jeopardize his security under the circumstances with any man, unless that man were already as much involved in the crime as himself. It would add weight to the argument to remember that it is Polonius, moreover, who puts an end to the acting of the Mouse-trap when the King rises too agitated to stop the performance by word of mouth himself.

> OPH.   The King rises.
> HAM.   What, frighted with false fire?
> QUEEN.   How fares my lord?
> POL.   Give o'er the play.
>
> III, ii, 276 seq.

The accusation against Polonius as an accomplice in the murder has been maintained by a few critics,[44] and, we believe, with reason. As a matter of fact, as has already been remarked (see page 238), Ophelia's mad scene would seem to contain fairly conclusive proof of his cooperation in the killing of Hamlet's father.

It is nevertheless undeniable that Shakespeare has preferred to leave this point in the background of the play, so that we are never more than dimly aware of it as a possibility. He had two chief reasons for underplaying Polonius' guilt:

1. He did not want to burden the portrait of Polonius to the extent that he must cease to be a source of comedy in the play—as he must if we consciously think of him as co-conspirator in the murder.

2. Polonius' complicity is not important to the plot. It is rather part of the story's background, and therefore does not merit undue prominence. (Shakespeare is always remarkable in knowing when to avoid unnecessary explanations. He knew that in plays where every trifling detail is explained and given full attention, the background tends to disappear altogether, everything moves up to the foreground, and the picture loses dimension.)

Shakespeare plainly wished us to do no more than strongly suspect Polonius of nefariousness. Since he chose to imply rather than to represent his complicity, it devolves upon us to feel vaguely about the whole matter too, but to feel strongly that Polonius is a repulsive old man, whose death causes pity not for himself, but for the reckless Prince who must perforce pay a heavy price for it.*

* Counterbalancing the popular overkindly view of Polonius' character is a particularly mad one of the German critic Flathe, who finds: that the whole "Polonius family" is a collection of heartless, ruthless, ambitious creatures, more important to the play than Claudius; that they are all straining for royal power; that Ophelia has no love for Hamlet but falls in with her father's machinations because she wishes to be

LAERTES

Laertes is a chip off the old block. Did an early death not cut him off in time, what Polonius is he would become. The unattractiveness of his character does not strike us so forcibly, however, because he is a young man. He has some of the dash, hence some of the charm, of youth; he is young enough to be capable of passionate emotion; the genuineness of his love for his father and sister indicates potentialities superior to Polonius. That capacity for love prevents our detesting him.

But he is undoubtedly headed the same way as his father. His moral strictures to Ophelia are identical with those of Polonius, and proceed from the same narrow limitations of values. He, too, cannot believe in Hamlet's sincerity of love only because the latter is a prince; he, too, defines virtue for his sister in terms of her maidenhead; he, too, believes it best for her to distrust her emotions till the marriage-knot has been safely tied. And he, too, believes in one code of morals for his sister and another for himself. When Ophelia, heeding his warning, recommends his advice to himself to live chastely too, he brushes her off with:

> O, fear me not.
> I, iii, 51

While he has already displayed his father's penchant for sermonizing her, he is not at all disposed to be lectured to by her, however briefly.

But it is on his return to Denmark that his unpleasanter side is exposed to us. How differently from Hamlet he goes about avenging a father's murder! His recklessness, unsupported by either the intelligence or the noble-mindedness of a Hamlet, precipitates him into the vilest sort of behavior. It is clear that the chief ingredient in his furious need of revenge is his concern about the world's opinion of him if he does not at once kill—anybody—in retaliation:

Queen; that they all use Hamlet's madness for their own ends, and play upon it; that when Hamlet ceases to love Ophelia, Polonius' furious ambition blinds him to the fact to the length that he brings about his own death; that Ophelia loses her mind because her father's death puts an end to *her* hopes for the throne, etc., etc.[45]

QUEEN.   Calmly, good Laertes.
LAER.   That drop of blood that's calm proclaims me
                bastard,
        Cries cuckold to my father. . . .

                                                    IV, v, 116 seq.

This regard for the esteem of others causes him to feel the lack of
ceremony attending his father's burial as almost as great a catastrophe
as the old man's death itself:

                his obscure burial—
        No trophy, sword, nor hatchment o'er his bones,
        No noble rite nor formal ostentation—
        Cry to be heard, as 'twere from heaven to
                earth . . .

                                                    IV, v, 213 seq.

His grief is real enough; but he is making a fuss partly because he
feels it expected of him. His attitude is in marked contrast to Hamlet's indifference to the opinion of others.

Rash without nobility or a desire for justice, he is no match for
Claudius. Though storming the palace with a rabble, and ready to
take the King's life in revenge, he is quickly wound around the monarch's little finger, and before he knows it is apologizing for his
threats.

When Claudius presently identifies Hamlet as the slayer of
Polonius, we see Laertes at his worst. He is unconcerned with the
facts—Hamlet, after all, did not deliberately commit murder—and
is anxious only to get even, no matter how dishonorably. He would
be willing to cut the Prince's throat even in a church, is willing to
jeopardize his own immortal soul, will stoop to the most nefarious
means—as long as he succeeds in killing Hamlet. While Hamlet cannot think of using any method of vengeance inconsistent with his
own dignity, Laertes, having no such commodity, is prepared to
employ any means. The King's plan of arranging for an unbated
sword in the fencing match is vile enough, but it is Laertes who at
once offers to anoint his sword with a mortal poison, a scheme
worthy of the lowest kind of villain. Laertes is, of course, not that;
our disgust with his methods is somewhat tempered by the sincerity

of his anguish. Nevertheless, his proneness to base trickery reveals capacities for unlimited treachery.

His virility is only of the obvious kind, the kind his father has approved of, but it lacks any moral stature. When Hamlet publicly apologizes for his conduct at Ophelia's grave, Laertes, did he possess any quality, must feel ashamed of the part he has agreed to play, and is still in time to renounce it. Instead, he hypocritically pretends to accept Hamlet's friendly overtures at the very moment he knows his murderous purposes are in a matter of minutes to make an end of the other.

The best of him is his strong family feeling. But even here, though he wins our sympathy, we must feel the same distaste that is Hamlet's for his melodramatic display of emotion at his sister's grave. The emotion is sincere, but experience teaches us that those who can make a great show of feeling on such occasions are never those who feel most deeply. Unlike Hamlet, he weeps easily. He feels as deeply as he can, but the very excess of his exhibition points to a quick recovery.

What he is, Polonius in all likelihood once was. Thus are we forced to judge him.*

* E. K. Ilyin has made available the record of a conversation held in French between Gordon Craig and Stanislavski in 1909 on the stage of the Moscow Art Theatre, where the young Craig had been invited to stage *Hamlet*. The discussion, taken down in Russian by a co-producer of Stanislavski's, is quite amusing to read not only because Craig's discomfort is obvious (possibly it was owing to the annoyance of seeing his words being transcribed as they came out) but also because his opinions about Polonius and his two children are very lively. Almost the first thing he says is: "Laertes is basically nothing but a little Polonius" (almost our own very words for years before the article was printed). Stanislavski expresses surprise that there should be anything "different" about that family. Yes, Craig assures him, "a fatuous stupid family." Ophelia too? "I am afraid so. She must be both stupid and lovely at the same time. . . . Like the whole family . . . she is a terrible nonentity. . . . All the advice that Laertes and his father give Ophelia shows their extraordinary pettiness and insignificance." Stanislavski simply cannot conceive of such an Ophelia; how can she be such a fool as Craig describes her? "Perhaps she was frightened by a boy on a fence who made faces at her." [46]

HORATIO

It is Shakespeare's practice in many of his tragedies to include among the persons of the drama a man close to the central character, a man of less magnificence than the hero but also without his short-comings, a man of less genius but greater balance of character, re-markable in the play's setting for his loyalty, soundness of judgment, and humanity—the individual in the drama who represents the norm of human conduct at its best, a man who is the salt of the earth. In *Romeo and Juliet* he is Benvolio, always bespeaking moderation and calm reflection; in *King Lear* he is Kent, rugged, frank, loving, speaking out when no one else dares speak the truth; in *Antony and Cleopatra* he is Enobarbus, rough soldier, mincing no words, stoop-ing to no flattery when his commander is bent on self-destruction; in *Hamlet* he is Horatio. The dramatic employment of these char-acters is another demonstration of Shakespeare's cunning as an artist. For it is against the boundless good sense and loving concern of these men that we best gauge the excesses of the more gifted hero.

From the very beginning Horatio's is the voice of sane judg-ment in the tragedy. In the opening scene, we find Horatio politely skeptical about the existence of ghosts:

> Tush, tush, 'twill not appear.
>
> I, i, 30

Despite the desultoriness of Craig's remarks, his are the only opinions about the three we have ever been able to be in full accord with. It is too bad he has nothing to say about Hamlet or any of his problems—though he is unintentionally droll about the Prince's relations to Rosen-crantz and Guildenstern. "They were good friends at school," he says, and then adds inaccurately, "that is why he sent for them, to have the chance of renewing their friendship." Stanislavski is quick to remind him that it was Claudius who sent for them. "Yes," counters Craig, "but they were brought up together." "Lots of people are brought up together! There's a great difference between being brought up together and being friends." Cornered, Craig blunders badly: "Quite right. When they found out that Hamlet had not inherited the throne they went over to the King."

(Craig, by the way, finds Desdemona "rather stupid," but adores Cordelia and Imogen.)

But, though rational, he does not push his rationality, as so many do, to the point of fanaticism. There is no need for Hamlet to assert to him that there are more things in heaven and earth than are dreamt of in philosophy, for Horatio is not so foolish as to deny the evidence of his senses even if he cannot account for what they perceive.* The Ghost appears, and its appearance puts an end to Horatio's skepticism:

> Before my God, I might not this believe
> Without the sensible and true avouch
> Of mine own eyes.
>
> I, i, 56–58

Reason dictates doubt about such matters; but good sense requires accepting the evidence, even when it defies logic.

Thus, throughout the play, Horatio's quiet voice continues to urge intelligence and moderation upon Hamlet and anyone else he speaks to. It is characteristic of him, when the Queen dreads having to see Ophelia in her madness, that he should remind her that there are more important considerations than her own thinness of skin:

> 'Twere good she were spoken with, for she may strew
> Dangerous conjectures in ill-breeding minds.
> Let her come in.†
>
> IV, v, 14–16

He is a man of few words, and his friendship with Hamlet is so perfect that they need none. Whatever Hamlet has to impart, he understands at once. When Hamlet's affection one time starts to

---

* They tell a story, not really amusing, but illustrative of the man of remorselessly logical mind—than whom no one is ever, probably, more unbalanced. Such a one—he was a German, of course—met an American traveler at Cairo, and said, "Young man, I suppose you came the canal through?" "No," said the American. "Then you came the river down?" "No," said the American. "Then you came the desert across?" "No," said the American. "In that case, my friend," said the German haughtily, "you haff not yet arrived."

† The 1604 edition of the play assigns these lines to Horatio, the 1623 edition (plainly in error) to the Queen. The advice has the very sound of Horatio's good judgment.

pour out in words, Horatio, who needs no reassurance, tries to intercept the flow:

> HAM. Horatio, thou art e'en as just a man
>   As e'er my conversation coped withal.
> HOR. O, my dear lord,—
>
> III, ii, 59–61

He never fears to disagree with his friend. He indicates his feeling
that Hamlet has been unjust to Rosencrantz and Guildenstern (V,
i, 56); when the Prince quarrels with Laertes at Ophelia's grave, it
is Horatio who murmurs:

> Good my lord, be quiet.
> V, i, 288

And when Hamlet, revolted at the insensitiveness of the gravedigger
who can sing an idiotic song quite cheerfully while shoveling up a
skull that once tenanted a human brain, asks:

> Has this fellow no feeling of his business, that he sings at
> grave-making?

Horatio in a terse line reminds him that since the world cannot dispense with gravemakers, we must expect them in self-defense to
harden themselves if they are to endure their necessary work:

> Custom hath made it in him a property of easiness.

Hamlet is quick to catch the gentle reproof implied by his friend,
and handsomely acknowledges the thoughtlessness of his over-ex-
quisite revulsion:

> 'Tis e'en so. The hand of little employment hath the
> daintier sense.
>
> V, i, 73 seq.

Again, in the same scene, when the sight of Yorick's skull generates
a train of gloomy thoughts in the Prince:

> To what base uses we may return, Horatio! Why may
> not imagination trace the noble dust of Alexander, till he
> find it stopping a bung-hole?

Horatio gently warns his friend that there is neither intellectual nor spiritual profit in indulging the mind in morbid speculations of that kind:

> Twere to consider too curiously, to consider so.
>
> V, i, 223 seq.

It is part of wisdom to recognize as insoluble the mysteries of life and death, and not to dissipate the health of the mind in attempting to answer the unanswerable. There are enough questions which we can answer.

At the end of the tragedy, the survival of this perfectly balanced, admirable man among the living forms a significant part of the *katharsis*. After Hamlet's death, with a man of Horatio's stamp still in the world, we feel some justification in the race's continuing its hard struggle against evil.

ROSENCRANTZ AND GUILDENSTERN

While Hamlet's two old schoolfellows have not the beauty, modesty, humanity, or sensitiveness of Horatio's intelligence, there is no warrant in the play for their being represented, as they constantly are on the stage, as a pair of reptiles.

They were never as close to the Prince as Horatio, but the evidence is that among his friends they have shared the next place in his affections. It is unthinkable that a man as quick and intuitive as Hamlet, who misses no look of the eye or intonation of the voice, would have made friends of two "smirking and bowing, . . . assenting, wheedling, flattering" knaves such as Goethe describes them as being,[47] and the world conceives them to be. Such could not have come within a mile of intimacy with Hamlet.

They seem to be the not very profound but agreeable, jolly good fellows we all number among our acquaintances. The three of them must have had many good times together, and it is on the basis of their capacity for drawing him "on to pleasures" that the King has pretended to send for them. We all retain people dear to us because they have been "of so young days brought up" with us, and this was their sort of friendship with Hamlet. He could not be more delighted than he is to see them, when they first arrive (II, ii, 228 seq.). If they were treacherous by nature, Hamlet would have been the first to know it, and the last to greet them with such obvious pleasure. It is in the very nature of their relationship that they should be the bearers of the news of the theatrical world and also herald the arrival of the actors in town.

But Hamlet assuredly turns against them, remorselessly and finally. Before their first interview in the play is ended he, who has welcomed them as best of friends, parts from them as among the most contemptible of his foes. Nothing in the play is more subtly demonstrated than this alteration in his feelings. (See page 201.) When Hamlet feels he must distrust them, it is the last in the series of his disenchantments with those he has loved. But that he feels this does not mean that he feels it justly.

As a matter of fact, poor Guildenstern and Rosencrantz are the unlucky victims of circumstance in the play. It is their misfortune to become enmeshed quite innocently in the struggle between Hamlet and the King. Their original intent was honorable. They have been asked, as good friends, to do what they can to divert Hamlet and try to discover what it is that afflicts him, and to find out whether there be anything that Claudius as a loving father can do that lies within his remedy (II, ii, 18). The Queen has seconded this plea of the King, adding that Hamlet has much talked of them,

> And sure I am two men there are not living
> To whom he more adheres.

The King, of course, means to use them because his own uneasy mind wishes to discover what can be the cause of Hamlet's discontented conduct. But they honestly believe that Claudius is anxious to help their friend—why should they not? When the King and Queen both inform them that Hamlet is "transformed," there is no reason why they should not credit what has been told them or entertain any suspicion of Claudius's motives. Had they been bosom-friends to Hamlet, like Horatio, the case might have been different.

When they meet their friend, they therefore look for signs of his mental aberration, and soon enough find them—since they know nothing of Hamlet's problem or misery. All they can see is that Hamlet's mother and stepfather are so concerned over his well-being that they themselves have been expressly sent for. Yet he speaks of

Denmark as a prison—he, the heir-apparent! Their poor friend is in a bad way.

They have, in short, with the best of intentions, undertaken a mission better declined. No one can play the spy on a friend—for no matter what high-minded ends—with honor. It is an office they should have refused.

They have, unluckily for them, simple, unsubtle minds. They cannot comprehend Hamlet's sudden detestation of them—unless it be on the grounds of madness. It is with the sorrow of despised friendship that Rosencrantz overcomes his pride to ask sincerely:

> Good, my lord, what is the cause of your distemper? You do surely bar the door upon your own liberty if you deny your griefs to your friend.

The lines cry out the man's sincerity. Hamlet's curt answer evokes another response from his old friend which bespeaks his mystification:

HAM.   Sir, I lack advancement.
ROS.   How can that be, when you have the voice of the
      King himself for your succession in Denmark?
                       III, ii, 350 seq.

Loathing them, Hamlet refuses to be forthright with them again, nor will he afford them an opportunity to prove the honesty of their friendship.

In the end they are put to death without justice. They have no knowledge that the sealed documents they bear to the English King command Hamlet's death. In their eyes the flight to England is a measure for Hamlet's protection after his murder of Polonius. Claudius can have appeared to them only in the light of a patient father whose love for Hamlet, like theirs, has been rejected because of their friend's warped mind. But for Hamlet, rash man, capable of being as monstrously unjust as he is nobly desirous of being honorable, it is enough that they bear the commission for his execution. And so without a tremor he sends them to their death.

It indeed proves catastrophic for these two that they should, though innocent, come

> Between the pass and fell incensed points
> Of mighty opposites.
>
> V, ii, 61–2

Men of their rather commonplace, if agreeable, stamp are ever in
danger of disaster when they make friends with a man of Hamlet's
volcanic character. The atmosphere hovering about genius is always
charged with lightning.

Luckless pair! Victims of the machinations of Claudius and the
rashness of Hamlet, they have since been doomed to be even more
the victims of the misunderstanding of critics, directors, and actors!

REFERENCES IN CHAPTER VI

1. E. E. Stoll, *Hamlet: an Historical and Comparative Study* (Minneapolis, 1919), p. 27.
2. H. R. Walley, "Shakespeare's Conception of 'Hamlet'" in *Publications of the Modern Language Association* XLVIII (Sept., 1933), p. 797.
3. C. F. E. Spurgeon, *Shakespeare's Imagery and What It Tells Us* (New York, 1935), pp. 316–20.
4. F. Fergusson, *The Idea of a Theater* (Garden City, 1953), p. 145.
5. R. Loening, *Die Hamlet-Tragödie Shakespeares* (Stuttgart, 1893), p. 22.
6. C. D. Stewart, *Some Textual Difficulties in Shakespeare* (New Haven, 1914), pp. 204–29.
7. G. R. Foss, *What the Author Meant* (London, 1932), pp. 12–26.
8. F. Gilchrist, *The True Story of Hamlet and Ophelia* (Boston, 1889), p. 21.
9. J. Masefield, *William Shakespeare* (London, 1930), p. 158.
10. J. Q. Adams, *Hamlet* (Boston, 1929), p. 193.
11. L. B. Campbell, *Shakespeare's Tragic Heroes* (Cambridge, England, 1930), p. 115.
12. J. Q. Adams, *op. cit.*, p. 182.
13. A. C. Bradley, *Shakespearean Tragedy* (London, 1929), p. 169.
14. J. Masefield, *op. cit.*, p. 161.
15. H. M. Jones, *The King in Hamlet* (Austin, Texas, 1918).
16. G. L. Kittredge, *Hamlet* (Boston, 1939), pp. xviii–xix.
17. A. C. Bradley, *op. cit.*, pp. 168–9.
18. J. W. Draper, "Queen Gertrude" in *Revue Anglo-américaine* XII (1934), pp. 20–34.

19. A. L. Bartholomew, "Queen Gertrude" in *Shakespeariana* III (1886), pp. 451–4.
20. S. Johnson, *The Plays of Shakespeare* (London, 1765), Vol. VIII, p. 311.
21. "T. C.," "Letters on Shakespeare" in *Blackwood's Magazine* (Feb., 1818), p. 511.
22. F. T. Vischer, *Kritische Gänge* (Stuttgart, 1861), Vol. II, p. 98.
23. H. H. Furness, *Hamlet* (Philadelphia, 1918), Vol. II, p. 173.
24. J. D. Wilson, *What Happens in Hamlet* (New York, 1936), p. 101.
25. A. C. Bradley, *op. cit.*, p. 103.
26. *Ibid.*, p. 153.
27. *Ibid.*, p. 158.
28. J. W. von Goethe, *Wilhelm Meister* (translated by T. Carlyle) (Boston, 1851), Vol. I, Book V, p. 296.
29. H. Coleridge, *Essays and Marginalia* (London, 1851), Vol. I, p. 166.
30. Anon., "Hamlet" in *Quarterly Review* LXXIX (1847), p. 334.
31. G. G. Gervinus, *Shakespeare Commentaries* (translated by Miss Burnett) (London, 1863), Vol. II, p. 151.
32. A. W. Schlegel, *Letters on Art and Dramatic Literature* (translated by J. Black), (London, 1815), Vol. II, p. 194.
33. E.g., M. Huhner, *Shakespeare's Hamlet* (New York, 1952), p. 150.
34. H. H. Furness, *op. cit.*, Vol. II, pp. 286–7.
35. Sir A. Quiller-Couch, *Shakespeare's Workmanship* (London, 1919), pp. 209–10.
36. J. Q. Adams, *op. cit.*, p. 238.
37. J. D. Wilson, *op. cit.*, p. 103.
38. S. de Madariaga, *On Hamlet* (London, 1948), p. 36.
39. *Ibid.*, p. 40.
40. *Ibid.*, p. 41.
41. *Ibid.*, p. 59.
42. *Ibid.*, p. 56.
43. H. H. Furness, *op. cit.*, Vol. II, p. 285.
44. R. Limberger, *Polonius* (Berlin, 1908).
    E. Reichel, "Polonius" in *Magazin für Literatur* LXIX (Feb. 10 and Feb. 17, 1900), pp. 163–6; 179–82.
45. J. L. F. Flathe, *Shakespeare in Seiner Wiklichkeit* (Leipzig, 1863), Vol. I, pp. 37–151.
46. E. K. Ilyin, "Gordon Craig's Mission to Moscow" in *Theatre Arts* (May, 1954), pp. 78–9; 88–90.
47. J. W. von Goethe, *op. cit.*, Vol. I, Book V, p. 357.

*The Tragedy of Hamlet,
Prince of Denmark*

Editor's Foreword to the Text of the Play

IN THE FOOTNOTES which accompany the present text of *Hamlet*, we shall rarely concern ourselves with the discussion of variant readings and emendations of the text. These matters, fascinating in themselves, have little bearing on our correct understanding of the plot, the characterization, and the tragic conflict; and I do not propose to indulge my own interest in them at the expense of the general reader's patience. We are happily in the position of being able to accept the received text of the play without having, like many scholars, to insist on alterations to advance our theories of the action or of the temperament of the characters. Only here and there will the question of a correct reading be raised, and then it will be to endorse a time-honored editing. In the matter of text, we find it more honorable not to be in haste to suggest changes; in a very few cases there will be a choice between accepted readings, and we shall call attention to them only because one of the alternatives is flagrantly wrong.

A few words about the text of *Hamlet* are in order before we approach the play. There are three early editions of *Hamlet* to which all modern printings of it are indebted:

¶ The First Quarto, of 1603, a "pirated" edition giving a badly distorted version of the play, abridged and confused, and in some details closer to Belleforest's story (i.e., to Kyd's lost play, one assumes) than to Shakespeare's play. Nevertheless, the First Quarto has been of some use in settling some textual questions.

¶ The Second Quarto, of 1604, running over with misprints, but on the whole an authoritative edition.

¶ The First Folio, of 1623, the first collected edition of Shakespeare's plays, made by his friends and fellow-actors, John Heminges and Henry Condell, seven years after the dramatist's death. The *Hamlet* here printed was copied from a manuscript different from that which supplied the text for the Second Quarto, and carries its own quota of printer's errors. Despite its imperfections, however, the First Folio wears the authority of sponsorship by members of Shakespeare's acting-company, and therefore bears equal weight with the Second Quarto in establishing the correct text. Many lines of the play as they appear in the First Folio are unquestionably superior to those of the Second Quarto.

The First Folio contains 85 lines not in the Second Quarto, and omits 218 lines that are in it. *Hamlet* is an extraordinarily long play even for the age in which it was written (one might say of it, as Schumann said of Schubert's Ninth Symphony, that it is "of heavenly length"), and Shakespeare apparently during the years following the 1604 publication made such cuts as he found possible to make. The First Folio undoubtedly gives us the acting-version of Shakespeare's troupe as the text stood in 1623. The 218 lines omitted are, by and large, passages which could be cut from any performance of *Hamlet* without jeopardy to the health of the tragedy. (We shall note most of these passages as we come upon them.) In a play of such dimensions, 218 lines are, of course, proportionately few indeed.

All good modern editions of the work inevitably include the 85 lines from the First Folio and the 218 from the Second Quarto; as for the rest of the play, a modern editor must use his discretion in selecting his reading from one or the other edition when they differ. The task is not so Promethean as is sometimes pretended; where differences exist the choice is either not crucial or else clearly dictated by judgment and taste. In some instances the reading of the otherwise inferior First Quarto is the arbiter in the matter.

The many misconceptions about *Hamlet* have had relatively nothing to do with these textual variations. Rather must we accuse the wholesale amputations of large sections of the play for public performances, as the leading cause of confusion. The truth is that ever since the Restoration theatre began the practise of drastically cutting *Hamlet*, the public has rarely been permitted to see and hear the play as Shakespeare wrote it. We have said that the 218 lines which Shakespeare's company had found dispensable may safely be omitted from the tragedy without great loss; we ought now to add that those comparatively few lines are almost the *only* lines that can be so omitted. If this is true, then my contemporaries have only once been privileged to witness something resembling the play Shakespeare wrote, and that was when Mr. Maurice Evans gave his uncut version of *Hamlet*. The excited reaction of the public to those performances indicates that the perpetuation of erroneous ideas concerning *Hamlet* is intimately connected with the presentation only of cut (and therefore perverted) versions of the tragedy. On the occasion of Mr. Evans's production, even though the direction attempted little more than to exploit the surface meaning of individual scenes without relevance to the whole design, the drama-critics all acclaimed Mr. Evans's "new" interpretation of the hero—although they were rather vague about identifying what that interpretation was! They did note that Mr. Evans seemed to make him a "more active" Prince than they were accustomed to. Everyone seemed to feel this was a new *Hamlet*. All that was actually new about the production was that for the first time in many a decade the lines that Shakespeare had written were at last to be heard in their fullness. Naturally the resulting play was "new!" Every *Hamlet* the critics had seen before Mr. Evans's had necessarily been a distorted one because of the annihilation of whole portions of the tragedy. Not because of any profound understanding of the play, but because the lines at least were there, was Mr. Evans's the first (and, to date, the last) attempt in our time to give the play as Shakespeare conceived it.

"Despite the notable success of Maurice Evans's uncut revival, nearly all Shakespeare's plays have proved too long for the endurance of most audiences," says Mr. Hazelton Spencer, as we have already noted (p. 115). "Why Shakespeare," he continues, "who almost lived in the theatre, habitually wrote in excess of its requirements is a pretty question." * An equally pretty question is how, knowing those "requirements" well enough to become the most successful dramatist of his time, Shakespeare contrived to write so much "in excess" of the artistic "requirements" of his theatre that

* H. Spencer, *The Art and Life of William Shakespeare* (New York, 1940), p. 309.

he created not for his age but for all time. If we knew the answer to that question, instead of writing books about Shakespeare Mr. Spencer and I would doubtless be writing our own tragedies! Is it not just possible that Shakespeare gauged correctly the length of each of his masterpieces? that he made the length of each conform to the "requirements" of his art rather than to a modern director's guess of the possible "endurance of most audiences?"

Besides, how long should a tragedy be? If the function of tragedy were no more than to supply amusement for the interim between an early dinner and an after-theater snack, we could readily reply as Broadway does: "Any play (consider the servant-problem and the traffic in restaurants!) should not begin before 8:40—and even that is hard to make! We must also be granted time off for at least two ten-minute intermissions for a cigarette and—our chief reason for attending the theater—an interchange of opinion of the merits of the performance. Naturally it is only reasonable to expect the play to be over by 10:50 (do not forget the scarcity of taxis, the commuter-train schedules, and the rush for tables at Sardi's!), though for a masterpiece we will suffer waiting for a taxi or a table—a masterpiece may end ten minutes later, at 11 P.M., but no later!"

Well, it is too unfortunate, but *Hamlet* cannot be trimmed to *these* requirements. Its members, to be sure, are forever being lopped off: we have even had a *Hamlet* without a Guildenstern and Rosencrantz, and another in which Ophelia is never buried. The convenience of the public is thus ever being flattered, while Shakespeare's meaning is flouted.

Are we to conclude from the dramatist's success in his own day, despite his writing in excess of its stage's requirements, that after all the butcher, the baker, and the candlestick-maker of Shakespeare's age had greater endurance for things of beauty, that his audiences were not immune to the high purposes of tragedy? If our more enlightened times understood the high function of tragedy, if tragedy were not meant for a higher role than that of affording an evening's diversion or of occasioning an invaluable exchange in the smoking-rooms of personal impressions of actors' performances—if tragedy were permitted to play its purifying part in our civic life, the case would need no arguing. But we live in a period which has sanctioned Miss Webster's twenty-minute versions of Shakespeare's plays for audiences at the New York World's Fair, an age which is not at all shocked when all of an hour is deemed sufficient for the broadcast of a Shakespearean masterwork.

Obviously every work of art must be as long as it needs to be. It is safe to assume that the world's greatest dramatist possessed the knowledge of managing that. The *Henry IV* plays, *Henry V*, *Hamlet*, *Othello*, and *Lear* (to mention some of his longer plays) own no peers, too long though they be for the endurance of most audiences!

In the arts no attribute partakes less of the absolute than that of length. *Vanity Fair* and *The Egoist*, for all their pages, are immeasurably briefer in their effect than many a novelette that could be mentioned; *Paradise Lost* seems much shorter than *Peter Bell*. The relativity of length was forcibly demonstrated years ago during several seasons' attendance at the Wagner-cycle at the Metropolitan Opera House. During the regular subscription nights *Götterdämmerung, Parsifal, Die Meistersinger*, and *Tristan* had quite tedious and long-winded spots, though the performances were each cut down by an hour and more. But at the special Wagner-cycle performances, where they were presented uncut, often with the same casts, they seemed never a note too long. A performance lasting more than an hour longer than the cut version inevitably became a swifter one. In short, one decided, Wagner knew more about the ideal length for his masterpieces than his editors!

For like reasons Mr. Evans's uncut performances were the most rapid of contemporary *Hamlet*s. Certainly, only the full play can reveal the design of the author. Mr. Alan Dent justifies his admitted "lack of compunction" in hacking out whole sections of *Hamlet* for the cinema on the grounds that there is a "fundamental difference between the two mediums" of stage and screen; and he thus explains his omission of Guildenstern and Rosencrantz: "The two, who seemed hardly worth the killing have been killed before their first appearance." * This was doubtless a very witty piece of assassination on Mr. Dent's part, but he might be asked why, if there are such enormous disparities in the technique of stage and screen he wished to adapt a stage-play to the screen at all? If the differences are fundamental, why not leave, untampered with, works written for the stage? If Shakespeare made his own work out of an old tale, why

* A. Dent, *Hamlet, The Film and the Play* (London, 1948), Preface.

could not Mr. Dent write his own *Hamlet* too if he was determined to make a new story out of Shakespeare's?

There are those, of course, who feel that any *Hamlet*, no matter how mutilated, is better than none, just as there are those who feel that it is better to have a svelte enlivening of a melody from Tschaikowski's *Romeo and Juliet Overture* by a jazz-band than no Tschaikowski at all. But a mutilated *Hamlet* or *Romeo and Juliet Overture* does no service either to Shakespeare or Tschaikowski; a jazz-band which can get the man in the street to whistle an imitation of a Tschaikowski "tune" is bringing him not an inch closer to true musical appreciation; just so, a travesty of Shakespeare's meaning in a cut version of *Hamlet* brings no one an inch closer to an understanding of one of the world's greatest tragedies.

In the stage presentation of Shakespeare some compromise with public requirements could be achieved by approximating closer than we do Elizabethan stage conditions. In Shakespeare's day there was no problem of scene-changes or the lowering and raising of curtains; scene followed scene without interruption or intermission. If we would learn to dispense with all but the merest indication of scenery so that there need be no pause between scenes, we might still have an intermission or two (since we *must* have them!) without the play's lasting beyond midnight. It is true that conditions in this respect have much improved during the last few decades, but the scene-designer is still too much in evidence for the play's health. A Shakespearean play presented in something like the Elizabethan manner can be given uncut without greatly exceeding the usual theatre hours; we know also that so directed, it always gains immeasurably in speed and power.

In our edition of *Hamlet* we have dared to employ two kinds of innovation:

¶ 1. In lieu of further long and elaborate discussions, we have added stage directions and emotional cues to facilitate and make more vivid the reading of the play. (*These have been printed in italics and enclosed in parentheses.*) And it is precisely because we object strongly to the common procedure of superimposing meanings foreign to the author's clear intention, that we have been thus bold. It is to be hoped that every one of these new stage-directions and cues will be quickly seen to be called for by the lines of the play. Indeed, we anticipate that these new directions and cues will immediately elucidate the lines themselves. We also indulge the hope that this text may provide the beginning for a tradition to restore the *Hamlet* that Shakespeare wrote to the stage.

¶ 2. For the same reasons we have also italicized here and there a word or phrase in the dialogue. Though this practice has never before been attempted, we believe, in adopting it we have wished to point up many a dramatic effect always bypassed in the theatre, and sometimes of considerable dramatic moment. We repeat: we have never once done this, we feel, without the sanction of the line itself.

It should further be noted that in our text:

¶ 3. Words or passages not to be found in the Folios are printed within Roman brackets. As has been remarked, many of these passages might well be omitted from stage performances, as they are omitted in the Folios.

¶ 4. The received, traditional stage directions are printed in italics without parentheses or brackets—except for the familiar [*Aside*].

B.G.

The Tragedy of Hamlet, Prince of Denmark

DRAMATIS PERSONÆ

CLAUDIUS, *King of Denmark.*

HAMLET, *son to the late, and nephew to the present King.*

POLONIUS, *Lord Chamberlain.*

HORATIO, *friend to Hamlet.*

LAERTES, *son to Polonius.*

VOLTIMAND,
CORNELIUS,
ROSENCRANTZ,
GUILDENSTERN, } *courtiers.*
OSRIC,
A GENTLEMAN,

MARCELLUS, } *officers.*
BERNARDO,

FRANCISCO, *a soldier.*

REYNALDO, *servant to Polonius.*

A Priest.

Players.

Two Clowns, grave-diggers.

FORTINBRAS, *Prince of Norway.*

A Captain.

English Ambassadors.

GERTRUDE, *Queen of Denmark, and mother to Hamlet.*

OPHELIA, *daughter to Polonius.*

Ghost of Hamlet's Father.

Lords, Ladies, Officers, Soldiers, Sailors, Messengers, and other Attendants.

SCENE: *Elsinore, Denmark.*

ACT FIRST

Elsinore. A platform before the castle. (Midnight.)

Francisco at his post. Enter to him Bernardo. (Both men are tense.)

BER. (*Perceiving Francisco's form; nervously.*)   Who's there?

FRAN. (*Equally on edge.*)   Nay, answer *me*. Stand, and unfold [1] yourself.

BER.   Long live the king!

FRAN.   Bernardo?

BER.   He.

FRAN.   You come most carefully upon your hour.

BER.   'Tis now struck twelve. Get thee to bed, Francisco.

FRAN.   For this relief much thanks. 'Tis bitter cold,
And I am sick at heart.

BER.   Have you had quiet guard?

FRAN.   Not a mouse stirring.   10

BER.   Well, good-night.
If you do meet Horatio and Marcellus,
The rivals [2] of my watch, bid them make haste.
Enter Horatio and Marcellus.

FRAN.   I think I hear them. (*On his way out advancing toward them.*)
Stand! Who's there?

HOR.   Friends to this ground.

MAR.   And liegemen to the Dane.[3]

FRAN.   Give you good-night.

MAR.   O, farewell, honest soldier.
Who hath reliev'd you?

FRAN.   Bernardo has my place.
Give [4] you good-night.   *Exit.*

MAR.   Holla! Bernardo!

BER.   Say,
What, is Horatio there?

HOR. (*With quiet humor.*)   A piece of him.

BER.   Welcome, Horatio; welcome, good Marcellus.   20

HOR.   What, has this thing appear'd again to-night?

BER.   I have seen nothing.

MAR.   Horatio says 'tis but our fantasy,
And will not let belief take hold of him

---

[1] disclose.   [2] partners.   [3] Danish king.   [4] God give.

Touching this dreaded sight, twice seen of us;
Therefore I have entreated him along
With us, to watch the minutes of this night,
That if again this apparition come,
He may approve [5] our eyes and speak to it.

HOR. (*Sceptically.*)   Tush, tush, 'twill not appear.

BER.   Sit down a while,
And let us once again assail your ears,   31
That are so fortified against our story,
What we two nights have *seen*.

HOR.   Well, sit we down,
And let us hear Bernardo speak of this.

BER.   Last night of all,
When yond same star that's westward from the pole
Had made his [6] course to illume that part of heaven
Where now it burns, Marcellus and myself,
The bell then beating one,—
Enter the Ghost.

MAR. (*Excitedly.*)   Peace, break thee off! Look, where it comes again!

BER.   In the same figure, like the King that's dead.   41

MAR.   Thou art a scholar; [7] speak to it, Horatio.

BER.   Looks it not like the King? Mark it, Horatio.

HOR.   Most like; it harrows me with fear and wonder.

BER.   It would be spoke to.

MAR.   Question it, Horatio.

HOR.   What art thou that usurp'st this time of night,
Together with that fair and warlike form
In which the majesty of buried Denmark [8]
Did sometimes march? By heaven I charge thee, speak!

MAR.   It is offended.

BER.   See, it stalks away!   50

HOR.   Stay! Speak, speak! I charge thee, speak!   *Exit Ghost.*

MAR.   'Tis gone, and will not answer.

BER.   How now, Horatio! *you* tremble and look pale!

[5] corroborate.

[6] The old form of the neuter possessive. *Its* is a newer word.

[7] Scholars, because of their knowledge of Latin, were held best qualified to speak to spirits, who were thought to prefer that language. Horatio, of course, does not proceed to use Latin, but Shakespeare here is acknowledging a popular tradition.

[8] The King of Denmark. In Shakespeare's plays the monarch is often referred to by the name of his country.

Is not this something more than fantasy?
What think you on't?

HOR.   Before my God, I might not this believe
Without the sensible [9] and true avouch
Of mine own eyes.[10]

MAR.   Is it not like the King?

HOR.   As thou art to thyself.
Such was the very armour he had on   60
When he the ambitious Norway combated.
So frown'd he once, when, in an angry parle,
He smote the sledded Polacks [11] on the ice.
'Tis strange.[12]

MAR.   Thus twice before, and jump [13] at this dead hour,
With martial stalk hath he gone by our watch.

HOR.   In what particular thought to work I know not;
But, in the gross and scope of my opinion,
This bodes some strange eruption to our state.

MAR.   Good now,[14] sit down, and tell me, he that knows,   70
Why this same strict and most observant watch
So nightly toils [15] the subject [16] of the land,
And why such daily cast of brazen cannon,
And foreign mart for implements of war;
Why such impress of shipwrights, whose sore task
Does not divide the Sunday from the week.
What might be toward, that this sweaty haste
Doth make the night joint-labourer with the day,
Who is't that can inform me?

HOR.   That can I;
At least, the whisper goes so. Our last king,   80
Whose image even but now appear'd to us,
Was, as you know, by Fortinbras of Norway,
Thereto prick'd on by a most emulate pride,
Dar'd to the combat; in which our valiant Hamlet—
For so this side of our known world esteem'd him—
Did slay this Fortinbras; who, by a seal'd compact,
Well ratified by law and heraldry,

[9] of the senses.   [10] See pp. 294–295.
[11] The Poles, who use sledges. It has been suggested that the line should
read "his leaded pole-axe."
[12] It is important to remember that this word was once a powerful one. A
thing was then "strange" to the point of being almost incredible.
[13] exactly.   [14] (an exclamation).   [15] makes toil.   [16] subjects.

Did forfeit, with his life, all those his lands
Which he stood seiz'd on,[17] to the conqueror;
Against the which, a moiety competent [18]
Was gaged by our king; which had return'd
To the inheritance of Fortinbras,
Had he been vanquisher; as, by the same covenant,
And carriage of the article design'd,
His fell to Hamlet. Now, sir, young Fortinbras,
Of unimproved mettle hot and full,
Hath in the skirts of Norway here and there
Shark'd [19] up a list of landless resolutes,[20]
For food and diet, to some enterprise
That hath a stomach in't; which is no other—
As it doth well appear unto our state—
But to recover of us, by strong hand
And terms compulsative, those foresaid lands
So by his father lost; and this, I take it,
Is the main motive of our preparations,
The source of this our watch, and the chief head
Of this post-haste and romage [21] in the land.
[BER.[22]   I think it be no other but e'en so.
Well may it sort that this portentous figure
Comes armed through our watch, so like the King
That was and is the question of these wars.
HOR.   A mote it is to trouble the mind's eye.
In the most high and palmy [23] state of Rome,
A little ere the mightiest Julius fell,
The graves stood tenantless and the sheeted dead
Did squeak and gibber in the Roman streets.

. . . . .[24]

As stars with trains of fire and dews of blood,
Disasters [25] in the sun; and the moist star
Upon whose influence Neptune's empire stands

---

[17] possessed of (legal term).   [18] an equivalent portion.
[19] Shakespeare makes a verb out of the noun "shark."   [20] desperadoes.
[21] rummage.
[22] Lines 108–125 are not in the Folio. All such passages are indicated in this text by being enclosed in Roman brackets. Most of them might be omitted in a production of the play. See Editor's Foreword to the Text of the Play.
[23] flourishing.   [24] A line seems to have been lost here.
[25] signs of disaster.

Was sick almost to doomsday with eclipse.   120
And even the like precurse of fierce events,
As harbingers preceding still the fates
And prologue to the omen [26] coming on,
Have heaven and earth together demonstrated
Unto our climatures and countrymen.]
Re-enter Ghost.
(*Breaking off.*) But soft, behold! Lo, where it comes again!
(*With determination.*) I'll cross it, though it blast me. Stay, illusion!
(*In a kind of incantation.*) If thou hast any sound, or use of voice,
Speak to me;
If there be any good thing to be done   130
That may to thee do ease and grace to me,
Speak to me;
If thou art privy to thy country's fate,
Which, happily, foreknowing may avoid,
O speak!
Or if thou hast uphoarded in thy life
Extorted treasure in the womb of earth,
For which, they say, you spirits oft walk in death,
Speak of it; stay, and speak!   *Cock crows.*
          Stop it, Marcellus.
MAR. Shall I strike at it with my partisan? [27]   140
HOR. Do, if it will not stand.
BER.   'Tis here!
HOR.   'Tis here!
MAR. 'Tis gone!   *Exit Ghost.*
We do it wrong, being so majestical,
To offer it the show of violence;
For it is, as the air, invulnerable,
And our vain blows malicious mockery.
BER. It was about to speak, when the cock crew.
HOR. And then it started like a guilty thing
Upon a fearful summons. I have heard,
The cock, that is the trumpet to the morn,   150
Doth with his lofty and shrill-sounding throat
Awake the god of day; and, at his warning,
Whether in sea or fire, in earth or air,
The extravagant [28] and erring [29] spirit hies

[26] calamity.   [27] pike.   [28] escaping (literally "wandering about").
[29] wandering.

To his confine; and of the truth herein
This present object made probation.[30]

MAR.   It faded on the crowing of the cock.
Some say that ever 'gainst that season comes
Wherein our Saviour's birth is celebrated,
The bird of dawning singeth all night long;   160
And then, they say, no spirit can walk abroad;
The nights are wholesome; then no planets strike,[31]
No fairy takes,[32] nor witch hath power to charm,
So hallow'd and so gracious [33] is the time.

HOR.   So have I heard and do in part believe it.
But, look, the morn, in russet mantle clad,
Walks o'er the dew of yon high eastern hill.
Break we our watch up; and, by my advice,
Let us impart what we have seen to-night
Unto young Hamlet; for, upon my life,   170
This spirit, dumb to us, will speak to him.
Do you consent we shall acquaint him with it,
As needful in our loves, fitting our duty?

MAR.   Let's do't, I pray; and I this morning know
Where we shall find him most conveniently.   *Exeunt.*

SCENE II

A room of state in the castle. (Later that same morning.)
Flourish. Enter the King, Queen, Hamlet, Polonius, Laertes, Ophelia,
Lords, and Attendants. (Hamlet alone wears the black of mourning.)
KING. (*With urbanity and well-modulated warmth.*)   Though yet of
        Hamlet our dear brother's death
The memory be green, and that it us befitted
To bear our hearts in grief, and our whole kingdom
To be contracted in one brow of woe,
Yet so far hath discretion fought with nature
That we with wisest sorrow think on him
Together with remembrance of ourselves.
Therefore our sometime sister, now our queen,
The imperial jointress [1] of this warlike state,
Have we, as 'twere with a defeated joy,—   10
With one auspicious and one dropping eye,
With mirth in funeral and with dirge in marriage,

[30] proof.   [31] exert evil influence.   [32] no wicked fairy bewitches.
[33] full of divine grace.   [1] See pp. 192–193.

In equal scale weighing delight and dole,—
Taken to wife; nor have we herein barr'd
Your better wisdoms, which have freely gone
With this affair along. For all, our thanks.
Now follows that you know: young Fortinbras,
Holding a weak supposal of our worth,
Or thinking by our late dear brother's death
Our state to be disjoint and out of frame,   20
Colleagued [2] with the dream of his advantage,
He hath not fail'd to pester us with message
Importing the surrender of those lands
Lost by his father, with all bonds of law,
To our most valiant brother. So much for him.
Enter Voltimand and Cornelius.
Now for ourself and for this time of meeting,
Thus much the business is: we have here writ
To Norway,[3] uncle of young Fortinbras,—
Who, impotent and bed-rid, scarcely hears
Of this his nephew's purpose,—to suppress   30
His further gait herein, in that the levies,
The lists and full proportions, are all made
Out of his subject; and we here dispatch
You, good Cornelius, and you, Voltimand,
For bearing of this greeting to old Norway;
Giving to you no further personal power
To business with the king, more than the scope
Of these delated [4] articles allow.   *Giving a paper.*
Farewell, and let your haste commend your duty.

[COR.] ⎫
VOL.   ⎬ In that and all things will we show our duty.   40

KING.   We doubt it nothing; heartily farewell.

                          Exeunt Voltimand and Cornelius.
(*With great cordiality.*) And now, Laertes, what's the news with
     you?
You told us of some suit; what is't, Laertes?
You cannot speak of reason to the Dane,
And lose your voice. What wouldst thou beg, Laertes,
That shall not be my offer, not thy asking?
The head is not more native to the heart,

---

[2] (refers to "supposal" of line 18).   [3] the King of Norway.
[4] detailed.

The hand more instrumental to the mouth,
Than is the throne of Denmark to thy father.[5]
What wouldst thou have, Laertes?

LAER.   Dread my lord,   50
Your leave and favour to return to France;
From whence though willingly I came to Denmark
To show my duty in your coronation,
Yet now, I must confess, that duty done,
My thoughts and wishes bend again towards France
And bow them to your gracious leave and pardon.[6]

KING.   Have you your father's leave? What says Polonius?

POL.   He hath, my lord, [wrung from me my slow leave
By laboursome petition, and at last
Upon his will I seal'd my hard consent.]   60
I do beseech you, give him leave to go.

KING.   Take thy fair hour, Laertes. Time be thine,
And thy best graces spend it at thy will!
(*With a show of great affection.*) But now, my cousin Hamlet, and
    my son,—

HAM. [*Aside.*]   A little more than kin,[7] and less than kind.[8]

KING.   How is it that the clouds still hang on you?

HAM.   Not so, my lord; I am too much i' the sun.[9]

[5] See pp. 288–290.   [6] permission.
[7] (i.e., Claudius is both uncle and "father").
[8] human. Hamlet is remembering that the marriage is incestuous. See pp. 195–196.
[9] Hamlet here indulges a many-sided pun:
a. in answer to the King's "How is it that the clouds still hang on you,"—the surface meaning—"For my own part I am not mourning enough."
b. in answer to the King's preceding speech (line 64)—"You call me 'son' a little too much."
c. "I am too much the son of my father to be a son to you."
d. "This court is far too gay to please me."
e. "I am too much in the limelight of your attention."
f. "I am fallen from felicity into a bad state." (This would be a reference to the old proverb, "Out of heaven's blessing to the warm sun." Kent says of Lear,

> "Good king, that must approve the common saw,
>   Thou out of heaven's benediction comest
>   To the warm sun!"
>   *Lear*, II, ii, 167 seq.

and Beatrice, on her cousin's betrothal, says of herself with a sigh,

QUEEN.   Good Hamlet, cast thy nighted colour off,
And let thine eye look like a friend on Denmark.
Do not for ever with thy vailed [10] lids   70
Seek for thy noble father in the dust.
Thou know'st 'tis common; all that lives must die,
Passing through nature to eternity.

HAM. (*Bitingly*.)   Ay, madam, it is common.

QUEEN. (*Unconscious of Hamlet's rudeness.*)   If it be,
Why seems it so particular with thee?

HAM. (*Indignantly*.)   Seems, madam! Nay, it *is;* I know not
"seems."
'Tis not alone my inky cloak, good mother,
Nor customary suits of solemn black,
Nor windy suspiration of forc'd breath,
No, nor the fruitful [11] river in the eye,   80
Nor the dejected haviour of the visage,
Together with all forms, moods, *shows* of grief,
That can denote me truly. These indeed seem,
For they are actions that a man might play;
But I have that within which passeth [12] show,
These but the trappings and the suits of woe.

KING. (*Pocketing the insult; in an unctuous voice.*)   'Tis sweet and com-
mendable in your nature, Hamlet,
To give these mourning duties to your father.
But, you must know, your father lost a father;
That father lost, lost his; and the survivor bound
In filial obligation for some term   90
To do obsequious sorrow. (*Sorrowfully*.) But to persever
In obstinate condolement is a course
Of impious stubbornness; 'tis *unmanly* grief;

"Good Lord, for alliance! Thus goes every one to the world but I,
and I am sunburnt; I may sit in a corner, and cry heigh-ho for a
husband!"

Much Ado, II, i, 330 seq.)

How many of these six possible rebuffs to the King could Hamlet have consciously meant? Well, since he is a genius, let us allow him to have intended
at least three. And like all clever people, and even those who are not particularly
clever, he has given expression to wit which turns out to be even wittier than
intended. The reader is free to choose which meanings Hamlet deliberately
aimed at Claudius.

[10] downcast.   [11] ever-ready to bear tears.   [12] surpasses.

It shows a will most incorrect [13] to heaven,
A heart unfortified, a mind impatient,
An understanding simple and unschool'd
For what we know must be, and is as common
As any the most vulgar thing to sense.
Why should we in our peevish opposition   100
Take it to heart? Fie! (*With religiosity.*) 'tis a fault to heaven,
A fault against the dead, a fault to nature,
To reason most absurd, whose common theme
Is death of fathers, and who still hath cried,
From the first corse till he that died to-day,
"This must be so." We pray you, throw to earth
This unprevailing [14] woe, and think of us
As of a father; [15] for, let the world take note,
You are the most immediate to our throne,
And with no less nobility of love   110
Than that which dearest father bears his son,
Do I impart towards you. For your intent
In going back to school in Wittenberg,
It is most retrograde to our desire;
And we beseech you, (*With fatherly affection.*) bend you to remain
Here in the cheer and comfort of our eye,
Our chiefest courtier, cousin, and (*Since Hamlet objects being called "son."*) our son.

QUEEN.   Let not thy mother lose her prayers, Hamlet.
I prithee, stay with us; go not to Wittenberg.

HAM.   I shall in all my best obey *you*, madam.   120

KING. (*Smothering his annoyance.*)   Why, 'tis a loving and a fair reply.
Be as ourself in Denmark. Madam, come;
This gentle and unforc'd accord of Hamlet
Sits smiling to my heart; in grace whereof,
No jocund health that Denmark drinks to-day,
But the great cannon to the clouds shall tell,
And the King's rouse [16] the heavens shall bruit again,
Re-speaking earthly thunder. Come away.

Flourish. Exeunt all but Hamlet.

[13] undisciplined.   [14] unavailing.
[15] No doubt the King enjoys saying this since he well knows Hamlet's dislike of him. Before the Court, Hamlet has no choice but to listen to the hypocrisy that he alone apprehends.
[16] deep draught.

HAM. (*With violent exasperation.*)   O,[17] that this too too solid [18] flesh
        would melt,
    Thaw, and resolve itself into a dew!   130
    Or that the Everlasting had not fix'd
    His canon 'gainst self-slaughter! [19] O God! God!
    How weary, stale, and unprofitable,
    Seems to me all the uses of this world!
    Fie on't! oh fie, fie! 'Tis an unweeded garden,
    That grows to seed; things rank and gross in nature
    Possess it merely.[20] That it should come to this!
    But two months dead! Nay, not so much, not two.
    So excellent a king; that was, to this,
    Hyperion to a satyr; so loving to my mother   140
    That he might not beteem [21] the winds of heaven
    Visit her face too roughly. Heaven and earth!
    Must I remember? Why, she would hang on him,

[17] See pp. 194–195.
[18] The Folio reads "solid," the Second Quarto "sallied." "Sallied" has been
generally pronounced either an error for "solid" or a variant spelling of it.
George Macdonald and later J. Dover Wilson have argued that "sallied" is a
misprint for "sullied," and prefer that reading, the latter scholar maintaining
that Hamlet feels "his very flesh corrupted by what his mother has done"
(*What Happens in Hamlet*, p. 42). This emendation seems to us irrelevantly
morbid. Hamlet at this time does not know that his mother has been an
adulteress; and he could hardly feel *his* flesh sullied by *her* marriage, no matter
how much he loathes Claudius or how incestuous he might hold the marriage
to be. Moreover, "solid" makes perfect sense. Where that is the case, it is unsound to suggest any changes in text.
[19] Incredibly enough, these first lines of the soliloquy have often been taken
to mean that Hamlet is contemplating suicide. (See pp. 101–102.) H. B. Charlton
thinks they prove that the Prince is "passively longing to be dead;" the only
reason Hamlet does not commit suicide is because of the Everlasting's canon
against it; thus, to Charlton, Hamlet is like a "young poet" longing beside a
pool "for the eternal quiet of its depths," but keeping "to the bank" because
"the water might be too cold" (*Shakespearean Tragedy*, pp. 91–92).
    On the contrary, Hamlet is the sort of man who, if he wished to kill
himself, would do so, the Everlasting's canon notwithstanding, and not talk
about it. This brief reference to the peace of death is merely a product of the
Prince's impatience. Why should it appear extraordinary that an energetic man,
allied to a situation he has not made and cannot alter—his mother's marriage
—should cry out in sheer exasperation: "O God, I wish I were dead! For
twopence I'd give up the ghost"—and then proceed, as Hamlet does proceed,
to the matter that is troubling him? It is not people who have lost the desire
to live, it is certainly not suicidal maniacs who say such things, but those who
are very much in love with life.
    [20] wholly.   [21] permit.

As if increase of appetite had grown
By what it fed on; and yet, within a month,—
Let me not think on't!—Frailty, thy name is woman!—
A little month, or e'er [22] those shoes were old
With which she followed my poor father's body,
Like Niobe, all tears,—why she, even she—
O God! a beast, that wants discourse [23] of reason,   150
Would have mourn'd longer—married with mine uncle,
My father's brother, but no more like my father
Than I to Hercules; [24] within a month,
Ere yet the salt of most unrighteous tears
Had left the flushing [25] of her galled [26] eyes,
She married. O, most wicked speed, to post
With such dexterity to incestuous [27] sheets!
It is not, nor it cannot come to good.—
But break [28] my heart, for I must hold my tongue.
Enter Horatio, Marcellus, and Bernardo.

HOR.   Hail to your lordship!

HAM.   (*Automatically, without looking at the newcomers.*)   I am glad
       to see you well.   160
      (*Suddenly aware that it was Horatio's voice which greeted him.*)
       Horatio!—or I do forget myself.

HOR.   The same, my lord, and your poor servant ever.

HAM.   Sir, my good friend; I'll change that name with you.
      And what make you from Wittenberg, Horatio? [29]
      Marcellus?

MAR.   My good lord!

HAM.   I am very glad to see you. [*To Ber.*] Good even, sir.—
      But what, in faith, make you from Wittenberg?

HOR.   A truant disposition, good my lord.

HAM.   I would not hear your enemy say so,   170
      Nor shall you do mine ear that violence,
      To make it truster of your own report

---

[22] "or e'er" is a strong expression for "before."   [23] faculty.

[24] Surely no weakling, no man who habitually shrinks from action, would dream of comparing himself to Hercules; he would sooner hang himself. Only a very strong man would chance the comparison. The mightiest of men need not hesitate to think himself less mighty than Hercules.

[25] redness.   [26] inflamed.   [27] See pp. 195–196.

[28] "break" is possibly subjunctive.

[29] Hamlet is delightedly surprised that his friend has come to Elsinore unexpectedly.

Against yourself. I know you are no truant.
But what is your affair in Elsinore?
(*The "great cannon" speaks to the clouds, as Claudius has promised
   it should at his "jocund" drink. Hamlet's thoughts are re-
   directed to the sources of his grief.*) We'll teach you to drink
deep ere you depart.

HOR. My lord, I came to see your father's funeral.

HAM. I pray thee, do not mock me, fellow-student.
I think it was to see my mother's wedding.

HOR. Indeed, my lord, it followed hard upon.

HAM. Thrift, thrift, Horatio! The funeral bak'd-meats   180
Did coldly furnish forth the marriage tables.
Would I had met my dearest [30] foe in heaven
Ere I had ever seen that day, Horatio!
My father!—Methinks I see my father.

HOR. (*Startled by Hamlet's words.*)   Oh, where, my lord?

HAM. (*Astounded at the question.*)   In my mind's eye, Horatio.

HOR. I saw him—once; he was a goodly king.

HAM. He was a *man*, take him for all in all,
I shall not look upon his like again.

HOR. (*Quietly.*)   My lord, I think I saw him yesternight.

HAM. Saw? (*Incredulous.*) Who?   190

HOR. My lord, the King your father.

HAM. (*Still disbelieving.*)   The King my father!

HOR. Season your admiration [31] for a while
With an attent ear, till I may deliver,
Upon the witness of these gentlemen,
This marvel to you.

HAM.   For God's love, let me hear.

HOR. Two nights together had these gentlemen,
Marcellus and Bernardo, on their watch,
In the dead waste and middle of the night,
Been thus encount'red. A figure like your father,
Arm'd at all points [32] exactly, cap-a-pie,[33]   200
Appears before them, and with solemn march
Goes slow and stately by them. Thrice he walk'd
By their oppress'd and fear-surprised eyes,

[30] bitterest.   [31] astonishment.
[32] The variant reading is "Arm'd at point," which would mean the same:
"completely."
[33] from head to foot (from the French).

Within his truncheon's [34] length; whilst they, distill'd
Almost to jelly with the act [35] of fear,
Stand dumb and speak not to him. This to me
In dreadful secrecy impart they did,
And I with them the third night kept the watch;
Where, as they had deliver'd, both in time,
Form of the thing, each word made true and good,   210
The apparition comes. (*Noting that Hamlet is still not convinced.*)
    I *knew* your father;
These hands are not more like.

HAM.   But where was this?

MAR.   My lord, upon the platform where we watch'd.

HAM.   Did you not *speak* to it?

HOR.   My lord, I did;
But answer made it none. Yet once methought
It lifted up it [36] head and did address
Itself to motion, like as it would speak;
But even then the morning cock crew loud,
And at the sound it shrunk in haste away,
And vanish'd from our sight.

HAM. (*Still not quite believing.*)   'Tis very strange.   220

HOR. (*Assuringly.*)   As I do live, my honour'd lord, 'tis true,
And we did think it writ down in our duty
To let you know of it.

HAM.   Indeed, indeed, sirs. But this troubles me.
Hold you the watch to-night?

MAR. }
BER. }   We do, my lord.

HAM.   Arm'd,[37] say you?

MAR. }
BER. } Arm'd, my lord.

HAM.   From top to toe?

MAR. }
BER. }   My lord, from head to foot.

HAM.   Then saw you not his face?

HOR.   O, yes, my lord; he wore his beaver [38] up.   230

HAM.   What, look'd he frowningly?

---

[34] A staff, the truncheon was the sign of military authority.   [35] action.
[36] "It," like "his," is to be found in Shakespeare as the possessive for the neuter.
[37] i.e., the Ghost.   [38] visor.

HOR.   A countenance [39] more
  In sorrow than in anger.

HAM.   Pale, or red?

HOR. Nay, very pale.

HAM.   And fix'd his eyes upon you?

HOR. Most constantly.

HAM. (*In an impetuous outburst.*) I would I had been there!

HOR. It would have much amaz'd you.

HAM. (*Abstractedly.*) Very like, very like. Stay'd it long?

HOR. While one with moderate haste might tell [40] a hundred.

MAR.
      }Longer, longer.
BER.

HOR. Not when I saw't.

HAM.   His beard was grizzly? No?   240

HOR. It was, as I have seen it in his life,
  A sable silver'd.

HAM. (*With sudden resolve.*) I will watch to-night;
  Perchance 'twill walk again.

HOR.   I warrant you it will.

HAM. If it assume my noble father's person,
  I'll speak to it, though hell itself should gape
  And bid me hold my peace.[41] I pray you all,
  If you have hitherto conceal'd this sight,
  Let it be tenable [42] in your silence still;
  And whatsoever else shall hap to-night,
  Give it an understanding, but no tongue.   250
  I will requite your loves. So, fare ye well.
  Upon the platform 'twixt eleven and twelve,
  I'll visit you.

ALL.   Our duty to your honour.

HAM. (*With great courtesy.*) Your *love*, as mine to you; farewell.

                           Exeunt [all but Hamlet].

  My father's spirit in arms! All is not well;
  I doubt [43] some foul play.[44] Would the night were come!
  Till then [45] sit still, my soul. Foul deeds will rise,
  Though all the earth o'erwhelm them, to men's eyes.   *Exit.*

---

[39] an expression.   [40] count.   [41] See pp. 151–157.   [42] held.   [43] suspect.
[44] Hamlet is sure that something is wrong. But, of course, he has no idea or suspicion that a murder has been committed. In Elizabethan English "foul play" would have applied to any kind of nefariousness.
[45] Impetuous Hamlet cannot bear waiting even until night comes!

SCENE III

> *A room in Polonius's house. (Later the same day.)*
> *Enter Laertes and Ophelia.*

LAER.   My necessaries are embark'd, farewell;
And, sister, as the winds give benefit
And convoy is assistant, do not sleep,
But let me hear from you.

OPH.   Do you doubt that?

LAER.   For Hamlet and the trifling of his favours,
Hold it a fashion and a toy [1] in blood,
A violet in the youth of primy [2] nature,
Forward,[3] not permanent, sweet, not lasting,
The [perfume and] suppliance [4] of a minute;
No more.

OPH. (*Dubiously.*)   No more but so?

LAER. (*Sententiously.*)   Think it no more: 10
For nature crescent [5] does not grow alone
In thews [6] and bulk, but, as this temple [7] waxes,
The inward service of the mind and soul
Grows wide withal. Perhaps he loves you now,
And now no soil nor cautel [8] doth besmirch
The virtue of his will; but you must fear,
His greatness [9] weigh'd, his will is not his own;
For he himself is subject to his birth.
He may not, as unvalued persons do,
Carve for himself, for on his choice depends   20
The sanity and health of the whole state;
And therefore must his choice be circumscrib'd
Unto the voice and yielding of that body
Whereof he is the head. Then, if he says he loves you,
It fits your wisdom so far to believe it
As he in his particular act and place
May give his saying deed; which is no further
Than the main voice of Denmark goes withal.
Then weigh what loss your honor may sustain
If with too credent ear you list his songs,   30
Or lose your heart, or your chaste treasure open
To his unmast'red importunity.

---

[1] caprice.   [2] (of the springtime).   [3] early.   [4] pastime.   [5] growing.
[6] sinews.   [7] (the body).   [8] deceit.   [9] his rank, as Prince of the realm.

Fear it, Ophelia, fear it, my dear sister,
And keep you in the rear of your affection,
Out of the shot and danger of desire.
The chariest maid is prodigal enough,
If she unmask her beauty to the moon.
Virtue itself scapes not calumnious strokes.
The canker [10] galls the infants of the spring
Too oft before the buttons [11] be disclos'd,   40
And in the morn and liquid dew of youth
Contagious blastments are most imminent.
Be wary then, best safety lies in fear;
Youth to itself rebels, though none else near.

OPH.   I shall the effect of this good lesson keep,
As watchman to my heart. But, good my brother,
Do not, as some ungracious [12] pastors do,
Show *me* the steep and thorny way to heaven,
Whilst, like a puff'd and reckless libertine,
Himself the primrose path of dalliance treads,   50
And recks not his own rede. [13]

LAER.   (*Brushing off her concern.*)   O, fear me not.
Enter Polonius.
I stay too long: but here my father comes.
A double blessing is a double grace;
Occasion smiles upon a second leave.

POL.   Yet here, Laertes? Aboard, aboard, for shame!
The wind sits in the shoulder of your sail,
And you are stay'd for. There; (*Laertes kneels for his father's bless-
      ing*) my blessing with you!
And these few precepts in thy memory
See thou character. [14] Give thy thoughts no tongue, [15]
Nor any unproportion'd thought his act.   60
Be thou familiar, but by no means vulgar. [16]
The friends thou hast, and their adoption tried,
Grapple them to thy soul with hoops of steel;
But do not dull thy palm with entertainment
Of each new-hatch'd, unfledg'd comrade. Beware
Of entrance to a quarrel; but being in,
Bear't that the opposed may beware of thee.
Give every man thine ear, but few thy voice;

[10] caterpillar.   [11] buds.   [12] (without grace).   [13] advice.   [14] inscribe.
[15] See pp. 284–287.   [16] i.e., don't consort with ordinary people.

Take each man's censure,[17] but reserve thy judgement.
Costly thy habit as thy purse can buy,   70
But not express'd in fancy; rich, not gaudy;
For the apparel oft proclaims the man,
And they in France of the best rank and station
Are most select and generous chief in that.
Neither a borrower nor a lender be;
For loan oft loses both itself and friend,
And borrowing dulls the edge of husbandry.[18]
This above all: to thine own self be true,
And it must follow, as the night the day,
Thou canst not then be false to any man.   80
Farewell; my blessing season [19] this in thee!

LAER.   Most humbly do I take my leave, my lord.

POL.   The time invites you; go, your servants tend.[20]

LAER.   Farewell, Ophelia, and remember well
What I have said to you.

OPH.   'Tis in my memory lock'd,
And you yourself shall keep the key of it.

LAER.   Farewell.   *Exit.*

POL.   What is't, Ophelia, he hath said to you?

OPH.   So please you, something touching the Lord Hamlet.

POL.   Marry, well bethought.   90
'Tis told me, he hath very oft of late
Given private time to you, and you yourself
Have of your audience been most free and bounteous.
(*Reprovingly.*) If it be so—as so 'tis put on me,[21]
And that in way of caution—I must tell you,
You do not understand yourself so clearly
As it behoves my daughter and your honour.
What is between you? Give me up the truth.

OPH.   He hath, my lord, of late made many tenders
Of his affection to me.   100

POL.   (*Sneeringly.*) Affection! pooh! You speak like a green girl,
Unsifted [22] in such perilous circumstance.
Do you believe his *tenders*,[23] as you call them?

OPH.   (*Worried.*)   I do not know, my lord, what I should think.

POL.   Marry, I'll teach you: think yourself a baby
That you have ta'en his tenders for true pay,

[17] opinion.   [18] economy.   [19] temper.   [20] await.
[21] called to my attention.   [22] untried.   [23] offers.

Which are not sterling. Tender [24] yourself more dearly,
Or—not to crack the wind of the poor phrase,
Running it thus—you'll tender [25] me a fool.

OPH. (*Shocked.*)   My lord, he hath importun'd me with love   110
In *honourable* fashion.

POL. (*With mockery.*)   Ay, fashion you may call it. Go to, go to.

OPH.   And hath given countenance to his speech, my lord,
With almost all the holy vows of heaven.

POL.   Ay, springes [26] to catch woodcocks.[27] I do know,
When the blood burns, how prodigal the soul
Lends the tongue vows. These blazes, daughter,
Giving more light than heat, extinct in both
Even in their promise, as it is a-making,
You must not take for fire. From this time, daughter,   120
Be somewhat scanter of your maiden presence.
Set your entreatments [28] at a higher rate
Than a command to parley.[29] For Lord Hamlet,
Believe so much in him, that he is young,
And with a larger tether may he walk
Than may be given you. In few,[30] Ophelia,
Do not believe his vows; for they are brokers,[31]
Not of that dye which their investments [32] show,
But mere implorators of unholy suits,
Breathing like sanctified and pious bawds,   130
The better to beguile. This is for all:
I would not, in plain terms, from this time forth,
Have you so slander [33] any moment leisure
As to give words or talk with the Lord Hamlet.
Look to't, I charge you. Come your ways.

OPH.   I shall obey, my lord.[34]   *Exeunt.*

SCENE IV

   The platform. (*Midnight of the second day.*)
   Enter Hamlet, Horatio, and Marcellus.

HAM.   The air bites shrewdly; it is very cold.

---

[24] regard.   [25] give.   [26] snares.
[27] The woodcock was held to be the most foolish of birds because most
easily caught.
[28] Polonius here draws an analogy between a woman defending her virtue
and a town being besieged by the enemy.
[29] a conference.   [30] in short.   [31] panders.   [32] attire.   [33] misuse.
[34] And she does! See p. 280.

HOR.   It is a nipping and an eager [1] air.

HAM.   What hour now?

HOR.   I think it lacks of twelve.

MAR.   No, it is struck.

HOR.   Indeed? I heard it not. Then it draws near the season
　　　Wherein the spirit held his wont to walk.
　　　A flourish of trumpets, and two pieces go off within.
　　　What does this mean, my lord?

HAM.   The King doth wake [2] to-night and takes his rouse,
　　　Keeps wassail,[3] and the swaggering up-spring [4] reels;
　　　And, as he drains his draughts of Rhenish down,　　　　　　10
　　　The kettle-drum and trumpet thus bray out
　　　The triumph of his pledge.

HOR.   Is it a custom?

HAM.   Ay, marry, is't,
　　　But to my mind, though I am native here
　　　And to the manner born, it is a custom
　　　More honour'd in the breach than the observance.
　　　[5] [This heavy-headed revel east and west
　　　Makes us traduc'd and tax'd [6] of other nations.
　　　They clepe [7] us drunkards, and with swinish phrase
　　　Soil our addition; [8] and indeed it takes　　　　　　　20
　　　From our achievements, though perform'd at height,
　　　The pith and marrow of our attribute.[9]
　　　So, oft it chances in particular [10] men,
　　　That for some vicious mole [11] of nature in them,
　　　As, in their birth—wherein they are not guilty,
　　　Since nature cannot choose his [12] origin—
　　　By their o'ergrowth of some complexion [13]
　　　Oft breaking down the pales and forts of reason,
　　　Or by some habit that too much o'er-leavens

---

[1] sharp.　　[2] holds revel.

[3] (from the Anglo-Saxon *wes hal*—a toast—"may you be in health").

[4] a boisterous dance.

[5] This passage, lines 17–38, not in the Folio, is one of the most clearly superfluous in the play. Mr. Olivier's movie, which omitted vast sections of the play, included most of this. Worse yet, the lines from "So, oft it chances" through "From that particular fault" were quoted at the opening of the film in a ghostly voice as the theme of the story, with the gratuitous appended motto:

　　　This is the tragedy of a man who could not make up his mind.

[6] censured.　　[7] call.　　[8] title.　　[9] reputation.　　[10] individual.
[11] blemish.　　[12] its.　　[13] of some part of their temperament.

The form of plausive [14] manners, that these men,   30
Carrying, I say, the stamp of one defect,
Being nature's livery, or fortune's star,—
His virtues else—be they as pure as grace,
As infinite as man may undergo—
Shall in the general censure take corruption
From that particular fault. The dram of eale [15]
Doth all the noble substance often dout [16]
To his own scandal.]
Enter Ghost.

HOR. (*With awe.*)   Look, my lord, it comes!
HAM.   Angels and ministers of grace defend us!
Be thou a spirit of health or goblin damn'd,[17]   40
Bring with thee airs from heaven or blasts from hell,
Be thy intents wicked or charitable,
Thou com'st in such a questionable [18] shape
That I will speak to thee. I'll call thee Hamlet,
King, father, royal Dane. O, answer me!
Let me not burst in ignorance, but tell
Why thy canoniz'd [19] bones, hearsed in death,
Have burst their cerements; [20] why the sepulchre,
Wherein we saw thee quietly inurn'd,
Hath op'd his ponderous and marble jaws,   50
To cast thee up again. What may this mean,
That thou, dead corse, again in complete steel
Revisits thus the glimpses of the moon,
Making night hideous, and we fools of nature
So horridly to shake our disposition
With thoughts beyond the reaches of our souls?
Say, why is this? Wherefore? What should we do?

Ghost beckons Hamlet.

HOR.   It beckons you to go away with it,
As if it some impartment did desire
To you alone.
MAR.   Look, with what courteous action   60
It wafts you to a more removed ground.
But do not go with it.
HOR.   No, by no means! [21]

---

[14] pleasing.   [15] evil.   [16] do out, put out.   [17] See pp. 153–156.
[18] inviting question.   [19] buried with all due ceremonial rites.
[20] burial clothes.   [21] See pp. 156–157. Note lines 69–74, below.

HAM.   It will not speak; then will I follow it. (*He begins to move toward the Ghost.*)

HOR. (*Putting a restraining hand on Hamlet's arm.*)   Do not, my lord.

HAM.   Why, what should be the fear?
I do not set my life at a pin's fee,
And for my soul, what can it do to that,
Being a thing immortal as itself?
It waves me forth again. (*Disengaging himself from Horatio's hold.*)
I'll follow it.

HOR.   What if it tempt you toward the flood, my lord,
Or to the dreadful summit of the cliff   70
That beetles o'er his base into the sea,
And there assume some other horrible form,
Which might deprive your sovereignty of reason
And draw you into madness? Think of it.
[The very place puts toys of desperation,
Without more motive, into every brain
That looks so many fathoms to the sea
And hears it roar beneath.]

HAM.   It wafts me still.
(*Beginning to move toward the Ghost again.*) Go on, I'll follow
thee. (*Horatio and Marcellus each seize an arm of Hamlet and
hold him back.*)

MAR.   You shall not go, my lord.

HAM.   Hold off your hand.   80

HOR. (*Firmly.*)   Be rul'd; you shall not go.

HAM. (*With anguish.*)   My fate cries out,
And makes each petty artery in this body
As hardy as the Nemean lion's [22] nerve.
Still am I call'd. Unhand me, gentlemen.
(*Fiercely.*) By heaven, I'll make a ghost [23] of him that lets [24] me!
(*Throwing them off.*)
I say, away!—Go on, I'll follow thee.   *Exeunt Ghost and Hamlet.*

HOR.   He waxes desperate with imagination.

MAR.   Let's follow. 'Tis not fit thus to obey him.

HOR.   Have after. To what issue will this come?

MAR.   Something is rotten in the state of Denmark. [25]   90

---

[22] One of the labors of Hercules was to fetch the Nemean lion's skin.
[23] Even at such a moment Hamlet can make such a pun!   [24] hinders.
[25] At least one idiot in every audience can be counted upon to laugh at
this line of Marcellus. There must in all justice be a particularly deep pit of

HOR.   Heaven will direct it.[26]

MAR.   Nay, let's follow him.   *Exeunt.*

SCENE V

> *Another part of the platform. (Some few hours later.)*
> *Enter Ghost* [1] *and Hamlet.*

HAM.   Where wilt thou lead me? Speak, I'll go no further.

GHOST.   Mark me.

HAM.   I will.

GHOST.   My hour is almost come,
When I to sulphurous and tormenting flames [2]
Must render up myself.

HAM.   Alas, poor ghost!

GHOST.   Pity me not, but lend thy serious hearing
To what I shall unfold.

HAM.   Speak; I am bound to hear.

GHOST *(Firmly.)*   So art thou to *revenge*,[3] when thou shalt hear.

HAM. *(Astounded.)*   What!

GHOST.   I *am* thy father's spirit,
Doom'd for a certain term to walk the night,   10
And for the day confin'd to fast in fires,
Till the foul crimes done in my days of nature
Are burnt and purg'd away.[4] But that I am forbid
To tell the secrets of my prison-house,
I could a tale unfold whose lightest word
Would harrow up thy soul, freeze thy young blood,
Make thy two eyes, like stars, start from their spheres,
Thy knotty and combined locks to part

Hell reserved for the half-wit who first decided to make comic capital out
of the expression. (By his side there must be a place for one other, the ass
who decided that the opening measures of Chopin's superb *Marche Funèbre*
from the Sonata in B flat minor are funny too.) The unfortunate actor is
these days reduced to mumbling this line so that it is barely heard, so that
some fool will not titter.

    [26] (the issue).   [1] See pp. 151–159.   [2] of purgatory.

    [3] This is the first intimation Hamlet has had that there is anything to avenge.

    [4] Hamlet's father has died without the opportunity of receiving the last
rites of the Church. His spirit is atoning in purgatory for such sins as a mortal
is likely to commit. He is not to be thought of as having been in any way
criminal. (See lines 76–79, below.) Hamlet's hate for his father's murderer
will hereafter be doubled when he remembers that the murder prevented his
father from making his peace with Heaven (III, iii, 80 seq.).

And each particular hair to stand on end,
Like quills upon the fretful porpentine.[5]   20
But this eternal blazon [6] must not be
To ears of flesh and blood. List, Hamlet, O, list!
If thou didst ever thy dear father love—

HAM.   O God! [7]

GHOST.   Revenge his foul and most unnatural murder.

HAM. (*Horror-struck.*)   *Murder?*

GHOST.   Murder most foul, as in the best it is,
But this most foul, strange, and unnatural.

HAM. (*Passionately.*)   Haste me to know't, that I, with wings as swift
As meditation or the thoughts of love,   30
May sweep to my revenge.

GHOST.   I find thee apt;
And duller shouldst thou be than the fat weed [8]
That roots [9] itself in ease on Lethe [10] wharf,
Wouldst thou not stir in this. Now, Hamlet, hear.
It's given out that, sleeping in mine orchard,
A serpent stung me; so the whole ear of Denmark
Is by a forged process [11] of my death
Rankly abus'd; but know, thou noble youth,
The serpent that did sting thy father's life
Now wears his crown.

HAM.   O my prophetic soul!   40
Mine uncle! [12]

GHOST.   Ay, that incestuous, that adulterate beast,
With witchcraft of his wit, with traitorous gifts,—
O wicked wit and gifts, that have the power
So to seduce!—won to his shameful lust
The will of my most seeming-virtuous queen.
O Hamlet, what a falling-off was there!
From me, whose love was of that dignity
That it went hand in hand even with the vow
I made to her in marriage, and to decline   50
Upon a wretch whose natural gifts were poor

---

[5] porcupine.   [6] disclosure of what eternity is like.
[7] Note the brilliant dramaturgy which is involved in Hamlet's heartfelt cry. This interruption of his isolates the next line from the preceding lines of the Ghost's speech, and causes this line which follows to stand alone in all its shocking power.
[8] the asphodel.(?)   [9] This is the Quarto reading. The Folio reads "rots."
[10] the river of forgetfulness.   [11] official story.   [12] See footnote p. 110.

To those of mine!
But virtue, as it never will be moved,
Though lewdness court it in a shape of heaven
So lust, though to a radiant angel link'd,
Will sate itself in a celestial bed
And prey on garbage.
But, soft! methinks I scent the morning's air.
Brief let me be. Sleeping within mine orchard,
My custom always in the afternoon,   60
Upon my secure [13] hour thy uncle stole,
With juice of cursed hebenon [14] in a vial,
And in the porches of mine ears did pour
The leperous distilment; whose effect
Holds such an enmity with blood of man
That swift as quicksilver it courses through
The natural gates and alleys of the body,
And with a sudden vigour it doth posset [15]
And curd, like eager droppings into milk,
The thin and wholesome blood. So did it mine,   70
And a most instant tetter bark'd [16] about,
Most lazar-like, with vile and loathsome crust,
All my smooth body.
Thus was I, sleeping, by a brother's hand
Of life, of crown, and queen, at once dispatch'd;
Cut off even in the blossoms of my sin,
Unhousel'd,[17] disappointed,[18] unanel'd,[19]
No reckoning made, but sent to my account
With all my imperfections on my head.

HAM.   O, horrible! O, horrible! most horrible!   80
GHOST.   If thou hast nature in thee, bear it not;
Let not the royal bed of Denmark be
A couch for luxury [20] and damned incest.
But, howsoever thou pursuest this act,
Taint not thy mind, nor let thy soul contrive
Against thy mother aught.[21] Leave her to heaven
And to those thorns that in her bosom lodge,
To prick and sting her. Fare thee well at once!

---

[13] unsuspecting.   [14] the juice of the yew or of the ebony.
[15] curdle. The "eager droppings" of the next line are vinegar droppings.
[16] encrusted as if with a bark.   [17] without having received the Eucharist.
[18] unprepared.   [19] without extreme unction.   [20] lechery.   [21] See p. 142.

The glow-worm shows the matin to be near,
And 'gins to pale his uneffectual fire.   90
Adieu, adieu! Hamlet, remember me.   *Exit.*

HAM. (*Staggering about like a drunken man.*)   O all you host of heaven!
    O earth! What else? [22]
And shall I couple hell? O, fie! Hold, my heart,
And you, my sinews, grow not instant old,
But bear me stiffly up. Remember thee!
(*His hands clutching at his temples.*) Ay, thou poor ghost, while
    memory holds a seat
In this distracted globe.[23] Remember thee!
Yea, from the table of my memory
I'll wipe away all trivial fond records,
All saws [24] of books, all forms, all pressures [25] past,   100
That youth and observation copied there,
And thy commandment all alone shall live
Within the book and volume of my brain,
Unmix'd with baser matter. Yes, yes, by heaven!
O most pernicious woman!
O villain, villain, smiling, damned villain!
My tables,[26] my tables,—meet it is I set it down!
That one may smile, and smile, and be a villain! [27]
At least I'm sure it may be so in Denmark.
So, uncle, there you are. Now to my word; [28]   110
It is "Adieu, adieu! remember me." [29]
I have sworn't.[30]

MAR. ⎫
      ⎬ (*Within.*)   My lord, my lord!
HOR. ⎭

MAR.   (*Within.*)   Lord Hamlet!

---

[22] See pp. 142–143.   [23] head.   [24] maxims.   [25] impressions.

[26] tablets. These were used for jotting down memoranda. Most modern
critics conceive of Hamlet as here actually writing down the next line. Bradley
thinks him to be making the notation in a spirit of "desperate jest" (*Shakespearean Tragedy*, pp. 409–412). Adams calls the act "more or less silly," but
justified as a product of Hamlet's exhaustion (*Hamlet*, p. 216). It seems pref-
erable to think of Hamlet as referring to the "tablets" of his memory. He has
just said:

> Yea, from the table of my memory
> I'll wipe away all trivial fond records . . .

[27] Thinking of Claudius' urbanity and calm manipulation of everyone's
allegiance, Hamlet here unconsciously touches upon the vastness of the task
before him.

[28] motto.   [29] (the Ghost's last words).   [30] See pp. 142–143.

HOR.   (*Within.*)   Heaven secure him!
HAM.   So be it! [31]
MAR.   (*Within.*)   Illo, ho, ho,[32] my lord!
HAM.   Hillo, ho, ho, boy! Come, bird, come.
       Enter Horatio and Marcellus.
MAR.   How is't, my noble lord?
HOR.   What news, my lord?
HAM.   O, wonderful!
HOR.   Good my lord, tell it.
HAM.   (*Bursting with the Ghost's revelations, and eager to impart them
           to his friend.*)   No, you'll reveal it.
HOR.   Not I, my lord, by heaven.
MAR.   Nor I, my lord.   120
HAM.   How say you, then, would heart of man once think it?—
       But you'll be secret?
HOR. ⎱
MAR. ⎰   Ay, by heaven, my lord.

HAM.   (*In a rush of words, about to disclose what he has heard.*)   There's
           ne'er a villain dwelling in all Denmark—(*He halts just in time.
           With characteristic impetuosity he was about to tell all and
           conceivably ruin his case before he had even taken the time
           to assess it! He looks in dazed bewilderment at both men, claps
           his hand over his mouth to dam the current, and staggers away,
           mumbling.*)

       But he's an arrant knave.[33]
HOR.   (*A little offended at Hamlet's suddenly breaking off the confidence.*)
           There needs no ghost, my lord, come from the grave
       To tell us this.
HAM.   (*Evasively.*)   Why, right, you are i' the right.
       And so, without more circumstance [34] at all,
       I hold it fit that we shake hands and part;
       You, as your business and desires shall point you,
       For every man has business and desire,
       Such as it is; and for mine own poor part,   130
       Look you, I'll go pray.
HOR.   These are but wild and whirling words, my lord.
HAM.   (*Perceiving that his belated precaution is hurting his best friend;*

---

[31] Amen! (to Horatio's preceding line).
[32] This is the call of a falconer to his hawk. Hence Hamlet's next line.
[33] These minutes are not thus generally understood. See pp. 142–144.
[34] circumlocution.

with warm apology.)   I'm sorry they offend you, heartily;
Yes, faith, heartily.

HOR. (*Like the true friend he is, reassuringly.*)   There's no offence, my
lord.

HAM.   Yes, by Saint Patrick, but there is, Horatio,
And much offence too. Touching this vision here,
It is an honest ghost,[35] that let me tell you.
(*Atoning to Marcellus too.*)   For your desire to know what is be-
tween us,
O'ermaster't as you may. And now, good friends,   140
As you are friends, scholars, and soldiers,
Give me one poor request.

HOR.   What is't, my lord? We will.

HAM.   Never make known what you have seen to-night.[36]

HOR. ⎱ My lord, we will not.
MAR. ⎰

HAM. (*Insistent.*)   Nay, but swear't.

HOR.   In faith,
My lord, not I.[37]

MAR.   Nor I, my lord, in faith.

HAM.   Upon my sword.[38]

MAR. (*Taking umbrage, since he has already given his word.*)   We have
sworn, my lord, already.

HAM. (*Not to be denied, urgently.*)   Indeed, upon my sword, indeed.

GHOST.   Swear!   *Ghost cries under the stage.*[39]

HAM.   Ah, ha, boy! say'st thou so? Art thou there, truepenny? [40]   150
Come on; you hear this fellow in the cellarage.
Consent to swear.

HOR.   Propose the oath, my lord.

[35] Hamlet is here only too eager to believe that the Ghost was no demon.
Later he understands the importance of making sure of what the Ghost has
told him.

[36] Having so nearly made a grave mistake himself, he pledges them to
silence on what they have witnessed.

[37] i.e., I'll not make known what I have seen tonight.

[38] Oaths were often made upon a sword because of the cruciform of the
hilt. Moreover, the hilt sometimes had a cross engraved upon it or the name
"Jesus."

[39] This segment of the scene, because of its supernatural effects, may very
well be a carry-over from Kyd's play; if it is, Shakespeare has employed it
well to continue to the end of the act the nightmarish tone of the whole
scene's proceedings.

[40] honest old fellow—a deliberately slangy expression.

HAM.   Never to speak of this that you have seen.
         Swear by my sword.

GHOST. (*Beneath.*)   Swear.

HAM.   *Hic et ubique?* [41] Then we'll shift our ground.
         Come hither, gentlemen,
         And lay your hands again upon my sword.
         Never to speak of this that you have heard,
         Swear by my sword.   160

GHOST. (*Beneath.*)   Swear.

HAM.   Well said, old mole! Canst work i' the earth so fast?
         A worthy pioneer! [42] Once more remove, good friends.

HOR.   O day and night, but this is wondrous strange! [43]

HAM.   And therefore as a stranger give it welcome.
         There are more things in heaven and earth, Horatio,
         Than are dreamt of in our [44] philosophy.
         But come;
         Here, as before, never, so help you mercy,
         How strange or odd soe'er I bear myself,—   170
         As I perchance hereafter shall think meet
         To put an antic disposition on [45]—
         That you, at such time seeing me, never shall,
         With arms encumb'red thus, or this headshake,
         Or by pronouncing of some doubtful phrase,
         As "Well, we know," or "We could, an if we would,"
         Or "If we list to speak," or "There be, an if they might,"
         Or such ambiguous giving out, to note
         That you know aught of me,—this not to do,
         So grace and mercy at your most need help you,   180
         Swear.

GHOST. (*Beneath.*)   Swear.

HAM.   Rest, rest, perturbed spirit! (*They swear.*) So, gentlemen,
         With all my love I do commend me to you.

---

[41] here and everywhere (Latin). The Ghost, like the Devil, seems to be everywhere at once.

[42] digger.

[43] Hamlet's behavior seems "strange" to Horatio only because neither he nor Marcellus have been hearing the ghostly voice. As in III, iv, it is a ghost's privilege to be seen or heard only by those he chooses for the honor.

[44] The Quartos read "your." The meaning would be about the same in either case, for "your" would be meant impersonally.

[45] See pp. 144–148 for a full discussion of this. It is the pledge of secrecy, not the "antic disposition," which is the core of the passage.

And what so poor a man as Hamlet is
May do, to express his love and friending to you,
God willing, shall not lack. Let us go in together; [46]
And still your fingers on your lips, I pray.
The time is out of joint;—O cursed spite,
That ever I was born to set it right! [47]   190
Nay, come, let's go together.   *Exeunt.*

ACT SECOND

SCENE I

    A room in Polonius's house. (Some two months later.)
Enter Polonius and Reynaldo.

POL. Give him this money and these notes, Reynaldo.

REY. I will, my lord.

POL. You shall do marvellous wisely, good Reynaldo,
Before you visit him, to make inquiry
Of his behaviour.

REY.   My lord, I did intend it.

POL. Marry,[1] well said, very well said. Look you, sir,
Inquire me first what Danskers [2] are in Paris,
And how, and who, what means, and where they keep,
What company, at what expense; and finding
By this encompassment and drift of question   10
That they do know my son, come you more nearer
Than your particular demands will touch it.
Take you, as 'twere, some distant knowledge of him,
As thus, "I know his father and his friends,
And in part him." Do you mark this, Reynaldo?

REY. (*Bored.*) Ay, very well, my lord.

POL. "And in part him; but," you may say, "not well.

[46] As they are about to go off, the others stand aside in respectful attendance.
But Hamlet will not have it: they are his friends and will "go in together."

[47] It is odd that this couplet has so often been cited to show Hamlet's
indisposition toward action. But, after all, he does say that he *was born* to
set things right. And, as we shall see, he will at the first possible moment
attempt to do something in that direction. (A parallel instance: Wilson says
that after reading Gregg on *Hamlet*, he realized he "had been born" to answer
him. Result: not procrastination, but Wilson's *What Happens in Hamlet!*)

[1] (an expletive).   [2] Danes.

But, if't be he I mean, he's very wild,
Addicted so and so;" and there put on him
What forgeries you please; marry, none so rank   20
As may dishonour him,—take heed of that;
But, sir, such wanton,[3] wild, and usual slips
As are companions noted and most known
To youth and liberty.

REY.   As gaming, my lord?
POL.   Ay, or drinking, fencing, swearing, quarrelling,
Drabbing;[4] you may go so far.
REY. (*Astonished.*)   My lord, that would dishonour him.
POL.   Faith, no, as you may season it in the charge.
You must not put another scandal on him,
That he is open to incontinency.[5]   30
That's not my meaning. But breathe his faults so quaintly[6]
That they may seem the taints of liberty,
The flash and outbreak of a fiery mind,
A savageness in unreclaimed blood,
Of general assault.[7]
REY. (*Protesting.*)   But, my good lord,—
POL.   Wherefore should you do this?
REY.   Ay, my lord,
I would know that.
POL.   Marry, sir, here's my drift,
And, I believe, it is a fetch of warrant:[8]
You laying these slight sullies on my son,
As 'twere a thing a little soil'd i' the working,[9]
Mark you,   40
Your party in converse, him you would sound,
Having ever seen in the prenominate crimes
The youth you breathe of guilty, be assur'd
He closes with you[10] in this consequence;
"Good sir," or so, or "friend," or "gentleman,"
According to the phrase and the addition[11]
Of man and country.
REY.   Very good, my lord.
POL.   And then, sir, does he this—he does—

---

[3] such slips as are common to a spoiled young man.   [4] visiting prostitutes.
[5] visiting prostitutes regularly.   [6] whisper his faults so delicately.
[7] common to all young men.   [8] a warrantable stratagem.
[9] soiled by his experiences.   [10] he agrees with you.   [11] title.

What was I about to say? [By the mass,] I was about
    to say something. Where did I leave? [12]

REY. (*Grimly.*)   At "closes in the consequence," at "friend or
so," and "gentleman."

POL.   At "closes in the consequence," ay, marry.
He closes with you thus: "I know the gentleman.
I saw him yesterday, or t'other day,
Or then, or then, with such and such; and, as you say,
There was he gaming; there o'ertook in 's rouse; [13]
There falling out [14] at tennis;" or, perchance,
"I saw him enter such a house of sale," [15]   60
Videlicet, a brothel, or so forth.
(*Triumphantly.*) See you now
Your bait of falsehood takes this carp [16] of truth;
And thus do we of wisdom and of reach,[17]
With windlasses [18] and with assays of bias,[19]
By indirections find directions out.
So by my former lecture and advice,
Shall you my son. You have me, have you not?

REY. (*With a sigh.*)   My lord, I have.

POL.   God buy you; fare you well.

REY. (*Anxious to depart.*)   Good my lord.   70

POL.   Observe his inclination in [20] yourself.

REY.   I shall, my lord.

POL.   And let him ply his music.

REY.   Well, my lord.

POL.   Farewell!   *Exit Reynaldo.*[21]

---

[12] Kittredge: Just because Polonius gets befuddled here, we should not be
led "to undervalue the wisdom of his advice to his son" (*Hamlet*, p. 176). (!!)
If this were so, it might be asked why Shakespeare took the trouble to show
us how dull, contemptible, and dim-witted he is in this conversation with
Reynaldo.
    [13] overcome with drink.   [14] quarreling.   [15] a brothel.
    [16] The carp is a big fish. "With just this little bit of a lie we can catch a
great amount of truth."
    [17] far seeing.   [18] roundaboutness.
    [19] a term from bowling. The ball is thrown in a curved, not a direct, line.
    [20] for.
    [21] It is only because we know that Laertes has been for some time in
Paris that we have now any indication that some time has elapsed since Act I.
In no place in Act II is there any reference made as to how much time has
passed since Hamlet's interview with the Ghost. In short, Shakespeare does
not want us to think of the time element here at all. See pp. 177–180.

Enter Ophelia.

     How now, Ophelia! what's the matter?

OPH. Alas, my lord, I have been so affrighted!

POL. With what, in the name of God?

OPH. (*In terror.*) My lord, as I was sewing in my chamber,[22]
  Lord Hamlet, with his doublet all unbrac'd,[23]
  No hat upon his head, his stockings foul'd,
  Ungart'red, and down-gyved [24] to his ankle,   80
  Pale as his shirt, his knees knocking each other,
  And with a look so piteous in purport
  As if he had been loosed out of hell
  To speak of horrors,—he comes before me.

POL. Mad [25] for thy love?

OPH.   My lord, I do not know,
  But truly, I do fear it.

POL.   What said he?

OPH. He took me by the wrist and held me hard;
  Then goes he to the length of all his arm,
  And, with his other hand thus o'er his brow,
  He falls to such perusal of my face   90
  As he would draw it. Long stay'd he so.
  At last, a little shaking of mine arm,
  And thrice his head thus waving up and down,
  He rais'd a sigh so piteous and profound
  That it did seem to shatter all his bulk [26]
  And end his being. That done, he lets me go;
  And, with his head over his shoulder turn'd,
  He seem'd to find his way without his eyes,
  For out o' doors he went without their help,
  And, to the last, bended their light on me.   100

POL. [Come,] go with me, I will go seek the King.
  This is the very ecstasy [27] of love,
  Whose violent property [28] fordoes [29] itself
  And leads the will to desperate undertakings
  As oft as any passion under heaven
  That does afflict our natures. I am sorry,—

---

 [22] See pp. 196–199. [23] unlaced.
 [24] slipped down to the ankle like "gyves"—i.e., fetters.
 [25] This is the first time anyone speaks of Hamlet as mad. Polonius may
very well be the author of that idea. See pp. 147–150.
 [26] frame. [27] madness. [28] nature. [29] destroys.

(*Sternly.*) What, have you given him any hard words of late?

OPH.   No, my good lord, but, as you did command,
I did repel his letters and deni'd
His access to me.[30]

POL.   That hath made him mad.   110
I am sorry that with better heed and judgement
I had not quoted [31] him. I fear'd he did but trifle
And meant to wreck thee; but beshrew my jealousy! [32]
By heaven, it is as proper to our age [33]
To cast [34] beyond ourselves in our opinions
As it is common for the younger sort
To lack discretion. Come, go we to the King.
This must be known, which, being kept close, might move
More grief to hide than hate to utter love.[35]   119
[Come.]   *Exeunt.*

SCENE II

   A room in the castle. (*The same day.*)
   Flourish. Enter King, Queen, Rosencrantz, Guildenstern, with others.

KING.   Welcome, dear Rosencrantz and Guildenstern!
Moreover that we much did long to see you,
The need we have to use you did provoke
Our hasty sending. Something have you heard
Of Hamlet's transformation; so I call it,
Since not the exterior nor the inward man
Resembles that it was. What it should be,
More than his father's death, that thus hath put him
So much from the understanding of himself,
I cannot dream of. I entreat you both,   10
That, being of so young days brought up with him
And since so neighbour'd to his youth and humour,

---

[30] Note that Shakespeare here quite plainly informs us what Ophelia's treatment of Hamlet has been since I, iii.

[31] observed.   [32] suspicion.   [33] i.e., people of my years.   [34] to go too far.

[35] These two lines are the most difficult in the play. The meaning seems to be: "This love of Hamlet's must be made known—i.e., to the King and Queen—which, if we keep it secret (close) might cause more grief if concealed (to hide) than anger (hate) if we tell it." Polonius is certain that the King and Queen will never approve of a marriage between Hamlet and Ophelia because of the difference in their rank. Gertrude, we see presently, has no such objection.

That you vouchsafe your rest [1] here in our court
Some little time; so by your companies
To draw him on to pleasures, and to gather
So much as from occasions you may glean,
[Whether aught, to us unknown, afflicts him thus,]
That, open'd, lies within our remedy.

QUEEN.   Good gentlemen, he hath much talk'd of you;
And sure I am two men there are not living   20
To whom he more adheres.[2] If it will please you
To show us so much gentry [3] and good will
As to expend your time with us a while
For the supply and profit [4] of our hope,
Your visitation shall receive such thanks
As fits a king's remembrance.

ROS. (*Graciously.*)   Both your Majesties
Might, by the sovereign power you have of us,
Put your dread pleasures more into command
Than to entreaty.

GUIL. (*Warmly.*)   We both obey,
And here give up ourselves, in the full bent   30
To lay our services freely at your feet,
To be commanded.[5]

---

[1] agree to remain.   [2] See pp. 297–298.   [3] courtesy.
[4] support and realization.
[5] See pp. 266–267. Claudius' words to Hamlet's friends have been no less astute than revealing. At no time does Claudius ever believe Hamlet mad; he would be much more at his ease if he had reason to think that. He has insinuated by the word "transformation" that Hamlet is unbalanced, without his actually saying so. And what would not Claudius give to know what it is "more than his father's death" that is disturbing Hamlet!

How has Hamlet been "transformed"? We have seen him behaving with incivility toward his mother and with insolence toward the King before the whole Court; and we have seen Claudius respond only with sorrowful patience. The disclosures of the Ghost, and complexities of his problem, his old hate for Claudius, his disgust (greater than ever) at the marriage, and his newer distress over Ophelia's apparent desertion of him, have naturally done nothing to cause the Prince to be more gracious or less caustic to the King and Queen. The Court, knowing no detail of his multiple causes of anguish, will inevitably have been buzzing about the oddity of his conduct—all the more so since, as we later learn, he has in the past been a model of elegance and charm. Hamlet's "transformation" has, in short, been one only of degree: he is now more ungracious, more insolent, more ironic than ever. And thus the rumors have begun to grow.

The King's tolerance of his nephew's ill temper will have only given

KING. Thanks, Rosencrantz and gentle Guildenstern.

QUEEN. Thanks, Guildenstern and gentle Rosencrantz,[6]
And I beseech you instantly to visit
My too much changed son. Go, some of ye,
And bring the gentlemen where Hamlet is.

GUIL. Heavens make our presence and our practices
Pleasant and helpful to him!

QUEEN.   Amen!

> *Exeunt Rosencrantz, Guildenstern, and some Attendants.*
> *Enter Polonius.*

POL. The ambassadors from Norway, my good lord,   40
Are joyfully return'd.

KING. (*Smiling.*) Thou still [7] hast been the father of good news.[8]

POL. (*Radiant at the flattery.*) Have I, my lord? Assure you, my good
liege,
I hold my duty as I hold my soul,
Both to my God and to my gracious king.
And I do think, or else this brain of mine
Hunts not the trail of policy [9] so sure
As it hath us'd to do, that I have found
The very cause of Hamlet's lunacy.

KING. O, speak of that; that I do long to hear.   50

POL. Give first admittance to the ambassadors.
My news shall be the fruit [10] to that great feast.

KING. Thyself do grace to them, and bring them in.   *Exit Polonius.*
He tells me, my sweet queen, that he hath found

---

wings to the whispers. The more incomprehensible Hamlet's bad grace in the
presence of the King's forbearance, the better for Claudius. By calling such
conduct a "transformation," he not only plays safe, he exhibits anew his loving
tenderness for Hamlet. Hamlet's two friends can see Claudius only as a concerned parent, anxious to draw his son on to gaiety. From the King's point
of view, there is everything to profit and nothing to lose. Hamlet may very
well confide in his old friends: if the source of Hamlet's rudeness is not the
fratricide, Claudius' chief worry is laid; if by some miracle Hamlet has learned
something of his father's murder, Claudius will be armed against his nephew
by that knowledge but, on the other hand, has nothing to fear if Rosencrantz
and Guildenstern are let into the secret. Such a story told to his friends would
sound preposterous enough to make Hamlet seem indeed transformed!

[6] These two lines are probably spoken together. Claudius and Gertrude
would naturally each first address the young man standing nearer.

[7] always.

[8] Kittredge interprets the line as showing that "both the King and the
Queen have a genuine affection" for Polonius (*Hamlet*, p. 180). See pp. 287-290.

[9] statesmanship.   [10] dessert.

The head and source of all your son's distemper.

QUEEN. (*Moodily.*)   I doubt [11] it is no other but the main,[12]
His father's death and our o'erhasty marriage.
Re-enter Polonius, with Voltimand and Cornelius.

KING.   Well, we shall sift him.—Welcome, my good friends!
Say, Voltimand, what from our brother Norway?

VOLT.   Most fair return of greetings and desires.   60
Upon our first,[13] he sent out to suppress
His nephew's levies, which to him appear'd
To be a preparation 'gainst the Polack,
But, better look'd into, he truly found
It was against your Highness. Whereat grieved,
That so his sickness, age, and impotence
Was falsely borne in hand,[14] sends out arrests [15]
On Fortinbras; which he, in brief, obeys,
Receives rebuke from Norway, and in fine
Makes vow before his uncle never more   70
To give the assay of arms against your Majesty.
Whereon old Norway, overcome with joy,
Gives him three thousand crowns in annual fee,
And his commission to employ those soldiers,
So levied as before, against the Polack;
With an entreaty, herein further shown,   *Giving a paper.*
That it might please you to give quiet pass
Through your dominions for his enterprise,
On such regards [16] of safety and allowance [17]
As therein are set down.

KING.   It likes us well;   80
And at our more consider'd time [18] we'll read,
Answer, and think upon this business.
Meantime we thank you for your well-took labour.
Go to your rest; at night we'll feast together.
Most welcome home!   *Exeunt Voltimand and Cornelius.*

POL.   This business is well ended.
(*With self-satisfaction and forensic flourish.*) My liege, and madam,
   to expostulate [19]

---

[11] suspect.   [12] main thing.
[13] as soon as we began to speak with him.   [14] deluded.
[15] summons.   [16] pledges.
[17] (your) permission (for the troops to pass through Denmark).
[18] time for more consideration.   [19] discuss.

What majesty should be, what duty is,
Why day is day, night night, and time is time,
Were nothing but to waste night, day, and time;
Therefore, since brevity is the soul of wit [20] _____   90
And tediousness the limbs and outward flourishes,
I will be brief. Your noble son is mad. ⌒
Mad call I it; for, to define true madness,
What is't but to be nothing else but mad?
(*Becoming befuddled.*) But let that go.

QUEEN. (*A little impatiently.*)   More matter, with less art.

POL.   Madam, I swear I use no art at all.[21]
That he is mad, 'tis true; 'tis true 'tis pity,
And pity 'tis 'tis true. A foolish figure!
But farewell it, for I will use no art.
(*Beginning anew.*) Mad let us grant him then; and now remains   100
That we find out the cause of this effect,
Or rather say, the cause of this *de*fect,
For this effect defective comes by cause.
Thus it remains, and the remainder thus.
Perpend.
(*With a new start.*) I have a daughter—have whilst she is mine—
Who, in her duty and obedience, mark,
Hath given me this. Now gather, and surmise.   *Reads the letter.*
"To the celestial and my soul's idol, the most beautified Ophe-   110
lia,"—
(*With a grimace.*) That's an ill phrase, a vile phrase; "beautified"

---

[20] (This from Polonius!)

[21] i.e., My eloquence is natural, not studied. This speech in which Polonius reveals his theory of Hamlet's lunacy seems to have inspired to a degree the style in which Dr. Ernest Jones reveals *his;* we quote from *four successive* paragraphs of Chapter III from his *Hamlet and Oedipus:* "In short. . . . We have, therefore, to take up the argument again. . . . The extensive experience of the psychoanalytic researches . . . has amply demonstrated. . . . In other words. . . . In order therefore to gain a proper perspective it is necessary briefly to inquire. . . . Experience shows. . . . One may formulate the following generalization. . . . Biologically stated. . . . It being understood that the term. . . . It is for this reason that. . . . This merely says that. . . . The apparent exceptions to this rule need not be here explained. . . . Further. . . . Hence. . . . A little consideration . . . will make it comprehensible. . . . It only remains to add the obvious. . . . We have here the explanation. . . . On the surface, of course. . . . Bearing these considerations in mind. . . . It should now be evident. . . ."

is a vile phrase. But you shall hear. Thus: "In her excellent white
bosom, these." [22]

QUEEN.   Came this from Hamlet to her?

POL. (*Disliking to be hurried and having his dramatic effects ruined.*)
Good madam, stay a while. I will be faithful.   *Reads.*

> "Doubt thou the stars are fire,
>   Doubt that the sun doth move,
>   Doubt truth to be a liar,
>   But never doubt I love.[23]

"O dear Ophelia, I am ill at these numbers. I have not art to   120
reckon my groans; but that I love thee best, O most best,
believe it. Adieu.

>   Thine evermore, most dear lady,
>   Whilst this machine [24] is to him,

>   HAMLET."

This in obedience hath my daughter show'd me,
And more above,[25] hath his solicitings,
As they fell out by time, by means, and place,
All given to mine ear.

KING.   But how hath she
Receiv'd his love

POL. (*Taking umbrage.*)   What do you think of me?

KING. (*Smoothing him down.*)   As of a man faithful and honourable.   130

POL. (*Basking in the compliment.*)   I would fain prove so. But what
        might you think,
When I had seen this hot love on the wing,—
As I perceiv'd it, I must tell you that,
Before my daughter told me,[26]—what might you,
Or my dear Majesty your queen here, think,
If I had play'd the desk or table-book,[27]
Or given my heart a winking,[28] mute and dumb,
Or look'd upon this love with idle [29] sight,

---

[22] a usual ending for a familiar letter; like our "Yours."
[23] Hamlet is not much of a hand at verse—as the next line proves he knows.
[24] body. (The word he uses would itself show Hamlet's authorship!)
[25] besides.
[26] (Polonius insists on getting full credit for keenness of perception.)
[27] i.e., if I had shut it up within myself.
[28] "Connive" means literally "to wink at."
[29] For the sake of a later reference, please notice that the word "idle"
means here (as usually) "idle."

What might you think? No, I went round [30] to work,   140
And my young mistress thus I did bespeak:
"Lord Hamlet is a prince, out of thy star.
This must not be"; and then I precepts gave her,
That she should lock herself from his resort,
Admit no messengers, receive no tokens.
Which done, she took the fruits of my advice; [31]
And he, repulsed—a short tale to make—
Fell into a sadness, then into a fast,
Thence to a watch, thence into a weakness,
Thence to a lightness, and, by this declension,
Into the madness whereon now he raves,   150
And all we wail for.

KING. (*To the Queen.*)   Do you think 'tis this?

QUEEN. (*Hopefully.*)   It may be, very likely.

POL. (*His wisdom challenged.*)   Hath there been such a time—I'd fain
      know that—
That I have positively said, " 'Tis so,"
When it prov'd otherwise? [32]

KING.   Not that I know.

POL. Take this from this (*drawing a finger across his throat to suggest
      decapitation*), if this be otherwise.
If circumstances lead me, I will find
Where truth is hid, though it were hid indeed
Within the centre.[33]

KING.   How may we try it further? [34]

---

[30] The Elizabethans said "round" where we should say "direct" or "directly."

[31] Note again this clear explanation of Hamlet's later treatment of Ophelia. The only mystery connected with that treatment is why everyone has made a mystery of it!

[32] See pp. 288–290.   [33] (of the earth).

[34] At this juncture Wilson introduces a new stage direction which, unless we can abolish it, is already well on the way to becoming a traditional one in performances of the play. Finding Shakespeare's lines inadequate to explain Hamlet's treatment of Ophelia when next they meet (a difficulty we do not ourself experience), Wilson concludes that Hamlet must overhear the scheme while Polonius is proposing it. Therefore just before the King's

    "How may we try it further?"

Wilson inserts:

    (*Hamlet, disorderly attired and reading a book, enters the lobby by
      the door at the back; he hears voices from the chamber and
      pauses beside one of the curtains, unobserved.*)

POL.   You know, sometimes he walks for hours [35] together   160
         Here in the lobby.
QUEEN.   So he has, indeed.
POL.   At such a time I'll loose my daughter to him.
         Be you and I behind an arras [36] then;
         Mark the encounter. If he love her not

Then, a few lines further down, where Hamlet in the received texts has here-tofore entered "reading on a book," Wilson alters the direction to:

(Hamlet comes forward, his eyes on the book.) (*Hamlet*, pp. 43-44.)

Though this editing is indeed a work of supererogation, it is all important in Wilson's eyes: "Hamlet's accidental discovery of the intention to spy upon him has a bearing much wider than his attitude towards Ophelia. Indeed, the manner in which it eases the general working of the plot is strong testimony in its favour . . . It constitutes the mainspring of the events that follow in acts 2 and 3; it renders the nunnery scene playable and intelligible as never before; it adds all kinds of fresh light and shade to the play scene. In a word . . . (it) means the restoration of a highly important piece of the dramatic structure." (*What Happens in Hamlet*, p. 108).

To this enthusiastic appraisal it is necessary to dissent. We find Wilson's new stage direction adding nothing to the plot that has not always been there without it, no new light or shade. On the contrary, it renders the nunnery scene truly unplayable and unactable—as we shall see. John Gielgud's own experience—he was the first to introduce Hamlet's "overhearing" upon the boards—is eloquent of the fatuity of the device." See pp. 15-16.

There is, indeed, every objection to be made against this "recovered" stage-direction, as Wilson boldly names it. Aside from its superfluity and its tendency to confuse matters, it is itself esthetically indefensible, for it makes the overhearing suggested purely *accidental*—unlike the eavesdropping to which Hamlet is subjected. In truth, if *any* significant part of the action had been made to hinge upon such an *accidental* overhearing, the nobility of the entire work must have been irreparably damaged. The device, therefore, would actually be worse than superfluous: for the purposes of tragedy it would be unpardonably vulgar.

Another objection to Wilson's direction will not have escaped the notice of the reader. He would have Hamlet enter "disorderly attired"—apparently only because he has so appeared in Ophelia's room. Wilson slips this in without any warrant from the lines in the remainder of the scene, and is certainly guilty of imposing upon the audience's vision a spectacle Shakespeare never intended.

If our protests against this innovation have been strenuous it is because, despite Mr. Gielgud's acknowledgment of the failure of his experiment with it, most productions since his have incorporated it. It is distressingly possible that many theatergoes are now unaware, therefore, that Shakespeare never meant Hamlet to overhear Polonius's little plot.

[35] The usual reading is "four hours." But Elizabethan spelling having been as frivolous as it was, it is quite possible that simply "for hours" was meant.
[36] tapestry.

And be not from his reason fallen thereon,
Let me be no assistant for a state,
But keep a farm and carters.

KING.   We will try it.

Enter Hamlet, reading on a book.

QUEEN.   But look where sadly the poor wretch comes reading.

POL.   Away, I do beseech you, both away.
I'll board [37] him presently. [38]

Exeunt King, Queen and Attendants.
O, give me leave,   170

How does my good Lord Hamlet?

HAM.   Well, God-a-mercy.

POL.   (*As though addressing an imbecile.*)   Do you know me, my lord?

HAM.   Excellent well; you are a fishmonger. [39]

POL.   Not I, my lord.

HAM.   Then I would you were so honest a man.

POL.   Honest, my lord!

HAM.   Ay sir. To be honest, as this world goes, is to be one man
pick'd out of ten thousand.

POL.   That's very true, my lord.   180

HAM.   For if the sun breed maggots in a dead dog, being a good
kissing carrion,—Have you a daughter?

POL.   I have, my lord.

HAM.   Let her not walk i' the sun. [40] Conception is a blessing, but

---

[37] accost.   [38] at once.

[39] Coleridge sensibly interpreted the remark to mean that Hamlet is aware
Polonius has come to fish out his secret. But Kittredge objects to this on the
grounds that fishmongers do not catch fish; they sell them (*Hamlet*, p. 185).
The objection is hardly valid. All over the world the men who catch fish
often do sell them.

On the authority of a few examples of Elizabethan popular usage not
directly related to the word *fishmonger*, other scholars have glossed the word
as "bawd." The whole idea is preposterous; according to Adams, for instance,
Hamlet is thus expressing his fear that Claudius has designs on Ophelia's innocence and that Polonius is quite ready to sell his daughter's virtue (*Hamlet*,
pp. 238–239). No matter how much Hamlet detests Polonius or is disillusioned
in Ophelia, there is no reason why he should think of the old man as a procurer
or the girl as a wanton; the rest of the play will show him as much in love
with her as ever. The verb *fish*, meaning "to use artifice to obtain a thing,
solicit an opinion," was already in use (*Oxford Eng. Dict.*, IV, p. 256), and
Chaucer employed it to signify the getting by artifice (Idem, p. 257). Good
dramatic sense is best served by understanding Hamlet to mean: "I know you
well enough. You've come to fish."

[40] To decipher Hamlet's meaning, we must bear in mind two things: ac-

not as your daughter may conceive.[41] Friend, look to't. (*Hamlet
returns to his book.*)

POL. [*Aside.*]   How say you by that? Still harping on my daughter.
Yet he knew me not at first; he said I was a fishmonger. He is
far gone, far gone. And truly in my youth I suff'red much   190
extremity for love; very near this. I'll speak to him again.
—What do you read, my lord?

HAM. (*Without looking up.*)   Words, words, words.

POL.   What is the matter,[42] my lord?

HAM.   Between who?[43] (*Hamlet returns anew to his book.*)

POL.   I mean, the matter you read, my lord.

HAM. (*Half-angry, half-amused.*)   Slanders, sir;[44] for the satirical
slave says here that old men have grey beards, that their faces
are wrinkled, their eyes purging thick amber or plum-tree gum,   200
and that they have a plentiful lack of wit (*In irritation Hamlet
advances on Polonius in a mock-threatening way; Polonius begins to back off from him, bowing and scraping to placate him.*),
together with weak hams;[45] all which, sir, though I most powerfully and potently believe, yet I hold it not honesty to have it
thus set down; (*Polonius becomes involved in his robe and be-*

---

cording to the now-discarded theory of abiogenesis, organisms found in putrid
matter were thought to have sprung spontaneously from it through heat; and
Hamlet, once more quibbling on the word "sun" (See footnote on I, ii, 67),
is referring ironically to the "sun of the King's presence," that is, Claudius'
sycophantic court. What he is saying then is: If the sun can cause the birth
of maggots in a dead dog, a carrion ripe for the decaying kiss of the hot sun
("being a good kissing carrion")—what can happen to a daughter of yours
at this court? Let her avoid the corrupting place for (as you yourself would
demonstrate) everything corrupts in the King's presence.

[41] Hamlet perceives that Polonius comprehends nothing of what he is
saying, and therefore adds: Understanding ("conception") is a blessing indeed.
Then he bitterly appends: But not the kind of conception your daughter might
have if she remains at court. The late John Macy years ago told us of a similar
pun perpetrated by Mark Twain. In London Mark was being feted at a dinner
which was also attended by a prominent woman-writer, who was also an
ardent feminist. "Mr. Clemens," she said, "here are you, America's leading
humorist, and here am I, England's. You are a man and I am a woman. Now
tell me honestly, is there any real difference between us?" Thoughtfully Mark
answered, "Madam, I cannot conceive."

[42] subject matter.

[43] Hamlet pretends to misunderstand Polonius's use of the word "matter."

[44] It would appear that it is Juvenal's Tenth Satire which Hamlet is reading.
But the applicability of the passage to Polonius is obvious.

[45] a reference to Polonius' bowing and scraping.

gins to stumble; *Hamlet concludes with a suppressed laugh in which there is some pity for the old simpleton.*) for you your-self, sir, should be old as I am, if like a crab you *could* go back-ward.[46]

POL. [*Aside.*] Though this be madness, yet there is method in't.— Will you walk out of the air, my lord?

HAM.   Into my grave?   210

POL.   Indeed, that is out o' the air. [*Aside.*] How pregnant some-times his replies are! a happiness that often madness hits on, which reason and sanity could not so prosperously be deliver'd of.[47] I will leave him, and suddenly contrive the means of meet-ing between him and my daughter.—My honourable lord, I will most humbly take my leave of you.

HAM. (*With elaborate sarcasm.*)   You cannot, sir, take from me any-thing that I will more willingly part withal,—[*Aside*] except   220 my life, my life.

POL.   Fare you well, my lord.

HAM. (*Wearily.*)   These tedious old fools!
   Enter Rosencrantz and Guildenstern.

POL. (*Although Hamlet is not invisible!*)   You go to seek my Lord Hamlet? There he is.

ROS. (*To Polonius.*)   God save you, sir!

                                                                Exit Polonius.

GUIL.   Mine honour'd lord!

ROS.   My most dear lord!

HAM. (*With joy.*)   My excellent good friends! How dost thou, Guildenstern? Oh, Rosencrantz! Good lads, how do ye both?   230

ROS.   As the indifferent children of the earth.[48]

GUIL.   Happy, in that we are not over-happy.
   On Fortune's cap we are not the very button.

HAM.   Nor the soles of her shoe?

ROS.   Neither, my lord.

HAM.   Then you live about her waist, or in the middle of her fa-vour?

GUIL.   Faith, her privates we.

[46] Kittredge's explanation is more philosophical than our stage direction: Old people cannot be blamed for being old; if they could walk backward "they would quickly return to a time of life" when none of the things Hamlet has quoted from his book "would be true" (*Hamlet*, p. 186). In the Olivier film no explanation was suggested, since Hamlet was walking about upon an elevation at the height of Polonius' head!

[47] (Surely not Polonius' reason and sanity!)   [48] i.e., "fair to middling."

HAM. In the secret parts of Fortune? Oh, most true; she *is* a strumpet. What's the news? 240

ROS. None, my lord, but that the world's grown honest.

HAM. Then is doomsday near. But your news is not true. Let me question more in particular. What have you, my good friends, deserved at the hands of Fortune, that she sends you to prison hither?

GUIL. (*Exchanging glances with Rosencrantz.*) Prison, my lord?

HAM. (*Bitterly.*) Denmark's a prison.

ROS. (*With an embarrassed laugh.*) Then is the world one. 250

HAM. A goodly one, in which there are many confines, wards, and dungeons, Denmark being one o' the worst.

ROS. (*Trying to be light.*) We think not so, my lord.

HAM. Why, then, 'tis none to you; for there is nothing either good or bad, but thinking makes it so. To me it is a prison.

ROS. (*To bring the mood back to the agreeable.*) Why, then, your ambition makes it one. 'Tis too narrow for your mind.

HAM. (*Hamlet's feelings have altered: he has been thrust out of his pleasure at seeing his old friends into a recollection of his wretched circumstances.*) O God, I could be bounded in a 260 nutshell and count myself a king of infinite space, were it not that— I have bad dreams.

GUIL. (*Bent on pleasantries.*) Which dreams indeed are ambition, for the very substance of the ambitious is merely the shadow of a dream.

HAM. A dream itself is but a shadow.

ROS. Truly, and I hold ambition of so airy and light a quality that it is but a shadow's shadow.

HAM. Then are our beggars bodies, and our monarchs and outstretch'd heroes the beggars' shadows. (*Hamlet gives up his* 270 *rather lame attempts at recapturing the gaiety of their meeting.*) Shall we to the court? for, by my fay,[49] I cannot reason.[50] (*Hamlet begins to move toward the exit, inviting his friends to accompany him.*)

ROS ⎱
GUIL. ⎰ We'll wait upon you.

HAM. No such matter. I will not sort you with the rest of my servants, for, to speak to you like an honest man, I am most dreadfully attended. But in the beaten way of friendship, what make you at Elsinore?

[49] faith.　　[50] See pp. 199–202.

ros. (*Trying to sound innocent, as indeed he is.*)   To visit you, my lord; no other occasion.

ham. (*Reacting to "To visit you, my lord," with great cordiality.*) Beggar that I am, I am even poor in thanks, but I thank you: and sure, dear friends, my thanks are too dear a halfpenny. (*He stops, suddenly struck with that "no other occasion" and looks searchingly at the other two.*) Were you not sent for? (*They are too abashed to answer. Hamlet begins to be infuriated.*) Is it your own inclining? Is it a free visitation? Come, deal justly with me. Come, come. Nay, speak.

guil. (*Confused.*)   What should we say, my lord?

ham. (*Sardonically.*)   Why, anything, but to the purpose! You *were* sent for; and there is a kind of confession in your looks which your modesties have not craft enough to colour. I know the good king and queen have sent for you.

ros. (*Desperately.*)   To what end, my lord?

ham.   That *you* must teach *me*. But let me conjure you, by the rights of our fellowship, by the consonancy of our youth, by the obligation of our ever-preserved love, and by what more dear a better proposer could charge you withal, be even and direct with me, whether you were sent for or no!

ros. [*Aside to Guil.*]   What say you?

ham. [*Aside.*]   Nay, then, I have an eye of you.—If you love me, hold not off.

guil. (*Shame-facedly.*)   My lord, we were sent for.

ham. (*Vindictively.*)   I will tell you *why;* so shall my anticipation prevent [51] your discovery,[52] and your secrecy to the King and Queen moult no feather. I have of late—but wherefore I know not—lost all my mirth, forgone all custom of exercise; and indeed it goes so heavily with my disposition that this goodly frame, the earth, seems to me a sterile promontory, this most excellent canopy, the air, look you, this brave [53] o'erhanging firmament, this majestical roof fretted with golden fire, why, it appears no other thing to me than a foul and pestilent congre-

280

290

300

310

---

[51] anticipate.

[52] disclosure. It is now forever too late for Guildenstern and Rosencrantz. The rashness which is part of Hamlet's charm and genius, is also his besetting vice. Their yielding to his reminder of the rights of friendship avails them nothing, though in all justice it should clear the air between them. But he has already dealt his affection for them its deathblow.

[53] magnificent.

gation of vapours. What a piece of work is a man! How noble
in reason! How infinite in faculty! In form and moving how
express [54] and admirable! In action how like an angel! In apprehension how like a god! The beauty of the world! The paragon   320
of animals! [55] And yet, to me, what is this quintessence of
dust? [56] Man delights not me, (*Seeing Rosencrantz smile, he
flares up.*)—no, nor woman neither, though by your smiling
you seem to say so.

ROS. (*Taken aback at Hamlet's anger.*)   My lord, there was no such
stuff in my thoughts.

HAM. (*Furiously.*)   Why did you laugh then, when I said, "Man
delights not me"?

ROS.   To think, my lord, if you delight not in man, what lenten
entertainment [57] the players shall receive from you. We coted [58]   330
them on the way, and hither are they coming to offer you
service.

HAM. (*Suddenly enthusiastic at the prospect of seeing the players
again.*)   He that plays the king shall be welcome; his majesty
shall have tribute of me; the adventurous knight shall use his
foil and target; [59] the lover shall not sigh gratis; the humorous [60]
man shall end his part in peace; the clown shall make those
laugh whose lungs are tickle o' the sere; [61] and the lady shall say
her mind freely, or the blank verse shall halt [62] for't. What
players are they? [63]

                                                                          340

[54] particularly fitted to perform his (noblest) functions.

[55] Lines 315-321 prove how far from pessimism is Hamlet's natural bent.
They might stand as a perfect statement of the Renaissance view of the endless
potentialities of mankind. See pp. 251-252.

[56] He turns to bitter thoughts again. Even these good friends, he believes,
fail him now, and are willing to play the spy against him.

[57] lean reception.   [58] overtook.   [59] shield.   [60] eccentric.

[61] The "sere" was the lever between the trigger and the tumbler of a gun.
To be "tickle" is to be delicately adjusted. A gun which was "tickle o' the
sere" would go off at the least touch. Hamlet is describing those foolish members of the audience who will go off into gales of laughter at the crook of a
finger.

[62] limp.

[63] The talk which follows has little, if anything, to do with the action
of the play. But for that reason it has its own especial interest. At such moments,
when Shakespeare halts his play to speak on extraneous matters, we listen with
particular attention, for then we know that *he* (who almost never does so)
is speaking directly to us. Shakespeare here vents his annoyance at the recent
vogue for child-actors, the success of whom had seriously crippled business
at his own theater. Their high-pitched voices, heard in their own playhouse,

ROS. Even those you were wont to take delight in, the tragedians of the city.

HAM. How chances it they travel? Their residence, both in reputation and profit, was better both ways.

ROS. I think their inhibition comes by the means of the late innovation.

HAM. Do they hold the same estimation they did when I was in the city? Are they so follow'd? 350

ROS. No, indeed, they are not.

HAM. How comes it? Do they grow rusty?

ROS. Nay, their endeavour keeps in the wonted pace; but there is, sir, an aery [64] of children, little eyases, [65] that cry out on the top of question, [66] and are most tyrannically clapp'd for't. These are now the fashion, and so berattle the common stages—so they call them—that many wearing rapiers are afraid of goose-quills and dare scarce come thither. 360

HAM. What, are they children? Who maintains 'em? How are they escoted? [67] Will they pursue the quality [68] no longer than they can sing? Will they not say afterwards, if they should grow themselves to common players, [69]—as it is most like, if their means are no better—their writers do them wrong, to make them exclaim against their own succession? [70]

ROS. Faith, there has been much to do on both sides, and the nation holds it no sin to tarre [71] them to controversy. There was for a 370 while no money bid for argument [72] unless the poet and the player went to cuffs in the question. [73]

HAM. Is't possible?

GUIL. O, there has been much throwing about of brains.

HAM. Do the boys carry it away?

ROS. Ay, that they do, my lord; Hercules and his load too. [74]

---

had become a serious threat to adult professionals; moreover, the dramatists writing for these precocious youngsters were using them as mouthpieces for attacks on the regular players.

[64] a nest of the young of eagles or hawks.　[65] unfledged hawks.

[66] cry out the dialogue in a shrill voice.　[67] supported.

[68] profession. These children were originally choirboys.

[69] i.e., when their voices change and they can no longer be choirboys. They may then have to continue, when adult, as actors.

[70] future. "Aren't their writers doing them an injustice in forcing them to ruin their future profession?" They can be child actors, after all, only for a few years.

[71] egg on.　[72] plot of a play.　[73] dialogue of a play.

[74] Hercules took upon his shoulders the globe from Atlas, while the latter

HAM.   It is not strange; for mine uncle is King of Denmark, and   380
   those that would make mows at him while my father lived, give
   twenty, forty, [fifty,] an hundred ducats apiece for his picture
   in little.[75] ['Sblood,] [76] there is something in this more than
   natural, if philosophy could find it out.

                                              Flourish for the Players.

GUIL.   There are the players.

HAM.   Gentlemen, you are welcome to Elsinore. Your hands, come.
   (*With elaborate pretence at civility.*) The appurtenance of welcome is fashion and ceremony.[77] Let me comply with you in
   the garb,[78] lest my extent to the players, which, I tell you, must   390
   show fairly outward, should more appear like entertainment
   than yours. You are welcome; (*with contempt*) but my uncle-
   father and aunt-mother are deceiv'd.

GUIL.   In what, my dear lord?

HAM.   I am but mad north-north-west.[79] When the wind is southerly
   I know a hawk from a handsaw.[80]
   Enter Polonius.

POL.   Well be with you, gentlemen!

HAM.   [*Aside to them.*] Hark you, Guildenstern, and you too, at
   each ear a hearer: that great baby you see there is not yet out   400
   of his swathing-clouts.

---

went to fetch for him the golden apples of the Hesperides. Hercules carrying
the globe was the sign of the Globe Theater, where this play was being performed. See footnote 63, above.

[75] miniature. One director had Hamlet at this speech rip off the miniatures
of Claudius which Rosencrantz and Guildenstern were wearing on a chain
about their necks, and hurl them in their faces. A good piece of business, no
doubt, but rather silly. There is no reason why the young men should be
adorned with Claudius' portrait—they are not in love with him! Indeed, in
some productions of *Hamlet* there is a downright epidemic of wearing miniatures on chains; Hamlet wears one of his father—Gertrude, Rosencrantz, and
Guildenstern each one of the new King—and sometimes Ophelia, Polonius
and even Laertes of unidentified persons. This is surely too much of a good thing.

[76] God's blood.

[77] The right accompaniment to welcome is form and ceremony.

[78] Allow me to include you in the proper forms.

[79] the smallest deviation possible from north on the compass. I.e., "I'm just
a little bit off!"

[80] It is generally believed that "handsaw" is a corruption for "hernshaw"
—a heron. I.e., the bird flying with the south wind (to the north) flies away
from the sun; thus the observer has not the sun in his eyes. "When the sun
is not in my eyes I can tell a bird of prey from an innocent heron." (He knows
his erstwhile friends now for what they are.)

ROS.   Happily he is the second time come to them, for they say an old man is twice a child.

HAM.   I will prophesy he comes to tell me of the players; mark it. (*Aloud, as though in the middle of a conversation with the other two.*) You say right, sir; for o' Monday morning 'twas so indeed.

POL.   My lord, I have news to tell you.

HAM.   (*Wheeling about to face Polonius.*)   My lord, I have news to tell *you.* When Roscius was an actor in Rome,—   410

POL.   The actors are come hither, my lord.

HAM.   Buzz, buzz! [81]

POL.   Upon mine honour,—

HAM.   "Then came each actor on his ass," [82]

POL.   (*Pedantically.*)   The best actors in the world, either for tragedy, comedy, history, pastoral, pastoral-comical, historical-pastoral, tragical-historical, tragical-comical-historical-pastoral, scene individable,[83] or poem unlimited; [84] Seneca [85] cannot be too heavy, nor Plautus [86] too light. For the law of writ [87] and   420 the liberty,[88] these are the only men.

HAM.   O Jephthah, judge of Israel,[89] what a treasure hadst thou!

POL.   What a treasure had he, my lord?

HAM.   Why,

> "One fair daughter, and no more,[90]
> The which he loved passing well."

[81] At Oxford this was the cry when someone began to tell a story everyone already knew.

[82] probably a line from an old ballad. Hamlet implies that if the actors are come hither upon Polonius' honor, then each actor has come upon an ass.

[83] with unity of place and time.

[84] paying no heed to unity of place and time.

[85] the Roman author of tragedies, whose sententious plays were much revered during the Renaissance.

[86] the Roman author of comedies, very popular at the universities during the Renaissance. Shakespeare's *The Comedy of Errors* is indebted for its plot to his *Menaechmi.*

[87] the three unities of place, time, and action.

[88] the ignoring of the three unities.   [89] See Judges xi.

[90] To tease Polonius Hamlet cites an old ballad on Jepthah. It would be well to bear the lines in mind during the ensuing dialogue:

> "I read that many yeares ago,
>   When Jeptha, Judge of Israel,
> Had one fair Daughter, and no moe,
>   Whom he loved passinge well,
>   And as by lot, God wot,

POL. [*Aside.*]   Still on my daughter.

HAM.   Am I not i' the right, old Jephthah?

POL.   If you call me Jephthah, my lord, I *have* a daughter that I   430
love passing well.

HAM.   Nay, that follows [91] not.

POL.   What follows, then, my lord?

HAM.   Why,

"As by lot, God wot,"

and then, you know,

"It came to pass, as most like it was,"—

(*Getting bored with this.*) The first row of the pious chanson
will show you more,[92] for look where my abridgements [93]
come.

Enter four or five Players.

(*With lively friendliness.*) You're welcome, masters, welcome   440
all. I am glad to see thee well.[94] Welcome, good friends. O, my
old friend! Thy face is valanc'd [95] since I saw thee last; com'st
thou to *beard* me in Denmark? What, my young lady and
mistress! [96] By'r lady, your ladyship is nearer heaven than when
I saw you last, by the altitude of a chopine.[97] Pray God, your
voice, like a piece of uncurrent gold,[98] be not crack'd within
the ring. Masters, you are all welcome. We'll e'en to't like
French falconers—fly at anything we see; we'll have a speech   450
straight. Come, give us a taste of your quality; [99] come, a passionate speech.

1. PLAY.   What speech, my lord?

HAM.   I heard thee speak me a speech once, but it was never acted;
or, if it was, not above once. For the play, I remember, pleas'd

---

It came to passe, most like it was,
Great warres there should be,
And who should be the chiefe but he, but he . . ."

[91] He is playing on the word. He means "that isn't the next line."

[92] The first line of the religious ballad will explain all this to you:

"I read that many years ago."

[93] The Players are his abridgments because they cut his talk short.

[94] In the Olivier movie this line was addressed to a poodle. Very original!

[95] fringed (with a beard).

[96] said, of course, to a young man. There were no female actors on the
Elizabethan stage.

[97] a stilt attached to the bottom of a shoe to increase a woman's height—
not dissimilar to the modern "platform shoes" which women have been wearing.

[98] unfit for currency because cracked.   [99] profession.

not the million; 'twas caviare to the general; [100] but it was—as I
receiv'd it, and others, whose judgement in such matters cried
in the top of mine [101]—an excellent play, well digested in the   460
scenes, set down with as much modesty as cunning. I remember,
one said there were no sallets [102] in the lines to make the matter
savoury, nor no matter in the phrase that might indict the
author of affectation; but call'd it an honest method, [as wholesome as sweet, and by very much more handsome than fine.[103]]
One speech in it I chiefly lov'd; 'twas Æneas' tale to Dido, and
thereabout of it especially where he speaks of Priam's slaughter.
If it live in your memory, begin at this line: let me see, let me   470
see—
"The rugged Pyrrhus, like the Hyrcanian beast," [104]
—It is not so. It *begins* with Pyrrhus:—
"The rugged Pyrrhus, he whose sable arms,[105]

[100] the general theater-audience.   [101] superior in authority to mine.
[102] spicy passages. The word means "salads."   [103] overdone.
[104] the Asian ("Hyrcanian") tiger.
[105] The quoted passage has occasioned considerable commentary. No play
exists from which the passage could have been taken. It has been argued that
it comes from a lost play of Chapman's (J. M. Robertson, *Shakespeare and
Chapman*, London, 1917, pp. 215-218), of Ben Jonson's (C. W. Wallace in
Englischen Studien XLIII, 1911, pp. 378-379), of Shakespeare's (H. D. Gray in
Modern Language Review XV, 1920, pp. 217-322)—or from Kyd's *Hamlet*
(F. Radebrecht in *Englischen Studien*, LII, 1918, pp. 327-341). But the stylistic
resemblances to a passage in *The Tragedy of Dido*, written by Marlowe with
additions by Nashe, are so obvious that scholarly opinion generally grants that
it was of that play Shakespeare was thinking. The following extracts from
Marlowe's play will indicate the similarity of tone:
AEN:

> I rose,
> And looking from a turret, might behold
> Yong infants swimming in their parents bloud,
> Headles carkasses piled vp in heapes,
> Virgins halfe dead dragged by their golden haire,
> And with maine force flung on a ring of pikes . . .
> At last came Pirrhus fell and full of ire,
> His harnesse dropping bloud, and on his speare
> The mangled head of Priams yongest sonne,
> And after him his band of Mirmidons,
> With balles of wilde fire in their murdering pawes . . .
> And at Ioues Altar finding Priamus,
> About whose withered necke hung Hecuba,
> Foulding his hand in hers, and ioyntly both
> Beating their breasts and falling on the ground,
> He with his faulchions poynt raisde vp at once, . . .

> Threatning a thousand deaths at euery glaunce . . .
> This butcher whil'st his hands were yet held vp,
> Treading vpon his breast, strooke off his hands . . .
> At which the franticke Queene leapt on his face,
> And in his eyelids hanging by the nayles,
> A little while prolong'd her husbands life:
> At last the souldiers puld her by the heeles,
> And swong her howling in the emptie ayre,
> Which sent an eccho to the wounded King:
> Whereat he lifted vp his bedred lims,
> And would haue grappeld with Achilles sonne,
> Forgetting both his want of strength and hands,
> Which he disdaining whiskt his sword about,
> And with the wind thereof the King fell downe:
> Then from the nauell to the throat at once;
> He ript old Priam. . . .

ANNA: O what became of aged Hecuba? . . .
ACHA: What happened to the Queene we cannot shewe.
> (II, i, 486–589—ed. C. F. T. Brooke, Oxford, 1925, pp. 405–408)

This may indeed be Marlowe, though not at his best.

But the passage quoted in *Hamle* has evoked some peculiarly insensitive comment. Read for their literal meaning, the lines in our play seem, of course, extraordinarily inflated. For this reason Pope decided that Shakespeare was being "ironical" at the "bombast" of a contemporary (quoted in Furness, Vol. I, p. 180). Steevens seconded this judgment so far as to construe Hamlet's praise of the speech as according "very well with the character of madness, which, before witnesses, he thought it necessary to support (Furness, Vol. I, p. 182). Many modern scholars concur in believing that Shakespeare is here ridiculing a contemporary; as Wilson puts it, the passage is a parody of Marlowe's style (*Hamlet*, p. 186).

Such a view should be shocking to all esthetic considerations, and Coleridge's answer to those who have held it is to be endorsed: "The fancy that a burlesque was intended sinks below criticism" (*Essays and Lectures*, London, 1907, p. 149). The reasons are plentiful:

¶ 1. Hamlet has lauded the passage with superlatives. Though it "pleased not the million," it was in his opinion and the opinion of others whose judgment exceeded his, "an excellent play, well digested. . . , set down with as much modesty as cunning," a play free of affectation, honest, wholesome, sweet, and handsome. And this particular speech he "chiefly loved."

¶ 2. After such an introduction why should the dramatist proceed to give us a satirical passage?

¶ 3. What would be the artistic value of ridicule at this moment of the tragedy?

¶ 4. It is from this same passage that Hamlet is to receive his inspiration of presenting the Mouse-trap before Claudius, Gertrude and the Court. It is unthinkable that the leading dramatic fact of Act Two—the fact which does most to advance the plot—should emanate from a passage in parody. Moreover, not only must the passage itself be seriously intended, but Hamlet's admiration of it must have been sincerely meant. The all-important conception of the Mouse-trap can come to Hamlet only if he too is most serious in everything concerning this play on Dido.

¶ 5. Why should Shakespeare ridicule Marlowe, to whom he owed so much, and who had by this time been dead for a number of years—when several years earlier he had paid the deceased poet a graceful tribute:

> "Dead shepherd, now I find thy saw of might,
> 'Who ever loved that loved not at first sight?' "

—a direct quotation from Marlowe's beautiful narrative, *Hero and Leander?* When Shakespeare was of a mind to ridicule the shortcomings of his fellow-writers, he preferred to find fitter targets than the greatest of his predecessors.

How, then, are we to account for the unquestionably inflated quality of the lines in Hamlet's favored quotation? It is quite beside the point to defend the serious intent of the speech by such considerations as Bradley advances: "Does not Shakespeare elsewhere write bombast? The truth is that the two defects of style in the speech are the very defects we do find in his writings. When he wished to make his style exceptionally high he always ran some risk of bombast. And he was even more prone to the fault which in this speech seems to me the more marked, a use of metaphors which sound . . . grotesque. There are many places in Shakespeare worse than the speech of Æneas" (*Shakespearean Tragedy*, p. 416). If this were the truth, and we should emphatically deny it when applied to any except a few of Shakespeare's earliest works, it would still not explain why *Hamlet*, written with perfection throughout, should suddenly become uncontrolled in its writing for this extended section, and for this section alone.

Stoll makes the case against Shakespeare even more damagingly: "That he was like many poets not a sure critic of his own or others' works, appears from Hamlet's warm words of praise for the turgid and bombastic lines about Pyrrhus and Hecuba which the Player at his request repeats for him" (*Shakespearean Studies*, New York, 1942, p. 29). This is a cliché whose demise is centuries over-due. It has been a solace for ages to bookreviewers, commentators, and pedagogues particularly, to pretend that the critical faculty is opposed to the creative, that the great creators are touchingly childlike in their critical ineptitude, that the poet does pretty well in his poetry but that he had better leave the serious business of criticism to more capable hands. The ghost of that idea should have been laid more than three hundred years ago when Ben Jonson observed that criticism is not only the business of a poet but the business of a very good poet at that. The great names in the history of literary criticism will bear out Jonson's contention (he was using the word *poet* to cover all kinds of literary "makers"—in prose as well as verse). Only the names of Aristotle and Longinus among the ancients do not figure as creators as well as literary critics; the others are Aristophanes, Plato and Horace. After them the most important writers on literary criticism include great creators like Dante, Boccaccio, Sidney, Jonson, Dryden, Pope, Johnson, Lessing, Goethe, Wordsworth, Coleridge, Lamb, Hazlitt, De Quincey, Arnold, Hugo, Flaubert, Pater. Such creators cannot be described as "not a sure critic" of their own or others' works!

Shakespeare's motives have been, though briefly, already suggested by Coleridge: the dramatist had somehow in employing the Æneas speech to achieve a "contrast between *Hamlet* and the play in *Hamlet*." (*loc. cit.*) That

> Black as his purpose, did the night resemble
> When he lay couched in the ominous horse,[106]
> Hath now this dread and black complexion smear'd
> With heraldry more dismal. Head to foot
> Now is he total gules,[107] horribly trick'd [108]
> With blood of fathers, mothers, daughters, sons,   480
> Bak'd and impasted with the parching streets,

is to say, if we the audience are to accept the noble blank verse of Shakespeare's own play as representing "real life," obviously the same blank verse will not do to represent verse quoted from a drama in that play. Shakespeare has the identical problem to solve when the Mouse-trap is presented before Claudius; to make it seem like a play, he will not be able to use the blank verse which forms the body of *Hamlet;* in the later scene he will solve the problem by using the artifice of rhyme. Artifice, in short, is called for to lift a play within a play out of its environing verse. In the present scene Shakespeare employs the artifice of a highly inflated speech for the purpose. It is simply a device for achieving perspective.

Why, then, did he choose to compose a Marlovian passage? For there can be little doubt that Shakespeare himself wrote this passage, with the intent of making it sound like a passage that Christopher Marlowe *might have written.* Well, he might have been moved by either of the following reasons, neither of which excludes the other:

¶ 1. He might not have had a copy of *Dido* available. During the fever of composition he perhaps was too impatient to wait until he could come by one, and therefore decided to compose a passage that would sound like a scene he remembered from that play.

¶ 2. He may have been paying Marlowe tribute by composing something in his predecessor's style. So Schumann paid a charming tribute to Chopin in the midst of his *Carnaval,* inventing not only a lovely Chopinesque passage but also (a little roguishly) some odd fingering such as the Polish master had introduced in his editing. We have already noted an earlier tribute by Shakespeare to Marlowe; why need we construe this Marlovian passage as ridicule? Hamlet's praise, which prefaces it, is enough indication of how we are to feel about it. Read it aloud, fairly. Whatever may be said of its vocabulary, its music is far from contemptible: it has the noble, majestic march of Marlowe's syllables. As a poet Marlowe was above all a noble musician—the first, and perhaps the only, poet to discover the kind of music Milton was later to orchestrate more fully; even when Marlowe's ideas are childishly extravagant, the music of his lines can be enthralling. And it is this quality of Marlowe's work which Shakespeare is projecting in the Æneas speech.

These suggestions are, of course, beyond possiblity of documentation; but so, for that matter, are the coarse imputations of parodying. At such moments is it beyond the criteria of "good scholarship" to yield to the dictates of esthetic fitness?

[106] (the Trojan horse).   [107] red.   [108] adorned.

That lend a tyrannous and damned light
To their vile murders. Roasted in wrath and fire,
And thus o'er sized [109] with coagulate gore,
With eyes like carbuncles, the hellish Pyrrhus
Old grandsire Priam seeks."
[So, proceed you.]

POL. (*To ingratiate himself with Hamlet.*) 'Fore God, my lord, well
spoken, with good accent and good discretion.

I. PLAY.   "Anon he finds him   490
Striking too short at Greeks. His antique [110] sword,
Rebellious to his arm, lies where it falls,
Repugnant to command. Unequal match,
Pyrrhus at Priam drives, in rage strikes wide,
But with the whiff and wind of his fell [111] sword
The unnerved [112] father falls. Then senseless Ilium,[113]
Seeming to feel his blow, with flaming top
Stoops to his [114] base, and with a hideous crash
Takes prisoner Pyrrhus' ear; for, lo! his sword,
Which was declining on the milky head   500
Of reverend Priam, seem'd i' the air to stick.
So, as a painted tyrant, Pyrrhus stood
And, like a neutral to his will and matter,[115]
Did nothing.
But, as we often see, against some storm,
A silence in the heavens, the rack [116] stand still,
The bold winds speechless and the orb below
As hush as death, anon the dreadful thunder
Doth rend the region; [117] so, after Pyrrhus' pause,
Aroused vengeance sets him new a-work;   510
And never did the Cyclops' hammers [118] fall
On Mars his [119] armour forg'd for proof eterne [120]
With less remorse than Pyrrhus' bleeding sword
Now falls on Priam.
Out, out, thou strumpet Fortune! All you gods,
In general synod take away her power!
Break all the spokes and fellies [121] from her wheel,

---

[109] pasted **over**.   [110] quaintly designed, or, possibly, old.   [111] fierce.
[112] feeble.   [113] Troy's citadel.   [114] its.
[115] his purpose and its accomplishment.   [116] storm clouds.   [117] sky.
[118] The Cyclopes acted as workmen in the smithy for Vulcan.   [119] Mars's.
[120] eternal resistance.   [121] wheel's rim.

And bowl the round nave [122] down the hill of heaven
As low as to the fiends!"

POL. (*Bored.*) This is too long.   520

HAM. (*Angrily.*) It shall to the barber's, with your beard. Prithee,
say on; [123] he's for a jig [124] or a tale of bawdry, or he sleeps.
Say on; come to Hecuba. [125]

1. PLAY. "But who, O, who had seen the mobled [126] queen"—[127]

HAM. (*Impressed.*) "The mobled queen"!

POL. (*Hoping to win Hamlet's approval.*) That's good; "mobled queen"
is good.

1. PLAY. "Run barefoot up and down, threat'ning the flame
With bisson rheum,[128] a clout [129] about that head
Where late the diadem stood, and for a robe,   530
About her lank and all o'er-teemed loins,[130]
A blanket, in the alarm of fear caught up;—
Who this had seen, with tongue in venom steep'd,
'Gainst Fortune's state would treason have pronounc'd.
But if the gods themselves did see her then,
When she saw Pyrrhus make malicious sport

---

[122] hub.

[123] Hamlet's anger at Polonius' interruption proves his deep concentration
on what the player is reciting, and that alone is at variance with the theory
that the passage could be meant satirically. Could Shakespeare have intended
that *we* react to it in the same way that stupid Polonius does—i.e., be bored
by it?

Shakespeare had, of course, an important dramatic reason for the old
man's interruption. Having dismissed it, Hamlet will turn with augmented
intensity to listen to the player. And it is the next line which contains the
phrase that is to give him his all-important idea. By this device, the dramatist
accounts for the impact of the line on Hamlet, and at the same time isolates the
line itself.

[124] Following the performance of a serious play, a jig was often performed
to satisfy the most vulgar members of the audience. The jigs were farcical skits
and ballads.

[125] Queen of Troy.   [126] muffled.

[127] Hamlet is struck forcibly by the expression. See pp. 202–203. (The
meaninglessness of the Olivier movie achieved its nadir in this scene. The whole
recitation of the Marlovian passage was cut out, beginning with "I heard thee
speak me a speech once." Thus there was no "mobled queen" and thus no
motivation for the Mouse-trap. We never learned how or why Hamlet thought
of presenting it. Hence, the bulk of the next soliloquy was omitted too, and
about all that remained of it was Hamlet's rushing into a spot of light crying
"The play's the thing!" while he pirouetted about like a ballet-dancer.)

[128] blinding tears.   [129] cloth.

[130] loins exhausted from the bearing of children.

In mincing with his sword her husband's limbs,
The instant burst of clamour that she made,
Unless things mortal move them not at all,
Would have made milch [131] the burning eyes of heaven, 540
And passion [132] in the gods."

POL. (*Finding a new excuse to put an end to the recital.*) Look,
whe'er he has not turn'd his colour and has tears in's eyes.
Pray you, no more.

HAM. (*Now so excited that he is willing to let Polonius terminate the
recitation.*) 'Tis well; I'll have thee speak out the rest soon.
Good my lord, will you see the players well bestow'd? Do ye
hear? Let them be well us'd, for they are the abstracts and brief
chronicles of the time; after your death you were better have
a bad epitaph than their ill report while you lived. 550

POL. My lord, I will use them according to their desert.

HAM. (*Indignantly.*) God's bodykins, man, better! Use every man
after his desert, and who should scape whipping? Use them
after your own honour and dignity. The less they deserve, the
more merit is in your bounty.[133] Take them in.

POL. Come, sirs. *Exit.*

HAM. Follow him, friends; we'll hear a play tomorrow.[134] 560
Exeunt all the Players but the First.

Dost thou hear me, old friend? Can you play "The Murder
of Gonzago"? [135]

I. PLAY. Ay, my lord.

HAM. We'll ha't to-morrow night. You could, for a need, study

---

[181] yielding milk—i.e., tears.   [132] powerful feelings.

[133] This philosophy, much akin to Portia's, is the one by which Hamlet
would live, if but permitted to. His own graciousness and warmth towards
his social inferiors prove how profoundly these sentiments emanate from his
nature.

[134] The sudden acceleration of tempo in the brief passage that follows, in
his dismissal of Rosencrantz and Guildenstern, and in his detaining the First
Player for but a few moments, makes clear that Hamlet has been projected
into a state of great excitement. He is anxious to be alone—and Shakespeare
is anxious to have him alone, so that we may learn what thing it is that has
caused this new ferment.

[135] Adams, who will have Hamlet the victim of melancholia, ascribes
Hamlet's purpose in giving the play only to "malicious pleasure," which he
names a symptom of the disease. The Prince presents the piece only "to
annoy" Claudius, and his added passage is intended merely to make some
further pointed thrusts at the King, for Hamlet "has no doubt whatsoever" of
Claudius' guilt (*Hamlet*, p. 244).

a speech of some dozen or sixteen lines, which I would set down
and insert in't,[136] could ye not?

1. PLAY.   Ay, my lord.

HAM.   Very well. Follow that lord,—and look you mock him not.   570
(*Exit 1. Player.*) My good friends, I'll leave you till night. You
are welcome to Elsinore.

ROS.   Good my lord!

                              Exeunt Rosencrantz and Guildenstern.
HAM.   Ay, so, God buy ye.—Now I am alone.[137]

[136] probably the speech of Lucianus III, ii, 266 seq.

[137] Adams concludes at this point that Hamlet is moved to soliloquize
from a need of self-denunciation at two months of "absolutely inexcusable"
delay (It cannot too much be emphasized that during the soliloquy the audience has as yet only the vaguest idea of how much time has elapsed—is indeed
unaware of any delay at all!) and an equal need of finding excuses to "justify
that delay." But Hamlet cannot find a reason. Even his scheme of "playing
the madman" has been rendered "absurd" by the plain fact of "two months'
inactivity," despite his having no "smallest doubt" about his father's death
and the identity of the murderer (*Hamlet*, pp. 244-247).

When Hamlet soliloquizes we must always, before we examine the out-
pouring of his words, remember the occasion for them, the dramatic occurrence
which has fathered the emotion. And that occurrence, that dramatic fact, is
Hamlet's decision to present *The Murder of Gonzago* before the King and
Queen. The "mobled queen" has engendered a series of ideas which give him
at last a means of testing the Ghost's veracity and the guilt of Claudius and
Gertrude. His reckless nature operates upon his feverish anticipation of that
test, and causes him to open with a torrent of violence. Why? Because he
cannot wait until tomorrow to put the test into practise. His violence is an
outlet for his impatience.

But the torrent is *not*, as generally interpreted, chiefly a flood of self-
condemnation. (Kittredge: "Hamlet rages against himself for stupid inactivity . . . He has done nothing to avenge his father and seems incapable
of doing anything"—*Hamlet*, p. 203.) It is much more a condemnation of his
outrageous fortune. Able in will, courage, intelligence, and determination to
sweep with "wings as swift as meditation' into action, he has been propelled
into a situation in which common sense and justice both have prescribed his
making no move. Only too eager to believe Claudius a culprit, only too ready
to avenge, he has no proof that there is anything to avenge or that the man
he hates is guilty. Whatever his impulses would have him believe, he has not
dared to yield to their promptings—has had, rather, to smother the demands
of his blood for action until the moment arrive when he is free to act, knowing then his cause just and the criminal identified. The evidence for our so
interpreting him is in his very words.

He begins with the actor. Here was a man reliving in his recitation a
mere "fiction," a mere dream of strong emotions—yet speaking with "broken
voice," "tears in his eyes," his whole being giving expression to a counter-
feited passion. What would he do, asks Hamlet, had he my motives for
suffering? Ah, he would then speak with such overwhelming feeling as

O, what a rogue and peasant slave am I!
Is it not monstrous that this player here,

"would drown the stage with tears," and "make mad the guilty" among those
who heard him! Yet I am forced to go about as though I were living in a
dream, my very cause denied life, and am in a position where I may not even
open my lips! No, not open them to speak of the death of my royal father!
Can it be that I am a coward? What opportunity has my courage to express
itself? Does anyone give me an open chance to fight with him? ("Who calls
me villain," etc.—i.e., Who insults me, who attacks me, so that I may leap to
fight with him? Hamlet's meaning, of course, is that no one is doing any
of these things; no one offers the challenge to prove his mettle.) No. Nevertheless, I suppose I must have become "pigeon-livered" or I should have killed
this bloody, pitiless ("remorseless"), treacherous, lecherous, unnatural ("kindless") villain by this! (Hamlet, knowing well that he is no coward, castigates
himself with the charge that even if there *were* anything he could have done,
he probably would have failed to do it. But we are not to be so superficial as
to take this impatient charge against himself literally. In a moment he will
completely exonerate himself from this impetuous self-accusation. He *is* doing
something, and has, moreover, seized the first opportunity that has presented
itself to do something.)

He continues: What a fool I am to waste myself cursing this wretch
as though I were a common harlot or kitchen wench! Is it not pretty that I,
prompted—perhaps by heaven, perhaps by hell—to avenge my dear father,
must relieve my heart with mere words! But, enough of this; let's get to
work ("About, my brain").

And now he reveals to the audience his plan of presenting the Mouse-trap
—his reckless impatience to do which, has been responsible for the violence of
his preceding lines. Ever since the player's reference to the "mobled queen"
his active mind has been busy. He has passed beyond his original inspiration,
which was to decipher his mother's nature, to the more pressing issue of exposing Claudius, and thereby proving the truth of all the Ghost has uttered.
I have heard, he observes, that "guilty creatures" at a play have been so much
struck by the reflection on the stage of their own misdeeds that they have at
once ("presently") publicly proclaimed their crimes. I shall have the players
perform something like the murder of my father, and watching Claudius's
reactions closely, I shall quickly know whether I am on the right track. (That
is, at best, Hamlet's play may cause Claudius openly to confess his guilt; at
the least, Hamlet will know whether Claudius is guilty.) After all,

> "The spirit that I have seen
> May be a devil,"

and the devil is always ready to flatter the prejudices of mortals when they
are most unarmed. Perhaps because I am only too willing to believe Claudius
a murderer, because my thoughts have been dark and bitter since my father's
death, the apparition sought me out only to involve me in crime, and lead
me to my eternal damnation.

I *must* be patient; before I proceed I must have grounds more conclusive
("relative") than the words of a ghost. It is the play with which, if Claudius is
guilty, I shall entrap him!

But in a fiction, in a dream of passion,[138]
Could force his soul so to his own conceit
That from her working all his visage wann'd,   580
Tears in his eyes, distraction in's aspect,
A broken voice, and his whole function suiting
With forms to his conceit? [139] And all for nothing!
For Hecuba!
What's Hecuba to him, or he to Hecuba,
That he should weep for her? What would he do,
Had he the motive and the cue for passion
That I have? He would drown the stage with tears
And cleave the general ear with horrid speech,
Make mad the guilty and appall the free,[140]   590
Confound the ignorant, and amaze indeed
The very faculty of eyes and ears.
Yet I,
A dull and muddy-mettled rascal, peak
Like John-a-dreams, unpregnant of my cause,
And can say nothing; [141] no, not for a king,

[138] powerful feelings.   [139] imagination.   [140] (from guilt).
[141] In the phrases:

      "unpregnant of my cause,
  And can say nothing,"

which we have rendered in footnote 137 above as we understand them, lie embedded two crucial matters:

1. "Unpregnant" is glossed by Kittredge as "with no real sense of" (*Hamlet*, p. 203) and by Wilson as "not stirred to action"; (*Hamlet*, p. 289) both examples of the practise common to scholars of defining language to agree with a preconceived theory. But Wilson does admit that the word means literally "unimpregnated," which is a far cry from his glossing of it.

The *Oxford Dictionary* accepts the meaning of simply "not pregnant," and lists no earlier example than our line. As for "pregnant," the usage is old in its physiological sense, and the phrase "pregnant woman" is listed (as used in 1545). (*Oxford Dictionary*, VII, p. 1272) Since the literal meaning disdained by Wilson is the most concrete and therefore the most poetical, we submit that it represents Shakespeare's meaning here. Hamlet is saying that his "cause" lies within him waiting to be impregnated by the proof or the event which can quicken it into life.

2. Bradley is the spokesman for those who cannot find, as did Werder, any *external* reasons why Hamlet should not have killed Claudius immediately after the revelations of the Ghost, and who therefore look only to Hamlet's weakness as the source of his "delay." These scholars, of course, in overlooking the all-important question of the reliability of the Ghost, leave out of account one of the chief elements of the plot, an element which is plenti-

Upon whose property [142] and most dear life
A damn'd defeat was made. Am I a coward?
Who calls me villain, breaks my pate across,
Plucks off my beard and blows it in my face,   600
Tweaks me by the nose, gives me the lie i' the throat
As deep as to the lungs, who does me this?
Ha!
['Swounds,] I should take it; for it cannot be
But I am pigeon-liver'd and lack gall
To make oppression bitter, or ere this
I should have fatted all the region kites [143]
With this slave's offal. Bloody, bawdy villain!
Remorseless,[144] treacherous, lecherous, kindless [145] villain!
O, vengeance!   610
Why, what an ass am I! Sure, this is most brave,
That I, the son of a dear father murdered,
Prompted to my revenge by heaven and hell,
Must,[146] like a whore, unpack my heart with words,
And fall a-cursing, like a very drab,
A scullion!
Fie upon't! Foh! About, my brain! I have heard
That guilty creatures sitting at a play
Have by the very cunning of the scene
Been struck so to the soul that presently   620
They have proclaim'd their malefactions;

---

fully in evidence during more than the first half of the play. But Bradley
gives his reasons for refusing to look elsewhere than to Hamlet's "melancholia" for an understanding of the plot; his leading objection is: "From beginning to end of this play, Hamlet never makes the slightest reference to
any external difficulty" (*Shakespearean Tragedy*, p. 95).

This is simply not true. Even though the Elizabethan audience would have
required no reminder that no one could kill a king without some public
reason (just as it would have required no reminder about the possible demonic
nature of the Ghost), there *are*, nevertheless, several references made by Hamlet
to external forces rendering vengeance impossible—all of them missed by
Bradley. And the first two of them are in these lines. Hamlet says his cause is
unpregnant—that is, that it awaits the necessary occasion. And he also remarks
that he *can* say nothing about his cause (*not* that he does say nothing!)—
that is, that he is forced to keep silence when everything in him cries out
to be heard.

[142] self.   [143] kites (bird of prey) of the sky.   [144] pitiless.   [145] inhuman.
[146] Another instance overlooked by Bradley. Hamlet does not say that he
does unpack his heart with words, but that he *must* unpack it so (i.e., because
of restraining circumstance).

For murder, though it have no tongue, will speak
With most miraculous organ. I'll have these players
Play something like the murder of my father
Before mine uncle. I'll observe his looks;
I'll tent [147] him to the quick. If he but blench,[148]
I know my course.[149] The spirit that I have seen
May be the devil; and the devil hath power
To assume a pleasing shape; [150] yea, and perhaps
Out of my weakness and my melancholy,   630
As he is very potent with such spirits,
Abuses [151] me to damn me. I'll have grounds
More relative [152] than this. The play's the thing
Wherein I'll catch the conscience of the King.

                                                                        Exit.

[147] probe.   [148] flinch.

[149] It would be interesting to know what precisely the scholars have made out of "If he but blench I know my course," but they have avoided comment upon it. Yet a correct understanding of the word "course" might strangle many a false interpretation. "If Claudius but flinch I know my course." What does Hamlet mean? The *Oxford Dictionary* (II, pp. 1087–88) lists several meanings for the word, any one of which would give the line significance:

  a. "Onward movement in a particular path" (first use in 1290).
  b. "The action or practise of coursing, or pursuing game with hounds" (first use by Chaucer).
  c. "The line along which anything runs or travels" (first use in 1380).
  d. "The direction . . . towards which a ship sails" (first use in 1553).
  e. "A line of personal action, way of acting, method of proceeding" (first use in 1583).

Meanings *a* and *c* are close; *d* and *e* not at all so—yet all four would yield more or less the sense we have given—"I shall know whether I am on the right track." Hamlet's very next lines,

         "The spirit I have seen," etc.

strongly confirm the weight we attach to the word. Meaning *b*, however, is the strongest, most athletic of all and one is strongly tempted to prefer it.

[150] Curiously enough, Coleridge quoted merely as a parallel passage from Sir Thomas Browne's *Religio Medici:* "I believe—that those apparitions and ghosts of departed persons are not the wandering souls of men, but the unquiet walks of devils, prompting and suggesting us unto mischief, blood and villainy" (*Essays and Lectures on Shakespeare*, p. 150) without reflecting on what it reveals about earlier beliefs in ghosts. Had he reflected on his quotation, he would have been compelled to abandon his theory!

[151] deceives.   [152] convincing.

ACT THIRD

SCENE I

A room in the castle. (The next day.) [1]
Enter King, Queen, Polonius, Ophelia, Rosencrantz,
and Guildenstern.

KING.   And can you, by no drift of circumstance,[2]
  Get from him why he puts on [3] this confusion,
  Grating so harshly all his days of quiet
  With turbulent and dangerous lunacy?

ROS.   He does confess he feels himself distracted;
  But from what cause he will by no means speak.

GUIL.   Nor do we find him forward to be sounded,
  But, with a crafty madness, keeps aloof
  When we would bring him on to some confession
  Of his true state.

QUEEN.   Did he receive you well?   10

ROS.   Most like a gentleman.

GUIL.   But with much forcing of his disposition.

ROS.   Niggard of question; [4] but, of our demands,
  Most free in his reply.

QUEEN.   Did you assay him
  To any pastime? [5]

ROS.   Madam, it so fell out, that certain players
  We o'er-raught [6] on the way; of these we told him,
  And there did seem in him a kind of joy
  To hear of it. They are about the court,
  And, as I think, they have already order   20
  This night to play before him.

POL.   'Tis most true.

---

[1] With this scene begins the longest day of the action, a succession of
events that do not terminate until the small hours of the morning (IV, iv).
Before this day has ended Hamlet will know that it was an "honest" Ghost,
but he will also have wrought tragic damage to himself.

[2] roundaboutness.

[3] Note that Claudius' words betray, though he pretends to be saying otherwise, that he knows perfectly well that Hamlet is not insane.

[4] conversation.

[5] Characteristically, the Queen is anxious only that things go smoothly.

[6] overtook.

And he beseech'd me to entreat your Majesties
To hear and see the matter.

KING. (*Prepared to make peace with Hamlet, if possible.*)   With all my
        heart; and it doth much content me
To hear him so inclin'd.
Good gentlemen, give him a further edge,
And drive his purpose on to these delights.

ROS.   We shall, my lord.

                              Exeunt Rosencrantz and Guildenstern.

KING.   Sweet Gertrude, leave us too,
For we have closely [7] sent for Hamlet hither,
That he, as 'twere by accident, may here   30
Affront [8] Ophelia.
Her father and myself, lawful espials,
Will so bestow ourselves that, seeing unseen,
We may of their encounter frankly judge,
And gather by him, as he is behaved,
If't be the affliction of his love or no
That thus he suffers for.

QUEEN.   I shall obey you.
And for your part, Ophelia, I do wish
That your good beauties be the happy cause
Of Hamlet's wildness. So shall I hope your virtues   40
Will bring him to his wonted way again,
To both your honours.

OPH.   Madam, I wish it may.

                                            Exit Queen.

POL. (*Placing her.*)   Ophelia, walk you here. Gracious, so please ye,
We will bestow ourselves. (*To Ophelia. Putting a prayerbook in
        her hands.*) Read on this book,
That show of such an exercise may colour [9]

---

[7] privately.   [8] confront.

[9] Attention must be called to the use of this word in this line (because of
a highly important moment later in this act). Despite its being glossed quite
differently by modern editors, we insist that what Polonius is saying is: "That
show of such an exercise may afford a good *reason* for your being alone."
The *Oxford Dictionary* lists *colour* as a noun as having meant since 1380, "allegeable ground or reason" (*Oxford Dictionary* II, p. 638). The fitness of that
meaning is so clear in this line as to require no further argument. We should
not trouble to quarrel with Wilson's "disguise" (*Hamlet*, p. 266) or Kittredge's
"give a specious pretext to" (*Hamlet*, p. 207) since their definitions constitute
differences from "reason" by no means crucial in this speech. But the meaning

Your loneliness. We are oft to blame in this,—
'Tis too much prov'd—that with devotion's visage
And pious action we do sugar o'er
The devil himself.

KING.   O, 'tis true!

[*Aside.*] How smart a lash that speech doth give my conscience! 50
The harlot's cheek, beautied with plast'ring art,
Is not more ugly to the thing that helps it
Than is my deed to my most painted word.
Oh heavy burden! [10]

POL.   I hear him coming. Let's withdraw, my lord.[11]

Exeunt King and Polonius.

Enter Hamlet.

HAM.   To be, or not to be: that is the question.[12]
Whether 'tis nobler in the mind to suffer
The slings and arrows of outrageous fortune,
Or to take arms against a sea of troubles,
And by opposing end them. To die; to sleep;   60
No more; and by a sleep to say we end

---

of "colour" is going to prove highly crucial in III, iv, 130; in that line neither Wilson's nor Kittredge's definition will have meaning, while we shall insist (quite without precedent) that the word again will mean "allegeable ground or reason," as it does here.

Such too is its meaning when King Hal excoriates Scroop:

> All other devils that suggest by treasons
> Do botch and bungle up damnation
> With patches, colours, and with forms being fetched
> From glistering semblances of piety. (*Henry V*, II, ii, 114–17)

and such too when Cleopatra upbraids Antony:

> Nay, pray you, seek no colour for your going,
> But bid farewell and go. (*Antony and Cleopatra*, I, ii, 32–3)

[10] Shakespeare accomplishes two ends with Claudius' aside: it is time that the *audience* be made certain of the King's guilt, and these lines so apprizing us tighten our concentration, as the contest between Hamlet and him approaches its moment of greatest intensity; also, Claudius' being able to feel the prick of conscience makes us aware that, murderer though he is, he is not a monster, and for the first time we feel a twinge of sympathy for him. (In the Olivier movie, however, this effect was canceled because Claudius eyed Ophelia holding her prayer book as though her very innocence of appearance were moving him to consider appropriating her for his bed!)

[11] In the Elizabethan theater, the inner stage, a space curtained off at the back of the stage proper, is the regular place for "overhearing." To it Polonius and Claudius now retire.

[12] See pp. 203–212.

The heart-ache and the thousand natural shocks
That flesh is heir to. 'Tis a consummation [13]
Devoutly to be wish'd. To die; to sleep;—
To sleep? Perchance to dream! Ay, there's the rub;[14]
For in that sleep of death what dreams may come,
When we have shuffl'd off this mortal coil,[15]
Must give us pause. There's the respect [16]
That makes calamity of so long life.
For who would bear the whips and scorns of time,   70
The oppressor's wrong, the proud man's contumely,
The pangs of dispriz'd love, the law's delay,
The insolence of office, and the spurns
That patient merit of the unworthy takes,
When he himself might his quietus make [17]
With a bare bodkin? [18] Who would fardels [19] bear,
To grunt and sweat under a weary life,
But that the dread of something after death,
The undiscovered country [20] from whose bourn
No traveller returns, puzzles the will   80
And makes us rather bear those ills we have
Than fly to others that we know not of?
Thus conscience [21] does make cowards of us all;
And thus the native hue of resolution
Is sicklied o'er with the pale cast [22] of thought,
And enterprises of great pith and moment
With this regard [23] their currents turn awry,
And lose the name of action.—(*Suddenly aware of her presence.*)
    Soft you now!
The fair Ophelia! (*In chastened mood, gently.*) Nymph, in thy
    orisons
Be all my sins rememb'red. [24]

OPH.   Good my lord,   90
    How does your honour for this many a day?
HAM.   I humbly thank you, (*A little dispiritedly.*) well, well, well.
OPH.   My lord, I have remembrances of yours
    That I have longed long to re-deliver.
    I pray you, now receive them.

---

[13] See p. 210.   [14] hindrance, a term from bowling.
[15] fuss.   [16] consideration.
[17] settle his accounts (i.e., put an end to his troubles).   [18] poniard.
[19] burdens.   [20] See pp. 211–212.   [21] conscious thought.   [22] shade.
[23] i.e., the thought of something after death.   [24] See pp. 212–222.

HAM. (*In a pained voice, rejecting what she offers to return.*) No, no;
    I never gave you aught.

OPH. (*Taking him literally.*) My honour'd lord, I know right well you
      did,
    And, with them, words of so sweet breath compos'd
    As made the things more rich. Their perfume lost,
    Take these again; for to the noble mind   100
    Rich gifts wax poor when givers prove unkind.
    There, my lord.

HAM. (*Smarting from the wounds of rejected love, and not crediting
      his ears.*) Ha, ha! are you honest?* [25]

OPH. My lord!

HAM. Are you fair?

OPH. What means your lordship?

HAM. (*Angry now, but chiefly with himself for having just for-
    gotten what her apparent rejection of him has been.*) That if
    you be honest and fair, your honesty should admit no discourse
    to your beauty.

OPH. (*Taking refuge in tears.*) Could beauty, my lord, have better
    commerce than with honesty? [26]   110

HAM. Ay, truly; for the power of beauty will sooner transform
    honesty from what it is to a bawd than the force of honesty can
    translate beauty into his likeness. (*Construing her tears as
    hypocritical; ironically.*) This was sometime a paradox,[27] but
    now the time gives it proof. (*With all the hurt of thwarted
    love.*) I did love you once.

OPH. (*Confounded, sobbing.*) Indeed, my lord, you made me
    believe so.

HAM. (*Unable to bear her tears.*) You should not have believ'd
    me, for virtue cannot so inoculate our old stock [28] but we shall
    relish of it. (*Partly out of wounded pride, partly out of pity.*)
    I loved you not.   120

OPH. I was the moré deceived.

HAM. (*More and more gently.*) Get thee to a nunnery; why
    wouldst thou be a breeder of sinners? I am myself indifferent
    honest, but yet I could accuse me of such things that it were

[25] chaste.

[26] Ophelia thinks Hamlet has been using "honest" in the sense of "telling
the truth."

[27] i.e., "You don't catch my meaning! You *will* play the injured innocent
to the last, won't you?"

[28] cannot change the sinful nature we have inherited from Adam.

better my mother had not borne me. I am very proud, revengeful, ambitious, with more offences at my beck than I have
thoughts to put them in, imagination to give them shape, or time
to act them in. What should such fellows as I do crawling be-   130
tween heaven and earth? We [29] are arrant knaves all; believe
none of us. Go thy ways to a nunnery. (*He turns away abruptly
and begins to leave. Polonius, who has been peeking out from
time to time, is unprepared for Hamlet's sudden move, and does
not withdraw without being seen by Hamlet.[30] Hamlet is now
in a perfect fury with Ophelia.*) Where's your father?

[29] (men).

[30] This manner of presenting this moment of the drama may have been
fairly traditional before Wilson's *What Happens in Hamlet* was published. That
scholar implies that it was, to his displeasure. He is happy to think that his
suggestion of Hamlet's overhearing Polonius before Polonius overhears *him,*
"rids us of the traditional stage-business of Polonius exposing himself to the
eye of Hamlet and the audience, which has hitherto been the only way open
to stage managers of putting any meaning at all into the scene. It is a trick
at once crude and inadequate: crude because the chief councillor of Denmark
is neither stupid nor clumsy(!!), and to represent him so . . . is to degrade
intrigue to buffoonery; inadequate, because it only tells Hamlet of one, whereas
his words clearly lose a great deal of their force if he is not known to be
conscious of the presence of two (pp. 132–33)."

Of course, we agree to none of this. Polonius *is* stupid and clumsy—and
has already plentifully demonstrated that he is. Peeking out at the lovers is just
what this fumbling busybody would do. Nor is the device crude, since it is
strictly in keeping with his character. Certainly the "buffoonery" it involves
is of the kind we are treated to nearly every time he is on the stage. Indeed,
as we have had occasion to observe on pages 238–240, Shakespeare has so woven
his play that this "buffoonery" is one of the ever-present threads in it. Nor
is this "buffoonery," as managed by the dramatist, less harmonious with the
prevailing tone of the play than would be the "intrigue" Wilson offers, an
intrigue which, being merely theatrical, is distant enough from true tragedy.
As to Hamlet's having to know that there are two eavesdroppers, that presents
no difficulty at all. The Prince, with his quick and rash intuitiveness, once he
is aware of Polonius's presence, knowing the councilor a hireling of Claudius,
will guess that the King may very well be there too. And even if Claudius
is not there, Hamlet knows, everything said will be carried straight back to
him. The audience's knowing the King to be there renders it easy on the stage
—once Hamlet catches sight of the withdrawing head and end of robe—to
grant the Prince's immediate apprehension.

Wilson, who finds this simple and natural solution of the passage a crude
and inadequate trick, has had a remarkably "stagy" solution for the preceding
act, where he would have Hamlet enter to overhear Polonius's plot. As the old
man speaks of Hamlet's often walking in the lobby (II, ii, 159), "we may imagine
him jerking a thumb over his shoulder towards the inner stage. . . . Words
and the action are a direct invitation to the spectators to look in that direction;
and as they do, Hamlet enters the inner-stage from the door at the back, his

OPH. At home, my lord.

HAM. (*Addressing himself directly to Polonius.*) Let the doors be shut upon him, that he may play the fool nowhere but in's *own* house. (*Furiously.*) Farewell! (*He moves again toward the exit.*)

OPH. O, help him, you sweet heavens!

HAM. (*Returning, her tears now evoking in him only cold wrath.*) If thou dost marry, I'll give thee this plague for thy dowry: be thou as chaste as ice, as pure as snow, thou shalt not escape 140 calumny. Get thee to a nunnery, go. Farewell! Or, if thou wilt needs marry, marry a fool; for wise men know well enough what monsters you make of them. To a nunnery, go, and quickly too. Farewell! (*Again, about to leave.*)

OPH. O heavenly powers, restore him!

HAM. (*Returning again to spit out in exacerbation.*) I have heard of your [31] paintings too, well enough. God has given you one face, and you make yourselves another. You jig,[32] you amble,[33] 150 and you lisp and nick-name God's creatures and make your wantonness your ignorance.[34] Go to, I'll no more on't; it hath made me mad. I say, we will have no more marriages. Those that are married already, (*once more addressing himself to where Polonius is hiding*) all but *one*, shall live; the rest shall keep as they are. To a nunnery, go. *Exit.*

OPH. (*Not knowing what Hamlet has seen, and convinced that he is mad.*) O, what a noble mind is here o'erthrown!
The courtier's, soldier's, scholar's, eye, tongue, sword;
The expectancy and rose of the fair [35] state, 160
The glass of fashion and the mould [36] of form,
The observ'd of all observers, quite, quite down!
And I, of ladies most deject and wretched,
That suck'd the honey of his music vows,
Now see that noble and most sovereign reason,
Like sweet bells jangled out of tune and harsh;
That unmatch'd form and feature of blown [37] youth

---

eyes upon a book" (p. 106). Unfortunately, Wilson has, since he wrote his book, had little cause for complaint. John Barrymore's was the last Hamlet on Broadway (memory could be at fault here) we recollect performing the scene in the way we have described. Soon came Mr. Gielgud, adopting Wilson's stage direction, and since then there have been no peeking Poloniuses.

[31] (i.e., women's).   [32] walk with jigging gait.   [33] (i.e., affectedly).
[34] excuse your wantonness on the grounds of ignorance.
[35] fair because of Hamlet.   [36] model.   [37] full-blown.

Blasted with ecstasy.[38] O, woe is me,
To have seen what I have seen, see what I see! [39]
Re-enter King and Polonius.

KING. *Love!* his affections do not *that* way tend;   170
Nor what he spake, though it lack'd form a little,[40]
Was not like madness. There's something in his soul
O'er which his melancholy sits on brood,
And I do doubt [41] the hatch and the disclose
Will be some danger; which for to prevent,[42]
I have in quick determination
Thus set it down: he shall with speed to England
For the demand of our neglected tribute.[43]
Haply the seas and countries different
With variable objects [44] shall expel   180
This something-settled matter in his heart,
Whereon his brains still beating puts him thus
From fashion of himself. What think you on't?

POL. It shall do well; but yet do I believe
The origin and *commencement* of this grief
Sprung from neglected love.[45] How now, Ophelia!
You need not tell us what Lord Hamlet said;
We heard it all. My lord, do as you please,
But, if you hold it fit, after the play
Let his queen mother all alone entreat him   190
To show his griefs. Let her be round [46] with him,
And I'll be plac'd, so please you, in the ear
Of all their conference. If she find him not,[47]
To England send him, or confine him where
Your wisdom best shall think.

KING.   It shall be so.   195
Madness in great ones must not unwatch'd go.[48]   *Exeunt.*

---

[38] madness.   [39] (Poor Ophelia has seen nothing of what she has seen!)
[40] (Claudius is unaware, of course, that Hamlet's sudden swerving into violence was owing to his catching that glimpse of Polonius.)
[41] fear.   [42] come ahead of.   [43] See pp. 223-224.
[44] variety of things to be seen.
[45] (Polonius is unwilling to give up his point!)   [46] direct.
[47] does not discover (the root of Hamlet's behavior).
[48] (The King for all his diplomacy is always giving himself away to us. He has strongly stated his conviction that there is nothing unbalanced about Hamlet; nevertheless, he pretends to think otherwise, a policy well-calculated to be a defense for himself should Hamlet become obstreperous.)

SCENE II

A hall in the castle. (Later the same day.)
Enter Hamlet and Players.

HAM. Speak the speech, I pray you, as I pronounc'd it to you,
trippingly on the tongue;[1] but if you mouth it, as many of your

---

[1] The most exciting scene in the play opens with a passage which might serve as gospel to actors and interpreters in general. Here again (as in II, ii, 343 seq.) Shakespeare is talking to us, this time on a matter of never-failing interest, a topic on which nobody could be a greater authority, the art of interpretation. Hamlet's advice to the players has the slenderest thread of connection with the plot: he naturally wishes *The Murder of Gonzago* to be given as effectively as possible to insure the fruits he hopes to reap from it. Dramatically speaking, the passage could be briefer. Nevertheless, only a churl would wish it any shorter, for these fifty lines are as encyclopedic as they are fundamental. It is a recurring matter of chagrin that the actor speaking these lines of Hamlet normally violates every principle contained in them while he delivers the passage!

Speak the lines, Hamlet counsels, "trippingly on the tongue"—what is known on the stage as "throwing the line away—" that is, don't overemphasize, don't caress each syllable. If you insist upon doing that, I'd just as soon have the town crier bawl out my lines. And don't use too many gestures.

These vices Hamlet admonishes against are still in evidence whenever Shakespeare is presented today, as though it were inconceivable that his lines could be spoken humanly; the mouthing and over-gesticulation, however, have disappeared when our contemporary dramatists are presented on the boards. Earlier in our century these habits constituted, we believe, the "grand style" in acting. The year of our birth precluded our being able to see more than a very few of the leading actors of the period preceding and including the First World War, and even those we did see, by the time we saw them, were in their old age. We remember a performance of *Œdipus Tyrannus* by Sir Martin Harvey in which he swooped up and down the scale in a fashion to inspire the envy of a coloratura soprano, and one of *King Lear* in which Robert Mantell thundered until he was breathless. And the only occasion we saw the Divine Sarah, in a solo recitation, was dreadfully disenchanting; the exhibition we witnessed was fearful; despite the handicap of an artificial limb she managed to cover every inch of a large stage, and her arms were in constant motion in emulation of a windmill. We prefer to believe that what we saw during that last American tour of hers could not have been representative of her art. Though at second hand we feel that we know pretty well the style current on Broadway for the first two decades of the twentieth century; for we had an uncle who "saw all the plays." He never missed a Saturday night, we have been told, and on the regular Sunday gatherings of the family he was very easily persuaded to re-enact the stirring passages he had heard the night before, to the immense delight of his adoring sisters and their children. Frequently he would give extended encores by digging into his repertory of the great moments created by thespians long since dead. Thus we were privileged to witness the imitation of the styles, minutely studied by

players do, I had as lief the town-crier spoke my lines.[2] Nor do
not saw the air too much with your hand, thus, but use all
gently; for in the very torrent, tempest, and, as I may say, the
whirlwind of passion, you must acquire and beget a temperance
that may give it smoothness.[3] O, it offends me to the soul to see
a robustious periwig-pated fellow tear a passion to tatters,[4] to   10

---

our uncle, not only of Forbes-Robertson, Barrett, Beerbohm Tree, Martin
Harvey, Matheson Lang, Robert Mantell, David Warfield, E. H. Sothern, and
Otis Skinner, but of Henry Irving, Edwin Booth, and Joseph Jefferson as well.
We certainly gathered the impression that none of these worthies had been
sparing of gesture or melodramatic intonation. When all these gentlemen had
taken their final curtain calls and we were busy adulating a newer generation
of stars, our uncle, of course, dismissed the newer mode of acting as anemic
and without style.

One imagines that the newer manner of understatement, which one is
now accustomed to (except in our Shakespeare!), was more or less evolved
through the example of Duse. When she made her return appearance during
the last year of her life, we were inspired to do one of the few sensible things
we've ever done: for three weeks no professor saw us in our college classes,
for we went during that period to see every one of her performances. We had
never seen, we have never since seen, anything approaching the magic of her
acting. The beauty of that quiet fragile voice, the glow of her inner fire
carried across the vast reaches of the old Century Theatre up to the gallery
where we were seated. There was such intensity in the air that, we think,
if a pin had been dropped everyone in the audience would have jumped in
fright. Yet she kept her register within a narrow range, and employed very
few gestures. But every modulation of her voice and every movement of her
eloquent frame were charged with meaning. We remember her sitting in a
chair for some twenty minutes with hardly more visual variation than an
occasional lift of the hand, and still holding us spellbound; then when she at
last rose to walk to a table the dramatic significance of that move was almost
unbearably poignant. We saw her in good plays and bad plays, we saw her
enact roles from that of a maiden to that of an aged grandmother, and we
have never seen the breath of life so much given to women on the stage as
she bestowed on each. Yet no one could have more completely followed
Hamlet's injunction to "use all gently."

While the preceding paragraphs were in press, we were reading Bernard
Shaw's *Dramatic Criticism* from the *Saturday Review*. On June 8, 1895 he
speaks of the "rarity" of Duse's gigantic, intellectual "energy" as against "the
mere head steam needed to produce Bernhardtian explosions." Bernhardt "has
nothing but her own charm"; Duse "gives you . . . the charm . . . belonging
to the character she impersonates."

[2] i.e., at the top of his lungs.

[3] These are some of the profoundest words ever spoken on the art of
interpretation. The interpreter must always stand a little bit apart from the
emotions he is projecting, must not dare himself to participate in them. It is
the audience who is to feel these emotions, and he is inevitably cut off from
experiencing them, except by reflection from the audience. Knowing what

his own responses to the work he interprets have been, he as an artist must acquire the means of arousing those same responses. It is for this cause that the greatest performers, once they have decided on the means, give identical performances night after night. Only the inferior depend on the inspiration of the moment. For them the moment rarely arrives. Pavlova once said that she had to know the precise pinpoint on the stage where her toe was to alight.

The pianist who becomes involved in the whirling emotions of the last movement of the *Sonata Appassionata* will never survive to the end. He will deliver not those emotions but a chaos of sound; his fingers instead of obeying him will run away with him and the music. The Isolda and Tristan who become caught up in that prolonged (though not a note too long) witchery of love in the second act of Wagner's music-drama, cannot continue to sing but must indeed sink back to revel silently in their moonlit passion. The actor who allows himself for one minute to become encompassed in the violence of Lear's heartbreak could not endure to the final curtain, but must collapse (as we have seen a veteran actor do) on the stage incoherently. King Lear's is one of the most difficult of all roles to enact just because it is so difficult for the interpreter to keep sufficiently aloof from the maelstrom of its lines: the actor's problem here is to achieve the violence of volcanic passion without feeling it within himself—and the role begins *fortissimo* and ascends from there! In the very whirlwind of passion, the actor must acquire a temperance that will give that whirlwind full utterance.

'In our own time it has become a question as to whether or not understatement on the stage has not been carried to the point where it ceases to be acting at all. We have learned the lesson far too well. If we no longer tear a passion to tatters, we pretend that the conveying of any emotion is somehow indecent. Actors now sin in being entirely too natural, entirely too much themselves. They saunter on and off the stage as though they were drifting in and out of our parlors. One is grateful to the man who avoids making a scene in one's parlor, but no thanks are due to the actor who never makes one on the stage. That is what he is there for! A friend of ours once observed that you can always tell when the universally admired Miss X has reached the high point of the drama, for at that moment her nostrils begin to quiver! One takes no pleasure in watching actors as they shuffle or lounge about the stage in their own natural walk, stand limply, hold a hand in a pocket, scratch their heads or noses, fuss with their hair—as the whim may seize them. On the stage every gesture or move must have a meaning. If a man scratches his nose we at once try to find a meaning in it, if he lounges about we wish to understand the meaning of that—though in a parlor such actions mean nothing more than ill-breeding. In their talk, too, actors are too tame. A number of them have made a career out of the questionable virtue of speaking throughout an evening in monotone. They talk in the most casual of tones as though nothing being said were worth getting excited about. What they forget is that, in the theater, if nothing worth getting excited about is being said, there is also nothing worth listening to. To create the effect of even the casual, no actor himself can be casual. As in all art, a certain degree of heightening is necessary to the best interpretation. The arts do not attempt a carbon copy of life but an imitation of its values. Imitation involves selectivity, and selectivity means heightening. Thus, a musician playing Chopin's *Berceuse* very rags, to split the ears of the groundlings,[5] who for the most part are capable of nothing but inexplicable dumb-shows [6] and noise. I could have such a fellow whipp'd for o'erdoing Termagant.[7] It out-herods Herod.[8] Pray you, avoid it.

---

must stop short of the naturalism which makes the lullaby so pervasive as to put the audience *en masse* to sleep. An actor performing the role of a bore, must make that bore interesting; he must stop short of the naturalism which makes the bore so convincing that the audience walks out. By the very terms of its existence effective theater can never be truly naturalistic. Its only realism is the illusion of reality. Rob the theater of illusion and you rob it of drama.

For, as Hamlet remarks, the whole "purpose of playing . . . both at the first and now, was and is, to hold, as 'twere, the mirror up to nature." Emphatically stated, yet few phrases have been more distorted in esthetic discussion than the last. Holding "the mirror up to nature" has been cited as a justification for all kinds of literary crimes, including the writing of the naturalistic novel. It seems to have escaped notice, however, that to "hold the mirror up to nature" is to indulge in a practise obverse to naturalism. When you hold the mirror up to her, you do not catch nature in a net, you catch rather her reflection.

Indeed, though Shakespeare is plainly speaking only of the arts of the dramatist and actor (both included in the term "playing"), the figure of speech is so powerful and accurate that it may be applied to the method of all the arts. The arts are not concerned with catching Henry Jones and/or Mary Smith in a net so that we may know them as they really are and as they entirely are. That would be an enterprise both futile and useless. Futile, because Henry Jones and Mary Smith, being only themselves, will always retain an element of mystery decipherable neither to themselves nor to anyone else, retain some secret springs of motive and action the sources of which must be forever untraceable. And useless, because much of what we may know of Henry Jones and Mary Smith is uninteresting and valueless to know. But what is always possible, interesting, and valuable to know of them are their peculiar manifestations and variations of our common humanity. These we may catch by holding the mirror up to their actions. And what the mirror of art catches is, unlike life itself, complete, interesting, and decipherable.

The analogy of the mirror is quite perfect. For art, as we have said, because it is selective, is more vivid than life. So is the reflection in the mirror. The rose in the vase reflected in the mirror is a more vivid rose than the flower in the vase on the dresser before the mirror. The rose in the mirror is more vivid because it is selected out of the numerous details of the room, is heightened because it is cut off from the room by the frame of the mirror, while the rose on the dresser is part of a continuity in the room which the eye restlessly takes in without being able to isolate the flower from its incongruous environment. The rose in the mirror, more vivid than the "real" rose, gives a greater illusion of reality. Such is the paradox of art. The rose on the dresser is to the rose in the mirror as life is to art.

Now, what is it that the mirror of drama would reflect? Hamlet brilliantly explains:

"To show virtue her own feature, scorn her own image, and the

1. PLAY.   I warrant your honour.

HAM.   Be not too tame neither, but let your own discretion be your
tutor. Suit the action to the word, the word to the action; with   20
this special observance, that you o'erstep not the modesty of
nature. For anything so overdone is from the purpose of playing, whose end, both at the first and now, was and is, to hold,
as 'twere, the mirror up to nature; to show virtue her own
feature, scorn her own image, and the very age and body of
the time his form and pressure. Now this overdone, or come
tardy off, though it make the unskilful laugh, cannot but make
the judicious grieve; [9] the censure [10] of the which one must, in   30
your allowance, o'erweigh a whole theater of others. O, there
be players that I have seen play, and heard others praise, and
that highly, not to speak it profanely, that, neither having the
accent of Christians nor the gait of Christian, pagan, nor man,
have so strutted and bellowed that I have thought some of Na-

---

very age and body of the time his form and pressure" (i.e., the time's
very appearance and shape).

Thus Shakespeare is at one with Aristotle in understanding character (*ethos*)
in tragedy to mean a man's "moral constitution," and the function of tragedy
to exhibit that moral constitution in action. The mirror of drama does not
wish to reflect the meaningless routine of a man's life—his itinerary on his
daily way to work, what he eats for breakfast or lunch, whom he says "Good
morning" to, whether the five dollars in his pocket are in one bill or a particular assortment of coins and notes—unless there be a revealing meaning in
any of these details. The mirror of drama is far less concerned with why a
man found his way into a room than with *how* he behaves when he gets
there, what moral traits he reveals there, whether he is weak or strong, generous
or mean, loving or hating, giving or taking. Psychologists and anthropologists
notwithstanding, the concern of literature "at the first and now, was and is,"
with ethical values.

[5] those of the audiences who were in the pit, the cheapest location in
the playhouse.

[6] pantomime.

[7] The medieval romances, conceiving the Muslims to be idol-worshippers,
invented among other gods for them Termagant, who was a quarrelsome deity.

[8] Herod was a familiar character in the old plays, and it was his business
to rage and threaten generally. In one of the plays in which he figures, he is
directed to rage on the wagon (i.e., the wagon used for the stage) "and in
the street also."

[9] The imitation of life upon the stage, Hamlet continues, if overdone or
lamely contrived, can, of course, be counted upon to move the rowdier elements of the audience to laughter.

[10] opinion.

ture's journeymen had made men and not made them well,
they imitated humanity so abominably.[11]

1 PLAY. I hope we have reform'd that indifferently [12] with us, sir.   40
HAM.   O, reform it altogether. And let those that play your clowns
speak no more than is set down for them; [13] for there be of
them that will themselves laugh to set on some quantity of
barren spectators to laugh too, though in the mean time some
necessary question of the play be then to be considered. That's

[11] Shakespeare thought he was punning here. "Abominable" was then in-
correctly thought to derive from the Latin *ab homine*, i.e., away from what
is natural to man.
[12] fairly well.
[13] The clowns of Shakespeare's day were often the idols of the vulgar,
and were quite willing to sacrifice the quality of a work by playing up to
the lowest tastes of the audience. Many stories have come down to us demonstrating the astonishing freedom clowns sometimes appropriated to themselves with the text of the drama. They would mimic the serious business of
the plot, improvise lines, and generally contrive to hold the stage longer than
the dramatist intended. The corrupt First Quarto of our play assigns to
Hamlet a fuller explanation of what is meant:

> "And then you have some again that keeps one suit
> Of jests as a man is known by one suit of
> Apparel, and gentlemen quotes his jests down
> In their tables, before they come to the play, as thus:
> 'Cannot you stay till I eat my porridge?' and 'You owe me
> A quarter's wages,' and 'My coat wants a cullison,'
> And 'Your beer is sour,' and blabbering with his lips,
> And thus keeping in his cinquepace of jests,
> When, God knows, the warm clown cannot make a jest
> Unless by chance, as the blind man catcheth a hare:
> Masters, tell him of it."

This passage itself reads like someone's rather stupid improvisation, and
bears no marks of Shakespeare's authorship or the sort of speech he assigns
to Hamlet. We ourselves have long believed that this tampering by clowns
with the text may be the reason why Marlowe's *Doctor Faustus*, alone among
his works, reads like such a discouraging mixture of inspired imagination and
tasteless vulgarity. Everywhere else Marlowe's work is singularly free from
attempts at humor. The pagan radiance of his lines is of a kind that implies
he probably owned no sense of humor, and his first play boasts in its prologue
that it will have no traffic with "such conceits as clownage keeps in pay." But
their clowns the Elizabethan audience would have. The slapstick passages
in *Faustus,* so inconsistent with the dignity of the rest of the play, might well
be elaborations of the clowns, and these improvisations (if they were that)
would easily have found their way into the text when the play was at last
published.

villanous, and shows a most pitiful ambition in the Fool that
uses it.[14] Go, make you ready. *Exeunt Players.* 50
Enter Polonius, Rosencrantz, and Guildenstern.
How now, my lord! Will the King hear this piece of work?

POL. And the Queen too, and that presently.[15]

HAM. Bid the players make haste.

Exit Polonius

Will you two help to hasten them?

ROS. ⎱
GUIL. ⎰ We will, my lord.

Exeunt Rosencrantz and Guildenstern.

HAM. What ho! Horatio.
Enter Horatio.

HOR. Here, sweet lord, at your service.

HAM. (*Putting his hand on Horatio's shoulder; affectionately.*) Horatio,
thou art e'en as just a man
As e'er my conversation [16] cop'd withal. 60

HOR. (*Embarrassed.*) O, my dear lord,—

HAM. Nay, do not think I flatter,
For what advancement may I hope from thee
That no revenue hast but thy good spirits
To feed and clothe thee? Why should the poor be flatter'd?
No, let the candied tongue lick absurd pomp,
And crook the pregnant hinges of the knee
Where thrift may follow fawning. Dost thou hear?
Since my dear soul was mistress of my choice
And could of men distinguish, her election

---

[14] It has ever been lamentably true that it is the "pitiful ambition" of clowns
(professional clowns or unconscious ones) to gauge their success with the audience by the amount of mirth they can provoke, without regard to the appro-
priateness of laughter to the subject in hand. There is a school of public
speakers who could not think of beginning a funeral oration without some
funny anecdote, and we have all seen actors who will deliberately burlesque
their lines or business in order to amuse the vulgar. There is always present
"some quantity of barren spectators" who are ready to laugh if you crook your
finger at them, and it is an ancient trick that any actor can begin to laugh
without reason, knowing that these same barren folk will laugh along with
him. This conduct is indeed "villanous."

We have permitted ourselves, by Shakespeare's own delightful example, the
luxury of divagation. With him we now return to his play.

[15] at once. [16] human relationship.

Hath seal'd thee for herself; [17] for thou hast been   70
As one, in suffering all, that suffers nothing,
A man that Fortune's buffets and rewards
Hath ta'en with equal thanks; and blest are those
Whose blood and judgement are so well commingled,
That they are not a pipe for Fortune's finger
To sound what stop [18] she please. Give me that man
That is not passion's slave,[19] and I will wear him
In my heart's core, ay, in my heart of heart,
As I do thee. (*Embarrassed, too, by this display of deep affection,
     he stops short.*)—Something too much of this.—
There is a play to-night before the King.   80
One scene of it comes near the circumstance
Which I have told thee [20] of my father's death.
I prithee, when thou seest that act a-foot,
Even with the very comment of thy soul
Observe mine uncle. If his occulted guilt
Do not itself unkennel [21] in one speech,
It *is* a damned ghost that we have seen,
And my imaginations are as foul
As Vulcan's stithy.[22] Give him heedful note;
For I mine eyes will rivet to his face,   90
And after we will both our judgements join
To censure [23] of his seeming.

HOR.   Well, my lord.
If he steal aught the whilst this play is playing,
And scape detecting, I will pay the theft.
Danish march. A flourish. Enter King, Queen, Polonius, Ophelia,

---

[17] See pp. 261–262.
[18] On wind instruments the pitch is fixed by the various stops.
[19] the victim of strong feelings. Himself a slave of his own sufferings and
deep emotions, Hamlet knows how to value a man like Horatio, who can be
depended upon to exert judgment in a crisis, and not (like himself) be carried
away by impulse.
[20] (obviously, sometime between I, v and II, i).
[21] Shakespeare's phrasing of these phrases is psychologically masterful.
"Occulted" is used in the pure Latin sense of "hidden." To "unkennel" is to
force a fox or a dog out of his lodging. Hamlet is saying that he hopes to
force Claudius out into the open, but his words reveal that what he especially
anticipates is that, as a result of witnessing that scene, Claudius will *publicly*
proclaim himself a murderer.
[22] smithy.   [23] to form a judgment.

Rosencrantz, Guildenstern, and other Lords attendant, with the guard carrying torches.

HAM.   They are coming to the play; (*separating himself from Horatio, and moving off*) I must be idle.[24] Get you a place.

KING. (*Very amicably.*)   How fares [25] our cousin [26] Hamlet?

HAM.   Excellent, i' faith,—of the chameleon's dish.[27] I eat [28] the air, promise-cramm'd. You cannot feed capons so.   100

KING.   I have nothing with this answer, Hamlet; these words are not mine.

HAM.   No, nor mine now.[29] (*To Polonius.*) My lord, you play'd once i' the university, you say?

[24] The word here means "idle"! See pp. 224–227 for the meaning of the ensuing passage.

[25] (i.e., How are you feeling?).

[26] relative.

[27] The chameleon was thought to require no food—i.e., to live on air.

[28] Hamlet pretends to understand the King's "fare" in the sense of "dine."

[29] i.e., I've done with them. Scholars have been fairly unanimous in construing the preceding passage as meaning absolutely nothing but the nonsense invented by one pretending lunacy. In truth, at no point in the play does Hamlet talk with livelier and more dramatic pertinancy. It is the case, of course, that Claudius does not apprehend Hamlet's meanings, for the good reason that Claudius knows nothing of Hamlet's purposes in the presentation of the play. The Prince speaks to him in double meanings, the real significance of which he enjoys knowing is clear only to himself (to Horatio, too, if he is within earshot, and to us, if we are alert!). But it is absurd to pretend that this double-talk is a manifestation of assumed lunacy, when everything said is so powerfully cogent and apropos.

Shakespeare has used this same device elsewhere, notably in a scene between Juliet and her mother. It is early morning, and Romeo has just left her, after their wedding night, to go into banishment. The poor girl has had hardly a minute to release her misery in tears, when Lady Capulet appears before her in a benign mood to bring news of the forthcoming marriage to Paris. Seeing her daughter's flood of weeping, she interprets the tears as shed for the dead Tybalt:

"Evermore weeping for your cousin's death?
What, wilt thou wash him from his grave with tears?"

She is unaware that Juliet has even met Romeo. Juliet, thinking of Romeo, answers:

"Yet let me weep for such a feeling loss."

Confident that she understands the girl's emotions, her mother goes on:

"Well, girl, thou weep'st not so much for his death
As that the villain lives which slaughtered him."

Stung by the word, Juliet cries angrily:

"What villain, madam?"

POL. That I did, my lord, and was accounted a good actor.
HAM. And what did you enact?

Lady Capulet answers:

> "That same villain, Romeo."

Murmuring to herself that her husband is no villain, Juliet again speaks with double-meaning:

> "God pardon him! I do, with all my heart,
> And yet no man like he doth grieve my heart."

She would have her mother think by "no man like he" that she is not weeping for Romeo; her private meaning is that the man she weeps for, Romeo, is no such villain as her mother has described him. The strain continues:

> "LADY CAP. That is because the traitor murderer lives.
> JUL.   Aye, madam, from the reach of these my hands.
>   Would none but I might venge my cousin's death!"

While her mother believes her to be talking like a loyal Capulet, Juliet is to herself stating her loyalty to Romeo. Lady Capulet, complacently on the wrong scent, informs her daughter that she plans to send someone to Mantua after Romeo to poison him,

> "And then I hope thou wilt be satisfied."

Juliet's response is so spoken that her mother is to connect *dead* with *him;* she herself means it to be connected with *my poor heart:*

> "Indeed I never shall be satisfied
> With Romeo till I behold him—dead—
> Is my poor heart so for a kinsman vexed."

And her mother's plan to send a poisoner to Mantua gives her sudden hope that this may be a means of communicating with her husband:

> "Madam, if you could find out but a man
> To bear a poison, I would temper it,
> That Romeo should, upon receipt thereof,
> Soon sleep in quiet."

Lady Capulet takes this to mean that Juliet would like to mix a poison that would quickly send Romeo to his final rest; to Juliet *temper* and *sleep in quiet* have far different intent. The poor girl concludes her passage of double talk in an ironic vein:

> "Oh, how my heart abhors
> To hear him named and cannot come to him,
> To wreak the love I bore my cousin
> Upon his body that hath slaughtered him!"
>   (*Romeo and Juliet*, III, v, 70–103)

In anyone else's hands this scene would be painfully artificial; in Shakespeare's it is highly dramatic and moving.

No one thus far has accused Juliet of pretending lunacy before her mother when she speaks in these double meanings. Hamlet is doing something quite analogous in this conversation with Claudius.

POL. I did enact Julius Cæsar. I was kill'd i' the Capitol; Brutus kill'd me.[30]

HAM. It was a brute part of him to kill so capital a calf there. 110
(*Turning away from Polonius.*) Be the players ready?

ROS. Ay, my lord, they stay upon your patience.

QUEEN. (*In a sudden access of motherly affection—perhaps Hamlet has decided to be reasonable after all?*) Come hither, my good Hamlet, sit by me.

HAM. No, good mother, here's metal more attractive.[31]

Lying down at Ophelia's feet.

---

[30] Wilson waxes fantastic over this line. Why, he asks, does Hamlet "lead Polonius on to speak of the assassination of Julius Caesar?" (*What Happens in Hamlet*, p. 139). Because Hamlet intends to assassinate Claudius, and Polonius's answer will "remind his uncle and the court of a famous precedent for the assassination of tyrants" (p. 180). If Hamlet did meditate assassination, why on earth should he wish to forewarn his victim? And what need has he of establishing the precedent before killing his uncle? To win Claudius's approval? Though poor Hamlet is never allowed by the scholars to have any fun with Polonius (and is always perforce being either crazy or threatening in his jokes), Wilson goes further here in making Hamlet clairvoyant. All Hamlet has asked is,

"And what did you enact?"

How was Hamlet to know in advance what Polonius's answer would be? *They* never went to school together! For all Hamlet knows, the old man might respond that he had enacted Andrew Merrygreek or Gammer Gurton.

The whole point of the exchange to Hamlet, of course, has been to break off the dangerous talk he was having with Claudius; Shakespeare, too, had another motive—to hold in check a moment the rising suspense with the little jest Hamlet employs to terminate the conversation with Polonius.

[31] How should this scene be staged? It is customary to place the King, Queen and Court on one side of the stage; Hamlet and Ophelia on the other; and the players in the centre. Horatio is sometimes seen on the King's side, sometime on Hamlet's. The arrangement, on first thought, might appear adequate, and it has Prof. Wilson's endorsement. Realizing that Horatio must watch the King too, he would place him near Hamlet and Ophelia. But that location, though it is better than the impractical one near the King, is bad too. Anyone who can think in terms of theater will understand it to be true that from the moment the audience has heard Hamlet and Horatio agree to study the King's face so that they can compare later what they have seen, it will be inevitably expected that they will each take opposite posts of observation. That is "theater."

Actually the whole plan is unsatisfactory. It is foolish to place the performance of *The Murder of Gonzago* centrally. The mere fact of its being a performance will involve movement among the players, and movement on stage powerfully draws the eye of the audience. The players have no need of the extra advantage of the most commanding situation on the stage. More im-

POL. (*To the King.*)   O, ho! Do you mark that?
HAM.   Lady, shall I lie in your lap? [32]

---

portantly, we are not half so much interested in what they are performing as in the reactions of three people during that performance, Claudius, Gertrude, and Hamlet.

Above everything else we are concerned now with Claudius's behavior. No less than Hamlet and Horatio do we wish to study him intently. It is Claudius who ought to be in the centre of the stage, so we may watch every fleeting expression on his face. By his side, naturally, will be Gertrude; and around the monarchs, Polonius and the Court will cluster. Hamlet and Ophelia will be on one side of the stage—Hamlet closer to downstage center—and the players on the other side. Horatio, for dramatic reasons, should be placed near the players. Thus Hamlet and Horatio, on opposite sides of the stage, would form the base of a large triangle of which Claudius and Gertrude would be the apex, the focus of all eyes.

We cannot be positive how this was staged in Shakespeare's theater, but if the King and Queen were to be seen on their thrones—and one imagines that is where the audience would expect to see them—then they would have occupied the central position on the stage by necessity. The only place where the thrones could have been made ready for them was behind the curtain covering the inner stage; the curtain would have been drawn and the thrones revealed. It was not possible to drag a pair of thrones in and out on the Elizabethan stage, and the inner stage was serviceable for this and many other similar uses.

[82] His mother's invitation has not suited Hamlet's purposes; he needs a better observation post, and so he chooses to lie at Ophelia's feet. To cancel any suspicion his brief but dangerously revealing exchange with Claudius (lines 95–100) may have generated in the King, Hamlet begins to bandy jests with Ophelia in a careless manner. It is here that the worthy scholars are so much shocked by the indecency of his language to her—here, and in his other passages with her during the enactment of the Mouse-trap—and we have already quoted their explanations as to why he treats her "like a prostitute." This scholarly point of view is incredibly naïve. Many of Shakespeare's heroines, lovely girls all, speak or enjoy hearing jests on the *risqué* side. As, indeed, why should they not, since morality has never been a valid criterion for humor or wit? Shakespeare's was an age, not unlike our own in this respect, in which women did not have to listen through keyholes to enjoy racy sallies, did not have to faint at them to prove their superior moral constitution. There is nothing in the lines indicating that Ophelia takes offence, or that it is through his bawdy language that Hamlet wishes to insult her. On the contrary, it will be noted that innocent as Ophelia unquestionably is, she understands his little indecencies only too well. Indeed, as one might expect these excessively good girls to do, it is she who first gives his words a less than innocent interpretation. That she has no mid-Victorian revulsion from the bawdy is later demonstrated. In her insanity she sings a song which is as naughty as anything Hamlet ever says to her, but it has not the alleviating virtue of being amusing. It is, in fact, a rather revolting song, and she could not sing it if she had not learned it! There is, therefore, no reason why when she says,

"You are merry, my lord,"

OPH.   No, my lord.   120

HAM.   I mean, my head upon your lap?

OPH.   Ay, my lord.

HAM.   Do you think I meant country matters? [33]

OPH.   I think nothing, my lord.

HAM.   That's a fair thought to lie between maid's legs.

OPH.   What is, my lord?

HAM.   Nothing.

OPH.   You are merry, my lord.

HAM.   Who, I?   130

OPH.   Ay, my lord.

HAM.   (*With renewed bitterness.*)   O God, your only jig-maker.[34]
       What should a man do but *be* merry? For, look you, how
       cheerfully my mother looks, and my father died within's two
       hours.[35]

---

she should not be saying it with a happy laugh, delighted, as she must be, to
find her lover in good humor again.

Madariaga notes that she does not object to Hamlet's words. But his explanation is that she is a "flirt with no particular inhibition about anything."
Actually, he is sure, she has been unchaste and has already surrendered her
virginity to Hamlet. (*On Hamlet* pp. 43, 51).

[33] improprieties.

[34] writer of comic ballads.

[35] Gertrude, because Hamlet seems inclined to be agreeable for a change, is
looking particularly radiant tonight; but the more cheerful she looks, the more
afflicted he feels. Surprisingly, actors usually shout this line across the stage
straight at Gertrude's head. But Hamlet surely would do no such thing; his
very conversing with Ophelia is to create the impression that nothing special
is afoot tonight; he is now on guard against himself, and would do nothing
here to ruin the success of his play. If Gertrude and Claudius heard his insult,
it would put them too much on the alert. He is anxious to seem at present
unconcerned with them.

Yet, Wilson thinks Hamlet "certainly intends his mother to hear it all,"
without explaining why (*What Happens in Hamlet*, p. 182). In the cinema-
version of Olivier it was performed in this way, and Gertrude squirmed, as
well she might. But that is a curious way for Hamlet to carry out his plan
of being "idle"—unless you insist on making that mean "crazy."

Wilson also thinks that the *look you* is an invitation for the Court to look
at Gertrude, and for the audience to perceive that Gertrude, Claudius, and
Polonius are busily whispering among themselves, and therefore will fail to see
the dumb-show that is soon to be presented (p. 183). Wilson's account of the
dialogue between Hamlet and Ophelia is the product of an over-operative
imagination, we fear: "Hamlet continues to play up to Jephthah in the conversation with his daughter. His language to Ophelia, outrageous as it is, is in keeping with the part of a love-distraught swain; and her gentle forbearance of
his conduct shows that she regards him as a madman and sees nothing strange

OPH. Nay, 'tis twice two months, my lord.[36]

HAM. (*Caustically.*)   *So long?* Nay then, let the devil wear black,
for I'll have a suit of sables.[37] O heavens! die two months ago,
and not forgotten yet? Then there's hope a great man's memory   140
may outlive his life—half a year! But, by'r lady, he must build
churches then, or else shall he suffer *not* thinking on, with the
hobby-horse, whose epitaph is "For, O, for, O, the hobby-horse
is forgot." [38]

Hautboys play. The dumb-show enters.[39]

Enter a King and Queen very lovingly, the Queen embracing him.[40]
She kneels and makes show of protestation unto him. He takes her up

---

in the form which his dementia takes. Her father too, so far from being
shocked, is actually gleeful, for every word that is uttered in this strain estab-
lishes his theory upon a firmer basis. And, as the conversation proceeds, the
old man winks and nods in triumph to the King" (p. 182).

[36] This is the line which enables us to calculate the interval of time since
the end of Act I. Ophelia is very clever! When Hamlet has said bitterly that
his father died some two hours ago, she proves that she knows better. To
Hamlet her correction implies that she deems it quite suitable for his mother
to be merry four months after his father's death.

[37] i.e., I'll give up wearing mourning. But Hamlet is also punning on the
word *sable*, which means "black."

[38] The hobby-horse was used in morris-dances. The phrase itself seems to
have been proverbial for deploring the passing of the good old days.

[39] See p. 227.

[40] There is no record of the existence of such a play as *The Murder of
Gonzago;* but Dowden and Sarrazin (*Jahrbuch der deutschen Shakespeare
Gesellschaft*, XXXI, 1895, pp. 169–76) have each unearthed the account of an
actual murder in Italy involving a Gonzaga (*sic*), one in 1538, the other in
1592. Wilson raises the unimportant question as to how the players happen to
possess in their repertory a drama which so closely parallels Claudius's crime
(*What Happens in Hamlet*, p. 139), and thinks Shakespeare went to elaborate
lengths to cover up so inexplicably convenient a coincidence (pp. 141–44). But
the matter presents no greater difficulty than is posed in many other Shakespearean plays—*King Lear*, for example, which has a considerable number of
such coincidences—and it is a question that need trouble no one. Shakespeare
wisely wastes no time accounting for trifling details which have to do with the
logic of everyday fact and nothing to do with the realities of artistic truth. He
required the presence of *The Murder of Gonzago* in the troupe's repertory,
and so put it there without apology. We readily accept the coincidence when
confronted with it. *Hamlet* owns enough of important complexities without
concerning itself over trivialities.

But there is something unusual in the way the players present their play.
The Murder of Gonzago is given first as a brief pantomime, and immediately
after that it is begun all over again in dialogue. There was, of course, nothing
exceptional in the offering of a dumb-show in the eyes of Shakespeare's contemporaries; they were not unfamiliar with such pantomimes. But they had never
seen a dumb-show of this unique type. There is none on record which

and declines his head upon her neck; lays him down upon a bank of flowers. She, seeing him asleep, leaves him. Anon comes in a fellow, takes off his crown, kisses it, and pours poison in the King's ears, and exit. The Queen returns, finds the King dead, and makes passionate action. The poisoner, with some two or three Mutes, comes in again, seeming to lament with her. The dead body is carried away. The poisoner woos the Queen with gifts; she seems loath and unwilling a while, but in the end accepts his love.[41]   *Exeunt.*

OPH. What means this, my lord?

HAM. (*Pretending to concentrate on Ophelia.*)   Marry, this is mich-
     ing mallecho;[42] that means mischief.

OPH. Belike this show imports the argument[43] of the play?   150
     Enter Prologue.

HAM. (*Gaily.*) We shall know by this fellow. The players cannot
     keep counsel,[44] they'll tell all.

OPH. Will they tell us what this show meant?

HAM. Ay, or any show that you'll show him. Be not you asham'd
     to show, he'll not shame to tell you what it means.

OPH. (*Tittering; in mock reproval.*) You are naught,[45] you are
     naught. I'll mark the play.

---

presents in advance of the dialogue the exact and complete plot of the play
to ensue.

This singularity has raised two questions about the performance of *The
Murder of Gonzago:* Why does Shakespeare cause the players to present the
story twice?—an interesting query. And how is it that Claudius, having once
seen in the dumb-show what the plot of the dialogue is to be, allows the performance to proceed?—an incredibly unimaginative query. We have already
answered both these questions on pages 227–231. In connection with the first
of these questions, it might be added that Shakespeare faced another analogous
problem in this play—that is, the problem of providing the audience a background for understanding what is happening at a given moment on the stage.
When later Hamlet will commit the fatal error of killing Polonius, it will be
necessary for the audience to understand at that moment all that the Prince has
lost in that rash act. Shakespeare's device for providing us with a background
for gauging the gravity of the deed is to reiterate in advance of it Claudius's
intention of sending Hamlet off to England; when the Prince kills Polonius,
we immediately know that Hamlet will now have to leave the country and
thus has forfeited all his gains. In the instance of *The Murder of Gonzago*, in
order that we understand the King's breaking, we must have a knowledge of
the close similarity of the play's plot to the Ghost's narrative. Shakespeare's
solution of these dramatic problems are interesting examples of how far art
may have to go in the direction of artifice in order to achieve the illusion of
reality.

[41] See p. 229.   [42] sneaking mischief.   [43] plot.   [44] keep a secret.
[45] naughty.

PRO. For us, and for our tragedy,
      Here stooping to your clemency,   160
      We beg your hearing patiently.   *Exit.*

HAM. (*Laughing.*)   Is this a prologue, or the posy of a ring? [46]

OPH. 'Tis brief, my lord.

HAM. As woman's love.
      Enter two Players, King and his Queen.

P. KING. Full thirty times hath Phœbus' cart [47] gone round
      Neptune's salt wash [48] and Tellus' orbèd ground,[49]
      And thirty dozen moons with borrowed sheen [50]
      About the world have times twelve thirties been,
      Since love our hearts and Hymen [51] did our hands
      Unite commutual in most sacred bands.   170

P. QUEEN. So many journeys may the sun and moon
      Make us again count o'er ere love be done!
      But, woe is me, you are so sick of late,
      So far from cheer and from your former state,
      That I distrust [52] you. Yet, though I distrust,
      Discomfort you, my lord, it nothing must;
      For women's fear and love holds quantity,
      In neither aught, or in extremity.
      Now, what my love is, proof hath made you know;
      And as my love is siz'd, my fear is so.   180
      [Where love is great, the littlest doubts are fear;
      Where little fears grow great, great love grows there.]

P. KING. Faith, I must leave thee, love, and shortly too.
      My operant [53] powers their functions leave [54] to do;
      And thou shalt live in this fair world behind,
      Honour'd, belov'd; and haply one as kind
      For husband shalt thou—

P. QUEEN.   O, confound the rest! [55]
      Such love must needs be treason in my breast!
      In second husband let me be accurst!
      None wed the second but who kill'd the first.   190

HAM. [*Aside.*]   Wormwood, wormwood!

P. QUEEN. The instances [56] that second marriage move
      Are base respects [57] of thrift, but none of love.

[46] a motto engraved on a ring.   [47] the Sun's chariot.   [48] the sea.
[49] the earth.   [50] (light borrowed from the sun).   [51] god of marriage.
[52] fear for.   [53] vital.   [54] cease.
[55] (the remainder of what you were going to say).   [56] motives.
[57] considerations.

A second time I kill my husband dead,
When second husband kisses me in bed.

P. KING.   I do believe you think what now you speak,
But what we do determine oft we break.
Purpose is but the slave to memory,
Of violent birth, but poor validity; [58]
Which now, like fruit unripe, sticks on the tree,   200
But fall unshaken when they mellow be.
Most necessary 'tis that we forget
To pay ourselves what to ourselves is debt.[59]
What to ourselves in passion we propose,
The passion ending, doth the purpose lose.
The violence of either grief or joy
Their own enactures [60] with themselves destroy.
Where joy most revels, grief doth most lament;
Grief joys, joy grieves, on slender accident.[61]
This world is not for aye, nor 'tis not strange   210
That even our loves should with our fortunes change,
For 'tis a question left us yet to prove,
Whether love lead fortune, or else fortune love.
The great man down, you mark his favourite flies;
The poor advanc'd makes friends of enemies.
And hitherto [62] doth love on fortune tend,
For who not needs shall never lack a friend;
And who in want [63] a hollow friend doth try,
Directly seasons him [64] his enemy.
But, orderly to end where I begun,   220
Our wills and fates do so contrary run
That our devices [65] still are overthrown;
Our thoughts are ours, their ends none of our own.
So think thou wilt no second husband wed;
But die thy thoughts when thy first lord is dead.

P. QUEEN.   Nor earth to me give food, nor heaven light!
Sport and repose lock from me day and night!
[To desperation turn my trust and hope!
An anchor's cheer [66] in prison be my scope!]
Each opposite that blanks [67] the face of joy   230

---

[58] value.   [59] that which we owe because we have determined to do.
[60] fulfillment.   [61] cause.   [62] thus far.   [63] (when he is suffering want).
[64] (converts him into).   [65] plans.   [66] an anchorite's fare.
[67] makes white.

Meet what I would have well and it destroy!
Both here and hence [68] pursue me lasting strife,
If, once a widow, ever I be wife!

HAM. (*To Gertrude.*)   If she should break it now!

P. KING.   'Tis deeply sworn. Sweet, leave me here a while.
My spirits grow dull, and fain I would beguile
The tedious day with sleep.   *Sleeps.*

P. QUEEN.   Sleep rock thy brain,
And never come mischance between us twain!   *Exit.* [69]

HAM. (*Unable to decipher his mother; pointedly ignoring Claudius.*)
Madam, how like you this play?

QUEEN. (*To whom this is only another play.*)   The lady protests too
much, methinks. [70]   240

HAM.   O, but she'll keep her word.

KING. (*In a turmoil of fear, breaking silence despite himself.*)   Have
you heard the argument? Is there no offence in't?

HAM. (*This is what he has been waiting for. For the first time he
looks straight at Claudius. Loudly.*)   No, no, they do but jest,
poison in jest. No offence i' the world.

KING. (*Losing his self-control.*)   What do you call the play?

HAM. (*He must break the King's nerves, and also prevent him from
stopping the performance. Exultantly, with lightning-rapidity.*)
The Mouse-trap. Marry, how? Tropically. [71] This play is the
image of a murder done in *Vienna*. [72] *Gonzago* is the duke's
name; [73] his wife, *Baptista*. [74] You shall see anon. 'Tis a knavish   250
piece of work, but what o' that? Your Majesty and we that have
free souls, it touches *us* not. Let the gall'd jade wince, *our*
withers are unwrung.
Enter Lucianus.

---

[68] this world and the world to come.

[69] Shakespeare has written *The Murder of Gonzago* in rhyme to set it off
from the rest of the play. His own play is in blank verse varied with prose:
that combination is to give us the illusion of life. If the play within the play
was to seem like one, he had to give it some artifice, such as that of rhyme,
so it could take proper perspective in the work.

[70] Though Gertrude's casual attitude makes her a riddle to Hamlet, we
can understand her position easily enough. A happily and respectably married
woman now, she has forgotten the unhappy days of her adultery. But more:
this play has to do with the murder of a queen's husband by the lady's lover—
and she knows of no murder connected with her life. Why should she think
the play applies to her?

[71] by figure of speech.   [72] (*not* Denmark).   [73] (*not* Hamlet).

[74] (*not* Gertrude).

This is one Lucianus, nephew to the king.

OPH.   You are a good chorus, my lord.

HAM.   (*Elaborately seeming to look away from Claudius.*)   I could interpret [75] between you and your love, if I could see the puppets dallying.

OPH.   You are keen, my lord, you are keen.

HAM.   It would cost you a groaning to take off my edge.[76]   260

OPH.   Still better, and worse.

HAM.   So you must take your husbands.[77] Begin, murderer; pox, leave thy damnable faces and begin. Come, "the croaking raven doth bellow for revenge." [78]

LUC.   Thoughts black, hands apt, drugs fit, and time agreeing;
Confederate season,[79] else no creature seeing.
Thou mixture rank, of midnight weeds collected,
With Hecate's ban [80] thrice blasted, thrice infected,
Thy natural magic and dire property   270
On wholesome life usurp immediately.

Pours the poison in to the sleeper's ears. (*Claudius begins to crack, and starts to rise, despite himself.*)

HAM.   (*Wildly spitting out anything that comes into his head, hoping to make Claudius talk.*)   He poisons him i' the garden for's estate. His name's Gonzago; the story is extant, and writ in choice Italian. You shall see anon how the murderer gets the love of Gonzago's wife.[81]

OPH.   The King rises.

HAM.   What, frighted with false fire?

QUEEN.   How fares my lord?

POL.   Give o'er the play.[82]

KING.   (*Brokenly, the King staggers from his seat and stumbles out.*)
Give me some light. Away! [83]   280

---

[75] (like the man at the puppet shows, explaining the pantomimic action of the puppets). But Hamlet is also making a ribald pun on "puppets," which signified "the breasts," vulgarly. Ophelia understands the indecency.

[76] another piece of ribaldry.

[77] An alternate reading is "mistake" for "must take."

[78] A quotation from an old play.

[79] the time cooperating.   [80] the curse of the goddess of Hell.

[81] According to Kittredge, Hamlet delivers these lines "without any show of excitement," as though he were only "explaining the play" to innocent spectators (*Hamlet*, p. 229).

[82] Note that it is Polonius who stops the performance, and perhaps saves the King from overtly confessing!

[83] On grounds difficult to imagine, Wilson would have Claudius rush

"shrieking from the room" (*What Happens in Hamlet*, p. 150). He also considers the King's exit to be the "turning-point" of the play (p. 200). To that one must object that although at this moment Hamlet is sure of the King's guilt and Claudius is aware of Hamlet's knowledge of the crime, their basic dramatic relationship to each other is not altered. Hamlet is still the hunter and Claudius still the hunted. It is the killing of Polonius which reverses that relationship.

In Mr. Olivier's movie, the whole Court observed Claudius's terrified reaction to *The Murder of Gonzago* rather than the play itself, and seemed to understand that he had been guilty of such a murder. The courtiers became infected with Claudius's fright—why?—and general pandemonium ensued. To complete the riot, Hamlet seized upon a torch, and scared the entire assemblage out of the chamber.

Not wishing to interrupt the preceding pages with many footnotes on Wilson's interpretation of the play scene, we have chosen to summarize his ideas concerning it in this place. They must be noticed for the reason that his work on *Hamlet* retains a prestige second to none. His ingeniousness is commendable; but his conception of the play scene, if followed, would drain from the most exciting scene in the tragedy every drop of dramatic power with which it is so plentifully charged.

His whole thinking about *Hamlet* revolves about this scene; he calls it "the climax and crisis of the whole drama." He objects to the fact that stage performances tend to subordinate the dumb-show and the dialogue following, so as to cause the audience to concentrate on Hamlet and Claudius (p. 138). He apparently deems *The Murder of Gonzago* itself of equal importance. Though the presentation of the little play has been largely exempt in the past from difficulties in the minds of commentators, Wilson asks eleven questions concerning it:

¶ 1. How do the players happen to have in their repertory a play figuring a crime paralleling Claudius'?
¶ 2. Why does Hamlet instruct the First Player, before the play is given, on the art of acting?
¶ 3. Why is the dumb-show given?
¶ 4. Why does Claudius seem undisturbed during the dumb-show?
¶ 5. Why is the Player Poisoner the *nephew* and not the brother of his victim?
¶ 6. Why do the courtiers later assume that Hamlet has threatened Claudius with death?
¶ 7. What is the meaning of "I eat the air, promise-crammed?"
¶ 8. Why does Hamlet "lead Polonius on" to speak of the murder of Julius Caesar?
¶ 9. To whom and to what does "miching mallecho" refer?
¶10. Why does *The Murder of Gonzago* have a prologue?
¶11. Why does Hamlet utter "that extraordinary remark," "The croaking raven doth bellow for revenge?" (p. 139)

To the answering of these, Wilson devotes sixty pages of *What Happens in Hamlet* (pp. 138–197).

Every one of these questions, with the exception of the third, invents a difficulty or mystery that does not exist in *Hamlet*. Is it not, moreover, wilful to be exercised (in the first question) over the resemblance of the crime in *The Murder of Gonzago* to Claudius's, and then proceed to find a new mysteriousness (in the fifth) because of the circumstance that the Player Poisoner is a nephew, rather than a brother, to the King—thus making the resemblance *not* complete? Is it not obvious that it served Shakespeare's purpose to make the situations not identical, so that the presence of the piece in the actors' repertory would seem less of a coincidence? and that it serves Hamlet's purpose too, so that Claudius might by the difference in detail be made the more confused? Yet out of that difference in detail, Wilson constructs an edifice truly monumental. According to him, the Player Poisoner is a *nephew* because Hamlet wishes King, Queen, and courtiers to identify him, Hamlet, with the murderer! This is Hamlet's threat to them all—a warning that he intends to assassinate his uncle! (pp. 170–71) Why Hamlet would go so far out of his way to prepare his uncle for being murdered, is not explained. Indeed, Wilson deliberately negates Hamlet's expressed motive in presenting the play, by some curious reasoning. Hamlet, he says, is particularly anxious that the courtiers should *not* know of his father's murder because "the family honour of the House of Denmark forbade any disclosure of the truth" (p. 172). (This, despite Hamlet's avowed hope that he could "unkennel" the King's guilt!) Why, you may ask, does Hamlet present his play at all, in that case? Wilson's response is that the Prince wishes to prove Claudius's guilt to himself alone; at the same time he is notifying the world that he will soon assassinate his uncle! Wilson's answers to several other of his questions are made to fortify this elaborate notion.

But none of these eleven questions, except the third, has any validity. By this we have accounted for the points raised in questions 1, 2, 3, 4, 5, 7, and 8. The matter raised in question 6 does not exist in the play at all. The answers to questions 9, 10, and 11 are embarrassingly simple:

¶ 9. "miching mallecho" (which means "sneaking mischief") is a reply to Ophelia's query as to the meaning of the dumb-show. The plot exhibited in pantomime, as well as Claudius's crime, was each a piece of sneaking mischief. "That means mischief," Hamlet continues, with a play on the word *that*; i.e., *mallecho* means "mischief," and so does Hamlet's presentation of the play.

¶10. Many Elizabethan plays, including several of Shakespeare's, had prologues. Why not this one?

¶11. This "extraordinary remark" is born of Hamlet's frenzied excitement. He sees Claudius is near the breaking-point, and he quotes a line from an old play, urging the Player Poisoner to get on with his performance.

As for the entire scene's chief business, the unmasking of Claudius, Wilson answers Mr. Greg's question as to why the King should remain unmoved by the dumb-show (not at all the case, of course), by asserting that Claudius is at the time occupied in private conversation with Polonius and Gertrude, and therefore fails to see the pantomime (*Modern Language Review*, XIII, 1918, pp. 129–56). His proof for this remarkable interpretation is that if Claudius had seen the dumb-show, he would not ask Hamlet,

"Have you heard the argument?" (Athenaeum, July 1918, pp. 303–7).

He further interprets Hamlet's agitated aside,

"Wormwood, wormwood!"

ALL.   Lights, lights, lights!

Exeunt all but Hamlet and Horatio.

HAM.   (*Exultant over his success.*) [84]   Why, let the strucken deer go
weep,
The hart ungalled play;
For some must watch, while some must sleep,—
So runs the world away.

Would not this, sir, and a forest of feathers—if the rest of my
fortunes turn Turk with me—with two Provincial roses [85] on
my raz'd [86] shoes, get me a fellowship in a cry [87] of players, sir?

HOR.   Half a share.

HAM.   A whole one, I.   290

For thou dost know, O Damon [88] dear,
This realm dismantled was

---

as provoked by Gertrude's flinching, and as delivered straight at his mother
because he now knows her guilty (*What Happens in Hamlet*, p. 189). Thereafter, when Hamlet asks her,

"Madam, how like you this play?"

Wilson hears her stammering in her reply,

"The lady protests too much, methinks."

And, despite the fact that by then Claudius has heard most of *The Murder of
Gonzago*, Wilson thinks he still has no suspicion of what Hamlet is up to
when he asks his nephew,

"What do you call this play?" (p. 190),

and that Hamlet's feverish remarks about the scene's being laid in Vienna, the
murdered duke's name being Gonzago, and so forth, are successful in allaying
Claudius's mounting distrust of the play! Hamlet's hectic words as the King
at last rises,

"His name's Gonzago; the story is extant,"

are interpreted as "meaningless, pointless, in their bland suavity" (pp. 191–2).
Wilson's direction of the play scene would leave all of it but the last minute
empty of dramatic interest. His Claudius, moreover, is a slow-witted dullard,
one must conclude, his Gertrude quite capable of being honest with herself,
his Hamlet neurotically eager to ruin his plans. These three belong to some
other play than ours.

[84] (though he has not realized that the better half of his anticipated harvest,
the King's public acknowledgment of guilt, has not been his).

[85] damask roses.

[86] slashed. (The players have always been noted for their gaudy dress.)

[87] pack.

[88] Damon and Pythias are the most celebrated of all loyal friends. The
reference shows Hamlet's deep love for Horatio.

Of Jove himself; and now reigns here
A very, very—pajock.[89]

HOR. You might have rhym'd.[90]

HAM. O good Horatio, I'll take the ghost's word for a thousand pound. Didst perceive?

HOR. Very well, my lord.

HAM. Upon the talk of the poisoning?   300

HOR. I did very well note him.

Re-enter Rosencrantz and Guildenstern.

HAM. Ah, ha! Come, some music! Come, the recorders! [91]
      (*Still in exhilaration.*) For if the king like not the comedy—
      (*Seeing Rosencrantz and Guildenstern coming, he changes his rhyme and ends lamely. He deliberately turns his back on them.*) Why then, belike, he likes it not, perdy.[92]
      Come, some music!

GUIL. Good my lord, vouchsafe me a word with you.

HAM. (*Wheeling about; in scorn.*) Sir, a whole history.

GUIL. The King, sir,—   310

HAM. (*Eagerly.*) Ay, sir, what of him?

GUIL. Is in his retirement marvellous distemper'd.

HAM. (*Ironically.*) With drink, sir?

GUIL. No, my lord, rather with choler.[93]

HAM. (*Witheringly.*) Your wisdom should show itself more richer to signify this to his *doctor;* for, for *me* to put him to his purgation would perhaps plunge him into *far more choler.*

GUIL. (*Uncomprehending.*) Good my lord, put your discourse   320
      into some frame, and start not so wildly from [94] my affair.

HAM. (*With insulting docility.*) I am tame, sir; pronounce.

GUIL. The Queen, your mother, in most great affliction of spirit, hath sent me to you.

HAM. (*Sneeringly.*) You are welcome.

GUIL. (*Offended.*) Nay, good my lord, this courtesy is not of the

[89] Hamlet was about to say "ass," but thinking better of it said "pajock" (peacock) instead, possibly because that bird was noted for its cruelty.

[90] i.e., have said "ass."

[91] The recorder is a wind instrument; a kind of glorified shepherd's pipe.

[92] by God. Hamlet might have intended to say something like, "Why then, belike, he's guilty as can be," before he saw Rosencrantz and Guildenstern approaching.

[93] an attack of bile.

[94] *From* was the strongest of the prepositions, possessing almost the force of a verb.

right breed. (*Standing on his dignity*.) If it shall please you to
make me a wholesome answer I will do your mother's commandment; if not, your pardon and my return shall be the end
of my business.   330

HAM. (*Bitterly*.)   Sir, I cannot.

GUIL.   What, my lord?

HAM.   Make you a wholesome answer.[95] My wit's diseas'd. But, sir,
such answers as I *can* make, you shall command, or, rather, as
you say, my *mother*. (*Brusquely*.) Therefore no more, but to
the matter. My mother, you say,—

ROS.   Then thus she says: your behaviour hath struck her into
amazement and admiration.[96]

HAM.   O *wonderful son*, that can so astonish a mother! But is there   340
no sequel at the heels of his mother's admiration? [Impart.]

ROS.   She desires to speak with you in her closet [97] ere you go to
bed.

HAM.   We shall obey, were she ten times our mother.[98] (*Contemp-
tuously*.) Have you any further *trade* with us? [99]

ROS. (*Wounded, pleading*.)   My lord, you once did love me.

HAM.   So I do *still*, by these pickers and stealers! [100]

ROS. (*Making a final attempt to revive their old relationship*.)   Good
my lord, what is your cause of distemper? You do surely bar   350
the door upon your own liberty if you deny your griefs to
your friend.

HAM. (*Vaguely*.)   Sir, I lack advancement.[101]

ROS.   How can that be, when you have the voice of the King himself for your succession in Denmark?

HAM.   Ay, but "While the grass grows,"—the proverb is something musty.[102]

[95] i.e., You *know* my wit's diseased, don't you?

[96] astonishment. This does not refer, says Kittredge, to "anything Hamlet
had said or done during the play scene"! (*Hamlet*, p. 231)

[97] private room.

[98] Hamlet does not need the Queen's invitation. He would insist upon seeing
her, after her undecipherable conduct at the play, even if she refused to give
him audience.

[99] Hamlet uses the royal "we," to put a distance between himself and his
erstwhile friends.

[100] these ten fingers of mine.

[101] Hamlet's private meaning is that they stand in the way of his prosecuting
vengeance. They take him literally, and voice what would be the point of view
of the average Dane: "Why should you be dissatisfied? Hasn't the King himself declared publicly his voice for your succession to the crown?"

[102] "the silly horse he starves," is the rest of the proverb. But Hamlet does

Re-enter one with a recorder.

O, the recorder! Let me see.—To withdraw with you: (*taking*   360
Guildenstern aside)—why do you go about to recover the wind
of me,[103] as if you would drive me into a toil? [104]

GUIL. (*Upset.*)   O, my lord, if my duty be too bold, my love is too
unmannerly.

HAM. (*Not troubling even to consider his apology.*)   I do not well
understand that. Will you play upon this pipe? (*Offering the
recorder to him.*)

GUIL.   My lord, I cannot.

HAM. (*Insistent.*)   I *pray* you.

GUIL.   Believe me, I cannot.

HAM.   I do *beseech* you.   370

GUIL.   I know no touch of it, my lord.

HAM. (*Furiously.*)   'Tis as easy as lying. Govern these ventages [105]
with your finger and thumb, give it breath with your mouth,
and it will discourse most excellent music. Look you, these are
the stops. (*He plays upon it.*)

GUIL.   But these cannot *I* command to any utterance of harmony.
I have not the skill.

HAM.   Why, look you now, how unworthy a thing you make of
me! You would play upon *me*, you would seem to know *my*   380
stops, you would pluck out the heart of my mystery, you
would sound me from my lowest note to the top of my compass; and there is much music, excellent voice, in this little
organ, yet cannot you make *it* [speak. 'Sblood,] do you think
that I am easier to be play'd on than a pipe? Call me what instrument you will though you can fret [106] me, you cannot play
upon me.[107]

---

not care to discuss his affairs with enemies, as he conceives them to be, and
seizes upon the entrance of a servant with the recorder he has called for,
as an occasion for denouncing Guildenstern.

[103] a term from hunting: to force the animal to run with the wind so that
it may not scent its hunter.

[104] trap.   [105] the stops.

[106] one of the ridges across the finger board of a stringed instrument, such
as the lute, to aid the fingers in stopping the strings at the right point. Hamlet
is punning on the word, of course.

[107] This recorder scene is another example of Shakespeare's incredible
modernity of mind. Earlier this night Hamlet has spoken to Horatio in praise
of those men who

"are not a pipe for Fortune's finger
To sound what stop she please." (III, ii, 75-6)

Enter Polonius.

God bless you, sir.   390

POL.   My lord, the Queen would speak with you, and presently.

HAM.   Do you see that cloud that's almost in shape like a camel?

POL.   By the mass, and it's like a camel, indeed.

HAM.   Methinks it is like a weasel.

POL.   It is *back'd* like a weasel.

HAM.   Or like a whale?

POL.   Very like a whale.

HAM.   *Then* [108] will I come to my mother by and by.[109] *[Aside.]*   400
They fool me to the top of my bent.[110]—I will come by and by.

POL.   I will say so.   *Exit.*

HAM.   (*Annoyed.*) "By and by" is easily said. Leave me, friends.
                                              Exeunt all but Hamlet.[111]

'Tis now the very witching time of night
When churchyards yawn and hell itself breathes out
Contagion to this world. Now could I drink hot blood,
And do such bitter business as the day
Would quake to look on. Soft! now to my mother.   410
O heart, lose not thy nature! Let not ever

The image has been germinating in the realm of Hamlet's subconscious mind and now reappears in full bloom as the substance of an entire scene. We believe this has never been noted. Were it a solitary instance in Shakespeare's work, we should consider it unintended. But there are similar examples in the other plays.

[108] We take this word to imply by sarcastic overtone: "And *I'm* the one who's supposed to have the disordered mind?" Kittredge thinks otherwise: it is, he says, a "false appearance of logic" employed as part of his pretended lunacy (*Hamlet*, p. 233)!

[109] at once.

[110] We consider Kittredge's glossing of this line one of the choicest pieces of perversion of meaning in the history of commentary on this play: "They indulge my folly—humour me in my supposed madness—as completely as I can wish" (*Hamlet*, p. 233). The meaning of *bent* in this line comes from archery, and signifies "power"; in this sense it appears a number of times in Shakespeare; in II, ii, 30 (for example) Guildenstern has so used it. Hamlet is here saying: "They fool me to the limits of my power (or endurance)."

[111] Left alone, Hamlet has a brief but important soliloquy—important, because it prepares us for his fatal error soon to be committed in Gertrude's chamber. He is plainly in a very dangerous mood, as he himself knows. The rashness in his nature has been fed by the success of his play. Now he could drink hot blood and do the most dreadful of deeds. As he goes to his mother, he tries to pacify the violence raging in his veins. He clearly fears himself. No matter how he must shame her with words, let not his soul consent to punish her with death!

The soul of Nero [112] enter this firm bosom;
Let me be cruel, not unnatural.
I will *speak* daggers to her, but *use* none.
My tongue and soul in this be hypocrites;
How in my words soever she be shent [113]
To give them seals [114] never, my soul, consent!   *Exit.*

SCENE III

    *A room in the castle. (The King's private chamber, a few
        minutes before the conclusion of the preceding scene.)*
    Enter King, Rosencrantz, and Guildenstern.

KING.   I like him not,[1] nor stands it safe with us [2]
To let his madness range. Therefore prepare you.
I your commission will forthwith dispatch,
And he to England shall along with you.
The terms of our estate may not endure
Hazard so dangerous as doth hourly grow
Out of his lunacies.

GUIL.   We will ourselves provide.
Most holy and religious fear it is
To keep those many many bodies safe
That live and feed upon your Majesty.   10

ROS.   The single and peculiar [3] life is bound
With all the strength and armour of the mind
To keep itself from noyance,[4] but much more
That spirit upon whose weal depends and rests
The lives of many. The cease of majesty [5]
Dies not alone, but, like a gulf,[6] doth draw
What's near it with it. It is a massy wheel,
Fixed on the summit of the highest mount,
To whose huge spokes ten thousand lesser things
Are mortis'd and adjoin'd; which, when it falls,   20
Each small annexment, petty consequence,
Attends the boisterous ruin. Never alone
Did the King sigh, but with a general groan.

KING.   Arm you, I pray you, to this speedy voyage,

---

[112] who killed his mother, Agrippina.   [113] shamed.
[114] to execute them, put them into action. Deeds are "executed" by putting
seals upon them.
   [1] (i.e., the way he is behaving).   [2] (the royal *we*).   [3] individual.
[4] injury.   [5] the king's death (decease).   [6] whirlpool.

For we will fetters put upon this fear,
Which now goes too free-footed.[7]

ROS. }
GUIL. }   We will haste us.

                        Exeunt Rosencrantz and Guildenstern.

Enter Polonius.

POL.   My lord, he's going to his mother's closet.
Behind the arras [8] I'll convey myself,
To hear the process. I'll warrant she'll tax him home; [9]
And, as you said,[10] and wisely was it said,   30
'Tis meet that some more audience than a mother,
Since nature makes them partial, should o'er hear
The speech, of vantage.[11] Fare you well, my liege.
I'll call upon you ere you go to bed,
And tell you what I know.[12]

KING.   Thanks, dear my lord.

                                       Exit Polonius.

---

[7] It is possible that at this point the King has as yet no nefarious intentions toward Hamlet. During his soliloquy, which follows shortly, though it is the longest passage in the scene, he has nothing to say about Hamlet's death. While he is being so anguishingly honest with God, would he not include his murderous purposes against Hamlet if he had any then? At this moment he is probably interested only in hustling Hamlet out of the country.

And the audience, on its part, does not believe that he will succeed in doing this—surely not when Hamlet's cause has recently been so much advanced. The King himself may very well doubt his ability to make Hamlet go. His repetition of the desire to be rid of Hamlet's presence, however, will arm the audience with an awareness of the gravity of Hamlet's error in the next scene. It is likely that Claudius does not think of killing off his nephew until the slaying of Polonius reveals to him how much his own life is in jeopardy.

[8] The Elizabethan audience would at once know that Polonius was going to hide behind the curtain that shut off the inner stage.

[9] severely reprove him.

[10] Actually, of course, this was Polonius' suggestion.

[11] i.e., from a place of vantage.

[12] Thus, once again we are confronted with the question of how wicked "kind old" Polonius may in truth be. Claudius is now absolutely certain that Hamlet knows he is the murderer of the late king. He can also be fairly sure that Hamlet will not fail to speak of that fact to Gertrude (else, why the eavesdropping?). Would so cunning and able a monarch as this be willing now to entrust anyone with the mission of listening to such damning revelations by Hamlet? Obviously not—unless what will be revealed would prove no news to the eavesdropper. Claudius's reliance on Polonius to learn what is likely to be incriminating to the murderer is strong indication that Polonius must have been, to some degree, an accomplice in the murder. That he makes no overt reference to it to the King is what one should expect from an unscrupulous and servile politician. In a later scene, his guilt will be almost certified.

O, my offence is rank, it smells to heaven; [13]
It hath the primal eldest curse upon't,
A brother's murder.[14] Pray can I not,
Though inclination be as sharp as will.
My stronger guilt defeats my strong intent,   40
And, like a man to double business bound,
I stand in pause where I shall first begin,
And both neglect. What if this cursed hand
Were thicker than itself with brother's blood,
Is there not rain enough in the sweet heavens
To wash it white as snow? Whereto serves mercy
But to confront the visage of offence? [15]
And what's in prayer but this twofold force,
To be forestalled ere we come to fall,[16]
Or pardon'd being down? [17] Then I'll look up;   50
My fault is past. But, O, what form of prayer
Can serve my turn? [18] "Forgive me my foul murder"?
That cannot be; since I am still possess'd
Of those effects for which I did the murder,
My crown, mine own ambition, and my queen.
May one be pardon'd and retain the offence?
In the corrupted currents [19] of this world
Offence's gilded hand may shove by justice,
And oft 'tis seen the wicked prize itself
Buys out the law.[20] But 'tis not so above.   60

[13] Alone, Claudius kneels to pray, and that twinge of sympathy we for a moment felt for him (III, i, 50 seq.) now blossoms into something like pity. The man is a murderer, a sensualist, a corrupted materialist; but he is capable of honesty with himself. And his honesty moves us strangely. He knows his offence is rank, smells to heaven, and bears the curse of Cain upon it. He wishes to implore heaven for forgiveness, but he knows empty words cannot avail him. How can he be forgiven his brother's murder when he retains the prizes for which he committed that murder: his crown and the love of his wife? It is to God that his words are addressed, and his words reveal that it was not ambition alone which fostered his criminality, that his love of Gertrude was equally a mainspring. He knows that no matter how much he has succeeded in deluding the world and buying its allegiance, heaven cannot be deceived. His distress is deep and terrible. Shakespeare nowhere proves himself more the great poet than in this soliloquy (particularly in lines 68–72), which moves us in our own despite.

[14] Cain's murder of Abel.   [15] but to confront the offender's guilt.
[16] "Lead us not into temptation."
[17] "Forgive us our trespasses."   [18] See pp. 267–269.   [19] occurrences.
[20] The prize, which was won through evil, made it possible to purchase injustice.

There is no shuffling, there the action lies [21]
In his [22] true nature; and we ourselves compell'd,
Even to the teeth and forehead of our faults,
To give in evidence. What then? What rests?
Try what repentance can. What can it not?
Yet what can it when one cannot repent?
O wretched state! O bosom black as death!
O limed soul,[23] that, struggling to be free,
Art more engag'd! Help, angels! Make assay!
Bow, stubborn knees, and, heart with strings of steel,   70
Be soft as sinews of the new-born babe!
All may be well.   *Kneels.*[24]

Enter Hamlet. (*On the inner stage, on his way to his mother's
room. Seeing the King at prayer, he pauses.*) [25]

HAM.   Now might I do it pat, now he is praying.
And now I'll do't. (*Whipping out his sword.*)—And so he goes
            to heaven;
And so am I reveng'd? That would be scann'd.
A villain kills my father, and for that,
I, his sole son, do this same villain send
To heaven.
Oh, this is hire and salary, not revenge.
He took my father grossly,[26] full of bread,[27]   80
With all his crimes broad [28] blown, as flush as May;
And how his audit stands who knows save Heaven?
But in our circumstance [29] and course of thought
'Tis heavy with him. And am I then reveng'd,
To take him in the purging of his soul,
When he is fit and season'd for his passage?
No!
Up, sword, and know thou a more horrid hent.[30] (*Replacing his
            sword in its scabbard.*)

---

[21] "action lies"—in the legal sense of "suit brought."   [22] its.
[23] The image is of a bird caught in birdlime. As it struggles to free itself
it becomes only the more entrapped.
[24] On the Elizabethan stage, the King was probably seen kneeling on the
stage proper, and Hamlet was seen through the opened curtains at the rear,
passing along the space of the inner stage, on his way to his mother's chamber.
[25] See pp. 180–183.   [26] before he had the chance to repent.
[27] in the midst of worldly pleasures.   [28] full.
[29] gauging as well as one can from our circumstances.
[30] seizure. The figure here seems to be the tearing of the ploughshare

When he is drunk asleep, or in his rage,
Or in the incestuous pleasure of his bed, 90
At gaming, swearing, or about some act
That has no relish of salvation in't,—
Then trip him, that his heels may kick at heaven,
And that his soul may be as damn'd and black
As hell, whereto it goes. My mother stays.
This physic [31] but prolongs thy sickly days.

Exit.

KING. (*Rising.*)   My words fly up, my thoughts remain below.
Words without thoughts never to heaven go.

SCENE IV

The Queen's closet (a few minutes before the conclusion of the preceding scene.)
Enter Queen and Polonius.

POL.   He will come straight.[1] Look you lay home to him.
Tell him his pranks have been too broad to bear with,
And that your Grace hath screen'd and stood between
Much heat and him. I'll silence [2] me e'en here.
Pray you, be round [3] with him.

HAM. (*Dangerously excited.*) [*Within.*]   Mother, mother, mother!
QUEEN.   I'll warrant you, fear me not. Withdraw,
I hear him coming.

Polonius hides behind the arras.

Enter Hamlet.

HAM. (*Harshly.*)   Now, mother, what's the matter?
QUEEN. (*In the role of the sorrowing mother.*)   Hamlet, thou hast thy
father much offended.
HAM.   Mother, you have *my* father much offended. 10
QUEEN. (*Not understanding him, annoyed.*)   Come, come, you answer
with an idle [4] tongue.
HAM.   Go, go, you question with a *wicked* tongue.
QUEEN. (*Indignant at his manner.*)   Why, how now, Hamlet!
HAM.   What's the matter now?
QUEEN. (*Mustering dignity.*)   Have you forgot me?

---

through the soil; so Hamlet's sword will tear through Claudius' flesh, when the
right moment comes.
   [31] medicine (which saves your life at the moment).
   [1] directly.   [2] hide quietly.   [3] forthright.
   [4] Note that again "idle" means "idle"!

HAM. (*Bitterly and explosively.*)   No, by the rood,[5] not so.
   You are the Queen, your (*Spacing the words.*) husband's brother's
       wife;
   And—would you were not so—you are my mother.[6]

QUEEN. (*Starting for the door.*)   Nay, then, I'll set those to you that
   can speak.

HAM. (*Seizing her by the wrist, and forcing her to sit down and listen.*)
       Come, come, and sit you down. (*She struggles to free herself
       from his grasp.*) You shall not budge.
   You go not till I set you up a glass
   Where you may see the inmost part of you.   20

QUEEN. (*In a panic now, convinced that he will do her some bodily
       harm.*)   What wilt thou do? Thou wilt not murder me?
   (*Losing her head, she shrieks in terror.*) Help, help, ho!

POL. (*Behind.*)   What, ho! help, help, help!

HAM. (*Drawing.*) How now! A rat? Dead, for a ducat, dead!
                  Kills Polonius through the arras.[7]

POL. (*Behind.*) O, I am slain!

QUEEN.   O me, what hast thou done?

HAM.   Nay, I know not.
   Is it the King? [8]

QUEEN.   O, what a rash and bloody deed is this!

HAM.   A bloody deed! Almost as bad, good mother,
   As kill a king, and marry with his brother.

QUEEN. (*Not in the least understanding him.*)   As kill a king?

HAM.   Ay, lady, 'twas my word.   30
            Lifts up the arras and discovers Polonius.
   (*Seeing it is Polonius, disgustedly.*) Thou wretched, rash, intruding
       fool, farewell!
   I took thee for thy better. Take thy fortune.
   Thou find'st to be too busy is some danger.
   (*Turning back to his mother.*)—Leave wringing of your hands.
       Peace! Sit you down,

---

[5] the Cross.
[6] The Folio reads: "But would you were not so. You are my mother." Our
reading here is based upon the Second Quarto, as slightly amended by Pope.
[7] See pp. 190-191.
[8] This climactic deed of Hamlet exhibits his tragic rashness. He has killed
first and then asks afterwards who his victim is. Had he reflected for but a
moment, he must have remembered that this could not have been the King,
for he left Claudius praying in the adjoining chamber a few moments ago!
This impetuous act will enable Claudius to send Hamlet off to England.

And let me wring your *heart;* for so I shall,
If it be made of penetrable stuff,
If damned custom have not braz'd [9] it so
That it is proof [10] and bulwark against sense.

QUEEN. (*Self-righteously.*) What have *I* done, that thou dar'st wag thy
    tongue
In noise so rude against me?

HAM. (*With passion.*)   Such an act   40
That blurs the grace and blush of modesty,
Calls virtue hypocrite, takes off the rose
From the fair forehead of an innocent love
And sets a blister [11] there, makes marriage-vows
As false as dicers' oaths; O, such a deed
As from the body of contraction [12] plucks
The very soul, and sweet religion makes
A rhapsody of words. Heaven's face doth glow,
Yea, this solidity and compound mass,[13]
With tristful visage, as against the doom,[14]   50
Is thought-sick at the act.

QUEEN.   Ay me, *what* act,
That roars so loud and thunders in the index? [15]

HAM.   Look here, upon this picture, and on this,
The counterfeit presentment of two brothers.[16]

---

[9] covered with brass.   [10] proofed against feeling.   [11] brand of the harlot.
[12] the marriage contract.   [13] the earth.
[14] as if the Day of Judgment were approaching.
[15] Originally the index (table of contents) was placed at the beginning of the book. Here the meaning would correspond to "prologue."
[16] Though the employment of the visible is generally wise on the stage, there is a question of delicacy in the old tradition of having in the Queen's private apartment two paintings or tapestries to represent her former and present husbands (the "counterfeit presentment of two brothers"). Modern sensibilities must find them shocking, though Rowe's edition of the play (1709) has a print showing half-length portraits of the two kings. During the Restoration it was common for Hamlet "to produce from his pocket two pictures in little of his father and uncle, not much bigger than large coins." It is inconceivable that Hamlet would carry around the portrait of a man he so much detests. Edwin Booth made use of two miniatures, "taking one from his own neck, and the other from his mother's." Rossi not only tore the miniature from Gertrude's neck, but dashed it to the ground and stamped upon it in a fine Italian frenzy. The modern craze in productions of *Hamlet* for equipping everyone with a miniature about his neck, has naturally encouraged the use of them for this scene. Holman's idea was not bad: there was a painting of Claudius on the wall, and Hamlet produced a miniature of his father "from

See, what a grace was seated on this brow:
Hyperion's curls, the front [17] of Jove himself,
An eye like Mars, to threaten or command,
A station [18] like the herald Mercury
New-lighted on a heaven-kissing hill,
A combination and a form indeed,   60
Where every god did seem to set his seal,
To give the world assurance of a man.
This *was* your husband. (*As Hamlet proceeds in his denunciations,
    there is an air of desperateness in what he says, as of a man
    fighting at the last ditch. While he is speaking, he realizes that
    he has committed an irremediable mistake, and he hurries on
    as though he has no time to waste.*) Look you now what
    follows:
Here *is* your husband, like a mildew'd ear,
Blasting his [19] wholesome brother.[20] Have you eyes?
Could you on this fair mountain leave to feed,
And batten [21] on this moor? Ha! have you eyes?
You cannot call it love, for at your age
The hey-day in the blood is *tame*, it's *humble*,
And waits upon the judgement; and what judgement   70
Would step from this to *this*? [Sense [22] sure you have,
Else could you not have motion; [23] but sure, that sense
Is apoplex'd; for madness would not err,
Nor sense to ecstasy [24] was ne'er so thrall'd
But it reserv'd *some* quantity of choice,
To serve in such a difference.] What devil was't
That thus hath cozen'd you at hoodman-blind? [25]
[Eyes without feeling, feeling without sight,
Ears without hands or eyes, smelling sans [26] all,
Or but a sickly part of one true sense   80
Could not so mope.[27]]
O shame! where is thy blush? Rebellious hell,
If thou canst mutine in a matron's bones,

---

his bosom." But Irving and Salvini, following a suggestion of Fitzgerald's, were,
we think, soundest of all in having the two pictures "seen with the mind's eye
only" (Furness, *Variorum Hamlet*, p. 290).
[17] forehead.   [18] posture.   [19] its.
[20] a reference to the dream of Pharoah, Genesis XLI.   [21] fatten.
[22] feeling.   [23] the ability to move.   [24] madness.   [25] blindman's buff.
[26] without.   [27] be so dull.

To flaming youth let virtue be as wax,
And melt in her own fire. Proclaim no shame
When the compulsive ardour gives the charge,[28]
Since frost [29] itself as actively doth burn
And reason panders will.[30]

QUEEN. (*Unable to bear this image of herself.*)

                                  O Hamlet, speak no more!
Thou turn'st mine eyes into my very soul,
And there I see such black and grained [31] spots   90
As will not leave their tinct.

HAM. (*Seeing he is making an impression on her, he increases his
       violence.*)   Nay, but to live
In the rank sweat of an enseamed [32] bed,
Stew'd in corruption, honeying and making love
Over the nasty sty,—

QUEEN.   O, speak to me no more!
These words like daggers enter in mine ears.
No more, sweet Hamlet! [33]

HAM.   A murderer and a villain!
A slave that is not twentieth part the tithe [34]
Of your precedent lord! A vice [35] of kings!
A cutpurse of the empire and the rule,
That from a shelf the precious diadem stole,   100
And put it in his pocket! [36]

QUEEN. (*Holding her hands over her ears.*) No more!
Enter Ghost.[37]

HAM.   A king of shreds and patches,—(*Seeing the Ghost.*)
Save me, and hover o'er me with your wings,
You heavenly guards! What would your gracious figure?

QUEEN. (*With a sigh of relief.*) Alas, he's *mad!* [38]

---

[28] attacks.   [29] old age.
[30] reason plays the pander to desire.   [31] ingrained.   [32] greasy.
[33] See p. 272.   [34] the tenth.   [35] clown.
[36] i.e., Claudius is a pickpocket who stole the unguarded crown.
[37] See pp. 231–235.
[38] The Queen now is convinced that she has been taking too seriously the accusations of her poor mad son. With a sigh she throws off the whole load of guilt she has begun to feel, and assumes the more agreeable task of sorrowing for her unhappy deranged Hamlet.

That Hamlet alone sees and hears the Ghost in this scene is in no way unusual; it was a ghost's prerogative to single out one person, in the midst of many, as an audience. It suited the Ghost's purposes to appear to all the men at the opening of the play; yet in I, v, only Hamlet is permitted to hear its

HAM.   Do you not come your tardy son to chide,
       That, laps'd in time and passion, lets go by
       The important acting of your dread command?
       O, say!

GHOST.   Do not forget! This visitation   110
       Is but to whet thy almost blunted [39] purpose.
       But, look, amazement on thy mother sits.
       O, step between her and her fighting soul.
       Conceit [40] in weakest bodies strongest works.
       Speak to her, Hamlet.

HAM.   How is it with you, lady?

QUEEN.   (*Pityingly*.)   Alas, how is't with *you*,
       That you do bend your eye on vacancy
       And with the incorporal air do hold discourse?
       Forth at your eyes your spirits wildly peep,
       And, as the sleeping soldiers in the alarm,[41]   120
       Your bedded hair, like life in excrements,[42]
       Start up and stand on end. O gentle son,
       Upon the heat and flame of thy distemper
       Sprinkle cool patience. Whereon do you look?

HAM.   On *him*, on *him*! Look you, how pale he glares!
       His form and cause conjoin'd, preaching to stones,
       Would make them capable.[43] (*To the Ghost.*) Do not look upon me,
       Lest with this piteous action you convert
       My stern effects; then what I have to do
       Will want true colour,[44] tears perchance for blood.   130

QUEEN.   To whom do you speak this?

HAM.   Do you see nothing there?

QUEEN.   Nothing at all, yet all that is I see.

"Swear!" Here the Ghost's purposes require its being unseen by Gertrude.

Nevertheless, the situation has occasioned much comment. The fact that the Queen does not see or hear the Ghost has been used, naturally, to prove that the apparition is a figment of Hamlet's imagination—which, in turn, would prove him truly deranged. Wilson, however, has a novel explanation: Gertrude cannot see the figure of her late husband because of the adultery she has committed, is indeed "cut off" from seeing him (*What Happens in Hamlet*, pp. 254-55).

[39] See p. 233.   [40] imagination.   [41] call to arms.

[42] The hair and the nails were the "excrements" (literally, "outgrowths") of the body.

[43] (of understanding).

[44] See pp. 234-235. "Color" means "reason," "justification."

HAM.   Nor did you nothing hear?

QUEEN.   No, nothing but ourselves.

HAM.   Why, look you there! Look, how it steals away!
My father, in his habit [45] as he lived!
Look, where he goes, even now, out at the portal!

                                                Exit Ghost.

QUEEN.   This is the very coinage of your brain.
This bodiless creation ecstasy [46]
Is very cunning in.

HAM.   Ecstasy! [47]
My pulse, as yours, doth temperately keep time,   140
And makes as healthful music.[48] It is *not madness*
That I have uttered. Bring me to the test,
And I the matter will re-word, which madness
Would gambol from. (*A sudden suspicion comes over him. Can it
    be that she is discounting everything he has said because she
    believes him mad?*) Mother, for love of grace,
Lay not that flattering unction [49] to your soul,
That not *your trespass*, but *my madness* speaks.
It will but skin and film the ulcerous place,
Whilst rank corruption, mining [50] all within,
Infects unseen. Confess yourself to Heaven;
Repent what's past, avoid what is to come,   150
And do not spread the compost on the weeds,
To make them rank. (*For his father's sake, he kneels to ask her
    pardon for his asperities; but he is too honest to sound more
    penitent than he can feel.*) Forgive me this my virtue,
For in the fatness of these pursy [51] times
Virtue itself of vice must pardon beg,
Yea, curb [52] and woo for leave to do him good.

---

[45] clothes.   [46] madness.   [47] See pp. 150–151.

[48] Hamlet has this time heard the charge of his being mad just once too
often, and passionately tries to make clear to her that he is perfectly sane.
Oddly enough, scholars have never raised what would prove an embarrassing
question: If Hamlet, as they have so long maintained, has been deliberately
pretending to be mad (the critics, it will be remembered, have construed his
disordered appearance in Ophelia's room, his jokes with Polonius, his sarcasms
to Ophelia and the King and his mother and Rosencrantz and Guildenstern,
and so forth, as intended to convince Claudius that he is mad), *why should he
be at such pains to undeceive his mother?* The question is the more pertinent
in that he will soon ask her *not* to reveal to the King that he really is sound
of mind!

[49] ointment.   [50] undermining.   [51] short-winded—i.e., fat.   [52] kneel.

QUEEN. (*Assuming anew the part of the broken-hearted mother of a
          mad son.*)   O Hamlet, thou hast cleft my heart in twain.[53]

HAM. (*Poor Hamlet! It is not, as he imagines, from remorse or guilt that
          her heart is cleft.*)   O, throw away the worser part of it,
      And live the purer with the other half.[54]
      Good-night; but go not to mine uncle's bed.
      Assume a virtue, if you have it not.   160
      [That monster, custom, who all sense doth eat,
      Of habits devil, is angel yet in this,
      That to the use of actions fair and good
      He likewise gives a frock or livery,
      That aptly is put on.] [55] Refrain to-night,
      And that shall lend a kind of easiness
      To the next abstinence; [the next more easy;
      For use almost can change the stamp of nature,
      And either master the devil or throw him out,
      With wondrous potency.] Once more, good-night; (*She looks so
          sorrowfully at him that he misreads her thoughts.*)   170
      And when you are desirous to be blest,
      I'll blessing beg of you. For this same lord,

                                                          Pointing to Polonius.

      I do repent; but Heaven hath pleas'd it so,
      To punish me with this and this with me,
      That I must be their [56] scourge and minister.
      I will bestow him, and will answer well
      The death I gave him.[57] So, again, good-night.
      (*More gently.*) I must be cruel, only to be kind.
      Thus bad begins and worse remains behind.
      [One word more, good lady.]

QUEEN.   What shall I do?   180

HAM.   Not this, by no means, that I bid you do:
      (*The very thought of her love-making causes him to vent his long-*

----

[53] See pp. 272–273.

[54] Gertrude has, of course, recovered her own self-esteem. (In the Olivier
movie, however, Hamlet would seem really to have awakened his mother's
conscience; for after this scene a barrier is set up between her and Claudius, and
each is beheld going his own heartsick way alone for the rest of the play.) It
is almost unbearably painful to observe Hamlet, unaware that nothing he now
says is making any impression on her, effectively following up, as he thinks,
his lecture.

[55] easy to wear.   [56] "Heaven" is usually conceived as a plural.

[57] For some minutes Hamlet has realized the heavy penalty he will have
to pay for the folly of killing Polonius—the forfeiture of all he has accomplished.

accumulated disgust.) Let the bloat king tempt you again
  to bed,
Pinch wanton on your cheek, call you his mouse,
And let him, for a pair of reechy kisses,
Or paddling in your neck with his damn'd fingers,
Make you to ravel all this matter out,
That I essentially am not in madness,
But mad in craft.[58] 'Twere good you let him know;
For who, that's but a queen, fair, sober, wise,
Would from a paddock,[59] from a bat, a gib,[60]   190
Such dear concernings hide? Who would do so?
No, in despite of sense and secrecy,
Unpeg the basket on the house's top,
Let the birds fly, and like the famous ape,
To try conclusions,[61] in the basket creep,
And break your own neck down.[62]

QUEEN. Be thou assur'd, if words be made of breath,
And breath of life, I have no life to breathe
What thou hast said to me.[63]

HAM. I must to England; you know that?

QUEEN.   Alack,   200
I had forgot. 'Tis so concluded on.

HAM. [There's letters seal'd, and my two schoolfellows,
Whom I will trust as I will adders fang'd,
They bear the mandate. They must sweep my way,
And marshal me to knavery. Let it work;
For 'tis the sport to have the enginer [64]
Hoist [65] with his own petar; [66] and 't shall go hard

---

[58] A moment's reflection will make it clear that this is not tantamount to a confession that he *has* been playing the madman. His one objective here is to keep Claudius convinced now that his nephew is insane (an opinion which Claudius never has held—though Hamlet does not know that). Hamlet is aware that by this late date it would be impossible to unravel his well-established reputation for acting like a madman. The only important thing, now that he has killed Polonius, is that everyone should continue in the error.

[59] toad.

[60] tomcat. The word is a contraction of "Gilbert," which was a common name for a male cat.

[61] experiments.

[62] This is some old popular story, now lost to us, though the details of it may be glimpsed from this passage.

[63] In all fairness to her, it must be said that she keeps this promise.

[64] engineer.   [65] blown up.

[66] a metal cone filled with explosives, used to destroy walls and gates.

But I will delve one yard below their mines,
And blow them at the moon. O, 'tis most sweet,
When in one line two crafts directly meet.]   210
This man shall set me packing.[67]
I'll lug the guts into the neighbour room.
Mother, good-night. Indeed this counsellor
Is now most still, most secret, and most grave,
Who was in life a foolish prating knave.
Come, sir, to draw toward an *end* with you.[68]
Good-night, mother.

>   *Exeunt severally, Hamlet tugging in Polonius.*

ACT FOURTH

SCENE I

>   *A room in the castle.* (*Immediately after the preceding scene.*) [1]
> *Enter King, Queen, Rosencrantz, and Guildenstern.*

KING.   There's matter [2] in these sighs; these profound heaves
You must translate; 'tis fit we understand them.
Where is your son?

QUEEN.   [Bestow this place on us a little while.]

>   *Exeunt Rosencrantz and Guildenstern.*

Ah, my good lord, what have I seen to-night!

KING.   What, Gertrude? How does Hamlet?

QUEEN.   Mad as the seas and wind, when both contend
Which is the mightier. In his lawless fit,
Behind the arras hearing something stir,
He whips his rapier out, and cries, "A rat, a rat!"   10
And, in his brainish [3] apprehension, kills
The unseen good old man.

[67] a pun upon "plotting," and "going away quickly." The senseless killing of Polonius will require his going out of the country now; it will also mean that he must devise some new plan of action to achieve revenge.

[68] He does not spare Polonius this final derisive pun. Hamlet still has not forgiven him for having been killed by him!

[1] There is no intermission of time between the end of Act III and the opening of Act IV; and the first three scenes of this act follow immediately upon one another. For this reason some editors would prefer to print them as Scenes v, vi, and vii of the preceding act. The longest day of the action began with III, i, and does not end until IV, iv.

[2] some meaning.   [3] brainsick.

KING.   O heavy deed!
  It had been so with us,[4] had we been there.
  His liberty is full of threats to all,
  To you yourself, to us, to every one.
  Alas, how shall this bloody deed be answered? [5]
  It will be laid to us,[6] whose providence [7]
  Should have kept short, restrain'd, and out of haunt,
  This mad young man. But so much was our love,
  We would not understand what was most fit,   20
  But, like the owner of a foul disease,
  To keep it from divulging,[8] let it feed
  Even on the pith of life. Where is he gone?
QUEEN. To draw apart the body he hath kill'd,
  O'er whom his very madness, like some ore
  Among a mineral of metals base,
  Shows itself pure; he weeps for what is done.[9]
KING. O Gertrude, come away!
  The sun no sooner shall the mountains touch,
  But we will ship him hence, and this vile deed   30
  We must, with all our majesty and skill,
  Both countenance and excuse. Ho, Guildenstern!
  Re-enter Rosencrantz and Guildenstern.
  Friends both, go join you with some further aid.
  Hamlet in madness hath Polonius slain,
  And from his mother's closet hath he dragg'd him.
  Go seek him out; speak fair, and bring the body
  Into the chapel. I pray you, haste in this.
      Exeunt Rosencrantz and Guildenstern.
  Come, Gertrude, we'll call up our wisest friends
  To let them know both what we mean to do
  And what's untimely done; [so, haply, slander] [10] 40
  [Whose whisper o'er the world's diameter,

[4] Claudius knows the sword was meant for him. But he says nothing to refute the attribution of lunacy to Hamlet or to wound his wife's motherly concern. The genuineness of his love for her is always beyond question. He pretends to fear that the Prince's madness is now a threat to the safety of everyone, and blames himself for not having kept his nephew under restraint.
[5] accounted for. [6] the royal "we." [7] foresight.
[8] being brought to light.
[9] Gertrude tries to mitigate her son's crime by this uncharacteristic picture of Hamlet. Possibly, being Gertrude, she prefers to believe that what she is saying is true.
[10] "so, haply, slander," is a conjecture of Capell to fill out the incomplete line. Most editors have adopted it. The next lines are not in the First Folio.

As level [11] as the cannon to his blank,[12]
Transports his poisoned shot, may miss our name,
And hit the woundless air.] O, come away!
My soul is full of discord and dismay.

                                                        Exeunt.

SCENE II

>   *Another room in the castle. (Immediately after the preceding*
>   *scene.)*
>   *Enter Hamlet.*

HAM. Safely stowed.

ROS. } (*Within.*)   Hamlet! Lord Hamlet!
GUIL.

HAM. What noise? Who calls on Hamlet? (*Bored, and half-amused.*) O, here they come.[1]
Enter Rosencrantz and Guildenstern.

ROS. What have you done, my lord, with the dead body?

HAM. Compounded it with dust, whereto 'tis kin.

ROS. Tell us where 'tis, that we may take it thence
And bear it to the chapel.

HAM. Do not believe it.

ROS. Believe what?   10

HAM. That I can keep *your* counsel [2] and not mine *own*. Besides, to be demanded [3] of a *sponge!* [4] What replication should be made by the son of a king? [5]

ROS. Take you me for a sponge, my lord?

HAM. Ay, sir, that soaks up the King's countenance, his rewards, his authorities. But such officers do the King best service in the end. He keeps them, as an ape doth nuts, in the corner of his jaw; first mouth'd, to be last swallowed. When he needs   20

---

[11] as level in aim.   [12] its target.

[1] When Mr. Evans, enacting the title role in his uncut *Hamlet,* saw his schoolfellows approach, at this line he graphically projected the idea that he was about to pretend insanity by seizing a lock of his hair and, to the vast amusement of the audience, bringing it down over his eyes. But though the line is sardonic enough, nothing occurs in this scene which can be construed as sounding lunatic.

[2] secrets.   [3] asked.

[4] At first he seems to mean that they have come to soak up all the information they can. Soon he elaborates on the word.

[5] Again he stands on his princely rank (which with others he is never prone to do) just to put a distance between them. Note the formality of his language.

what you have glean'd, it is but squeezing you, and, sponge, you shall be dry again.

ROS.   I understand you not, my lord.

HAM.   I am glad of it. A knavish speech sleeps in a foolish ear.

ROS.   My lord, you must tell us where the body is, and go with us to the King.

HAM.   The body *is* with the King, but the King is *not* with the body.[6] The King is a thing—

                                                                              30

GUIL. (*Scandalized.*)   A thing, my lord!

HAM.   Of nothing. Bring me to him. Hide fox, and all after.[7]

                                                                Exeunt.

SCENE III

> *Another room in the castle. (Immediately following the preceding scene.)*
> *Enter King and two or three.*

KING. I have sent to seek him, and to find the body.
How dangerous is it that this man goes loose!
Yet must not we put the strong law on him.
He's lov'd of the distracted multitude,
Who like not in their judgement, but their eyes,
And where 'tis so, the offender's scourge is weigh'd,
But never the offence. To bear all smooth and even,
This sudden sending him away must seem

[6] Steevens long ago gave an intelligent explanation of this line: "The body is in the King's house (i.e., the present King's) yet the King (i.e., he who should have been king) is not with the body. Intimating that the usurper is here, the true king in a better place" (*Variorum Hamlet*, I, p. 316).

Other interesting possibilities have been suggested; Caldecott thought that the second half of the line might mean that Claudius "is not lying with Polonius" (Ibidem); Wilson extends this idea by interpreting the line to mean that Polonius' body is "in the next world" with the elder Hamlet, but Claudius "has not yet joined him there" (*Hamlet*, p. 219). But Kittredge thinks it a line of sheer nonsense, "designed to carry off Hamlet's pretence of madness" (*Hamlet*, p. 251). And Adams interprets it in the same way, with an incredible qualification: this is "the first time in the play" that Hamlet makes any attempt to "convince others of his madness" (*Hamlet*, p. 292). Is not this rather too late for pretended madness to begin asserting itself? Adams' remark reminds us of the extent to which the theory of assumed lunacy is hard put to it to find little scraps here and there to lend it credence.

[7] This is a phrase from the old game of Hide-and-Seek, and in that connotation would mean, "Catch me if you can!" But the word "fox" appears often in Elizabethan drama as a word for "sword." Hamlet may thus be also addressing his sword, patting the scabbard, and meaning, "Be patient for a while, and hide; your time will come."

Deliberate pause.[1] Diseases desperate grown
By desperate appliance are relieved,   10
Or not at all.
Enter Rosencrantz.
                    How now! What hath befallen?

ROS.   Where the dead body is bestow'd, my lord,
We cannot get from him.

KING.   But where is he?

ROS.   Without, my lord, guarded, to know your pleasure.

KING.   Bring him before us.

ROS.   Ho, Guildenstern! bring in my lord.
Enter Hamlet and Guildenstern.

KING.   Now, Hamlet, where's Polonius?

HAM.   (*With deep bitterness.*)   At supper.[2]

KING.   At supper! Where?

HAM.   Not where he *eats*, but where he is *eaten*. A certain convoca-   20
tion of [politic] worms are e'en at him.[3] Your worm is your
only emperor for diet. We fat all creatures else to fat us, and we
fat ourselves for maggots. Your fat king and your lean beggar
is but variable service,[4] two dishes, but to one table; that's the
end.

[KING.   Alas, alas!

HAM.   A man may fish with the worm that hath eat of a king, and
eat of the fish that hath fed of that worm.]   30

KING.   What dost thou mean by this?

HAM.   Nothing but to show you how a king may go a progress[5]
through the guts of a beggar.

KING.   Where is Polonius?

HAM.   In heaven; send thither to see. If your messenger find him
not there, seek him i' the other place *yourself*.[6] But indeed, if
you find him not [within] this month, you shall nose him as
you go up the stairs into the lobby.   40

KING.   Go seek him there.

                                        To some Attendants.

[1] thought.
[2] Knowing there is no further postponement of the penalty he must pay,
Hamlet finds relief momentarily in a barrage of insults heaped upon Claudius.
[3] The Elizabethan audience would naturally remember the Diet of Worms
in the recent past.
[4] may be served in various ways.
[5] A stately journey made by the monarch, accompanied by the Court,
through the realm to see and hear the conditions of the country. Queen
Elizabeth made a number of them.
[6] What Hamlet is wittily saying is: "Go to Hell."

HAM. (*Drily.*)   He will *stay* till ye come.

Exeunt Attendants.

KING.   Hamlet, this deed of thine, for thine especial safety,—
    Which we do tender, as we dearly grieve
    For that which thou hast done,—must send thee hence
    With fiery quickness; therefore prepare thyself.
    The bark is ready, and the wind at help,
    The associates tend, and everything is bent
    For England.

HAM.   For England?

KING.   Ay, Hamlet.

HAM. (*Savagely.*)   *Good!*

KING.   So *is* it, if thou knew'st our purposes.

HAM.   I see a *cherub* that sees *them*.[7] But, come, for England! Fare- 50
    well, dear mother.[8]

KING.   Thy loving *father*, Hamlet.

HAM.   My mother. Father and mother is man and wife, man and
    wife is one flesh, and so, my mother. Come, for England!   *Exit.*

KING.   Follow him at foot, tempt him with speed aboard.
    Delay it not; I'll have him hence to-night.
    Away! for everything is seal'd and done
    That else leans on the affair. Pray you, make haste.

Exeunt Rosencrantz and Guildenstern.

    And, England,[9] if my love thou hold'st at aught,— 60
    As my great power thereof may give thee sense,
    Since yet thy cicatrice looks raw and red
    After the Danish sword, and thy free awe [10]
    Pays homage to us—thou mayst not coldly set [11]
    Our sovereign process,[12] which imports at full,
    By letters conjuring to that effect,
    The present [13] death of Hamlet. Do it, England;
    For like the hectic [14] in my blood he rages,
    And thou must cure me. Till I know 'tis done,
    Howe'er my haps,[15] my joys were ne'er begun.   *Exit.*[16] 70

[7] i.e., I know how angelic your purposes are!

[8] Kittredge: "The maddest speech that Hamlet has yet made" (*Hamlet*, p. 252)!!

[9] the King of England.   [10] the awe which you freely feel.   [11] (aside).

[12] instructions.   [13] instant.   [14] fever.

[15] whatever my fortune. It is to be noted that since Gertrude is not present Claudius is free for the first time to vent his hatred of his nephew.

[16] Olivier's film by omitting Rosencrantz and Guildenstern omitted some of the most significant parts of the action. One never had any feeling that Hamlet

SCENE IV

A plain in Denmark. (The same day.)
Enter Fortinbras, a Captain, and army, marching.[1]

FOR. Go, captain, from me greet the Danish king.
Tell him that, by his license, Fortinbras

---

had embarked for England. It is odd that such huge portions should have been
cut from the cinema version. Years before the picture was made, we read in a
recent study of the distinguished actor, Mr. Olivier agreed with the director,
Mr. Tyrone Guthrie, that it was revolting that *Hamlet* must be cut to suit
the "convention of a two and a half hour's entertainment" in the theater. A
cut *Hamlet*, he felt, could never be the play Shakespeare wrote; "the thought
of this awful sacrilege produced a brooding silence" (F. Barker, *The Oliviers*,
1953, pp. 143–44). Yet when it came to making the film, the venture was described by Mr. Olivier and his new colleagues as "a simplified essay in *Hamlet*,"
and "if it was to be a *good* film, it was necessary to be quite ruthless . . . It
must be easy to follow, which meant that they would have to discard ir-
relevancies of plot" (p. 301). Such a decision might have well called anew
for a brooding silence!

[1] At last we are privileged to see Fortinbras, though only for a minute or
two. We have heard him discussed, early in the play, as a brave soldier who
boldly took arms to avenge his father's death, and was able to do so because
the world knew the circumstances of the latter's slaying in open combat. Shakespeare will need Fortinbras for the end of his play, and therefore introduces
him to us, so that when he appears during the concluding minutes of the tragedy
we need not look upon him as an unknown newcomer.

It would be fair to say that this was Shakespeare's chief purpose in writing
this short scene. He had, however, another dramaturgical reason for writing
it. On the Elizabethan stage there was no curtain that might descend to show
the passage of time, when it was important that the audience be aware of such
an interval, or a shift of locale to another place; Shakespeare's method, exhibited
far more copiously in other plays than *Hamlet*, was to compose a "separation
scene"—a short scene not important to the plot, at the end of which we can
feel either that some time has elapsed since the last significant event or that the
setting has changed. As printed in the Second Quarto, we here see Hamlet on
his way to the seaport, at the ending of the "long day" which began with Act
Three. The next we shall hear of him enough time will have elapsed for his
having sailed towards England, been intercepted by the pirates, and returned
to Denmark.

Although Hamlet has an interesting soliloquy in this scene, his presence
in it, for the first time in any scene, must be pronounced as of secondary
importance. It is noteworthy that the acting version of this scene which Shakespeare's company gave to the world in 1623, cuts Hamlet out entirely—thus
making it purely a "separation scene." The First Folio, that is, gives only the
eight lines of dialogue between Fortinbras and the Captain. Knowing Shakespeare's purposes well, his fellow actors, in casting about for the comparatively
few lines that could be spared from *Hamlet* to shorten the performance, decided—very possibly with Shakespeare's permission (if indeed he did not make

Claims the conveyance [2] of a promis'd march
Over his kingdom. You know the rendezvous.
If that his Majesty would aught with us,
We shall express our duty in his eye; [3]
And let him know so.

CAP.   I will do't, my lord.

FOR.   Go softly on.

                     Exeunt Fortinbras and Soldiers.

[Enter Hamlet, Rosencrantz, and others.

HAM.   Good sir, whose powers [4] are these?

CAP.   They are of Norway, sir.   10

HAM.   How purpos'd, sir, I pray you?

CAP.   Against some part of Poland.

HAM.   Who commands them, sir?

CAP.   The nephew to old Norway, Fortinbras.

HAM.   Goes it against the main [5] of Poland, sir,
Or for some frontier?

CAP.   Truly to speak, and with no addition,
We go to gain a little patch of ground
That hath in it no profit but the name.[6]
To pay five ducats, five, I would not farm it; [7]   20
Nor will it yield to Norway or the Pole
A ranker rate, should it be sold in fee.[8]

HAM.   Why, then the Polack never will defend it.

CAP.   Yes, it is already garrison'd.

HAM.   Two thousand souls and twenty thousand ducats
Will not debate the question of this straw.[9]
This is the imposthume [10] of much wealth and peace,
That inward breaks, and shows no cause without [11]
Why the man dies. I humbly thank you, sir.

CAP.   God buy you,[12] sir.   *Exit.*

ROS.   Will't please you go, my lord?   30

HAM.   I'll be with you straight. Go a little before.

                     Exeunt all except Hamlet.

---

the cut himself)—to omit all but the opening eight lines of this scene. We must therefore conclude that Hamlet's soliloquy in this scene, the only one omitted from the First Folio, is the only unimportant one in the play.

[2] convoying (of Fortinbras' troops through Denmark).   [3] presence.
[4] forces.   [5] i.e., all.   [6] (of glory).   [7] (on a lease).   [8] outright.
[9] trifle.   [10] abscess.   [11] externally.
[12] God be with you; hence, "Goodbye."

How all occasions do inform against me,[13]
And spur my dull revenge! What is a man,
If his chief good and market of his time
Be but to sleep and feed? A beast, no more.
Sure, He that made us with such large discourse,[14]
Looking before and after, gave us not
That capability and god-like reason
To fust [15] in us unus'd.[16] Now, whether it be
Bestial oblivion,[17] or some craven scruple   40
Of thinking too precisely on the event,[18]—

[18] Alone, Hamlet soliloquizes. Again we must first ask what are the events
which have fostered his present state of mind. He has ruined his cause through
his reckless killing of Polonius. Now he is being hurried into exile because in
slaying Polonius he surrendered the guidance of reason, which for so long
he had patiently followed.

What is a man, he asks, if he live but to sleep and feed? No more than
a beast. (These lines are usually taken to be a self-castigation for insufficient
action. But the very next passage gives the lie to such an interpretation. Hamlet
is blaming himself for not having used his reason enough!) Surely, when God
gave us the faculty of reasoning ("discourse"), with the power to envision
cause and effect of our actions ("looking before and after"), He did not give us

"That capability and god-like reason
To fust in us unused."

When I forgot to use that divine faculty and acted on blind impulse, I was
guilty of behaving like a beast.

Or, perhaps, on the other hand, I have worried *too much* about the outcome ("event") of killing Claudius before the time was ripe? (With his characteristic rashness, the curse of which will not leave him till death—which
will, indeed, cause his death—Hamlet, now that everything seems lost, regrets
that he has not been rasher! Had he been, he feels, Claudius at all odds would
now be dead and the problem ended.) Here is Fortinbras leading an army
boldly and mocking whatever may be the outcome of his exploit ("makes
mouths at the invisible event")—all for a trifle, "for an egg-shell." His example shows that when honor is at stake true nobility will find justification
in quarreling over a straw. (Whereas, with a murder to avenge, Hamlet has
had to bide his time, has had first to be sure that the Ghost's word was de-
pendable before he could even think of vengeance.)

"O, from this time forth,
My thoughts be bloody, or be nothing worth!"

Hamlet has begun by recognizing his tragic percipitance, but in the end
bitterness provokes him to the unreasonable conclusion that he must henceforth surrender himself yet more to the dictates of passion! (Several of the
remarks in this soliloquy are new instances, overlooked by Bradley, of Hamlet's
references to external difficulties with which his vengeance has to cope.)

[14] power of reasoning.   [15] grow mouldy.   [16] See p. 262.
[17] the forgetfulness of a beast.   [18] outcome.

A thought which, quarter'd, hath but one part wisdom
And ever three parts coward,—I do not know
Why yet I live to say, "This thing's to do,"
Sith [19] I have cause and will and strength and means
To do't. Examples gross [20] as earth exhort me;
Witness this army of such mass and charge
Led by a delicate and tender prince,
Whose spirit with divine ambition puff'd
Makes mouths [21] at the invisible event,   50
Exposing what is mortal and unsure
To all that fortune, death, and danger dare,
Even for an egg-shell. Rightly to be great
Is not to stir without great argument,
But greatly to find quarrel in a straw
When honour's at the stake.[22] How stand I then,
That have a father kill'd, a mother stain'd,
Excitements of my reason and my blood,
And let all sleep, while to my shame I see
The imminent death of twenty thousand men,   60
That for a fantasy and trick [23] of fame
Go to their graves like beds, fight for a plot
Whereon the numbers cannot try the cause,
Which is not tomb enough and continent [24]
To hide the slain? [25] O, from this time forth,
My thoughts be bloody, or be nothing worth!]   *Exit.*

SCENE V

> *Elsinore. A room in the castle. (Some days later.)*
> *Enter Queen, Horatio and a Gentleman.*

QUEEN. (*Evasively.*)   I will not speak with her.[1]

[GENT.]   She is importunate, indeed distract.
Her mood will needs be pitied.

QUEEN. (*Defending herself against seeing Ophelia.*)   What would she
have?

[GENT.]   She speaks much of her father; says she hears

---

[19] since.   [20] obvious.   [21] disdains.
[22] It is a sign of greatness not to stir for every trifle, but rather to stir
at once when honor is in question.
[23] trifle.   [24] what which contains.
[25] not large enough to hold the soldiers who will be slain in the fight.
[1] See p. 270.

There's tricks [2] i' the world, and hems, and beats her heart,
Spurns enviously [3] at straws,[4] speaks things in doubt
That carry but half sense. Her speech is nothing,[5]
Yet the unshaped use of it [6] doth move
The hearers to collection.[7] They aim at it
And botch the words up fit to their own thoughts;   10
Which, as her winks, and nods, and gestures yield them,
Indeed would make one think there would be thought,
Though nothing sure, yet much unhappily.

[HOR.]   'Twere good she were spoken with, for she may strew
Dangerous conjectures in ill-breeding minds.[8]

QUEEN.   (*Grudgingly.*)   Let her come in.   *Exit Gentleman.*
[*Aside.*] To my sick soul, as sin's true nature is,
Each toy seems prologue to some great amiss;
So full of artless [9] jealousy [10] is guilt,
It spills [11] itself in fearing to be spilt.   20
Enter Ophelia, distracted.[12]

OPH.   Where is the beauteous majesty of Denmark?
QUEEN.   How now, Ophelia!
OPH.   (*Sings.*)

                    "How should I your true love know [13]
                              From another one?
                         By his cockle hat and staff,
                              And his sandal shoon."

QUEEN.   Alas, sweet lady, what imports this song?
OPH.   Say you? Nay, pray you, mark.
                    (*Sings.*) "He is dead and gone, lady,
                              He is dead and gone;   30
                         At his head a grass-green turf
                              At his heels a stone."

       Enter King.
QUEEN.   Nay, but, Ophelia,—

---

[2] plots.   [3] spitefully.   [4] trifles.   [5] without purpose.
[6] the formless way she speaks.   [7] inference.   [8] minds which breed evil.
[9] unreasonable.   [10] suspicion.   [11] destroys.

[12] The corrupt First Quarto has an interesting direction for her entrance.
She is to come in "playing on a Lute, and her haire downe singing."

[13] We perceive that Hamlet and his exile are uppermost in her scattered
thoughts from her reference to the lover's hat decorated with a cockle shell
—the sign of a pilgrim who has been overseas to the shrine of St. James of
Compostella. The second stanza of this old ditty shows her brooding over
the death of her father, without whose domineering will she is now lost.

OPH. Pray you, mark.

 (*Sings.*) "White his shroud as the mountain snow,"—

QUEEN. Alas, look here, my lord.

OPH. (*Sings.*)

  "Larded with sweet flowers;
  Which bewept to the grave did not go
  With true-love showers."

KING. How do you, pretty lady? 40

OPH. Well, God 'ild [14] you! They say the owl was a baker's daughter. [15] Lord, we know what we are, but know not what we may be. God be at your table!

KING. Conceit [16] upon her father.

OPH. Pray you, let's have no words of this, but when they ask you what it means, say you this: [17]

  (*Sings.*) "To-morrow is Saint Valentine's day,
   All in the morning betime, [18]

---

[14] yield (i.e., reward).

[15] a reference to an old Gloucestershire tale. Jesus went into the shop of a baker, asking for bread, and was given some by the woman who owned the shop. Her daughter upbraided her for her generosity, and was thereupon transformed to an owl.

[16] imagination.

[17] Her second song, as Halliwell observed, "alludes to the custom of the first girl seen by a man . . . this day (i.e., St. Valentine's Day) being considered his Valentine or true-love." The tradition is engaging, but this song makes anything but charm out of it.

It is not so much the indecency of the third stanza—much bawdier than anything Hamlet has uttered, though without any of the wit with which he charges his merriment—as the disgusting morality of the last stanza which makes the lyric distasteful. Though such words and ideas come as a surprise to us when sung by Ophelia, the touch is a masterstroke. One is strangely moved to deep pity for the poor mad girl, completely at the mercy of her wandering mind. But where can she have learned such a song? It has been suggested by several critics that Ophelia in her childhood must have had a nurse something like Juliet's who taught it to her. We fancy, however, that this is too extreme even for such a nurse. It sounds much more the kind of thing which the chaste and suppressed Ophelia might have picked up unintentionally from having heard her young spark of a brother, with his set of values inculcated by his father, sing it around the house; she was expected, we assume, not to hear it, being a good girl, but heard it whether she wished to or not—perhaps with horror, perhaps with some confused excitement; at any rate it sank deep into her consciousness. That is our guess, though there is no way of proving it right or wrong. If it is right, her singing such a song in her madness becomes all the more pathetic.

[18] early.

And I a maid at your window,   50
　　To be your Valentine.

"Then up he rose and donn'd his clothes,
　　And dupp'd [19] the chamber door;
　　Let in the maid, that out a maid
　　　　Never departed more."

KING.　Pretty Ophelia!

OPH.　Indeed, la, without an oath I'll make an end on't.
　　"By gis,[20] and by Saint Charity,
　　　　Alack! and, Fie for shame!   60
　　Young men will do't, if they come to't;
　　　　By Cock,[21] they are to blame.

"Quoth she, 'Before you tumbled me,
　　You promis'd me to wed.'
'So would I ha' done, by yonder sun,
　　And thou hadst not come to my bed.' " [22]

KING.　How long hath she been thus?

OPH.　I hope all will be well. We must be patient; but I cannot
choose but weep, to think they should lay him i' the cold
ground. My brother shall know of it; and so I thank you for   70
your good counsel. Come, my coach! [23] Good-night, ladies;
good-night, sweet ladies; good-night, good-night.   *Exit.*

KING.　(*Touched.*)　Follow her close; give her good watch, I pray you.
　　　　　　　　　　　　　　　　　　　　　　　　　Exeunt some.

O, this is the poison of deep grief; it springs
All from her father's death. O Gertrude, Gertrude,
When sorrows come, they come not single spies,
But in battalions. First, her father slain;
(*Careful to make her believe he is affectionately concerned for
　　Hamlet.*) Next, your son gone; and he most violent author   80
Of his own just remove; the people muddied,
Thick and unwholesome in their thoughts and whispers,
For good Polonius' death; and we have done but greenly

---

[19] opened (from "do ope").　　[20] by Jesus.
[21] an indecent and even sacrilegious pun. Vulgarly "by God" became "by
Cock."
[22] See pp. 281–282.
[23] She departs, as though she were leaving some gay festivities.

In hugger-mugger [24] to inter him; poor Ophelia
Divided from herself and her fair judgement,
Without the which we are pictures, or mere beasts;
Last, and as much containing as all these,
Her brother is in secret come from France,
Feeds on his wonder, keeps himself in clouds,
And wants not buzzers [25] to infect his ear   90
With pestilent speeches of his father's death,
Wherein necessity, of matter beggar'd,[26]
Will nothing stick [27] our persons to arraign
In ear and ear. O my dear Gertrude, this,
Like to a murdering-piece,[28] in many places
Gives me superfluous death.   *A noise within.*
Enter a Messenger.

QUEEN.   Alack, what noise is this?
KING.   Where are my Switzers? Let them guard the door.
What is the matter?
MESS.   Save yourself, my lord!
The ocean, overpeering of his list,[29]
Eats not the flats with more impetuous haste   100
Than young Laertes, in a riotous head,
O'erbears your officers. The rabble call him lord;
And, as the world were now but to begin,
Antiquity forgot, custom not known,
(The ratifiers and props [30] of every word,)
They cry, "Choose we! Laertes shall be king!"
Caps, hands, and tongues applaud it to the clouds,
"Laertes shall be king, Laertes king!"
QUEEN.   How cheerfully on the false trail they cry!
O, this is counter,[31] you false Danish dogs!   110
Enter Laertes armed; Danes following.

KING.   The doors are broke.   *Noise within.*
LAER.   Where is this king? Sirs, stand you all without.
DANES.   No, let's come in.
LAER.   I pray you, give me leave.

---

[24] secretly.   [25] people who whisper in his ears.
[26] i.e., having no facts to go on.   [27] not at all hesitate.
[28] cannon which is so loaded as to scatter its shot.   [29] its boundary.
[30] Antiquity and custom are the "ratifiers and props."
[31] A hound hunting in the wrong direction is running "counter."

DANES.   We will, we will.

                                          They retire without the door.

LAER.   I thank you; keep the door. O thou vile king,
   Give me my father!

QUEEN.   Calmly, good Laertes.

LAER.   That drop of blood that's calm proclaims me bastard,
   Cries cuckold to my father, brands the harlot
   Even here, between the chaste unsmirched brows
   Of my true mother.[32]

KING.   (*Calmly, as though talking to a child.*)   What is the cause,
      Laertes,
                                                                    120
   That thy rebellion looks so giant-like? (*Laertes makes a threaten-
      ing move toward Claudius. The Queen rushes between them,
      restraining Laertes.*)
   Let him go, Gertrude; do not fear our person.
   There's such divinity doth hedge a king,
   That treason can but peep to what it would,
   Acts little of his [33] will. Tell me, Laertes,
   Why thou art thus incens'd. Let him *go*, Gertrude.
   Speak, man.

LAER. (*Raging.*)   Where's my father?

KING.   Dead.

QUEEN. (*Quickly.*)   But not by him.

KING.   Let him demand his fill.

LAER.   How came he dead? I'll not be juggl'd with.
                                                                    130
   To hell, allegiance! Vows, to the blackest devil!
   Conscience and grace, to the profoundest pit!
   I dare damnation. To this point I stand,
   That both the worlds [34] I give to negligence,
   Let come what comes; only I'll be reveng'd
   Most throughly for my father.

KING. (*With a touch of mockery.*)   Who shall *stay* you?

LAER.   My will, not all the world.

---

[32] See p. 291.   [33] its.
[34] this world and the next. Herein Laertes differs from Hamlet. The Prince
would not have vengeance unless it be just; he would make sure that the object
of his revenge is guilty before he could undertake to punish him. Laertes is
willing to kill almost anybody as long as he can be "most thoroughly" re-
venged for his father. Honor is no consideration to him. Hamlet would not
forfeit his immortal soul for the mere satisfaction of causing the death of no
matter whom in exchange for his father's.

And for my means, I'll husband them so well,
They shall go far with little.[35]

KING.   Good Laertes,
   If you desire to know the certainty   140
   Of your dear father's death, is't writ in your revenge
   That, swoopstake,[36] you will draw both friend and foe,
   Winner and loser?

LAER.   None but his enemies.

KING. (*Almost with derision.*)   Will you *know* them then?

LAER.   To his good friends thus wide I'll ope my arms,
   And like the kind life-rend'ring pelican,[37]
   Repast them with my blood.

KING. (*Patronizingly.*)   Why, now you speak
   Like a good child and a true gentleman.
   That I am guiltless of your father's death,
   And am most sensibly in grief for it,   150
   It shall as level [38] to your judgement pierce
   As day does to your eye.

               A noise within: "Let her come in!"

Re-enter Ophelia.

LAER.   How now! what noise is that? (*Overwhelmed at his sister's state,*
     and bursting into tears.)
   O heat, dry up my brains! Tears seven times salt
   Burn out the sense and virtue [39] of mine eye!
   By heaven, thy madness shall be paid by weight
   Till our scale turns the beam. O rose of May!
   Dear maid, kind sister, sweet Ophelia!
   O heavens! is't possible, a young maid's wits
   Should be as mortal as an old man's life?   160
   Nature [40] is fine in love, and where 'tis fine,

---

[35] This short speech is in itself enough of an answer to one of the chief
difficulties Bradley raises: If there were any external difficulties in Hamlet's
bringing the King to justice, "why does Shakespeare exhibit Laertes quite
easily raising the people against the King?" Why could Hamlet not have done
the same thing? (*Shakespearean Tragedy*, p. 95). It is not the *people* whom
Laertes has raised against Claudius, but a small rabble. The uprising, such as
it is, is put down in a few minutes by Claudius through sheer personal efficiency.
And in this speech Laertes makes it clear that he knows that he has no real
force behind him.

[36] indiscriminately.

[37] It was thought that the pelican fed its young on its own blood and therefore this bird was proverbially cited as the kindest of creatures.

[38] with as direct aim.   [39] power.   [40] human nature.

It sends some precious instance of itself
After the thing it loves.[41]

OPH. (*Sings.*)

> "They bore him barefac'd on the bier;
> Hey non nonny, nonny, hey nonny;
> And on his grave rains many a tear,"—

Fare you well, my dove!

LAER.   Hadst thou thy wits and didst persuade revenge,
It could not move thus.

OPH. (*She imagines she's at a spinning wheel.*)   You must sing,
"Down a-down, and you call him a-down-a." O, how the wheel   170
becomes it![42] It is the false steward, that stole his master's
daughter.[43]

LAER.   This nothing's more than matter.[44]

OPH. (*To Laertes.*)   There's rosemary, that's for remembrance;
pray, love, remember; and there is pansies, that's for thoughts.[45]

LAER.   A document[46] in madness, thoughts and remembrance fitted.

OPH. (*To Claudius.*)   There's fennel for you, and columbines;   180
there's rue for you, and here's some for me; we may call it
herb of grace o' Sundays. O, *you* (*to Gertrude*) must wear
your rue with a difference. There's a daisy. I would give you
some violets, but they wither'd all when my father died. They
say he made a good end,—

(*Sings.*) "For bonny sweet Robin is all my joy."

LAER.   Thought[47] and affliction, passion,[48] hell itself,
She turns to favour[49] and to prettiness.

OPH. (*Sings.*)

> "And will he not come again?
> And will he not come again?   190
> No, no, he is dead;
> Go to thy death-bed;
> He never will come again.

---

[41] Dr. Johnson: "Love, says Laertes, is the passion by which nature is most
exalted and refined, and as substances refined and subtilised, easily obey any
impulse, or follow any attraction, some part of nature, so purified and refined,
flies off after the attracting object, after the thing it loves."
[42] keeps time with the tune.
[43] Possibly the subject of a ballad of which she has been singing a fragment.
[44] (This aimless talk of Ophelia's tells more of her sufferings than could
coherent speech.)
[45] See pp. 236–238.   [46] lesson.   [47] melancholy.   [48] suffering.
[49] attractiveness.

> "His beard as white as snow,
> All flaxen was his poll.
> He is gone, he is gone,
> And we cast away moan.
> God ha' mercy on his soul!"

And of all Christian souls, I pray God. God buy ye. *Exit.* 200

LAER. (*Weeping.*) Do you see this, you gods?

KING. (*Gently.*) Laertes, I must commune with your grief,
Or you deny me right. Go but apart,
Make choice of whom your wisest friends you will,
And they shall hear and judge 'twixt you and me.
If by direct or by collateral hand
They find us touch'd, we will our kingdom give,
Our crown, our life, and all that we call ours,
To you in satisfaction; but if not,
Be you content to lend your patience to us, 210
And we shall jointly labour with your soul
To give it due content.[50]

LAER. (*Apologizing.*) Let this be so.
His means of death, his obscure burial—
No trophy,[51] sword, nor hatchment[52] o'er his bones,
No noble rite nor formal ostentation[53]—
Cry to be heard, as 'twere from heaven to earth,
That I *must* call't in question.

KING. So you shall;
And where the offence is let the great axe fell.
I pray you, go with me. *Exeunt.*

SCENE VI

Another room in the castle. (*The same day.*)
Enter Horatio with an Attendant.

HOR. What are they that would speak with me?

ATT. Sailors, sir. They say they have letters for you.

HOR. Let them come in. *Exit Attendant.*
I do not know from what part of the world
I should be greeted, if not from Lord Hamlet.
Enter Sailor.

SAIL. God bless you, sir.

[50] Gertrude is present. The King is therefore guarded in his promise to Laertes that he will not stand in the way of vengeance.
  [51] memorial.   [52] tablet with coat of arms.   [53] ceremony.

HOR.   Let Him bless thee too.

SAIL.   He shall, sir, an't please Him. There's a letter for you, sir
—it comes from the ambassador that was bound for England—   10
if your name be Horatio, as I am let to know it is.

[HOR.] (*Reads.*) "Horatio, when thou shalt have overlook'd this,
give these fellows some means to the King; they have letters for
him. Ere we were two days old at sea, a pirate of very warlike
appointment gave us chase. Finding ourselves too slow of sail,
we put on a compelled valour. In the grapple I boarded them.
On the instant they got clear of our ship, so I alone became
their prisoner. They have dealt with me like thieves of mercy,[1]   20
but they knew what they did: I am to do a good turn for them.
Let the King have the letters I have sent, and repair thou to me
with as much haste as thou wouldest fly death. I have words
to speak in your ear will make thee dumb, yet are they much
too light for the bore[2] of the matter. These good fellows will
bring thee where I am. Rosencrantz and Guildenstern hold their
course for England; of them I have much to tell thee. Farewell.   30

        "He that thou knowest thine,

                                                        HAMLET."

Come, I will give you way for[3] these your letters;
And do't the speedier, that you may direct me
To him from whom you brought them.

                                                        Exeunt.

SCENE VII

        Another room in the castle. (*The same day.*)
        Enter King and Laertes.

KING.   Now must your conscience my acquittance seal;
And you must put me in your heart for friend,
Sith you have heard, and with a knowing ear,
That he which hath your noble father slain
Pursu'd my life.

LAER.   It well appears. But tell me
Why you proceeded not against these feats,[1]
So crimeful and so capital in nature,

---

[1] Hamlet's courage in leading the attack on the pirates, "boarding their ship
single-handed," and "negotiating his release" comes as a "surprise" to Adams
(*Hamlet*, p. 307).
    [2] caliber.   [3] make it possible for you to deliver.
    [1] acts.

> As by your safety, wisdom, all things else,
> You mainly were stirr'd up.

KING.   O, for two special reasons,
> Which may to you, perhaps, seem much unsinew'd,   10
> And yet to me they are strong.[2] The Queen his mother
> Lives almost by his looks; and for myself—
> My virtue or my plague, be it either which—
> (*With embarrassment.*) She's so conjunctive to my life and soul,
> That, as the star moves not but in his sphere,
> I could not but by her.[3] The other motive
> Why to a public count [4] I might not go,
> Is the great love the general gender [5] bear him;[6]
> Who, dipping all his faults in their affection,
> Would, like the spring that turneth wood to stone,   20
> Convert his gyves [7] to graces; so that my arrows,
> Too slightly timb'red for so loud a wind,
> Would have reverted to my bow again,
> And not where I had aim'd them.

LAER. (*Bitterly.*)   And so have I a noble father lost,
> A sister driven into desperate terms,
> Whose worth, if praises may go back again,[8]
> Stood challenger on mount of all the age
> For her perfections. But my revenge will come.

KING. (*Firmly.*)   Break not your sleeps for that. You must not think   30
> That we are made of stuff so flat and dull
> That we can let our beard be shook with danger
> And think it pastime. You shortly shall hear more.[9]
> I lov'd your father, and we love ourself,
> And that, I hope, will teach you to imagine—
> *Enter a Messenger with letters.*
> How now! What news?

MESS.   Letters, my lord, from Hamlet.

---

[2] See pp. 268–269.

[3] This half-ashamed confession of love for the Queen is sincere. For some reason or other, men can speak publicly of their affection for their wives only as though it were a kind of crime.

[4] judgment.   [5] common people.

[6] Many scholars have built much on this remark of the King's; it may be the truth or it may not be the truth. We have no evidence for or against it.

[7] fetters.   [8] (to what she was like before her present condition).

[9] He expects soon to be able to please Laertes with news of Hamlet's death in England.

This to your Majesty; this to the Queen.

KING. (*Astonished*).   From Hamlet! Who brought them?

MESS.   Sailors, my lord, they say; I saw them not.

They were given me by Claudio. He receiv'd them   40
[Of him that brought them].

KING.   Laertes, you shall hear them.

Leave us.   *Exit Messenger.*

(*Reads.*) "High and mighty, You shall know I am set naked on
your kingdom. To-morrow shall I beg leave to see your kingly
eyes, when I shall, first asking your pardon thereunto, recount
the occasions of my sudden and more strange return.

                                                    HAMLET."

What should this mean? Are all the rest come back?   50
Or is it some abuse,[10] or no such thing? [11]

LAER.   Know you the hand? [12]

KING.   'Tis Hamlet's character. "Naked!" [13]
And in a postscript here, he says, "*alone.*"
(*Staggered by the turn of events.*) Can you advise me?

LAER.   I'm lost in it, my lord. (*Gloating.*) But let him come.
It warms the very sickness in my heart
That I shall live and tell him to his teeth,
"Thus didest thou."

KING.   If it be so,[14] Laertes,—
As how should it be so? [15] How otherwise? [16]—
Will you be rul'd by me?

LAER.   [Ay, my lord,]   60
If so you'll not o'errule me to a peace.

KING.   To thine *own* peace. If he be now return'd,
As checking [17] at his voyage, and that he means
No more to undertake it, I will work him
To an exploit, now ripe in my device,
Under the which he shall not choose but [18] fall;
And for his death no wind of blame shall breathe,

---

[10] deception.   [11] is it a fantasy?   [12] handwriting.
[13] The King does not miss the threat in the word "naked." On the surface
the word implies that Hamlet is arriving without resources. But Hamlet (and
Shakespeare) expect that an immediate association with "naked" will be "sword,"
as the King reads the letter. Something like that must be implied by the King's
singling out the word for repetition because it impressed him.
[14] if Hamlet is returned.   [15] though it's too incredible to be possible.
[16] But here's his letter in evidence.   [17] refusing to continue.
[18] cannot help.

But even his mother [19] shall uncharge the practice [20]
And call it accident.
[LAER.   My lord, I will be rul'd;
The rather, if you could devise it so   70
That *I* might be the organ.
KING.   It falls [21] right.
You have been talk'd of since your travel much,
And that in Hamlet's hearing, for a quality
Wherein, they say, you shine. Your sum of parts
Did not together pluck such envy from him
As did that one, and that, in my regard,
Of the unworthiest siege.[22]
LAER.   What part is that, my lord?
KING.   A very riband in the cap of youth,
Yet needful too; for youth no less becomes
The light and careless livery that it wears   80
Than settled age his sables [23] and his weeds,[24]
Importing health and graveness.[25]] Two months since,
Here was a gentleman of Normandy;—
I've seen myself, and serv'd against, the French,
And they can well on horseback; but this gallant
Had witchcraft in't. He grew unto his seat,
And to such wondrous doing brought his horse,
As he had been incorps'd [26] and demi-natur'd
With the brave beast. So far he pass'd [27] my thought,
That I, in forgery [28] of shapes and tricks,   90
Come short of what he did.
LAER.   A Norman, was't?
KING.   A Norman.
LAER.   Upon my life, Lamound.
KING.   The very same.
LAER.   I know him well. He is the brooch [29] indeed
And gem of all the nation.
KING.   He made confession of you,
And gave you such a masterly report

---

[19] Note that regard for his wife is still paramount in Claudius' thoughts.
[20] believe the plot not to be one.   [21] (circumstances are).
[22] lowest rank.   [23] dignified attire.   [24] clothes.
[25] The "light and careless livery" of youth import "health"; the "sables"
and "weeds" of "settled age" import "graveness."
[26] of one body with.   [27] surpassed.   [28] invention.   [29] ornament.

For art and exercise [30] in your defence,[31]
And for your rapier most especially,
That he cried out, 'twould be a sight indeed   100
If one could match you. [The scrimers [32] of their nation,
He swore, had neither motion, guard, nor eye,
If you oppos'd them.] Sir, this report of his
Did Hamlet so envenom with his envy [33]
That he could nothing do but wish and beg
Your sudden coming o'er to play with him.
Now, out of this—

LAER.   What out of this, my lord?

KING (*With rhetorical effectiveness.*)   Laertes, was your father dear to
        you?
    Or are you like the painting of a sorrow,
    A face without a heart?

LAER. (*Impatiently.*)   Why ask you this?   110

KING.   Not that I think you did not love your father,
    But that I know love is begun by time,
    And that I see, in passages of proof,[34]
    Time qualifies the spark and fire of it.
    [There lives within the very flame of love
    A kind of wick or snuff [35] that will abate it,[36]
    And nothing is at a like goodness still;
    For goodness, growing to a plurisy,[37]
    Dies in his own too much.[38] That we would do,
    We should do when we would; for this "would" changes,   120
    And hath abatements and delays as many
    As there are tongues, are hands, are accidents;
    And then this "should" is like a spendthrift sigh,[39]
    That hurts by easing. But, to the quick o' the ulcer:—]
    Hamlet comes back. What would you undertake,
    To show yourself your father's son in deed
    More than in words?

LAER. (*Savagely.*)   To cut his throat i' the church.

---

[30] in theory and practice.   [31] sword practice.   [32] fencers.
[33] We can readily believe that Hamlet anticipated the pleasure of fencing
with a man of Laertes' skill. It is, of course, inconceivable that he could have
felt any malice ("envy") at the admiration Laertes has won in France.
    [34] instances in experience.   [35] charred wick of a lamp.   [36] kill the flame.
[37] excess.   [38] excess.
[39] According to medieval medicine, every sigh cost a drop of blood.

KING. (*Sanctimoniously.*)   No place, indeed, should murder sanctuarize;
    Revenge should have no bounds. But, good Laertes,
    Will you do this, keep close within your chamber?   130
    Hamlet return'd shall know you are come home.
    We'll put on [40] those shall praise your excellence
    And set a double varnish on the fame
    The Frenchman gave you, bring you in fine together
    And wager on your heads. He, being remiss,[41]
    Most generous [42] and free from all contriving,
    Will not peruse the foils, so that, with ease,
    Or with a little shuffling, you may choose
    A sword unbated,[43] and in a pass of practice [44]
    Requite him for your father.

LAER.   I will do't;   140
    And, for that purpose, I'll anoint my sword.
    I bought an unction [45] of a mountebank,[46]
    So mortal that, but dip a knife in it,
    Where it draws blood no cataplasm [47] so rare,
    Collected from all simples [48] that have virtue [49]
    Under the moon, can save the thing from death
    That is but scratch'd withal. I'll touch my point
    With this contagion, that, if I gall [50] him slightly,
    It may be death.

KING.   Let's further think of this,
    Weigh what convenience both of time and means   150
    May fit [51] us to our shape.[52] If this should fail,
    And that our drift look through [53] our bad performance,
    'Twere better not assay'd; therefore this project
    Should have a back or second, that might hold
    If this should blast in proof.[54] Soft! let me see.
    We'll make a solemn wager on your cunnings,—
    I ha't!
    When in your motion you are hot and dry—
    As make your bouts more violent to that end—

[40] instigate.   [41] careless.
[42] It is dreadful to hear how completely Claudius can count on using Hamlet's best qualities against him.
[43] unblunted. The blades used for the sport of fencing were blunted.
[44] a treacherous ("of practice") thrust.   [45] ointment.   [46] quack.
[47] poultice.   [48] herbs.   [49] power.
[50] scratch.   [51] be suitable.   [52] plans.   [53] expose itself through.
[54] burst in the test.

And that he calls for drink, I'll have prepar'd him   160
A chalice for the nonce,[55] whereon but sipping,
If he by chance escape your venom'd stuck,[56]
Our purpose may hold there.
Enter Queen.

                                     How, sweet queen!

QUEEN.   One woe doth tread upon another's heel,
So fast they follow. Your sister's drown'd, Laertes.

LAER.   Drown'd! O, where?

QUEEN.   There is a willow grows aslant a brook,[57]
That shows his hoar leaves in the glassy stream.
There with fantastic garlands did she come
Of crow-flowers, nettles, daisies, and long purples   170
That liberal [58] shepherds give a grosser name,[59]
But our cold [60] maids do dead men's fingers call them;
There, on the pendent boughs her coronet weeds
Clamb'ring to hang, an envious [61] sliver broke,
When down her weedy trophies and herself
Fell in the weeping brook. Her clothes spread wide,
And, mermaid-like, a while they bore her up;
Which time she chanted snatches of old tunes,
As one incapable [62] of her own distress,
Or like a creature native and indued [63]   180
Unto that element. But long it could not be

---

[55] purpose.   [56] thrust.

[57] This is the only passage in the entire play written in a manner characteristic of Shakespeare's earlier plays, where he often was willing to halt the progress of his drama for the sake of lyrical description. It is so beautifully written that one feels ill-natured in making an objection to it. Yet the fact is that Gertrude's narrative remains an embarrassment to every actress who must speak it, it is so much out of tempo with the rest of the play. The passage itself is informed with the most moving kind of delicacy and sweetness, and the Queen's words are replete with tenderness for the poor girl who knew not how to save herself when she lost hold of the branch and fell into the brook.

By tragic irony Ophelia's death may very well have been responsible for hastening the death of Mrs. Charles Dante Gabriel Rossetti. She posed "for hours long in a tub of water" in drenched Elizabethan costume for the celebrated "Ophelia" of the painter John Everett Millais (Frances Winwar, *Poor Splendid Wings*, 1933, p. 74). Her health was probably permanently undermined by the experience.

[58] licentious.

[59] Malone: "One of the grosser names Gertrude had a particular reason to avoid,—*the rampant widow*."

[60] chaste.   [61] malicious.   [62] insensible.

[63] endowed with the properties of.

> Till that her garments, heavy with their drink,
> Pull'd the poor wretch from her melodious lay
> To muddy death.

LAER.   Alas, then, is she drown'd?

QUEEN. Drown'd, drown'd.

LAER. (*Weeping.*) Too much of water hast thou, poor Ophelia,
> And therefore I forbid my tears. But yet
> It is our trick. Nature her custom holds,
> Let shame say what it will; when these are gone,
> The woman will be out. Adieu, my lord;   190
> I have a speech of fire that fain would blaze,
> But that this folly douts [64] it.   *Exit.*

KING.   Let's follow, Gertrude.
> How much I had to do to calm his rage!
> Now fear I this will give it start again,
> Therefore let's follow.   *Exeunt.*

ACT FIFTH

SCENE I

> *A churchyard. (The next day.)*
> *Enter two Clowns with spades and pickaxes.*[1]

1. CLO.[2] Is she to be buried in Christian burial that wilfully seeks
    her own salvation? [3]

2. CLO. I tell thee she is, and therefore make her grave straight.[4]
    The crowner [5] hath sat on her,[6] and finds it Christian burial.

1. CLO. How can that be, unless she drown'd herself in her own
    defence? [7]

2. CLO. Why, 'tis found so.

---

[64] puts out ("do out").   [1] See p. 238.   [2] (the Sexton).

[3] We hear from these two clowns the same kind of illiterate and pretentious argument that still can be heard any day in London outside Hyde Park or in New York at Union Square. This pair, in common with all of Shakespeare's stupid clowns (as distinguished from the brilliant ones like Feste, Touchstone, and the Fool in *Lear*), frightfully confuse language. The Sexton is shocked that anyone who wilfully sought her "own salvation" (he means "damnation") should be allowed Christian burial (which is denied to suicides).

[4] straightway.

[5] coroner. The second clown is a young laborer, acting as the Sexton's helper.

[6] on her case.

[7] The clown irrelevantly brings up the fact that one may kill in self-defence.

1. CLO. It *must* be *"se offendendo,"* [8] it cannot be else. For here
         lies the point: if I drown myself wittingly, it argues an act, and
         an act hath three branches; it is, to act, to do, and to perform;[9]
         argal,[10] she drown'd herself wittingly.

2. CLO. Nay, but hear you, goodman delver,—

1. CLO. (*Wishing not to be interrupted.*)   Give me leave. (*He begins
         to dramatize the argument.*) Here lies the water; good. Here
         stands the man; good. If the man go to this water and drown him-
         self, it is, will he, nill [11] he, he goes,—mark you that? But if the
         water come to him and drown him, he drowns not himself; argal,
         he that is not guilty of his own death shortens not his own life.

2. CLO. (*Impressed.*)   But is this law?

1. CLO. Ay, marry, is't; crowner's quest [12] law.

2. CLO. (*Voicing social protest.*)   Will you ha' the truth on't? If
         this had not been a gentlewoman, she should have been buried
         out o' Christian burial.

1. CLO. (*Nodding his head in agreement.*)   Why, there thou say'st;
         and the more pity that great folk should have countenance [13]
         in this world to drown or hang themselves, more than their
         even [14] Christian. Come, my spade. There is no ancient gentle-
         men but gardeners, ditchers, and grave-makers; they hold up
         Adam's profession.

2. CLO. (*Surprised.*)   Was he a *gentleman?*

1. CLO. (*Impressively.*)   He was the first that ever bore arms.

2. CLO. Why, he had none.

1. CLO. What, art a heathen? How dost thou understand the Scrip-
         ture? The Scripture says Adam digg'd; could he dig without
         arms? I'll put another question to thee. If thou answerest me
         not to the purpose, confess thyself [15]—

2. CLO. (*Protesting.*)   Go to.

1. CLO. What is he that builds stronger than either the mason, the
         shipwright, or the carpenter?

2. CLO. The gallows-maker; for that frame outlives a thousand
         tenants.

1. CLO. I like thy wit well, in good faith. The gallows does well;
         but how does it well? It does well to those that do ill. Now,
         thou dost ill to say the gallows is built stronger than the church,

---

[8] He means "se defendendo," i.e., "self-defence."
[9] He *does* sound like Polonius!
[10] for "ergo," a term which in logic means "hence."   [11] will he not.
[12] inquest.   [13] authority.   [14] fellow-.
[15] "Confess thyself and be hanged"—a proverbial expression.

argal, the gallows may do well to thee. To't again, come.

2. CLO. (*Scratching his head.*)   "Who builds stronger than a mason, a shipwright, or a carpenter?"

1. CLO.   Ay, tell me that, and unyoke.[16]

2. CLO. (*Eyes alight.*)   Marry, *now* I can tell.

1. CLO.   To't.

2. CLO. (*He has lost it.*)   Mass, I cannot tell.

    Enter Hamlet and Horatio, afar off.

1. CLO.   Cudgel thy brains no more about it, for your dull ass will not mend his pace with beating; and, when you are ask'd this question next, say "a grave-maker"; the houses that *he* makes lasts till doomsday. Go, get thee to Yaughan; [17] fetch me a stoup [18] of liquor.

                                  Exit 2. Clown.

    He digs, and sings.

        "In youth, when I did love, did love,[19]

          Methought it was very sweet,

       To contract, O, the time for-a my behove,

         O, methought, there was nothing meet."

HAM. (*Shuddering.*)   Has this fellow no feeling of his business, that he sings at grave-making? [20]

HOR. (*With quiet reproof.*)   Custom hath made it in him a property [21] of easiness.

HAM. (*Apologetically.*)   'Tis e'en so. The hand of little employment *hath* the daintier sense.

1. CLO. (*Sings.*)

        "But age, with his stealing steps,

          Hath claw'd me in his clutch,

[16] unharness (your wit).

[17] It has been conjectured that Yaughan was a well-known tavern-keeper in London near the Globe Theatre, and this seems more than likely. In his plays, no matter what their locale, Shakespeare made little pretense of being outside England of his own day. Such a reference familiar to every member of the audience would only make the play more vividly present to them.

[18] cup.

[19] On the Elizabethan stage the representation of the grave was peculiarly easy to manage. The stage itself was erected at about the level of a man's chest. With the trap door open on stage, the Sexton, jumping into it to continue his digging, was actually standing on *terra firma,* and his shoulders and head could be clearly seen above the floor of the stage. He sings a bungled version of a silly old song, printed in 1557 in Tottel's *Miscellany* as "The Aged Lover Renounceth Love."

[20] The irritability of the remark shows that Hamlet is feeling edgy.

[21] quality.

And hath shipped me intil [22] the land,
As if I had never been such."

Throws up a skull.

HAM. (*His own begins to ache at the sight.*) That skull had a
tongue in it, and could sing once. How the knave jowls [23] it to
the ground, as if it were Cain's jaw-bone,[24] that did the first
murder! It might be the pate of a politician,[25] which this ass
now o'erreaches; [26] one that would circumvent God, might it
not?

HOR.   It might, my lord.

HAM.   Or of a courtier, which could say, "Good morrow, sweet   90
lord! How dost thou, good lord?" This might be my lord such-
a-one, that prais'd my lord such-a-one's horse, when he meant
to beg it; might it not?

HOR.   Ay, my lord.

HAM.   Why, e'en so; and now my Lady Worm's; chapless,[27] and
knock'd about the mazzard [28] with a sexton's spade. Here's fine
revolution, if we had the trick to see't. Did these bones cost no
more the breeding, but to play at loggats [29] with 'em? Mine   100
ache to think on't.

I. CLO. (*Sings.*)   "A pick-axe, and a spade, a spade
                          For and [30] a shrouding sheet;
                       O, a pit of clay for to be made
                          For such a guest is meet."

Throws up another skull.

HAM.   There's another. Why might not that be the skull of a
lawyer? Where be his quiddits [31] now, his quillets,[32] his cases,
his tenures,[33] and his tricks? Why does he suffer this rude
knave now to knock him about the sconce [34] with a dirty   110
shovel, and will not tell him of his action of battery? Hum!
This fellow might be in's time a great buyer of land, with his
statutes, his recognizances, his fines, his double vouchers, his
recoveries.[35] Is this the fine [36] of his fines,[37] and the recovery

---

[22] in to.   [23] dashes.
[24] Tradition had it that Cain killed Abel with the jaw-bone of an ass.
[25] plotter.   [26] circumvents.   [27] jawless.   [28] (a bowl), slang for "head."
[29] a game played with little logs.   [30] moreover.   [31] quiddities.
[32] subtleties.   [33] possessions in real estate.   [34] (a helmet), slang for "head."
[35] These are all legal terms.
[36] end. This is the beginning of a four-sided pun.   [37] legal processes.

of his recoveries, to have his fine [38] pate full of fine [39] dirt?
Will his vouchers vouch him no more of his purchases, and
double ones too, than the length and breadth of a pair of inden-
tures? [40] The very conveyances of his lands will hardly lie in   120
this box, and must the inheritor [41] himself have no more, ha?

HOR. Not a jot more, my lord.

HAM. Is not parchment made of sheep-skins?

HOR. Ay, my lord, and of calf-skins too.

HAM. They are sheep and calves that seek out assurance in that.[42]
I will speak to this fellow. Whose grave's this, sir?

1. CLO. Mine, sir.

(*Sings.*) "O, a pit of clay for to be made
            For such a guest is meet."   130

HAM. I think it be thine indeed, for thou liest in't.

1. CLO. You lie out on't, sir, and therefore it is not yours. For my
part, I do not lie in't, and yet it is mine.

HAM. Thou dost lie in't, to be in't and say 'tis thine. 'Tis for the
dead, not for the quick,[43] therefore thou liest.

1. CLO. (*Blandly.*) 'Tis a quick lie, sir; 'twill away again, from me
to you.   140

HAM. What man dost thou dig it for?

1. CLO. For no man, sir.

HAM. What *woman*, then?

1. CLO. For none, neither.

HAM. Who is to be buried in't?

1. CLO. One that *was* a woman, sir; but, rest her soul, she's dead.

HAM. How absolute the knave is! We must speak by the card,[44] or
equivocation will undo us. By the Lord, Horatio, these three   150
years I have taken note of it; the age is grown so picked [45] that
the toe of the peasant comes so near the heels of our courtier,
he galls [46] his kibe.[47] How long hast thou been a grave-maker?

1. CLO. Of all the days i' the year, I came to't that day that our
last king Hamlet o'ercame Fortinbras.

HAM. How long is that since?

1. CLO. Cannot you tell that? Every *fool* can tell that. It was the
very day that young Hamlet was born; he that was mad,[48] and   160
sent into England.

---

[38] elegant, or, possibly, clever.   [39] thin.   [40] contracts.   [41] owner.
[42] safety in legal parchments.   [43] the living.   [44] precisely.   [45] finical.
[46] rubs.   [47] chilblain.
[48] Hamlet's reputation for insanity is now common among the people.

HAM.   Ay, marry, why was he sent into England?

1. CLO.   Why, because 'a was mad. He shall recover his wits there;
or, if he do not, it's no great matter there.

HAM.   Why?

1. CLO.   'Twill not be seen in him there; there the men are as mad
as he.   170

HAM.   How came he mad?

1. CLO.   Very strangely, they say.

HAM.   How "strangely"?

1. CLO.   Faith, e'en with losing his wits.

HAM.   Upon what ground?

1. CLO.   Why, here in Denmark. I have been sexton here, man and
boy, thirty years.[49]

[49] This settles the question of Hamlet's age. If the Sexton "came to" his
job of grave-maker the day Hamlet was born, and has been at it thirty years,
Hamlet must be thirty. See p. 250. Despite the quibbles of scholars there is
no possibility of ignoring the Sexton's precise declarations. Moreover, as if
to fortify the fact that Hamlet is thirty, a little further on we are told that
Yorick, the King's jester, carried Hamlet a thousand times on his back and
that Yorick "has lain in the earth three and twenty years." We are not asked to
imagine that Yorick carried the Prince in swaddling clothes on his back, or
that when the jester's days of carrying Hamlet were over, Yorick kicked up
his heels and died. Hamlet remembers him well; indeed, remembers well the
jester's gibes, gambols, songs, and "flashes of merriment, that were wont to
set the table on a roar." If Hamlet is thirty—i.e., was seven at Yorick's death
—he was bright enough as a child to have noted that much of the jester's merry-
making!

But the scholars have generally felt that if Hamlet is a young man, thirty
is too old an age for him—an objection we do not understand, particularly
when it comes, as often it does, from greybeards. The Devrients insisted that
Hamlet must be "in his minority" to be credible (Deutscher *Bühnen und
Familien Shakespeare*, 1873, p. 9). Furnivall was convinced that he could not
be "past twenty" when the play begins, and that Shakespeare altered his conception of Hamlet's age in the later portion of the play, because thirty seemed
"the right age for him then" (*Variorum Hamlet*, I, p. 391). Minto saw him
as seventeen (*Idem*, p. 392). Marshall imagined him nearer twenty than thirty
(*Ibidem*). Kittredge believes the "thirty" a misprint or miscopying for twenty
(*Hamlet*, p. xvii). Wilson, although conceding that it would be better to think
of him as thirty, since Shakespeare says so, feels that that age does "not tally
with the impression of youth and inexperience which Hamlet gives us at
the opening of the play" (*Hamlet*, pp. 236-37). Many other scholars have felt
a discrepancy, and have laid it to Shakespeare's carelessness with small details.
It may be objected to them, however, that in this case Shakespeare is so very
specific about Hamlet's age (see text above) that he can be charged on this
subject with anything but carelessness.

Dowden, who is willing to concede that Hamlet might be as young as
twenty-five or twenty-six, but no younger, is interesting in his confutation of

HAM.   How long will a man lie i' the earth ere he rot?

1. CLO.   (*Interested, now that his professional opinion is sought.*)   I'
faith, if he be not rotten before he die—as we have many pocky   180
corses now-a-days, that will scarce hold the laying in—he will
last you some eight year or nine year. A tanner will last you
nine year.[50]

HAM.   Why he more than another?

1. CLO.   Why, sir, his hide is so tann'd with his trade that he will
keep out water a great while, and your water is a sore decayer
of your whoreson dead body. (*Lifting out a skull.*) Here's a
skull now; this skull has lain in the earth three and twenty   190
years.

HAM.   Whose was it?

1. CLO.   A whoreson mad fellow's it was. Whose do you think
it was?

HAM.   Nay, I know not.

1. CLO.   A pestilence on him for a mad rogue! 'A pour'd a flagon
of Rhenish on my head once. This same skull, sir, was Yorick's
skull, the King's jester.

HAM.   This?   200

1. CLO.   E'en that.

HAM.   Let me see. (*Takes the skull.*) Alas, poor Yorick![51] I knew

---

Hamlet's being twenty or younger: Shakespeare's notion of the dividing line
between boyhood and young adulthood for men is somewhere between twenty-
one and twenty-five. Cymbeline's two sons, "boys just ready to be men" are
twenty-three and twenty-two; Troilus, "a beardless youth," is just under
twenty-three; Henry V ascended the throne at twenty-six. In *Much Ado*
we read of hot bloods between "fourteen and five-and-thirty." In the *Sonnets*
the poet "names forty (not thirty) as the age when time has marred the face"
(*The Academy, New Series* VIII, Dec. 1875, p. 651). We should like to add
to the defense of Hamlet's being thirty and no younger (aside from the fact
that Shakespeare tells us twice that he is no younger), that at thirty a man is
still a young man, and that, on the other hand, there is no hint of precocity
in Hamlet's brilliance of intellect. The depth and power of his observation, the
majesty and solemnity of his noblest thoughts—imply a degree of maturity
impossible to a youth in his twenties.

To conclude the matter: if Shakespeare tells us Hamlet is thirty, it is
wiser to revise one's own notions than to revise Shakespeare's.

[50] We once had occasion to reflect on the modernity of this passage. We
found ourself on a train, surrounded in the coach by many undertakers who
were returning from a convention. (Undertakers, it seemed, had their conventions too.) They talked freely and loudly, and their chief topic of conversation was "Corpses I Have Known."

[51] One's heart bleeds for the actor who must manage to get over this line

him, Horatio; a fellow of infinite jest, of most excellent fancy. He hath borne me on his back a thousand times. And now how abhorred in my imagination it is! My gorge rises at it. Here hung those lips that I have kiss'd I know not how oft. Where be your gibes now, your gambols, your songs, your flashes of merriment, that were wont to set the table on a roar? Not one ²¹⁰ now, to mock your own grinning? Quite chop ⁵²-fallen? Now get you to my lady's chamber, and tell her, let her paint an inch thick, to this favour ⁵³ she must come. Make her laugh at *that*. Prithee, Horatio, tell me one thing.

HOR.   What's that, my lord?

HAM.   Dost thou think *Alexander* look'd o' this fashion i' the earth? ⁵⁴

HOR.   E'en so.   ²²⁰

HAM.   And smelt so? Pah!

                                                                    Puts down the skull.

HOR.   E'en so, my lord.

———

without provoking the mirth of some members of the audience. Although a great English novelist is perhaps not a little responsible for casting the light of the ludicrous on a perfectly respectable line, and though we yield to no one in our affection for the prose of Lawrence Sterne, we fancy that the crime merits the heaping on of a few extra shovels of coal in Purgatory—if there be coals there. Most actors resort either to mumbling or omitting the words, and we fear are to be forgiven.

⁵² mouth-.   ⁵³ a pun. "Favour" also meant "face."

⁵⁴ Hamlet's thoughts in this scene are, for the first time, truly morbid. Perhaps the site of the churchyard itself, the callousness of the sexton, the careless tossing up of skulls are cause enough for his present sombre bent. But something else may also be involved. In the next scene we shall learn that Hamlet has returned prepared at last to unmask Claudius. The day of reckoning is at hand, and the Lord alone knows what cataclysms will be involved in it. Hamlet feels that heaviness of heart we all know before our facing a long-awaited crucial event. The depression of his thoughts, moreover, is from Shakespeare's point of view artistically perfect as an appropriate prelude to the funeral of Ophelia.

Even the great Alexander, conqueror of the world, Hamlet reflects, looked and smelled no better than poor Yorick after he had lain some years in the ground. Why may not the imagination follow the adventures of noble Alexander's dust until it find it mixed with horse-dung to stop a brewer's beer-barrel? With his unfailing stability, Horatio warns his friend that to go into such matters is to waste one's ingenuity profitlessly. The riddles of whence we come and whither we go are not for a mortal's solving, and no good can result from pretending to read them. But Hamlet will indulge his mood, and traces the post-mortem career of that "imperial Caesar," touching off his speculation with a piece of impromptu verse-making.

HAM.   To what base uses we may return, Horatio! Why may not
imagination trace the noble dust of Alexander, till he find it
stopping a bung-hole?

HOR.   'T were to consider too curiously, to consider so.

HAM.   No, faith, not a jot; but to follow him thither with modesty
enough and likelihood to lead it; as thus: Alexander died, Alex-   230
ander was buried, Alexander returneth into dust, the dust is
earth, of earth we make loam, and why of that loam whereto he
was converted might they not stop a beer-barrel?

> "Imperial Cæsar, dead and turn'd to clay,
>   Might stop a hole to keep the wind away.
>   O, that that earth, which kept the world in awe,
>   Should patch a wall to expel the winter's flaw!"

But soft! but soft! Aside! Here comes the King,   240

Enter Priests, etc., in procession; King, Queen, Laertes, and a Coffin,
with Lords attendant.

The Queen, the courtiers. Who is that they follow?
And with such maimed rites? This doth betoken
The corse they follow did with desperate hand
Fordo [55] it [56] own life. 'Twas of some estate. [57]
Couch we a while, and mark.

Retiring with Horatio.

LAER.   (*With choked voice.*)   What ceremony else?

HAM.   That is Laertes, a very noble youth. Mark.

LAER.   (*Insistent.*)   What ceremony else?

PRIEST.   Her obsequies have been as far enlarg'd
As we have warrantise. [58] Her death was doubtful, [59]   250
And, but that great command [60] o'ersways the order,
She should in ground unsanctified have lodg'd
Till the last trumpet; for charitable prayer,
Shards, [61] flints, and pebbles should be thrown on her
Yet here she is allow'd her virgin rites, [62]
Her maiden strewments, and the bringing home [63]
Of bell and burial.

LAER.   Must there no more be done?

PRIEST.   No more be done.
We should profane the service of the dead

---

[55] destroy.   [56] its.   [57] rank.   [58] authority.
[59] It was not clear whether her death was accidental or suicidal.
[60] (the King and Queen's).   [61] potsherds.
[62] The First Folio reads "rites," the Quartos "crants" (i.e., "garland").
[63] (to the grave).

To sing such requiem and such rest to her   260
As to peace-parted [64] souls.

LAER. (*Weeping.*)   Lay her i' the earth,
And from her fair and unpolluted flesh
May violets spring! I tell thee, churlish priest,
A minist'ring angel shall my sister be,
When thou liest howling.

HAM. (*Overwhelmed.*)   What, the fair Ophelia! [65]

QUEEN.   Sweets to the sweet; farewell!

> *Scattering flowers.*

I hop'd thou shouldst have been my Hamlet's wife.
I thought thy bride-bed to have deck'd, sweet maid,
And not to have strew'd thy grave.[66]

LAER. (*With violent denunciation.*)   O, treble woe
Fall ten times treble on that cursed head   270
Whose wicked deed thy most ingenious sense [67]
Depriv'd thee of! Hold off the earth a while,
Till I have caught her once more in mine arms.

> *Leaps in the grave.*

Now pile your dust upon the quick [68] and dead,
Till of this flat a mountain you have made
To o'ertop old Pelion,[69] or the skyish head
Of blue Olympus.

HAM. (*Advancing.*)   What is he whose grief
Bears such an emphasis, whose phrase of sorrow
Conjures the wand'ring stars [70] and makes them stand

---

[64] -departed.

[65] Wilson considers the exclamation a proof of Hamlet's indifference to Ophelia, because the word "fair" is "remote, almost callous;" Hamlet, Wilson feels, "could hardly have said less" if it were the burial of a "pretty daughter of his washerwoman" (*What Happens in Hamlet*, p. 269). Yet, in his preceding speech, Laertes, speaking from the depths of affection, uses exactly the same word! See pp. 212–213.

[66] When Ophelia was alive and in trouble, Gertrude preferred not to see her. Now that the girl is beyond mortal help, the Queen can luxuriate in tender words over her corpse. Her "I hoped thou shouldst have been my Hamlet's wife" is a knife in Laertes.

[67] keen mind.   [68] live.

[69] The Giants of antique lore piled Mt. Ossa on high Mt. Pelion in an effort to scale Olympus, and Laertes seems rhetorically to be attempting the same. It is not that his sincerity is in question; but human experience is that it is rarely those who feel the deepest who make such scenes at a funeral. His words sting Hamlet into revealing his presence.

[70] planets.

Like wonder-wounded hearers? This is I,   280
  Hamlet, the Dane!   *Leaps into the grave.*
LAER. (*Seizing him by the throat.*)   The devil take thy soul!
                                                 Grappling with him.
HAM.   Thou pray'st not well.[71]
  I prithee, take thy fingers from my throat,
  For, though I am not splenitive [72] and rash,
  Yet have I something in me dangerous,
  Which let thy wiseness fear. Away thy hand!
KING.   Pluck them asunder.
QUEEN.   Hamlet, Hamlet!
[ALL.   Gentlemen,—

---

[71] What prompts Hamlet to do this? Madariaga, who apparently detests Hamlet, interprets the action as owing to Hamlet's unwillingness "to be out-done by Laertes at anything," (*On Hamlet*, p. 24) and Hamlet's *I loved Ophelia* a little further on as "words which were certainly not meant to convey to anyone in his senses that Hamlet loved Ophelia; but merely that he was ready to outdo Laertes in anything" (p. 38). Wilson believes that this later remark of Hamlet's is an expression not of love but of "self-reproach that love is absent; he is careful to say, 'I *loved* Ophelia.'" (*What Happens in Hamlet*, p. 270).

That Hamlet uses the past tense is not really noteworthy. Hamlet has been accused by Laertes of being responsible by his "wicked deed" for driving her out of her mind; his thought here, in answer to Laertes, is that when she died it was not because she had lost his love—that he still loved her. Moreover, when he says he *loved* her he does not necessarily imply that he has ceased to do so. At this moment Hamlet is much too agitated to be "careful" about anything he says. He explains to Horatio in the next scene that Laertes's parade of grief put him "into a towering passion" at Ophelia's grave. But the impulse comes from a deeper source than anger or annoyance. It was but a few minutes ago that he learned of Ophelia's death; this terrible blow is made the fiercer by his realizing that her death may have been voluntary; a moment later Laertes is charging her death to him. Had Hamlet Laertes's facility in weeping or ability publicly to expose his misery in a flow of rhetoric, he too might break out into tears or rant. But he is not made of such stuff. Stunned at learning of Ophelia's end, Hamlet cannot bear the theatricality of her brother's leaping into the grave and "conjuring the wandering stars" with extravagant words. The violence of his leaping into the grave after Laertes—Hamlet is ever moved to *do*—is *his* characteristic mode of expressing his inner grief, which he is too proud to put more emotionally into words than those which he presently utters, and which are themselves a full explanation of the act:

> "I loved Ophelia. Forty thousand brothers
>   Could not, with all their quantity of love,
>   Make up my sum."

Anyone who cannot hear the restrained voice of his deep sorrow in the cadences of that speech is unfamiliar with the workings of the proud heart.

[72] excitable.

HOR.]   Good my lord, be quiet.

The Attendants part them, and they come out of the grave.

HAM.   Why, I will fight with him upon this theme

    Until my eyelids will no longer wag.   290

QUEEN. (*Thinking him insane.*) O my son, what theme?

HAM.   I lov'd Ophelia. Forty thousand brothers

    Could not, with all their quantity of love,

    Make up my sum. What wilt *thou* do for her?

KING.   O, he is mad, Laertes.

QUEEN.   For love of God, forbear him.

HAM.   ['Swounds,] show me what thou'lt do.

    Woo't [73] weep? Woo't fight? [Woo't fast?] Woo't tear thyself?

    Woo't drink up eisel? [74] Eat a crocodile?

    I'll do't. Dost thou come here to *whine*?   300

    To outface me with leaping in her grave?

    Be buried quick with her, and so will I;

    And, if thou prate of mountains, let them throw

    Millions of acres on us, till our ground,

    Singeing his pate against the burning zone,

    Make Ossa like a wart! [75] Nay, an thou'lt *mouth*,

    I'll rant as well as thou.

[QUEEN.] (*Who only wants everyone to be agreeable, sentimentally.*)

                    This is mere madness,

    And thus a while the fit will work on him.

    Anon, as patient as the female dove,

    When that her golden couplets are disclos'd,   310

    His silence will sit drooping.

HAM.   Hear you, sir,

    What is the reason that you use me thus? [76]

---

[73] wilt thou.   [74] vinegar.

[75] If bombast is in order, Hamlet can give Laertes a run for his money.

[76] Rash Hamlet! He has killed the man's father, but because he has always liked Laertes and never nourished an unkind thought of him, he can be outraged at Laertes's hatred for him. Wilson surely goes too far when he says that we must "love" Hamlet "for his attitude towards Laertes" (*What Happens in Hamlet*, p. 274). Love Hamlet we must, but *in spite of*, not because of, the flagrant recklessness which makes him forget that Laertes now has no more reason to love him than he himself has to love Claudius. Later in the day, however, he will have thought over this unreasonableness, and will confess to Horatio:

> "I am very sorry, good Horatio,
> That to Laertes I forgot myself;
> For, by the image of my cause, I see
> The portraiture of his. I'll court his favors."

I lov'd you ever. But it is no matter.
Let Hercules himself do what he may,
The cat will mew and dog will have his day.   *Exit.*
KING.   I pray you, good Horatio, wait upon him.

Exit Horatio.

(*To Laertes.*) Strengthen your patience in our last night's speech;
We'll put the matter to the present push.[77]
Good Gertrude, set some watch over your son.
This grave shall have a *living* [78] monument.   320
An hour of quiet shortly shall we see;
Till then, in patience our proceeding be.

Exeunt.

SCENE II

A hall in the castle. (Later the same day.)
Enter Hamlet [1] *and Horatio.*

For that we can love him—that all too uncommon personal dignity and integrity which move him, once he knows he has been at fault, to be the first
to admit it.

[77] instant test.

[78] The King means a *double entente;* for Gertrude and the Court: "an
enduring monument"; for Laertes: "the living Hamlet shall be sacrificed as an
atonement for Ophelia's death."

[1] It is, of course, the same Hamlet we have known throughout the play
who has come back to Denmark. We take the trouble to say this only because
the newest school of *Hamlet*-criticism—the most pretentious and annoying on
record—stresses the conviction that he returns a changed man. This alteration
in him is "by general consent" held to be revealed in the speech he makes to
Horatio in this final scene, "Not a whit; we defy augury," etc. (lines 230–35),
and this general consent takes these words to be "the crux of the play"
(S. F. Johnson in *Shakespeare Quarterly* III, 1952, p. 192).

It is peculiarly vexing to be compelled to confute a point of view based
on the *naïf* belief that in a great tragedy (one of the very longest, in this
case, extant) the crux could occur some fifteen minutes before the final curtain! Such a notion can be held only in complete indifference to or ignorance
of the fundamentals of dramatic structure. In a highly theatrical melodrama it
is conceivable that what is most crucial occur just before the conclusion of the
play; the scope of tragedy makes such a sensational arrangement impossible.
Moreover, this speech (as the reader will note when he comes to it) has no
cardinal importance to the plot, is not directly related to any action of Hamlet's,
but is rather the expression of his mood at the moment. Nevertheless, this
school of critics finds the speech as proof that Hamlet at the end is entirely
changed as a result of "the events associated with his abortive voyage to England" (p. 199). Before leaving Denmark, to put their views briefly, Hamlet
was enmeshed in his merely earthly reasoning; when he comes back it is with
the realization that "reason is not enough"; he is now prepared to act as the
instrument of Providence (*Ibidem*).

HAM. So much for this, sir; *(taking back a paper from Horatio)* now
let me see the other.[2]
 You do remember all the circumstance?
HOR. Remember it, my lord!
HAM. Sir, in my heart there was a kind of fighting,
That would not let me sleep. Methought I lay

Hardin Craig ("rightly," it has been pronounced) (p. 195) has analyzed
the tragedy in the light of the morality plays (*Shakespeare Quarterly*, I, 1950,
pp. 64–72); he thinks the struggle in *Hamlet* is not the classic one between
reason and passion, but between "passion and a self-mastery which leads to
indifference to the blows of fortune" (*An Interpretation of Shakespeare*, 1948,
p. 182). Theodore Spencer finds Hamlet at the end no longer passion's slave
but a man resigned, a man at last "aware of the world's order" (*Shakespeare
and the Nature of Man*, 1945, p. 108). According to John Paterson, Hamlet
concludes as no longer a "hysterial personality" because he has at last won
"to a clear apprehension of the truth" (*Shakespeare Quarterly*, II, 1951, p. 54).
Quoting the *fall of a sparrow* passage, Bertram Joseph declares that Hamlet
achieves at last "a glimpse of himself as a fragment in a mighty pattern"
(*Conscience and the King*, 1953, p. 140). All of this is, to be sure, very lofty,
but none of it speaks the language of drama.

The point of view has been most explicitly stated, perhaps, by Mr. S. F.
Johnson and Roy Walker. The former says: Hamlet's experiences at sea
"are symbolic of the power of fate . . . (Rubbish! They are symbolic of
nothing. They are themselves! It was Hamlet, not Fate, who overcame the
pirates and persuaded them to do his bidding—as far as a merely terrestrial
intelligence can see!) Before he left Denmark . . . all occasions informed
against him; while at sea all occasions informed in his favor"; Hamlet ends
by becoming the ready "instrument of an inscrutable Providence to whom
man is of more value than many sparrows"; his is now "a willing compliance
with the workings of heaven" (*op. cit.*, pp. 199–206). Walker puts it rather
more mystically: Hamlet eventually comes to believe "that he was an instrument of Providence, heaven's scourge and minister, and that what was required of him was acceptance and obedience to his own nature in all its complexities and contradictions" (*The Time Is Out of Joint*, 1948, p. 143).

If this be drama and upon *Hamlet* proved, then Shakespeare never writ!
It is the same Hamlet we have always known who returns to Denmark, but
he comes back in a very different situation from the one in which he left
the country. Then he was a man who had ruined his cause by recklessness, an
exile hurried off because of his folly from the one place where it was his wish
and business to be. Now he has returned with a new lease on vengeance.
Fate directed the pirate ship across his path, and he was quick to seize the
opportunity, and by his own initiative bent circumstance his way. He has in
his possession certain documents which may well clear his road of all its
former obstacles to his goal. Has he learned by bitter experience the necessity
of curbing that rashness which brought him once to the verge of catastrophe,
now that he has a second chance?

[2] This is the reading of the First Folio; the Second Quarto has:
 "now shall you see the other."

For our interpretation, which follows, the only difference between the two readings would be a question of whether Hamlet himself first glances at the paper or immediately hands it to Horatio. There has been almost no comment on this line, and I suppose Kittredge's explanation of it is the accepted one: *So much for this* refers to "certain early incidents of the voyage" which Hamlet has been relating to Horatio; *the other* refers to "the rest of the story" (*Hamlet*, p. 283). But this seems to us to be an undue straining of the meaning of very simple words. Kittredge, like most editors, prefers the Quarto reading, since it alone would fit his understanding of the line. We cannot imagine what the Folio reading means to others. M. Gide, too conscientious a reader of the commentators, we fear, contrives to straddle both Folio and Quarto readings, and imparts the accepted vagueness of meaning to his rendition:

> *Suffit pour cette affaire, Monsieur;*
> *à présent nous allons étudier l'autre.* (*Hamlet*, 1945, p. 255)

Our own understanding of the line is based upon our usual premise that in a play, of two possible interpretations, the one more concretely allied to meaningful action is the better. Hamlet has been showing his friend some of the papers involved. He takes one back and hands him another. Thus, by a vivid appeal to our visual sense Shakespeare at once projects the telling idea that Hamlet has in his possession something important, even before we know what it is he has.

His account is thrilling. Aboard ship he was restless at night and could not sleep. Impulsively he got up, groped his way through the darkness to his schoolfellows' packet, carried his burden back to his cabin, unsealed the King's commission, and read Claudius's commands that the English monarch, immediately upon reading the document,

"No, not to stay the grinding of the axe,"

should cause Hamlet's head to be struck off.

We are so much excited by his graphic account that we may have overlooked a detail in his prologue to it. As he is setting the scene for the moment when it occurred to him that he ought to inspect Claudius's message to the King of England, he describes the notion as "rashly" conceived. But was it truly so? He well knew that Claudius's purposes in sending him to England, whatever they were, were not cherubic. It was, rather than rashness, good judgment that he suspect his uncle of nefarious intent.

But in the most recent of his soliloquies, as he was being rushed out of the country, Hamlet in his bitterness at himself had decided to embrace henceforth a policy of recklessness:

"O, from this time forth
My thoughts be bloody, or be nothing worth!"

Despite his long self-restraint, one unplanned sword-thrust had undone him. But his ill-considered conclusion after that act was, not to resolve to be even more patient, but, hereafter to abjure all thought of consequences when prompted to violence. His craving to exercise that energy which, since his first talk with the Ghost, he has had to keep pent up, was at last satisfied in his encounter with the pirates. Recklessness then served him well. It was rash of him to board the pirate-ship alone and take on a crew of cut-throats single-handed; and this time his rashness bore excellent fruit. In his exhilaration

Worse than the mutines [3] in the bilboes.[4] Rashly,—
And prais'd be rashness for it; let us know
Our indiscretion sometimes serves us well
When our deep plots do pall;[5] and that should teach us
There's a divinity that shapes our ends,   10
Rough-hew [6] them how we will,—

HOR.   That is most certain.

HAM.   Up from my cabin,
My sea-gown scarf'd about me, in the dark
Grop'd I to find out them; had my desire;
Finger'd their packet; and in fine withdrew
To mine own room again, making so bold,
My fears forgetting manners,[7] to unseal
Their grand commission; where I found, Horatio,—
O royal knavery!—an exact command,
Larded [8] with many several sorts of reason   20
Importing Denmark's health and England's too,
With, ho! such bugs [9] and goblins in my life,
That, on the supervise,[10] no leisure bated,[11]
No, not to stay the grinding of the axe,
My head should be struck off.

HOR.   Is't possible?

---

over the success of that free play of will at sea, he now can say to Horatio:

> "And praised be rashness for it; let us know
> Our indiscretion sometimes serves us well."

If, in the midst of the speed of his opening narrative here, we could pause to reflect upon the import of what he is saying, we should have good cause to be worried on his account. He has already nearly lost his life because of rashness and ruined his plan of vengeance. And at this very moment, while he is narrating his adventures to his friend and praising rashness just because for once its consequences were not tragic, his life is in double jeopardy! We are the more alarmed that as he pays tribute to that

> "divinity that shapes our ends"

he admits that he has already bungled (rough-hewn) his cause ("end") through that same rashness which he is busy praising. (Florio's little dictionary of 1598 thus defines the Italian *abbozzare:* "to rough hew any first draught, to bungle ill-favouredly" [*Variorum Shakespeare* I, p. 414].)

[3] mutineers.   [4] stocks.   [5] fail.
[6] bungle. See last sentences in Note 2 above.
[7] This is an endearing touch. Although he was saving his life in opening the letter, Hamlet instinctively feels a little ashamed for the breach of decency involved in peering into other people's correspondence.
[8] decorated.   [9] bugbears.   [10] perusal.   [11] deducted.

HAM.   Here's the commission; read it at more leisure.
    But wilt thou hear me how I did proceed?

HOR.   I beseech you.

HAM.   Being thus be-netted round with villainies,—
    Ere I could make a prologue to my brains,   30
    They had begun the play,—I sat me down,
    Devis'd a new commission, wrote it fair.[12]
    I once did hold it, as our statists do,
    A baseness to write fair,[13] and labour'd much
    How to forget that learning; but, sir, now
    It did me yeoman's service. Wilt thou know
    The effect of what I wrote?

HOR.   Ay, good my lord.

HAM. (*Satirically.*)   An earnest conjuration from the King,
    As England was his faithful tributary,
    As love between them as the palm should flourish,
    As Peace should still her wheaten garland wear   40
    And stand a comma [14] 'tween their amities,
    And many such-like *as*-es of great charge,
    That, on the view and know of these contents,
    Without debatement further, more or less,
    He should the bearers put to sudden death,
    Not shriving time allow'd.

HOR.   How was this seal'd?

HAM.   Why, even in that was Heaven ordinant.
    I had my father's signet in my purse,
    Which was the model [15] of that Danish seal;   50
    Folded the writ up in form of the other,
    Subscrib'd it, gave't the impression,[16] plac'd it safely,
    The changeling never known. Now, the next day
    Was our sea-fight; and what to this was sequent
    Thou know'st already.

HOR. (*Grimly.*)   So Guildenstern and Rosencrantz go to't.

HAM. (*Refusing to feel any guilt.*)   Why, man, they did make *love* to
       this employment;
    They are not near my conscience.[17] Their defeat [18]

---

[12] legible.

[13] (it being well enough for a clerk to write "fair" but not a nobleman or prince).

[14] link.   [15] copy.   [16] (of the seal).

[17] (any more than was Polonius after Hamlet had slain him!) Hamlet's indifference to the fate of his victims, once he is convinced they have been

Doth by their own insinuation grow.
'Tis dangerous when the baser nature comes   60
Between the pass [19] and fell [20] incensed points
Of mighty opposites.[21]

HOR.   Why, what a king is this!

HAM.   Does it not, thinks't thee, stand me now upon [22]—
He that hath kill'd my king and whor'd my mother,
Popp'd in between the election and my hopes,
Thrown out his angle for my proper life,
And with such cozenge—is't not perfect conscience,[23]
To quit him with this arm? And is't not to be damn'd,
To let this canker of our nature [24] come
In further evil? [25]   70

HOR.   It must be shortly known to him from England
What is the issue of the business there.

HAM.   It will be short; the interim is mine,
And a man's life's no more than to say "One."
But I am very sorry, good Horatio,
That to Laertes I forgot myself;
For, by the image of my cause, I see
The portraiture of his.[26] I'll court his favours.
But, sure, the bravery [27] of his grief did put me
Into a tow'ring passion.

HOR.   Peace! who comes here?   80

Enter young Osric.[28]

---

treacherous to him, is another manifestation of his rashness. From this central
quality of his make-up spring his most reprehensible as well as his most
loveable traits.

[18] ruin.   [19] thrust.   [20] fierce.   [21] opponents.

[22] The King's commission, in his possession, is proof that Claudius has
attempted Hamlet's life. It will, in addition, explain to the Court the King's
behavior at *The Murder of Gonzago*. And both will lend credibility to charges
on the late King's murder. Hamlet can therefore conclude that now it is time
and "perfect conscience" to kill Claudius, and Horatio spurs him in that resolve
by reminding him that he has not much time. Soon Claudius is bound to hear
from England.

[23] I.e., would it now clearly be not tainting my soul to avenge my father?
[24] this cancer of humanity.   [25] proceed to further mischief.

[26] Hamlet realizes now that he has been unfair to Laertes, and understands
the similarity of their positions as men whose fathers have been secretly
murdered.

[27] bravado.

[28] At this point broad comedy is for the last time introduced again with
the appearance of young Osric. It is safe to conclude from the great frequency

OSR. Your lordship is right welcome back to Denmark.

HAM. I humbly thank you, sir.—Dost know this water-fly?

HOR. No, my good lord.

HAM. (*He intends Osric to hear him. Osric is incapable of being offended.*) Thy state is the more gracious, for 'tis a vice to know him. He hath much land, and fertile; let a beast be lord of beasts, and his crib shall stand at the King's mess.[29] 'Tis a chough,[30] but, as I say, spacious in the possession of dirt.   90

OSR. (*Waving his hat about, affectedly.*) Sweet lord, if your lordship were at leisure, I should impart a thing to you from his Majesty.

HAM. (*Mockingly adopting the same idiom.*) I will receive it with all diligence of spirit. (*Changing to a rough tone.*) Put your bonnet to his right use; 'tis for the *head.*[31]

OSR. (*Insisting on being deferential.*) I thank your lordship, 'tis *very* hot.

HAM. No, believe me, 'tis very cold; the wind is northerly.

OSR. It is indifferent cold, my lord, indeed.   100

HAM. Methinks it is very sultry and hot for *my* complexion.

OSR. Exceedingly, my lord; it is very sultry,—as 'twere,—I cannot tell how. But, my lord, his Majesty bade me signify to you that he has laid a great wager on your head. Sir, this is the matter,—

---

with which Shakespeare adverts to the subject, that the dramatist had little patience with the artificiality in speech and dress which were epidemic in his day. The exchange between Hamlet and Osric is particularly droll, and is equalled in its satire only by the best pages in which Molière mocks hilariously the pretentiousness of the false elegance of Louis XIV's days. Osric, who can say nothing except with inflated affectation, is completely unaware of Hamlet's ridicule because the Prince deliberately apes his manner. Osric, indeed, seems to enjoy the conversation very much, as though he feels he is holding discourse with someone who really appreciates grandiloquence.

But Osric is something more than an affected fop. He is a young opportunist, and like most opportunists impervious to insult. Worse than that, he is quite ready to lend himself to the base designs of the King. Since it will be he who will offer the weapons to Hamlet and Laertes, he must be commissioned to see to it that one particular sword is reserved for the latter's use only. Hamlet has him well gauged as annoying as a gnat ("water-fly"), a creature with wide holdings in land, and therefore dear to Claudius's heart. It is a privilege, says Hamlet, not to know Osric.

From the young courtier's first words we can almost hear the effeminate artificiality of his voice.

[29] table.   [30] jackdaw—a silly bird.

[31] Osric knows that good manners dictate his removing his hat in the

HAM. I beseech you, remember—
Hamlet moves him to put on his hat.

OSR. (*Protesting.*) Nay, in good faith; for mine *ease*, in good faith. [Sir, here is newly come to court Laertes, believe me an absolute gentleman, full of most excellent differences,[32] of very soft society and great showing; indeed, to speak feelingly of him, he is the card or calendar of gentry, for you shall find in him the continent [33] of what part a gentleman would see.

HAM. (*Outdoing Osric's hyperbolic style.*) Sir, his definement suffers no perdition in you; though, I know, to divide him inventorially would dizzy the arithmetic of memory, and yet but yaw [34] neither, in respect of [35] his quick sail. But, in the verity of extolment, I take him to be a soul of great article; and his infusion of such dearth and rareness, as, to make true diction of him, his semblable [36] is his mirror; and who else would trace him, his umbrage,[37] nothing more.

OSR. (*With admiration for this elegance.*) Your lordship speaks most infallibly of him.

HAM. (*Maintaining the inflated style.*) The concernancy,[38] sir? Why do we wrap the gentleman in our more rawer breath?

OSR. (*Lost at last.*) Sir?

HOR. (*Amused.*) Is't not possible to understand in another tongue? [39] You will do't, really.

HAM. What imports the nomination of this gentleman?

OSR. (*Forced to be direct.*) Of Laertes?

HOR. His purse is empty already. All's golden words are spent.

HAM. (*Grimly.*) Of him, sir.

OSR. (*Beginning in the high style anew.*) I know you are not ignorant—

HAM. (*Who has had enough of this.*) I would you did, sir; yet, in faith, if you did, it would not much approve [40] me. Well, sir?]

OSR. You are not ignorant of what excellence Laertes is—

[HAM. I dare not confess that, lest I should compare with him in excellence; but to know a man well were to know himself.

---

presence of his social superior. But Hamlet wants no subservience from a creature he despises.
   [32] distinctive excellences.   [33] sum.   [34] be steering wildly.
   [35] as regards.   [36] only true resemblance.   [37] shadow.
   [38] How does this concern us?   [39] Can't we talk English?
   [40] "it would not be much to my credit"—Clarendon.

osr. I mean, sir, for his weapon; but in the imputation [41] laid on him by them, in his meed [42] he's unfellowed.]   150

ham. What's his weapon?

osr. Rapier and dagger.

ham. That's *two* of his weapons; but well.

osr. (*Nothing can change this magpie.*) The King, sir, has wag'd with him six Barbary horses, against the which he has impon'd, as I take it, six French rapiers and poniards, with their assigns, as girdle, hanger, or so. Three of the carriages, in faith, are very dear to fancy, very responsive to the hilts,[43] most delicate carriages, and of very liberal conceit.[44]   160

ham. What call you the carriages?

[hor. I knew you must [45] be edified by the margent [46] ere you had done.]

osr. The carriages, sir, are the hangers.[47]

ham. The phrase would be more germane to the matter, if we could carry *cannon* by our sides; I would it might be hangers till then. But, on: six Barbary horses against six French swords, their assigns, and three liberal-conceited carriages; that's the French bet against the Danish. Why is this "impon'd," as you call it?   170

osr. The King, sir, hath laid that in a dozen passes between you and him, he shall not exceed you three hits; he hath laid on twelve for nine; and that would come to immediate trial, if your lordship would vouchsafe the answer.

ham. How if I answer no?

osr. I mean, my lord, the opposition of your person in trial.

ham. Sir, I will walk here in the hall; if it please his Majesty, 'tis the breathing time [48] of day with me. Let the foils be brought, the gentleman willing, and the King hold his purpose, I will win for him if I can; [49] if not, I'll gain nothing but my shame and the odd [50] hits.   180

---

[41] reputation.   [42] merit.   [43] matching in design.   [44] imagination.
[45] you'd have to.   [46] marginal note (i.e., footnote).
[47] straps for the carrying of a sword.   [48] (when I take my exercise).
[49] See p. 263.
[50] Because no previous commentator interprets Hamlet's purposes in this scene as we interpret them, it has never been suggested before that Hamlet is making a very important pun here on the word *odd*. To Osric he is saying, of course, that if he should lose the match he will be the gainer in nothing but disgrace and the extra hits. But to Horatio, to himself, and to us he is

osr.   Shall I re-deliver you e'en so?

ham.   (*Ironically*).   To this effect, sir; after what flourish your nature will.

osr.   I commend my duty to your lordship.

ham.   *Yours, yours!* (*Exit Osric.*) He does well to commend it   190
himself; there are no tongues else for 's turn.

hor.   This lapwing runs away with the shell on his head.[51]

ham.   He did comply with [52] his dug [53] before he suck'd it. Thus
has he, and many more of the same bevy that I know the drossy
age dotes on, only got the tune of the time and outward habit
of encounter; a kind of yesty [54] collection, which carries them
through and through the most fond [55] and winnowed opinions;   200
and do but blow them to their trials, the bubbles are out.
[*Enter a Lord.*

lord.   My lord, his Majesty commended him to you by young
Osric, who brings back to him, that you attend him in the
hall. He sends to know if your pleasure hold to play with
Laertes, or that you will take longer time.

ham.   I am constant to my purposes; they follow the King's pleas-

---

using the word *odd* in the not unfamiliar sense of "not taken into account," as:

> "There are yet missing of your company
> Some few odd lads that you remember not."
> —*The Tempest*, V, i, 255

and thus is saying, Even if I do lose the match, I may make some hits which
the King little counts upon—that is, *in any case* the match will be profitable
for it will serve as the occasion for his revenge against Claudius.

We suggest that Hamlet accepts the offer to fence with Laertes because it
will be an excuse for bringing the Court together, and that he intends immediately after the match is over to avenge his father's murder, to expose
Claudius as a murderer, and to justify his vengeance by producing the documents relative to his own ordered execution. He knows his time is short—and,
in truth, it turns out to be shorter than he could possibly have anticipated, for
before the scene is over the English Ambassador will arrive with the tidings
that Rosencrantz and Guildenstern have been killed. He intends, then, to act
this very hour. He is now in a position to know it "perfect conscience" to
do the deed; he is assured that there is no longer a question of tainting his
mind, for he *has* proof. And this is what he darkly signifies when he speaks
of the "odd hits" he counts upon winning, no matter how he fares in the
fencing-match. Having heard his talk about the King's commission and having
seen the document in his hands, we are prepared to have him use it.

[51] This youngster is pretty precocious.   [52] pay compliments to.
[53] his mother's teat.   [54] frothy.   [55] foolish.

ure. If his fitness speaks, mine is ready, now or whensoever, 210
provided I be so able as now.[56]

LORD. The King and Queen and all are coming down.

HAM. In happy time.

LORD. The Queen desires you to use some gentle entertainment to
Laertes before you fall to play.

HAM. She well instructs me.]   *Exit Lord.*

HOR. You will lose this wager, my lord.[57]

HAM. I do not think so; since he went into France, I have been in
continual practice.[58] I shall win at the odds.[59] (*Suddenly* 220
depressed.) But thou wouldst not think how ill all's here about
my heart.[60] But it is no matter.

[56] It is incomprehensible that the threat in this can have been thus far
completely overlooked by commentaries. If Hamlet does not have a double
meaning in what he says here, what was Shakespeare's reason for penning the
lines? Beneath the surface of his words, Hamlet's meaning is, for *our* ears
and his private satisfaction: My purposes of avenging my father have not
changed in the least; my purposes of avenging him pursue the King through
the paths his pleasure took him (his adultery with Gertrude and his murder
of Hamlet's father for the sake of possessing her and the crown); I am ready
for those purposes right now, and I shall be ready for them at any other time
the King prefers—provided that the time he chooses will find me as well-
equipped to wreak my just revenge as I am at this minute. This is Hamlet's
usual way of speaking—one meaning for the person addressed, another for
himself, Horatio, and us.

As if to underline his expectations that the fencing-match will provide the
witnesses he needs for taking the kind of vengeance he requires, the nobleman informs him that

"all are coming down."

"In happy time," says Hamlet. Everything is arranging itself perfectly for his
purposes.

[57] Horatio thinks Hamlet's ability with the foils not equal to Laertes'.

[58] This would imply that Hamlet has done other things besides moping—
or as some would have it, cutting insane capers—since his interview with the
Ghost!

[59] This is, we think, a pun of triple meaning:

¶ 1. I shall win because the odds (twelve hits required of Laertes and only
nine of Hamlet) are in my favor.

¶ 2. I shall win the odd hits that the King is not counting upon (the same
meaning as in his speech to Osric).

¶ 3. I shall win at all odds (i.e., in any case) because I shall revenge myself
upon Claudius within this hour.

[60] Hamlet is conscious of a sense of oppression about the heart. He may feel
this, as most of us do, because he at last faces a long-awaited and all-important
trial in his undertaking. In his case, where the taking of a life will be involved

HOR. (*Alarmed.*)   Nay, good my lord,—

HAM.   It is but foolery; but it is such a kind of gain-giving,[61] as
would perhaps trouble a woman.

HOR.   If your mind dislike anything, obey it. I will forestall their
repair hither, and say you are not fit.

HAM.   Not a whit; we defy augury.[62] There's a special providence   230
in the fall of a sparrow.[63] If it be now, 'tis not to come; if it be
not to come, it will be now; if it be not now, yet it will come;
the readiness is all. Since no man has aught of what he leaves,
what is't to leave betimes? [64] [Let be.]

   *Enter King, Queen, Laertes, Osric, Lords, and other Attendants
with foils and gauntlets; a table and flagons of wine on it.*

KING.   Come, Hamlet, come, and take this hand from me.

   The King puts Laertes's hand into Hamlet's.

HAM.   Give me your pardon, sir.[65] I've done you wrong,
But pardon't, as you are a gentleman.

---

and the outcome for himself not at all predictable, it is the more comprehensible. Like most of us, he is inclined to interpret the feeling as a premonition.
And perhaps, indeed, it is a forewarning. There are more things in heaven
and earth than are dreamt of in our science, and only the earthiest of us deny
that such forebodings come occasionally to most men. Certainly, even so
level-headed a man as Horatio is, knows enough from his experience, to be
somewhat alarmed:

   "If your mind dislike anything, *obey* it."

(How often have most of us had occasion to wish we had followed that
sage counsel!) He will be glad to postpone the match for his friend. But
Hamlet will not give in to such misgivings which, with male blindness, he
describes as such "as would perhaps trouble a woman." He chooses to summon
that stoicism which most of us rely upon when an inner voice, which we
interpret as weakness, prompts us to halt in our steps. "There's a special
providence in the fall of a sparrow." Every man must be ready for all things
that may come his way. Since none of us can foretell what our futures would
be, why should we nurse the fear of an early death?

   There is, then, a premonition of death within him. Or is it only because
he anticipates dealing death to the King himself? There is no time for Horatio
to argue the matter, for the King, the Queen, and the courtiers come in.

   [61] misgiving.   [62] omens.   [63] See Matthew x: 29 and Luke xii: 6.

   [64] Since no man has aught of what he leaves behind, what is it to leave
(i.e., die) early?

   [65] It is only the rarest of men who are equal to the honorableness of these
words. Yet Samuel Johnson interprets everything Hamlet says here as false,
and wishes "Hamlet had made some other defence." Kittredge answers that
"Hamlet's particular falsehood here is inseparable from the general falsehood
involved" in his pretending to be mad (*Hamlet*, p. 293).

This presence [66] knows,
And you must needs have heard, how I am punish'd   240
With sore distraction. What I have done
That might your nature, honour, and exception
Roughly awake, I here proclaim was madness.
Was't Hamlet wrong'd Laertes? Never Hamlet! [67]
If Hamlet from himself be ta'en away,
And when he's not himself does wrong Laertes,
Then Hamlet does it not, Hamlet denies it.
Who does it, then? His madness. If't be so,
Hamlet is of the faction that is wrong'd;
His madness is poor Hamlet's enemy.   250
Sir, in this audience,
Let my disclaiming from a purpos'd evil
Free me so far in your most generous thoughts,
That I have shot mine arrow o'er the house
And hurt my brother.[68]

LAER.   I am satisfied in nature,
Whose motive, in this case, should stir me most
To my revenge; but in my terms of honour
I stand aloof, and will no reconcilement,
Till by some elder masters of known honour
I have a voice [69] and precedent of [70] peace,   260
To keep my name ungor'd. But till that time,
I do receive your offer'd love like love,
And will not wrong it.

HAM.   I embrace it freely,
And will this brother's wager frankly play.
Give us the foils. Come on.[71]

[66] royal presence.
[67] Everyone here, says Hamlet, knows I am sorely distracted. If I've done anything to offend you, I must have been mad. If it was madness to have hurt you, then you must believe it was Hamlet's madness, not Hamlet, who is the offender.

He knows that there would be no point in attempting to unwind the tangled web of the courtiers' misconceptions concerning him. Besides, he wishes to say not a word in the presence of Claudius more than what is necessary to win Laertes's forgiveness. For in a little while they all will learn the whole truth from his lips, when he flashes out his documents and takes his vengeance on Claudius. After that Laertes will surely understand what has been the nature of the "sore distraction" with which Hamlet has been "punished."

[68] See pp. 240–241.   [69] opinion.   [70] for making.
[71] See pp. 240–244 and 263.

LAER   Come, one for me.

HAM.   I'll be your foil,[72] Laertes; in mine ignorance
        Your skill shall, like a star i' the darkest night,
        Stick fiery off [73] indeed.

LAER.   You mock me, sir.

HAM.   No, by this hand.

KING.   Give them the foils, young Osric.[74] (*Deliberately distracting Ham-
        let's attention so that Osric can direct Laertes to the right
        foil.*) Cousin Hamlet,   270
        You know the wager?

HAM.   Very well, my lord.
        Your Grace hath laid the odds o' the weaker side.[75]

KING.   I do not fear it, I have seen you both;
        But since he is better'd, we have therefore odds.

LAER.   This is too heavy, let me see another. (*He chooses the foil in-
        dicated by Osric.*)

HAM.   (*Choosing carelessly.*)   This likes me well. These foils have all a
        length?   *They prepare to play.*

OSR.   Ay, my good lord.

KING.   (*Excitedly.*)   Set me the stoups of wine upon that table.
        If Hamlet give the first or second hit,
        Or quit in answer of the third exchange,   280
        Let all the battlements their ordnance fire.
        The King shall drink to Hamlet's better breath,
        And in the cup an union [76] shall he throw,
        Richer than that which four successive kings
        In Denmark's crown have worn. Give me the cups,
        And let the kettle [77] to the trumpets speak,
        The trumpet to the cannoneer without,
        The cannons to the heavens, the heaven to earth,
        "Now the King drinks to Hamlet." Come, begin;
        And you, the judges, bear a wary eye.   290

HAM.   Come on, sir.

LAER.   Come, my lord.   *They play.*

HAM.   One.

LAER.   No.

HAM.   Judgement.

---

[72] setting for a gem (a pun).   [73] stand out brilliantly.
[74] It is impossible that Osric is not privy to the King's treachery against
Hamlet.
[75] See pp. 241–242.   [76] a fine pearl.   [77] kettledrum.

OSR.   A hit, a very palpable hit.

LAER. (*Reluctant to do his best.*)   Well; again.

KING. (*Seeing that Hamlet is doing too well.*) Stay, give me drink.
    Hamlet, this pearl [78] is thine;
  Here's thy health! Give him the cup. (*He sends the poisoned
    goblet down to Hamlet.*)

                        Trumpets sound, and shot goes off within.

HAM. (*Brushing aside the proffered goblet.*)   I'll play this bout first;
    set it by a while. (*The servant stands aside with the goblet.*)
  Come. (*They play.*) Another hit; what say you?

LAER.   A touch, a touch, I do confess.

KING.   Our son shall win.

QUEEN.   He's fat,[79] and scant of breath.

  (*Delighted at her son's exhibition of prowess, she quits her place
    to play again the loving mother—this time fatally. She comes
    to him and affectionately wipes his brow with her handker-
    chief.*) Here, Hamlet, take my napkin, rub thy brows. (*Ex-
    citedly, she takes the cup from the servant and raises it to
    toast Hamlet.*)

  The Queen carouses to thy fortune, Hamlet.   300

HAM.   Good madam!

KING. (*With a shout.*)   Gertrude, do not drink!

QUEEN.   I will, my lord; I pray you, pardon me. (*She drinks deeply,
    then offers the cup to Hamlet.*)

KING. [*Aside.*]   It is the poison'd cup; it is too late.

HAM.   I dare not drink yet, madam; by and by.

QUEEN.   Come, let me wipe thy face.

LAER. (*Desperately.*)   My lord, I'll hit him now.

KING. (*Anguished.*)   I do not think't.

LAER. [*Aside.*]   And yet 'tis almost 'gainst my conscience.

[78] From Hamlet's later reference to it, it would appear that the "union"
is actually the poison.
    In Mr. Olivier's movie there seemed to be *many* plays within the play!
At least, the courtiers were moved to applause on the slightest excuse. They
applauded Hamlet's apology to Laertes, and now applauded Claudius when
he threw the "pearl" into the goblet.
    [79] This line becomes ludicrous on our stage when we are treated to a
Hamlet who is but a wisp of a man. Not that the word implies that Hamlet is
corpulent! It would be used in the same way today, as any frequenter of a
men's gymnasium knows, to mean "out of practice" or "soft." Indeed, it is
usually the men who keep in good trim who disgustedly will call every ounce
they accumulate on their physiques "fat." But the point is that a stage Hamlet
ought to be at least muscular-looking.

HAM. (*In high spirits.*)   Come, for the third, Laertes; you but dally.

I pray you, pass with your best violence.   310

I am afeard you make a wanton [80] of me.

LAER.   Say you so? Come on.   *They play.*

OSR.   Nothing, neither way.

LAER.   Have at you now!

Laertes wounds Hamlet; then, in scuffling, they change rapiers.[81]

KING.   Part them; they are incens'd.

HAM.   Nay, come, again.

Hamlet wounds Laertes. The Queen falls.

OSR.   Look to the Queen there! Ho!

HOR.   They bleed on both sides. How is't my lord!

OSR.   How is't, Laertes?

LAER.   Why, as a woodcock [82] to mine own springe, Osric;

I am justly kill'd with mine own treachery.

[80] spoiled child.

[81] The last minutes of the match have elicited a variety of comment and exposition. See pp. 242–243.

Wilson gives a scholarly and full account of the three bouts, though we cannot agree with him that Hamlet's successful hits are owing to the Prince's superiority with the foils; we believe they are due to the element of decency, not quite extinguished in Laertes's make-up, which renders it difficult for him to fight his best in so nefarious a match, and we think Hamlet's

I am afeard you make a wanton of me

proves as much. Wilson's interesting and valid suggestion as to how Laertes manages to wound Hamlet is, he informs us, the idea employed by Irving in 1878. According to this direction, Hamlet is relaxing a moment after the third bout; suddenly Laertes in "open foul play" lunges at him and cuts him on the arm. This arrangement was adopted in Mr. Olivier's movie to good effect. Next, Wilson continues, acknowledging his indebtedness to Mr. Evan John for the conception, Hamlet, infuriated, closes with Laertes, "beats aside his dagger with the dagger in his own left hand, and suddenly dropping to the ground the foil in his right, seizes with the empty hand the hilt of the sword he covets and wrests it from his enemy's grasp. . . . He pauses in ironical courtesy to allow Laertes to pick up the discarded foil" (*What Happens in Hamlet*, pp. 285–86). This makes good theater. If we prefer the scene as executed by the late John Barrymore, it is only because we think that made rather better theater—though one could not forget that it was very much in the Barrymore manner! We also prefer to think that Laertes wounds Hamlet *during* the third bout, rather than treacherously after it, for the latter way makes Laertes entirely too depraved; when Shakespeare gave him the aside,

"And yet 'tis almost 'gainst my conscience"

it is clear the dramatist wished to soften our attitude towards Laertes for the few minutes of life remaining to him. See pp. 240–244.

[82] the type foolish bird.

HAM. How does the Queen?

KING. She swounds to see them bleed.

QUEEN. No, no, the drink, the drink,—O my dear Hamlet,— 320
The drink, the drink! I am poison'd. *Dies.*

HAM. O villainy! Ho! let the door be lock'd:
Treachery! (*Fumbling in his doublet for the document.*) Seek it
out.[83]

LAER. It is *here*, Hamlet. Hamlet, thou art slain.
No medicine in the world can do thee good;
In thee there is not half an hour of life.
The treacherous instrument is in thy hand,
Unbated and envenom'd. The foul practice
Hath turn't itself on me. Lo, here I lie,
Never to rise again. Thy mother's poison'd. 330
I can no more:—the King, the King's to blame.

HAM. The point envenom'd too!
Then, venom, to thy work. *Hurts the King.*

ALL. Treason! treason!

KING. O, yet defend me, friends; I am but hurt.

HAM. (*Forcing the remainder of the drink down the King's throat.*)
Here, thou incestuous, murderous, damned Dane,
Drink off this potion! Is thy *union* here?
Follow my mother! *King dies.*

LAER. He is justly served;
It is a poison temp'red [84] by himself.
Exchange forgiveness with me, noble Hamlet. 340
Mine and my father's death come not upon thee,
Nor thine on me! *Dies.*

HAM. Heaven make thee free of it! (*The poison has begun its work.*)
I follow thee.
I am dead, Horatio. Wretched queen, adieu! [85]
You that look pale and tremble at this chance,
That are but mutes or audience to this act,
Had I but time—as this fell sergeant, Death,
Is strict in his arrest—O, I could tell you—

[83] We suggest, but do not insist, that at this line Hamlet reaches into his
doublet to extract his document as a prelude to the revelation of Claudius's
guilt. But Laertes's next words prevent his proceeding, for he learns, and
begins to feel, that his time is running out.

[84] mixed.

[85] With the clutch of death about his throat, Hamlet's only thought is
the importance of the world's understanding why he had to kill Claudius.

   But let it be. Horatio, I am dead;
   Thou liv'st. Report me and my cause aright   350
   To the unsatisfied.
HOR.   Never believe it.
   I am more an antique Roman than a Dane;
   Here's yet some liquor left. (*Quickly seizing the goblet.*)
HAM. (*Seizing on the goblet too.*) As thou 'rt a man,
   Give me the cup. Let go! By heaven, I'll have't! (*He wrenches it
    free from Horatio's grasp.*)
   O good Horatio, what a wounded name,
   Things standing thus unknown, shall live behind me!
   If thou didst ever hold me in thy heart,
   Absent thee from felicity a while
   And in this harsh world draw thy breath in pain
   To tell my story.   *March afar off, and shot within.*
      What warlike noise is this?   360
OSR. Young Fortinbras, with conquest come from Poland,
   To the ambassadors of England gives
   This warlike volley.
HAM.   O, I die, Horatio;
   The potent poison quite o'er-crows [86] my spirit.
   I cannot live to hear the news from England,
   But I do prophesy the election lights
   On Fortinbras; he has my dying voice.
   So tell him, with the occurrents, more and less,
   Which have solicited [87]—The rest is silence.   *Dies.*
HOR. Now cracks a noble heart. Good-night, sweet prince, 370
   And flights of angels sing thee to thy rest!
   Why does the drum come hither?   *March within.*
   Enter Fortinbras [88] *and the English Ambassador, with drum, colours,*
and Attendants.

[86] overcomes.

[87] His last breath is expended on the prime concern that all the facts be known. Fortinbras must be apprized of everything which has occasioned Hamlet's final deed. But he can say no more. "The rest is silence." Hamlet dies without being certain whether or not the world will understand the justice of his vengeance. That is his final anguish.

[88] At the risk of irritating the reader by interfering at such a moment— yet, after all, our endeavor has not been to re-write Shakespeare's masterpiece, but only to make it clear and to enrich the reader's enjoyment of it—we wish to make a few observations on the closing passage.

  It would be fair to say that Shakespeare's original purpose in bringing in Fortinbras and his men was to meet the need of having the four corpses now

FORT.   Where is this sight?

HOR.   What is it ye would see?
If aught of woe or wonder, cease your search.

FORT.   This quarry [89] cries on [90] havoc.[91] O proud death,
What feast is toward [92] in thine eternal cell,
That thou so many princes at a shot
So bloodily hast struck?

AMB.   The sight is dismal,
And our affairs from England come too late.
The ears are senseless that should give us hearing,   380
To tell him his commandment is fulfill'd,
That Rosencrantz and Guildenstern are dead.
Where should we have our thanks?

HOR.   Not from his [93] mouth,
Had it the ability of life to thank you.
He never gave commandment for their death.
But since, so jump [94] upon this bloody question,
You from the Polack wars, and you from England,
Are here arrived, give order that these bodies

---

on stage conveyed off. In the Elizabethan theater there was no curtain
that might be brought down across the front of the proscenium to conceal
them when the play is over. Fortinbras's presence answered the need reasonably.
So much for the necessity. But Shakespeare was ever an artist, as we have said,
to make much virtue out of necessity, and he has put the last minutes of the
tragedy to superb esthetic uses. It is not the function of tragedy to leave the
audience devastated at the end, but rather to leave it purged, chastened, more
deeply aware of the tragic lot and dignity of the race. Fortinbras's presence
conjoined with Horatio's sends us back into the world with a sense that despite
all the havoc we have witnessed, things are no longer rotten in Denmark. If
the noblest has perished, so have all the evil-doers, and affairs have been left in
the hands of good and courageous men. Goodness, we understand, cannot go
down to defeat. If life have meaning it is in the living itself, in that struggle
in which goodness in the long eventuality must survive the temporary triumph
of evil. In the communication of this *katharsis*, Shakespeare has given us for
the final passages poetry of the most exalted order.

We have at least once witnessed a *Hamlet* in which the actor-manager
dispensed with everything after Hamlet's last line, and brought the curtain
down on Hamlet's death. The effect was as if an orchestral conductor should
decide to cut from Richard Strauss's *Death and Transfiguration* the sublimely
aspiring final pages. We never were more aware of the superb artistry of Shakespeare than on that sorry occasion. For as the play now stands, we must reason
not the need which occasioned the entrance of Fortinbras. Without him the
play would lack its crowning touch.

[89] heap of slain.   [90] cries out.   [91] indiscriminate slaughter.
[92] in preparation.   [93] (the King's).   [94] exactly.

High on a stage to be placed to the view;
And let me speak to the yet unknowing world   390
How these things came about. So shall you hear
Of carnal, bloody, and unnatural acts,
Of accidental judgments, casual slaughters,
Of deaths put on by cunning and forc'd cause,
And, in this upshot, purposes mistook
Fallen on the inventors' heads: all this can I
Truly deliver.

FORT.   Let us haste to hear it,
And call the noblest to the audience.
For me, with sorrow I embrace my fortune.
I have some rights of memory in this kingdom,   400
Which now to claim, my vantage doth invite me.

HOR. (*Solemnly.*) Of that I shall have also cause to speak,
And from his [95] mouth whose voice will draw on more.[96]
But let this same be presently perform'd
Even while men's minds are wild, lest more mischance,
On plots and errors, happen.

FORT.   Let four captains
Bear Hamlet, like a soldier, to the stage,
For he was likely, had he been put on,
To have prov'd most royally; and, for his passage,[97]
The soldiers' music and the rites of war   410
Speak loudly for him.
Take up the bodies. Such a sight as this
Becomes the field, but here shows much amiss.
Go, bid the soldiers shoot.
*Exeunt marching, bearing off the dead bodies; after which a peal of
ordnance are shot off.*

[95] (Hamlet's).
[96] be seconded by others. The Quartos read "draw no more."
[97] death.

Index

Italic figures indicate important passages

APOLLO EDITIONS